LIFESPAN COGNITION

MECHANISMS OF CHANGE

EDITED BY

Ellen Bialystok
Fergus I. M. Craik

OXFORD

UNIVERSITY PRESS

2006

UNIVERSITY PRESS

Oxford University Press, Inc., publishes works that further
Oxford University's objective of excellence
in research, scholarship, and education.

Oxford   New York
Auckland   Cape Town   Dar es Salaam   Hong Kong   Karachi
Kuala Lumpur   Madrid   Melbourne   Mexico City   Nairobi
New Delhi   Shanghai   Taipei   Toronto

With offices in
Argentina   Austria   Brazil   Chile   Czech Republic   France   Greece
Guatemala   Hungary   Italy   Japan   Poland   Portugal   Singapore
South Korea   Switzerland   Thailand   Turkey   Ukraine   Vietnam

Copyright © 2006 by Ellen Bialystok, Fergus I.M. Craik

Published by Oxford University Press, Inc.
198 Madison Avenue, New York, New York 10016
www.oup.com

Oxford is a registered trademark of Oxford University Press

Library of Congress Cataloging-in-Publication Data

Lifespan cognition : mechanisms of change / edited by Ellen Bialystok, Fergus I.M. Craik.
p.   cm
ISBN-13: 978-0-19-516953-9
ISBN 0-19-516953-0
1. Cognition—Age factors.   2. Aging—Psychological aspects.   I. Bialystok, Ellen.
II. Craik, Fergus I. M.
BF724.55.C63L54 2005
153—dc22
2005009305

1 3 5 7 9 8 6 4 2

Printed in the United States of America
on acid-free paper

Preface

Interdisciplinary! The word is heard often in academic circles. It is a state of affairs appreciated by students, encouraged by funding agencies, beloved by university administrators, yet often treated with reserve and suspicion by scholars and scientists themselves. One reason for this negative reaction is the desire of researchers to pursue their goals in a focused and single-minded fashion. But what if two groups of researchers in the same discipline who are asking the same basic questions have so little contact and shared resources that they each create their own methodologies and establish their own knowledge systems, profiting little if at all from the efforts of the other group? This, we believe, is the situation for researchers in cognitive development and cognitive aging. Our purpose in editing this book is to contribute to a resolution of this divide through the model of interdisciplinary research, in which unique skills are blended to create a richer and more powerful set of ideas and methods to address a common problem.

Because communication between the groups is so rare, the division between researchers in development and aging takes on the proportions of that between such pairs as physicists and chemists, linguists and philosophers, or economists and geographers. In these latter cases, however, the differences are obvious—academic convention has placed these scholars in different departments, often in different buildings, calling for an effort of will for interaction to take place. The term *interdisciplinary* is recognition of this effort, and the fruits of those collaborations are admired and respected. Normally, researchers in cognitive development and cognitive aging live together, yet without some special incentive there has been little reason to walk down the corridor. We believe that collaborations between these groups of researchers are not only desirable but also *necessary* for the evolution of a comprehensive model of cognitive lifespan development.

Our proposal is to create a bridge between these two areas of specialization to gain a perspective on issues and processes that transcend their differences. Our interest is in the problem of change. How do the cognitive skills that constitute our mental lives evolve across the lifespan? The components of cognition mature through childhood, building in sophistication and complexity, to construct the machinery of the adult mind. Eventually these same processes begin to wane, dimming in their clarity and becoming compromised in their precision. A set of important and scientifically exciting questions may be asked about the nature of these processes and mechanisms that drive cognitive change across the lifespan.

We offer this volume as part of the growing enterprise concerned with integrating the insights of researchers who endeavor to understand cognitive change at the two ends of the life course. We invited pairs of authors to write complementary chapters on a set of central topics in cognitive psychology—attention, memory, language, problem solving, and so on—with one member of each pair working in child development and one working in cognitive aging, and then asked Shu-Chen Li and Paul B. Baltes to describe the main issues from the lifespan perspective. The paired authors were asked to present the main issues on either the developmental or aging side of their allotted topics, to respond to some of the comments raised by the researcher on the other side of the lifespan, and to reflect on the implications for lifespan psychology and the search for mechanisms of cognitive change. Not surprisingly, the nature of these interactions varied substantially, with some pairs of authors embracing converging views and others arguing for the need for more independent explanations at the two life stages. Our intention was not to propose a solution but to create a dialogue in which researchers concerned with cognitive change can share insights and amalgamate resources. Our greatest hope is that these opening exchanges will fuel a conversation that takes on its own energy. Our greatest reward will be an increase in the number of walks down these previously untraveled corridors.

We have been supported by many individuals and institutions in this project, and we are grateful to all of them for their roles in bringing the work to completion. Our research, and the time to work on this manuscript, has been funded by grants from the Natural Sciences and Engineering Research Council of Canada (NSERC) to each of us, and by a grant from the Canadian Institutes of Health Research (CIHR) to us jointly. We are indebted to the Rotman Research Institute and to its director, Donald Stuss, for providing the context in which the collaboration took place and for supporting our work on it. Jane Logan took on the responsibilities as editorial assistant and brought the chapters into their final forms. Catharine Carlin at Oxford University Press provided the support and resources for the book to be published. Most important, we thank our colleagues and students with whom we have worked and who have shaped our ideas on these issues. In the end, however, it is our families who have allowed us the time and space to immerse ourselves in these ideas and follow them wherever they led. To them we are deeply grateful.

Contents

Contributors   ix

1. On Structure and Process in Lifespan
   Cognitive Development   3
   FERGUS I. M. CRAIK
   ELLEN BIALYSTOK

2. Neural Bases of Cognitive
   Development   15
   MARGOT J. TAYLOR

3. Brain Changes in Aging:
   A Lifespan Perspective   27
   RANDY L. BUCKNER
   DENISE HEAD
   CINDY LUSTIG

4. Four Modes of Selection   43
   JAMES T. ENNS
   LANA M.TRICK

5. Aging and Attention   57
   ARTHUR F. KRAMER
   JUTTA KRAY

6. The Early Development
   of Executive Functions   70
   ADELE DIAMOND

7. The Aging of Executive Functions   96
   KAREN DANIELS
   JEFFREY TOTH
   LARRY JACOBY

8. Working Memory in Children:
   A Cognitive Approach   112
   GRAHAM J. HITCH

9. Working Memory Across
   the Adult Lifespan   128
   DENISE C. PARK
   DORIS PAYER

10. Children's Memory Development: Remembering the Past and Preparing for the Future 143
PETER A. ORNSTEIN
CATHERINE A. HADEN
HOLGER B. ELISCHBERGER

11. Aging and Long-Term Memory: Deficits Are Not Inevitable 162
ROSE T. ZACKS
LYNN HASHER

12. Development of Representation in Childhood 178
KATHERINE NELSON

13. Representation and Aging 193
DEBORAH M. BURKE

14. The Emergentist Coalition Model of Word Learning in Children Has Implications for Language in Aging 207
ROBERTA MICHNICK GOLINKOFF
KATHY HIRSH-PASEK

15. Language in Adulthood 223
SUSAN KEMPER

16. Language Meaning and Form Disorders 239
MAUREEN DENNIS

17. Language Disorders in Aging 253
DAVID CAPLAN
GLORIA WATERS

18. Patterns of Knowledge Growth and Decline 264
FRANK KEIL

19. Aging of Thought 274
TIMOTHY A. SALTHOUSE

20. Inter- and Intra-individual Differences in Problem Solving Across the Lifespan 285
ROBERT S. SIEGLER

21. Variability in Cognitive Aging: From Taxonomy to Theory 297
ULMAN LINDENBERGER
TIMO VON OERTZEN

22. Intelligence and Cognitive Abilities as Competencies in Development 315
DAMIAN P. BIRNEY
ROBERT J. STERNBERG

23. The Lacunae of Loss? Aging and the Differentiation of Cognitive Abilities 331
PATRICK RABBITT
MIKE ANDERSON

24. Cognitive Developmental Research from Lifespan Perspectives: The Challenge of Integration 344
SHU-CHEN LI
PAUL B. BALTES

Author Index 365
Subject Index 383

Contributors

MIKE ANDERSON
School of Psychology
University of Western Australia
Crawley
Australia
mike@psy.uwa.edu.au

PAUL B. BALTES
Max Planck Institute for Human Development
Berlin
Germany
baltes@mpib-berlin.mpg.de

ELLEN BIALYSTOK
Department of Psychology
York University
Toronto, ON
Canada
ellenb@yorku.ca

DAMIAN P. BIRNEY
Psychology Department
University of Sydney
Sydney
Australia
damianb@psych.usyd.edu.au

RANDY L. BUCKNER
Department of Psychology
Washington University
St. Louis, MO
USA
rbuckner@artsci.wustl.edu

DEBORAH M. BURKE
Department of Psychology
Pomona College
Claremont, CA
USA
dmb04747@pomona.edu

DAVID CAPLAN
Massachusetts General Hospital
Boston, MA
USA
dcaplan@partners.org

FERGUS I. M. CRAIK
Rotman Research Institute
Baycrest Centre for Geriatric Care
Toronto, ON
Canada
fcraik@rotman-baycrest.on.ca

KAREN DANIELS
Department of Psychology
University of North Carolina—
    Wilmington
Wilmington, NC
USA
danielsk@uncw.edu

MAUREEN DENNIS
The Hospital for Sick Children
Toronto, ON
Canada
maureen.dennis@sickkids.ca

ADELE DIAMOND
University of British Columbia
Vancouver, BC
Canada
Adele.Diamond@ubc.ca

HOLGER B. ELISCHBERGER
Psychology Department
University of North Carolina
Chapel Hill, NC
USA
holger@email.unc.edu

JAMES T. ENNS
Department of Psychology
University of British Columbia
Vancouver, BC
Canada
jenns@psych.ubc.ca

ROBERTA MICHNICK GOLINKOFF
Psychology Department
University of Delaware
Newark, DE
USA
roberta@udel.edu

CATHERINE A. HADEN
1035 Damen Hall
Loyola University
Chicago, IL
USA
CHADEN@wpo.it.luc.edu

LYNN HASHER
Department of Psychology
University of Toronto
Toronto, ON
Canada
hasher@psych.utoronto.ca

DENISE HEAD
Department of Psychology
Washington University
St. Louis, MO
USA
dhead@artsci.wustl.edu

KATHY HIRSH-PASEK
Department of Psychology
Temple University
Philadelphia, PA
USA
khirshpa@temple.edu

GRAHAM J. HITCH
Department of Psychology
University of York
York
UK
g.hitch@psych.york.ac.uk

LARRY JACOBY
Department of Psychology
Washington University
St. Louis, MO
USA
lljacoby@artsci.wustl.edu

FRANK KEIL
Department of Psychology
Yale University
New Haven, CT
USA
frank.keil@yale.edu

SUSAN KEMPER
Department of Psychology
University of Kansas
Lawrence, KS
USA
skemper@ukans.edu

ARTHUR F. KRAMER
Department of Psychology
University of Illinois at Urbana-Champaign
Champaign, IL
USA
akramer@cyrus.psych.uiuc.edu

JUTTA KRAY
Department of Psychology
Saarland University
Saarbrücken
Germany
J.Kray@mx.uni-saarland.de

SHU-CHEN LI
Max Planck Institute for Human Development
Berlin
Germany
shuchen@mpib-berlin.mpg.de

ULMAN LINDENBERGER
Max Planck Institute for Human Development
Berlin
Germany
lindenberger@mpib-berlin.mpg.de

CINDY LUSTIG
Department of Psychology
University of Michigan
Ann Arbor, MI
USA
clustig@umich.edu

KATHERINE NELSON
City University of New York
New York, NY
USA
knelson@gc.cuny.edu

PETER A. ORNSTEIN
Psychology Department
University of North Carolina
Chapel Hill, NC
USA
peter_ornstein@unc.edu

DENISE C. PARK
Department of Psychology
University of Illinois
Champaign, IL
USA
denisep@uiuc.edu

DORIS PAYER
Department of Psychology
University of Illinois
Champaign, IL
USA
payer@s.psych.uiuc.edu

PATRICK RABBITT
Department of Psychology
University of Manchester
Manchester
United Kingdom
rabbitt@psy.man.ac.uk

TIMOTHY A. SALTHOUSE
Department of Psychology
University of Virginia
Charlottesville, VA
USA
salthouse@virginia.edu

ROBERT S. SIEGLER
Department of Psychology
Carnegie Mellon University
Pittsburgh, PA
USA
rs7k+@andrew.cmu.edu

ROBERT J. STERNBERG
Department of Psychology
Yale University
New Haven, CT
USA
robert.sternberg@yale.edu

MARGOT J. TAYLOR
The Hospital for Sick Children
Toronto, ON
Canada
margot.taylor@sickkids.ca

JEFFREY TOTH
Department of Psychology
University of North Carolina—
    Wilmington
Wilmington, NC
USA
tothj@uncw.edu

LANA M. TRICK
Department of Psychology
University of Guelph
Guelph, ON
Canada
trick@psy.uoguelph.ca

TIMO VON OERTZEN
Department of Mathematics
Saarland University
Saarbrücken
Germany
timovoe@gmx.de

GLORIA WATERS
Boston University, Sargent College
Boston, MA
USA
gwaters@acs-pop.bu.edu

ROSE T. ZACKS
Psychology Building
Michigan State University
East Lansing, MI
USA
zacksr@msu.edu

LIFESPAN COGNITION

On Structure and Process in Lifespan Cognitive Development

Fergus I. M. Craik

Ellen Bialystok

John Macnamara ended his book *Names for Things* with the following observation:

> I know of no evidence that the minds of children and adults differ structurally. In this book we have seen considerable evidence that even to learn names for things, a modest part of what the very young child learns even in language, they must be structurally equivalent. That, together with the strategic wisdom of taking two mysteries as one (the null hypothesis) commends the conclusion that they are equivalent. (1982, p. 236)

There is nothing apparently radical in Macnamara's conclusion about the structural similarity of the minds of children and adults, but the insight contradicts a considerable portion of the research examining cognitive change across the lifespan. The practical assumption in this research appears to be that the minds of children and adults are different entities. For the most part, researchers in cognitive development investigate the emergence of cognitive abilities from birth until about 10 or 12 years old, and researchers in cognitive aging confine their inquiries to adults beyond the age of about 60 years. In both cases, although more so in cognitive aging, comparisons are also made with the performance of high-functioning young adults, usually university undergraduates, from whom deviations in performance are measured. Attempts to integrate these bodies of research into a single function that traces cognitive changes from the rapid increases in childhood, through the more subtle variations in adulthood, to the slower but inevitable deterioration in many of these processes with aging, are extremely rare. And yet, if the minds of children and adults were "structurally equivalent," then one would expect continuity in the genesis and decline of cognitive function across the lifespan.

Some official acknowledgement of the mandate to study cognitive change across the entire lifespan is found in the textbooks that circumscribe the fields for novice students. For example, in an introductory textbook on developmental psychology, Shaffer, Wood, and Willoughby (2002) define development as the "systematic continuities and changes in an individual that occur between conception . . . and death" (p.2). Within this broad view, some texts situate child development as a subset of developmental psychology within a more specific age band. For example, Berk (2000) defines developmental psychology as including "all changes we experience throughout the lifespan" but child development as addressing "those factors that influence the dramatic changes in young people during the first two decades of life" (p. 4). Other textbooks take a more bifurcated view of the processes of development and aging. Birren and Schroots (1996) note that "the psychology of aging is grounded in a two-stages-of-life perspective; the two stages, development and aging, are usually thought of as two successive processes of change in time, with the transition point or apex at maturity" (p.9). It is this latter view that defines most of the research conducted on the development and decline of cognitive functions across the lifespan.

In spite of this division of labor, the fields of developmental psychology and cognitive aging share a concern for formulating content descriptions of cognitive change over time, rely on similar theories to explain the nature of these changes and the reasons for their evolution, and employ comparable methodologies to detect such changes and situate them in descriptions of performance of the stable state. These commonalities are formidable and set both fields apart from the main enterprise of cognitive psychology that is concerned with description and theory of performance in the stable state. Our purpose in this book is to explore the possibility of integrating these fields to produce a more unified description of change that can constitute the basis of a lifespan approach to cognition.

An integrated account of lifespan cognitive change would benefit both developmental psychology in its endeavor to explain the emergence of cognitive skill and cognitive aging in its study of the decline of cognitive function with age. The common reference point for both of these fields has been the psychology of young adults, perhaps the most widely studied group in all of psychology, and understanding what precedes and follows that utopian state of cognitive efficiency would undoubtedly inform those models as well. The necessity to extract principles and methods that operate across the lifespan would inevitably refine our understanding of basic cognitive processes at all stages of life.

Consider some potential benefits more specifically. A lifespan account would provide a dynamic view of cognition and create a richer context for descriptions of the stable state usually studied in cognitive psychology. One example is the contribution to cognitive theorizing that would follow from considering the role of variability, a factor that is fundamental to descriptions of cognitive performance. Variability in performance has been assigned a crucial role in explaining the nature of cognitive change both for children (Siegler, Chapter 20, this volume) and older adults (Lindenberger & von Oertzen, Chapter 21, this volume). But there is also variability in adult performance even when the focus is not on mechanisms of change, and in those cases the variability is often treated as noise in the data. Understanding the function of variability when cognitive performance is more obviously in transition would contribute importantly to understanding the role of variability when transition is not the main interest. In general, cognitive models that are based on the explanation of how change takes place are also better able to explain variability—the question of why a participant performs better on day 2 than on day 1 has some parallels with the question of why a child performs better at 6 years than at 5 years, or why an adult performs better at 20 years than at 60 years.

Another example of the potential to provide richness to models of adult cognitive performance is the research that shows the centrality of the rise (Golinkoff & Hirsh-Pasek, Chapter 14, this volume) and fall (Kemper, Chapter 15, this volume) of language abilities on cognitive performance. Unlike earlier structuralist models of language that isolated linguistic processing from other cognitive skills, current theorizing places language abilities in an integrated network of cognitive processes. In spite of this, adult cognitive psychology pays little attention to the linguistic abilities of participants and how those abilities potentially interact with the cognitive processes under investigation. However, the dramatic changes in language competencies across the lifespan and the impact of those changes on performance indicate that more attention should be paid to the role of language proficiency in cognitive functioning, even during young adulthood when those abilities are relatively stable.

A lifespan approach to cognitive change would facilitate the enterprise of relating specific aspects of cognitive processing to changes in brain functions. There is a growing interest in both cognitive development and cognitive aging in understanding the complex relations between cognitive functions and brain structures. In both fields, tremendous progress has been made in both situating specific cognitive functions to brain structures and, more importantly, in understanding changes in those functions in terms of organic changes taking place in the brain at different points in the lifespan. These analyses have been enabled by new research revealing details of the growth (Taylor, Chapter 2, this volume) and contraction (Buckner, Head, & Lustig, Chapter 3, this volume) of brain structure and function over time. Ultimately, the changes documented for the emergence of cognitive function and the changes noted with the decline of cognitive function need to be specified in the same brain as follows a specific trajectory across the lifespan. For example, research has shown that the growth of executive functions in childhood (Diamond, Chapter 6, this volume) and their decline with aging (Daniels, Toth, & Jacoby, Chapter 7, this volume) are clearly related to structural changes in the frontal lobes in childhood and older adults, respectively. Changes at both ends of the lifespan emerge in concert with physical changes in the same brain. Finding commonality in the process of change would assist the task of relating those changes to structural changes that are taking place in the brain at different points in time.

Finally, discovering commonalities between development and aging can point to fundamental processes in cognitive change. The concept of change is among the most difficult targets of scientific inquiry; by definition, change is that which does not stand still. Mathematicians needed to invent calculus as an entirely new way of conceptualizing relations in order to capture the descriptions of change that were not conveyed in standard algebraic formulas. Similarly, researchers concerned with both development and aging struggle to create models that are sufficiently complex to incorporate the nonlinear dimensions that characterize the changes in cognitive processing that occur at different points in the lifespan. More shared resources and more cross-fertilization from work in the field focused on the opposite end of the lifespan would undoubtedly facilitate all these researchers in this difficult but crucial enterprise.

What do current research results tell us about the similarities and differences between cognitive growth and decline? This question is answered in large part by the following chapters, but we precede these detailed descriptions with a brief examination of some basic issues in these inquiries. Judgments about the relative similarity or uniqueness of development and aging depend on the perspective one takes to describe performance and the grain of the analysis that is used to examine change at these two points in the lifespan. The broadest perspective is to consider the relation between the mind and the world at these different ontogenetic stages. In this view, one can explore the relative influence of exogenous factors given by the environment and endogenous factors given by the biological structure of the mind on development. A more precise description based on a more fine-grained analysis comes from the perspective that examines the structure of the mind itself, identifying its component abilities and exploring the changing relationships among those abilities. This view, while focused exclusively on the structure of the mind, nonetheless considers a wide and diffuse range of cognitive functions. Finally, the most detailed perspective places only a select set of cognitive processes under scrutiny—for example, the executive functions—and examines their lifespan evolution under the most detailed lens. From all these perspectives, systematic and coherent cognitive changes can be described across the lifespan. In all cases, however, the trajectory uncovered to represent that lifespan development is somewhat different and the mechanisms underlying those dynamics are most certainly different. Therefore, the pattern of development and decline of cognitive abilities depends on the observation perspective one takes and the size of the lens through which one peers. We shall illustrate these differences by describing the evidence from three perspectives that progressively narrow the lens and sharpen the focus: context and performance, differentiation-dedifferentiation, and representation and control. In each case, we consider whether there is evidence for developmental growth and decline; and if so, whether the rise and fall are symmetrical and whether the patterns of change can be traced to the same underlying mechanisms.

THE ROLE OF CONTEXT

A number of developmental theorists have stressed the crucially supportive roles played by physical, psychological, and social contexts on various aspects of the child's intellectual performance. Piaget (1959), for example, described the processes of intellectual maturation as involving a gradual detachment from the "here and now," enabling the older child to deal with abstractions, and with past and future events. In the present volume, Ornstein, Haden, and Elischberger (Chapter 10) describe how the young child's conversation is "scaffolded" by the mother's promptings, a type of contextual support that becomes less necessary as verbal abilities develop. Similarly, Vygotsky (1978) argued that social structures serve to support thinking by moving children beyond the level they could achieve by functioning alone, a view significantly expanded and explicated by Rogoff (1990). In an influential work, Bruner (1983) argued that Chomsky's innate language acquisition device (LAD) could not on its own lead a child into linguistic competence without the cooperation of the language acquisition support system (LASS). The LASS was the experiential and interactive context in which the child encountered language and assumed at least shared responsibility with the biological biases for the child's mastery of language. In all these cases, children's cognitive development is inextricably tied to the environment in which those abilities are learned and expressed.

There is good evidence to suggest that this developmental trend reverses in the course of aging such that older adults show progressively greater reliance on environmental and schematic support (Craik, 1983, 1986). Examples of the importance of environmental support include anecdotal reports of older people becoming confused and somewhat cognitively impaired (usually temporarily) after moving from their familiar home surroundings into assisted housing or a nursing home. In the laboratory, the memory performance of older adults typically shows differential benefits of context reinstatement and of recognition over recall (see Craik, 1983, 2002; Craik & Jennings, 1992, for details). Older adults are also supported in their behavior by relying on the context provided by past learning and ingrained habits. Thus, for example, older adults benefit more than do their younger counterparts from an increase in the meaningful relatedness of word pairs in a paired-associate learning paradigm (Naveh-Benjamin, Craik, Guez, & Kreuger, 2005).

Another way of characterizing the role of context in lifespan developmental is to consider the support provided through a sort of "mental context"—that is, the conceptual schemas that have been built up through habit and experience in specific environmental contexts. Successful performance reflects an optimal balance between environmentally driven (bottom-up) and schematically driven (top-down) processes and, crucially, by interactions *between* these sets of processes. In both childhood and older adulthood

this balance may become distorted, however, with individuals relying more heavily on the habitual schemas constructed through experience. That is, there can be an overreliance on habit. The classic A-not-B error in which an infant continues to search for a toy in an obsolete location in spite of seeing it hidden in a new place has traditionally been interpreted as evidence for a failure of object permanence (Piaget, 1954). Diamond (2002; Chapter 6, this volume), however, argues that the child is overrelying on a habitual response that successfully located the toy on previous occasions, and the new information from the environment is insufficient to overrule the previous scheme. Cognitive behaviors of older adults are similarly dominated by habit; this point has been well documented by studies from Larry Jacoby's lab (see Daniels, Toth, & Jacoby, Chapter 7, this volume).

The decreasing reliance on schematic and environmental support in the developing child and the increasing reliance in the aging adult reflect the growth and decline, respectively, of the biological systems that underpin and enable a variety of cognitive abilities. The consequence of this change in dependency is different for the two groups, however. For children, the decreasing reliance on such supports allows them to respond flexibly and adaptively to specific situations; that is, their behavior is governed by an intelligent appreciation of the current situation in light of relevant past experiences. For older adults, the increasing reliance on contextual support has both positive and negative implications. It is positively adaptive in that performance decrements that would otherwise occur are prevented or at least ameliorated. However, a negative consequence of this reliance on past learning and habitual responding is that the person's thoughts and actions become more stereotyped and predictable; adaptive as long as the environmental and social contexts remain stable and unchanging, but poorly adapted and inflexible in new surroundings.

It is generally agreed that the adaptive, self-initiated forms of control found in young adulthood are mediated by the frontal lobes, which are among the last parts of the brain to develop fully and among the first to deteriorate in the course of aging (Gogtay et al., 2004; Raz et al., 1997). Pathology of the frontal lobes is therefore associated with a loss of flexibility and an undue dependence on the current context. Patients who have suffered frontal damage can show "utilization behaviors" in which their actions are unduly controlled and driven by external stimulation. For example, such patients will continue to eat when plates of food are continually presented, or will automatically start to sew when materials are placed in their laps (Lhermitte, Pillon, & Serdaru, 1986). In such extreme cases, the external environment has gone from providing support to being overly controlling. The reliance on environmental support may be particularly salient when aging is accompanied by pathology. An early Alzheimer patient, for example, may not be able to describe the steps involved in writing a bank check but can carry out the various procedures capably and fluently (and with full knowledge of the implications!) when placed in the appropriate context.

Baltes and his colleagues have recently stressed the idea of co-constructivism—the notion that while most researchers have emphasized the role of the brain in determining mental processes and behaviors, it is equally true that the developing brain is itself shaped and molded by specific circumstances, experiences, successes, and failures (Baltes & Smith, 2004). We strongly endorse this transactional view of relations between brain function and the physical and social worlds, but would simply add that the nature of these brain–world interactions changes through the lifespan from a dominance of world-to-brain transactions in childhood to an eventual dominance of brain-to-world transactions in old age.

DIFFERENTIATION–DEDIFFERENTIATION

A second perspective on lifespan changes in cognition is to examine organizational differences in the mind at different stages of life. Specificity of representation is an aspect of lifespan development that appears to increase throughout childhood and then decrease in the course of aging. The evidence comes largely from behavioral studies of developmental changes in language, concept formation, and memory, but these traditional sources have been augmented recently by findings from cognitive neuroscience (Cabeza, 2002; Casey, Thomas, Davidson, Kunz, & Franzen, 2002). In the area of language development, children first acquire and name concepts at the basic object level (Brown, 1958; Clark, 1993); further development serves both to differentiate that basic level into specific exemplars and to fuse the object in question with similar objects to form more abstract concepts at a higher level (Karmiloff-Smith, 1992). Thus the initial learning of "dog" is both differentiated into spaniel, terrier,

collie, and so on, and linked with cat, horse, and pig to form the concepts of mammals and animals. Studies of children's memory reveal a developmental trend in that recall of both specific detail and overall gist increase substantially as children age (Brainerd & Reyna, 1990).

Another example of the differentiation of children's knowledge representations into more detailed and increasingly organized categories is in the knowledge base revealed in their problem-solving ability, such as performance on Piaget and Inhelder's (1958) balance beam problem. In the task, children observe while different weights are placed at the ends of a balance scale in which the balancing arm has been fixed in place. The problem is to decide which (if either) end of the arm will go down when the stabilizing block is removed. In detailed research with children learning to solve this problem, Siegler (1978) has shown that children begin with simple rules based on one feature, such as the number of weights on each side, and increasingly add more rules that include more information and more detail about the nature of the weights. These rules incorporate increasingly detailed representations of the stimuli, providing a richer base upon which to solve the problem.

These developmental trends are mirrored in studies of aging, where it has been found that recall of gist is relatively unaffected between the ages of 20 and 70, but the recall of specific detail is markedly impaired in groups of older adults (Dixon, Hultsch, Simon, & von Eye, 1984). It is also well established that recollection of the source of acquired information (seen on TV? read in a newspaper? told by a friend?) is more affected by aging than is recall of the information itself (McIntyre & Craik, 1987; Schacter, Kaszniak, Kihlstrom, & Valdiserri, 1991). Similarly, several studies have shown that recall of context is particularly impaired in older adults (Spencer & Raz, 1995). Older people also have great difficulty in retrieving names (Cohen & Burke, 1993; James, 2004). Putting these various memory problems together, Craik (2002) suggested that the common feature might be a greater age-related difficulty in accessing very specific representations (e.g., names and contexts in which events occurred) than in accessing information that is represented at a higher, more general level.

Paul Baltes and his colleagues (Baltes, Cornelius, Spiro, Nesselroade, & Willis, 1980; Baltes, Lindenberger, & Staudinger, 1998) have suggested that the developmental processes underlying differentiation in children are mirrored in older adulthood by processes of "dedifferentiation" (see also Rabbitt & Anderson, Chapter 23, this volume). One type of evidence is that different cognitive abilities intercorrelate to a much higher degree in children and in older adults than in younger adults (Li et al., 2004), suggesting that good cognitive performance in childhood and old age is more attributable to some general ability (g, for example, or fluid intelligence) than to specific abilities or experiential factors. The fractionation of that common ability in young adulthood—that is, the differentiation of cognition—reflects the impact of exogenous factors on the growth of knowledge. Baltes and Lindenberger (1997) have also shown that sensory-motor losses (e.g., in audition, vision, and grip strength) correlate highly with age-related losses in various aspects of cognitive performance. As one possible explanation of this dramatically unexpected finding, they suggested that some common cause underlies the correlated drop in such a wide range of physical and intellectual abilities, with the result that abilities are less differentiated in older than in younger adults. The nature of this common cause, however, is still a matter of active debate.

The notion that abilities are "functionally closer" in the aging brain and are therefore more vulnerable to mutual interference was suggested speculatively by Marcel Kinsbourne some 25 years ago (Kinsbourne, 1980). Recent evidence from brain imaging studies has supported the idea that the neural representations of cognitive function become more specific and delimited as children develop, but then they dedifferentiate and are less focally represented in older adulthood. For example, Casey and her colleagues have shown that performance of a simple stimulus-response compatibility task is mediated by brain regions that are more diffuse in children aged 7–11 years than in young adults (Casey et al., 2002). In older adults this trend is reversed; cognitive processes such as inhibition (Colcombe, Kramer, Erickson, & Scalf, in press) and memory retrieval (Park & Gutchess, 2004) are largely represented unilaterally in young adults, but bilaterally in older adults. This pattern of an age-related decrease in the specificity of cortical representation has also been attributed to a compensatory adjustment of brain function—the recruitment of additional resources from the corresponding area in the opposite hemisphere (Cabeza, 2002; Grady et al., 1995). Similarly, a recent study by Park and colleagues (Park et al., 2004) provides interesting evidence that

areas of the ventral visual cortex are specialized to process specific patterns (e.g., faces, houses, chairs) in young adults, but show significantly less neural specialization for these stimulus categories in older adults. In our view, the growing consensus is that mental representations become more specified and focally represented as children develop, and that the processes of dedifferentiation result in a reversal of this trend in the course of aging. These focal representations are more specialized than the general abilities from which they develop and the undifferentiated representations to which they eventually return.

The observed processes of dedifferentiation may be neither compensatory nor adaptive but rather reflect a less efficient central nervous system, in the same way as less stable and less speedy walking and running in older adults is not truly adaptive in any sense, but simply reflects less efficient musculature and motor control. The present evidence on this point is mixed, with some studies finding that greater degrees of bilateral representation in older adults are associated with better performance and are therefore compensatory (e.g., Cabeza, 2002) but with other studies finding the opposite relationship (e.g., Colcombe et al., in press). One logical difficulty with the compensatory view is that bilaterality decreases from childhood to maturity, and this trend toward unilateral representation is related to higher levels of cognitive performance. If *bilaterality* relates to better performance in the elderly (the compensatory view), then somewhere in the lifespan the relation between bilaterality and cognitive performance reverses—not impossible, but unlikely in our view.

REPRESENTATION AND CONTROL

Most theorists agree that cognitive performance draws on two rather different systems, one being a relatively stable repository of stored knowledge and experience, the other being a more flexible set of processes that deal with new problems and with the acquisition of new information. This distinction has been captured under such headings as *fluid versus crystallized intelligence* (Horn, 1994; Rabbitt & Anderson, Chapter 23, this volume) or *mechanics versus pragmatics of intelligence* (Li & Baltes, Chapter 24, this volume). The distinction between the knowledge base and the control processes that operate on it provide a clear case of asymmetry in the lifespan trajectory. Both the knowledge base and the control processes continue to develop substantially during childhood, adolescence, and young adulthood; at older ages, however, knowledge holds up (provided the information is accessed and used from time to time), but control processes decline in efficiency.

The development of knowledge representations and control processes in children is well documented and not controversial. Specifications for the development of knowledge in young children have been studied from a variety of perspectives, including the impact of expertise, or specialized knowledge (Chi, 1978), and the cognitive reorganization and effect on problem solving that take place as knowledge accrues (Carey, 1985). This line of research is critically examined also by Nelson (Chapter 12, this volume). A major outcome of development is the straightforward acquisition and representation of knowledge in many different domains and the increasing *organization* of these representations into coherent schematic structures having different levels of specificity and abstraction (Karmiloff-Smith, 1992). Similarly, the executive control functions develop throughout childhood, beginning at about 5 years of age (Diamond, 2002; Diamond, Chapter 6, this volume; Zelazo, Muller, Frye, & Marcovitch, 2003). Mastery of these processes is linked to the maturation of the frontal lobes, the last region of the brain to become myelinated.

The correlated and progressive development of these two processes in children is not mirrored in aging. The representation of knowledge is relatively unaffected by the processes of normal aging, and is even considered by some theorists to undergo continuing positive development, resulting in the perceived wisdom of older people (e.g., Baltes, Staudinger, Maercker, & Smith, 1995). At the very least, the representation of knowledge (semantic memory) is spared relative to such other cognitive processes as episodic memory, working memory, and executive processes (e.g., Burke, Chapter 13, this volume; Light 1992). What does appear to change is the *accessibility* to stored knowledge, with older adults experiencing progressively greater difficulty in the retrieval of information they demonstrably *know*, as illustrated by its retrieval at a later date or in response to cues and prompts. Retrieval of proper names seems particularly vulnerable to age-related loss (Cohen & Burke, 1993; James, 2004; but see also Maylor, 1997), although it is possible that names are examples of highly specific information, including the original source of remembered information and the contextual details of a remembered episode (Craik, 2002). In summary, the difficulties with knowledge utilization in children appear to be largely due to the incomplete *acquisition* of relevant knowledge, its representation, and its organization. The problems for the elderly, in contrast, appear more to do with inefficient *accessibility* to knowledge that is still "there" in some sense. It would be interesting to see whether there is a genuine lifespan parabola—a continuous rise and then fall—in the contextual specificity of knowledge utilization. Such an outcome would mean that children first learn new information or a new skill in a specific context and can use it only in that context, they gradually extend its generality and scope to new contexts, and this increasing generality unwinds in old age, so that the ability to exercise skills and access knowledge becomes restricted to specific contexts once again.

The age-related decline in executive process functioning is well documented. Older adults are less able to deploy inhibitory processes effectively, with the result that processing is more vulnerable to interference and may be less precisely focused and directed (Hasher & Zacks, 1988; Hasher, Zacks, & May, 1999). Extending this idea, Jacoby and his colleagues have argued that older people are also less able to *accentuate* specific types of processing to enhance them when required; the resulting deficit is one of overall cognitive control, not merely of inhibition (Daniels, Toth, & Jacoby, Chapter 7, this volume). The notion of executive control of cognitive processing is often discussed and illustrated under the heading of *working memory*. The original formulation of this concept (Baddeley & Hitch, 1974) emphasized its temporary storage aspects, but later versions have linked working memory to attention and executive processes (e.g. Cowan, 1999; Engle & Kane, 2004). Indeed, Baddeley himself has commented that he might well have labeled the concept *working attention* (Baddeley, 1993). In this context, many studies have shown age-related decrements in working memory (see Craik & Jennings, 1992, for review) and these may be interpreted as showing impairments in control.

PATTERNS OF DEVELOPMENT AND DECLINE

Does cognitive aging simply reflect cognitive development in reverse? Evidence from the three perspectives cited in the present chapter, and those developed at greater length in succeeding chapters, make it clear that the issue is much more complex. There are certainly striking instances of inverted U-shaped patterns across the lifespan, the most obvious being the increasing speed of cognitive processing as children develop (e.g., Kail, 1991) and the general slowing associated with aging (e.g., Cerella, 1985; Salthouse, 1996). Another salient example of the mirror-image pattern is executive control, whose development is chronicled by Diamond (Chapter 6, this volume). The age-related decline in inhibitory control is also well documented (Hasher & Zacks, 1979, 1988) as is its rise and fall across the lifespan (Dempster, 1992).

An important point to consider regarding lifespan trajectories of cognitive skills is the level of detail incorporated into various descriptions. It seems unlikely, for example, that attentional control is a single entity. Just as theorists have distinguished between automatic and controlled aspects of information processing, so too they will further subdivide the broad category of controlled processing into task- and context-specific components that show different lifespan trajectories. A more complete description of cognitive changes across the lifespan, therefore, will need to incorporate more detail and more complexity into the account and explain those details in ways that acknowledge both the similarity and the diversity of cognitive performance at different times of life.

Some examples of the need to impose finer distinctions on broad processes are found in studies of visual search. Trick and Enns (1998), for example, found that the ability to detect conjunction targets (defined by two features) increased through childhood and decreased again in the course of aging, but the ability to perform a single feature search improved early in life and then remained stable throughout adulthood. Similarly, in a large-scale study examining search processes across the lifespan, Hommel, Li, and Li (2004) reported that simple feature searches took three times as long as a simple reaction-time (RT) task for children, but that this difference was no greater in older adults than it was in younger adults. In contrast, the increases in RT associated with increasing the number of distractors and with target-absent compared with target-present trials were roughly equivalent for children and young adults but substantially longer for older adults. The authors conclude that, in spite of clear similarities between the performance of children and older adults, there are differences specific to aspects of information processing. For example,

children's difficulties appear to be related to the mere presence of distracting items, whereas older adults exhibit both a general decline in speed and a more cautious decision-making style, shown in their particularly long RTs in target-absent trials. The growth of attentional control processes in children may be linked primarily to a mechanics-related growth of myelination, whereas age-related declines in the same functions may be related both to a decline in mechanics (neural degeneration) and to pragmatic experiential factors such as an increased tendency to conservatism and caution in decision-making situations.

Similar results that called for more detailed explanations of lifespan change in visual search were reported by Williams, Ponese, Schachar, Logan, and Tannock (1999). They found that RT on a two-choice task fell from young children to young adults and then rose in older adults, but the time taken to stop a response after stimulus presentation remained relatively stable throughout the lifespan. Similarly, the study by Hommel et al. (2004) found that visual search rates were comparatively slow during both childhood and old age, but that this apparent symmetry masked the effects of a variety of factors that behaved *asymmetrically* across different age groups. These studies show that even the apparently homogeneous process of visual search comprises a number of different components that show different behavioral effects depending on such features as the depth and complexity of the processing operations demanded by the task in question. Thus, attentional control processes may resemble other similarly broad constructs such as working memory in being umbrella terms for families of processing operations whose exact form and characteristics vary substantially depending on the nature of the task, the materials, and the participant.

These examples from studies of visual search point to the need for more detailed descriptions to form the basis for a lifespan framework. One point to emphasize is the level of analysis applied to the behavior; behaviors that look similar at a surface level of analysis may be carried out by very different mechanisms. As an example, McIntosh and colleagues (McIntosh et al., 1999) had younger and older adults carry out a short-term visual memory task while in the positron emission tomography (PET) scanner. The results showed that both age groups performed the task equally well and that they activated many of the same brain regions, but the patterns of connections among activated regions differed markedly between the age groups. The authors concluded that the new network seen in adults might have evolved to compensate for the reduced interactions between areas most active in younger adults. Another example is the reduction in speed of processing found in children and older adults relative to young adults. Slow rates of processing could stem from a number of causes, including the degree of myelination, synaptic density and aborization, the burden of vascular lesions, and the number of areas required to perform the task in question (Raz, 2000). Equivalent slowing in children and older adults is likely attributable to different mixes of these factors, with the first two dominating performance in children and the second two coming progressively into play in the course of aging. Finally, Bialystok and colleagues (Bialystok et al., 2005) found that monolingual and bilingual young adults performed the Simon task with relatively equivalent speed, but that the two groups recruited different frontal regions, with the bilinguals relying more on areas associated with language processing. These examples point to the need to include other levels of analysis in conjunction with behavioral observation to detect aspects of performance that may diverge even when observable behavior remains constant.

The related notions of plasticity, adaptation, and compensation are central to understanding lifespan changes in cognitive processing. Brain plasticity underlies learning and it is clearly an aspect of development that does *not* first rise and then fall across the lifespan. Children are extremely efficient learners of new information but this general ability declines through adulthood and old age (Hultsch & Dixon, 1990). Nonetheless, learning is eminently possible at all ages, and much current research in aging is directed at exploring the limitations of this plasticity and investigating ways to optimize learning at different stages of life (Kramer, Larish, Weber, & Bardell, 1999; Schaie & Willis, 1986). We alluded earlier to neuroimaging studies that have shown bilateral activations in older adults during episodic memory retrieval—cognitive operations that are predominantly localized in the right hemisphere in younger adults (e.g., Cabeza, 2002). Such findings are often interpreted as signaling compensatory brain mechanisms, but in our view a simpler account is that the bilaterality reflects a reversion to a less complex manner of functioning, given such age-related changes as demyelination, cell loss, and loss of connectivity. More generally, although human optimism urges us to believe that all change is for the better, a more cautious view suggests that

many of the neurological changes associated with aging may not be biologically intended or evolutionarily selected, but rather reflect optimal ways for the neural machinery to function given the reduced state of its component parts.

On a related point, it may be important to distinguish between biological compensation and social compensation in aging. While biological compensation may reflect less efficient or less well-coordinated neural components, social compensation may reflect more truly compensatory age-related changes in preferences, goals, and motives (Isaacowitz, Charles, & Carstensen, 2000; Staudinger & Pasupathi, 2000). Age-related changes in cognition at both ends of the developmental spectrum should be construed within a framework delineating a set of goals and values. There may also be compensatory activities that are reasonably classifiable as cognitive, such as wearing glasses and hearing aids to compensate for declining sensory efficiency and leaving Post-it notes on the fridge or computer to compensate for memory failures. The richness and complexity of this topic is well covered in a collection of chapters on age-related compensation edited by Dixon and Bäckman (1995).

In conclusion, questions of what develops and what declines across the lifespan form the subject matter of the present book. Perhaps our main point in setting the scene for the subsequent chapters is that these questions must be answered in the context of specific levels of analysis and description. What seems like a smoothly continuous rise and fall of performance at one level may break down into a variety of different underlying cognitive and neurological mechanisms at other levels. In our view no one level is more correct or has greater reality than any other; rather, any final theory of lifespan development will have to show how variables at one level map onto variables at adjacent levels. Our hope is that the present attempt to initiate a dialogue between researchers in the cognitive development and cognitive aging fields will illuminate the mechanisms of development and decline and illustrate the complex ways in which development and aging are related.

References

Baddeley, A. D. (1993). Working memory or working attention? In A. Baddeley & L. Weiskrantz (Eds.), *Attention: Selection, awareness and control* (pp. 152–170). New York: Oxford University Press.

Baddeley, A., & Hitch, G. (1974). Working memory. In G. Bower (Ed.), *The psychology of learning and motivation* (pp. 47–90). New York: Academic Press.

Baltes, P. B., Cornelius, S. W., Spiro, A., Nesselroade, J. R., & Willis, S. L. (1980). Integration versus differentiation of fluid/crystallized intelligence in old age. *Developmental Psychology, 6,* 625–635.

Baltes, P. B., & Lindenberger, U. (1997). Emergence of a powerful connection between sensory and cognitive functions across the adult life span: A new window to the study of cognitive aging? *Psychology and Aging, 12,* 12–21.

Baltes, P. B., Lindenberger, U., & Staudinger, U. M. (1998). Life-span theory in developmental psychology. In W. Damon (Ed.-in-Chief) & R. M. Lerner (Vol. Ed.), *Handbook of child psychology: Vol. 1. Theoretical models of human development* (pp. 1029–1041). New York: Wiley.

Baltes, P.B., & Smith, J. (2004). Lifespan psychology: From developmental contextualism to developmental biocultural co-constructivism. *Research on Human Development, 1,* 123–144.

Baltes, P. B., Staudinger, U. M., Maercker, A., & Smith, J. (1995). People nominated as wise: A comparative study of wisdom-related knowledge. *Psychology and Aging, 10,* 155–166.

Berk, L. E. (2000). *Child development.* Needham Heights, MA: Allyn & Bacon.

Bialystok, E., Craik, F.I.M., Grady, C., Chau, W., Ishii, R., Gunji, A., & Pantev, C. (2005). Effect of bilingualism on cognitive control in the Simon task: Evidence from MEG. *NeuroImage, 24,* 40–49.

Birren, J. E., & Schroots, J. F. (1996). History, concepts, and theory. In J. E. Birren & K. W. Schaie (Eds.), *Handbook of the psychology of aging* (pp. 2–23). San Diego: Academic Press.

Brainerd, C. J., & Reyna, V. F. (1990). Gist is the grist: fuzzy-trace theory and the new intuitionism. *Developmental Review, 10,* 3–47.

Brown, R. (1958). How shall a thing be called? *Psychological Review, 65,* 14–21.

Bruner, J. (1983). *Child's talk: Learning to use language.* New York: W.W. Norton.

Cabeza, R. (2002). Hemispheric asymmetry reduction in older adults. *Psychology and Aging, 17,* 85–100.

Carey, S. (1985). *Conceptual change in childhood.* Cambridge, MA: MIT Press.

Casey, B. J., Thomas, K. M., Davidson, M. C., Kunz, K., & Franzen, P. L. (2002). Dissociating striatal and hippocampal function developmentally with a stimulus-response compatibility task. *The Journal of Neuroscience, 22,* 8647–8652.

Cerella, J. (1985). Information-processing rates in the elderly. *Psychological Bulletin, 98,* 67–83.

Chi, M. (1978). Knowledge structures and memory development. In R. S. Siegler (Ed.), *Children's thinking: What develops?* (pp. 73–96). Hillsdale, NJ: Lawrence Erlbaum Associates.

Clark, E. V. (1993). *The lexicon in acquisition.* New York: Cambridge University Press.

Cohen, G., & Burke, D. M. (1993). Memory for proper names: A review. *Memory, 1,* 249–263.

Colcombe, S. J., Kramer, A. F., Erickson, K.I., & Scalf, R. (in press). The implications of cortical recruitment and brain morphology for individual differences in cognitive performance in aging humans. *Psychology and Aging.*

Cowan, N. (1999). An embedded-processes model of working memory. In A. Miyake & P. Shah (Eds.), *Models of working memory* (pp. 62–101). New York: Cambridge University Press.

Craik, F. I. M. (1983). On the transfer of information from temporary to permanent memory. *Philosophical Transactions of the Royal Society of London Series B-Biological Sciences, B302,* 341–359.

Craik, F. I. M. (1986). A functional account of age differences in memory. In F. Klix & H. Hagendorf (Eds.), *Human memory and cognitive capabilities, mechanisms, and performances* (pp. 409–422). Amsterdam: Elsevier.

Craik, F.I.M. (2002). Human memory and aging. In L. Bäckman & C. von Hofsten (Eds.), *Psychology at the turn of the millennium* (pp. 261–280). Hove, UK: Psychology Press.

Craik, F.I.M., & Jennings, J. M. (1992). Human memory. In F.I.M. Craik & T. A. Salthouse (Eds.), *The handbook of aging and cognition* (pp. 51–110). Hillsdale, NJ: Lawrence Erlbaum Associates.

Dempster, F. N. (1992). The rise and fall of the inhibitory mechanism: Toward a unified theory of cognitive development and aging. *Developmental Review, 12,* 45–75.

Diamond, A. (2002). Normal development of prefrontal cortex from birth to young adulthood: Cognitive functions, anatomy and biochemistry. In D. T. Stuss & R. T. Knight (Eds.), *Principles of frontal lobe function* (pp. 466–503). London: Oxford University Press.

Dixon, R. A., & Bäckman, L. (1995). *Compensating for psychological deficits and declines.* Mahwah, NJ: Lawrence Erlbaum Associates.

Dixon, R. A., Hultsch, D. F., Simon, E. W., & von Eye, A. (1984). Verbal ability and text structure effects on adult age differences in text recall. *Journal of Verbal Learning and Verbal Behavior, 23,* 569–578.

Engle, R. W., & Kane, M. J. (2004). Executive attention, working memory capacity and a two-factor theory of cognitive control. In B. Ross (Ed.), *The psychology of learning and motivation, 44,* 145–199. New York: Elsevier.

Gogtay, N., Giedd, J. N., Lusk, L., Hayashi, K. M., Greenstein, D., Vaituzis, A. C., Nugent, T. F., Hermon, D. H., Clasen, L. S., Toga, A.W., Rapoport, J. L., & Thompson, P. M. (2004). Dynamic mapping of human cortical development during childhood through early adulthood. *Proceedings of the National Academy of Sciences USA, 101*, 8174–8179.

Grady, C. L., McIntosh, A. R., Horwitz, B., Maisog, J. M., Ungerleider, L. G., Metis, M. J., Pietrini, P., Schapiro, M. B., & Haxby, J. V. (1995). Age-related reduction in human recognition memory due to impaired encoding. *Science, 269*, 218–221.

Hasher, L., & Zacks, R. T. (1979). Automatic and effortful processes in memory. *Journal of Experimental Pscyhology: General, 108*, 356–388.

Hasher, L. & Zacks, R. T. (1988). Working memory, comprehension, and aging: A review and a new view. In G. Bower (Ed.), *The psychology of learning and motivation* (Vol. 22, pp. 193–225). New York: Academic Press.

Hasher, L., Zacks, R. T., & May, C. P. (1999). Inhibitory control, circadian arousal, and age. In D. Gopher & A. Koriat (Eds.), *Attention and performance XVII. Cognitive regulation of performance: Interaction of theory and application* (pp. 653–675). Cambridge, MA: MIT Press.

Hommel, B., Li, K. Z., & Li, S. (2004). Visual search across the life span. *Developmental Psychology, 40*, 545–558.

Horn, J. (1994). Theory of fluid and crystallized intelligence. In R. J. Sternberg (Ed.), *Encyclopedia of intelligence* (Vol. 1, pp. 443–451). New York: Macmillan.

Hultsch, D., & Dixon, R. A. (1990). Learning and memory in aging. In J. E. Birren & K. W. Schaie (Eds.), *Handbook of the psychology of aging* (3rd ed., pp. 258–274). New York: Academic Press.

Isaacowitz, D. M., Charles, S. T., & Carstensen, L. L. (2000). Emotion and cognition. In F.I.M. Craik & T. A. Salthouse (Eds.), *The handbook of aging and cognition* (2nd ed., pp. 593–631). Mahwah, NJ: Lawrence Erlbaum Associates.

James, L. E. (2004). Meeting Mr. Farmer versus meeting a farmer: Specific effects of aging on learning proper names. *Psychology and Aging, 19*, 515–522.

Kail, R. (1991). Developmental change in speed of processing during childhood and adolescence. *Psychological Bulletin, 109*, 490–501.

Karmiloff-Smith, A. (1992). *Beyond modularity: A developmental perspective on cognitive science.* Cambridge, MA: MIT Press.

Kinsbourne, M. (1980). Attentional dysfunctions and the elderly: Theoretical models and research perspectives. In L.W. Poon, J. L. Fozard, L. S. Cermak, D. Arenberg & L. W. Thompson (Eds.), *New directions in memory and aging* (pp. 113–129). Hillsdale, NJ: Lawrence Erlbaum Associates.

Kramer, A. F., Larish, J. F., Weber, T. A., & Bardell, L. (1999). Training for executive control: Task coordination strategies and aging. In D. Gopher & A. Koriat (Eds.), *Attention and Performance: XVII* (pp. 617–652). Cambridge, MA: MIT Press..

Lhermitte, F., Pillon, B., & Serdaru, M. (1986). Human autonomy and the frontal lobes I: Imitation and utilization behavior, a neuropsychological study of 75 patients. *Annals of Neurology, 19*, 326–334.

Li, S. C., Lindenberger, U., Hommel, B., Aschersleben, G., Prinz, W., & Baltes, P. B. (2004). Life span transformations in the couplings among intellectual abilities and constituent cognitive processes. *Psychological Science, 15*, 155–163.

Light, L. L. (1992). The organization of memory in old age. In F.I.M. Craik & T. A. Salthouse (Eds.), *The handbook of aging and cognition* (pp. 111–165). Hillsdale, NJ: Lawrence Erlbaum Associates.

Macnamara, J. (1982). *Names of things: A study of human learning.* Cambridge, MA: MIT Press.

Maylor, E. A. (1997). Proper name retrieval in old age: Converging evidence against disproportionate impairment. *Aging, Neuropsychology, and Cognition, 4*, 211–226.

McIntosh, A. R., Sekuler, A. B., Penpeci, C., Rajah, M. N., Grady, C. L., Sekuler, R., & Bennett, P. J. (1999). Recruitment of unique neural systems to support visual memory in normal aging. *Current Biology, 9*, 1275–1278.

McIntyre, J. S., & Craik, F.I.M. (1987). Age differences in memory for item and source information. *Canadian Journal of Psychology, 41*, 175–192.

Naveh-Benjamin, M., Craik, F.I.M., Guez, J., & Kreuger, S. (2005). Divided attention in younger and older adults: Effects of strategy and relatedness on memory performance and secondary task costs. *Journal of Experimental Psychology: Learning, Memory and Cognition, 31*, 520–537.

Park, D. C., & Gutchess, A. H. (2004). Long-term memory and aging: A cognitive neuroscience perspective. In R. Cabeza, L. Nyberg, & D. C. Park (Eds.), *Cognitive neuroscience of aging: Linking cognitive and cerebral aging* (pp. 218–245). New York: Oxford University Press.

Park, D. C., Polk, T. A., Park, R., Minear, M., Savage, A., & Smith, M. R. (2004). Aging reduces neural specialization in ventral visual cortex. *Proceedings of the National Academy of Sciences USA, 101*, 13091–13095.

Piaget, J. (1954). *The construction of reality in the child.* New York: Basic Books.

Piaget, J. (1959). *The language and thought of the child.* London: Routledge & Kegan Paul.

Piaget, J., & Inhelder, B. (1958). *The growth of logical thinking from childhood to adolescence.* New York: Basic Books.

Raz, N. (2000). Aging of the brain and its impact on cognitive performance: Integration of structural and functional findings. In F.I.M Craik & T. A. Salthouse (Eds.), *The Handbook of Aging and Cognition* (2nd ed., pp. 1–90). Mahwah, NJ: Lawrence Erlbaum Associates.

Raz, N., Gunning, F. M., Head, D., Dupuis, J. H., McQuain, J. M., Briggs, S. D., Thornton, A. E., Loken, W. J., & Acker, J. D. (1997). Selective aging of human cerebral cortex observed in vivo: Differential vulnerability of the prefrontal gray matter. *Cerebral Cortex, 7,* 268–282.

Rogoff, B. (1990). *Apprenticeship in thinking: Cognitive development in social context.* New York: Oxford University Press.

Salthouse, T. A. (1996). The processing speed theory of adult age differences in cognition. *Psychological Review, 103,* 403–428.

Schacter, D. L., Kaszniak, A. W., Kihlstrom, J. F., & Valdiserri, M. (1991). The relation between source memory and aging. *Psychology and Aging, 6,* 559–568.

Schaie, K. W., & Willis, S. L. (1986). Can intellectual decline in the elderly be reversed? *Developmental Psychology, 22,* 223–232.

Shaffer, D. R., Wood, E., & Willoughby, T. (2002). *Developmental psychology: Childhood and adolescence.* Toronto: Thomson.

Siegler, R. S. (1978). The origins of scientific reasoning. In R. S. Siegler (Ed.), *Children's thinking: What develops?* (pp. 109–149). Hillsdale, NJ: Lawrence Erlbaum Associates.

Spencer, W. D., & Raz, N. (1995). Differential effects of aging on memory for content and context: A Meta-Analysis. *Psychology and Aging, 10,* 527–539.

Staudinger, U. M., & Pasupathi, M. (2000). Life-span perspectives on self, personality, and social cognition. In F.I.M Craik & T. A. Salthouse (Eds.), *The handbook of aging and cognition* (2nd ed., pp. 633–688). Mahwah, NJ: Lawrence Erlbaum Associates.

Trick, L., & Enns, J. (1998). Life span changes in attention: The visual search task. *Cognitive Development, 13,* 369–386.

Vygotsky, L. S. (1978). *Mind in society: The development of higher psychological processes.* Cambridge, MA: Harvard University Press.

Williams, B., Ponesse, J., Schachar, R., Logan, G. D., & Tannock, R. (1999). Development of inhibitory control across the life span. *Developmental Psychology, 25,* 205–213.

Zelazo, P. D., Muller, U., Frye, D., & Marcovitch, S. (2003). The development of executive function in early childhood. *Monographs of the Society for Research in Child Development, 68,* Serial No. 274.

2

Neural Bases of Cognitive Development

Margot J. Taylor

At birth an infant's brain and central nervous system contain all the components found in an adult brain, just as the newborn's body has all the parts in the right places, but the growth and development over infancy and childhood are as remarkable for the brain as for the body. Understanding the development of brain structure and function is critical to understanding the development of cognitive abilities. In this chapter I will first review the basic physiological maturation of the brain and then link these changes with some examples of cognitive development.

PHYSIOLOGICAL MEASURES
OF BRAIN DEVELOPMENT

At full-term birth, an infant's brain is about 300–350 grams, 15% of body weight. Over the first year of life the brain weight more than doubles, largely accounted for by a doubling of the hemispheric surface. The adult cortical surface area is reached within the sec-

ond year of life. Brain growth is then slower over childhood, but continues until late adolescence when it achieves the adult weight of between 1350 g and 1500 g (approximately 3% of body weight). Thus, the brain size increases by a factor of 4 or 5, yet all the neurons and glial cells ($\sim$ 10 billion (10^9) neurons and 10^{12} glial cells) are present and neuronal migration is completed at birth. This remarkable augmentation in size and volume is due to myelination and synaptogenesis.

In adults the brain consumes 20% of the body's oxygen. During infancy the metabolic needs of the brain increase dramatically after birth, being at least double that of adults' in the first years of life and reaching a maximum of 50% of the body's oxygen around 6 years of age (Morgan & Gibson, 1991). There is subsequently a plateau period over childhood and then a gradual decrease until adulthood. These phases are linked with synaptogenesis and with the proliferation of arborization in early childhood, the high plateau period reflecting a critical period when synaptic excess and a high rate of connectivity is seen, related to the acquiring of skills and the forming of stable synaptic connections. Starting in pre-adolescence and continuing during adolescence, when synaptic growth is replaced by synaptic pruning, the metabolic needs decline. Maturational changes are also seen in relation to neural receptors such as the GABAA complex, which includes the receptors for GABA, the most common inhibitory neurotransmitter in the brain. Across brain regions, these receptors are maximal at the youngest age tested (2 years of age) and decrease exponentially until adulthood. This is in contrast to glucose metabolism levels that are highest from 4–10 years and show regional variation that correlates positively with synaptic density (Chugani, 1998). The GABAA changes are not uniform, with the visual cortex and medial temporal lobe structures showing larger decreases than basal ganglia and anterior cortical regions (Chugani et al., 2001); only the decline in synaptic density in the visual cortex parallels the GABAA receptor decrease with age. As with myelination and glucose metabolism (Yakolev & Lecours, 1967; Chugani, Phelps & Mazziotta, 1987), subcortical structures reach adult GABAA values earlier than the cortex. Various metabolic levels also covary with synaptic development or progressive increases in white matter over childhood (e.g., Horska et al., 2002).

MYELINATION—WHITE MATTER MATURATION

Myelin, a fatty sheath that surrounds and insulates a large proportion of both peripheral and central nerve fibers, allows rapid conduction through the nervous system. The process of myelination has long been linked with cognitive development and is a clearly identifiable, quantitative change in the brain that occurs over a protracted period.

Although all neurons and brain regions undergo myelination, they do not develop at the same rate or at the same time. Myelination of the spinal cord and lower brain stem structures starts early in the prenatal period (20 to 26 weeks gestational age), while more rostral subcortical structures (e.g., middle cerebellar peduncle) begin closer to term. Myelin is barely present in cortical regions in the newborn, and even in the major cortical fiber tracts (e.g., corpus callosum, optic radiation) the myelination process starts only at or after term (for a review see Majovski, 1989) and can continue until the end of childhood (Rajapakse et al., 1996). Once myelination starts, it can be completed

rapidly, in a matter of weeks, or can extend over periods of many years. The rate of myelination varies with brain regions (see figure 1 from Yakolev & Lecours, 1967), which explains why it is a valid, albeit crude index of regional brain development (Konner, 1991). Magnetic resonance imaging (MRI) now provides excellent measures of white matter maturation, reflecting the rapid early changes, but also the extensive slower changes throughout adolescence (Paus et al., 2001), with steady increases in white matter density and volume.

Basic sensory development is relatively rapid, and the sensory pathways are among the first to myelinate. For the primary sensory system in humans, vision, the sensory fibers are largely myelinated by 1 year of life, while the acoustic radiation is not myelinated until at least 3 years of age, linked with the protracted development of language in humans (Brody, Kinney, Kloman, & Gilles, 1987; Paus et al., 1999). The somatosensory pathways mature over longer periods, the upper limb before the lower limb (as reflected by the development of fine finger movements before walking). Myelination occurs from caudal to rostral structures; brain stem portions of the pathways that support early reflexes mature prior to the cortical radiations, which in turn precede the myelination of the primary cortical regions. The classically considered association areas in the parietal cortex myelinate throughout the teenage years, with the frontal regions continuing to show increases in myelination into at least the third decade of life (Bartzokis et al., 2001).

Unmyelinated pathways function, but with incomplete or without myelination their maintainable rate of firing is slower, conduction is slower, refractory period is longer, synchronization is reduced, and cross talk is higher. All of these effects are typical of what can be seen in neurophysiological measures of sensory-evoked potentials in young infants (Taylor, 1993a), and are consistent with the behavior of young infants and children before they develop the motor coordination and speed of processing typical of older children.

GRAY MATTER MATURATION

The cortical layers are formed by 6 months gestational age, although final differentiation continues throughout childhood and well into adulthood. The cortical layers that receive primary afferent input and give rise to efferent fibers (layers 4, 5, 6) have a more rapid maturation than layers implicated in higher cognitive function (layers 2, 3; Huttenlocher & Dabholkar, 1997). In adults all cortical areas have similar synaptic density; however, as seen with myelination, the development of gray matter volumes varies by region and changes in a nonlinear fashion with age. Most brain areas studied show an increase in gray matter over pre-adolescence and adolescence with peaks seen at around 11.5 years for frontal areas, 11 years for parietal areas, and 16.5 years for temporal regions before the decrease due to pruning starts (Giedd et al., 1999). Occipital gray matter did not show a decline before 22 years of age. Sowell, Thompson, Tessner, and Toga (2001) also reported continued changes over adolescence in the dorsal areas of the frontal lobes and in the temporo-occipital junction, with reductions in gray matter density. They found cortical thinning; decrease in gray matter was particularly marked in the frontal regions, which, associated with synaptic pruning, leaves more efficient connections. Across these and earlier studies, the overall decrease in gray matter with age is balanced by the increase in white matter with myelination, producing no loss of brain volume between adolescence and adulthood.

Sex differences are consistently found in developmental studies, with relatively less loss of gray matter in girls and relatively greater white matter development in boys (De Bellis et al., 2001; Giedd, Castellanos, Rajapakse, Vaituzis & Rapoport, 1997; Rajapakse et al., 1996). There are also structural developmental differences, with boys having relatively larger amygdala and putamen, for example, and girls having larger caudate and hippocampal nuclei (Caviness, Kennedy, Richelme, Radamacher, & Filipek, 1996; Giedd et al., 1996; Sowell, Trauner, Gamst, & Jernigan, 2002) that may be linked with the pubertal hormonal influences on brain maturational processes (De Bellis et al., 2001). A number of these papers have suggested that the sexually dimorphic patterns of brain development, such as greater loss of gray matter in boys, could be associated with psychiatric disorders (e.g., schizophrenia) that have adolescent onsets with differential sex ratios (for a review see Durston et al., 2001). Sex differences in cognitive skills, such as generally higher verbal skills in girls and spatial skills in boys, have also been linked recently with differential brain regional development (Yurgelun-Todd, Killgore & Cintron, 2003; Blanton et al., 2004), as seen in adults (Gur et al., 1999).

FUNCTIONAL MEASURES OF NEURAL DEVELOPMENT OVER CHILDHOOD

Measures of brain structure in children are limited, as they classically came from postmortem studies. More recently, structural neuroimaging techniques have provided confirmatory and additional information of brain structure that is being increasingly correlated with behavioral measures (see Thomas, 2003, for a review). Neuroimaging studies using event-related potentials (ERPs) have been in the literature for several decades now, being the most adapted to developmental studies. The latency of the components reflects speed of processing (and is linked with myelination and efficiency of neuronal transmission) while amplitudes of the components are associated with cortical activation, with the suggestion that larger activation likely reflects greater or more widespread neuronal involvement. There is a recent upsurge in the use of these methods for investigating cognitive development, in part because of more sophisticated analyses that can determine the spatial location of the electrical sources. There is also a generally increased interest in developmental issues in the neurosciences, as it becomes obvious that to understand our capacities as adults we need to understand how they develop, from birth through to old age. Other neuroimaging studies are only more recently being completed in children, using such methods as positron emission tomography (PET), and particularly structural and functional MRI. Although these neuroimaging techniques provide excellent structural information, in the functional studies good spatial localization, the timing of these activations is missing. A major feature of cognitive development is increased speed of processing, which occurs ubiquitously but far from uniformly, and changes in the localization of function. The combination of techniques providing spatial as well as temporal data is producing tremendous advances in our understanding of lifelong developmental changes in the neural substrates of cognition.

EXPERIENCE AND DEVELOPMENTAL CHANGES

Although myelination can be affected by experience, it generally follows a genetically programmed course of development. In contrast, the development in gray matter is largely dependent upon experience. With synaptic proliferation over the neonatal and early childhood years, there is an excess of synaptic connections. This exuberant growth is an adaptive mechanism; as with the development of skills and capacities over childhood, the neural networks that are used become stable while the synaptic connections that are not used disappear and lose their function by adulthood. This produces the adaptability or plasticity of the child's brain, which allows the acquisition of skills important for that child depending on his or her environment, and the addition of further skills over childhood as needs demand. Plasticity also enables the restoration of cognitive function subsequent to brain injury (e.g., Chugani, Muller, & Chugani, 1996; Hertz-Pannier et al., 2002), and is seen as underlying the development of exceptional skills, such as early musical virtuosity (Pantev et al., 2003). Impairments of neuronal plasticity—the synaptic overgrowth and subsequent pruning—are the basis of devastating neurodevelopmental disorders such as Rett syndrome (Johnston, 2001).

It is generally assumed that, because of the plasticity seen in normal development—the capacity for learning many complex skills and talents over childhood—recovery after brain injury is greater in children than in adults. However, early studies that reported plasticity of recovery of function in children used primarily outcome measures of language and did not adequately separate out age and etiologies (see Ewing-Cobbs, Barnes, & Fletcher, 2003, for a review). The commonly believed dictum that the younger the age at the time of brain injury the better does not always hold. For example, pre-school children who suffer traumatic brain injury (as from a motor vehicle accident) that produces diffuse brain insult show greater long-term impairment in language skills and executive functions than school-age children who suffer comparable injury (Slomine et al., 2002; Levin, 2003). This is suggested to be due to skills in the midst of a rapid developmental period being more susceptible to brain damage than skills that are more established (Ewing-Cobbs et al., 2003). Children with early brain damage, congenital brain malformations, or cognitive difficulties not due to specific brain injury (such as specific language impairment (SLI)) show differing patterns of cognitive deficits and can show long-term dysfunction (e.g., Bishop, 2000; Vargha-Khadem, Gadian, & Mishkin, 2001; Ewing-Cobbs et al., 2003). In contrast, children with focal brain insults generally show remarkable recovery back to performance levels within normal range. These are the cases that have

provided the basis for the model of plasticity of function in children. It is also notable that language development appears unaffected by early focal brain damage, regardless of the side of brain lesion (see a special issue of *Brain and Language*, 88, 2004, for a series of articles on plasticity and development of language). These studies demonstrate impressive plasticity in children in the circumstance of focal brain injury, but a more mixed picture is seen with diffuse injury or diffuse dysfunction.

There is an interesting comparison of neural dysfunction in development and in aging with the frontal-striatal circuit. This circuit, which is implicated in deficits in executive function and attention in elderly adults (Buckner, Head, & Lustig, Chapter 3, this volume), is strongly linked to attention deficit hyperactivity disorder (ADHD) in children. ADHD is the most common psychiatric developmental disturbance, most frequent in boys, and a number of studies have shown smaller basal ganglia (caudate, putamen, and globus pallidus) and smaller frontal lobes in ADHD boys (e.g., Aylward et al., 1996; Overmeyer et al., 2001; Sowell et al., 2003). Functional neuroimaging studies also show deficits in frontal-striatal activation patterns in ADHD (e.g., Durston et al., 2003; Yeo et al., 2003), which are most often reported to be right-sided, suggesting right frontal-striatal dysfunction. The effects are unlikely to be due to maturational delay (Durston et al., 2003), as larger gray matter volumes are seen in younger children and ADHD children have both gray and white matter decreases relative to age-matched controls. The presence of differing brain anomalies for boys and girls with ADHD (Baving, Laucht, & Schmidt, 1999; Yeo et al., 2003) further suggests an underlying developmental disturbance that interacts with the differing patterns of neural developmental by sex. This disorder, in the context of the current book, raises several intriguing questions. As the symptoms of ADHD tend to decrease with age, is this an example of compensation? Are children who have suffered ADHD in childhood more likely to experience the cognitive deficits associated with frontal-striatal deterioration with aging, or are they less likely to owing to developing alternate networks or strategies? Anomalies in this circuit produce atypical and difficult behavioral patterns in children and decline in this network is one of the major causes of cognitive dysfunction in normal aging; the combined study of these two populations may provide valuable insights into both processes.

FUNCTIONAL CHANGES
WITH DEVELOPMENT

The early maturation of the senses is critical as the development of cognitive processes relies on the raw material of the sensory stimuli. ERP studies of sensory function show that the basic sensory pathways are mature in the first 2 to 6 years of life (Taylor, 1993a). More interesting, however, is the protracted development of the cognitive functions related to attention, interpretation, and memory of incoming sensory information. I will review briefly two areas of cognitive processing—face processing and language—as examples of relations between neuronal and cognitive development.

NEURAL CORRELATES OF THE
DEVELOPMENT OF FACE PROCESSING

The visual system is the most rapidly developing of the sensory systems, with remarkable increases in visual abilities over the first years of life that correlate with its rapid myelination and synaptogenesis. The most critical visual stimulus for our social interactions is the human face; from birth, infants prefer faces to other objects and acquire knowledge of faces quickly (Johnson & de Haan, 2001). Nevertheless, the amount of information that a face contains is considerable, and the skill in recognizing hundreds of faces as well as subtle expressions takes most of childhood to acquire (for reviews see Chung & Thompson, 1995; de Haan, Johnson, & Halit, 2003; Taylor, Batty, & Itier, 2004). The initial ERP studies of face processing demonstrated the sensitivity of the N170 component to faces (Bentin, Allison, Puce, Perez, & McCarthy, 1996), while later studies have examined both the P1 and the N170, which reflect, respectively, early stages of holistic, or global processing, and configural processing of faces (Itier & Taylor 2002; Taylor, 2002). N170 putative precursors are seen in young infants, with sources in occipital and lateral posterior temporal cortices, and the developmental pattern reflects a gradual specialization of face processing toward upright human faces (de Haan et al., 2003). The rapid, global processing of upright compared to inverted faces is seen on the P1 from 4 years of age (Taylor, Edmonds, McCarthy, & Allison, 2001), while the sensitivity to the configural manipulation of inversion is seen at 12 months of age (de Haan et al., 2003; Halit et al., 2003) and in both implicit

and explicit tasks in childhood (e.g., Taylor et al., 2001; Itier & Taylor, 2004a, b). The sources of these components arise from the ventral visual pathways, with contributions from the posterior and inferior temporal as well as from the medial and superior temporal regions (Allison, Puce, Spencer, & McCarthy, 1999; McCarthy, Puce, Belger, & Allison, 1999; Haxby, Hoffman, & Gobbini, 2000; Itier & Taylor, 2004c), with typically greater activation from the right hemisphere areas. The sensitivity of the ERP components to faces from infancy suggests that the neural networks involved in face processing are present early in life, although the relative implication of contributing regions likely varies as a function of the type of facial stimuli and age (Taylor et al., 2001, 2004). However, these neural networks, particularly in the right hemisphere, require appropriate experience to develop normally, as even an early period of impairment can have long-lasting effects on face processes (Le Grand, Mondloch, Maurer, & Brent, 2003).

The latency of the face-sensitive ERP components decreases steadily across childhood, long past the myelination of the primary visual system, and reflects the continuing myelination in the ventral pathway and association areas. Decreases in ERP amplitudes are thought to index a reduction in cortical activation; as the child's experience and skill increase, less neuronal involvement is required, consistent with greater efficiency and stability in neuronal networks with synaptic pruning. The decrease in P1 amplitude with age suggests that the holistic processing of faces matures early and becomes steadily more restricted in cortical activation from age 4 through to adulthood. In contrast, the N170 first decreases in amplitude during childhood and then increases in adolescence, likely due to several more dispersed functions gradually merging with development (Taylor et al., 2004). This is supported by distributional changes with age in the ERP components, as well as by a recent fMRI study. Passarotti et al. (2003) showed that with a face-identification task the children showed much more extensive fMRI activation than adults, which nevertheless included the principal areas activated to faces in the adult group. Thus, for children there is greater cortical involvement for a task, which with age contracts down to the more focal activations seen in adults. Task performance is not necessarily disparate between children and adults, but the cortical areas recruited alter. This process appears to continue throughout the lifespan, as in older adults the areas activated for face processing also differ from those seen in young adults; older adults recruit greater prefrontal activity in more difficult tasks than do young adults (Grady, 2002), while reduced activation has been reported for more posterior and subcortical areas in older than in younger adults (Iidaka et al., 2002).

As the frontal lobes show the most long-lasting myelin changes with age, they are frequently targeted for developmental investigations. Working memory tasks show large age effects (e.g., Cycowitz, 2000; Thomas et al., 1999) that correlate with behavioral performance (Klingberg, Forssberg, & Westerberg, 2002), although differences among types of processing—for example, visually or verbally mediated—are already present in young children (Kwon, Reiss, & Menon, 2002). Thus, studies reflect increased activation in frontal and parietal-frontal networks with age, which is suggested to index greater capacity and stability for working memory tasks, but not necessarily qualitative changes in task performance.

Frontal lobe involvement in the recognition of faces has also been investigated over childhood; again, although strategies do not appear to differ with age, there are continued and significant changes in measures of frontal processing that are task sensitive (Itier & Taylor, 2004a, b). As is seen in the sensory systems, function precedes myelination; the frontal lobes myelinate until the third decade of life yet mnemonic strategies can be in place from 8 years of age. Children perform more poorly than adults but appear to process faces similarly (Itier & Taylor, 2004a; Kolb, Wilson, & Taylor, 1992).

Processing of emotions from facial expressions is critical to normal social development, with psychiatric disorders almost universally including an aspect of emotional dysfunction (Davidson & Slagter, 2000). As with other aspects of facial information, there is protracted development in the acquisition of adult levels of facial emotional processing (Kolb et al., 1992). An important correspondence between myelination and development of this behavior is seen between the rather late myelination of the limbic system (it starts after birth) and development of an understanding and use of emotions (Konner, 1991). Most aspects of the limbic tracts myelinate between the first and third year of life (Brody et al., 1987; Yakolev & Lecours, 1967). This pattern of myelination is linked with the onset of social smiling in the third month of life, critical for interpersonal relationships, and the development of attachment behavior

around 9–15 months of age. The understanding (not just imitating) of basic facial expressions is not in place until the third year of life, while the development of the short latency, automatic processing of facial emotions seen in adults (Batty & Taylor, 2003) is not evident in children until mid-teenage years (Batty & Taylor, in press), suggesting the need for extensive experience before the neural correlates of this aptitude develop. Subcortical activation of limbic structures with emotional face stimuli has been reported with fMRI studies (Thomas et al., 2001; Lobaugh, Gibson, & Taylor, 2004) in children in mid-childhood, demonstrating the presence of these aspects of the neural networks, consistent with the earlier maturation of caudal rather than rostral structures. As seen with the recognition of facial identity, where frontal activation shows adultlike patterns despite its physical immaturity, the frontal ERPs to emotional faces also show a similar pattern in children and adults (Batty & Taylor, in press).

Early in childhood there is a differentiation between negative and positive emotions, with longer latencies to negative expressions suggesting greater difficulty in their detection or processing. Aging adults also show poorer performance with detection of negative facial emotions (e.g., Phillips, MacLean, & Allen, 2002; Sullivan & Ruffman, 2004) that is independent of perceptual or cognitive abilities or the understanding of emotions. In children this is hypothesized to be due to less experience with the subtleties of emotional expressions and less exposure to negative expressions such as fear and sadness. In aging adults this decrease is linked with asymmetrical decreases in activation in the limbic system (Iidaka et al., 2002). Thus although the behavioral effects may be similar, the causal influences are believed to be disparate.

NEURAL CORRELATES OF THE DEVELOPMENT OF LANGUAGE SKILLS

As with face processing there is an early and strong predisposition for language in human infants, with evidence of early stages of acquisition starting at 3 months of age. The sensory developmental patterns of auditory processing show protracted changes through childhood, even for simple stimuli (e.g., Pang & Taylor, 2000; Ponton, Eggermont, Kwong, & Don, 2000). There are, however, few studies of early language acquisition. As with other fields of cognitive research, children from 1 to 3 years of age are the most difficult to study, as they usually prefer not to sit still and do not yet have the understanding to follow instructions for task performance.

ERP investigations of language have been completed in 13-, 17-, and 20-month-old infants assessing words that were either known or unknown (Mills & Neville, 1997). Clear differences in the ERPs, starting at 200 ms (N200) that were widespread bilaterally over the brain, were seen in the 13–17-month-olds between the recognized words and unknown words. By 20 months of age, differences between the toddler's known vocabulary and unknown words were also evident from the N200 wave, although the activations from known words were larger and localized to left temporal and parietal electrodes. This suggests widespread activation to language in the early stages of word acquisition, which very rapidly becomes more focal and precise. When the distributions were compared within the two age groups of children, as a function of when they started to talk, more localized (specialized) brain activity was associated with increased language comprehension. In 20-month-old children with left-sided focal brain lesions, who had normal-for-age language, the N200 showed the same sensitivity to known and unknown words, but over right hemisphere sites. Children with poor language abilities and left focal lesions had ERPs with delayed and bilaterally distributed components (Mills, Coffey-Corina, & Neville 1994). Thus, early ERP components (P100 and N200) to words appear to be sensitive to level of language acquisition as well as reflecting normal or atypical lateralization with age.

An interesting corollary to the lateralization of language to the left hemisphere is seen with deaf individuals who use sign language that relies on visual spatial location and movement, which in proficient signers also localizes to the left hemisphere. This argues for the central role of the left hemisphere for the underlying neurobiology of language, independent of the modality of the language (Neville & Bavelier, 1998).

Only a few studies have investigated normal language processing over childhood, despite its continued development at least through adolescence. In an fMRI study of verbal fluency, children from 8 years of age showed a much greater extent of activation than adults, but as seen with faces, the activation also included the primary areas seen typically in adults (Gaillard et al., 2000). The authors argued that the

children activated similar regions, but the more widespread activation still allowed formation of neural circuits for language and continuing plasticity even in mid-childhood.

The lateralization of language to the left hemisphere includes written language. Reading involves a network of brain regions (Pugh et al., 2000) including the left inferior frontal, inferior temporo-occipital, and parieto-temporal regions. These areas were activated in young children (6–8 years of age) learning to read; all but two were strongly left lateralized, suggesting similar neural networks in both beginning and adult readers (Gaillard, Balsamo, Ibrahim, Sachs, & Xu, 2003). ERP studies of reading-related tasks show larger amplitude over left than right hemisphere sites from 7 years of age (Taylor, 1993b) while more challenging reading tasks show increasing left lateralization with age (Holcomb, Coffey, & Neville, 1992; Taylor & Eals, 1996), suggesting continued specialization with age. Consistent with the infant work that suggests early lateralization for language function, the presence of left-lateralized reading activation in children from 6 and 7 years of age underlines the stability of this neural network in normal development. This makes its adaptability in brain-injured children all the more remarkable.

Like compensation in adulthood, compensation in childhood refers to skills using atypical cognitive strategies and/or atypical brain regions; but rather than being a strategy to maintain function with decreasing resources as for aging adults, in children it refers to the development of function. Compensation is seen systematically in developmental dyslexia, which includes increased activation in frontal and/or right hemisphere regions during reading, in attempts to compensate for the failure to engage the processes of the left posterior areas. Neuroimaging studies in dyslexia often show right-sided lateralization for reading. This suggests that the left hemisphere neural circuits normally used are dysfunctional, the strategies employed diverge to such an extent that the left hemisphere network is not recruited, or there is aberrant connectivity in the neural network for reading (see Démonet, Taylor, & Chaix, 2004, for a review). In dyslexic children anomalous lateralization can be reversed with remedial training (e.g., Papanicolaou et al., 2003), although studies have not yet explained why 10% of otherwise normal children need to invoke compensatory mechanisms to learn to read.

CHANGES IN BRAIN STRUCTURE AND
FUNCTION ACROSS THE LIFESPAN

Brain volume increases by a factor of at least 4 over childhood, but has no correlation with intelligence or with the maintenance of cognitive function in old age (Staff, Murray, Deary, & Whalley, 2004). Education and intellectual challenges, which are important factors in the development of neuronal networks and guide synaptic pruning, are factors that help protect against cognitive decline in old age. Neural networks are formed by experience over childhood, and Elman (1993) has argued that adultlike networks are not capable of acquiring some of the multifaceted abilities (in his example, language), but limited capacity systems that themselves develop with training are most appropriate for mastering these complex cognitive capacities. The development of these skills does not appear to be a finite process, as experience continues to have an effect on cognitive abilities and strategies through to old age. The cognitive function of language, for example, is a skill that can show continued development, as evidenced by writers and orators who often improve their abilities through to old age.

Over childhood there is generally an increasing specificity of function. For example, the widespread cortical activation seen in children to faces and language, and in visual search and response tasks, becomes more focal toward adulthood (Passarotti et al., 2003; Gaillard et al., 2000; Booth et al., 2003); amygdala activation to emotional stimuli decreases between children and adults (Thomas et al., 2001). However, there is regional variation in this, as is seen for most aspects of brain development: activation of the frontal and parietal lobes appears to increase with age, in both ERP and fMRI measures (Itier & Taylor, 2004b; Klingberg et al., 2002; Kwon et al., 2002). This suggests differential maturational curves as a function of the type of cognitive process; the more basic "essential" aspects of cognition activate large areas in early childhood and show increasing specialization with age, and thus one could speculate they would also have greater options of plasticity, while more abstract and mnemonic functions that require the associative and frontal cortical regions seem to show increased development and activation with age and experience into early adulthood.

In aging populations, memory and attention skills have been intensely studied, as they show some of the most marked changes with age, and thus considerable research has been devoted to frontal lobe function in the elderly (see Buckner et al., Chapter 3, this volume; Zacks & Hasher, Chapter 11, this volume). Neuroimaging studies have shown greater frontal and prefrontal activation in older adults when task performance is high. These changes are consistent with compensatory activation and an apparent decrease of specialization of function (Grady & Craik, 2000; Cabeza, Anderson, Locantore, & McIntosh, 2002; Cabeza et al., 2004) and alteration in cortical connectivity or strategies to maintain performance levels (Grady, McIntosh, & Craik, 2003). This suggests a level of brain plasticity that extends into old age, as these compensatory mechanisms appear similar to what is seen in developmental dyslexia, for example. This allows the speculation that developmental changes do not end in early or even mid-adulthood, but continue in different forms throughout the lifespan in normal aging. The remarkable capacities in childhood for the acquisition of skills and abilities are during an intense period of brain development, but more subtle modification of function is maintained throughout life in the cognitively active.

CONCLUSIONS

Brain maturational changes that are largely programmed (increases in brain size, myelination, synaptogenesis, etc.) underlie the basic developmental milestones, but other influences on brain development (experience, learning, lesions) are more critical in terms of cognitive development. The largest physical changes in the brain occur in the first years of life and vary significantly with brain region and functions, yet considerable physical maturation is evident through to the end of adolescence, and more subtle changes continue through adulthood. Associated cognitive development also occurs throughout the lifespan, with the greatest cognitive milestones in childhood, which reflect the changes in brain structure and functions. Cognitive processes show very protracted transformation, however, with early perceptual skills being in place much earlier than the complex utilization of the perceptual input, as seen in face processing and language, which continue to improve through adulthood. Cognitive function itself shapes the brain, as it is function that guides synaptic pruning, which in turns sculpts gray matter and modifies neural networks, allowing the refinement of skills and their adaptability over the lifespan.

References

Allison, T., Puce, A., Spencer, D. D., & McCarthy, G. (1999). Electrophysiological studies of human face perception. I: Potentials generated in occipito-temporal cortex by face and non-face stimuli. *Cerebral Cortex, 9*(5), 415–430.

Aylward, E. H., Reiss, A. L., Reader, M. J., Singer, H. S., Brown, J. E., & Denckla, M. B. (1996). Basal ganglia volumes in children with attention-deficit hyperactivity disorder. *Journal of Child Neurology, 11*(2), 112–115.

Bartzokis, G., Beckson, M., Lu, P. H., Nuechterlein, K. H., Edwards, N., & Mintz, J. (2001). Age-related changes in frontal and temporal lobe volumes in men: a magnetic resonance imaging study. *Archives of General Psychiatry, 58*(5), 461–465.

Batty, M., & Taylor, M. J. (2003). Early processing of the six basic facial emotional expressions. *Cognitive Brain Research, 17*(3), 613–620.

Batty, M. Taylor, M. J. (in press). Development of the perception of facial emotional expressions. Manuscript in preparation. *Developmental Science.*

Baving, L., Laucht, M., & Schmidt, M. H. (1999). Atypical frontal brain activation in ADHD: Preschool and elementary school boys and girls. *Journal of the American Academy of Child and Adolescent Psychiatry, 38*(11), 1363–1371.

Bentin, S., Allison, T., Puce, A., Perez, E., & McCarthy, G. (1996). Electrophysiological studies of face perception in humans. *Journal of Cognitive Neuroscience, 8*, 551–565.

Blanton, R. E., Levitt, J. G., Peterson, J. R., Fadale, D., Sporty, M. L., Lee, M., To, D., Mormino, E. C., Thompson, P. M., McCracken, J. T., & Toga, A. W. (2004). Gender differences in the left inferior frontal gyrus in normal children. *Neuroimage, 22*(2), 626–636.

Bishop, D. V. (2000). How does the brain learn language? Insights from the study of children with and without language impairment. *Developmental Medicine and Child Neurology, 42*(2), 133–142.

Booth, J. R., Burman, D. D., Meyer, J. R., Lei, Z., Trommer, B. L., Davenport, N. D., Li, W., Parrish, T. B., Gitelman, D. R., & Mesulam, M. M. (2003). Neural development of selective attention and response inhibition. *Neuroimage, 20*(2), 737–751.

Brody, B. A., Kinney, H. C., Kloman, A. S., & Gilles, F. H. (1987). Sequences of human post-natal myelination in human infancy. I. An autopsy study of myelination. *Journal of Neuropathology and Experimental Neurology, 46*, 283–301.

Cabeza, R., Anderson, N. D., Locantore, J. K., & McIntosh, A. R. (2002). Aging gracefully: compensatory brain activity in high-performing older adults. *Neuroimage, 17*(3), 1394–1402.

Cabeza, R., Daselaar, S. M., Dolcos, F., Prince, S. E., Budde, M., & Nyberg, L. (2004). Task-independent and task-specific age effects on brain activity during working memory, visual attention and episodic retrieval. *Cerebral Cortex, 14*(4), 364–375.

Caviness, V. S., Jr., Kennedy, D. N., Richelme, C., Rademacher, J., & Filipek, P. A. (1996). The human brain age 7–11 years: a volumetric analysis based on magnetic resonance images. *Cerebral Cortex, 6*(5), 726–736.

Chugani, D. C., Muzik, O., Juhasz, C., Janisse, J. J., Ager, J., & Chugani, H. T. (2001). Postnatal maturation of human GABAA receptors measured with positron emission tomography. *Annals of Neurology, 49*(5), 618–626.

Chugani, H. T. (1998). A critical period of brain development: studies of cerebral glucose utilization with PET. *Preventative Medicine, 27*(2), 184–188.

Chugani, H. T., Muller, R. A., & Chugani, D. C. (1996). Functional brain reorganization in children. *Brain Development, 18*(5), 347–356.

Chugani, H. T., Phelps, M. E., & Mazziotta, J. C. (1987). Positron emission tomography study of human brain functional development. *Annals of Neurology, 22*(4), 487–497.

Chung, M. S., & Thomson, D. M. (1995). Development of face recognition. *British Journal of Psychology, 86*(Pt 1), 55–87.

Cycowicz, Y. M. (2000). Memory development and event-related brain potentials in children. *Biological Psychology, 54*(1–3), 145–174.

Davidson, R. J., & Slagter, H. A. (2000). Probing emotion in the developing brain: Functional neuroimaging in the assessment of the neural substrates of emotion in normal and disordered children and adolescents. *Mental Retardation and Developmental Disabilities Research Review, 6*(3), 166–170.

De Bellis, M. D., Keshavan, M. S., Beers, S. R., Hall, J., Frustaci, K., Masalehdan, A., Noll, J., & Boring, A. M. (2001). Sex differences in brain maturation during childhood and adolescence. *Cerebral Cortex, 11*(6), 552–557.

de Haan, M., Johnson, M. H., & Halit, H. (2003). Development of face-sensitive event-related potentials during infancy: A review. *International Journal of Psychophysiology, 51*, 45–58.

Démonet, J.-F., Taylor, M. J., & Chaix, Y. (2004). Developmental dyslexia. *Lancet, 363*, 1451–1460.

Durston, S., Hulshoff Pol, H. E., Casey, B. J., Giedd, J. N., Buitelaar, J. K., & van Engeland, H. (2001). Anatomical MRI of the developing human brain: what have we learned? *Journal of the American*

Academy of Child and Adolescent Psychiatry, 40(9), 1012–1020.

Durston, S., Tottenham, N. T., Thomas, K. M., Davidson, M. C., Eigsti, I. M., Yang, Y., Ulug, A. M., & Casey, B. J. (2003). Differential patterns of striatal activation in young children with and without ADHD. *Biological Psychiatry, 53*(10), 871–878.

Elman, J. L. (1993). Learning and development in neural networks: The importance of starting small. *Cognition, 48*(1), 71–99.

Ewing-Cobbs, L., Barnes, M. A., & Fletcher, J. M. (2003). Early brain injury in children: development and reorganization of cognitive function. *Developmental Neuropsychology, 24*(2–3), 669–704.

Gaillard, W. D., Balsamo, L. M., Ibrahim, Z., Sachs, B. C., & Xu, B. (2003). fMRI identifies regional specialization of neural networks for reading in young children. *Neurology, 60*(1), 94–100.

Gaillard, W. D., Hertz-Pannier, L., Mott, S. H., Barnett, A. S., LeBihan, D., & Theodore, W. H. (2000). Functional anatomy of cognitive development: fMRI of verbal fluency in children and adults. *Neurology, 54*(1), 180–185.

Giedd, J. N., Blumenthal, J., Jeffries, N. O., Castellanos, F. X., Liu, H., Zijdenbos, A., Paus, T., Evans, A. C., & Rapoport, J. L. (1999). Brain development during childhood and adolescence: A longitudinal MRI study. *Nature Neuroscience, 2*(10), 861–863.

Giedd, J. N., Castellanos, F. X., Rajapakse, J. C., Vaituzis, A. C., & Rapoport, J. L. (1997). Sexual dimorphism of the developing human brain. *Progress in Neuropsychopharmacology and Biological Psychiatry, 21*(8), 1185–1201.

Giedd, J. N., Snell, J. W., Lange, N., Rajapakse, J. C., Casey, B. J., Kozuch, P. L., Vaituzis, A. C., Vauss, Y. C., Hamburger, S. D., Kaysen, D., & Rapoport, J. L. (1996). Quantitative magnetic resonance imaging of human brain development: ages 4–18. *Cerebral Cortex, 6*(4), 551–560.

Grady, C. L. (2002). Age-related differences in face processing: A meta-analysis of three functional neuroimaging experiments. *Canadian Journal of Experimental Psychology, 56*(3), 208–220.

Grady, C. L., & Craik, F. I. M. (2000). Changes in memory processing with age. *Current Opinion Neurobiology, 10*(2), 224–231.

Grady, C. L., McIntosh, A. R., & Craik, F. I. M. (2003). Age-related differences in the functional connectivity of the hippocampus during memory encoding. *Hippocampus, 13*(5), 572–586.

Gur, R. C., Turetsky, B. I., Matsui, M., Yan, M., Bilker, W., Hughett, P., & Gur, R. E. (1999). Sex differences in brain gray and white matter in healthy young adults: correlations with cognitive performance. *Journal of Neuroscience, 19*(10), 4065–4072.

Halit, H., de Haan, M., & Johnson, M. V. (2003). Cortical specialisation for face processing: face-sensitive event-related potential components in 3-and 12-month-old infants. *Neuroimage, 19*(3), 1180–1193.

Haxby, J. V., Hoffman, E. A., & Gobbini, M. I. (2000). The distributed human neural system for face perception. *Trends in Cognitive Science, 4*(6):223–233.

Hertz-Pannier, L., Chiron, C., Jambaque, I., Renaux-Kieffer, V., Van de Moortele, P. F., Delalande, O., Fohlen, M., Brunelle, F., & Le Bihan, D. (2002). Late plasticity for language in a child's non-dominant hemisphere: a pre- and post-surgery fMRI study. *Brain, 125*(Pt 2), 361–372.

Holcomb, P. J., Coffey, S. A., & Neville, H. J. (1992). Visual and auditory sentence processing: A developmental analysis using event-related brain potentials. *Developmental Neuropsychology, 8*, 203–241.

Horska, A., Kaufmann, W. E., Brant, L. J., Naidu, S., Harris, J. C., & Barker, P. B. (2002). In vivo quantitative proton MRSI study of brain development from childhood to adolescence. *Journal of Magnetic Resonance Imaging, 15*(2), 137–143.

Huttenlocher, P. R., & Dabholkar, A. S. (1997). Regional differences in synaptogenesis in human cerebral cortex. *Journal of Comparative Neurology, 387*(2), 167–178.

Iidaka, T., Okada, T., Murata, T., Omori, M., Kosaka, H., Sadato, N., & Yonekura, Y. (2002). Age-related differences in the medial temporal lobe responses to emotional faces as revealed by fMRI. *Hippocampus, 12*(3), 352–362.

Itier, R. J., & Taylor, M. J. (2002). Inversion and contrast polarity reversal affect both encoding and recognition processes of unfamiliar faces: A repetition study using ERPs. *NeuroImage, 15*, 353–372.

Itier, R. J., & Taylor, M. J. (2004a). Face recognition memory and configural processing: A developmental ERP study using upright, inverted, and contrast-reversed faces. *Journal of Cognitive Neuroscience, 16*(3), 487–502.

Itier, R. J., & Taylor, M. J. (2004b). Effects of learning and configural changes on the development of face recognition processes. *Developmental Science, 7*(4), 469–487.

Itier, R. J., & Taylor, M. J. (2004c). Source analysis of the N170 to faces and objects. *Neuroreport, 15*(8), 1261–1265.

Johnson, M. H., & de Haan, M. (2001). Developing cortical specialization for visual-cognitive function: the case of face recognition. In J. McClelland and R. Siegler (Eds.), *Mechanisms of Cognitive Development: Behavioral and Neural Perspectives.*

(pp. 253–270). Mahwah, NJ: Lawrence Erlbaum Associates.

Johnston, M. V. (2001). Developmental disorders of activity dependent neuronal plasticity. *Indian Journal of Pediatrics, 68*(5), 423–426.

Klingberg, T., Forssberg, H., & Westerberg, H. (2002). Increased brain activity in frontal and parietal cortex underlies the development of visuospatial working memory capacity during childhood. *Journal of Cognitive Neuroscience, 14*(1), 1–10.

Kolb, B., Wilson, B., & Taylor, L. (1992). Developmental changes in the recognition and comprehension of facial expression: implications for frontal lobe function. *Brain and Cognition, 20*(1), 74–84.

Konner, M. (1991). Universals of behavioral development in relation to brain myelination. In K.R. Gibson & A.C. Petersen (Ed.), *Brain maturation and cognitive development* (pp. 181–223). New York: Aldine deGruyer.

Kwon, H., Reiss, A. L., & Menon, V. (2002). Neural basis of protracted developmental changes in visuospatial working memory. *Proceedings of the National Academy of Science, U.S.A., 99*(20), 13336–13341.

Le Grand, R., Mondloch, C. J., Maurer, D., & Brent, H. P. (2003). Expert face processing requires visual input to the right hemisphere during infancy. *Nature Neuroscience, 6*(10), 1108–1112.

Levin, H. S. (2003). Neuroplasticity following non-penetrating traumatic brain injury. *Brain Injury, 17*(8), 665–674.

Lobaugh, N. J., Gibson, E., & Taylor, M. J. (2004). Functional MRI of implicit emotional face processing in children. *Neuroimage, 22,* suppl. 1.

Majovski, L.V. (1989). Higher cortical functions in children: A developmental perspective. IN: C. R. Reynolds & E. Fletcher-Janzen, E. (Eds.), *Handbook of clinical child neuropsychology. Critical issues in neuropsychology* (pp. 41–67). New York: Plenum Press.

McCarthy, G., Puce, A., Belger, A., & Allison, T. (1999). Electrophysiological studies of human face perception. II: Response properties of face-specific potentials generated in occipitotemporal cortex. *Cerebral Cortex, 9*(5), 431–444.

Mills, D. L., Coffey-Corina, S. A., & Neville, H. J. (1994). Variability in cerebral organization during primary language acquisition. In G. Dawson & K. W. Fischer (Eds.), *Human behavior and the developing brain* (pp. 427–455). New York: Guilford Press.

Mills, D. L., & Neville, H. J. (1997). Electrophysiological studies of language and language impairment. *Seminars Pediatric Neurology, 4*(2), 125–134.

Morgan, B. G., & Gibson, K. R. (1991). Nutritional and environmental interactions in brain development.

In K.R.Gibson & A. C. Petersen (Ed.), *Brain maturation and cognitive development* (pp. 91–106). New York: Aldine deGruyter.

Neville, H. J., & Bavelier, D. (1998). Neural organization and plasticity of language. *Current Opinion in Neurobiology, 8*(2), 254–258.

Overmeyer, S., Bullmore, E. T., Suckling, J., Simmons, A., Williams, S. C., Santosh, P. J., & Taylor, E. (2001). Distributed gray and white matter deficits in hyperkinetic disorder: MRI evidence for anatomical abnormality in an attentional network. *Psychological Medicine, 31*(8), 1425–1435.

Pang, E. W., & Taylor, M. J. (2000). Tracking the development of the N1 from age three to adulthood: an examination of speech and non-speech stimuli. *Clinical Neurophysiology, 111,* 388–397.

Pantev, C., Ross, B., Fujioka, T., Trainor, L.J., Schulte, M., & Schulz, M. (2003). Music and learning-induced cortical plasticity. *Annals of the New York Academy of Science, 999,* 438–450.

Papanicolaou, A. C., Simos, P. G., Breier, J. I., Fletcher, J. M., Foorman, B. R., Francis, D., Castillo, E. M., & Davis, R. N. (2003). Brain mechanisms for reading in children with and without dyslexia: a review of studies of normal development and plasticity. *Developmental Neuropsychology, 24,* 593–612

Passarotti, A. M., Paul, B. M., Bussiere, J. R., Buxton, R. B., Wong, E. C., & Stiles, J. (2003). The development of face and location processing: An fMRI study. *Developmental Science, 6*(1), 100–117.

Paus, T., Collins, D. L., Evans, A. C., Leonard, G., Pike, B., & Zijdenbos, A. (2001). Maturation of white matter in the human brain: a review of magnetic resonance studies. *Brain Research Bulletin, 54*(3), 255–266.

Paus, T., Zijdenbos, A., Worsley, K., Collins, D. L., Blumenthal, J., Giedd, J. N., Rapoport, J. L., & Evans, A. C. (1999). Structural maturation of neural pathways in children and adolescents: In vivo study. *Science, 283*(5409), 1908–1911.

Phillips, L. H., MacLean, R. D., & Allen, R. (2002). Age and the understanding of emotions: Neuropsychological and sociocognitive perspectives. *Journal of Gerontology, 57*(6), P526–530.

Ponton, C. W., Eggermont, J. J., Kwong, B., & Don, M. (2000). Maturation of human central auditory system activity: Evidence from multi-channel evoked potentials. *Clinical Neurophysiology, 111*(2), 220–236.

Pugh, K. R., Mencl, W. E., Jenner, A. R., Katz, L., Frost, S. J., Lee, J. R., Shaywitz, S. E., & Shaywitz, B. A. (2000). Functional neuroimaging studies of reading and reading disability (developmental dyslexia). *Mental Retardation and Developmental Disabilities Research Review, 6*(3), 207–213.

Rajapakse, J. C., Giedd, J. N., Rumsey, J. M., Vaituzis, A. C., Hamburger, S. D., & Rapoport, J. L. (1996). Regional MRI measurements of the corpus callosum: A methodological and developmental study. *Brain Development, 18*(5), 379–388.

Slomine, B. S., Gerring, J. P., Grados, M. A., Vasa, R., Brady, K. D., Christensen, J. R., & Denckla, M. B. (2002). Performance on measures of executive function following pediatric traumatic brain injury. *Brain Injury, 16*(9), 759–772.

Sowell, E. R., Thompson, P. M., Tessner, K. D., & Toga, A. W. (2001). Mapping continued brain growth and gray matter density reduction in dorsal frontal cortex: Inverse relationships during postadolescent brain maturation. *Journal of Neuroscience, 21*(22), 8819–8829.

Sowell, E. R., Thompson, P. M., Welcome, S. E., Henkenius, A. L., Toga, A. W., & Peterson, B. S. (2003). Cortical abnormalities in children and adolescents with attention-deficit hyperactivity disorder. *Lancet, 362*(9397), 1699–1707.

Sowell, E. R., Trauner, D. A., Gamst, A., & Jernigan, T. L. (2002). Development of Cortical and subcortical brain structures in childhood and adolescence: a structural MRI Study. *Developmental Medicine and Child Neurology, 44*(1):4–16.

Staff, R. T., Murray, A. D., Deary, I. J., & Whalley, L. J. (2004). What provides cerebral reserve? *Brain, 127*(Pt 5):1191–1199.

Sullivan, S., & Ruffman, T. (2004). Emotion recognition deficits in the elderly. *International Journal of Neurosciences, 114*(3), 403–432.

Taylor, M. J. (1993a). Evoked potentials in paediatrics. In A. M. Halliday (Ed.), *Evoked potentials in clinicaltTesting* (2nd ed., Vol. 11, pp.489–521). London: Churchill Livingston.

Taylor, M. J. (1993b). Maturational changes in ERPs to orthographic and phonological tasks. *Electroencephalography and clinical Neurophysiology, 88*, 494–507.

Taylor, M. J. (2002). Non-spatial attentional effects on P1. *Clinical Neurophysiology, 113*(12), 1903–1908.

Taylor, M. J., Batty, M., & Itier, R. J. (2004). The faces of development: A review of early face processing over childhood. *Journal of Cognitive Science 16*, 1426–1442.

Taylor, M. J., & Eals, M. (1996). An event-related potential study of development using visual semantic tasks. *Journal of Psychophysiology, 10*, 125–139.

Taylor, M. J., Edmonds, G. E., McCarthy, G., & Allison, T. (2001). Eyes first! Eye processing develops before face processing in children. *Neuroreport, 12*(8), 1671–1676.

Thomas, K. M. (2003). Assessing brain development using neurophysiologic and behavioral measures. *Journal of Pediatrics, 143*(4 Suppl), S46–53.

Thomas, K. M., Drevets, W. C., Whalen, P. J., Eccard, C. H., Dahl, R. E., Ryan, N. D., & Casey, B. J. (2001). Amygdala response to facial expressions in children and adults. *Biological Psychiatry, 49*(4), 309–316.

Thomas, K. M., King, S. W., Franzen, P. L., Welsh, T. F., Berkowitz, A. L., Noll, D. C., Birmaher, V., & Casey, B. J. (1999). A developmental functional MRI study of spatial working memory. *Neuroimage, 10*(3 Pt 1), 327–338.

Vargha-Khadem, F., Gadian, D. G., & Mishkin, M. (2001). Dissociations in cognitive memory: the syndrome of developmental amnesia. *Philosophical Transactions of the Royal Society of London, B, Biological Sciences, 356*(1413), 1435–1440.

Yakolev, P. I., & Lecours, A. R. (1967). The myelogenetic cycles of regional maturation of the brain. In A. Minkowski (Ed.), *Regional development of the brain in early life* (pp. 3–70). Oxford: Blackwell.

Yeo, R. A., Hill, D. E., Campbell, R. A., Vigil, J., Petropoulos, H., Hart, B., Zamora, L., & Brooks, W. M. (2003). Proton magnetic resonance spectroscopy investigation of the right frontal lobe in children with attention-deficit/hyperactivity disorder. *Journal of the American Academy of Child and Adolescent Psychiatry, 42*(3), 303–310.

Yurgelun-Todd, D. A., Killgore, W. D., & Cintron, C. B. (2003). Cognitive correlates of medial temporal lobe development across adolescence: a magnetic resonance imaging study. *Perceptual Motor Skills, 96*(1), 3–17.

3

Brain Changes in Aging: A Lifespan Perspective

Randy L. Buckner

Denise Head

Cindy Lustig

Older adults differ in many ways from their younger selves. Change is always noted in hair color and thickness, muscle tone, and bone density. Sight and hearing become impaired, and actions are more difficult and slower than before. Cognitive changes are also prominent, with difficulties in attention and memory emerging frequently. Some causes of change are linked inextricably to our time on earth. For example, more hazards are encountered the longer we live. Hazards include diseases and stresses that directly affect the brain and systems that support brain function. However, even within relatively guarded environments, humans and other species undergo stereotyped aging trajectories that likely stem directly from genetic origins (Troen, 2003). It is remarkable that despite several billion attempts, not a single person has doubled the average modern lifespan. Change in aging undoubtedly arises from our fitness as an organism that fills a niche with a lengthy, but not infinite, life cycle. We are programmed for a developmental template that is expressed into adulthood and also into senescence.

In the present chapter, age-associated changes that affect the brain are discussed in the context of framing a general research approach to lifespan development. Discussion is separated into four sections. The first section focuses on global measures of structural brain change. The second section highlights distinct aging effects on frontal-striatal and medial temporal systems. These dissociable influences are discussed as possible causes for why executive (attentional) dysfunction and declarative memory difficulties are so common in aging. The third section focuses on functional brain imaging methods that both illuminate detrimental functional consequences of brain aging and also suggest functional responses that may be compensatory. In the final section, brain aging is considered within the broader context of lifespan development with a discussion of six possible ways early development can inform brain aging in senescence.

BRAIN CHANGE WITH AGING BEGINS EARLY AND PERSISTS ACROSS THE LIFESPAN

Brain volume reduction and ventricular enlargement are well-documented differences between old and young adults (e.g., Davis & Wright, 1977). What is less commonly appreciated is that brain volume reduction begins early in life and continues at a gradual, slow pace throughout adulthood, even in the absence of clinical impairment. Figure 3.1 shows brain volume differences during normal aging based on a cross-sectional MRI sample of 272 individuals. Volume decline is present and significant by age 30. Estimates from multiple MRI studies suggest brain volume decreases at about 0.2% per year throughout adult life, with an acceleration of volume loss in the oldest individuals (Fotenos, Snyder, Girton, Morris, & Buckner, 2005). In seniors, volume loss in nondemented aging is just under .5% per year, measured both with cross-sectional and longitudinal methods (Fotenos et al., 2005; Resnick, Pham, Kraut, Zonderman, & Davatzikos, 2003). By contrast, marked acceleration of volume loss is noted in the earliest stages of Alzheimer's disease, approximately doubling the rate of volume loss compared to that of age-matched controls (Fotenos et al., 2005; Jack et al., 2004; Schott et al., 2003).

Analyses that target different tissue types (gray versus white matter) in normal aging suggest that a large component of the lifelong global volume decline is due to reductions in gray matter volume (Good et al., 2001; Salat et al., 2004; Sowell et al., 2003). While there are clear age differences in white matter, as will be discussed in the next section, it may be of particular relevance to extended developmental processes that gray matter volume begins to decline in childhood, causing a shift in the ratio of gray-to-white matter after the age of about 10 (Courchesne et al., 2000; Pfefferbaum et al., 1994; Reiss, Abrams, Singer, Ross, & Denckla, 1996).

Taken collectively, these studies indicate that normal aging is associated with brain volume decline that begins surprisingly early in life, suggesting a component that is not pathological and that accelerates in old age, perhaps reflecting detrimental processes that emerge in late adulthood. Clinically apparent Alzheimer's disease leads to marked acceleration of volume loss. In the next section, we highlight two distinct forms of age-associated change that have selective anatomic patterns and may contribute to the global patterns noted above. In the final section, we return to the surprising finding that brain change in aging begins in early adulthood.

STRUCTURAL EVIDENCE SUGGESTS MULTIPLE FACTORS CONTRIBUTE TO COGNITIVE DECLINE IN ADVANCED AGING

While the constellation of observed cognitive changes in advanced aging eludes a simple, parsimonious

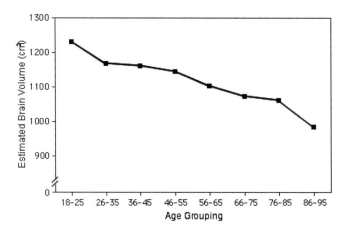

FIGURE 3.1. Brain volume declines across the adult lifespan with age-associated differences apparent by age 30, if not before. The graph plots cross-sectional brain volume from 272 individuals measured with structural MRI. Men and women are combined. (Adapted from tabular data of Fotenos et al., 2005.)

explanation (e.g., see Greenwood, 2000; Light, 1991; West, 1996), there is a recurring distinction between cognitive decline associated with executive and attention difficulties and that associated with declarative memory (for recent reviews, see Buckner, 2004; Hedden & Gabrieli, 2004). In the absence of dementia, studies of aging note difficulties on tasks that stress attention and executive abilities (Craik, Morris, Morris, & Loewen, 1990; Hasher & Zacks, 1988; Jennings & Jacoby, 1993; Moscovitch & Winocur, 1995). By contrast, clinical impairment in Alzheimer's disease begins with deficits in declarative memory, such as the inability to remember a short list of items. Recent behavioral analyses suggest that these two classes of deficit separate into distinct factors (see also Chapters 7 and 11, this volume). Using measures of performance on cognitive tasks, Salthouse and Ferrer-Caja (2003) suggest that a unitary, common influence leads to age differences on many abilities, including reasoning, memory, spatial processing, and speed, while a separate influence accounts for additional age-related effects on memory. In a similar vein, Glisky, Polster, and Routhieaux (1995) developed a two-factor framework for assessing cognitive function in aging, with one factor loading on tasks that tap executive function and a second factor on tasks that tap declarative memory function. Performance on further tests of memory was predicted based on which of the two factors an individual was better or worse.

Distinct factors in cognitive aging may arise from influences on separate anatomic circuits, with one involving the frontal cortex and basal ganglia and the other centered on the hippocampal formation and associated structures within the medial temporal lobe. These circuits are displayed in Figure 3.2. Prefrontal cortex contributes to attention and executive function. Damage to prefrontal cortex leads to various forms of planning deficit and executive dysfunction (Kolb & Wishaw, 1996). The basal ganglia are a set of subcortical nuclei that, through their anatomic connections, comprise part of a series of loops from the frontal cortex to the striatum (caudate and putamen) and globus pallidus, and then back to the frontal cortex through the thalamus (Alexander, DeLong, & Strick, 1986, Figure 3.2a). The basal ganglia thus receive information from cortical areas and project back to areas within frontal cortex, including prefrontal and motor cortex. The basal ganglia, however, do not directly control actions, as there are no direct connections between these nuclei and motor neurons. Because the caudate and putamen are the direct targets of frontal regions, this circuit is referred to as "frontal-striatal." While the functions of the frontal-striatal circuit are not well understood, current ideas include initiating and regulating thoughts and actions.

The second circuit involves the hippocampal formation and associated structures within the medial temporal lobe (Figure 3.2b). The hippocampal formation

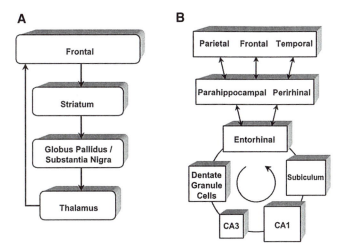

FIGURE 3.2. Schematic diagrams of brain systems hypothesized to be affected by aging. (A) The frontal-striatal circuit. (B) The hippocampal (medial temporal lobe) memory system. Behavioral, genetic, and structural findings suggest aging has dissociated effects on frontal-striatal and hippocampal structures (see text).

contains reciprocal projections to widespread regions of cortex through the perirhinal, entorhinal and parahippocampal cortex (Lavenex, Suzuki, & Amaral, 2002; Suzuki & Amaral, 1994). Within the hippocampal formation itself is a directional circuit by which information from the entorhinal cortex projects progressively through the dentate gyrus, CA3, CA1, and subiculum, and then back out through the entorhinal cortex. Human case studies and animal models of medial temporal damage have convincingly supported a role for these areas in declarative memory processing (for review see Squire, 1992), perhaps through their ability to arbitrarily and rapidly bind divergent inputs from widespread regions of cortex (Cohen & Eichenbaum, 1993).

The relevance of these two circuits to cognitive aging is that they appear separately susceptible to age-associated changes that lead to distinct kinds of cognitive decline (for comprehensive reviews of the full array of structural brain changes that accompany aging see Kemper, 1994; Raz, 2000). Changes in the frontal-striatal circuit may be preferentially related to reduced executive function in normal (nondemented) aging. These changes include anterior white matter damage and infarcts to subcortical structures, including the basal ganglia and thalamus, as well as changes in the function of the neurotransmitter systems that affect these regions. One hypothesis is that vascular compromise (small vessel disease), perhaps associated with hypertension, causes damage to the white matter structures responsible for the communication between neurons (DeCarli & Scheltens, 2002; Pantoni & Garcia, 1997; Pugh & Lipsitz, 2002; see also Söderlund, Nyberg, Adolfsson, Nilsson, & Launer, 2003). Anterior white matter and subcortical structures may be preferentially vulnerable. Preferential frontal atrophy of gray matter may also be an important factor (e.g., Raz et al., 1997) as well as striatal volume loss (Raz et al., 2003; see Rubin, 1999, for discussion).

Alterations in white matter have recently been explored using diffusion tensor imaging (DTI). DTI is a method that can measure water diffusion, which tends to be parallel along healthy white matter tracts because of their regular structure (much like water diffuses along the fibers of the long axis of a celery stalk) (LeBihan et al., 2001; Neil, Miller, Mukherjee, & Huppi, 2002). As white matter structure degrades, diffusion properties change, becoming more random and isotropic (as water diffusion would become more random if the fibers of the celery stalk were crushed).

Several DTI studies have noted age-associated differences in white matter that are present in nondemented aging and are preferential for anterior brain regions (Head et al., 2004; O'Sullivan et al., 2001; Pfefferbaum et al., 2000; see also Figure 3.3). For example, Head et al. (2004) measured diffusion properties within the anterior corpus callosum and frontal lobe white matter and noted significant differences between nondemented old and young adults. Furthermore, within the callosal regions, the anterior portions showed greater age-associated differences as compared to the most posterior region.

By contrast, damage to medial temporal structures is exhibited in Alzheimer's disease and may cause declarative memory dysfunction in aging, even before clinically apparent dementia is diagnosed. Prominent declarative memory impairment associated with Alzheimer's disease appears related to buildup of amyloid (extracellularly) and tau (intracellularly) in a pathological form (Golde, Eckman, & Younkin, 2000; Selkoe, 2001). One hypothesis is that amyloid deposits (plaques) and soluble forms of amyloid lead to neuronal dysfunction and cell death. Pathology begins in the medial temporal lobe and spreads outward to association cortex over time (Braak & Braak, 1991, 1997). The preferential vulnerability of medial temporal structures in the early stages of the disease may explain why prominent initial symptoms are memory impairment, and why MRI studies so consistently find medial temporal atrophy in patients with Alzheimer's disease (Jack, Petersen, O'Brien, & Tangalos, 1992; Killiany et al., 1993; see Jack & Petersen, 2000, for review). Symptoms advance to eventual global compromise as the disease progresses to include widespread regions of cortex.

Several lines of evidence further indicate that aging influences on frontal-striatal circuits dissociate from those affecting hippocampal and adjacent medial temporal structures. One source of evidence comes from rare genetic mutations that cause extreme forms of aging. Certain mutations have preferential effects on frontal-striatal circuits while others affect medial temporal structures. Cerebral autosomal dominant arteriopathy with subcortical infarcts and leukoencephalopathy (CADASIL) is a genetic form of dementia that is sometimes characterized by severe executive dysfunction (see Kalimo, Ruchoux, Viitanen, & Kalaria, 2002, for review). CADASIL is autosomal dominant; if an individual inherits the relevant gene, he or she will show the associated age-

Nondemented Aging   **Alzheimer Disease**

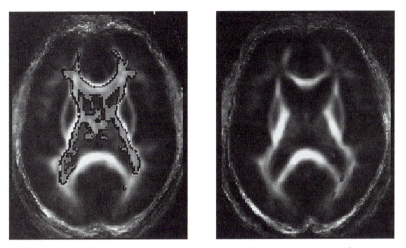

FIGURE 3.3. Age but not early-stage Alzheimer's disease associates with anterior differences in white matter as measured by diffusion tensor imaging (DTI). The image to the left shows differences in white matter when young and nondemented old adults are compared. Note the significant anterior white-matter differences. The image to the right shows differences between age-matched nondemented and demented older adults. Minimal additional differences are noted in anterior regions suggesting anterior white-matter differences are associated with aging and not accelerated in early stages of Alzheimer's disease. (Adapted from Head, et al., 2004.)

dependent pathology. In CADASIL, there is age-associated degeneration of the smooth muscle surrounding vessels that regulate blood flow in the brain resulting in white matter damage and, eventually, focal infarcts and stroke. Frontal and subcortical regions, including the basal ganglia and thalamus, show preferential vulnerability. By direct contrast, other genetic mutations, also of autosomal dominant form, affect protein metabolism in ways that cause amyloid and tau pathology, preferentially influencing medial temporal structures (causing early-onset forms of Alzheimer's disease; e.g., Goate et al., 1991). The existence of distinct genetic mutations that separately target frontal-striatal and hippocampal structures indicates they are susceptible to different age-associated vulnerabilities. Dissociation between frontal-striatal and hippocampal changes is also observed in common forms of aging, but the evidence is more circumstantial. For example, while prominent age-associated differences are observed in anterior white matter in nondemented aging, Head and colleagues (2004; 2005) recently observed that such differences are not accelerated in the early stages of Alzheimer's disease, even though clinically significant memory impair-

ment has begun (see Figure 3.3). The implication is that changes in anterior structures are present in aging but are not the cause of Alzheimer's disease. Jagust and colleagues (Wu, Mungas, Eberling, Reed, & Jagust, 2002) have recently provided additional evidence for dissociation and also an indication that the two factors combine their influences in cognitive aging. They explored the influence of only white matter damage, only hippocampal volume reduction, or their co-occurrence on the presence of cognitive dysfunction. Each predicted cognitive impairment; when they occurred together, more severe cognitive decline was observed than either would be expected to elicit in isolation. Specifically, individuals with hippocampal volume reduction *and* white matter damage were more likely to exhibit severe cognitive symptoms than the sum of their individual risk levels. In summary, distinct vulnerabilities in the brain are present and separately influenced by age. Mounting evidence suggests a distinction between factors that affect frontal-striatal circuits and those preferentially affecting the hippocampal formation and adjacent cortex within the medial temporal lobe. An open question has been the degree to which the changes reflect normal, nondemented aging versus changes characteristic of disease pathology, and whether such *qualitative* distinctions between "normal" and "pathological" aging are even meaningful. We return to this question in the last section of the chapter where lifespan development is considered.

FUNCTIONAL CHANGES OBSERVED IN ADVANCED AGING IMPLICATE DYSFUNCTION AND COMPENSATION

Imaging studies based on positron emission tomography (PET) and functional MRI (fMRI) provide insight into the functional consequences of brain aging and also the possible recruitment of compensatory processes. Both methods measure local blood flow change that indirectly reflects neuronal activity (Heeger & Ress, 2002; Raichle, 1987). By having adults of different ages and cognitive status perform tasks during imaging, functional activation patterns that associate with cognitive aging are observed. We discuss three findings that have been consistently observed across multiple studies.

Underrecruitment of Frontal Cortex in Advanced Aging

Older adults, including those with no signs of dementia, do not fully activate frontal regions to the same degree as younger adults under certain task conditions (e.g., Cabeza et al., 1997; Grady et al., 1995; Logan, Sanders, Snyder, Morris, & Buckner, 2002; Nyberg et al., 2003; see Park et al., in press, for review). The most consistent example of this phenomenon occurs in studies of memory encoding when information is intentionally committed to memory. During intentional memorization, young adults spontaneously recruit multiple frontal regions, including left prefrontal regions along the inferior frontal gyrus (near Broca's area) that play a role in verbal elaboration (e.g., Kapur et al., 1996; for reviews, see Buckner, Kelley, & Petersen, 1999; Fletcher & Henson, 2001). Such a finding is not surprising given that verbal elaboration is an effective memorization strategy and these frontal regions are used to flexibly retrieve words and their meanings. Of interest, older adults do not fully recruit these frontal regions during intentional memorization and memory performance suffers (Grady et al., 1995; Logan et al., 2002). For example, Grady and colleagues studied older adults memorizing faces. While activation in many regions was comparable between

older and younger adults, frontal cortex activity was significantly reduced.

A methodological concern in PET and fMRI studies is that underrecruitment might be an artifact of sample characteristics that confound measurement using these methods. Older adults, because of vascular compromise or other factors, may fail to elicit a comparable blood flow response that is the basis of PET and fMRI (D'Esposito, Deouell, & Gazzaley, 2003). However, control studies that explore responses during simple sensory and motor paradigms suggest that this confound is unlikely to account for the observed differences between younger and older adults (Buckner, Snyder, Sanders, Raichle, & Morris, 2000; D'Esposito, Zarahn, Aguirre, & Rypma, 1999; Huettel, Guezeldere, & McCarthy, 2001). A related possibility is that structural or physiological changes, as discussed in the previous section, have impaired frontal function to the point that the maximal level of recruitment in older adults is significantly lower than that in younger adults. Despite such an explanation's intuitive appeal, there is mounting evidence that mild frontal atrophy and white matter changes seen in normal older adults do not lead to a marked reduced potential for frontal recruitment (as measured by presently available PET and fMRI methods). Rather, markedly reduced frontal recruitment in normal aging appears to be context dependent and, to a large degree, reversible under supportive task conditions.

Logan and colleagues (2002) provide direct evidence that frontal underrecruitment is context dependent in normal aging. In a series of conditions using fMRI, they showed that the same individuals who failed to recruit appropriate frontal regions under intentional memory encoding conditions, where strategies must be developed and deployed spontaneously, nonetheless recruited the regions to nearly the same degree as younger adults when supportive task conditions were provided (Figure 3.4). The conclusion from this result is that frontal resources are available, at least to a larger degree than may be initially appreciated, and that structured tasks provide the context (environmental support) to maximize older adults' ability to use available frontal resources.

Preserved frontal recruitment under supportive conditions was replicated by Lustig and colleagues (2003; Lustig & Buckner, 2004) and generalized to older adults with very mild Alzheimer's disease. Not all studies have noted comparable recruitment in older and younger adults under supportive encoding conditions (for example, see Stebbins et al., 2002). The

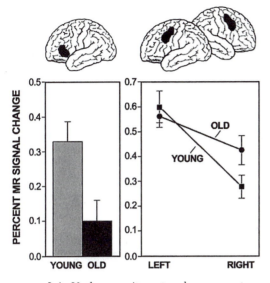

FIGURE 3.4. Under-recruitment and compensatory recruitment in advanced aging. The left panel displays under-recruitment of a left frontal region, along inferior frontal gyrus, implicated in verbal elaboration. During intentional memory encoding, young adults show strong activation in contrast to older adults who do not. This pattern is context-dependent. Supportive (structured) encoding conditions cause older adults to significantly increase recruitment (see text). The right panel displays compensatory recruitment during supportive task conditions. Strong recruitment is noted for both young and old adults. The older individuals show increased recruitment in right frontal regions that may represent a compensatory response (see text). (Figure adapted from Buckner, 2003.)

reasons for the variability remain unclear (see Park et al., in press, for a thoughtful discussion). Nonetheless, the presence of similar recruitment levels in younger and older adults in several studies tentatively suggests that frontal recruitment can occur under certain task conditions. As will be discussed more extensively in the final portion of this section, a common observation has been a paradoxical age-associated increase in recruitment in certain frontal regions, perhaps as a form of compensation.

Atypical Modulation of Default, Resting-State Networks in Alzheimer's Disease

Imaging studies of resting metabolism, using PET methods tailored to measure metabolism rather than blood flow, have observed that patients with Alzheimer's disease show reduced metabolism (hypometabolism). Reduced metabolism is particularly prominent (and consistently observed) in posterior parietal cortex and posterior cingulate (e.g., Benson et al., 1983; Leon et al., 2001; Loessner et al., 1995; Silverman et al., 2002). Functional imaging studies based on fMRI measures of blood flow properties have recently noted that individuals with Alzheimer's disease show differences in posterior cingulate activation, near retrosplenial cortex, that may be related to the declines in resting metabolism (Lustig et al., 2003). Differences in functional connectivity between posterior cortical regions and the medial temporal lobe have also been observed in Alzheimer's disease and even advocated as a marker for early diagnosis (Greicius, Srivastava, Reiss, & Menon, 2004).

An unresolved issue is whether differences in metabolism and resting activity in parietal and posterior cingulate cortex relate to the structural changes noted in the previous section—in particular those within the medial temporal lobe that are characteristic of Alzheimer's disease. A speculative answer to this question is that these posterior regions represent the cortical targets of medial temporal systems contributing to memory (Buckner, 2004). Medial temporal regions are a major source of projections to parietal cortex, prominently including zones near the posterior cingulate (Suzuki & Amaral, 1994; Vogt, Finch, & Olson, 1992), and their disruption leads to hypometabolism in both humans and animal models (Aupée et al., 2001; Meguro et al., 1999; Millien et al., 2002; Reed et al., 1999). As pathology associated with Alzheimer's disease affects medial temporal regions and progresses, a consequence might be the disruption of posterior cortical regions as observed in metabolic PET and fMRI studies. Further studies will be required to explore this tentative possibility.

Compensatory Recruitment Is a General Response to Cognitive Change in Advanced Aging

Activation increases have been observed in aging studies that may reflect compensation. Baltes (1997) defines compensation as a "response to loss in means (resources) used to maintain success or desired levels of functioning (outcomes)." The basic finding is that older adults, in a variety of cognitive tasks, show increased activation as compared to younger controls. Frontal increases are particularly common, with older adults often increasing recruitment in homologous regions in the nondominant hemisphere. For example, on language tasks that are strongly left lateralized in young adults, older adults tend to show bilateral recruitment patterns (Figure 3.4; for reviews see Cabeza, 2002; Grady & Craik, 2000; Park, Polk, Mikels, Taylor, & Marshuetz, 2001; Reuter-Lorenz, 2002). Increased recruitment has been demonstrated in individuals with Alzheimer's disease (Becker et al., 1996; Grady et al., 2003), individuals genetically at risk for Alzheimer's disease (Bookheimer et al., 2000), individuals with CADASIL (Reddy, De Stefano, Mortilla, Federico, & Matthews, 2002), individuals with stroke (Buckner, Corbetta, Schatz, Raichle, & Petersen, 1996), and nondemented older adults (Cabeza et al., 1997; Logan et al., 2002; Reuter-Lorenz et al., 2000). Thus, increased recruitment of brain regions appears to be a general response to conditions of neural compromise or strain.

Accumulating data further suggest increased recruitment may be a productive (compensatory) response in aging (Cabeza, Anderson, Locantore, & McIntosh, 2002; Grady et al., 2003; Rosen et al., 2002). Cabeza and colleagues, for example, selected two groups of older adults—those who performed similarly to younger adults on a battery of memory tests and those who performed worse. Bilateral activation of frontal cortex was observed in the older adults who performed well, in contrast to unilateral activation in those who performed badly, suggesting that increases in activation were compensatory in the older adults. This kind of finding goes against the alternative possibility that bilateral frontal recruitment is directly caused by (and not a productive response to) detrimental changes in aging (Cabeza, 2002; Logan et al., 2002).

An open question is whether there are specific age-associated causes that elicit increased recruitment. One possibility is that recruitment differences represent a general response to increasing task difficulty conveyed by any number of global factors that affect aging, including slowed processing (Salthouse, 1996) and perceptual difficulties (Lindenberger & Baltes, 1994). A second possibility is that, as frontal-striatal and medial temporal systems decline in aging, increased recruitment responds specifically to compensate, perhaps especially in prefrontal regions that control task processes. This second alternative, based on anatomic causes, is not independent from that described above in the context of cognitive abilities but encourages exploration of underlying physiological causes. By either idea, increased recruitment maintains a high level of performance in older adults in the presence of detrimental physiological changes. As task demands are increased or the pathological burden becomes severe (e.g., in Alzheimer's disease), cognitive differences may nonetheless emerge despite compensatory processes.

POSSIBLE RELATIONS BETWEEN DEVELOPMENT AND ADVANCED AGING

A major goal of this chapter is to frame discussion of brain change in the context of lifespan development. Many facets of cognitive aging are likely the extension of the developmental stages that occur prior to reaching maturity. Some connections have already been noted in the literature: reserve capacity in senescence probably relates to the success of development early in life (Stern, 2002). Vulnerability of brain systems in aging may link to their developmental course, as has been proposed by "first-in, last-out" models of brain aging that suggest structures late to mature are earliest to be affected by advanced aging (Raz, 2000). Other contact points are less obvious and speculative, such as the possibility that certain aspects of brain aging do not begin in late adulthood but rather reflect continuous processes that go on throughout life and simply did not evolve to be optimal in a modern world where being healthy into the seventh and eighth decades is a common occurrence. Along these lines, and at the risk of being too speculative, we revisit the interpretation of regional changes in gray matter in aging and suggest an alternative hypothesis based on the possibility of lifelong development.

Age-associated differences in gray matter volume prominently include frontal cortex and present across the cortex as a "patchwork of differential declines and relative preservation" (Raz, 2000). Implicit in discussions of cortical differences in aging has been a model: age-associated reductions in gray matter and other structures reflect a post-maturational, inherently detrimental process; if certain regions are affected and enough change exists, cognitive decline will result. We have leaned on such a model in our prior work (e.g., Head in Raz et al., 1997, and Buckner in Salat et al., 2004) and suspect, in most instances, this basic model will prove useful. There is, however, an alternative. Changing gray matter volumes may, in part, reflect the continuation of development and lifelong learning processes that sculpt cortical structures in an adaptive manner.

Consider Figure 3.5. The left panel shows age-associated gray matter differences across the entire cortical mantle (modified from Salat et al., 2004). The procedure used to make the image is based on collecting multiple high-contrast MRI images and measuring the thickness of the cortex. Differences in thickness are plotted across the brain with local regions showing large effects between young and old adults indicated by bright shading. Patterns of preservation and change are, to a large degree, consistent with prior ideas. For example, frontal regions show marked volume decline. However, surprisingly, the pattern is also remarkably similar to the pathway that participates in language reception and production. In particular, note the similarity between the regions showing thinning in aging and the regions implicated in the classic Wernicke-Geschwind model of language (Figure 3.5). The similarity may be purely coincidental. Nonetheless, it does cause one to wonder if there is a relation. Could certain components of age-associated brain change reflect the long-term sculpting of the nervous system? Is the pattern of thinning reflective of a pruning processes that occurs most in language pathways as a consequence of being highly verbal animals? To our knowledge, there are no strong data to argue for such an explanation, but it is nonetheless intriguing and quite different from the typical explanation given to structural changes in advancing age, which assumes detrimental processes that arise only long after the brain has matured. It is thus of interest that changes in cortical thickness begin early and are continuous in many regions across the adult age-span (Salat et al., 2004).

Discussing gray matter decline as the continuation of a lifelong developmental process highlights a broader issue: few theories consider changes observed in advanced aging as the extension, or alteration, of productive developmental processes. In what follows, six possible ways are described by which early developmental processes may inform changes in advanced aging. *Development* is used below in its broadest sense, referring to processes that induce neural change both in early, childhood development and in later life. We present these six possibilities as a beginning framework for exploring lifespan development (Table 3.1).

Continuous Adaptive Development

Processes of this form will cause change across the lifespan and are characterized by their positive influence on function. Continuation of dynamic plasticity within the cortex might be one such example, if it does indeed exist into late adulthood. Many biological processes potentially fall into this category. From a research perspective, the relevance of making this form of developmental process explicit is that, to the

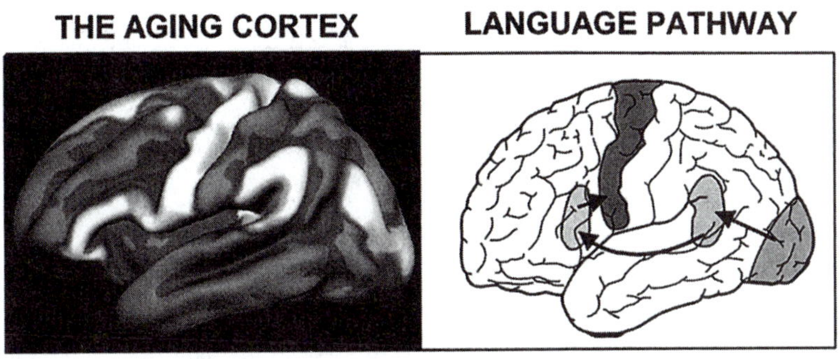

THE AGING CORTEX   **LANGUAGE PATHWAY**

FIGURE 3.5. Does lifelong cognitive activity sculpt the cortex? Age-associated cortical thinning is contrasted with the functional anatomy of the language pathway. The left panel displays a lateral surface of the brain. Cortical thickness differences between young and old adults are indicated by bright shading. Note the widespread thinning that prominently includes prefrontal cortex. (Adapted from Salat et al., 2004.) The right panel displays the classic Wernicke-Geschwind model of language processing (for word reading); the progression from visual regions to regions involved in language comprehension (Wernicke's area) and production (Broca's area and motor cortex) is noted with arrows. The similarity between regions implicated in language processing and cortical thinning with age is striking.

TABLE 3.1. Forms of lifespan development

Continuous Adaptive Development
  Allows productive change throughout life.

Maladaptive Consequences of Continuous Development
  Allows productive change early in life but then disturbs function in advanced aging.

Discontinued Development
  Productive early in life but then ceases or diminishes in advanced aging.

Accumulated Lesions
  Damage that gradually accumulates over time and disturbs function in advanced aging.

Emergent Maladaptive Development
  Change that emerges only in advanced aging that disturbs function.

Convergent Responses During Development
  Parallel responses to brain states in childhood and advanced aging.

---

degree such processes persist across the age span, in studies restricted to the adult age spectrum it may be easy to misattribute decline in cognition to lifelong processes that are adaptive. Certain forms of "atrophy" in advanced aging may actually be more appropriately characterized as the continuation of lifelong adaptive processes that facilitate learning. Explorations that contrast childhood development to that of advanced aging are well positioned to more clearly differentiate those brain processes that represent extensions of adaptive developmental processes from those that emerge as maladaptive processes in advancing age. Continuous adaptive developmental processes will be those that exist across the adult lifespan and aid function throughout.

Maladaptive Consequences of Continuous Development

Continuations of productive, age-associated developmental changes that reverse their utility in advanced aging fall into this category. As modern humans, we find ourselves in an odd evolutionary predicament. Having significantly modified our environment through health care and safety, most of us will live well beyond our reproductive fitness. Some biological processes that change or accumulate with age may have evolved to peak their utility well before senescence. It is presently unclear which, if any, developmental observations are of this form. A maladaptive conse-

quence might emerge from a biological process that is advantageous to an active organism at one point in its lifespan but then becomes detrimental at a later point. Evidence for this form of process would be the relation of a physiological process during development to positive function, and the directly opposite relation in advanced aging.

Discontinued Development

Discontinued developmental processes are those productive processes that are available in childhood and early adult development that decrease, or altogether cease, as age advances. Animal models suggest many kinds of processes that decline with age, ranging from repair mechanisms associated with white matter myelination (Peters et al., 1996), to processes associated with cell proliferation and neurogenesis (Kuhn, Dickinson-Anson, & Gage, 1996), to regulation of neurotransmitter systems (Arnsten, Cai, Murphy, & Goldman-Rakic, 1994). An understanding of aging phenomena may thus be informed by exploring the functional utility of developmental and other biological processes that are no longer available in advanced aging and whose long-term absence influences brain integrity.

Accumulated Lesions

Accumulated lesions refer to structural or cellular damage that is not repaired and accumulates with advancing age. White matter damage associated with subclinical infarcts is likely one such common example. An informal rule of thumb used by radiologists is that it is normal to observe one small asymptomatic lesion per decade of life. In a particularly careful study of nondemented older adults based on MRI, 65% of the adults over 75 showed white matter abnormalities (Ylikoski et al., 1995). Exposure to common forms of illness and injury that accompany advancing age may also be an important factor. Chronic stress is known to cause responses that disrupt plasticity and other cellular processes (McEwen, 2000). Furthermore, toxins either ingested or exposed during life may alter the nervous system or systems that support nervous system function. Fetal development researchers use the term *teratogen* to describe environmental agents that disturb proper development, such as observed in fetal alcohol syndrome. In adult development, alcohol and other ingested agents can influence the brain through their gradual and sometimes acute damaging effects on the nervous system (Fadda & Rossetti, 1998).

The research strategy best able to describe these forms of change will be to identify age-accumulated lesions, examine their risk factors, and explore their consequences on function. One place where comparison of child development and advanced aging may elucidate this form of change relates to susceptibility. Differential vulnerability to accumulated developmental lesions may be understood in the context of childhood development. For example, structures with the most protracted development, such as anterior white matter pathways, may be more susceptible to acquiring lesions in senescence. Similarly, the ability of the aging brain to tolerate lesions will, in part, relate to the reserve and robustness attained during early development. Lastly, discontinued development, as described in "Discontinued Development" above, may confer increased susceptibility to accumulated lesions.

Emergent Maladaptive Development

This form of process emerges only in advanced aging and is detrimental. Detrimental changes in the brain may result from the acquired state of the post-maturational brain or perhaps as an emergent result of interactions among age-dependent physiological and environmental factors. Pathology associated with Alzheimer's disease may reflect one such example. Assuming the proposed mechanisms are correct, proteins associated with amyloid may become toxic when a certain level is reached in adulthood that is not present, or more effectively tolerated, earlier in life. Antecedent progression may exist, but it is possible that, with some rare and minor exceptions, the toxic influences occur largely in late development and lead to cell death and gross anatomic atrophy only in older adults. The key element here is that the toxic influences of amyloid are not a significant factor until advanced aging. Emergent maladaptive developmental processes will affect the brain only in aging and perhaps not in all individuals. To some degree, this form of process shares similarities to that discussed above as "Maladaptive Consequences of Continuous Developmental Processes." The central difference is whether a novel, qualitatively distinct process emerges, such as a toxic form of amyloid that is separate from forms that convey productive function earlier in life.

Such processes are typically considered pathological when they lead to clinical impairment. Within nondemented older adults, maladaptive emergent processes likely influence cognition prior to impairment levels easily discerned as pathological.

Convergent Responses During Development

Convergent responses during development refers to the possibility of processes that independently emerge during early and late development because of the shared challenges that confront brain systems during those periods. Child development and advanced aging share a fundamental similarity: both represent periods of the lifespan when brain networks are not fully functioning. During childhood development, the brain is still calibrating itself for its intended environment. Functions are gradually coming online, tuning themselves, and expanding (see Chapters 2 and 6, this volume). In advanced aging, brain systems are degrading and being subjected to small and large lesions. For this reason, an interesting question is whether childhood development and advanced aging share similar functional responses to their incomplete states. Processes that reflect productive responses present both in childhood and late life, but not during other periods, will be candidates for convergent development.

One candidate is increased recruitment of frontal regions in advancing age, considered earlier as a possible compensatory response. Similar forms of increased recruitment to that observed in advanced aging also exist in childhood development. For example, Gaillard and colleagues (2000) observed extensive frontal recruitment in children during verbal fluency tasks as compared to young adults, including bilateral patterns of activation reminiscent of that present in older adults (see Casey, Giedd, & Thomas, 2000, for a recent review). Furthermore, Schlaggar et al. (2002) separated school-age children by whether their performance was similar to or worse than young adults. Those children with poor accuracy and slow responses showed increased frontal recruitment, along inferior frontal gyrus, suggesting a performance-dependent response in early development. Studies that directly compare childhood responses in difficult task situations to those of older adults may help us to understand if convergent responses solve challenges experienced at distinct developmental stages.

CONCLUSIONS

Cognition in advanced aging arises from initial brain development, the continuation of lifelong processes, and emergent processes in advanced aging. Six possible forms of lifespan developmental change are discussed above and listed in Table 3.1. In conclusion, we ask one final question to illustrate the ideas of this chapter: What might lifelong development look like in an individual? On the one hand, a satisfying answer cannot be given to this question. Too many factors are at work and too little is known about how they progress and interact. On the other hand, while not representing any true individual, a fictional answer can capture what a person's developmental life *might* look like. Figure 3.6 displays such a fictional person by plotting his lifetime changes in *cortical gray matter*.

Early childhood development begins with a rapid expansion of gray matter (Figure 3.6, A). After about age 10, perhaps due to learning or other origins, a gradual reduction in gray matter takes place that continues throughout adulthood into advanced aging. Superimposed on these extended developmental processes, lesions occur abruptly (C) and accumulate over time. As middle age is passed, continuation of otherwise beneficial processes causes antecedent accumulation of brain pathology (D) that leads to cell loss and clinical impairment in its end stages (E).

In response to these changes, available brain systems react. In early childhood, as functional abilities are rapidly developing, but not yet at optimal capacity, activity in available brain networks increases to accomplish task goals. During adolescence and mid-

dle age, efficiency increases. Tasks that were challenges during childhood become easy and reduced brain resources are required. As development progresses into advanced aging, brain activity is again increased, perhaps as a compensatory response.

As this fictional depiction of lifespan development illustrates, a complex landscape of change and response to change emerges from a continuous interplay of multiple factors. A lifespan perspective targets these complex interactions to understand the factors, and dependencies among factors, that give rise to our lifelong developmental course.

References

Alexander, G. E., DeLong, M. R., & Strick, P. L. (1986). Parallel organization of functionally segregated circuits linking basal ganglia and cortex. *Annual Review of Neuroscience, 9,* 357–381.

Arnsten, A. F. T., Cai, J. X., Murphy, B. L., & Goldman-Rakic, P. S. (1994). Dopamine D-1 receptor mechanisms in the cognitive performance of young-adult and aged monkeys. *Psychopharmacology, 116,* 143–151.

Aupée, A. M., Desgranges, B., Eustache, F., Lalevée, C., de la Sayette, V., Viader, F., et al. (2001). Voxel-based mapping of brain hypometabolism in permanent amnesia with PET. *NeuroImage, 13,* 1164–1173.

Baltes, P. B. (1997). On the incomplete architecture of human ontogeny: Selection, optimization, and compensation as foundation of developmental theory. *American Psychologist, 52,* 366–380.

Becker, J. T., Mintun, M. A., Aleva, K., Wiseman, M. B., Nichols, T., & DeKosky, S. T. (1996). Compensatory reallocation of brain resources supporting verbal episodic memory in Alzheimer's disease. *Neurology, 46,* 692–700.

Benson, D. F., Kuhl, D. E., Hawkins, R. A., Phelps, M. E., Cummings, J. L., & Tsai, S. Y. (1983). The fluorodeoxyglucose 18F scan in Alzheimer's disease and multi-infarct dementia. *Archives of Neurology, 40,* 711–714.

Bookheimer, S. Y., Stojwas, M. H., Cohen, M. S., Saunders, A. M., Pericak-Vance, M. A., Mazziotta, J. C., et al. (2000). Patterns of brain activation in people at risk for Alzheimer's disease. *New England Journal of Medicine, 343,* 450–456.

Braak, H., & Braak, E. (1991). Neuropathological staging of Alzheimer-related changes. *Acta Neuropathologica, 81,* 239–259.

Braak, H., & Braak, E. (1997). Staging of Alzheimer-related cortical destruction. *International Psychogeriatrics, 9*(Suppl. 1), 257–261.

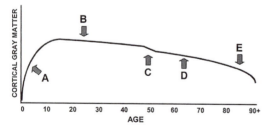

FIGURE 3.6. Lifespan development in a fictional person. Cortical gray matter changes are displayed with milestones labeled by letters (see text). This fictional person illustrates, heuristically, the kind of developmental landscape that might arise from the complex interactions among developmental factors listed in Table 3.1.

Buckner, R.L. (2003). Functional-anatomic correlates of control processes in memory. *Journal of Neuroscience, 23,* 3999–4004.

Buckner, R. L. (2004). Memory and executive function in aging and AD: Multiple factors that cause decline and reserve factors that compensate. *Neuron, 44,* 195–203.

Buckner, R. L., Corbetta, M., Schatz, J., Raichle, M. E., & Petersen, S. E. (1996). Preserved speech abilities and compensation following prefrontal damage. *Proceedings of the National Academy of Sciences, USA, 93,* 1249–1253.

Buckner, R. L., Kelley, W. H., & Petersen, S. E. (1999). Frontal cortex contributes to human memory formation. *Nature Neuroscience, 4,* 311–314.

Buckner, R. L., Snyder, A. Z., Sanders, A. L., Raichle, M. E., & Morris, J. C. (2000). Functional brain imaging of young, nondemented, and demented older adults. *Journal of Cognitive Neuroscience, 12* (Suppl. 2), 23–34.

Cabeza, R. (2002). Hemispheric asymmetry reduction in older adults: The HAROLD model. *Psychology and Aging, 17,* 85–100.

Cabeza, R., Anderson, N. D., Locantore, J. K., & McIntosh, A. R. (2002). Aging gracefully: Compensatory brain activity in high-performing older adults. *NeuroImage, 17,* 1394–1402.

Cabeza, R., Grady, C. L., Nyberg, L., McIntosh, A. R., Tulving, E., Kapur, S., et al. (1997). Age-related differences in neural activity during memory encoding and retrieval: A positron emission tomography study. *Journal of Neuroscience, 17,* 391–400.

Casey, B. J., Giedd, J. N., & Thomas, K. M. (2000). Structural and functional brain development and its relations to cognitive development. *Biological Psychology, 54,* 241–257.

Cohen, N. J., & Eichenbaum, H. (1993). *Memory, amnesia, and the hippocampal system.* Cambridge, MA: MIT Press.

Courchesne, E., Chisum, H. J., Townsend, J., Cowles, A., Covington, J., Egaas, B., et al. (2000). Normal brain development and aging: Quantitative analysis at *in vivo* MR imaging in healthy volunteers. *Radiology, 216,* 672–682.

Craik, F. I. M., Morris, L. W., Morris, R. G., & Loewen, E. R. (1990). Relations between source amnesia and frontal lobe functioning in older adults. *Psychology and Aging, 5,* 148–151.

Davis, P., & Wright, E. A. (1977). A new method for measuring cranial cavity volume and its application to the assessment of cerebral atrophy at autopsy. *Neuropathology and Applied Neurobiology, 3,* 341–358.

DeCarli, C., & Scheltens, P. (2002). Structural brain imaging. In T. Erkinjuntti & S. Gauthier (Eds.), *Vascular cognitive impairment.* London: Martin Dunitz Ltd.

D'Esposito, M., Zarahn, E., Aguirre, G. K., & Rypma, B. (1999). The effect of normal aging on the coupling of neural activity to the bold hemodynamic response. *NeuroImage, 10,* 6–14.

D'Esposito, M., Deouell, L. Y., & Gazzaley, A. (2003). Alterations in the BOLD fMRI signal with ageing and disease: A challenge for neuroimaging. *Nature Reviews Neuroscience, 4,* 863–872.

Fadda, F., & Rossetti, Z. L. (1998). Chronic ethanol consumption: From neuroadaptation to neurodegeneration. *Progress in Neurobiology, 56,* 385–431.

Fletcher, P. C., & Henson, R. N. A. (2001). Frontal lobes and human memory – Insights from functional neuroimaging. *Brain, 124,* 849–881.

Fotenos, A. F., Snyder, A. Z., Girton, L. E., Morris, J. C., & Buckner, R. L. (2005). Normative estimates of cross-sectional and longitudinal brain volume decline in aging and AD. *Neurology, 64,* 1032–1039.

Gaillard, W. D., Hertz-Pannier, L., Mott, S. H., Barnett, A. S., LeBihan, D., & Theodore, W. H. (2000). Functional anatomy of cognitive development – fMRI of verbal fluency in children and adults. *Neurology, 54,* 180–185.

Glisky, E. L., Polster, M. R., & Routhieaux, B. C. (1995). Double dissociation between item and source memory. *Neuropsychology, 9,* 229–235.

Goate, A., Chartier-Harlin, M. C., Mullan, M., Brown, J., Crawford, F., Fidani, L., et al. (1991). Segregation of a missence mutation in the amyloid precursor protein gene with familial Alzheimer's disease. *Nature, 349,* 704–706.

Golde, T. E., Eckman, C. B., & Younkin, S. G. (2000). Biochemical detection of A(isoforms: Implications for pathogenesis, diagnosis, and treatment of Alzheimer's disease. *Biochimica et Biophysica Acta, 1502,* 172–187.

Good, C. D., Johnsrude, I. S., Ashburner, J., Henson, R. N. A., Friston, K. J., & Frackowiak, R. S. J. (2001). A voxel-based morphometric study of aging in 465 normal adult human brains. *NeuroImage, 14,* 21–36.

Grady, C. L., & Craik, F. I. M. (2000). Changes in memory processing with age. *Current Opinions in Neurobiology, 10,* 224–231.

Grady, C. L., McIntosh, A. R., Beig, S., Keightley, M. L., Burian, H., & Black, E. (2003). Evidence from functional neuroimaging of a compensatory prefrontal network in Alzheimer's disease. *Journal of Neuroscience, 23,* 986–993.

Grady, C. L., McIntosh, A. R., Horwitz, B., Maisog, J. M., Ungerleider, L. G., Mentis, M. J., et al. (1995). Age-related reductions in human recognition memory due to impaired encoding. *Science, 269,* 218–221.

Greenwood, P. M. (2000). The frontal aging hypothesis evaluated. *Journal of the International Neuropsychological Society, 6,* 705–726.

Greicius, M. D., Srivastava, G., Reiss, A. L., & Menon, V. (2004). Default-mode network activity distinguishes Alzheimer's disease from healthy aging: Evidence from functional MRI. *Proceedings of the National Academy of Sciences, USA, 101,* 4637–4642.

Hasher, L., & Zacks, R. T. (1988). Working memory, comprehension, and aging: A review and a new view. In G. H. Bower (Ed.), *The psychology of learning and motivation: Advances in research and theory* (Vol. 22, pp.193–225). San Diego, CA: Academic Press.

Head, D., Buckner, R. L., Shimony, J. S., Williams, L. E., Akbudak, E., Conturo, T. E., et al. (2004). Differential vulnerability of anterior white matter in nondemented aging with minimal acceleration in dementia of the Alzheimer type: Evidence from diffusion tensor imaging. *Cerebral Cortex, 14,* 410–423.

Head, D., Snyder, A.Z., Girton, L.E., Morris, J.C., & Buckner, R.L. (2005). Frontal-hippocampal double dissociation between normal aging and Alzheimer's disease. *Cerebral Cortex, 15,* 732–739.

Hedden, T., & Gabrieli, J. D. E. (2004). Insights into the ageing mind: A view from cognitive neuroscience. *Nature Reviews Neuroscience, 5,* 87–96.

Heeger, D. J., & Ress, D. (2002). What does fMRI tell us about neuronal activity? *Nature Reviews Neuroscience, 3,* 142–151.

Huettel, S. A., Guezeldere, G., & McCarthy, G. (2001). Dissociating the neural mechanisms of visual attention in change detection using functional fMRI. *Journal of Cognitive Neuroscience, 13,* 1006–1018.

Jack, C. R., Jr., & Petersen, R. C. (2000). Structural imaging approaches to Alzheimer's disease. In L. F. M. Scinto & K. R. Daffner (Eds.), *Early diagnosis and treatment of Alzheimer's disease* (pp. 127–148). Totowa, NJ: Human Press.

Jack, C. R., Jr., Petersen, R. C., O'Brien, P. C., & Tangalos, E. G. (1992). MR-based hippocampal volumetry in the diagnosis of Alzheimer's disease. *Neurology, 42,* 183–188.

Jack, C. R., Jr., Shiung, M. M., Gunter, J. L., O'Brien, P. C., Weigand, S. D., Knopman, D. S., et al. (2004). Comparison of different MRI brain atrophy rate measures with clinical disease progression in AD. *Neurology, 62,* 591–600.

Jennings, J. M., & Jacoby, L. L. (1993). Automatic versus intentional uses of memory: Aging, attention, and control. *Psychology and Aging, 8,* 283–293.

Kalimo, H., Ruchoux, M. M., Viitanen, M., & Kalaria, R. N. (2002). CADASIL: A common form of hereditary arteriopathy causing brain infarcts and dementia. *Brain Pathology, 12,* 371–384.

Kapur, S., Tulving, E., Cabeza, R., McIntosh, A. R., Houle, S., & Craik, F. I. M. (1996). The neural correlates of intentional learning of verbal materials: A PET study in humans. *Cognitive Brain Research, 4,* 243–249.

Kemper, T. L. (1994). Neuroanatomical and neuropathological changes during aging and dementia. In M. L. Albert & J. E. Knoefel (Eds.), *Clinical neurology of aging* (2nd ed., pp.3–67). New York: Oxford University Press.

Killiany, R. J., Moss, M. B., Albert, M. S., Sandor, T., Tieman, J., & Jolesz, F. (1993). Temporal lobe regions on magnetic resonance imaging identify patients with early Alzheimer's disease. *Archives of Neurology, 50,* 949–954.

Kolb, B., & Whishaw, I. Q. (1996). *Fundamentals of human neuropsychology* (4th ed.). New York: W. H. Freeman.

Kuhn, H. G., Dickinson-Anson, H., & Gage, F. H. (1996). Neurogenesis in the dentate gyrus of the adult rat: Age-related decrease of neuronal progenitor proliferation. *Journal of Neuroscience, 16,* 2027–2033.

Lavenex, P., Suzuki, W. A., & Amaral, D. G. (2002). Perirhinal and parahippocampal cortices of the macaque monkey: Projections to the neocortex. *Journal of Comparative Neurology, 447,* 394–420.

LeBihan, D., Mangin, J. F., Poupon, C., Clark, C. A., Pappata, S., Molko, N., et al. (2001). Diffusion tensor imaging: Concepts and applications. *Journal of Magnetic Resonance Imaging, 13,* 534–546.

Leon, M. J., Convit, A., Wolf, O. T., Tarshish, C. Y., DeSanti, S., Rusinek, H., et al. (2001). Prediction of cognitive decline in normal elderly subjects with 2-[(18)F]fluoro-2-deoxy-D-glucose/poitron-emission tomography (FDG/PET). *Proceedings of the National Academy of Sciences, USA, 98,* 10966–10971.

Light, L. L. (1991). Memory and aging: Four hypotheses in search of data. *Annual Review of Psychology, 42,* 333–376.

Lindenberger, U., & Baltes, P. B. (1994). Sensory functioning and intelligence in old age: A strong connection. *Psychology and Aging, 9,* 339–355.

Loesnner, A., Alavi, A., Lewandrowski, K. U., Mozley, D., Souder, E., & Gur, R. E. (1995). Regional cerebral function determined by FDG-PET in healthy volunteers: Normal patterns and changes with age. *Journal of Nuclear Medicine, 36,* 1141–1149.

Logan, J. M., Sanders, A. L., Snyder, A. Z., Morris, J. C., & Buckner, R. L. (2002). Under-recruitment and nonselective recruitment: Dissociable neural mechanisms associated with aging. *Neuron, 33,* 827–840.

Lustig, C., Snyder, A. Z., Bhakta, M., O'Brien, K. C., McAvoy, M., Raichle, M. E., Morris, J.C., & Buckner, R.L. (2003). Functional deactivations: Change with age and dementia of the Alzheimer type. *Proceedings of the National Academy of Sciences, USA, 100,* 14504–14509.

Lustig, C., & Buckner, R.L. (2004). Preserved neural correlates of priming in old age and dementia. *Neuron, 40,* 865–875.

McEwen, B. S. (2000). The neurobiology of stress: From serendipity to clinical relevance. *Brain Research, 886,* 172–189.

Meguro, K., Blazoit, X., Kondoh, Y., Le Mestric, C., Baron, J.-C., & Chavoix, C. (1999). Neocortical and hippocampal glucose hypometabolism following neurotoxic lesions of the entorhinal and perirhinal cortices in the non-human primate as shown by PET: Implications for Alzheimer's disease. *Brain, 122,* 1519–1533.

Middleton, F. A., & Strick, P. L. (2001). A revised neuroanatomy of frontal-subcortical circuits. In D. G. Lichter & J. L. Cummings (Eds.), *Frontal-subcortical circuits in psychiatric and neurological disorders* (pp. 44–58). New York: Guilford Press.

Millien, I., Blazoit, X., Giffard, C., Mezenge, F., Insausti, R., Baron, J.-C., et al. (2002). Brain glucose hypometabolism after perirhinal lesions in baboons: Implications for Alzheimer disease and aging. *Journal of Cerebral Blood Flow and Metabolism, 22,* 1248–1261.

Moscovitch, M., & Winocur, G. (1995). Frontal lobes, memory, and aging. *Annals of the New York Academy of Sciences, 769,* 119–150.

Neil, J., Miller, J., Mukherjee, P., & Huppi, P. S. (2002). Diffusion tensor imaging of normal and injured developing human brain—A technical review. *NMR in Biomedicine, 15,* 543–552.

Nyberg, L., Sandblom, J., Jones, S., Stigsdotter-Neely, A., Magnus-Petersson, K., Ingvar, M., et al. (2003). Neural correlates of train-related memory improvement in adulthood and aging. *Proceedings of the National Academy of Sciences, USA, 100,* 13728–13733.

O'Sullivan, M., Jones, D. K., Summers, P. E., Morris, R. G., Williams, S. C., & Markus, H. S. (2001). Evidence for cortical "disconnection" as a mechanism of age-related cognitive decline. *Neurology, 57,* 632–638.

Pantoni, L., & Garcia, J. H. (1997). Pathogenesis of leukoaraiosis: A review. *Stroke, 28,* 652–659.

Park, D. C., Polk, T. A., Mikels, J. A., Taylor, S. F., & Marshuetz, C. (2001). Cerebral aging: Integration of brain and behavioral models of cognitive function. *Dialogues in Clinical Neuroscience, 3,* 151–165.

Park, D. C., & Gutchess, A. H. (2005). Long-term memory and aging: A cognitive neuroscience perspective. In R. Cabeza, L. Nyberg, & D. Park (Eds.), *Cognitive neuroscience of aging: Linking cognitive and cerebral aging* (pp. 218–245). New York: Oxford University Press.

Peters, A., Rosene, D. L., Moss, M. B., Kemper, T. L., Abraham, C. R., Tigges, J., et al. (1996). Neurobiological bases of age-related cognitive decline in the rhesus monkey. *Journal of Neuropathology and Experimental Neurology, 55,* 861–874.

Pfefferbaum, A., Mathalon, D. H., Sullivan, E. V., Rawles, J. M., Zipursky, R. B., & Lim, K. O. (1994). A quantitative magnetic resonance imaging study of changes in brain morphology from infancy to late adulthood. *Archives of Neurology, 51,* 874–887.

Pfefferbaum, A., Sullivan, E. V., Hedehus, M., Lim, K. O., Adalsteinsson, E., & Moseley, M. (2000). Age-related decline in brain white matter anisotropy measured with spatially corrected echo-planar diffusion tensor imaging. *Magnetic Resonance in Medicine, 44,* 259–268.

Pugh, K. G., & Lipsitz, L. A. (2002). The microvascular frontal-subcortical syndrome of aging. *Neurobiology, 23,* 421–431.

Raichle, M. E. (1987). Circulatory and metabolic correlates of brain function in normal humans. In F. Plum & V. Mountcastle (Eds.), *The handbook of physiology: Section 1. The nervous system: Vol. V. Higher Functions of the Brain: Pt. 1.* (pp. 643–674). Bethesda, MD: American Physiological Society.

Raz, N. (2000). Aging of the brain and its impact on cognitive performance: Integration of structural and functional findings. In F. I. M. Craik & T. A. Salthouse (Eds.), *The handbook of aging and cognition* (2nd ed., pp. 1–90). Mahwah, NJ: Erlbaum.

Raz, N., Gunning, F. M., Head, D., Dupuis, J. H., McQuain, J., Briggs, S. D., et al. (1997). Selective aging of the human cerebral cortex observed *in vivo*: Differential vulnerability of the prefrontal gray matter. *Cerebral Cortex, 7,* 268–282.

Raz, N., Rodrigue, K. M., Kennedy, K. M., Head, D., Gunning-Dixon, F., & Acker, J. D. (2003). Differential aging of the human striatum: Longitudinal evidence. *American Journal of Neuroradiology, 24,* 1849–1856.

Reddy, H., De Stefano, N., Mortilla, M., Federico, A., & Matthews, P. M. (2002). Functional reorganization of motor cortex increases with greater axonal injury from CADASIL. *Stroke, 33,* 502–508.

Reed, L. J., Marsden, P., Lasserson, D., Sheldon, N., Lewis, P., Stanhope, N., et al. (1999). FDG-PET analysis and findings in amnesia resulting from hypoxia. *Memory, 7,* 599–612.

Reiss, A. L., Abrams, M. T., Singer, H. S., Ross, J. L., & Denckla, M. B. (1996). Brain development, gender and IQ in children: A volumetric imaging study. *Brain, 119,* 1763–1774.

Resnick, S. M., Pham, D. L., Kraut, M. A., Zonderman, A. B., & Davatzikos, C. (2003). Longitudinal magnetic resonance imaging studies of older adults: A shrinking brain. *Journal of Neuroscience, 23,* 3295–3301.

Reuter-Lorenz, P. A. (2002). New visions of the aging mind and brain. *Trends in Cognitive Sciences, 6,* 394–400.

Reuter-Lorenz, P. A., Jonides, J., Smith, E. E., Hartley, A., Miller, A., Marshuetz, C., et al. (2000). Age differences in the frontal lateralization of verbal and spatial working memory revealed by PET. *Journal of Cognitive Neuroscience, 12,* 174–187.

Rosen, A. C., Prull, M. W., O'Hara, R., Race, E. A., Desmond, J. E., Glover, G. H., et al. (2002). Variable effects of aging on frontal lobe contributions to memory. *Neuroreport, 13,* 2425–2428.

Rubin, D. C. (1999). Frontal-striatal circuits in cognitive aging: Evidence for caudate involvement. *Aging, Neuropsychology, and Cognition, 6,* 241–259.

Salat, D. H., Buckner, R. L., Snyder, A. Z., Greve, D. N., Desikan, R. S., Busa, E., et al. (2004). Thinning of the cerebral cortex in aging. *Cerebral Cortex, 14,* 721–730.

Salthouse, T. A. (1996). The processing-speed theory of adult age differences in cognition. *Psychological Review, 103,* 403–428.

Salthouse, T. A., & Ferrer-Caja, E. (2003). What needs to be explained to account for age-related effects on multiple cognitive variables? *Psychology and Aging, 18,* 91–110.

Schlaggar, B. L., Brown, T. T., Lugar, H. M., Visscher, K. M., Miezin, F. M., & Petersen, S. E. (2002). Functional neuroanatomical differences between adults and school-age children in the processing of single words. *Science, 296,* 1476–1479.

Schott, J. M., Fox, N. C., Frost, C., Scahill, R. I., Janssen, J. C., Chan, D., et al. (2003). Assessing the onset of structural change in familial Alzheimer's disease. *Annals of Neurology, 53,* 181–188.

Selkoe, D. J. (2001). Alzheimer's disease: Genes, proteins, and therapy. *Physiological Reviews, 81,* 741–766.

Silverman, D. H., Gambhir, S. S., Huang, H. W., Schwimmer, J., Kim, S., Small, G. W., et al. (2002). Evaluating early dementia with and without assessment of regional cerebral metabolism by PET: A comparison of predicted costs and benefits. *Journal of Nuclear Medicine, 43,* 253–266.

Söderlund, H., Nyberg, L., Adolfsson, R., Nilsson, L. G., & Launer, L. J. (2003). High prevalence of white matter hyperintensities in normal aging: Relation to blood pressure and cognition. *Cortex, 39,* 1093–1105.

Sowell, E. R., Peterson, B. S., Thompson, P. M., Welcome, S. E., Henkenius, A. L., & Toga, A. W. (2003). Mapping cortical change across the human life span. *Nature Neuroscience, 6,* 309–315.

Squire, L. R. (1992). Memory and the hippocampus: A synthesis from findings with rats, monkeys, and humans. *Psychological Review, 99,* 195–231.

Stebbins, G. T., Carrillo, M. C., Dorfman, J., Dirksen, C., Desmond, J. E., Turner, D. A., et al. (2002). Aging effects on memory encoding in the frontal lobes. *Psychology and Aging, 17,* 44–55.

Stern, Y. (2002). What is cognitive reserve? Theory and research application of the reserve concept. *Journal of the International Neuropsychological Society, 8,* 448–460.

Suzuki, W. A., & Amaral, D. G. (1994). Perirhinal and parahippocampal cortices of the macaque monkey: Cortical afferents. *Journal of Computational Neurology, 350,* 497–533.

Troen, B. R. (2003). The biology of aging. *Mount Sinai Journal of Medicine, 70,* 3–22.

Vogt, B. A., Finch, D. M., & Olson, C. R. (1992). Functional heterogeneity in cingulate cortex: The anterior executive and posterior evaluative regions. *Cerebral Cortex, 2,* 526–535.

West, R. L. (1996). An application of prefrontal cortex function theory to cognitive aging. *Psychological Bulletin, 120,* 272–292.

Wu, C. C., Mungas, D., Eberling, J. L., Reed, B. R., & Jagust, W. J. (2002). Imaging interactions between Alzheimer's disease and cerebrovascular disease. *Annals of the New York Academy of Sciences, 977,* 403–410.

Ylikoski, A., Erkinjuntti, T., Raininko, R., Sarna, S., Sulkava, R., & Tilvis, R. (1995). White matter hyperintensities on MRI in the neurologically nondiseased elderly. *Stroke, 26,* 1171–1177.

4

Four Modes of Selection

James T. Enns

Lana M. Trick

The concept of selective attention is fundamental to understanding human behavior. And in everyday life, it is clear that there are marked differences in attention among individuals. Some have special talents and others face special challenges; individuals of different ages display predictably different capacities. Some of these differences reflect a genetically determined plan governing neural growth, maturation, and senescence, whereas others reflect specific positive events such as the acquisition of expertise and negative events such as pathology or injury. In this article we address three questions: What is attention? How does attention change during childhood? What are the consequences of these changes in daily life? We examine these questions primarily for the visual modality, although we believe that attention in other modalities follows similar principles.

A harsh reality that confronts all students of selective attention is that the literature is fragmented, making the study of individual differences a daunting task. This is especially true of individual differences that stem from human development and aging. The basic research on adults is carried on in isolation from the work on children and older adults. These literatures in turn make little contact with studies of special populations, and there is little communication between those doing basic and applied research. In this chapter we propose an ambitious new framework that has the potential to integrate our understanding of attentional performance in individuals of all kinds, both in how they perform experimental tasks and in how they perform common day-to-day tasks such as taking part in sports and driving.

We begin by describing the framework in broad terms. We then apply this framework to the study of age-related changes in children. In doing so, it will become clear that this framework is also useful in the study of senior citizens, as well as other special populations, such as persons with autism, elite athletes, and crash-prone automobile drivers. Our goal is to provide a way of understanding the sources not only of age-related change but also of stability, the origins of individual diversity, and the consistencies that define a common human nature.

To start, what is attention? If one examines the variety of tasks used to measure attention (e.g., covert orienting, visual search, filtering, multiple target tracking, dual tasks, and multiple action monitoring), it becomes clear that all measures require selection of one kind or another. Selection is needed because there is simply too much information for all of it to be used in the ongoing and timely control of action. Some signals must be selected while others are ignored, choices must be made, and priorities must be set. For these reasons, we define attention as *selection*.

It is also clear that there are different types of selection. It is our view that selective attention can best be understood in terms of a framework based on two fundamental dimensions (Trick, Enns, Mills, & Vavrik, 2004), as shown in Figure 4.1. The first concerns whether selection occurs with or without awareness. Selection without awareness has been variously called preattentive, inattentional, subconscious, unconscious, and unintentional. The key feature of this type of selection is that it is *automatic* (Shiffrin & Schneider, 1977), which is to say that selection is rapid, effortless, and without intention. Automatic selection is triggered by the presence of certain stimuli in the environment and runs to completion with little interference from other processes. Thus, some stimuli are selected even when the focus of conscious awareness is elsewhere or on another task.

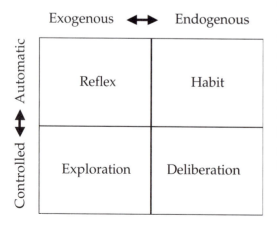

FIGURE 4.1. Four modes of selective attention, based on the two dimensions of automaticity – control (the degree of conscious control) and exogenous – endogenous (the extent of learning required).

Selection with awareness has been variously called attentive, conscious, or intentional. Stimuli that are selected in this way are given full perceptual analysis and transferred to working memory. This type of selection involves *control* (Shiffrin & Schneider, 1977), which is to say that selection is effortful and slow, but it can be started, stopped, or modified at will, a feature that makes this type of processing flexible and intelligent. Controlled processes can produce changes in explicit long-term memory through learning, and with adequate practice some types of controlled processes may even become automatic providing there is a fixed relationship between specific stimuli and responses (e.g., a search task where certain items are always targets and others are always distractors). The fundamental limitation is that only one controlled process can be conducted at a time.

The second dimension concerns the origin of the selective process. Some processes are innately specified, meaning that they do not need to be learned and are thus common to all. *Exogenous* selection occurs as a result of the way humans are built and is initiated by specific stimuli. In this case, external (exogenous) stimuli seem to trigger selection, but the reason they have this effect is based on the way the nervous system is organized. Specifically, there is an innate continuum of stimulus salience, with some types of stimuli more likely to receive exogenous selection than others.

Other processes are engendered by an individual's specific goals at a given time and are thus idiosyncratic and situation-specific. *Endogenous* selection results from what people know about an environment and what they want to achieve. People actively search the environment for information relevant to specific goals or intentions; they perform these tasks in ways that are consistent with their expectations and previous learning (endogenous factors). Expectancies may act as a *perceptual set*, causing people to look for specific objects at certain locations. A perceptual set can be advantageous because it directs viewers to goal-relevant information, but at the same time it impedes the perception of stimuli that do not conform to these expectations or goals.

FOUR MODES OF SELECTION

Figure 4.2 outlines the central features of each of the four modes of selection. Two of these modes involve automatic processes. *Reflexes* are innately specified

Reflex	**Habit**
• innately specified	• learned when goal repeated in specific environment
• triggered by stimuli given priority by the nervous system	• triggered by stimuli associated with specific goals in past
• unconscious, automatic, fast, obligatory, effortless	• unconscious, automatic, fast, obligatory, effortless
• avoided only with deliberation	• avoided only with deliberation
• emerges on a developmental timetable	• can emerge at any time
• stable once acquired	• can fade or be replaced at any time; strength varies with practice
Exploration	**Deliberation**
• innately specified generic goal for novel situations	• goal is internally generated and specific to the individual and context
• default mode for controlled processing	• occurs when individuals are carrying out specific goals in a specific context
• conscious, controlled, slow, optional, effortful	• conscious, controlled, slow, optional, effortful
• occurs when the only goal is exploration	• specific goals changed at will, but switches in goals take time
• generic goal easily replaced by specific goal (switch to deliberation)	• needed to overcome unwanted automatic processes
	• interferes with other deliberately selected goals

FIGURE 4.2. Aspects of each of the four modes of selective attention, including how it is acquired, what the triggering stimuli are, the degree of conscious control that is possible, and the stability of each mode over time.

and triggered by the presence of certain stimuli in the environment. In contrast, *habits* come into existence when the operations necessary to fulfill a certain goal are carried out so often in a certain context that they become automatic.

There are two critical differences between reflex and habit. First, though both are "triggered" by the presence of certain stimuli, the triggers for reflexes are innately specified (and common to all) whereas the triggers for habits are learned (and idiosyncratic, specific to an individual's learning history). Second, reflexes emerge on a developmental timetable and are stable once ac-

quired whereas habits can be formed at any time and can fade or be replaced at any time owing to lack of practice or new learning. Both can be problematic in that they may be triggered in situations where they are inappropriate, in which case processes involving deliberate selection will be required to compensate—processes that require time, effort, and planning.

The other two modes involve controlled processes. *Exploration* is the default mode for controlled processing, a type of selection carried out in the absence of specific goals. We argue that innate preferences set the default for what is attended when humans explore environments that they have no specific goals for or expectations about, environments lacking the stimulus triggers necessary to evoke reflex or habit. Exploration requires controlled processing because in most cases full object recognition requires attention. In contrast, *deliberation* involves the execution of a specific chosen attention-demanding process at the expense of other processes. It involves goals that reflect an individual's specific knowledge, plans, and strategies for a certain situation. Deliberate processing is noticeably effortful and time-consuming, but of all the modes of processing, it is the most flexible and responsive to new information because it is conscious and internally directed. Deliberate selection is also necessary when unwanted habits or reflexes must be brought under control.

AGE-RELATED CHANGES IN THE FOUR MODES OF SELECTION

This framework predicts that age-related change and individual variation will be more apparent in some modes of selection than in others. Three guiding principles emerge:

1. There is more age-related change in the two endogenous modes of selection (habit and deliberation) than in the two exogenous modes (reflex and exploration) because the former are driven by specific goals for certain situations. They are also more idiosyncratic because they reflect specific learning histories, which will vary as a function of age and experience. In contrast, the two exogenous modes represent innately specified default settings that give certain types of stimuli increased salience in a common way for all humans.

2. Age-related change is more evident in the two controlled modes of selection (exploration and deliberation) than in the two automatic modes (reflex and habit) because the areas of the brain mediating controlled processes (i.e., prefrontal cortex) are among the last to develop and the first to deteriorate with age. It is controlled processing that suffers first in the event of injury and pathology.

3. By combining the first two principles we can predict that, among the four modes of selection, reflexive selection will show the least change with age whereas deliberate selection will show the greatest variability and idiosyncrasy.

Because of the breadth of this framework, we cannot provide a comprehensive review of all relevant research. Instead, we will work through the four modes of selection, from the least to the most variable, highlighting findings that exemplify these principles. In each section we will begin with developmental research, but then also point to studies involving senior adults and finally other populations such as athletes and crash-prone drivers in which these same principles apply.

VISUAL REFLEXES

Among the most universal response tendencies of humans is orienting toward the location of an abrupt transient in illumination (Egeth & Yantis, 1997). Under everyday circumstances, such orienting is evident in movements of the body, head, and eyes to align the source of the new signal with the highly sensitive fovea (center) of the eye. This tendency is evident at birth (Colombo, 2001), and it persists through a wide variety of human neuropathologies, including autism (Burack, Enns, Stauder, Mottron, & Randolph, 1997), and Down syndrome (Serna & Carlin, 2001). It is also strongly present in the elderly (see Kramer & Kray, Chapter 5, this volume). Spatial orienting of this kind has the obvious adaptive advantage that it allows for the careful inspection of an object that appears abruptly in the visual field, either because the object is entering the same environment as the individual or because the individual has made an eye movement that brings the object into view.

Attention researchers often distinguish between the observable consequences of orienting, such as head and eye movements (called *overt orienting*), and the less directly observable orienting of the "mind's eye" toward the location of an abrupt visual signal (called *covert orienting*). Of the two, covert orienting is the more difficult to measure in many participant populations because it cannot be indexed by direct observation. The most common behavioral technique involves the participant's performing a primary task, such as target detection or discrimination, while the experimenter manipulates the visual events that precede the presentation of the target. For example, if the event that precedes a visual target is a brief presentation of a nontarget stimulus at the same location as the target, the response to the target is speeded and made more accurately. If the same event occurs at a nontarget location, it tends to slow target response and reduce accuracy.

The measurement of covert orienting is possible only for participants willing and able to perform a target detection or discrimination task. In the study of healthy human children, this usually means that the youngest studied age groups are 3–5 years of age (Enns & Brodeur, 1989; Randolph, 2002; Ristic, Friesen, & Kingstone, 2002). For many developmentally disabled populations, the lower age bound is considerable higher (Burack & Enns, 1997). Yet, within these constraints, the data have been quite consistent in showing that covert orienting differs little in the course of typical development across the lifespan and even differs little among the various special populations that have been tested (Plude, Enns, & Brodeur, 1994; Burack & Enns, 1997). In our own laboratory, we have also tested whether covert orienting is more strongly developed in participants who might be expected to have extra incentive or opportunity to engage in covert orienting in the course of their skilled activities. These include elite junior hockey players (Enns & Richards, 1997) and university athletes in swimming, track, soccer, and volleyball (Lum, Enns, & Pratt, 2002). So far, the answer has been no. The basic covert orienting reflex seems to be very stable even for these experts in orienting.

A second example of an important visual reflex is the strong tendency to orient spatial attention in the direction indicated by the eye gaze (Friesen & Kingstone, 1998), finger pointing (Langton & Bruce, 1999), or body posture (Langton, Watt, & Bruce, 2000) of another human who is being observed. For example, in the study by Friesen & Kingstone (1998), college-age observers performed a simple detection task in which the target could appear suddenly either on the left or the right of fixation. Importantly, a simple cartoon face preceded the target, with eyes drawn as simple open circles. Prior to the appearance of the target, the eyes suddenly acquired pupils (small black disks) that were shifted to either one side of the eyes (open circles) or the other. Although these shifts in eye gaze direction were randomly associated with target location, they nonetheless speeded target detection when the direction of gaze coincided with the target location.

This spontaneous sensitivity to the direction of gaze in a human face has been demonstrated in 10-week-old human infants (Hood, Willen, & Driver, 1998), adult chimpanzees (Povinelli & Eddy, 1996), and 3–5-year-old preschoolers (Ristic et al., 2002). In a study of preschoolers (Ristic et al., 2002), the only study in which the methods used with young children could be compared directly to those of adults, the children showed an even more robust tendency than the adults to orient in the direction of the gaze of the schematic face. Our interpretation is that the gaze orienting reflex is attenuated to some extent in older participants, in much the same way that older participants in developmental studies often show smaller effects of covert orienting to unpredictable luminance transients (Plude et al., 1994). In those studies, it has also been shown that the relative age ordering of the orienting effects can be reversed by making the luminance transient a predictive signal to the location of the target (Enns & Brodeur, 1989). We will have more to say about the modulation of visual reflexes in the upcoming section on deliberation.

Interestingly, adolescent individuals with autism who are diagnosed around the age of 2 years on the basis of failing to show typical effects of social interaction also fail to show gaze-directed cuing effects, at least for eye gaze cues that are nonpredictive (Ristic, Mottron, Iarocci, Burack, & Kingstone, 2002). However, these same individuals show eye gaze cuing effects when the eye direction is made to be highly predictive of the target location. This is in keeping with their relatively high visual-motor ability, when contrasted with their limited social skills. It is consistent with the anecdotal observations often made about individuals with autism—namely, that they treat other humans in the same utilitarian way as they treat other objects in their environment.

A final class of important visual reflexes can be found among the so-called visual-geometric illusions (Coren & Girgus, 1978). These are patterned stimulus events that lead to perceptions that are at odds with the actual physical conditions. We are surrounded by visual illusions at all times and for the most part we are oblivious to them. Perhaps the everyday illusions we pay least attention to are pictures. Photos, representational art, line drawings, and even cartoons are all examples of stimuli that evoke in us immediate and meaningful perceptions, usually of three-dimensional objects and scenes, even though they are completely flat and static reproductions of events. Pictures mimic, in some minimal respects, the important qualities of the physical conditions that usually give rise to our perceptions when we are viewing the three-dimensional world. They do this, and yet at the same time we can be acutely aware of the fact that we are viewing a flat picture in addition to having the meaningful experience evoked by the depicted objects. Gregory (1966) has aptly referred to this as the "dual reality" of picture perception.

Although there are many aspects of picture perception that depend on experience, we know that pictures evoke responses in infants that are often identical to the reactions evoked by the real object, such as their own mother (Spelke, 1990). In one of the most daring developmental experiments ever undertaken, Julian Hochberg and Virginia Brooks (1962) raised their son for the first 2 years of life with no exposure to pictures of any kind. They did this because they were so confident that picture perception was innate. The experiment was heroic because it meant that television, magazines, books, and product wrappers were not in his environment. On occasional rides in the car, his older sister was assigned the task of shielding his eyes from road signs. At the age of 2 years, the son passed the test of naming line-drawn objects with flying colors. The conclusion was that no special learning was required to recognize objects based only on a pictorial representation of their edges.

The developmental research on many other geometric illusions shows that some of them decrease in strength during childhood whereas others increase in strength (Coren & Girgus, 1978). It seems reasonable to assume, as was the case for covert orienting, that those that decrease in strength with age do so because other developmental processes permit the observer to understand and overcome the illusion. Interestingly, what the age-decreasing illusions have in common with each other is that they are based on the Gestalt principles of perceptual grouping. These principles allow the visual system to locate contours in images and to group them into clusters based on whether they are adjacent, similar, and can form continuous lines. This is clearly advantageous in most cases in our visual world, but research has shown that these principles lead to interesting illusions when the visual system examines simple displays on a flat surface (Enns & Girgus, 1985).

The research on driving also illustrates that not all illusions are confined to flat surfaces. For example, some roadway designs contribute to safety while others induce car accidents (Shinar, Rockwell & Malecki, 1980). Hills (1980) describes a "perceptual trap" created inadvertently when two nonconnected roads appeared to be coextensive from the driver's perspective. Drivers failed to notice the turn in the first road and sometimes drove right off the highway. The warning signs that were subsequently posted worked to some extent to prevent accidents, but for the present purposes the important point is that these signs were able to warn only of the illusion. They were not able to undo the illusion in the visual system of the drivers. Bringing reflexes under control requires valuable processing time, sustained mental effort, and the mechanisms involved in deliberate selection, and it is here both individual variation and age-related change are most evident, as we will discuss in that section.

VISUAL HABITS

When a goal is enacted repeatedly, carrying it out can become habitual and unconscious, and the processes associated with it eventually become effortless and almost impossible to prevent. Perhaps the visual habit that is most widespread and similar among individuals within the same language community is that of reading text. As those of us who can remember our own early childhoods can vouch, and as everyone with his or her own child can attest, reading is a slowly acquired skill that takes effort, training, and much practice. At the same time, the fact that we cannot turn this visual habit off once it has been learned is clearly illustrated in the famous Stroop effect (MacLeod, 1991); naming the ink color of words that spell incongruent color names is an effortful and slow task.

Research on color-naming Stroop effects in children shows that this is one task in which younger participants are actually better able than older participants to ignore task-irrelevant visual information (Schiller, 1966). This is because these younger participants are not yet reading as automatically as older participants and so the written words do not interfere as readily with the color-naming task. Indeed, when a Stroop task has been compared in good versus poor readers, it is the good readers who show the greatest interference (Comalli, Wapner, & Werner, 1962; Fournier, Mazzarella, Ricciardi, & Fingeret, 1975).

Words and other conventional visual symbols, such as arrows, have recently been shown to have a powerful influence on the orientation of visual attention. In one study, college-age participants were presented with symbols at the center of gaze prior to a simple visual search for the target letter X (Hommel, Pratt, Colzato, & Godijn, 2001). The X appeared randomly in 1 of 4 outline boxes, with the remaining boxes being filled with 3 different letters drawn randomly from the remainder of the alphabet. No-target trials occurred 20% of the time to ensure that the X was really found before the participant responded. A half second prior to the presentation of the target display, either an arrow pointing randomly to 1 of the 4 boxes, or the word *left, right, up* or *down* appeared randomly at the center of the display. Both of these kinds of signals, although they conveyed no reliable information to the participant, and although participants were instructed to ignore them, had a strong influence on the search for the X. Response times were reliably faster on those trials when the X appeared at the location corresponding to the arrow or word.

These findings indicate that, at least for adults, some directional symbols are so well rehearsed and familiar that their meaning cannot be ignored, just as the word spelling a color name interferes with actual color naming in the Stroop task. This was emphasized in a control experiment (Hommel et al., 2001) in which the arrows and words were made 80% predictive of the actual target location. The magnitude of the orienting effect was similar in the predictive and nonpredictive conditions, suggesting that these orienting effects were occurring for overlearned communicative symbols independently of the expectations of the participant.

A recent study tested for nonpredictive spatial cuing by centrally presented arrows in 4- and 5-year-old children (Ristic et al., 2002). The results showed that arrows were as effective as eye gaze in influencing the spatial direction of attention in children this young. Response times to the target object (cartoon snowman or cat) were faster when the target appeared in the location indicated by the central arrows. This shows that these young participants have already learned the visual habits associated with the meaning of an arrow. Future studies will need to test for possible habits associated with arrows in even younger participants, though it seems unlikely that infants will respond reliably and involuntarily to the direction indicated by an arrow. The Ristic et al. (2002) study also compared the responses of children in the arrow-cuing task with those of college students. As in some of the studies on visual reflexes described in the previous section, the orienting effect was larger in absolute terms for children, consistent with the idea that automatic responses are more difficult for young participants to modulate.

A final comparison that can be made concerning the Ristic et al. (2002) and the Kingstone and colleagues (Kingstone, Friesen, & Gazzaniga, 2000) study is the nonpredictive orienting shown by an individual (J.W.) who has had his corpus callosum surgically severed in order to treat intractable epilepsy. This surgery prevents the cortical information in one cerebral hemisphere from communicating directly with the other hemisphere. In the study by Kingstone and colleagues (2000), J.W. was tested with nonpredictive gaze cues, which are thought to orient attention via an innate reflex involving only the right cerebral hemisphere, which contains specialized neurons used in face processing. However, in the Ristic et al. (2002) study, involving a similar design, J.W. was tested with nonpredictive arrows, which are thought to require learning. In keeping with this expected pattern, J.W. showed an orienting effect only for left-sided targets (right hemisphere processing) when gaze cues were used, but showed an orienting effect for targets on both sides when arrows were used.

When it comes to finding attention-related variables to predict automobile crash risk, a good starting point is to look at the effects of experience. Inexperienced drivers are involved in more accidents per mile of exposure than any other group (McGwin & Brown, 1999). Some driving-related processes become automatic and habitual with practice, permitting experienced drivers to drive efficiently while performing other attention-demanding tasks (Shinar, Meir, & Ben-Shoham, 1998; Summala, Nieminen, & Punto, 1996; Wikman, Nieminen, & Summala, 1998). Some of these processes involve habits of selection that enable experienced drivers to know when, where, and how to look (Wikman et al., 1998) and these habits preserve driving performance in the face of age-related deficits in other types of processing. For example, although senior adults show greater performance deficits as a result of visual clutter, visual clutter does not have its usual deleterious effects in familiar environments (Ho, Caird, & Graw, 2001).

However, habits can also blind individuals to the unexpected. Langham, Hole, Edwards, and O'Neil (2002) compared experienced and inexperienced drivers in terms of their ability to notice police cars parked in a driving lane when the cars were parked in line or at an angle with the lane (unexpected and expected locations). Although the experienced drivers generally responded more quickly, they had difficulty detecting the police cars parked in line (unexpected orientation), putting the experienced drivers at greater risk for accidents. In contrast, inexperienced drivers detected parked police cars in either orientation equally well.

VISUAL EXPLORATION

Much of our important visual processing is done in the absence of a specific task or goal to accomplish. We often simply need to learn more about our visual environment, especially when it is new, before we are able to form more specific goals. Yet our visual system is not a blank slate. Some visual stimuli are processed preferentially, even when a person is exploring an unfamiliar environment, with no other goal than to gain new information. As everyone who has attended a museum or a shopping mall can attest, some visually guided actions are performed for no other reason than for the pleasure of manipulating a novel object. Yet this, too, is not arbitrary. Certain attributes can direct visual processing when the goal is primarily to explore.

Selection through exploration is the least researched of the four modes of attention. One of our purposes in highlighting it is to promote research in this area. The research we summarize is a small step in that direction.

One of the methods that hold great promise for studying visual exploration is the *oddball* visual search task. Unlike most visual search tasks, in which the participant is explicitly instructed to search for a specific target, oddball search involves looking for an unspecified target. In other words, there is a meta-level goal of finding an object or display item that doesn't "belong," but this search must be undertaken without the benefit of a search image or even a conceptual category that is known ahead of time.

Research with adults is very conclusive in showing that even for so called pop-out visual search tasks — such as searching for a red item among green items or searching for a vertical bar among horizontal bars — search time is influenced enormously by whether the observer knows ahead of time which feature will be the basis of the pop-out on any give trial (Wolfe, Butcher, Lee, & Hyle, 2003). That is, each of these searches is efficient, in the sense that the slope of response time over the number of display items is flat, but what is influenced greatly by foreknowledge of the target is the mean response time. It can be reduced by several hundred milliseconds if the specific feature

of the target is known in advance. This paradigm, therefore, seems ripe for developmental studies that examine age-related differences in known versus unknown pop-out search. If the exogenous (reflexive) visual processes of younger and older children are alike, then the main developmental differences should emerge in the known rather than the unknown conditions.

One of the important functions of exploration is to notify observers of changes in the environment, but what sort of changes attract attention? The *change detection task* (Rensink, 2002) is another method with potential to increase our understanding of exploration. This is a task in which two versions of the same scene are presented, either side by side or in rapid succession, and the participant's task is to determine what is different in one of the two scenes. Much recent research in this area has shown that even very large changes made to a scene can go unnoticed when there is more than an 80–millisecond blank period between scenes, when an eye movement is made during the inspection of a single scene, when a change in viewpoint occurs (e.g., movie cut), or when the sudden onset of the change is accompanied by the equivalent of "mud splats" that occur in nonchanging scene locations (Simons & Levin, 1997). The ability to detect changes under these conditions can, therefore, become an index of those changes that are attention getting (Scholl, 2000) as well as those objects that are attended because they occur to objects that are of central interest to the observer (Rensink, O'Regan & Clark, 1997). As such it is a rich testing ground for the processes involved in visual exploration.

We recently completed a study of change detection in healthy 7-, 9-, 11- and 27-year-old participants (Shore, Burack, Miller, Joseph, & Enns, 2004). The requirements of the task were carefully selected to ensure that none of the participant groups was at a disadvantage when it came to indicating a detection of the change. That is, instead of making verbal reports as in many studies of change detection, two different pictures were presented on each trial, each alternating over time with a second version of the picture that either contained a change or was identical to the first version. Participants were asked to indicate which of the two pictures being viewed was alternating over time with a different picture, and to indicate this decision with a button press corresponding to the side of the screen on which the change was occurring. The changes made to the pictures included shifts in object color, the deletion and reappearance of a main part, and a mirror-image orientation change from one view to the next.

The experiment was conducted with two different blank intervals between views of the pictures: a short blank of 50 milliseconds was intended to assess change detection when attention was summoned by sensory cues (motion transients and local flicker signal the change) and a longer blank of 250 milliseconds meant that change could be detected only by forming a representation of one picture and comparing it with the next picture. The results showed some age differences in the effects of the sensory cues to summon visual attention to the locations of change. In general, there was a 200–300 millisecond speedup in response time for each successive age group in the comparison of pictures separated by a 50-millisecond blank interval. In addition, changes involving mirror-image orientation of the pictures were detected more rapidly than changes involving color or a missing part, probably because a mirror-imaged picture differs most drastically and in the most locations from one version of a picture to the other. As such, these results for the 50-millisecond conditions simply replicate the findings that response times decrease with age and that abrupt transients in luminance, shape and color tend to orient attention to the locations of those transients.

The more interesting results for the question of visual exploration by children of different ages were revealed in the comparison of the 50- and 250-millisecond blank conditions. When these difference scores were used to index exploratory ability, additional age-related changes were found. In particular, the youngest participants (6–8-year-olds) were the slowest to detect change in the 250-millisecond condition, even after their relatively slow responses in the 50-millisecond condition were taken into account. For all the age groups thereafter, the additional time required in the 250-millisecond condition was approximately a constant of 300–400 milliseconds.

This improvement in change detection between the ages of 7 and 9 years is consistent with other documented developmental changes in attention. For instance, the largest changes in the ability to search for targets defined by the conjunction of two visual features occurs around the same age (Trick & Enns, 1998), as does the ability to ignore distractors (Enns, 1993) and the ability to orient attention voluntarily in response to a predictive cue (Enns & Brodeur, 1989). This concordance in the developmental trajectory for

exploratory and deliberate attentional functions gives further credence to the view, espoused in our framework (Figure 4.1), that these two functions are both governed by similar controlled cognitive processes.

Driving researchers were the first to notice the importance of exploratory selection. Hills (1980) noted that experienced drivers, when not fully taxed by the driving task, look away from the relevant driving-related information and explore roadside advertising, trees, and the local scenery. Although there have been periodic attempts to ensure that drivers look only at driving-relevant information, it is now commonly conceded that it is impossible to prevent exploratory selection (Coles & Hughes, 1984; Smiley, 1994). If driving does not require drivers' full attention, they direct their attention elsewhere. Normally this type of selection does not pose a significant problem because skilled drivers can readily refocus their attention and "shed" irrelevant information. The danger occurs when the driving situation changes suddenly. Attention switching may require a second or more, and any individual differences in exploration relate less to the tendency to explore than the ability to switch attention back and forth between exploration and tasks that require visual deliberation.

What determines the attraction of attention when an individual is exploring the environment without a specific goal? Preliminary work suggests that the *sensory conspicuity* of an object is increased by its retinal size, eccentricity, and contrast with the background (Cole & Hughes, 1984; Hughes & Cole, 1986). Efforts have been made to maximize the sensory conspicuity of safety-related signs, though conspicuity of an object depends on the number of other competing objects that are visible. Consequently, drivers are more likely to notice and remember the signs they see when driving at night than during the day (Shinar & Drory, 1983).

VISUAL DELIBERATION

Much of our visual activity involves the deliberate selection of a specific goal. This type of processing is the most flexible and therefore the most responsive to new information. It provides the opportunity to change behavior rapidly (typically within a half to a full second) in response to an oral command or the messages in visual symbols. The disadvantage of this type of processing is that it is difficult to perform more than one task at a time, presumably because there is a sharp limit on the information that a person can be consciously aware of at any one time (Endsley, 1995; Reason, 1990). Visual selection by deliberation is also noticeably effortful. This is manifest in self-report measures of cognitive strain and in such physiological measures as eye blink, heart rate and heart rate variability (Hancock, Wulf, & Thom, 1990; Richter, Wagner, Heger, & Weise, 1998).

In a laboratory for the study of visual orienting, visual deliberation is often indexed by a task in which participants orient their spatial attention deliberately in response to a cue. This response is then compared to a similar response that is made when no cue is being used or when the cue is being used in a reflexive or habitual way. There have been many studies on the ability of children of different ages to use a predictive cue to orient voluntarily toward the source of upcoming visual information. Reviews can be found in Plude et al. (1994) and Brodeur and Boden (2001).

Recently, work has also begun on the question of how rapidly children are able to switch from one visual task to another. In one study, children ages 7 to 15 years performed a two-target detection task in a rapid serial stream of visual shapes (Shapiro & Garrad-Cole, 2003). The first target was a blue triangle and the second was a red triangle. These target shapes appeared at random among other shapes that were presented at a rate of one per 100 milliseconds. The typical finding when college students perform this task is that accuracy on the first target is very high, but that there is a 500-millesecond period immediately after the appearance of the first target, in which the second target is missed. This is called the *attentional blink*. The main finding of the Shapiro and Garrad-Cole (2003) study was that this blink lasted longer for younger than for older children, revealing a relative deficit in their ability to switch rapidly from one visual item to the next. This general conclusion is consistent with other work on visual search in children (Trick & Enns, 1998).

One of the most important uses of deliberate visual processing involves the coordination of automatic and voluntary spatial orienting effects. Because of the structure of the eye, only visual events that are positioned near the fovea receive the most detailed spatial analysis of which human vision is capable. As a result, it is essential to orient the eyes appropriately to perceive the details in shape, motion, color, and texture that are associated with the event that summoned the at-

tention in the first place. Another importance of this coordination is that often there is more than one consideration to be made in coming to a decision to reorient. For example, it may be socially embarrassing to let your conversational partner know you are listening to another conversation and so you will want to keep your gaze fixed on the individual while your auditory attention is elsewhere. On the other hand, it can become dangerous, both for yourself and others, if you do not orient reflexively to unexpected sudden events when trying to drive safely. The skill of many athletes seems to reside in their ability to "fake out" their opponents with movements of their body and to not respond to similar false movements on the parts of their opponents.

The modulation of visual orienting reflexes by a voluntary intention to either respond quickly to the reflexively signaled events or to ignore these signals depending on their predictive value has now been the focus of several studies with elite athletes. A study by Enns and Richards (1997) tested younger and older elite junior hockey players in two conditions involving visual targets preceded by flash cues. In one condition the flashes were entirely random, meaning they were not predictive of the target location. In a second condition these same cues were highly reliable. The main finding was that the older players, as well as the more highly skilled players at all ages, showed a greater sensitivity to the predictability of these cues. Similar results have been reported for elite international water polo athletes and fencers, who were more sensitive to the predictive nature of flash cues than were elite international swimmers and nonathletes (Nougier, Ripoll, & Stein, 1989).

In an even more direct study of the coordination of competing sources of information for visual orienting, Lum et al. (2002) tested elite college athletes from two sports representing relatively static competitive visual environments (swimming, track) and from two sports representing more dynamic visual environments (soccer, volleyball). Within a block of trials during a target detection task, participants were given highly predictive central arrows well in advance of the target display, as well as nonpredictive flashes in closer temporal proximity to the target display. On any given trial, none of the cues may be presented, only one may be presented, or both were presented in either cooperative or competitive arrangement.

There were both sports-general and sports-specific effects. First, there was a tendency for all athletes to use the predictive arrow cues to greater effect than the nonathlete controls that were tested. However, when it came to the coordination of voluntary and reflexive cues, interesting sports-specific differences emerged. The athletes participating in static environments were best able to use the two cues in a cooperative fashion when they were in agreement about the target location and to ignore the flash cue when it contradicted the informative arrow cue. In contrast, the athletes from more dynamic environments were best able to inhibit visual reflexive orienting to the flashes under all conditions. Taken together, these findings suggest that skill and practice in specific visual environments alter the default arrangements concerning the coordination of visual orienting.

There are notable individual differences in deliberate selection, and these differences predict accident risk, particularly among senior drivers. Older drivers are disproportionately at risk for certain types of accident (Preusser, Williams, Ferguson, Ulmen, & Weinstein, 1998) and for missing information while driving (e.g., misreading signs, failing to notice a green arrow or green light, missing an exit on a highway; Aberg & Rimmo, 1998). There are a variety of age-related changes that might be at fault, including decreased sensory acuity and motor slowing, but it is the factors related to deliberate selection that correlate most with accident risk (Ball & Owsley, 1991; Klein, 1991; Parasuraman & Nestor, 1991). Laboratory studies of attention switching in seniors show that voluntary orienting becomes more difficult (Plude et al., 1994); visual search is slowed (Trick & Enns, 1998), the useful field of view is disproportionately reduced (Ball, Roenker, & Bruni, 1990; Pauzie, Gabaude, & Denis, 1998), and dual-task interference is exaggerated (e.g., McDowd & Craik, 1988; Parasuraman & Nestor, 1991). Consistent with our framework, it is the "hybrid" measures of performance—those that involve attention switching, serial visual search, and dual tasks—that best predict accident risk in driving seniors (Janke & Eberhard, 1998; Lundberg, Hakamies-Blomqvist, Almkuist, & Johansson, 1998; Owsley, Ball, Sloane, Roenker, & Bruni, 1991; Stutts, Stewart, & Martell, 1998; Wood, 1998).

CONCLUSION

This chapter provides a new framework for understanding attention in children, young and older adults, and other populations of related interest, including athletes and accident-prone drivers. Four modes of selection were identified, providing a rich means of assessing how individuals might differ from one another. Anchored in recent developments in the study of selective attention, this framework brings together some of the divergent threads in developmental research, as well as in research investigating performance on everyday tasks such as driving and participating in sports.

One of the main strengths of the framework is that it reduces confusion in the literature concerning the distinctions between automatic and controlled processes and also between exogenous and endogenous processes—distinctions that are often conflated. It is our view that this conflation occurs because of a confusion between the nature of a process (whether it requires conscious control or not) and its etiology (whether it arose through innate or learned processes). This conflation has led to needless controversy about some issues and complete neglect of others, in particular neglect of the importance of exploratory selection.

Applied to the development of attention in childhood, this framework provides a way of understanding both age-related stability and age-related change. Age-related change is more apparent in the two endogenous modes of selection (habit and deliberation), both of which depend on learning, than in the two exogenous modes (reflex and exploration), which rely on built-in tendencies. It is also more evident in the two controlled modes of selection (exploration and deliberation), which require conscious control, than in the two automatic modes (reflex and habit) that can occur without awareness. When these two trends are combined, it is clear that the exogenous automatic mode of selection (based on reflexive action) shows the greatest stability with age, whereas the endogenous controlled mode (deliberation) shows the greatest individual variability and therefore the largest developmental change. We believe this framework may also be fruitfully applied to the sparing and loss of selective function in older age, as summarized in Chapter 5 of this volume by Kramer and Kray.

References

Aberg, L, & Rimmo, P. (1998). Dimensions of aberrant driver behavior. *Ergonomics, 41*, 39–56.
Ball, K., & Owsley, C. (1991). Identifying correlates of accident involvement for the older driver. *Human Factors, 33*, 583–595.

Ball, K., Roenker, D., & Bruni, J. (1990). Developmental changes in attention and visual search through adulthood. In J. T. Enns (Ed.), *The development of attention: Research and theory* (pp. 489–508). North Holland: Elsevier.

Brodeur, D. A., & Boden, C. (2001). The effects of spatial uncertainty and predictability on visual orienting in children. *Cognitive Development, 15,* 367–382.

Burack, J. A., & Enns, J. T. (Eds.). (1997). *Attention, development, and psychopathology: A merging of disciplines.* New York: Guildford Press.

Burack, J. A., Enns, J. T., Stauder, J. E. A., Mottron, L., & Randolph, B. (1997). Attention and autism: Behavioral and electrophysiological evidence. In D. J. Cohen & F. R. Volkmar (Eds.), *Autism and pervasive developmental disorders: A handbook* (pp. 226–247). New York: Wiley.

Cole, B., & Hughes, P. (1984). A field trial of attention and search conspicuity. *Human Factors, 26,* 299–313.

Colombo, J. (2001). The development of visual attention in infancy. *Annual Review of Psychology, 52,* 337–367.

Comalli, P. E., Wapner, S., & Werner, H. (1962). Interference effects of Stroop color-word test in childhood, adulthood, and aging. *Journal of Genetic Psychology, 100,* 47–53.

Coren, S., & Girgus, J. S. (1978). *Seeing is deceiving: The psychology of visual illusions.* Hillsdale, NJ: Lawrence Erlbaum Associates.

Egeth, H. E., & Yantis, S. (1997). Visual attention: Control, representation, and time course. *Annual Review of Psychology, 48,* 269–297.

Endsley, M. (1995). Toward a theory of situation awareness in dynamic systems. *Human Factors, 37,* 32–64.

Enns, J. T. (1993). What can be learned about attention from studying its development? *Canadian Psychology, 34,* 271–281.

Enns, J. T., & Brodeur, D. (1989). A developmental study of covert orienting to peripheral visual cues. *Journal of Experimental Child Psychology, 48,* 171–189.

Enns, J. T., & Girgus, J. S. (1985). Perceptual grouping and spatial distortion: A developmental study. *Developmental Psychology, 21,* 241–246.

Enns, J. T., & Richards, J. R. (1997). Visual attentional orienting in developing hockey players. *Journal of Experimental Child Psychology, 64,* 255–275.

Fournier, P. A., Mazzarella, M. M., Ricciardi, M. M., & Fingeret, A. L. (1975). Reading level and locus of interference in the Stroop color-word task. *Perceptual & Motor Skills, 41,* 239–242.

Friesen, C. K., & Kingstone, A. (1998). The eyes have it! Reflexive orienting is triggered by nonpredictive gaze. *Psychonomic Bulletin & Review, 5,* 490–495.

Gregory, R. L. (1966). *Eye and brain.* New York: McGraw-Hill.

Hancock, P., Wulf, G., & Thom, D. (1990). Driver workload during differing driving maneuvers. *Accident Analysis and Prevention, 22,* 281–290.

Hills, B. (1980). Vision, visibility, and perception in driving. *Perception, 9,* 183–216.

Ho, G., Caird, J., & Graw, T. (2001). Visual search for traffic signs: The effects of clutter, luminance, and aging. *Human Factors, 43,* 194–207.

Hochberg, J., & Brooks, V. (1962). Pictorial recognition as an unlearned ability: A study of one child's performance. *American Journal of Psychology, 75,* 624–628.

Hommel, B., Pratt, J., Colzato, L., & Godjin, R. (2001). Symbolic control of visual attention. *Psychological Science, 12,* 360–365.

Hood, B. M., Willen, J. D., & Driver, J. (1998). Adult's eyes trigger shifts of visual attention in human infants. *Psychological Science, 9,* 131–134.

Hughes, P., & Cole, B. (1986). What attracts attention when driving? *Ergonomics, 29,* 377–391.

Janke, M., & Eberhard, J. (1998). Assessing medically impaired older drivers in a licensing agency setting. *Accident Analysis and Prevention, 30,* 347–361.

Kingstone, A., Friesen, C. K., & Gazzaniga, M. S. (2000). Reflexive joint attention depends on lateralized cortical connections. *Psychological Science, 11,* 159–166.

Klein, R. (1991). Age-related eye disease, visual impairment and driving in the elderly. *Human Factors, 33,* 521–525.

Langham, M., Hole, G., Edwards, J., & O'Neil, C. (2002). An analysis of "looked but failed to see" accidents involving parked police vehicles. *Ergonomics, 45,* 167–185.

Langton, S. R. H., & Bruce, V. (1999). Reflexive orienting to social attention signals. *Visual Cognition, 6,* 541–567.

Langton, S. R. H., Watt, R., & Bruce, V. (2000). Do the eyes have it? Cues to the direction of social attention. *Trends in Cognitive Sciences, 4,* 50–59.

Lum, J., Enns, J. T., & Pratt, J. (2002). Visual orienting in college athletes: Explorations of athlete type and gender. *Research Quarterly in Exercise and Sport, 73,* 156–167.

Lundberg, C., Hakamies-Blomqvist, L., Almkuist, O., & Johansson, K. (1998). Impairments of some cognitive functions are common in crash-involved older drivers. *Accident Analysis and Prevention, 30,* 371–377.

MacLeod, C. M. (1991). Half a century of research on the Stroop effect: An integrative review. *Psychological Bulletin, 109,* 163–203.

McDowd, J. M., & Craik, F. I. M. (1988). Effects of aging and task difficulty in divided attention performance. *Journal of Experimental Psychology: Human Perception and Performance, 14,* 267–280.

McGwin, G., & Brown, D. (1999). Characteristics of traffic crashes among young, middle-aged, and older drivers. *Accident Analysis and Prevention, 31,* 181–189.

Nougier, V., Ripoll, H., & Stein, J-F. (1989). Orienting of attention with highly skilled athletes. *International Journal of Sports Psychology, 20,* 205–223.

Owsley, C., Ball, K., Sloane, M., Roenker, D., & Bruni, J. (1991). Visual/cognitive correlates of vehicle accidents in older drivers. *Psychology and Aging, 6,* 403–415.

Parasuraman, R., & Nestor, P. (1991). Attention and driving skills in aging and Alzheimer's disease. *Human Factors, 33,* 539–557.

Pauzie, A., Gabaude, C., & Denis, J. (1998). Effect of a dynamic central task on the useful field of view: Investigation of visual and attentional abilities of elderly drivers. In A. G. Gale, I. D., Brown, C. M., Haslegrave, & S. P. Taylor (Eds.), *Vision in vehicles.* (Vol. VI, pp. 325–332). Amsterdam: Elsevier.

Plude, D., Enns, J. T., & Brodeur, D. A. (1994). The development of selective attention: A lifespan overview. *Acta Psychologica, 86,* 227–272.

Povinelli, D., & Eddy, T. (1996). Factors influencing young chimpanzees' recognition of "attention." *Journal of Comparative Psychology, 110,* 336–345.

Preusser, D., Williams, A., Ferguson, S., Ulmen, R., & Weinstein, H. (1998). Fatal crash risk for older drivers at intersections. *Accident Analysis and Prevention, 30,* 151–159.

Randolph, B. (2002). *Covert orienting across the lifespan.* Unpublished doctoral dissertation, McGill University, Department of Psychology, Montreal, Canada.

Reason, J. (1990). *Human Error.* Cambridge: Cambridge University Press.

Rensink, R. A. (2002). Change detection. *Annual Review of Psychology, 53,* 245–277.

Rensink, R. A., O'Regan, J. K., & Clark, J. J. (1997). To see or not to see: The need for attention to perceive changes in scenes. *Psychological Science, 8,* 368–373.

Richter, P., Wagner, T., Heger, R., & Weise, G. (1998). Psychophysiological analysis of mental load during driving on rural roads—A quasi-experimental field study. *Ergonomics, 41,* 593–609.

Ristic, J., Friesen, C. K., & Kingstone, A. (2002). Are eyes special? It depends on how you look at it. *Psychonmic Bulletin & Review, 9,* 507–513.

Ristic, J., Mottron, L., Iarocci, G., Burack, J., & Kingstone, A. (2002, November). Autism and reflexive orienting to gaze direction. Poster session presented at the International Meeting for Autism Research (IMFAR), Orlando, FL.

Schiller, P. H. (1966). Developmental study of color-word interference. *Journal of Experimental Psychology, 72,* 105–108.

Scholl, B. J. (2000). Attenuated change blindness for exogenously attended items in a flicker paradigm. *Visual Cognition, 7,* 377–396.

Serna, R., & Carlin, M. T. (2001). Guiding visual attention in individuals with mental retardation. In L. M. Glidden (Ed.), *International review of research in mental retardation* (Vol. 24, pp. 321–357). New York: Academic Press.

Shapiro, K., & Garrad-Cole, F. (2003). Age-related deficits and involvement of frontal cortical areas as revealed by the attentional blink. *Journal of Vision, 3,* 726a.

Shiffrin, R., & Schneider, W. (1977). Controlled and automatic human information processing: II. Perceptual learning, automatic attending, and a general theory. *Psychological Review, 84,* 127–190.

Shinar, D., & Drory, A. (1983). Sign registration in daytime and night time driving. *Human Factors, 25,* 117–122.

Shinar, D., Meir, M., and Ben-Shoham, I. (1998). How automatic is manual gear shifting? *Human Factors, 40,* 647–654.

Shinar, D., Rockwell, T., & Malecki, J. (1980). Effects of changes in driver perception on rural curve negotiation. *Ergonomics, 23,* 263–275.

Shore, D. I., Burack, J. A., Miller, D., Joseph, S., & Enns, J. T. (2004). Developmental trajectory of change-blindness using a flicker paradigm. Manuscript submitted for publication.

Simons, D. J., & Levin, D. T. (1997). Change blindness. *Trends in Cognitive Sciences, 1,* 261–267.

Smiley, A. (1994). *Driver distraction: A review of the literature.* Unpublished report prepared for Public Works Canada.

Spelke, E. S. (1990). Principles of object perception. *Cognitive Science, 14,* 29–56.

Stutts, J., Stewart, J., & Martell, C. (1998). Cognitive test performance and crash risk in an older population. *Accident Analysis and Prevention, 30,* 337–346.

Summala, H., Nieminen, T., & Punto, M. (1996). Maintaining lane position with peripheral vision during in-vehicle tasks. *Human Factors, 38,* 442–451.

Trick, L., & Enns, J. T. (1998). Lifespan changes in attention: The visual search task. *Cognitive Development, 13,* 369–386.

Trick, L. M., Enns, J. T., Mills, J., & Vavrik, J. (2004). Paying attention behind the wheel: A framework for studying the role of attention in driving. *Theoretical Issues in Ergonomic Science, 5,* 385–424.

Wikman, A., Nieminen, T., & Summala, H. (1998). Driving experience and time-sharing during in-car tasks on roads of different width. *Ergonomics, 41,* 358–372.

Wolfe, J. M., Butcher, S. J., Lee, C., & Hyle, M. (2003). Changing your mind: On the contributions of top-down and bottom-up guidance in visual search for feature singletons. *Journal of Experimental Psychology: Human Perception and Performance, 29,* 483–502.

Wood, J. (1998). Effect of aging and vision on measures of driving performance. In A.G. Gale, I. D., Brown, C. M., Haslegrave, & S. P. Taylor (Eds.), *Vision in vehicles* (Vol. VI, pp. 333–341). Amsterdam: Elsevier.

5

Aging and Attention

Arthur F. Kramer
Jutta Kray

In the present chapter we review and critique the scientific literature that has examined age-related changes in attention from young adulthood to old age. Owing to space limitations, the review will by necessity be both brief and selective. The theoretical issues and studies that we examine will, for the most part, be relatively recent—that is, within the past decade and a half. More extended reviews of the aging and attention literature can be found in Hartley (1992) and McDowd and Shaw (2000). At a global level, the chapter will focus on two different varieties of attention: selective and divided attention. In general, selective attention refers to the ability to both focus on information of relevance to the organism and exclude or ignore information that is task irrelevant. It is important to note, however, that selective attention is a dynamic set of processes since relevance is often contextually defined and what is relevant at one time can quickly become irrelevant depending on the task and environment. Divided attention entails the ability to concurrently attend and process information

from a wide area of the visual field or concurrently perform or switch among different skills or tasks (e.g., when driving an automobile this involves scanning for other vehicles and pedestrians, lane tracking and manual control of the vehicle, and so on).

When examining both selective and divided attention, we must consider that these processes may result from either goal-directed or stimulus-driven processes. Goal-directed attention refers to an individual's ability to intentionally and selectively process information in the environment. Central to the definition of goal-directed attention is that this form of attentional control relies on an observer's expectancies about events in the environment, knowledge of and experience with similar environments, and the ability to develop and maintain an attentional set for particular kinds of environmental events. In contrast, stimulus-driven attention entails the control of attention by characteristics of the environment, independent of an observer's intentions, expectancies, or experience. Indeed, it is often the case that goal-directed and stimulus-driven attentional processes interact (i.e., in either a cooperative or competitive fashion) to determine the focus of attention (see Chapter 4, this volume, for a similar conceptualization of attention). In the present chapter we will describe and critique research that has examined how these processes change over the adult lifespan.

COGNITIVE AND BRAIN AGING: CURRENT CONTEXT

Prior to delving into the literature on aging and attention, we take a brief detour to discuss recent views on the mechanism(s) that underlie age-related declines in cognition; this will provide a context in which changes in attentional processes can be interpreted. In general, cognitive aging has been viewed in terms of either changes in a variety of cognitive processes or as a change in a single mechanism that underlies performance across a wide range of tasks and skills. For example, it has been proposed that during aging there is a decline in the processing capacity needed to perform different tasks and skills (Salthouse, 1985), the ability to successfully inhibit task-irrelevant information in the immediate environment or in memory (Hasher & Zacks, 1988), the ability to rapidly process perceptual information (Salthouse, 1996), and the ability to maintain and operate on information in working memory (Craik & Byrd, 1982). Recently, models and mechanisms inspired by the study of neuroanatomical and neurophysiological changes over the adult lifespan have also been proposed (Braver et al., 2001; West, 1996).

A number of models have suggested that all or most of the age-related variance across a wide variety of laboratory and real-world tasks can be accounted for by a single mechanism, in many cases one of the mechanisms presented above. For example, Hasher and Zacks' (1988) original inhibitory deficit hypothesis was often interpreted as suggesting a general mechanism that could account for age-related slowing and other performance deficits across a wide variety of tasks. The same was the case for the perceptual processing deficit hypothesis (Salthouse, 1996). However, additional research has suggested that neither cognition (Kramer, Humphrey, Larish, Logan, & Strayer, 1994; West, 1996) nor brain function or structure (Braver et al., 2001; Raz, 2000) declines uniformly across the adult lifespan. Therefore, there is now some consensus that

different perceptual, cognitive, and motor processes exhibit different trajectories across the adult lifespan.

VISUAL SELECTIVE ATTENTION AND AGING

As described above, *selective attention* refers to the ability to both focus on information of relevance to the organism and exclude or ignore information that is task irrelevant. This can be accomplished by facilitating the processing of specific objects and/or inhibiting other task-irrelevant objects.

Spatial Cuing and Attention: Influence of Stimulus-Driven and Goal-Directed Factors

With respect to facilitative processing, several studies have examined potential age differences in cued spatial attention. In these paradigms attention is cued with either a peripheral onset that marks the future position of a task-relevant stimulus or a centrally presented symbolic cue (e.g., an arrow) that must be interpreted to discern the position of the imperative stimulus (Posner, 1980). The validity of the cue is also often manipulated such that some cues predict the location of the target with 100% accuracy while other cues are nonpredictive (e.g., a cue that appears at a target location 25% of the time in a display with four possible target locations). The combination of the location of the cue and its predictability is usually used to distinguish between exogenous (stimulus-driven) and endogenous (goal-directed) attentional cuing. Exogenous cuing is believed to lead to reflexive orienting of attention given the nonpredictive nature of the cues and use of peripheral onset cues that are known to capture attention (Yantis, 1996). Exogenous orienting leads to a rapid increase in facilitation in performance at the cued location, a rapid dissipation of the facilitation, and relative resistance to concurrent processing demands. On the other hand, endogenous cuing depends on deliberative or strategic orienting that results in a gradual and sustained facilitation of performance for objects at the cued location. As a result of these differences and others it has been suggested that distinct mechanisms underlie exogenous and endogenous orienting (Enns & Trick, Chapter 4, this volume; Müller & Rabbitt, 1989).

Although older adults clearly respond more slowly than young adults, studies have generally found age equivalence in the magnitude and time course of exogenous cuing effects (Folk & Hoyer, 1992; Gottlob & Madden, 1998; Hartley, Kieley, & Slabach, 1990) even when subjects are required to divide attention between two noncontiguous locations (Hahn & Kramer, 1995). Additionally, age equivalence has been found for inhibition of return (IOR) effects—that is, the slowed response time observed when a previously cued location has to be re-attended within 300 to 700 milliseconds after it was initially attended (Hartley & Kieley, 1995). Thus, it would appear that with respect to exogenous attention both facilitative and inhibitory processes are relatively age invariant.

Endogenous cuing effects, in terms of both their magnitude and their time course, have also been found to be similar for young and older adults (Folk & Hoyer, 1992; Lincourt, Folk, & Hoyer, 1997). However, there are some interesting qualifications for these effects. For example, Greenwood and Parasuraman (1999) found that older seniors (> 75 years of age) experienced difficulty in flexibly modifying the breadth of their attention in a display of multiple objects. Similarly, Madden, Connelly, and Pierce (1994) found age equivalence in shifting attention in the absence of distractors, but a performance deficit for older adults when required to shift attention in response to highly predictive cues in a display with multiple distractors. Thus, these data suggest that age-related differences in the ability to orient and reorient spatial attention might be (1) the result of inadvertent distractor processing, possibly due to inhibitory failures; and (2) more frequently observed with advanced age, where subclincal pathology may increase in frequency.

Selective Attention and Resistance to Distraction

A number of studies have examined the ability of young and old adults to focus attention on a predefined location of the visual field and ignore distractors that can prime an incorrect response. Many of these studies have been conducted with the response compatibility paradigm in which subjects are instructed to shift attention to a pre-cued location and ignore flanking distractors. The key manipulation is the relationship of the distractors to the target response. Some percentage of the distractors calls for the same response as the target while other distractors, if targets, require a different response. These conditions are referred to as *response compatible* and *response incompatible*, respectively, and the difference in response time between these conditions is interpreted as a metric of the ability to resist interference from task-irrelevant stimuli. Until recently, studies of age differences in the magnitude of the response compatibility effect have produced conflicting results, with some studies finding age equivalence (Kramer et al., 1994), some studies finding larger differences for older adults (Zeef, Sonke, Kok, Buiten, & Kenemans, 1996), and other studies finding smaller response compatibility effects for older adults (Madden & Gottlob, 1997).

There are several potential explanations for these discrepancies, including age-related acuity effects for the subset of studies in which the target was presented at the fovea and the distractors at different retinal eccentricities (Cerella, 1985). However, in a recent study Madden and Langley (2003) examined potential age-related discrepancies in the magnitude of the response compatibility effect within the context of Lavie's (1995) perceptual load theory of attention (see also Maylor & Lavie, 1998). Lavie argued that at high perceptual load, rejection of distractors is accomplished passively given that all attentional resources are engaged by task-relevant processing. However, at low perceptual load, when attentional resources are not fully engaged with task-relevant processing, rejection of distractors entails an active inhibitory process. Madden and Langley (2003) examined the hypothesis that deficient inhibitory processing associated with aging (Hasher & Zacks, 1988) will result in larger distractor effects for older adults at low perceptual loads. A secondary hypothesis concerned potential age-related differences in processing capacity (Maylor & Lavie, 1998). If older adults possess fewer attentional resources than younger adults, the influence of distractors should diminish more rapidly for older adults. Madden and Langley found evidence of larger response compatibility effects but similar changes in the magnitude of the response compatibility effect with diminishing perceptual load for older adults when the displays were presented briefly and the distractor was separated from the task-relevant stimuli. These data suggest that differences in inhibitory efficiency, but not attentional capacity, may explain the discrepancy in the results of previous studies with the response compatibility paradigm. However, it is important to point out that Madden and Langley found evidence of age equivalence in two other studies in which displays were presented for longer durations and the distractor was spatially integrated with the task-relevant stimuli. Thus, additional studies are needed to further define the boundary conditions for age-related inhibitory failures.

Two additional paradigms that have been employed in the study of aging and inhibitory processing in the service of understanding efficient selective attention are the Stroop task and the negative priming task. The Stroop task resembles the response compatibility paradigm, but the task-irrelevant and task-relevant aspects of the stimuli are integrated into the same object. In this paradigm subjects are often instructed to articulate the color in which a word is presented and the words can either be compatible with the ink color (i.e., the word *blue* printed in blue), neutral with respect to the ink color (i.e., the word *house* printed in blue), or incompatible with the ink color (i.e., the word *red* printed in blue). Response times increase when the ink color and the word meaning are incompatible.

It has generally been found that older adults show larger absolute interference effects than younger adults in the Stroop task (Dulaney & Rogers, 1994). However, in a recent meta-analysis of 20 Stroop studies, Verhaeghen and De Meersman (1998a) failed to find evidence for larger Stroop effects for older than for younger adults once general slowing had been taken into account. Such results might be interpreted as suggesting age equivalence in the ability to focus on one feature of an object (e.g., word color) while selectively ignoring another feature (e.g., word meaning) of the same object. However, two additional studies call this interpretation into question. Spieler, Balota, and Faust (1996), in a study of aging and Stroop performance, found disproportionate slowing in the incompatible word-color condition for the old adults. The increased response time (RT) for the older adults were the result of increased skew in the RT distribution rather than a shift in the entire RT distribution as a function of age. Such results led Spieler and colleagues to reject the general slowing account of the Stroop task.

Hartley (1993) took a different tack in his investigation of aging and Stroop interference. In this study he contrasted Stroop effects in which subjects either responded to the color when it was part of the word or in a condition in which a color block and word were physically separated. Hartley reasoned that previous research on spatial cuing suggests that older adults would show equivalent interference effects when the word and color were separated but that older adults may not be able to selectively focus on the color when the two features are integrated into a single object. Indeed, this was the case. Older adults were 22% slower in the color word task than in the color block task, while younger adults were only 12% slower. When viewed together, studies of Stroop effects appear to provide at least tentative support for an age-related change in the manner in which individuals attend to selective features of objects and ignore other features. Future research should examine whether the magnitude of this effect differs as a function of the perceptual load of the task (cf., Lavie, 1995) as well as the age and general level of cognitive function of the subject population (Greenwood & Parasuraman, 1999).

Finally, the negative priming paradigm has served as another test bed on which to examine age-related differences in selective inhibition. In the negative priming task, subjects are asked to respond to targets and ignore simultaneously presented distractor stimuli. The critical comparison is between trials in which a distractor from trial *n*-1 becomes a target on trial *n* (i.e., the ignored repetition [IR] condition) and trials in which different target and distractor stimuli are presented on trials *n* and *n*-1 (i.e., the control condition). In general, longer RTs are obtained in IR conditions than in control conditions, defining the negative priming effect. The negative priming effect is robust and has been obtained in a variety of tasks and for a number of stimulus and response types (for reviews see May, Kane, & Hasher, 1995; Neill & Valdes, 1996).

Initial aging studies found that older adults failed to produce a difference between IR and control conditions while younger adults responded more slowly to IR than control trials (Hasher, Stoltzfus, Zacks, & Rympa, 1991; Kane, Hasher, Stoltzfus, Zacks, & Connelly, 1994; Tipper, 1991). That is, young adults showed a negative priming effect while older adults did not. These initial results were interpreted as indicating a failure of selective inhibition by the older adults. However, more recent studies (Kieley & Hartley, 1997; Kramer et al., 1994; Kramer & Strayer, 2001; Sullivan & Faust, 1993; Sullivan, Faust, & Balota, 1995) have reported equivalent negative priming effects for young and old adults.

One potential problem in interpreting age-related similarities or differences in the negative priming effect is the lack of agreement with respect to underlying mechanisms. The two dominant models have focused on different underlying mechanisms to explain the negative priming effect. The distractor inhibition model proposed by Tipper (1985) suggests that negative priming is the result of a selective attention mechanism that inhibits the internal representations of distractor objects and thereby reduces access to response mechanisms. Although this is an efficient way to decrease the detrimental effect of the distractor on the prime trial (trial *n*-1), residual inhibition from the prime trial is hypothesized to impede performance when the object that was previously a distractor becomes a target on the probe trial (trial *n*). Thus, the distractor inhibition model suggests that the mechanisms underlying the negative priming effect are engaged during the processing of the prime trial when the internal representations of the distractor are inhibited to aid in the selection of the target.

By contrast, the episodic retrieval model (Neill, 1997) suggests that each time a stimulus is presented it produces a memory trace. One component of this memory trace is an indication of whether the stimulus served as a target or a distractor. When the stimulus is encountered again, the previously constructed memory trace is retrieved and performance is slowed if the information about the specific response is incompatible with the present action. Thus, within the episodic retrieval model, negative priming is the result of interference from action codes retrieved on the probe trial rather than inhibition of the internal representations of the distractor on the prime trial.

Finally, it has also been suggested that separate mechanisms underlie negative priming effects when location and identity of the stimulus are task relevant. Discrepancies in the aging literature have been attributed to age deficiencies in some but not other mechanisms that may be responsible for negative priming effects in different paradigms. It has been suggested that age-related deficits in negative priming will be observed only when the inhibitory selective attention mechanism is invoked to deal with identity-based judgments (Kane, May, Hasher, Rahhal, & Stoltzfus, 1997; May et al., 1995). However, this appears not to be the case. Verhaeghen and De Meersman (1998b) conducted a meta-analysis on 21 aging and inhibition studies and found that both young and old adults displayed significant negative priming effects, although the effects were larger for young than old for identity discrimination tasks. Verhaeghen and De Meersman speculated (see also Kramer et al., 1994) that the failure to observe more consistent negative priming effects for older adults might have been a result of the combination of small effects and small sample sizes—that is, a lack of power to detect such effects for older adults.

To briefly summarize the research on selective attention and distraction, it would appear that older adults fare best when attention can be spatially focused on the potential location of a target in advance of the presentation of a target and distractors, when there are few distractors in a display, and when the task at hand entails relatively high perceptual load. Older adults fare less well dealing with distracting events when they are part of the same object as the task-relevant events and when the identity of a distractor must be inhibited. Although no single theoretical framework appears capable of accounting for all of these effects, the literature would appear to suggest that a multitude of processes can be brought to bear in selectively focusing attention, some of which are more susceptible to aging (e.g., active vs. passive inhibition in Lavie's perceptual load model) than others.

VISUAL SEARCH AND AGING

Visual search, which entails the purposeful exploration of what often are cluttered environments, has been an important context in which to examine the influence of aging on goal-directed and stimulus-driven attention. Studies have, for the most part, found age equivalence in the ability to locate a target defined by a unique attribute among homogeneous distractors (e.g., a blue Honda Accord among red Honda Accords in an automotive dealer's lot). However, older adults have substantially more difficulty than young adults locating and identifying a target defined by a conjunction of features among heterogeneous distractors (e.g., a blue Honda Accord among red Honda Accords and blue Toyota Camrys). Interestingly, older adults perform better in a conjunction search when there is an asymmetry in the number of different types of distractors. That is, if the number of blue Toyota Camrys is held constant while the number of red Honda Accords increases with increasing numbers of distractors, both young and old adults will search selectively through the blue automobiles to find the blue Honda Accord. Each of these effects has been observed with colored letter stimuli in a classic study of aging and visual search conducted by Plude and Doussard-Roosevelt (1989).

Humphrey and Kramer (1997) extended the research of Plude and Doussard-Roosevelt (1989) by examining potential age-related differences in feature, conjunction, and triple conjunction search. Consistent with the earlier study, these researchers observed rapid and efficient search for both young and old adults in feature search and disproportionate search costs for older adults in conjunction search. Interestingly, both old and young adults showed similar performance benefits with the provision of an additional dimension to define a target in triple conjunction search. Thus, it may be the case that older adults can effectively use stimulus information to guide top-down search, but that they require more such information (such as the extra dimension in the triple conjunction task) than younger adults to do so.

Consistent with the research described above on distraction and focused attention, several visual search studies have also found that age-related deficits increase when the heterogeneity of distractors increases, making it more difficult to use top-down processes to distinguish the target from distractors (Folk & Lincourt, 1996; Madden, Pierce, & Allan, 1996). Age-related deficits in conjunction search have also been attributed to reductions in the flexibility of re-orienting attention in the visual field (Greenwood & Parasuraman, 1999) and a reduction in the breadth of attention for older as compared to younger adults (Scialfa, Thomas, & Joffe, 1994). Pringle, Irwin, Kramer, and Atchley (2001) observed a significant relationship between the estimated size of young and older adults' attentional fields (Owsley, Ball, Sloane, Roenker, & Bruni, 1991) and the number of eye movements required to find a change in a series of cluttered real-world driving scenes.

Recently a series of studies has examined potential age differences in visual marking. Visual marking is a form of top-down attentional prioritization in which new objects are favored in visual search (Watson & Humphreys, 1997). This phenomenon has been demonstrated in experiments in which one set of objects is presented followed after several hundred milliseconds by a second set of objects. The target, if present, always appears in the second set of objects. Despite the fact that the objects presented at different times are physically interspersed, Watson and Humphreys have shown that subjects can selectively ignore the first set of objects and focus their search on the second set of objects. Kramer and Atchley (2000) demonstrated that older adults were also capable of

selectively attending and searching through the new objects in order to speed search. However, while replicating Kramer and Atchley with stationary objects, Watson and Maylor (2002) discovered that older adults were not able to selectively prioritize the new objects in dynamic displays.

In summary, older adults can search just as rapidly as young adults when targets are defined by unique attributes, with relatively homogeneous distractors, and when sufficient information is available to define targets in multi-attribute conjunction tasks. However, older adults have difficulty searching with heterogeneous distractors in large cluttered displays and are less facile than young adults at using top-down prioritization strategies in dynamic displays

Despite these difficulties experienced by older adults in visual search, several recent studies have suggested that older adults can substantially improve their conjunction search (Batsakes & Fisk, 2000; Ho, Siakaluk, & Scialfa, 2003) and useful field of view or attentional field with practice (Ball, Beard, Roenker, Miller, & Griggs, 1988) and that high levels of search skills developed over the adult lifespan can moderate age-related deficits in search (Clancy & Hoyer, 1994). Therefore, the attentional processes that underlie visual search, and often decline in efficiency during the course of aging, are clearly amenable to practice and training. Furthermore, training effects have been linked to real-world skills, such as improvements in driving performance with expanded useful fields of view (Roenker, Cissell, Ball, Wadley, & Edwards, 2003).

AGING AND THE FLEXIBLE COORDINATION OF ATTENTION

The research discussed thus far has focused on the control and expression of attention to objects and locations in the visual field. However, there has also been a great interest in understanding potential age-related differences in the allocation and control of attention directed to internal events (e.g., encoding and retrieval of information from memory, selection and programming of responses, etc.) or some combination of internal and external events.

Task Switching and Aging

One paradigm in particular that has served as a test bed for examining age-related differences in coordinating the performance of multiple tasks is the task switching paradigm. Comparisons among three different conditions in this paradigm enable us to distinguish different control components and to determine interactions among them. In task-homogeneous blocks, participants perform the same task on every trial, while in task-heterogeneous blocks two (or more) tasks are intermixed. Task-heterogeneous blocks consist of two types of trials: switch trials, in which the task is different from the one in the preceding trial, and nonswitch trials, in which the task is the same as the task in the preceding trial.

In general, two processing time measures have been derived from this paradigm. *Specific* (or *local*) *switch costs* are defined as the difference in performance on nonswitching and switching trials within task-heterogeneous blocks (Meiran, 1996; Rogers & Monsell, 1995) and reflect the efficiency of cognitive processes concerned with the reconfiguration of task-specific stimulus-response mappings. Another type of switching cost, termed *general* (or *global*) *switch costs*, is defined as the difference in performance under task-homogeneous and task-heterogeneous conditions and reflects the effectiveness of cognitive processes needed to maintain task sets in working memory and also to select currently relevant task sets (Kray & Lindenberger, 2000).

Age Differences in Specific Switch Costs

Most studies have shown age effects in specific switch costs to be rather small or absent when age effects in general slowing are taken into account (Hartley et al., 1990; Kramer, Hahn, & Gopher, 1999; Kray & Lindenberger, 2000; Mayr, 2001; Salthouse, Fristoe, McGuthry, & Hambrick, 1998; but see Cepeda, Kramer, & de Sather, 2001; Kray et al., 2002). Kramer, Hahn, and Gopher (1999) found specific switch costs to be larger for older than for younger adults at the beginning of practice but found age-equivalent switching performance after three sessions of practice. Generally, both younger and older adults show a substantial reduction in specific switch costs when the time to prepare the next task increases either by increasing the cue-to-target interval (CTI) or by increasing the response-to-stimulus interval (RSI; Cepeda et al., 2001; Kramer, Hahn, & Gopher, 1999; Kray & Lindenberger, 2000; Meiran, Gotler, & Perlman, 2001). Interestingly, Kramer, Hahn, and Gopher (1999) found that older adults show no reduction in switch costs with an increase in the RSI when using a switching paradigm

in which participants had to switch on every fourth trial without explicit task cues. The finding supports the idea that older adults may be impaired in preparing for a task switch when the load on working memory is relatively high. On the other hand, older adults were able to improve their switching performance with practice to the same extent as younger adults when working memory load was low.

Age Differences in General Switch Costs

Studies of task switching have often found age effects to be much more pronounced in general than in specific switch costs (Kray & Lindenberger, 2000; Mayr, 2001). Importantly, older adults performance deficits in general switch costs remain reliable after controlling for age effects in general slowing (Cepeda et al., 2001). Further evidence for substantially larger general than specific switch costs for older adults was provided in a study by Mayr (2001). In this study Mayr contrasted several different possible explanations for larger general switch costs for older than younger adults. An important factor in the age-related increase in general switch costs was the amount of stimulus ambiguity and response overlap between task sets. These findings were interpreted in terms of an age-related deficit in the ability to differentiate between highly overlapping task-set representations, which leads to a tendency for older adults to update task sets in both nonswitching and in switching trials, resulting in relatively small specific switch costs and large general switch costs, whereas younger adults may need to employ this updating process only on switching trials (see also DiGirolamo et al., 2001). Other studies have found that age-related differences in general switch costs decrease with decreasing working memory load with the provision of external cues (Kray et al., 2002) or well practiced tasks (Bojko, Kramer, & Peterson, 2004). Thus, it would appear that both memory load and response ambiguity, which may both exacerbate memory demands, are the primary moderating factors in age-related differences in task switching performance.

Dual-Task Processing

Many of the studies that have examined age-related differences in the ability to concurrently perform two different tasks have found greater performance costs for older than younger adults (for reviews, see McDowd

& Shaw, 2000; Verhaeghen & Cerella, 2002). However, one important issue in cognitive aging is the question of whether the age-related decline in dual-task performance is related to *general slowing* in cognitive processing (e.g., Salthouse, 1991) or to specific slowing in the ability to share attention between two concurrent tasks. Taking this issue seriously, most of the recent studies on age differences in dual-task performance demonstrated a disproportional decline of dual-task performance in old age (Batsakes & Fisk, 2000; Kramer & Larish, 1996; Kramer, Larish, & Strayer, 1995; Kramer, Larish, Weber, & Bardell, 1999; Li, Lindenberger, Freund, & Baltes, 2001; Lindenberger, Marsiske, & Baltes, 2000; Mayr & Kliegl, 1993; McDowd & Craik, 1988; Tsang & Shaner, 1998).

An excellent method to deal with age differences in baseline performance is to adjust the dual-task conditions according to the performance of each subject under single-task conditions, but this procedure is very time-consuming. Thus far only a few studies have used this method to investigate age-related differences in dual-task performance (Batsakes & Fisk, 2000; Somberg & Salthouse, 1982). Li and colleagues (2001) adaptively trained and equated young and old adults in their performance on an episodic memory task and on a walking task prior to dual-task performance. Even after adjusting for individual differences in performance on the single tasks, significantly greater dual task costs were found for the older adults, but only in the memory domain and not in the sensorimotor domain. The authors suggest that older adults tend to prioritize the maintenance of walking abilities over the maintenance of memory abilities.

Another important issue is the interpretation of age-related performance differences in dual-task processing when there are age-related differences in the emphasis placed on each of the tasks. Most studies, therefore, have instructed the participants to give both tasks equal priority. An excellent but time-consuming way to examine potential age-related differences in assigning processing priorities to multiple tasks is to generate a performance-operating characteristic (POC) for each subject by using instructions that vary the relative emphasis on each of the tasks (Kramer et al., 1995; Somberg & Salthouse, 1982). When determining POC curves individually in younger and older adults in a highly demanding memory-span task, Salthouse, Rogan, and Prill (1984) found age differences to be more pronounced in dual-task performance than in single-task performance whereas the ability to allocate attention across the two tasks, indicated by similar POC curves, was preserved in old age (Kramer et al., 1995; Somberg & Salthouse, 1982).

Another important question is whether age differences in dual-task performance can be reduced or eliminated with practice on the tasks or by providing specific training strategies, and whether the ability to improve dual-task processing with increasing practice or training differs across age. A general finding is that both younger and older adults are able to improve dual-task processing during extended practice even when improvements in single-task performance are taken into account (Baron & Mattila, 1989; Batsakes & Fisk, 2000; Kramer & Larish, 1996; Kramer et al., 1995; Kramer, Larish, et al., 1999; Li et al., 2001; Lindenberger et al., 2000; Salthouse, Hambrick, Lukas, & Dell, 1996); nevertheless, age-related differences in dual-task processing often remain after extended practice (Kramer et al., 1995; Kramer & Larish, 1996; Salthouse et al., 1996). More controversial is whether age-related differences in dual-task costs can be reduced with training (Baron & Mattila, 1989; Batsakes & Fisk, 2000; Kramer, Larish, et al., 1999; Sit & Fisk, 1999. Interestingly, some studies report that older adults benefit more from increasing practice than younger adults (Batsakes & Fisk, 2000; Kramer et al., 1995). This appears to occur in situations in which specific training strategies such as adaptive training to shift processing priorities between tasks (Kramer et al., 1995; Kramer, Larish et al., 1999) or training to shift emphasis between speed and accuracy are employed (Baron & Mattila, 1989).

In a related line of research, age-related differences in dual-task processing have been examined in the psychological refractory period (PRP) paradigm. In the PRP paradigm two simple tasks are performed on the same trial. The trial usually begins with a warning signal. The stimulus for task 1 is then presented After a variable amount of time the stimulus for task 2 is presented, the onsets between the two tasks, termed stimulus onset asynchrony (SOA), vary between very short to long time intervals. Importantly, the subjects are usually instructed to respond to task 1 first and then respond to the second task. Mean reaction times and error rates are measured in both tasks. A typical finding using this paradigm is an increase in RT in task 2 when the SOA between the two tasks is decreased, called the PRP effect. On the other hand, the RT observed in task 1 should be unaffected when subjects follow the instructions to give the first task the higher priority.

The results obtained in the PRP paradigm with young and older adults have suggested that in general older adults show larger performance costs on task 2 than do younger adults. The differential age-related costs appear to be largely the result of interference between response selection and execution processes (Allen, Smith, Vires-Collins, & Sperry, 1998; Hartley & Little, 1999) and possibly also by differential strategies used to perform the two tasks (Glass et al., 2000).

In summary, while it seems clear that older adults have more difficulty in the performance of concurrent or closely spaced tasks than do younger adults, older adults are relatively proficient at shifting processing priorities between tasks when required. Older adults can also generally improve their ability to perform multiple tasks, in some cases to a greater extent than younger adults (Baron & Mattila, 1989; Kramer et al., 1995; Kramer, Larish, et al., 1999). However, future research will be necessary to further elucidate the mechanisms and strategies that underlie age-related differences in multitask processing as well as the generalizability of practice and training effects beyond the laboratory.

CONCLUSIONS, UNRESOLVED ISSUES, AND FUTURE DIRECTIONS

The results reviewed above suggest both age-related deficits and age-related sparing of different attentional processes. Older adults, much like young adults and children, perform well at spatial cuing tasks, especially under conditions in which attention is summoned by salient predictive and nonpredictive peripheral cues. Older adults also perform well, as compared to young adults, in visual-search tasks, particularly when targets are defined by unique features (such as color, orientation, or form) and when grouping may be used to segment conjunction targets from distractors. However, both young children (under 9 years of age) and older adults have difficulty finding conjunction targets when embedded among heterogeneous distractors. Interestingly, older adults do appear to be as capable as young adults of capitalizing on extra information that can be used to guide search in a goal-directed fashion in triple conjunction search. Whether young children can also benefit from additional information to guide atten-

tion in a goal-directed fashion in visual search is a question for future research.

As discussed by Enns and Trick (Chapter 4, this volume), young children show less interference in Stroop tasks than do young adults, presumably as a result of less proficient (and automatic) reading. Given these results one might expect that older adults will show a larger Stroop effect, assuming that they have many more years of reading experience than young adults. However, in general this is not the case (Verhaeghen & De Meersman, 1998a; but see Spieler et al., 1996). This failure to observe disproportionate Stroop effects for older as compared to younger adults could be the result of the development of asymptotic reading performance (and therefore automaticity of reading) by young adulthood. Other research with older adults suggests that inhibitory efficiency is decreased for older adults in some tasks (and presumably for some processes) but not in others (see Kramer et al., 1994). Clearly, more research is needed to examine both the nature of inhibitory processes in attention and memory and their changes across the lifespan.

The ability to divide attention between tasks also appears to improve from childhood to young adulthood and to decrease from young adulthood to old age. Interestingly these changes mimic the development and decline of prefrontal regions of the brain — brain areas that are extensively involved in multitask processing and task coordination (Braver et al., 2001; West, 1996). There is increasing evidence, however, that suggests that these changes are neither completely immutable nor inevitable. Cognitive training (e.g., Baron & Mattila, 1989; Kramer, Hahn, & Gopher, 1999) and other interventions such as fitness training programs (see Colcombe & Kramer, 2003; Kramer, Hahn, Cohen, et al., 1999) targeted to older adults can substantially improve task coordination and other attention skills. Indeed, recent data suggest that behavioral improvements are reflected in changes in brain function, as indexed by functional magnetic resonance imaging, which suggest more efficient cortical processing (Colcombe et al., 2004). Clearly, the extent to which such changes in attentional processes can be reduced during aging, and the manner in which plasticity is realized in the brain, is a important and fascinating topic for future studies.

Finally, both Chapter 4 and the present chapter have briefly described the relatively sparse literature that has examined the relationship between the efficiency of attentional processes, as measured in laboratory tasks, and attention in complex real-word tasks such as driving. Recent results are encouraging in that they suggest that laboratory-based training of attentional skills can generalize to driving performance (e.g., Roenker et al., 2003). However, we still have much to learn about how best to design real-world systems to aid in the direction of attention to task-relevant information (and away from distracting task-irrelevant information) and to optimize training programs to engender efficient stimulus-driven and goal-directed attention.

References

Allen, P. A., Smith, A. F., Vires-Collins, H., & Sperry, S. (1998). The psychological refractory period: Evidence for age differences in attentional time-sharing. *Psychology and Aging, 13,* 218–229.

Ball, K., Beard, B., Roenker, D., Miller, R., & Griggs, D. (1988). Age and visual search: Expanding the useful field of view. *Journal of the Optical Society of America, 5,* 2210–2219.

Baron, A., & Mattila, W. (1989). Response slowing of older adults: Effects of time-limit contingencies on single and dual-task performance. *Psychology and Aging, 4,* 66–72.

Batsakes, P. J., & Fisk, A. D. (2000). Age-related differences in dual-task visual search: Are performance gains retained? *Journal of Gerontology: Psychological Sciences, 55,* 332–342.

Bojko, A., Kramer, A. F., & Peterson, M. S. (2004). Age equivalence in switch costs for prosaccade and antisaccade tasks. *Psychology and Aging, 19,* 226–234.

Braver, T. S., Barch, D. M., Keys, B. A., Carter, C. S., Cohen, J. D., Kaye, J. A., Janowsky, J. S., Taylor, S. F., Yesavage, J. A., Momenthaler, M. S., Jagust, W. J., & Reed, B. R. (2001). Context processing in older adults: Evidence for a theory relating cognitive control to neurobiology in healthy aging. *Journal of Experimental Psychology: General, 130,* 746–763.

Cepeda, N. J., Kramer, A. F., & Gonzalez de Sather, J. C. M. (2001). Changes in executive control across the life span: Examination of task-switching performance. *Developmental Psychology, 37,* 715–730.

Cerella, J. (1985). Information processing rates in the elderly. *Psychological Bulletin, 98,* 67–83.

Clancy, S. M., & Hoyer, W. J. (1994). Age and skill in visual search. *Developmental Psychology, 30,* 545–552.

Colcombe, S., & Kramer, A. F. (2003). Fitness effects on the cognitive function of older adults: A meta-analytic study. *Psychological Science, 14,* 125–130.

Colcombe, S. J., Kramer, A. F., Erickson, K. I., Scalf, P., McAuley, E., Cohen, N. J., Webb, A., Gerome, G. J., Marquez, D. X., & Elavsky, S. (2004). Cardiovascular fitness, cortical plasticity, and aging. *Proceedings of the National Academy of Sciences, 101,* 3316–3321.

Craik, F. I. M., & Byrd, M. (1982). Aging and cognitive deficits: The role of attentional resources. In F. I. M. Craik & S. Trehub (Eds), *Aging and cognitive processes* (pp. 191–211). New York: Plenum.

DiGirolamo, G. J., Kramer, A. F., Barad, V., Cepeda, N. J., Weissman, D. H., Milham, M. P., Wszalek, T. M., Cohen, N. J., Banich, M. T., Webb, A., Belopolsky, A. V., & McAuley, E. (2001). General and task-specific frontal lobe recruitment in older adults during executive processes: A fMRI investigation of task switching. *Neuroreport, 12,* 2065–2072.

De Jong, R. (2001). Adult age differences in goal activation and goal maintenance. *European Journal of Cognitive Psychology, 13,* 71–89.

Dulaney, C., & Rogers, W. A. (1994). Mechanisms underlying reduction in Stroop interference with practice for young and old adults. *Journal of Experimental Psychology: Learning, Memory, and Cognition, 20,* 470–484.

Folk, C. L., & Hoyer, W. J. (1992). Aging and shifts of visual spatial attention. *Psychology and Aging, 7,* 453–465.

Folk, C. L., & Lincourt, A. E. (1996). The effects of age on guided conjunction search. *Experimental Aging Research, 22,* 99–118.

Frensch, P. A., Lindenberger, U., & Kray, J. (1999). Imposing structure on an unstructured environment: Ontogenetic changes in the ability to form rules of behavior under conditions of low environmental predictability. In A. Friederici & R. Menzel (Eds.), *Learning: Rule extraction and representation* (pp. 139–162). Berlin, Germany: De Gruyter.

Glass, J. M., Schumacher, E. H., Lauber, E. J., Zurbriggen, E. L., Gmeindl, L., Kieras, D. E., & Meyer, D. E. (2000). Aging and the psychological refractory period: Task-coordination strategies in young and old adults. *Psychology and Aging, 15,* 571–595.

Gottlob, L. R., & Madden, D. J. (1998). Time course of allocation of visual attention after equating for sensory differences: An age-related perspective. *Psychology and Aging, 13,* 138–149.

Greenwood, P. M., & Parasuraman, R. (1999). Scale of attentional focus in visual search. *Perception and Psychophysics, 61,* 837–855.

Greenwood, P. M., & Parasuraman, R. (2004). The scaling of spatial attention in visual search and its modification in healthy aging. *Perception & Psychophysics*, 66, 3–22.

Hahn, S., & Kramer, A. F. (1995). Attentional flexibility and aging: You don't need to be 20 years of age to split the beam. *Psychology and Aging, 10*, 597–609.

Hartley, A. A. (1992). Attention. In F. I. M. Craik & T. A. Salthouse (Eds.), *The handbook of aging and cognition* (pp. 3–49). Hillsdale, NJ: Lawrence Erlbaum Associates.

Hartley, A. A. (1993). Evidence for the selective preservation of spatial selective attention in old age. *Psychology and Aging, 3*, 371–379.

Hartley, A. A., & Kieley, J. M. (1995). Adult age differences of inhibition of return of visual attention. *Psychology and Aging, 10*, 670–683.

Hartley, A. A., Kieley, J. M., & Slabach, E. H. (1990). Age differences and similarities in the effects of cues and prompts. *Journal of Experimental Psychology: Human Perception and Performance, 16*, 523–537.

Hartley, A. A., & Little, D. M. (1999). Age-related differences and similarities in dual-task interference. *Journal of Experimental Psychology: General, 128*, 416–449.

Hasher, L., Stoltzfus, E. R., Zacks, R. T., & Rympa, B. (1991). Age and inhibition. *Journal of Experimental Psychology: Learning, Memory and Cognition, 17*, 163–169.

Hasher, L., & Zacks, R. T. (1988). Working memory, comprehension and aging: a review and a new view. In G. H. Bower (Ed.), *The psychology of learning and motivation* (Vol. 22, pp. 193–225). San Diego, CA: Academic Press.

Ho, G., Siakaluk, P. D., & Scialfa, C. T. (2003). Plasticity of feature-based selection in triple-conjunction search. *Canadian Journal of Experimental Psychology, 57*, 48–60.

Humphrey, D. G., & Kramer, A. F. (1997). Age differences in visual search for feature, conjunction, and triple-conjunction targets. *Psychology and Aging, 12*, 704–717.

Kane, M. J., Hasher, L., Stoltzfus, E. R., Zacks, R. T., & Connelly, S. L. (1994). Inhibitory attentional mechanisms and aging. *Psychology and Aging, 9*, 103–112.

Kane, M. J., May, C. P., Hasher, L., Rahhal, T., & Stoltzfus, E. R. (1997). Dual mechanisms of negative priming. *Journal of Experimental Psychology: Human Perception and Performance, 23*, 632–650.

Kieley, J. M., & Hartley, A. A. (1997). Age-related equivalence of identity suppression in the Stroop color-word task. *Psychology and Aging, 12*, 22–29.

Kramer, A. F., & Atchley, P. (2000). Age effects in the marking of old objects in visual search. *Psychology and Aging, 15*, 286–296.

Kramer, A. F., Hahn, S., Cohen, N., Banich, M., McAuley, E., Harrison, C., Chason, J., Vakil, E., Bardell, L., Boileau, R. A., & Colcombe, A. (1999). Aging, fitness, and neurocognitive function. *Nature, 400*, 418–419.

Kramer, A. F., Hahn, S., & Gopher, D. (1999). Task coordination and aging: Explorations of executive control processes in the task switching paradigm. *Acta Psychologica, 101*, 339–378.

Kramer, A. F., Humphrey, D. G., Larish, J. F., Logan, G. D., & Strayer, D. L. (1994). Aging and inhibition: Beyond a unitary view of inhibitory processing in attention. *Psychology and Aging, 9*, 491–512.

Kramer, A. F., & Larish, J. F. (1996). Aging and dual-task performance. In W. Rogers, A. D. Fisk, & N. Walkers (Eds.), *Aging and skilled performance: Advances in theory and application* (pp. 83–112). Mahwah, NJ: Lawrence Erlbaum Associates.

Kramer, A. F., Larish, J. F., & Strayer, D. L. (1995). Training for attentional control in dual task settings: A comparison of young and old adults. *Journal of Experimental Psychology: Applied, 1*, 50–76.

Kramer, A. F., Larish, J., Weber, T., & Bardell, L. (1999). Training for executive control: Task coordination strategies and aging. In D. Gopher & A. Koriat (Eds.), *Attention and performance XVII*. Cambridge, MA. MIT Press.

Kramer, A. F., & Strayer, D. L. (2001). Influence of stimulus repetition on negative priming. *Psychology and Aging, 16*, 580–587.

Kray, J., & Lindenberger, U. (2000). Adult age differences in task switching. *Psychology and Aging, 15*, 126–147.

Kray, J., Li, K. Z. H., & Lindenberger, U. (2002). Age-related changes in task switching components: The role of uncertainty. *Brain & Cognition, 49*, 363–381.

Lavie, N. (1995). Perceptual load as a necessary condition for selective attention. *Journal of Experimental Psychology: Human Perception and Performance, 21*, 451–468.

Li, K. Z. H., Lindenberger, U., Freund, A. M., & Baltes, P. B. (2001). Walking while memorizing: Age-related differences in compensatory behavior. *Psychological Science, 3*, 230–237.

Lincourt, A. E., Folk, C. L., & Hoyer, W. J. (1997). Effects of aging on voluntary and involuntary shifts of attention. *Aging, Neuropsychology and Cognition, 4*, 290–303.

Lindenberger, U., Marsiske, M., & Baltes, P. B. (2000). Memorizing while walking: Increase in dual-task costs from young adulthood to old age. *Psychology and Aging, 15*, 417–436.

Madden, D. J., Connelly, S. L., & Pierce, T. W. (1994). Adult age differences in shifting focused attention. *Psychology and Aging, 9*, 528–538.

Madden, D. J., & Gottlob, L. R. (1997). Adult age differences in strategic and dynamic components of focusing visual attention. *Aging, Neuropsychology and Cognition, 4,* 185–210.

Madden, D. J., & Langley, L. K. (2003). Age-related changes in selective attention and perceptual load during visual search. *Psychology and Aging, 18,* 54–67.

Madden, D. J., Pierce, T. W., & Allen, P. A. (1996). Adult age differences in the use of distractor homogeneity in visual search. *Psychology and Aging, 11,* 454–474.

May, C. P., Kane, M. J., & Hasher, L. (1995). Determinants of negative priming. *Psychological Bulletin, 118,* 35–54.

Maylor, E. A., & Lavie, N. (1998). The influence of perceptual load on age differences in selective attention. *Psychology and Aging, 13,* 563–573.

Mayr, U. (2001). Age differences in the selection of mental sets: The role of inhibition, stimulus ambiguity, and response-set overlap. *Psychology and Aging, 16,* 96–109.

Mayr, U., & Kliegl, R. (1993). Sequential and coordinative complexity: Age-based control limitations in figural transformations. *Journal of Experimental Psychology: Learning, Memory, and Cognition, 19,* 1297–1320.

McDowd, J. M., & Craik, F. I. M. (1988). Effects of aging and task difficulty on divided attention performance. *Journal of Experimental Psychology: Human Perception and Performance, 14,* 267–280.

McDowd, J. M., & Shaw, R. S. (2000). Attention and aging: A functional perspective. In F. I. M. Craik & T. A. Salthouse (Eds.), *Handbook of aging and cognition* (pp. 221–292). Mahwah, NJ: Lawrence Erlbaum Associates.

Meiran, N. (1996). Reconfiguration of processing mode prior to task performance. *Journal of Experimental Psychology: Learning, Memory, and Cognition, 22,* 1423–1442.

Meiran, N., Gotler, A. & Perlman, A. (2001). Old age is associated with a pattern of relatively intact and impaired task-set switching abilities. *Journal of Gerontology, Series B: Psychological Sciences and Social Sciences, 56,* 88–102.

Müller, H. J., & Rabbitt, P. M. A. (1989). Reflexive and voluntary orienting of visual attention: Time course of activation and resistance to interruption. *Journal of Experimental Psychology: Human Perception and Performance, 15,* 315–330.

Neill, W. T. (1997). Episodic retrieval in negative priming and repetition priming. *Journal of Experimental Psychology: Learning, Memory and Cognition, 23,* 1291–1305.

Neill, T., & Valdes, L. (1996). Facilitatory and inhibitory aspects of attention. In A. F. Kramer, M. G. H. Coles, and G. D. Logan (Eds.), *Converging operations in the study of visual selective attention* (pp. 77–106). Washington, DC: APA Press.

Owsley, C., Ball, K., Sloane, N., Roenker, D., & Bruni, J. (1991). Visual perceptual/cognitive correlates of vehicle crashes in older drivers. *Psychology and Aging, 6,* 403–415.

Plude, D., & Doussard-Rosselvet, J. (1989). Aging, selective attention, and feature integration. *Psychology and Aging, 4,* 98–105.

Posner, M. (1980). Orienting of attention. *Quarterly Journal of Experimental Psychology, 32,* 3–25.

Pringle, H., Irwin, D. E., Kramer, A. F., & Atchley, P. (2001). Relationship between attention and perceptual change detection in driving scenes. *Psychonomic Bulletin and Review, 8,* 89–95.

Raz, N. (2000). Aging of the brain and its impact on cognitive performance: Integration of structural and functional findings. In F. I. M. Craik & T. A. Salthouse (Eds.), *Handbook of aging and cognition* (pp. 1–90). Mahwah, NJ: Lawrence Erlbaum Associates.

Roenker, D. L., Cissell, G. M., Ball, K., Wadley, V. G., & Edwards, J. D. (2003). Speed of processing and driving simulator training result in improved driving performance. *Human Factors, 45,* 218–232.

Rogers, R. D., & Monsell, S. (1995). Costs of a predictable switch between simple cognitive tasks. *Journal of Experimental Psychology: General, 124,* 207–231.

Salthouse, T. A. (1985). Speed of behavior and its implications for cognition. In J. E. Birren & K. W. Schaie (Eds.), *Handbook of psychology of aging* (2nd ed., pp. 400–426). New York: Van Nostrand Reinhold.

Salthouse, T. A. (1991). *Theoretical perspectives on cognitive aging.* Hillsdale, NJ: Lawrence Erlbaum Associates.

Salthouse, T. A. (1996). General and specific speed mediation of adult age differences in memory. *Journal of Gerontology: Psychological Sciences, 51,* 30–42.

Salthouse, T. A., Rogan, J. D., & Prill, K. A. (1984). Division of attention: Age differences on a visually presented memory task. *Memory & Cognition, 12,* 613–620.

Salthouse, T. A., Fristoe, N. M., McGuthry, K. E., & Hambrick, D. Z. (1998). Relation of task switching to speed, age, and fluid intelligence. *Psychology and Aging, 13,* 445–461.

Salthouse, T. A., Hambrick, D. Z., Lukas, K. E., & Dell, T. C. (1996). Determinants of adult age differences on synthetic work performance. *Journal of Experimental Psychology: Applied, 2,* 1–25.

Scialfa, C. T., Thomas, D. M., & Joffe, K. M. (1994). Age differences in the Useful Field of View: An eye movement analysis. *Optometry and Vision Science, 71,* 1–7.

Sit, R. A., & Fisk, A. D. (1999). Age-related performance in a multiple-task environment. *Human Factors, 41,* 26–34.

Somberg, B. L. & Salthouse, T. A. (1982). Divided attention abilities in young and old adults. *Journal of Experimental Psychology: Human Perception and Performance, 8,* 651–663.

Spieler, D. H., Balota, D. A., & Faust, M. E. (1996). Stroop performance in healthy younger and older adults and in individuals with dementia of the Alzheimer type. *Journal of Experimental Psychology: Human Perception and Performance, 22,* 461–479.

Sullivan, M. P., & Faust, M. E. (1993). Evidence for identity inhibition during selective attention in older adults. *Psychology and Aging, 8,* 589–598.

Sullivan, M. P., Faust, M. E., & Balota, D. A. (1995). Identity negative priming in older adults and individuals with dementia of the Alzheimer type. *Neuropsychology, 9,* 537–555.

Tipper, S. P. (1985). The negative priming effect: Inhibitory priming by ignored objects. *The Quarterly Journal of Experimental Psychology, 37,* 571–590.

Tipper, S. (1991). Less attentional selectivity as a result of declining inhibition in older adults. *Bulletin of the Psychonomic Society, 29,* 45–47.

Tsang, P. S., & Shaner, T. L. (1998). Age, attention, expertise, and time-sharing performance. *Psychology and Aging, 13,* 323–347.

Verhaeghen, P., & Cerella, J. (2002). Aging, executive control, and attention: A review of meta-analyses. *Neuroscience and Biobehavioral Reviews, 26,* 849–857.

Verhaeghen, P., & De Meersman, L. (1998a). Aging and the Stroop effect: A meta-analysis. *Psychology and Aging, 13,* 120–126.

Verhaeghen, P., & De Meersman, L. (1998b). Aging and the negative priming effect: A meta-analysis. *Psychology and Aging, 13,* 435–444.

Watson, D. G., & Humphreys, G. W. (1997). Visual marking: Prioritizing selection for new objects by top-down attention inhibition of old objects. *Psychological Review, 104,* 90–122.

Watson, D. G., & Maylor, E. A. (2002). Aging and visual marking: Deficits for moving stimuli. *Psychology and Aging, 17,* 321–339.

West, R. L. (1996). An application of prefrontal cortex function theory to cognitive aging. *Psychological Bulletin, 120,* 272–292.

Yantis, S. (1996). Attentional capture in vision. In A. F. Kramer, M. G. H. Coles, & G. D. Logan (Eds.), *Converging operations in the study of visual selective attention* (pp. 45–76). Washington, DC: APA Press.

Zeef, E. J., Sonke, C. J., Kok, A., Buiten, M. M., & Kenemans, J. L. (1996). Perceptual factors affecting age-related differences in focused attention: Performance and psychophysiological analysis. *Psychophysiology, 33,* 555–565.

6

The Early Development
of Executive Functions

Adele Diamond

Executive function, also called *cognitive control* (Miller & Cohen, 2001); *effortful, conscious,* or *executive control*; or *supervisory attention* (Shallice, 1988), is required whenever going "on automatic" would be insufficient and especially when it would lead one astray. Classes of situations in which executive functions are required include (1) novel tasks and situations that require (2) concentration, (3) planning, (4) problem solving, (5) coordination, (6) change, (7) conscious choices among alternatives, or (8) overriding a strong internal or external pull.

Component cognitive abilities that constitute what collectively is known as *executive function* include the following:

1. *Inhibition,* that is, the ability to ignore distraction and stay focused, and to resist making one response and instead make another
2. *Working memory,* that is, the ability to hold information in mind and manipulate it
3. *Cognitive flexibility,* that is, the ability to flexibly switch perspectives, focus of attention, or response mappings

These abilities are crucial to all forms of cognitive performance. The ability to inhibit attention to distractors makes possible selective and sustained attention. The ability to inhibit a strong behavioral inclination helps make flexibility and change possible, as well as social politeness. Inhibition thus allows us a measure of control over our attention and our actions, rather than simply being controlled by external stimuli, our emotions, or engrained behavioral tendencies. The ability to hold information in mind makes it possible for us to remember our plans and others' instructions, to consider alternatives, and to relate one idea or datum to another, including relating the present to the future and the past. It is critical to our ability to see connections between seemingly unconnected items and to separate elements from an integrated whole; hence, it is critical to creativity, for the essence of creativity is to be able to disassemble and recombine elements in new ways, and to consider something from a fresh perspective.

While it is difficult to resist a natural inclination, after awhile executive function is no longer required to do that *as long as* one keeps within that same behavioral set. For example, on the classic Stroop task (MacLeod, 1991, 1992; Stroop, 1935), color words appear in the ink of another color (for example, the word *blue* might be printed in green ink). It is difficult to report the color of the ink, ignoring the word, but it is far easier to do that consistently than to switch back and forth between reporting the ink color and reporting the word. It is switching (resetting one's attentional focus, reorienting one's mindset) that is most difficult and epitomizes the twin needs for active maintenance (working memory) and inhibition, the hallmark of when concerted executive control is most clearly needed. Together, working memory and inhibition make it possible for us to quickly and flexibly adapt to changed circumstances, take the time to consider what to do next, and meet novel, unanticipated challenges.

There is strong evidence that areas of both dorsolateral and ventrolateral prefrontal cortex play a pivotal role in mediating executive functions. The evidence comes from a variety of sources, including brain-damaged patients (Barcelo & Knight, 2002; Koski & Petrides, 2001; Stuss, Floden, Alexander, Levine, & Katz, 2001; Stuss et al., 2000), functional neuroimaging of healthy adults (Braver, Reynolds, & Donaldson, 2003; Bunge, Ochsner, Desmond, Glover, & Gabrieli, 2001; Duncan & Owen, 2000; MacDonald, Cohen, Stenger, & Carter, 2000), studies using transcranial magnetic stimulation (TMS; Jahanshahi & Dirnberger, 1999; Mottaghy, Gangitano, Sparing, Krause, & Pascual-Leone, 2002), and studies of macaque monkeys (Diamond & Goldman-Rakic, 1985; Funahashi, Chafee, & Goldman-Rakic, 1993; Rainer, Assad, & Miller, 1998).

Executive function is not always needed when an action is complex and involves an intricate sequence. Novice dancers or athletes must concentrate hard and rely heavily on executive function, but expert dancers and athletes do not. Indeed, Miller, Verstynen, Raye, Mitchell, Johnson, and D'Esposito (2003) report that disrupting the functioning of dorsolateral prefrontal cortex impairs performance when a task is new and unfamiliar, but it improves performance when a task is familiar; presumably, thinking about what you are doing would get in the way of efficient performance.

THE FIRST YEAR OF LIFE

According to Piaget (1954), the first signs of what we would today call executive function are evident by 8–9 months of age (Sensorimotor Stage 4) and become consolidated over the next few months. When infants reach for a desired object, it is hard to tell if the external stimulus elicited an automatic reach or the intention was internally generated. However, when an infant searches for an object that is not visible, or acts on an object of no particular interest in order to obtain a desired object, then Piaget was willing to infer that intentionality was present and the action sequence had been truly goal-directed (i.e., executively controlled). The emergence of acting on one object to obtain another is also an example of creativity as Piaget pointed out: adapting a behavior (reaching and grasping) for an entirely new end (in order to obtain, not the object of the action, but for the first time as a means to obtaining a hidden or distant object). Piaget also took such means-end behavior to indicate planning, since infants seem to intentionally act on the covering or supporting object with the plan that this will make available the object they want.

My own work suggests that Piaget had this exactly right. Between 8 and 12 months of age, one sees the emergence of detour reaching (first around an opaque barrier and then around a transparent one; Diamond, 1988, 1990a, 1991; see Figure 6.1). Detour reaching requires holding a goal in mind, planning, and inhibiting the strong tendency to reach straight for the goal. Indeed, it requires reaching *away* from the goal object at the outset of the reach. Obviously, a detour reach requires more inhibition when the goal is visible than when it is not, hence detouring around a transparent barrier appears later. To come up with the plan of first reaching to the opening and then to the desired object, infants must grasp the connection between the opening and the desired object, even though these are spatially displaced. Indeed, the farther they are spatially displaced from one another, the later in the first year infants are able to come up with, and execute, the plan of reaching to the opening to obtain what they want.

Also between 8 and 12 months, infants are able to hold in mind for progressively longer periods where a desired object has been hidden, and are able to control their behavior so that they do not repeat a previously correct search that would now be wrong. Instead, they can now override the effects of previous

Detour reaching:
planning & inhibition

a

6 mos

9 mos
awkward
reach
note
looking

12mos

(*continued*)

FIGURE 6.1. Emergence of detour reaching around a transparent barrier. (*a*): Infant performing the object retrieval task. Top row: Infant of 6 months is not able to execute any detour reaching. Infants of this age reach exclusively through the side they are looking. Middle row: Infant of 9 months executes a detour reach to the side opening by leaning over to look in the opening and then remaining in that position (continuing to look in the opening) to execute the reach. This behavior is dubbed an "awkward reach" because it looks so awkward. Bottom row: Infant of 12 months executes a detour reach quickly and efficiently. No longer does the infant need to see through the opening before or during reaching there. NOTE: Photographs are screen captures.

A not B
= wm, inhib.

reinforcement to change their search behavior when the desired object's hiding place has changed (as shown by the body of work on the A-not-B task; Bell & Adams, 1999; Diamond, 1991; Gratch, 1975; Harris, 1987; Wellman, Cross, & Bartsch, 1987; see Figure 6.2).

What is happening in the brain that helps make possible these cognitive advances in the latter part of the first year? No one knows for sure. Monkeys with lesions of dorsolateral prefrontal cortex (DL-PFC) fail the detour-reaching object retrieval task and the A-not-b

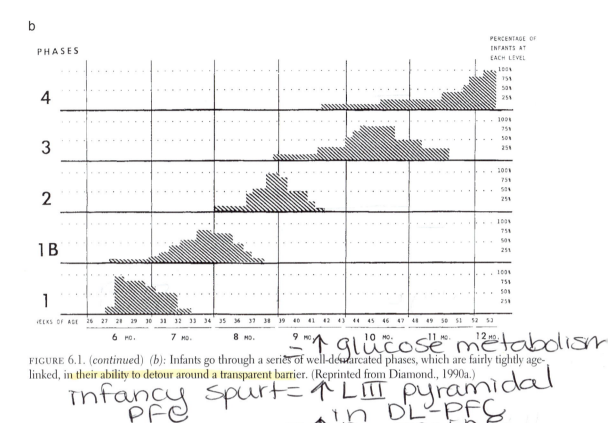

FIGURE 6.1. (*continued*) (*b*): Infants go through a series of well-demarcated phases, which are fairly tightly age-linked, in their ability to detour around a transparent barrier. (Reprinted from Diamond., 1990a.)

[handwritten annotations: → ↑ glucose metabolism; Infancy spurt= ↑ L III pyramidal PFC =↑ in DL-PFC =↑ dopamine]

B task in the same ways and under the same conditions as do human infants (Diamond, 1991; Diamond & Goldman-Rakic, 1989). In the human brain, dendrites of pyramidal neurons in layer III of DL-PFC undergo their most dramatic expansion between the ages of 7½ and 12 months (Koenderink, Ulyings, & Mrzljiak, 1994), exactly coinciding with the period of marked improvement on the A-not-B and object retrieval tasks. Pyramidal neurons in DL-PFC have relatively short dendritic extents at 7½ months, but reach their full mature extent by 12 months. The surface of the cell bodies of these pyramidal neurons also increases between 7½ and 12 months (Koenderink et al., 1994). The level of glucose metabolism in DL-PFC increases during this period as well, approximating adult levels by 1 year of age (Chugani & Phelps, 1986; Chugani, Phelps, & Mazziotta, 1987). One particularly important developmental change during this period might be increased levels of dopamine in DL-PFC. Dopamine is a particularly important neurotransmitter in prefrontal cortex and reducing dopamine in prefrontal cortex impairs performance on executive function tasks (Brozoski, Brown, Rosvold, & Goldman, 1979; Diamond, 2001; Sawaguchi &

Goldman-Rakic, 1991). During the period that infant rhesus macaques are improving on the A-not-B and object retrieval tasks, dopamine levels are increasing in their brain (Brown, Crane, & Goldman, 1976; Brown & Goldman, 1977), the density of dopamine receptors in prefrontal cortex is increasing (Lidow & Rakic, 1992), and the distribution within DL-PFC of axons containing the enzyme critical for the production of dopamine (tyrosine hydroxylase) is markedly changing (Lewis & Harris, 1991; Rosenberg & Lewis, 1995).

[handwritten: Dopa production enzyme]

THE SECOND YEAR OF LIFE

Not until almost 2 years of age (20–21 months; Diamond, 1990b; Diamond, Towle, & Boyer, 1994; Overman, Bachevalier, Turner, & Peuster, 1992) can infants succeed at a task called "delayed nonmatching to sample" (DNMS). First, a sample object is presented, which the child displaces to retrieve a small reward in the depression (or "well") beneath it. After a delay of 5–10 seconds, the sample and a novel object are presented, with the reward now in the well

[handwritten: 20 mos DNMS]

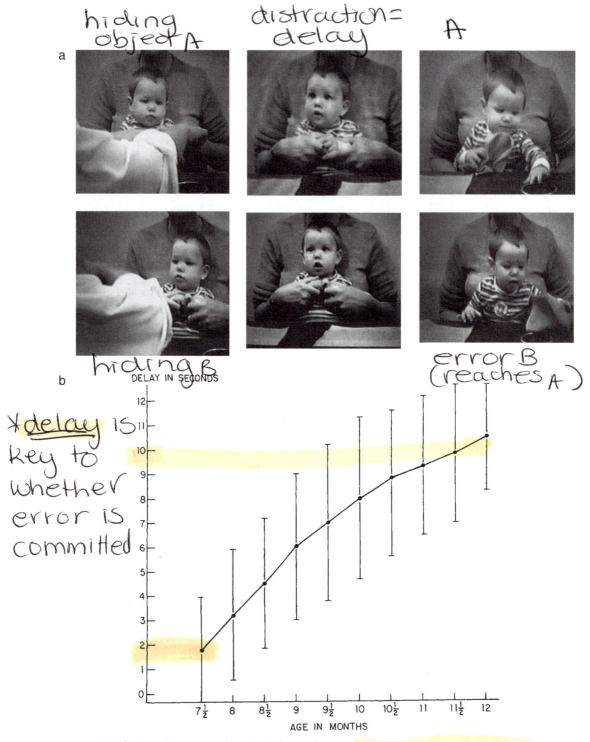

(handwritten annotations on figure: "hiding object A", "distraction = delay", "A", "hiding B", "error B (reaches A)", "delay is key to whether error is committed")

FIGURE 6.2. The A-not-B error in infants. *(a)*: Infant performing the A-not-B task devised by Jean Piaget. Top row: Trial at Well A: Infant watches as a desired object is hidden and both wells are covered simultaneously by identical covers. A brief delay of only seconds is imposed, during which the infant is restrained and distracted and not allowed to look toward the correct well. Then the infant is allowed to reach for the reward. The infant reaches correctly. Bottom row: Trial at Well B. The procedure is repeated but with the object hidden on the opposite side. Again the infant watches the hiding and the simultaneous covering. The same delay procedure is used. Then the infant is allowed to reach. The A-not-B error consists of the infant reaching correctly on the initial A trials, but erring on the B trial by going back to where the infant had previously been successful. *(b)*: Infants show a clear developmental progression in the length of the delay they can withstand on the A-not-B task. (Reprinted from Diamond, 1988 with the permission of Blackwell Publishing.) Note: Photographs are screen captures.

[Handwritten notes at top: DNMS = reward novel object/well (non-match to previous sample) = delay is issue too]

under the novel object. Thus, displacing the novel (nonmatching) object is rewarded. Many trials follow, each with a new sample and another novel object. Reaching to the novel stimulus is consistently rewarded, whether it is on the right or the left, is taller or shorter, or is more or less colorful than the sample. Once a child succeeds at the brief training delay, the delay is increased.

One might think that, since this task is a classic behavioral assay of the functions of the medial temporal lobe (Murray & Mishkin, 1998; Zola et al., 2000), and since success on it does not appear until late in infancy, the medial temporal lobe memory system must be late maturing. However, the problem for infants on this task is in "acquisition"—that is, understanding what correct performance entails, not retention at long delays (which is the problem for monkeys and adults with medial temporal lobe damage). Robust recognition memory at long delays is present well before 20–21 months (Brown, 1975; Dempster, 1985; Fagan, 1973). It is another ability required by the DNMS task that matures late.

The critical competence required for success on DNMS that young infants appear to lack is the ability to grasp the abstract rule-based relation between the stimulus and reward when there is no obvious physical connection between stimulus and reward. When

there is a physical connection, infants of only 9–12 months easily succeed. For instance, they succeed when the reward is "Velcroed" to the base of the stimulus (attached to, though detachable from, the stimulus), and still hidden beneath the stimulus when the stimulus is atop its well (Diamond, Churchland, Cruess, & Kirkham, 1999). They also succeed when the stimuli and rewards are attached to the same piece of apparatus and in the same visual field, even though not directly attached to one another and not spatially close together. Indeed, when the stimuli and rewards are parts of a single apparatus, even when the stimuli and rewards are several inches apart and the close temporal connection between pulling the stimulus and appearance of the reward is broken, infants succeed (Diamond, Lee, & Hayden, 2003). In the absence of the perception that the stimulus and reward are components of a single thing, even close spatial and temporal proximity are insufficient for infants of 12 months to succeed at DNMS (Shutts, Ross, Hayden, & Diamond, 2001; Diamond et al., 2003). For instance, infants fail even if the stimulus is directly in front or on top of the reward, and the reward pops up the instant the infant grasps the stimulus (see Figure 6.3). Physical connectedness appears to be necessary and sufficient for infants of 9–12 months to grasp the abstract principle connecting the stimuli and the rewards in the

*[Handwritten note: *physical connection*]*

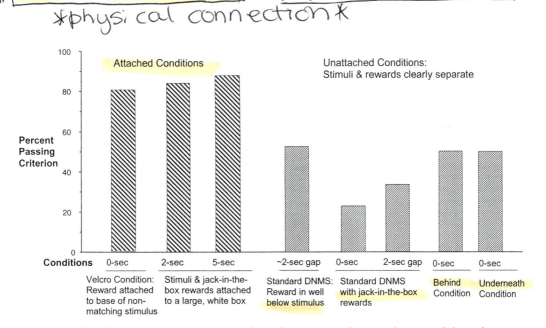

FIGURE 6.3. Delayed nonmatching to sample performance in infants as a function of physical connection, and temporal proximity, between stimulus and reward. (Based on data from Shutts, Ross, Hayden, & Diamond, 2001; Diamond et al., 2003.)

DNMS task. In its presence, neither close spatial or temporal proximity is needed. In its absence, even close spatial and temporal proximity are insufficient.

Physical connectedness also appears to be central to infants' ability to grasp conceptual connectedness. Aguiar and Baillargeon (2000) placed two cloths, one twice as long as the other, in front of 9-month-old infants. On the longer cloth, near its far end, sat a desired toy. Pulling the cloth brought the toy within reach. Equally far from the infant sat an identical toy behind the shorter cloth; pulling that cloth would not bring the toy within reach. After infants' initial success, if the locations of the shorter and longer cloths were reversed, 9-month-olds continued to succeed *if* the toy was attached to the longer cloth, but not if toy and cloth were not physically attached, though the toy was still on top of the cloth and spatially contiguous to it. In the former case (physical connection), infants correctly switched from pulling the cloth on side A to pulling the cloth on side B. In the latter case, 9-month-olds continued to the pull the cloth on side A. Evidently, physical attachment made a huge difference to the infants. Perhaps when the objects were attached, their synchrony of movement was exact, whereas when one was on top of the other unattached, the correlation was less precise. Synchrony of movement has long been known to be a powerful cue for infants in determining whether two things are part of one whole or are separate objects (Spelke, 1985; Vishton & Badger, 2003).

It may seem odd that physical attachment made such a big difference, but Jarvik (1953) found parallel results in rhesus macaques. When monkeys are trained on a color discrimination using two wells, one covered by a blue plaque and one by a red plaque, it can take a rhesus monkey 100 trials to learn the color discrimination. When Jarvik trained rhesus monkeys using bread as the reward (one slice injected with something that did not smell but tasted awful), the monkeys learned the color discrimination in one trial *if* there was a physical connection between stimulus and reward (the stimuli of red and green transparent celluloids pasted on top of the bread), but performed as poorly as in the standard procedure when the same stimuli were placed on top of the bread but were not attached.

DeLoache (1986) varied whether a reward was hidden in one of four distinctive containers, or whether the distinctive containers were mounted on top of plain boxes in which the rewards were placed.

For infants of 27 months, it did not matter. For 21-month-olds, however, it made a great difference. When the boxes were scrambled, 21-month-olds were 80% correct when the rewards were *in* the distinctive containers but only 35% correct when the distinctive containers *marked* where the rewards were hidden (the reward being in the box underneath). "[W]hen the same distinctive visual information was a less integral aspect of the hiding location, age differences appeared" (DeLoache, 1986, p. 123). Similarly, DeLoache and Brown (1983) found that infants of 18–22 months performed significantly better when a reward was hidden *in* a piece of furniture rather than *near* it. By 24–30 months, infants performed equally well in both conditions.

Thus, during the second year or year and a half of life, an important advance in executive function appears to be an improvement in the ability to grasp connections between physically connected things. Grasping such connections, and using them to deduce abstract rules, has been linked to the region of frontal cortex known as the *periarcuate region* in the monkey brain and the *inferior frontal junction* (IFJ) in the human brain (Derfuss, Brass, Neumann, & von Cramon, 2005). This region overlaps (a) the posterior portion of BA 44/45 (called *ventrolateral PFC* in monkeys and *inferior PFC* in humans) and (b) the anterior, ventral portion of BA8 (premotor cortex). This area is also called F5, includes Broca's area, and is where Rizzolatti and colleagues have identified mirror neurons (e.g., Rizzolatti & Fadiga, 1998). Wallis & Miller (2003) report that more cells in this periarcuate region than in any other frontal subregion encode the abstract delayed nonmatching and delayed matching rules. Such abstract rules were encoded earliest and most strongly in anterior premotor cortex invading the periarcuate. Indeed, earlier Kowalska, Bachevalier, & Mishkin (1991) and Rushworth, Nixon, Eacott, and Passingham (1997) had found that monkeys in whom ventrolateral PFC had been removed (as long as the lesions invaded the periarcuate, but not otherwise) were profoundly impaired at relearning the delayed matching or nonmatching to sample rule (even with no delay), needing over 10 times more trials post-operatively as pre-operatively or as controls; but once they grasped the rule, their performance showed no decline at longer and longer delays (i.e., the same profile as human infants: great difficulty abstracting the general rule, but no memory problem and therefore no delay-dependent deficits). Matsumoto, Suzuki, & Tanaka (2003) found that periarcuate neurons show higher activity during the phase when a monkey is learning the rule for correct performance on a task, whereas neurons in DL-PFC show less activity during learning. Bunge, Kahn, Wallis, Miller, & Wagner (2003) report that functional magnetic resonance imaging (fMRI) in human adults reveals that the posterior portion of inferior PFC extending into the IFJ appears to encode specific abstract rules, such as matching and non-matching. In an fMRI study of DNMS, Elliott & Dolan (1999) found increased activation in left anterior, ventral premotor cortex. In positron emission tomography (PET) studies, too, performance of delayed matching to sample has been shown to increase activation in right, posterior inferior PFC (Grady *et al.*, 1998) and selecting between actions on the basis of visual associative rules has been shown to increase activation of the IFJ (Brass & von Cramon, 2002; Toni et al, 2001).

THE PRESCHOOL PERIOD: 3–5 YEARS OF AGE

Between the ages of 3 and 7 years, and especially between 3 and 5 years, there are marked improvements in inhibition and cognitive flexibility, especially the flexibility to change perspectives. These cognitive advances are expressed in social cognition (theory of mind; Wimmer & Perner, 1983), moral development (Kohlberg, 1963), and on diverse cognitive tasks, such as the dimensional change card sort task (DCCS; Zelazo, Reznick, & Piñon, 1995), ambiguous figures (Gopnik & Rosati, 2001), appearance-reality (Flavell, Green & Flavell, 1986), false belief (Perner, Leekam, & Wimmer, 1987), Luria's tapping and hand tasks (Diamond & Taylor, 1996; Hughes, 1998), the day-night Stroop-like task (Gerstadt, Hong, & Diamond, 1994), conservation of liquid or number (Inhelder & Piaget, 1958), and go/no-go (Livesey & Morgan, 1991).

If one has "theory of mind," one is said to be able to infer what another person might know, think, believe, or want (another person's "mental state"), and to use that to accurately predict what the other person might do (Premack & Woodruff, 1978). Tasks that assess theory of mind generally require holding two things in mind about the same situation (the true state of affairs and the false belief of another person) and

inhibiting the impulse to give the veridical answer. That impulse likely comes from children's desire to show how smart they are (they followed everything that happened and know where the hidden object really is) and children's desire for the nice other person (or puppet) to succeed in finding the hidden object. Children must keep in mind where a hidden object has been moved to while the other person was not watching and where that other person last saw the object placed, and inhibit the inclination to say where the object really is, reporting the mistaken belief instead (see Figure 6.4). Children of 3 years typically fail such tests, but children of 4–5 years typically succeed (Wimmer & Perner, 1983; Flavell, 1999). Birch and Bloom (2003) propose that the errors of 3-year-olds on theory-of-mind tasks have their remnants in the "curse of knowledge" tendency seen in adults—the tendency to be biased by one's own knowledge and thus assume that another person, not privy to such knowledge, would still act in accord with it (e.g., Hinds, 1999; Kelley & Jacoby, 1996). Manipulations that reduce the perceptual salience of the true state of affairs (and hence the inhibitory demands) aid children of 3–4 years; for example, by telling children where the object has been moved to but not actually showing them (Zaitchik, 1991). So do manipulations that reduce inhibitory demand in other ways (see e.g., Carlson, Moses, & Hix,1998; Rice, Koinis, Sullivan, Tager-Flusberg, & Winner, 1997).

Success on theory-of-mind tasks emerges at roughly the same time as success on many cognitive tasks that assess executive functions, and performances on the latter and the former are correlated. This is true for performance on theory-of-mind tasks and (1) the DCCS task (Carlson & Moses, 2001; Perner, Lang, & Kloo, 2002), (2) the day-night Stroop-like task (Carlson & Moses, 2001; Hala, Hug, & Henderson, 2003), and (3) Luria's tapping (Hala et al., 2003) and hands (Hughes, 1998) tasks. Success on the day-night and similar tasks appears to precede and predict theory-of-mind success (Carlson, Mandell, & Williams, 2004; Flynn, O'Malley, & Wood, 2004; Hughes, 1998). Further, Kloo and Perner (2003) report that training on theory of mind improves performance on that and on the DCCS task, and training on the DCCS task improves performance on that and on theory of mind.

The moral reasoning of preschoolers of 2–4 years also reflects a seeming inability to consider two perspectives as potentially both having validity. Instead,

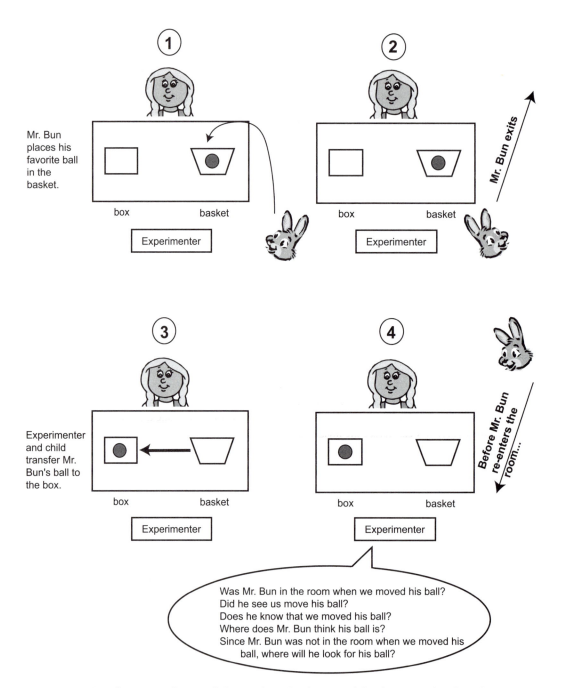

FIGURE 6.4. Illustration of a typical theory-of-mind task. Normal development of prefrontal cortex from birth to young adulthood: cognitive functions, anatomy, and biochemistry (Reprinted from Diamond, 2002 with the permission of Oxford University Press).

things are clearly right or wrong, and people are either good or bad. A parent or respected authority figure can do no wrong and therefore one should obey what the individual says and conform to the rules. Only very gradually do children begin to understand that even wise people can be wrong sometimes, good people can do things they are ashamed of, a person who does many bad things may still have good qualities, and different people may hold differing, yet reasonable opinions about the moral course of action in a given situation. Gilligan (1982) suggests that female moral development may differ from that of boys, but girls still need to overcome the tendency to see things as black or white: although it is right to help and care for others and wrong to be selfish, according to Gilligan, girls need to come to the realization that they will endanger the very relationships they are trying to preserve if they always deny their own needs in their attempt to be unselfish.

An ambiguous figure appears to be one thing (e.g., a duck or an old woman) from one perspective and something quite different from another perspective (e.g., a rabbit or a young woman). Even when informed of the alternatives in an ambiguous figure, children of 3 years remain stuck in their initial way of perceiving the figure; they cannot see the image from the other perspective (Gopnik & Rosati, 2001). Children of 3 years also have difficulty on appearance-reality tasks where, for example, they are presented with a sponge that looks like a rock. They typically report that it looks like a rock and really is a rock; children of 4–5 years correctly answer that it looks like a rock but really is a sponge (Flavell et al., 1986, 1993). The problem for the younger children appears to be in relating two conflicting identities of the same object (e.g., Rice et al., 1997) and in inhibiting the response that matches their perception. Manipulations that reduce perceptual salience on appearance-reality tasks, by removing the object during questioning, enable many more children of 3–4 years to succeed (e.g., Heberle, Clune, & Kelly, 1999).

In a second type of false-belief task, the true state of affairs (e.g., that pennies rather than M&M's are in an M&M's box) is at odds with the child's original belief that M&M's would be in the M&M's box. Once 3-year-olds see what is in the box, they insist that the answer to what is actually in the box and what they had earlier guessed is the same: they had thought all along that pennies were in the box (Perner et al., 1987).

Although adults typically succeed on these tasks, the difficulty in holding in mind two conflicting perspectives on the same thing and discomfort with ambiguity never completely disappear. Even adults often have difficulty accepting that good people (or good nations) sometimes act wrongly or that people who disagree with them might have a point (Van Hiel & Mervielde, 2003; Webster & Kruglanski, 1994). Even adults have difficulty representing more than one interpretation of an ambiguous figure at a time (Chambers & Reisberg, 1992). While adults do not claim that they earlier said that pennies were in an M&M's box, in analogous situations they claim that they earlier rated similarly unlikely outcomes as more probable than they actually had. This was named the "knew it all along" effect by Fischhoff (1977; Fischhoff, & Beyth, 1975); see also Hoffrage, Hertwig, and Gigerenzer (2000). I do not know of studies of the "curse of knowledge" or "knew it all along" in older adults, but if older adults have problems with inhibition, as some have claimed, then the prediction would be that they might be disproportionately prone to show these biases as they would be less able to inhibit them.

In the DCCS task, children are asked to sort a deck of cards first by one dimension (e.g., color) and then to switch and sort the same cards by another dimension (e.g., shape). No sorting card matches either model card on both color and shape; hence the correct sorting response for one dimension is necessarily the wrong response when sorting by the other dimension (see Figure 6.5). For example, a blue-truck stimulus card goes with a blue-star model card when sorting by color but goes with the red-truck model card when sorting by shape. By 3 years of age, children can sort the cards correctly by color or shape. However, when asked to switch sorting dimensions, 3-year-olds tend to continue to sort by the initially correct dimension, even though they can correctly indicate on each trial what the current sorting dimension is and how to sort according to it (Zelazo et al., 1995; Zelazo, Frye, & Rapus, 1996). By 4–5 years of age, that error disappears. This task, unlike the Wisconsin Card Sort Test (WCST), does not require participants to deduce which sorting criterion is currently correct because they are told, nor do they need to remember that over trials because they are reminded at the start of each trial, and when the sorting criterion changes, that change and the newly correct sorting dimension are pointed out to the participant and emphasized.

Sorting Boxes With Model Cards Affixed

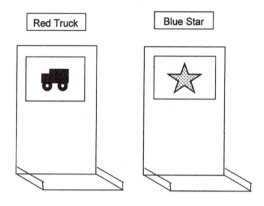

Red Truck

Blue Star

The Cards to be Sorted

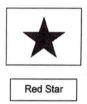

Red Star

Blue Truck

Model Cards

b

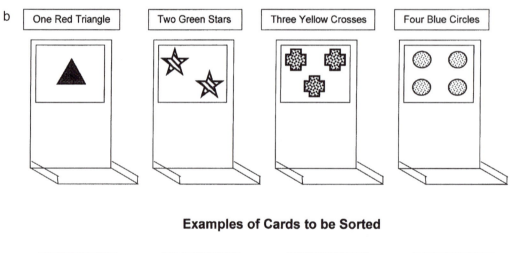

One Red Triangle

Two Green Stars

Three Yellow Crosses

Four Blue Circles

Examples of Cards to be Sorted

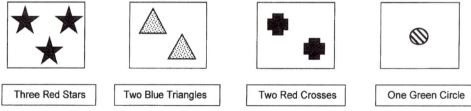

Three Red Stars

Two Blue Triangles

Two Red Crosses

One Green Circle

(continued)

80

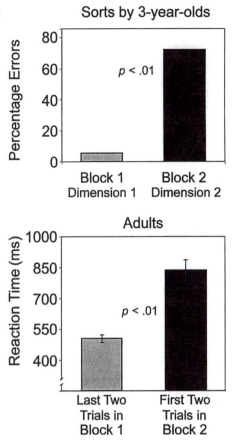

c

Sorts by 3-year-olds

Percentage Errors

$p < .01$

Block 1   Block 2
Dimension 1   Dimension 2

Adults

Reaction Time (ms)

$p < .01$

Last Two   First Two
Trials in   Trials in
Block 1   Block 2

FIGURE 6.5. (*a*): Illustration of the Dimensional Card Sort Task for preschoolers. There are 2 dimensions and 2 values per dimension. (*b*): Illustration of the Wisconsin Card Sort test for adults. There are 3 dimensions and 4 values per dimension. (Reprinted from Diamond, 2002 with the permission of Oxford University Press.) (*c*): Cost in switching from sorting by color or shape in Block 1 to sorting by the other dimension in Block 2. Three-year-olds can sort by either color or shape initially, but typically cannot switch to sort by the other dimensions. Adults can switch, but they are slower at sorting by the second dimension. Top: Percentage of 3-year-old children who sort incorrectly in Block 1 versus Block 2. Bottom: Reaction times for adults on the last 2 trials in Block 1 versus the first 2 trials in Block 2. (Reprinted from Diamond. & Kirkham, 2005 with permission of Blackwell Publishing.)

I think the problem for 3-year-olds on the DCCS task is in overcoming an inertial tendency—what Kirkham, Cruess, & Diamond (2003) have termed *attentional inertia*. Once a child of 3 years has focused on the "redness" of a red truck, it is difficult for the child to switch mindsets and focus on its "truckness." The child is not yet able to inhibit the inertial tendency to continue to focus on, and respond on the basis of, what had been relevant. Three-year-olds, who correctly point to where the trucks should go at the outset of a trial, run into a problem when they are handed a stimulus that is not only a truck but red, though the experimenter labels it along the relevant dimension only ("Here's a truck"). Sometimes 3-year-olds look at the stimulus and say, "But it's red"; typically they sort it with the red stars (the previously correct answer, but now the wrong response). Exactly analogous results obtain if the order is shape first and then color.

Increasing the perceptual salience of the previous dimension (and hence the inhibitory demand) impairs performance. For example, cards are normally sorted face down in the DCCS task. If they are sorted face up, the previously relevant dimension is visible on the sorted cards under each target when the rule changes, emphasizing the salience of the obsolete dimension. While almost all 4-year-olds succeed in the standard face-down condition, almost 50% of 4-year-olds fail the face-up condition (Kirkham et al., 2003).

Manipulations that reduce the inhibitory demand can dramatically increase the number of 3-year-olds who are able to successfully switch sorting dimensions. For example, redirecting attention to the currently relevant dimension by asking the child, rather than the experimenter, to label the card to be sorted according to the currently relevant dimension enables most 3-year-olds to succeed in switching (Kirkham et al., 2003; Towse, Redbond, Houston-Price, & Cook,

2000). Similarly, if the same color and shape are still present, but are not properties of the same object, the tendency to conceive of that object according to the previously correct perspective is no longer relevant and therefore does not need to be inhibited. Over 90% of 3–year-olds succeed if the sorting cards and model cards display the outline of a shape alongside a patch of color, even though each sorting card still matches one model card along one dimension and the other model card along the other dimension (Kloo & Perner, 2005). If shape outlines are used and the switch is a reversal (switch to sorting trucks with stars and stars with trucks), that does not require inhibiting attention to the previous relevant dimension and children of 3 years succeed (Brooks, Hanauer, Padowska, & Rosman, 2003; Perner & Lang, 2002).

The inertial tendency never completely disappears. Traces of it can be seen in the heightened reaction times of adults when asked to switch criteria and respond on the basis of another dimension (e.g., Monsell & Driver, 2000; Diamond & Kirkham, 2005). No matter how much warning adults are given about which dimension will be relevant on the upcoming trial, and no matter how long the time between the warning and when the stimulus appears, or how long the period between trials, adults are still slower to respond on trials where the relevant dimension switches than when it does not (Allport, Styles, & Hsieh, 1994; Meiran, 1996; Rogers & Monsell, 1995). Moreover, throughout a testing session of scores of trials, adults continue to sort faster by whichever criterion had been relevant first in their testing session (Diamond & Kirkham, 2005).

Luria's tapping test (Luria, 1966) requires remembering the rules, "Tap once when the experimenter taps twice, and tap twice when the experimenter taps once," and inhibiting the tendency to mimic what the experimenter does, making the opposite response instead. The greatest improvement in correct responding on this task occurs between 3½ and 4 years of age, and the greatest improvement in response speed occurs between 4½ and 5 years (Becker, Isaac, & Hynd, 1987; Diamond & Taylor, 1996; Passler, Isaac, & Hynd, 1985). Luria's hands test (used with children by Hughes, 1996, 1998) is quite similar (when the experimenter makes a fist, the child is to hold his or her pointer finger out straight; when the experimenter points that finger, the child is to make a fist) and that too is sensitive to developmental improvements between 3 and 5 years of age.

The day-night task has somewhat similar requirements. It requires remembering two rules (say "night" to a depiction of the sun, and "day" to the moon and stars) and inhibiting saying what the stimuli really represent. Children 3½ to 4½ years of age find the task very difficult; by the age of 6–7 years it is trivially easy. Improvement in the percentage of correct responses is relatively continuous from 3½ to 7 years of age, while improvement in response speed occurs primarily from 3½ to 4½ years (Gerstadt et al., 1994). However, children at least as young as 4 years *can* inhibit saying what these stimuli represent as long as the response to be inhibited is not related to the response to be activated. They can successfully say "dog" to a picture of the sun (or moon) and "pig" or "cat" to the other picture (Diamond, Kirkham, & Amso, 2002). The dog-pig manipulation teaches us that 4-year-olds *can* inhibit saying what a stimulus represents. The relation between the response to be activated and the response to be suppressed is key. It does not have to be a semantic relation either (contrary to what Diamond et al. [2002] had proposed). Simpson and Riggs (*submitted*) have shown that what matters is whether the prepotent response to Stimulus A (or B) is related to the correct response for Stimulus B (or A). For instance, if the stimuli are book and car (words *not* semantically related) and the correct responses are to say "car" when shown a picture of a book and to say "book" when shown a picture of a car, children show the same pattern of errors as on the "classic" day-night task (Gerstadt *et al.*, 1994).

Many of the advances of Piaget's "concrete operational" child of 5–7 years over a "preoperational" child of 3–4 years also reflect the development of the abilities to relate one thing to another and inhibit the strongest response of the moment. For example, children of 3 or 4 years fail tests of liquid conservation (they do not attend to both height and width, attending only to the most perceptually salient of the two dimensions) and they fail tests of perspective-taking where they must mentally manipulate a scene to indicate what it would look like from another perspective and must inhibit the tendency to give the most salient response (their current perspective). By 5 or 6 years, they can do these things (Flavell, 1963). Part of the difficulty posed by Piaget's liquid conservation task is the salience of the visual perception that the tall, thin container contains more liquid. Thus, placing an opaque screen between the child and the containers before the child answers enables younger children to perform better (Bruner, 1964).

A final example of a task on which dramatic improvements are seen between 3 and 5 years of age is go/no-go. Here, the child is to respond to one stimulus but withhold responding when another appears. Children 3–4 years old can correctly state the instructions, but they cannot inhibit responding to the no-go stimulus. Not until roughly 4½ years of age can they begin to curb errors of commission to the no-go stimulus (Livesey & Morgan, 1991; Tikhomirov, 1978; van der Meere & Stemerdink, 1999). This is not to say that continued improvements cannot be seen with age, especially when more rapid responding is required and/or the ratio of go to no-go responses is increased (Casey et al., 1997; van der Meere & Stemerdink, 1999). Even adults are rarely at ceiling. Conversely, with a slightly easier variant of the task, children of 3¾–4 years have been reported to perform at better than 90% correct (Jones, Rothbart, & Posner, 2003).

THE GRADE SCHOOL YEARS: EARLY CHILDHOOD

Between the ages of 5 and 11 years, improvements are evident in *cognitive flexibility* (especially flexibly switching back and forth), *working memory* (the ability to hold information in mind and work with it, manipulating, monitoring, or transforming it), and *speed*. (For a more extended discussion of developmental changes in working memory than provided here, see Chapter 8, this volume.) Tasks on which children show sharp improvements over this age period include the anti-saccade task, the Wisconsin Card Sort Test (WCST), the directional Stroop task, and span tasks. On the anti-saccade task, as soon as a target appears, participants are to look in the opposite direction (but matching the distance and angle). This requires inhibiting the strong tendency to look toward a target when it appears, the response that is correct on the pro-saccade trials. Children can barely do this at all until they are 6–7 years old and improve dramatically over the next few years, but do not reach peak performance until their early 20s (Luna et al., 2001; Munoz, Broughton, Goldring, & Armstrong, 1998). The WCST is one of the classic tests of prefrontal cortex function in adults (Stuss et al., 2000). The participant must deduce the sorting criterion, which can

be color, shape, or number, and must flexibly switch sorting rules without warning on the basis of feedback (the sorting dimension changes unannounced after every 6 or 10 consecutively correct sorts). Children show great improvements on this between 5 and 11 years but may still not reach adult levels until perhaps 20 years of age (Chelune & Thompson, 1987; Rosselli & Ardila, 1993; Welsh, Pennington, & Groisser, 1991).

Task-switching paradigms require that a participant flexibly switch back and forth between two rule sets and two sets of response mappings. In a paradigm devised by Meiran (1996), participants must indicate whether a cue is in the left or right half of a square or the top or bottom half of the square, one key being used to indicate left or top and the other to indicate right or down. On this task, by 4 years, children can begin to switch back and forth, but only poorly. The cost of having to switch back and forth was greatest for the youngest children and declined continuously through at least age 11. Even at the oldest age tested (11 years), children showed more of a reduction in speed and accuracy when they had to switch back and forth (compared to single-task blocks) than did adults (Cohen, Bixenman, Meiran, & Diamond, 2001). Another task-switching paradigm that has been used with children requires that they switch between identifying whether the stimulus display contains a 1 or a 3 (task A) and whether the number of digits displayed is 1 or 3 (task B). Hence, for task A, the correct response to a stimulus display of "1 1 1" is 1, but for task B for the same display the correct response is 3. As on Meiran's task, participants are cued on each trial. Cepeda, Kramer, and Gonzalez de Sather (2001) found that performance was better at 10–12 years than at 7–9 years, but did not reach peak levels until the early 20s. Development of the ability to flexibly switch starts early but continues for almost two decades.

Marked developmental advances between 5 and 11 years of age are consistently found on complex span tasks that require transforming information held in mind under high-interference conditions requiring inhibition (Dempster, 1985). For example, consider the counting span and spatial span tasks. On each trial of the counting span task (Case, Kurland, & Goldberg, 1982), a participant is asked to count a set of blue dots embedded in a field of yellow dots, touching each blue dot and enumerating it (see Figure 6.6a). Immediately thereafter, the participant is to give the answer for that display and the answers for all preceding displays in correct serial order. This requires (1) selective attention (inhibiting attention to the yellow dots); (2) holding information in mind while executing another mental operation (counting); (3) updating the information held in mind; and (4) temporal order memory (keeping track of the order of the totals computed across trials). In the spatial span task (Case, 1992) a participant inspects a 4 x 4 matrix on each trial, noting which cell is shaded (see Figure 6.6b). A filler pattern is then shown, and then a second 4 x 4 grid. The second grid is empty; the par-

ticipant is to point to the cell that had been shaded on that trial. Over several blocks of trials, the number of shaded cells gradually increases. Interference from prior trials and from the filler pattern is high. A meta-analysis by Case (1992) of 12 cross-sectional studies showed remarkably similar developmental progressions on both of these tasks (see Figure 6.6c). (Note also the remarkably similar developmental degradation during aging across letter, reading, and computation span tasks as illustrated in Figure 9.1a. Continuous and marked improvements are seen from 4½ to 8 years of age,

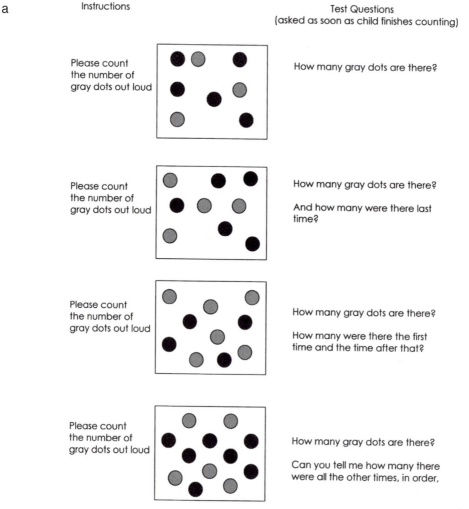

FIGURE 6.6. Two complex span tasks. (*a*): Sample of the kinds of trials presented on the counting span task. (Case et al., 1982.) (*b*): Sample of the kinds of trials presented in the spatial span task. (Stuss & Knight, 2002.) (*c*): Developmental progression in the number of items that can be held in mind on the two tasks. (Data from Crammond et al.,1992, for the counting span and Menna, 1989, for the spatial span.) (Reprinted from Diamond, 2002 with the permission of Oxford University Press.)

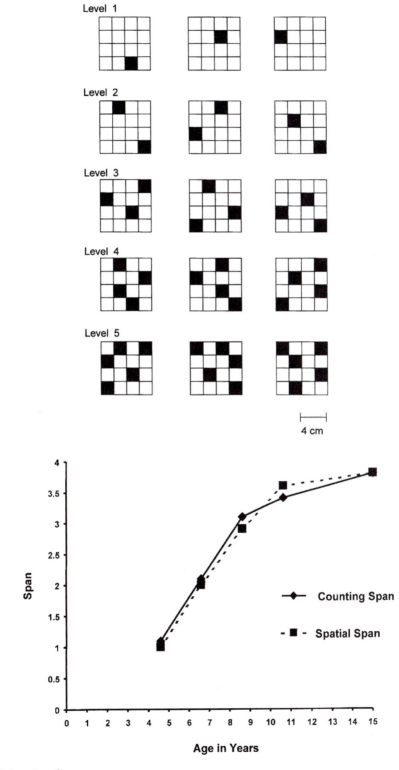

FIGURE 6.6. (*continued*)

continued, more gradual improvement until 10–11 years of age, and then much more gradual improvement thereafter.

The pattern span task is similar to the spatial span task except that several cells are shaded. First, the participant gets a quick look at the pattern. At test, one of the cells that had been shaded is now unshaded and the participant must point to that cell. The number of shaded cells increases until the participant's accuracy falls below criterion. Performance on this task also improves greatly between 5 and 11 years of age, when it starts to asymptote (Miles, Morgan, Milne, & Morris, 1996; Wilson, Scott, & Power, 1987). Finally, the listening span task (Daneman & Carpenter, 1980) requires processing of incoming information (auditorially presented sentences) while retaining, in correct temporal order, the final words of each preceding sentence. Performance on this improves from 6 years until at least 15 years and probably until the early 20s (Siegel, 1994).

Speed of processing is not considered an executive function, yet for reasons not fully understood, age-related improvements in the speed of processing account for a great deal of the age-related improvements on span tasks (Case et al., 1982; Hitch et al., 2001; Kail, 1992) and there is a strong, well-replicated relation between speed of processing and performance on executive function measures (Duncan, Burgess, & Emslie, 1995; Fry & Hale, 1996; Kail & Salthouse, 1994). Processing speed increases markedly until the early teens and continues improving, though more gradually, until early adulthood (Fry & Hale, 1996; Kail, 1991; Miller & Vernon, 1997). It might also be noted that processing speed slows markedly during aging and the decline in the speed of processing from early through late adulthood is highly correlated with the age-related decline in executive function performance (Salthouse, 1993; Salthouse & Meinz, 1995).

When I say that improvements in speed account for a large percentage of the variance in age-related improvements on span tasks, I am referring to findings such as the following: the faster people can repeat back the word they just heard, the more words they can hold in mind. As the speed of word repetition improves, so too does word-span memory. When the speed at which adults and 6-year-olds can repeat back words is equated by presenting adults with unfamiliar words, children and adults show equivalent word-span memory (Case et al., 1982). Similarly, when the speed at which adults and children can count is equated by requiring adults to count in a foreign language, equivalent counting-span memory is found in adults and 6-year-olds.

Item recognition speed also improves with age (Chi, 1977; Samuels, Begy, & Chen, 1975–1976), and the speed of item identification is related to the number of items (span) that can be held in mind and retrieved (Dempster, 1981). Individuals who have shorter naming times (within and between ages) have larger memory spans. People can generally name a digit faster than a word, and people generally have larger spans for digits than for words. Similarly, words can usually be identified faster than pictures, and people generally have larger spans for words than pictures (Mackworth, 1963). Chi (1977) found that when adults were allowed to view picture stimuli for only half as long as 5-year-olds (to offset the faster encoding speed of adults), the age difference in the number of pictures that could be held in mind was dramatically reduced.

The empirical relation between performance on complex span tasks and generalized speed of processing might be due to any number of reasons. Faster processing would mean that items do not need to be held in mind as long, for example. Faster processing and improved executive function performance may co-vary not because they are causally related but because they both reflect another factor, such as more efficient neural processing or improved signal-to-noise ratios; the latter could be either because of system-wide improvements in the nervous system (such as greater myelination) or because a better functioning prefrontal cortex improves signal-to-noise ratios for diverse neural regions, permitting faster and more efficient cognitive processing. It could be that both speed measures and complex span measures are sensitive to distraction and interference, so the relation between the two sets of measures is due to their common requirement for the exercise of inhibition. In any case, while a great deal of the variance in performance on complex span tasks can be accounted for by processing speed, controlling for speed does not eliminate all age-related differences in complex span performance (Hitch et al., 2001), so even if speed is a large part of the story, it is not the entire story.

TERMINOLOGY UNPACKED

Above, I have used the terms *executive function* and *working memory*—terms discussed in other chapters in this volume and widely used elsewhere, but sometimes

Handwritten annotations at top:
Adele:
WM → EF → Baddeley holding + manipulation
→ EF → inhibition + holding (AO)

used to mean quite different things. It might be helpful in closing to remind readers of the way in which those terms are used in this chapter and how that differs from the ways those terms are sometimes used by others.

Executive function, as I use the term, refers to occasions when conscious, cognitive control is required, and is the antithesis of occasions when going "on automatic" would suffice. The epitome of when executive control is required is when one's automatic inclinations provide no guidance or would lead one astray, as in novel situations or when things change. Executive function often involves inhibiting an automatic tendency and acting on information held in mind (what I have referred to as the conjunction of working memory and inhibition). Exercising executive function is not always beneficial; it can get in the way when acting "on automatic" is exactly what is required (e.g., "The Zen of Archery"; early in training disrupting lateral prefrontal function impairs performance, but disrupting lateral prefrontal function after a task is familiar can *improve* performance [Miller et al., 2003]).

In Chapter 7, (this volume), Daniels, Toth, and Jacoby discuss planning and problem solving as executive functions, whereas I am inclined to think of those as activities that require executive functions but not in themselves executive functions. Daniels et al. discuss the gambling task pioneered by Bechara and Damasio (Bechara, Damasio, Tranel, & Damasio, 1997; Bechara, Tranel, & Damasio, 2000) as an executive function measure. While it is true that the gambling task is a sensitive measure of the functions of orbital (ventromedial) prefrontal cortex, not all functions dependent on prefrontal cortex are executive, and the gambling task seems to me a prime example of that. When slower-operating, older systems can subserve gradually improved performance (as in the gambling task), executive function is not required. Orbital prefrontal cortex is the oldest area of prefrontal cortex and the most tied to the limbic system. Extinction has for years been held up as the epitome of a nonexecutive function, and extinction too is impaired by damage to orbital prefrontal cortex. There is general agreement, however, that executive function (or functions) is an umbrella term that covers a family of cognitive functions rather than a single function such as selective attention.

The term *working memory* has been used in even more varied senses than has executive function. Goldman-Rakic (1988) used the term to refer to holding information in mind, and I have generally focused

on that aspect of working memory as well. Baddeley (1992; Baddeley & Hitch, 1994) defined *working memory* as both holding information in mind and simultaneously manipulating or transforming it (maintenance + manipulation, or temporary storage + processing). Chapters 8 and 9 (this volume) rely heavily on this definition of working memory. Baddeley's perspective shares in common with my own that simply holding information in mind is not that taxing (unless the number of items becomes very large) and does not generally require involvement of dorsolateral prefrontal cortex. It is when holding information in mind must be combined with another operation, such as manipulation (which Baddeley has emphasized) or inhibition (which I have emphasized), ✗ that cognitive capacity is truly taxed and dorsolateral prefrontal cortex is required.

Another prominent model of working memory is that offered by Engle, who defines working memory as the ability to (1) maintain selected information in an active, easily retrievable form while (2) blocking or inhibiting other information from entering that active state (i.e., maintenance + inhibition; Conway & Engle, 1994; Kane & Engle, 2000, 2002). This shares much in common with the influential thinking of Hasher and Zacks (1988; Chapter 11, this volume), who have emphasized the inhibitory requirements of gating out irrelevant information from the mental workspace of working memory and deleting no-longer-relevant information from that limited-capacity workspace. Note that, to a large extent, the functions of holding information in mind and exercising inhibitory control, which I separate into working memory and inhibition components, are integrated in Engle's model under the term *working memory*. *Engle = WM = inhib.*

While some, such as Engle, myself, and Gernsbacher and Faust (1991), discuss holding information (activating relevant information) and inhibitory control (suppressing irrelevant information and disadvantageous action tendencies) as separate processes, others argue that activating the relevant information alone is sufficient. Computation models, in particular, have tended to support the latter perspective (Cohen, Dunbar, & McClelland, 1990; Kimberg & Farah, 1993; Munakata, 2001).

When people discuss individual differences, or age-related differences, in working memory, they are often referring to differences in performance on complex span tasks (see, e.g., Chapters 8 and 9 on working memory, this volume). As pointed out above, however, complex span tasks (including counting, spatial, or reading span tasks) require a great many abilities, such as holding information in mind, updating, temporally ordering the information held in mind, resisting attention to distractors, and performing operations such as counting or reading. They are not simple measures of working memory, unless working memory is so broadly defined as to include almost every mental operation. There is no question that these tasks tap executive functions. They are less informative, however, about which of the component functions required by the task are critical to the observed individual or age-related differences in performance. For example, although complex span tasks are generally interpreted as indices of working memory, individuals who are better at blocking out, or inhibiting, distracting information perform better on complex span tasks (Conway & Engle, 1994; Conway, Tuholski, Shisler, & Engle, 1999; Gernsbacher, 1993; Hasher & Zacks, 1988) as do individuals who perform better on tasks (such as the anti-saccade task) that impose minimal demands on memory (Kane, Bleckley, Conway, & Engle, 2001). Could the inhibitory requirement of complex span tasks be what is critical?

Jacoby's processing dissociation method (1991) and Posner's subtraction method (Posner, Petersen, Fox, & Raichle, 1988) are powerful approaches to understanding which of the component abilities required by a task is critical to observed performance differences or to observed neural correlates. Even tasks far simpler than complex span tasks require multiple abilities, and it is critical to establish which of those component abilities is the reason for someone's difficulty with the task (see the discussion above on the differences between the reason amnesic patients or monkeys with medial temporal lobe lesions fail the delayed nonmatching to sample task, and the reason infants fail the task). However, it is also critical to bear in mind that adding an additional cognitive requirement may also change the intensity or nature of the requirement(s) it is being added to. Take, for example, the Eriksen Flanker task, where you are to attend to the centrally presented stimulus, ignoring the flankers around it. When the flanking stimuli are irrelevant to the task, no response inhibition is required because no response is associated with the flankers and demands on attentional inhibition are minimal. When the flanking stimuli are relevant to the task and mapped to the opposite response from the center

stimulus (i.e., incompatible flankers), not only has a demand on response inhibition now been added, but the demand on attentional inhibition has also been increased.

Finally, distinctions between attentional control and working memory may be arbitrary and perhaps meaningless. Certainly, focusing on information held in mind for several seconds might as easily be called *focused* or *sustained attention* as working memory. The same prefrontal system that enables us to selectively remain focused on the information we want to hold in mind also helps us selectively attend to stimuli in our environment, tuning out irrelevant stimuli (e.g., Awh & Jonides, 2001; Barnes, Nelson, & Reuter-Lorenz, 2001; Casey et al., 2001). Individual differences in working memory capacity (using the Engle definition of working memory) correspond to individual differences in selective attention (Bleckley et al., 2003; Conway et al., 1999).

References

Aguiar, A., & Baillargeon, R. (2000). Perseveration and problem solving in infancy. In H. W. Reese (Ed.), *Advances in child development and behavior* (Vol. 27, pp. 135–180). San Diego: Academic Press.

Allport, A., Styles, E. A., & Hsieh, S. (1994). Shifting intentional set: Exploring the dynamic control of tasks. In C. Umilta & M. Moscovitch (Eds.), *Attention and performance XV* (pp. 421–452). Cambridge, MA: MIT Press.

Awh, E., & Jonides, J. (2001). Overlapping mechanisms of attention and spatial working memory. *Trends in Cognitive Science, 5,* 119–126.

Baddeley, A. (1992). Working memory. *Science, 255,* 556–559.

Baddeley, A. D., & Hitch, G. J. (1994). Developments in the concept of working memory. *Neuropsychology, 8,* 485–493.

Barcelo, F., & Knight, R. (2002). Both random and perseverative errors underlie WCST deficits in prefrontal patients. *Neuropsychologia, 40,* 349–356.

Barnes, L. L., Nelson, J. K., & Reuter-Lorenz, P. A. (2001). Object based attention and object working memory: Overlapping processes revealed by selective interference effect in humans. In C. Casanova & M. Ptito (Eds.), *Progress in brain research* (Vol. 134, pp. 471–481). Amsterdam: Elsevier Science.

Bechara, A., Damasio, H., Tranel, D., & Damasio, A. R. (1997). Deciding advantageously before knowing the advantageous strategy. *Science, 275,* 1293–1294.

Bechara, A., Tranel, D., & Damasio, H. (2000). Characterization of the decision-making deficit of patients with ventromedial prefrontal cortex lesions. *Brain, 123,* 2189–2202.

Becker, M. G., Isaac, W., & Hynd, G. W. (1987). Neuropsychological development of nonverbal behaviors attributed to "frontal lobe" functioning. *Developmental Neuropsychology, 3,* 275–298.

Bell, J. A., & Livesey, P. J. (1985). Cue significance and response regulation in 3– to 6– year old children's learning of multiple choice discrimination tasks. *Developmental Psychobiology, 18,* 229–245.

Bell, M. A., & Adams, S. E. (1999). Comparable performance on looking and reaching versions of the A-not-B task at 8 months of age. *Infant Behavior & Development, 22,* 221–235.

Birch, S., & Bloom, P. (2003). Children are cursed: An asymmetric bias in mental-state attribution. *Psychological Science, 14,* 283–286.

Bleckley, M. K., Durso, F. T., Crutchfield, J. M., Engle, R. W., & Khanna, M. M. (2003). Individual differences in working memory capacity predict visual attention allocation. *Psychonomic Bulletin & Review, 10,* 884–889.

Brass, M., & von Cramon, D. Y. (2002). The role of the frontal cortex in task preparation. *Cerebral Cortex, 12,* 908–914.

Braver, T. S., Reynolds, J. R., & Donaldson, D. I. (2003). Neural mechanisms of transient and sustained cognitive control during task switching. *Neuron, 39,* 713–726.

Brooks, P., Hanauer, J. B., Padowska, B., & Rosman, H. (2003). The role of selective attention in preschoolers' rule use in a novel dimensional card sort. *Cognitive Development, 117,* 1–21.

Brown, A. L. (1975). The development of memory: Knowing, knowing about knowing, and knowing how to know. In H. W. Reese (Ed.), *Advances in child development and behavior* (Vol. 10, pp. 103–152). New York: Academic Press.

Brown, R. M., Crane, A. M. & Goldman, P. S. (1976). Catecholamines in neocortex of rhesus monkeys: Regional distribution and ontogenetic development. *Brain Research, 124,* 576–580.

Brown, R. M., & Goldman, P. S. (1977). Catecholamines in neocortex of rhesus monkeys: Regional distribution and ontogenetic development. *Brain Research, 124,* 576–580.

Brozoski, T. J., Brown, R. M., Rosvold, H. E., & Goldman, P.S. (1979). Cognitive deficit caused by regional depletion of dopamine in prefrontal cortex of rhesus monkey. *Science, 205,* 929–932.

Bruner, J. S. (1964). The course of cognitive growth. *American Psychologist, 19,* 1–15.

Bunge, S. A., Kahn, I., Wallis, J. D., Miller, E. K., & Wagner, A. D. (2003). Neural circuits subserving the retrieval and maintenance of abstract rules. *Journal of Neurophysiology, 90,* 3419–3428.

Bunge, S. A., Ochsner, K. N., Desmond, J. E., Glover, G. H., & Gabrieli, J. D. (2001). Prefrontal regions involved in keeping information in and out of mind. *Brain, 124,* 2074–2086.

Carlson, S. M., Mandell, D. J., & Williams, L. (2004). Executive function and theory of mind: Stability and prediction from age 2 to 3. *Developmental Psychology, 40,* 1105–1122.

Carlson, S. M., & Moses, L. J. (2001). Individual differences in inhibitory control and children's theory of mind. *Child Development, 72,* 1032–1053.

Carlson, S. M., Moses, L. J., & Hix, H. R. (1998). The role of inhibitory processes in young children's difficulties with deception and false belief. *Child Development, 69,* 672–691.

Case, R. (1992). The role of the frontal lobes in the regulation of cognitive development. *Brain and Cognition, 20,* 51–73.

Case, R., Kurland, D. M., & Goldberg, J. (1982). Operational efficiency and the growth of short-term memory span. *Journal of Experimental Child Psychology, 33,* 386–404.

Casey, B., Forman, S., Franzen, P., Berkowitz, A., Braver, T., Nystrom, L., Thomas, K., & Noll, D. (2001). Sensitivity of prefrontal cortex to changes in target probability: A functional MRI study. *Human Brain Mapping, 13,* 26–33.

Casey, B. J., Trainor, R. J., Orendi, J. L., Schubert, A. B., Nystrom, L. E., Giedd, J. N., Castellanos, F. X., Haxby, J. V., Noll, D. C., Cohen, J. D., Forman, S. D., Dahl, R. E., & Rapoport, J. L. (1997). A developmental functional MRI study of prefrontal activation during performance of a go-no-go task. *Journal of Cognitive Neuroscience, 9,* 835–847.

Cepeda, N. J., Kramer, A. F., & Gonzalez de Sather, J. C. (2001). Changes in executive control across the life span: examination of task-switching performance. *Developmental Psycholgoy, 37,* 715–730.

Chambers, D., & Reisberg, D. (1992). What an image depicts depends on what an image means. *Cognitive Psychology, 24,* 145–174.

Chelune, G. J., & Thompson, L. L. (1987). Evaluation of the general sensitivity of the Wisconsin Card Sorting Test among younger and older children. *Developmental Neuropsychology, 3,* 81–89.

Chi, M. T. H. (1977). Age differences in memory span. *Journal of Experimental Child Psychology, 23,* 266–281.

Chugani, H. T., & Phelps, M. E. (1986). Maturational changes in cerebral function in infants determined by 18FDG positron emission tomography. *Science, 231,* 840–843.

Chugani, H. T., Phelps, M. E., & Mazziotta, J. C. (1987). Positron emission tomography study of human brain functional development. *Annals of Neurology*, 22, 487–497.

Cohen, J. D., Dunbar, K., & McClelland, J. L. (1990). On the control of automatic processes: A parallel distributed processing account of the Stroop effect. *Psychological Review*, 97, 332–361.

Cohen, S., Bixenman, M., Meiran, N., & Diamond, A. (2001, May). *Task switching in children*. Paper presented at the South Carolina Bicentennial Symposium on Attention, University of South Carolina, Columbia, SC.

Conway, A. R. A., & Engle, R. W. (1994). Working memory and retrieval: A resource-dependent inhibition model. *Journal of Experimental Psychology: General*, 123, 354–373.

Conway, A. R. A., Tuholski, S. W., Shisler, R. J., & Engle, R. (1999). The effect of memory load on negative priming: An individual differences investigation. *Memory and Cognition*, 27, 1042–1050.

Crammond, J. (1992). Analyzing the basic cognitive developmental processes of children with specific types of learning disability. In R. Case (Ed.), *The mind's staircase: Exploring the conceptual underpinnings of human thought and knowledge* (pp. 285–303). Hillsdale, NJ: Erlbaum.

Daneman, M., & Carpenter, P. (1980). Individual differences in working memory and reading. *Journal of Verbal Learning and Verbal Behavior*, 19, 450–466.

Daniels, K., Toth, J., & Jacoby, L. (2006). The aging of executive functions. In E. Bialystok & F. I. M. Craik (Eds.), *Lifespan cognition: mechanisms of change*. New York: Oxford University Press.

DeLoache, J. S. (1986). Memory in very young children: Exploitation of cues to the location of a hidden object. *Cognitive Development*, 1, 123–137.

DeLoache, J. S., & Brown, A. L. (1983). Very young children's memory for the location of objects in a large-scale environment. *Child Development*, 54, 888–897.

Dempster, F. N. (1981). Memory span: Sources of individual and developmental differences. *Psychological Bulletin*, 89, 63–100.

Dempster, F. N. (1985). Short-term memory development in childhood and adolescence. In C. J. Brainerd & M. Pressley (Eds.), *Basic processes in memory development: Progress in cognitive development research*. New York: Springer-Verlag.

Derfuss, J., Brass, M., Neumann, J., & von Cramon, D. Y. (2005). Involvement of the inferior frontal junction in cognitive control: Meta-analyses of switching and Stroop studies. *Human Brain Mapping*, 25, 22–34.

Diamond, A. (1985). The development of the ability to use recall to guide action, as indicated by infants' performance on A-not-B. *Child Development*, 56, 868–883.

Diamond, A. (1988). The abilities and neural mechanisms underlying A-not-B performance. *Child Development*, 59, 523–527.

Diamond, A. (1990a). Developmental time course in human infants and infant monkeys, and the neural bases, of inhibitory control in reaching. *Annals of the New York Academy of Sciences*, 608, 637–676.

Diamond, A. (1990b). Rate of maturation of the hippocampus and the developmental progression of children's performance on the delayed non-matching to sample and visual paired comparison tasks. *Annals of the New York Academy of Sciences*, 608, 394–426.

Diamond, A. (1991). Neuropsychological insights into the meaning of object concept development. In S. Carey & R. Gelman (Eds.), *The epigenesis of mind: Essays on biology and cognition* (pp. 67–110). Hillsdale, NJ: Lawrence Erlbaum Associates.

Diamond, A. (2001). A model system for studying the role of dopamine in prefrontal cortex during early development in humans. In C. Nelson & M. Luciana (Eds.), *Handbook of developmental cognitive neuroscience* (pp. 433–472). Cambridge, MA: MIT Press.

Diamond, A. (2002). Normal development of prefrontal cortex from birth to young adulthood: Cognitive functions, anatomy, and biochemistry. In D. T. Stuss & R. T. Knight (Eds.), *Principles of frontal lobe function* (pp. 466–503). New York: Oxford University Press.

Diamond, A., Churchland, A., Cruess, L., & Kirkham, N. Z. (1999). Early developments in the ability to understand the relation between stimulus and reward. *Developmental Psychology*, 35, 1507–1517.

Diamond, A., & Goldman-Rakic, P. S. (1985). Evidence for involvement of prefrontal cortex in cognitive changes during the first year of life: Comparison of performance of human infant and rhesus monkeys on a detour task with transparent barrier. *Society for Neuroscience Abstracts*, 11, 832.

Diamond, A., & Goldman-Rakic, P. S. (1989). Comparison of human infants and rhesus monkeys on Piaget's A-not-B task: Evidence for dependence on dorsolateral prefrontal cortex. *Experimental Brain Research*, 74, 24–40.

Diamond, A., & Kirkham, N. (2005). Not quite as grown-up as we like to think: Parallels between cognition in childhood and adulthood. *Psychological Science*, 16, 291–297.

Diamond, A., Kirkham, N., & Amso, D. (2002). Conditions under which young children CAN hold two rules in mind and inhibit a prepotent response. *Developmental Psychology, 38,* 352–362.

Diamond, A., Lee, E. -Y., & Hayden, M. (2003). Early success in using the relation between stimulus and reward to deduce an abstract rule: Perceived physical connectedness is key. *Developmental Psychology, 39,* 825–847.

Diamond, A., & Taylor, C. (1996). "Development of an aspect of executive control: Development of the abilities to remember what I said and to "Do as I say, not as I do." *Developmental Psychobiology, 29,* 315–334.

Diamond, A., Towle, C., & Boyer, K. (1994). Young children's performance on a task sensitive to the memory functions of the medial temporal lobe in adults, the delayed nonmatching-to-sample task, reveals problems that are due to non-memory-related task demands. *Behavioral Neuroscience, 108,* 659–680.

Duncan, J., Burgess, P., & Emslie, H. (1995). Fluid intelligence after frontal lobe lesions. *Neuropsychologia, 33,* 261–268.

Duncan, J., & Owen, A. M. (2000). Common regions of the human frontal lobe recruited by diverse cognitive demands. *Trends in Neuroscience, 23,* 475–483.

Elliott, R., & Dolan, R. J., (1999). Differential neural responses during performance of matching and nonmatching to sample tasks at two delay intervals. *Journal of Neuroscience, 19,* 5066–5073.

Fagan, J. F., III. (1973). Infants' delayed recognition memory and forgetting. *Journal of Experimental Child Psychology, 16,* 424–450.

Fischoff, B. (1977). Perceived informativeness of facts. *Journal of Experimental Psychology: Human Perception & Performance, 3,* 349–358.

Fischoff, B., & Beyth, R. (1975). "I knew it would happen": Remembered probabilities of once-future things. *Organizational Behavior & Human Decision Processes, 13,* 1–16.

Flavell, J. H. (1963). *The developmental psychology of Jean Piaget.* Oxford, England: Van Nostrand.

Flavell, J. H. (1986). The development of children's knowledge about the appearance-reality distinction. *American Psychologist, 41,* 418–425.

Flavell, J. H. (1993). The development of children's understanding of false belief and the appearance-reality distinction. *International Journal of Psychology, 28,* 595–604.

Flavell, J. H. (1999). Cognitive development: Children's knowledge about the mind. *Annual Review of Psychology, 50,* 21–45.

Flavell, J. H., Green, F. L., & Flavell, E. R. (1986). Development of knowledge about the appearance-reality distinction. *Monographs of the Society for Research in Child Development, 51,* 1–87.

Flynn, E., O'Malley, C., & Wood, D. (2004). A longitudinal, microgenetic study of the emergence of false belief understanding and inhibition skills. *Developmental Science, 7,* 103–115.

Fry, A. F., & Hale, S. (1996). Processing speed, working memory, and fluid intelligence: Evidence for a developmental cascade. *Psychological Science, 7,* 237–241.

Funahashi, S., Chafee, M. V., & Goldman-Rakic, P. S. (1993). Prefrontal neuronal activity in rhesus monkeys performing a delayed anti-saccade task. *Nature, 365,* 753–756.

Gernsbacher, M. A. (1993). Less skilled readers have less efficient suppression mechanisms. *Psychological Science, 4,* 294–298.

Gernsbacher, M. A., & Faust, M. E. (1991). The mechanism of suppression: A component of general comprehension skill. *Journal of Experimental Psychology, 17,* 245–262.

Gerstadt, C., Hong, Y., & Diamond, A. (1994). The relationship between cognition and action: Performance of 3 ½–7 year old children on a Stroop-like day-night test. *Cognition, 53,* 129–153.

Gilligan, C. (1982). *In a different voice: Psychological theory and women's development.* Cambridge, MA: Harvard University Press.

Goldman-Rakic, P. S. (1988). Cortical localization of working memory. In J. L. McGaugh & N. M. Weinberger & G. Lynch (Eds.), *Brain organization and memory: Cells, systems and circuits.* New York: Oxford University Press.

Gopnik, A., & Rosati, A. (2001). Duck or rabbit? Reversing ambiguous figures and understanding ambiguous representations. *Developmental Science, 4,* 175–183.

Grady, C. L., McIntosh, A. R., Bookstein, F., Horwitz, B., Rapoport, S. I., & Haxby, J. V. (1998). Age-related changes in regional cerebral blood flow during working memory for faces. *Neuroimage, 8,* 409–425.

Gratch, G. (1975). Recent studies based on Piaget's view of object concept development. In L. B. Cohen & P. Salapatek (Eds.), *Infant perception: From sensation to cognition* (Vol. 2, pp. 51–99). New York: Academic Press.

Hala, S., Hug, S., & Henderson, A. (2003). Executive function and false-belief understanding in preschool children: Two tasks are harder than one. *Journal of Cognition and Development, 4,* 275–298.

Hale, S. (1990). A global development trend in cognitive processing speed. *Child Development, 61,* 653–663.

Harris, P.L. (1987). Object permanence in infancy. In A. Slater & G. Bremner (Eds.), *Infant development.* Hillsdale, NJ: Lawrence Erlbaum Associates.

Hasher, L., & Zacks, R. T. (1988). Working memory, comprehension, and aging: A review and a new view. In G. H. Bower (Ed.), *The psychology of learning and motivation: Advances in research and theory* (Vol. 22, pp. 193–225). San Diego, CA: Academic Press.

Heberle, J., Clune, M., & Kelly, K. (1999, April). *Development of young children's understanding of the appearance-reality distinction.* Paper presented at the Society for Research in Child Development, Albuquerque, NM.

Hinds, P. J. (1999). The curse of expertise: The effects of expertise and debiasing methods on prediction of novice performance. *Journal of Experimental Psychology: Applied, 5,* 205–221.

Hitch, G. J. (2006). Working memory in children: A cognitive approach. In E. Bialystok and F. I. M. Craik (Eds.), *Lifespan cognition: Mechanisms of change.* New York: Oxford University Press.

Hitch, G. J., Howse, J. N., & Hutton, U. (2001). What limits children's working memory span? Theoretical accounts and applications for scholastic development. *Journal of Experimental Psychology: General, 130,* 184–198.

Hughes, C. (1996). Control of action and thought: Normal development and dysfunction in autism. *Journal of Child Psychology and Psychiatry, 37,* 229–236.

Hughes, C. (1998). Executive function in preschoolers: Links with theory of mind and verbal ability. *British Journal of Developmental Psychology, 16,* 233–253.

Hoffrage, U., Hertwig, R., & Gigerenzer, G. (2000). Hindsight bias: A by-product of knowledge updating? *Journal of Experimental Psychology: Learning, Memory, and Cognition, 26,* 566–581.

Inhelder, B., & Piaget, J. (1958). *The growth of logical thinking from childhood to adolescence* (A. Parsons & S. Milgram, Trans.). New York: Basic Books.

Jacoby, L. L. (1991). A process dissociation framework: Separating automatic from intentional uses of memory. *Journal of Memory and Language, 30,* 513–541.

Jahanshahi, M., & Dirnberger, G. (1999). The left dorsolateral prefrontal cortex and random generation of responses: Studies with transcranial magnetic stimulation. *Neuropsychologia, 37,* 181–190.

Jarvik, M. E. (1953). Discrimination of colored food and food signs by primates. *Journal of Comparative and Physiological Psychology, 46,* 390–392.

Jones, L. B., Rothbart, M. K., & Posner, M. I. (2003). Development of inhibitory control in preschool children. *Developmental Science, 6,* 498–504.

Kail, R. (1991). Development of processing speed in childhood and adolescence. In H. W. Reese (Ed.),

Advances in child development and behavior (Vol. 23, pp. 151–185). New York: Academic Press.

Kail, R. (1992). Processing, speed, speech rate, and memory. *Developmental Psychology, 28,* 899–904.

Kail, R., & Salthouse, T. A. (1994). Processing speed as a mental capacity. *Acta Psychologica, 86,* 199–225.

Kane, M. J., Bleckley, M., Conway, A. R., & Engle, R. W. (2001). A controlled-attention view of working-memory capacity. *Journal of Experimental Psychology: General, 130,* 169–183.

Kane, M. J., & Engle, R. W. (2000). Working-memory capacity, proactive interference, and divided attention: Limits on long-term memory retrieval. *Journal of Experimental Psychology, 26* (2), 336–358.

Kane, M. J., & Engle, R. W. (2002). The role of prefrontal cortex in working-memory capacity, executive attention, and general fluid intelligence: An individual-differences perspective. *Psychonomic Bulletin & Review, 9,* 637–671.

Kelley, C. M., & Jacoby, L. L. (1996). Adult egocentrism: subjective experience versus analytic bases for judgment. *Journal of Memory and Language, 35,* 157–175.

Kimberg, D. Y., & Farah, M. J. (1993). A unified account of cognitive impairments following frontal lobe damage: The role of working memory in complex, organized behavior. *Journal of Experimental Psychology, 122,* 411–428.

Kirkham, N., Cruess, L., & Diamond, A. (2003). Helping children apply their knowledge to their behavior on a dimension-switching task. *Developmental Science, 6,* 449–467.

Kloo, D., & Perner, J. (2003). Training transfer between card sorting and false belief understanding: Helping children understand conflicting descriptions. *Child Development, 74,* 1823–1839.

Kloo, D., & Perner, J. (2005). Disentangling dimensions in the dimensional change card sorting task. *Developmental Science, 8,* 44–56

Koenderink, M. J. T., Ulyings, H. B. M., & Mrzljiak, L. (1994). Postnatal maturation of the layer III pyramidal neurons in the human prefrontal cortex: A quantitative Golgi analysis. *Brain Research, 653,* 173–182.

Kohlberg, L. (1963). The development of children's orientations toward a moral order: I. Sequence in the development of moral thought. *Vita Humana, 6,* 11–33.

Koski, L., & Petrides, M. (2001). Time-related changes in task performance after lesions restricted to the frontal cortex. *Neuropsychologia, 39,* 268–281.

Kowalska, D. M., Bachevalier, J., & Mishkin, M. (1991). The role of the inferior prefrontal convexity in performance of delayed nonmatching-to-sample. *Neuropsychologia, 29,* 583–600.

Lewis, D. A., & Harris, H. W. (1991). Differential laminar distribution of tyrosine hydroxylase-immunoreactive axons in infant and adult monkey prefrontal cortex. *Neuroscience Letters, 125*, 151–154.

Lidow, M. S., & Rakic, P. (1992). Scheduling of monoaminergic neurotransmitter receptor expression in the primate neocortex during postnatal development. *Cerebral Cortex, 2*, 401–416.

Livesey, D. J., & Morgan, G. A. (1991). The development of response inhibition in 4- and 5-year-old children. *Australian Journal of Psychology, 43*, 133–137.

Luna, B., Thulborn, K. R., Munoz, D. P., Merriam, E. P., Garver, K. E., Minshew, N. J., Keshavan, M. S., Genovese, C. R., Eddy, W. F., & Sweeney, J. A. (2001). Maturation of widely distributed brain function subserves cognitive development. *Neuro-Image, 13*, 786–793.

Luria, A. R. (1966). *The higher cortical functions in man.* New York: Basic Books.

MacDonald, A. W., III, Cohen, J. D., Stenger, V. A., & Carter, C. S. (2000). Dissociating control processes of dorsolateral prefrontal cortex and anterior cingulate cortex with fMRI and the Stroop task. *Cognitive Neuroscience Society Annual Meeting Abstracts, 1*, 111.

Mackworth, J. F. (1963). The relation between the visual image and post-perceptual immediate memory. *Journal of Verbal Learning and Verbal Behavior, 2*, 75–85.

MacLeod, C. M. (1991). Half a century of research on the Stroop effect: An integrative review. *Psychological Bulletin, 109*, 163–203.

MacLeod, C. M. (1992). The Stroop task: The "gold standard" of attentional measures. *Journal of experimental psychology: General, 121*, 12–14.

Matsumoto, K, Suzuki, W, & Tanaka, K. (2003). Neuronal correlates of goal-based motor selection in the prefrontal cortex. *Science, 301(5630)*, 229–232.

Meiran, N. (1996). Reconfiguration of processing mode prior to task performance. *Journal of Experimental Psychology: Learning, Memory, and Cognition, 22*, 1423–1442.

Menna, R. (1989). *Working memory and development: An EEG investigation.* Toronto: University of Toronto.

Miles, C., Morgan, M. J., Milne, A. B., & Morris, E. D. M. (1996). Developmental and individual differences in visual memory span. *Current Psychology, 15*, 53–67.

Miller, B. T., Verstynen, T., Raye, C. L., Mitchell, K. J., Johnson, M. K., & D'Esposito, M. (2003). The role of dorsolateral PFC in refreshing just-activated information: A TMS study. Presented at the Society for Neuroscience Meeting, New Orleans, November, 2003. *Abstract Viewer/Itineray Planner. Society of Neuroscience, 287*, 211.

Miller, E. K., & Cohen, J. D. (2001). An integrative theory of prefrontal cortex function. *Annual Review of Neuroscience, 24*, 167–202.

Miller, L. T., & Vernon, P. A. (1997). Developmental changes in speed of information processing in young children. *Developmental Psychology, 33*, 549–554.

Monsell, S., & Driver, J. (Eds.). (2000). *Control of cognitive processes. Attention and performance XVIII.* Cambridge, MA: MIT Press.

Mottaghy, F. M., Gangitano, M., Sparing, R., Krause, B. J., & Pascual-Leone, A. (2002). Segregation of areas related to visual working memory in the prefrontal cortex revealed by rTMS. *Cerebral Cortex, 12(4)*, 369–375.

Munakata, Y. (2001). Graded representations in behavioral dissociations. *Trends in Cognitive Sciences, 5*, 309–315.

Munoz, D., Broughton, J., Goldring, J., & Armstrong, I. (1998). Age-related performance of human subjects on saccadic eye movement tasks. *Experimental Brain Research, 217*, 1–10.

Murray, E. A., & Mishkin, M. (1998). Object recognition and location memory in monkeys with excitotoxic lesions of the amygdala and hippocampus. *Journal of Neuroscience, 18*, 6568–6582.

Overman, W. H. (1990). Performance on traditional match-to-sample, nonmatch-to-sample, and object discrimination tasks by 12 to 32 month-old children: A developmental progression. *Annals of the New York Academy of Sciences, 608*, 365–393.

Overman, W. H., Bachevalier, J., Turner, M., & Peuster, A. (1992). Object recognition versus object discrimination: Comparison between human infants and infant monkeys. *Behavioral Neuroscience, 106*, 15–29.

Park, D. C. & Payer, D. (2006). Working memory across the adult lifespan. In E. Bialystok and F. I. M. Craik (Eds.), *Lifespan cognition: Mechanisms of change.* New York: Oxford University Press.

Passler, P. A., Isaac, W., & Hynd, G. W. (1985). Neuropsychological development of behavior attributed to frontal lobe functioning in children. *Developmental Neuropsychology, 4*, 349–370.

Perner, J., & Lang, B. (2002). What causes 3-year-olds' difficulty on the dimensional change card sort task? *Infant & Child Development, 11*, 93–105.

Perner, J., Lang, B., & Kloo, D. (2002). Theory of mind and self-control: More than a common problem of inhibition. *Child Development, 73*, 752–767.

Perner, J., Leekam, S. R., & Wimmer, H. (1987). Three-year-olds' difficulty with false belief: The case for a conceptual deficit. *British Journal of Developmental Psychology, 5*, 125–137.

Piaget, J. (1954). *The construction of reality in the child* (M. Cook, Trans.). New York: Basic Books.

Posner, M. I., Petersen, S. E., Fox, P. T., & Raichle, M. E. (1988). Localizations of cognitive operations in the human brain. *Science, 240*, 1627–1630.

Premack, D., & Woodruff, G. (1978). Does the chimpanzee have a theory of mind? *Behavioural and Brain Sciences, 1*, 515–526.

Rainer, G., Assad, W. F., & Miller, E. K. (1998). Selective representation of relevant information by neurons in the primate prefrontal cortex. *Nature, 393*, 577–579.

Rice, C., Koinis, D., Sullivan, K., Tager-Flusberg, H., & Winner, E. (1997). When 3-year-olds pass the appearance-reality test. *Developmental Psychology, 33*, 54–61.

Rogers, R. D., & Monsell, S. (1995). Costs of a predictable switch between simple cognitive tasks. *Journal of Experimental Psychology, 124*, 207–231.

Rosenberg, D., & Lewis, D. (1995). Postnatal maturation of the dopaminergic innervation of monkey prefrontal and motor cortices: A tyrosine hydroxylase immunohistochemical analysis. *The Journal of Comparative Neurology, 358*, 383–400.

Rosselli, M., & Ardila, A. (1993). Developmental norms for the Wisconsin Card Sorting Test in 5- to 12-year old children. *The Clinical Neuropsychologist, 7*, 145–154.

Rushworth, M. F. S., Nixon, P. D., Eacott, M. J., & Passingham, R. E. (1997). Ventral prefrontal cortex is not essential for working memory. *Journal of Neuroscience, 17*, 4829–4838.

Salthouse, T. A. (1993). Speed mediation of adult age differences in cognition. *Developmental Psychology, 29*, 722–738.

Salthouse, T. A., & Meinz, E. J. (1995). Aging, inhibition, working memory, and speed. *Journal of Gerontology Series B, Psychological Sciences and Social Sciences, 50*, 297–306.

Samuels, S. J., Begy, G., & Chen, C. C. (1975–1976). Comparison of word recognition speed and strategies of less skilled and more highly skilled readers. *Reading Research Quarterly, 11*, 72–86.

Sawaguchi, T., & Goldman-Rakic, P. S. (1991). D_1 dopamine receptors in prefrontal cortex: Involvement in working memory. *Science, 251*, 947–950.

Shallice, T. (1988). *From neuropsychology to mental structure*. Cambridge: Cambridge University Press.

Shutts., K., Ross, E., Hayden, M., & Diamond, A. (2001). *Grasping that one thing is related to another: Contributions of spatial contiguity, temporal proximity, and physical connection.* Presented at the Biennial Meeting of the Society for research in Child Development, Minneapolis, MN, April 2001.

Siegel, L. (1994). Working memory and reading: A lifespan perspective. *International Journal of Behavioural Development, 17*, 109–124.

Simpson, A., & Riggs, K. J. (2005). Factors responsible for performance on the day-night task: Response set or semantics? *Developmental Science, 8*, 360–371.

Spelke, E. S. (1985). Perception of unity, persistence, and identity: Thoughts on infants' conception of objects. In J. Mehler & R. Fox (Eds.), *Neonate cognition: Beyond the blooming buzzing confusion* (pp. 89–113). Hillsdale, NJ: Lawrence Erlbaum Associates.

Stroop, J. R. (1935). Studies of interference in serial verbal reactions. *Journal of Experimental Psychology, 18*, 643–662.

Stuss, D. T., Levine, B., Alexander, M. P., Hong, J., Palumbo, C., Hamer, L., Murphy, K. J., & Izukawa, D. (2000). Wisconsin Card Sorting Test performance in patients with focal frontal and posterior brain damage: Effects of lesion location and test structure on separable cognitive processes. *Neuropsychologia, 38*, 388–402.

Stuss, D. T., Floden, D., Alexander, M. P., Levine, B., & Katz, D. (2001). Stroop performance in focal lesion patients: Dissociation of processes and frontal lobe lesion location. *Neuropsychologia, 39*, 771–786.

Tikhomirov, O. K. (1978). The formation of voluntary movements in children of preschool age. In M. Cole (Ed.), *The selected writings of A.R. Luria* (pp. 229–269). White Plains, NY: M.E. Sharpe.

Toni, I., Ramnani, N., Josephs, O., Ashburner, J., & Passingham, R. E. (2001). Learning arbitrary visuomotor associations: Temporal dynamic of brain activity. *Neuroimage, 14*, 1048–1057.

Towse, J. N., Redbond, J., Houston-Price, C. M. T., & Cook, S. (2000). Understanding the dimensional change card sort: Perspectives from task success and failure. *Cognitive Development, 15*, 347–365.

van der Meere, J., & Stemerdink, N. (1999). The development of state regulation in normal children: An indirect comparison with children with ADHD. *Developmental Neuropsychology, 16*, 213–225.

Van Hiel, A., & Mervielde, I. (2003). The need for closure and the spontaneous use of complex and simple cognitive structures. *Journal of Social Psychology, 143*, 559–568.

Vishton, P. M., & Badger, A. N. (2003). *Infant Gestalt Perception and Object-Directed Reaching: Effects of Shape, Color, and Remembered Spatiotemporal Information.* Paper presented at the Society for Research in Child Development Biennial Meeting, Tampa, FL.

Wallis, J. D., & Miller, E. K. (2003). From rule to response: Neuronal processes in the premotor and prefrontal cortex. *Journal of Neurophysiology*. E-publication ahead of print; and personal communication.

Webster, D. M., & Kruglanski, A. W. (1994). Individual differences in need for cognitive closure. *Journal of Personality & Social Psychology, 67,* 1049–1062.

Wellman, H. M., Cross, D., & Bartsch, K. (1987). Infant search and object permanence: A meta-analysis of the A-not-B error. *Monographs of the Society for Research in Child Development, 51,* 1–67.

Welsh, M. C., Pennington, B. F., & Groisser, D. B. (1991). A normative-developmental study of executive function: A window on prefrontal function in children. *Developmental Neuropsychology, 7,* 131–149.

Wilson, J. T. L., Scott, J. H., & Power, K. G. (1987). Developmental differences in the span of visual memory for pattern. *British Journal of Developmental Psychology, 5,* 249–255.

Wimmer, H., & Perner, J. (1983). Beliefs about beliefs: Representation and constraining function of wrong beliefs in young children's understanding of deception. *Cognition, 13,* 103–128.

Zacks, R. T. & Hasher, L. (2006). Aging and long-term memory. In E. Bialystok and F. I. M. Craik (Eds.), *Lifespan cognition: Mechanisms of change.* New York: Oxford University Press.

Zaitchik, D. (1991). Is only seeing really believing? Sources of the true belief in the false belief task. *Cognitive Development, 6,* 91–103.

Zelazo, P. D., Frye, D., & Rapus, T. (1996). An age-related dissociation between knowing rules and using them. *Cognitive Development, 11,* 37–63.

Zelazo, P. D., Reznick, J. S., & Piñon, D. E. (1995). Response control and the execution of verbal rules. *Developmental Psychology, 31,* 508–517.

Zola, S. M., Squire, L. R., Teng, E., Stefanacci, L., Buffalo, E. A., & Clark, R. E. (2000). Impaired recognition memory in monkeys after damage limited to the hippocampal region. *Journal of Neuroscience, 20,* 451–463.

7

The Aging of Executive Functions

Karen Daniels

Jeffrey Toth

Larry Jacoby

For many young adults, the idea of retirement brings to mind carefree days of rest and relaxation. Yet, speak to any retiree and the discussion is likely to revolve around more complex issues such as how best to maintain one's health or financial security. As these two topics attest, old age can be a time that requires decisions as large in number and importance as those faced by much younger adults. The ability to make such decisions effectively has been attributed to *executive functions*—a loosely defined set of cognitive skills and processes that appear critical for complex thought and behavior. In this chapter, we explore the issue of how best to define and measure executive functions and their change with age. The dominant approach to measuring executive functions can be described as *task-based*. That is, one chooses a task or set of tasks that one believes taps executive functions (e.g., Stroop, A-not-B, Wisconsin Card Sort Test [WCST]) and then sees if performance on such tasks is sensitive to childhood development, frontal lobe damage, or aging. This approach has served the field well by delineat-

ing the scope of executive functions and identifying a set of candidate processes that appear fundamental in mediating complex thought and behavior (processes such as working memory, inhibition, and set shifting; see Diamond, Chapter 6, this volume). In this chapter, however, we argue that there are limitations with task-based approaches and propose instead a greater focus on underlying processes, as well as formal modeling of these processes.

Our discussion is organized as follows. We begin by describing the origin of the concept of executive functions, noting how the concept has been operationalized in both cognitive and neuropsychological studies in terms of performance on specific tasks. We cite some of the studies that have compared young and older adults on such tasks, but focus mainly on whether task-based research has been (or will be) able to answer two critical questions: First, whether there are multiple executive functions or only one superordinate function (i.e., the unity/diversity question; see Duncan, Johnson, Swales, & Freer, 1997; Miyake,

Friedman, Emerson, Witzki, & Howerter, 2000; Teuber, 1972); and, second, whether one or more of these functions decline with age (see Salthouse, Atkinson, & Berish, 2003; Wecker, Kramer, Wisniewski, Delis, & Kaplan, 2000). We find current answers to these questions unsatisfactory and trace our dissatisfaction to problems inherent with task-based approaches to executive functions, even those using latent-variable statistical techniques. As an alternative to task-based approaches, we next describe research and multinomial modeling done using the process-dissociation (PD) procedure. Although this research was initially directed at explaining age-related increases in various kinds of interference (proactive, Stroop, and retroactive), we argue that it is relevant to issues surrounding the concept of executive functions. As evidence for this relevance we describe research linking PD estimates of cognitive control to measures of fluid intelligence and metacognitive monitoring. We conclude with some general comments about how the PD approach can be combined with latent-variable techniques to better explicate the concept of executive functions and its change with age.

WHAT ARE EXECUTIVE FUNCTIONS?

The concept of executive functions has a long past, with its beginnings heavily influenced by neuropsychology (see Luria, 1966/1980; Stuss & Benson, 1986; Tranel, Anderson, & Benton, 1994). Historically, the concept can be traced to Hughling Jackson's (1884) hypothesis that "higher centers" of the brain controlled "lower centers"; to Jacobsen's work with monkeys (e.g., Jacobsen & Nissen, 1937) showing the importance of prefrontal cortex in holding information in mind and establishing a "mental set"; and to Goldstein's (e.g., 1936) notion of the "abstract attitude"—the ability to break down situations into their constituent parts (see Cronin-Golomb, 1990). However, most researchers would agree that the concept achieves its greatest importance with respect to the effects of frontal lobe damage on cognition, personality, and behavior—the case of Phineas Gage being the classic example (see Macmillan, 1986; Mesulam, 2002; Stuss & Benson, 1986; Stuss, Gow, & Heatherington, 1992).

As with Gage, damage to the prefrontal cortex produces an incredibly wide range of disturbances that encompass planning and organization, abstract

thought, complex decision making, the regulation of emotions and impulses, the sequencing of goal-directed behavior, and the monitoring of thought and action (see Fuster, 1989; Luria 1966/1980; Lyon & Krasnegor, 1996; Stuss & Benson, 1986). Additional descriptions could include the imposing of cognitive structure on ill-structured situations (Pribram, 1973), dealing with novel cognitive demands (Norman & Shallice, 1986), mediating between cognition and emotion in the context of risk (Damasio, 1998), and maintaining personal autonomy in the context of social interaction (Lhermitte, 1986). In line with these proposals, Mesulam (2002) describes frontal lobe processes as important for overcoming a "default mode" of information processing—a mode that reflects primitive, disinhibited behavioral tendencies including the triggering of automatic reactions and a preference for immediate gratification.

All of these descriptions appear to be capturing part of the "truth" of executive functions. Yet it should also be clear that the scope of these descriptions makes it difficult to pinpoint any central feature of such functions. Is there one fundamental ability that underlies all executive abilities, or does *executive functions* refer to a class of similar, but theoretically distinct processes? Most important, how can these functions be measured?

TASK-BASED APPROACHES TO MEASURING EXECUTIVE FUNCTIONS

As with most cognitive abilities, executive functions have been operationalized in terms of task performance, although the specific tasks employed have differed in neuropsychology (where the concern with executive processes emerged) and cognitive psychology. For the former, a major goal was to identify tasks sensitive to frontal-lobe damage, with little emphasis placed on underlying processes beyond their rough categorization as involving, say, "planning." Cognitive psychologists, in contrast, view underlying processes as paramount and, until late, were unconcerned with the neural systems mediating performance. This difference in emphasis has resulted in a hodgepodge of tasks in use today that are thought to require executive or frontal processes. In the next two sections, we provide brief summaries of research with these tasks, in the service of answering the two questions noted above: unity versus diversity and age effects.

Neuropsychological Tasks

Older adults perform more poorly than younger adults on many classic neuropsychological tests of executive function, including the Wisconsin Card-Sorting Task (WCST: e.g., Kramer, Humphrey, Larish, Logan, & Strayer, 1994; Parkin & Walter, 1992), the color-word Stroop task (e.g., Brink & McDowd, 1999; Cohn, Dustman, & Bradford, 1984), Trails B (e.g., Salthouse & Fristoe, 1995), tests of verbal fluency (see Salthouse et al., 2003), and several tower tasks (e.g., Ronnlund, Lovden, & Nilsson, 2001). Coupled with neuro-imaging studies showing changes in the structure and function of the frontal lobes with advancing age (see Prull, Gabrieli, & Bunge, 2000; Raz, 2000), these behavioral findings have led to a *frontal-lobe hypothesis* of cognitive aging (e.g., Albert & Kaplan, 1980; West, 1996). While likely true at some level, a problem with this hypothesis is its lack of specificity. The frontal lobe constitutes a large part of the brain and consists of anatomically specific regions that likely perform distinct cognitive functions; however, there is little consensus regarding the specific, age-related cognitive impairments that are associated with declines in frontal function.

Inconsistent behavioral findings with respect to the effects of age on neuropsychological tasks have also complicated our understanding of age-related changes in executive functioning. For example, numerous studies have either failed to find age-related effects on executive tasks (e.g., Boone, Miller, Lesser, Hill, & D'Elia, 1990) or have found observed effects to be eliminated when performance on nonexecutive-component processes such as perceptual/motor speed are taken into account (e.g., Fristoe, Salthouse, & Woodard, 1997; Parkin & Java, 1999; but see Dywan, Segalowitz, & Unsal, 1992). As well, correlations among neuropsychological measures of executive function are often small and nonsignificant (e.g., Burgess, Alderman, Evan, Emslie, & Wilson, 1998; Duncan et al., 1997; Lehto, 1996; Lowe & Rabbitt, 1997; Robbins et al., 1998), even among versions of the same basic task (e.g., Salthouse & Meinz, 1995; Shilling, Chetwynd, & Rabbitt, 2002). Although methodological limitations (small samples, low reliability) may partially explain these results, they are also consistent with two nonexclusive conclusions, both of which hint at problems with task-based approaches: First, that performance on "executive" tasks often reflects nonexecutive, idiosyncratic aspects of the task (aspects related to task materials and procedures, for example); and second, that the tasks are tapping distinct, separable forms of executive control.

Cognitive Tasks

Unlike neuropsychological tasks, modern cognitive tasks are designed to more precisely measure specific processes. Prominent among the tasks believed to measure executive-control processes are those that place large demands on working memory (e.g., span tasks, *n*-back); those that require the inhibition of pre-potent responses (e.g., Stroop, negative priming); and those that require the focusing, dividing, or switching of attention (e.g., task-switching paradigms). As with neuropsychological measures, older adults have been shown to perform more poorly than younger adults on a variety of tasks designed to tap these abilities (for reviews, see Park, 2000; Zacks, Hasher, & Li, 2000).

However, despite their intended specificity in terms of underlying processes, cognitive tasks appear vulnerable to many of the same empirical and interpretative limitations as neuropsychological tasks. For example, age-related deficits are often inconsistent across tasks, even those purported to measure a *single* executive function such as inhibition (see Kramer et al., 1994). As well, some age effects on executive-processing cognitive tasks are significantly reduced or eliminated when variance associated with more basic processes is first removed (e.g., Verhaeghen & De Meersman, 1998). More generally, although age-related declines in task performance are often interpreted as reflecting changes in *specific* executive processes, mediational analyses often show that the majority of decline can be accounted for by a common factor that is shared by all tasks, including tasks often considered "nonexecutive" (see Salthouse et al., 2003). Overall, then, while cognitive tasks arguably allow for a more process-specific analysis of executive functions, these tasks do not appear to get around the interpretive problems seen with neuropsychological tasks.

Part of the difficulty in interpreting relations among executive tasks and their changes with age may be traced to the more basic question of whether executive control reflects a single, unified ability or a family of distinct abilities. Some researchers have argued that executive control is very general (Duncan & Miller, 2002). Consistent with this perspective, Engle and colleagues have shown working memory tasks to predict a wide array of higher-order cognitive abilities, including comprehension, reasoning, and fluid intelligence (see Engle & Kane, 2004). Alternatively, dissociations among tasks, along with more theoretical considerations, have led other researchers to propose the existence of distinct executive processes (e.g., Miyake et al., 2000). Unfortunately, the few studies that have examined the validity of such fractionations have produced mixed results. For example, Salthouse et al. (2003) found little evidence that inhibition, updating (working memory), and time-sharing (switching) represent distinct aspects of executive control while Miyake et al. (2000) argued that very similar abilities (inhibition, updating, and shifting) were "clearly distinguishable" (p. 28).

Further complicating the picture, recent theorizing has hypothesized that each of the three executive processes described above can be further fractionated into constituent subprocesses. Thus, inhibition has recently been argued to consist of three distinct abilities: *access*, *deletion*, and *restraint* (Hasher, Zacks, & May, 1999; see also Friedman & Miyake, 2004). As well, at least two types of task-switching processes have been proposed—*local* (age insensitive) and *global* (age sensitive)—with a third switching-related measure (*focus switching*) on the horizon (see Verhaeghen, Cerella, Bopp, & Chandramallika, in press). Finally, it has been suggested that the executive control of working memory may reflect two distinct, interdependent mechanisms: *goal maintenance* and *conflict resolution* (Engle & Kane, 2004; Kane & Engle, 2003).

As should be apparent, the above studies and proposals paint a very complex picture of executive functions and their change with age. Such complexities have led some researchers to call for the development of new tasks that can more precisely measure relevant executive (sub-) processes (e.g., Conway, Kane, & Engle, 2003). However, as discussed in the next section, we question whether *any* task can achieve the level of process specificity required to answer the unity/diversity question, or the question of age-related changes in executive functions.

Executive Tasks and Executive Processes

A number of researchers have discussed the limitations with task-based approaches to defining and measuring executive functions (see especially Burgess, 1997; Rabbitt, 1997; Salthouse et al., 2003). One of the most worrisome is that ostensibly executive tasks are not process- or factor-pure in the sense that performance is determined not only by the targeted executive functions but also by one or more nonexecutive processes. As well, there is at least passing acknowledgment that, even if a task were process-pure, the measures obtained would still reflect variance associated with task materials and methods. Here we would like to further emphasize what could be called the *portion-of-variance* problem. In particular, there appears to be little concern with *how much* variability in task performance is due to executive processes relative to nonexecutive processes, despite the fact that this portion certainly differs across tasks and is also likely to change as a function of both practice and age (cf. Li et al., 2004).

Some of the problems associated with executive tasks can be addressed through latent-variable techniques. By reducing the impact of method-related variance, for example, and examining the relations among multiple tasks, these techniques have significantly broadened our understanding of executive functions (e.g., Miyake et al., 2000) and their change with age (e.g., Salthouse et al., 2003). Nevertheless, latent variables (and the conclusions they engender) are only as good as the measures used to estimate them; and, here again, basic problems with task-based measures emerge. One such problem is that latent-variable techniques are often predicated on the a priori selection of tasks thought to index-specific processes, yet there is often little agreement about the "true" process(es) involved.

Even more problematic, however, is the possibility that performance on executive tasks may be determined by more than one executive process. Most complex tasks—whether cognitive, neuropsychological, or real-world—are likely to reflect a number of executive-control processes, including planning, sequencing, shifting, monitoring, and error correction. Indeed, monitoring and error correction are particularly interesting as they are likely to play a role in a variety of tasks (cf. Garavan, Ross, Murphy, Roche, & Stein, 2002; Rabbitt, 2002). Thus, assuming complex tasks engage multiple processes, more than one of which may be plausibly described as "executive," to which latent factor does such a task belong? Task performance measures are usually used to define one factor; but if tasks engage multiple processes, then this approach would necessarily lose or mischaracterize the variance associated with these other executive processes. We believe a more appropriate strategy is to separate processes *within a task* prior to examining the relations of such processes to each other and to individual-difference variables such as age.

A PROCESS-DISSOCIATION APPROACH TO THE MEASUREMENT OF EXECUTIVE PROCESSES

The process dissociation (PD) procedure (Jacoby, 1991) was developed in the context of dual-process models of memory and attention that distinguish between cognitively controlled and more automatic bases for thought and action. Although not always described as such, we see *cognitive control* in the context of dual-process theories as being coextensive with *executive processes*. A key assumption underlying the PD procedure is that most tasks reflect a mixture of controlled and automatic processes. Thus, rather than associating executive processes with performance on particular tasks, the goal of the procedure is to isolate those aspects of *any* task that reflect executive control. We believe the strategy of isolating and measuring control *within* tasks, regardless of whether they are designated "executive," is an improvement over task-based approaches to the measurement of executive processes, especially given the likely possibility that tasks require multiple forms of control.

The PD approach has been quite successful in producing theoretically meaningful estimates of controlled and automatic processes as a function of variables generally agreed to be related to executive functions. In the context of memory, for example, both dividing attention at study and forcing faster responses at test have been shown to reliably decrease estimated recollection—a controlled form of memory—but to have no influence on estimated familiarity, a more automatic form of memory (e.g., Jacoby, 1999; Schmitter-Edgecombe, 1999; Toth, 1996). Aging has also been found to dissociate the two processes with older adults consistently showing lower estimates of recollection than younger adults, while estimates of familiarity are often equivalent in the two groups (e.g., Jacoby, 1999; Jennings & Jacoby, 1997). This pattern of results is consistent with theories suggesting that aging is associated with deficits in executive control, while more automatic processes remain relatively intact (e.g., Braver & Barch, 2002; Jacoby, Jennings, & Hay, 1996).

In this section, we describe research showing how the PD procedure has been used to estimate executive processes operating in memory and attention tasks. We then describe research from a new "I told you . . ." task to show how the procedure can be used to separate *multiple* executive processes operating within a single task. Next, we describe research showing that process estimates can be used as individual difference measures. We end by suggesting how the PD approach can be combined with latent-variable techniques to address questions about the unity versus diversity of executive functions and how such functions change with age.

Recollection as Executive Control over Proactive Interference

Proactive interference (PI) refers to an impairment in the ability to remember an item or event because of its similarity to other items or events that were encountered earlier. A classic laboratory paradigm of PI is the A-not-B task, often used in research with infants and young children (see Diamond, Chapter 6, this volume), although examples of PI in the everyday lives of adults can also be easily identified. In trying to remember the location of our keys, for example, PI can often lead us to initially search where we *usually* put our keys rather than where we put them most recently.

To explain PI, the PD approach distinguishes between recollection and automatic influences of memory expressed as *accessibility bias*. *Recollection* refers to a controlled use of memory whose impairment is largely responsible for age-related declines in memory. Recollection and accessibility bias serve as alternative bases for responding. The notion is that when people are unable to recollect a past event, they "guess" with the first response that comes to mind, thereby showing effects of accessibility bias. If this characterization is correct, then two predictions follow. First, PI can result from a decrease in recollection without a concomitant increase in accessibility bias. Second, PI can result from an increase in the accessibility of interfering information without a concomitant decrease in recollection of the target event.

To test these predictions, Jacoby, Debner, and Hay (2001) varied accessibility bias in an initial training phase by exposing young and older adults to pairs of associatively related words. Critically, each cue word was paired with two different responses and the probability of each pairing was varied over trials. For example, in a 75% condition, the typical response "bone" appeared with the cue word "knee" on 75%

of the training trials, whereas the atypical response "bend" appeared with the cue on only 25% of the trials. For a 50% condition, the two cue-response pairs were presented equally often. After training, participants were presented with short lists of to-be-remembered pairs followed by a cued-recall test for those pairs. Test trials consisted of a cue word and a fragmented version of the response ("knee b_n_") and participants were told to complete the fragment with the response presented in the immediately preceding study list, guessing if necessary. The fragments were such that they could be completed with *either* of the two responses paired with the cue in training.

For *congruent* test pairs, the response presented in the study list was the one presented most frequently during training ("bone"), making recollection and accessibility congruent in dictating the same response. As shown in Figure 7.1A, correct recall could result either from recollection (R) of the studied word or

when recollection failed, from reliance on the accessibility bias (A) developed during training: P (correct recall|congruent) = R + (1–R)A. For *incongruent* test pairs, in contrast, accessibility and recollection were placed in opposition by having participants study the response presented least frequently during training ("bend"). For these pairs, false recall (saying "bone" when "bend" was studied) would occur when participants failed to recollect the study pair, but instead relied on accessibility: P (false recall|incongruent) = (1–R)A.

Results reported by Jacoby and colleagues revealed dissociations that provided strong support for their dual-process model (see Table 7.1). Most important, in experiment 2, aging negatively influenced recollection (thereby increasing PI in the older adults) but left estimated accessibility bias unchanged. That is, older adults were less able to recollect the target response presented in the study list just prior to testing, but did

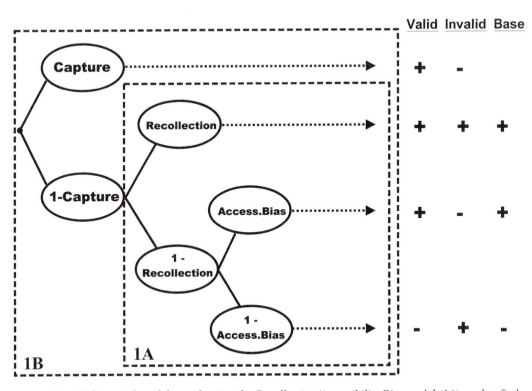

FIGURE 7.1. Multinomial model tree showing the Recollection/Accessibility-Bias model (1A) used to fit the data in Jacoby et al. (2005) and the Capture model (1B) used to fit the data in Jacoby et al. (2005). Branches lead to correct recall (+) and false recall (-) for valid (or congruent), invalid (or incongruent), and baseline conditions.

not differ from young adults in their reliance on accessibility bias when recollection failed. In contrast, the training manipulation (experiment 1) produced an opposite dissociation such that, relative to the 50% condition, training in the 75% condition increased accessibility bias (thereby increasing interference) but had no effect on a participant's ability to recollect the target information. These findings point to deficits in recollection, not inhibition, as the reason for older adults' increased susceptibility to PI.

Analogous findings were recently reported by Daniels (2003) in the context of working memory (WM). She found that individuals low in WM capacity as measured by span tasks ("low spans") showed elevated PI relative to individuals high in WM capacity ("high spans") a result also reported by Rosen and Engle (1998; Kane & Engle, 2000). However, just as Jacoby and colleagues (2001) found for older adults, Daniels found that the low spans' increased interference was entirely attributable to a selective decrease in recollection.

Note the implications of these findings for studies in which task-based measures of PI (i.e., observed performance in interference conditions) are entered into latent-variable analyses to identify "inhibitory" factors (cf. Friedman & Miyake, 2004). First, they show that nonexecutive processes such as accessibility bias are contributing to (contaminating) the index of PI. Second, they strongly imply that the resultant latent factor is inappropriately described as inhibitory because the relevant executive process—the process that determines whether and to what degree PI is exhibited—is not inhibition but recollection. The findings of Jacoby et al. (2001) and Daniels (2003) suggest

that more theoretical traction would be gained by using estimates of recollection as the basis for latent-variable analyses of PI.

Inhibitory Control in the Stroop Task

Although the PD procedure revealed no evidence of inhibitory processes in the control of PI (but see the work on RI, below), inhibitory-like processes do appear to be involved in performing the Stroop task. The Stroop task has been taken to represent a clear executive-control task because it requires the avoidance of habitual but goal-irrelevant responses (word reading) in favor of less-practiced but goal-relevant ones (naming the color in which the word appears). As noted earlier, older adults often demonstrate greater Stroop interference effects than younger adults. However, from a task-based perspective, it is difficult to tell whether elevated Stroop interference reflects decreased color naming, increased word-reading processes, or a combination of the two.

Using a model of Stroop performance that postulates independent processes of color naming and word reading (Lindsay & Jacoby, 1994), Spieler, Balota, and Faust (1996) showed that, once speed differences were taken into account, age-related deficits in Stroop performance could be completely described in terms of elevated word-reading estimates in older adults. A selective increase in estimated word reading has also been found for low-spans as compared to high-spans (Daniels, 2003). Although estimates of word reading likely reflect processes associated with word reading per se, age- and span-related increases in this parameter are also consistent with the idea of decreased in-

TABLE 7.1. Hits, false alarms (FAs), and process estimates for recall performance in Jacoby et al. (2001)

| | Recall | | Process Estimates | |
	Congruent (Hits)	Incongruent (FAs)	Recollection	Accessibility
Expt 1: PC				
PC50	.72	.32	.40	.54
PC75	.83	.40	.43	.69
Expt 2: Age				
Young	.80	.35	.44	.63
Old	.73	.44	.29	.62

hibitory efficiency (see Jacoby, McElree, & Trainham, 1999; Spieler et al., 1996) or, alternatively, with deficits in the ability to maintain the goal of color naming (see De Jong, 2001; Kane & Engle, 2003).

Executive Processes in a Retroactive-Interference ("I told you . . .") Paradigm

To this point, we have argued that the PD approach can purify measures of executive (and nonexecutive) processes operating in memory and attention tasks. However, one of the main reasons for advocating a PD approach to the study of executive processes is the possibility that tasks may often engage multiple executive processes (e.g., Garavan et al., 2002). In this section, we describe research using an "I told you . . ." procedure (Jacoby, Bishara, Hessels, & Toth, 2005) that we believe exemplifies such a task.

The "I told you . . ." procedure shares similarities with misinformation paradigms of the sort examined by Loftus (e.g., 1975) and others (e.g., Karpel, Hoyer, & Toglia, 2001). One of the reasons for our interest in misinformation effects is the possibility that such effects could be exploited to scam older adults. In one scam, for example, an unscrupulous repairman attempts to overcharge an older adult by falsely claiming, "I *told you* that it would cost X [a much higher price than was originally quoted], and you agreed to pay." The scam is most effective if its victim falsely remembers having agreed to pay the much higher price. In the research described below, we have found evidence suggesting that such a possibility is quite real—that a misleading cue, similar to a false "I told you . . ." claim, can result in older adults' showing levels of false remembering that are dramatically higher than those shown by younger adults. Moreover, such high levels of false remembering do *not* stem from age-related deficits in recollection of the sort found for PI (Jacoby et al., 2001); rather, they appear to reflect age differences in the likelihood of being "captured" by the false "I told you . . ." claim. Such capture appears to reflect an attention-related (inhibitory or goal-maintenance) deficit such that the "I told you . . ." claim preempts the older adult's attempt to recollect the relevant past event.

The general procedure for these experiments involves presenting pairs of related words for study (e.g., "knee bone"), with memory then tested by providing participants with a cued word along with a fragment of the response word ("knee b_n_"). The critical manipulation involved presenting a prime word just prior to presentation of the recall cue (word + fragment) pair. This prime was either the same as the target word (a *valid* prime: "bone"), an alternative to the target word (an *invalid* prime: "bend"), or a neutral nonword stimulus (a *baseline* prime: "&&&&").

In one experiment of this sort, young and older adults were required to give a response to each test cue, and then were asked to report on the basis of their response saying "remember," "familiar," or "guess." Similar to research by Gardiner and colleagues (Gardiner & Richardson-Klavehn, 2000), participants were to respond "remember" only when they could clearly recollect details of studying the target word. "Familiar" judgments were to be made when the participants *knew* that their response word was old but could not recollect details about studying it. Finally, "guess" judgments were to be made if the participants were purely guessing, with no idea of whether their response was the correct answer.

Results are shown in Table 7.2. Note that the recall performance of the young and older adults on neutral baseline trials was nearly identical (.70), a pattern achieved by giving older adults more study time for each word pair (3 seconds vs. 1 second). Nevertheless, despite this equivalence, performance on primed trials differed significantly for the young and older adults. For young adults, the interference produced by invalid primes was perfectly offset by the facilitation produced by valid primes; that is, performance in the prime conditions was symmetrical around that in the baseline condition. In contrast, the older adults showed a larger effect of the primes than did the young, and performance in the prime conditions was not symmetrical around baseline. The asymmetry would be expected if older adults were sometimes captured by the primes, thereby giving the prime as a response rather than engaging in recollection.

Consistent with this account, we fit the recall data from the above experiment with a multinomial model that combined the recollection/accessibility-bias (RA) model used by Jacoby et al. (2001) with an inhibition-deficit model of the sort used by Lindsay and Jacoby (1994) to describe Stroop performance. The combined model (Figure 7.1B) differs from the simpler RA model (Figure 7.1A) only in that a *capture* parameter precedes recollection. The notion is that being captured by a highly accessible response sacrifices the opportunity to engage in recollection in the same way

TABLE 7.2. Recall and "remember" judgments in Jacoby et al. (2005)

	Prime Condition		
	Valid	Neutral	Invalid
Target Recall			
Young	.89	.70	.51
Old	.93	.70	.31
Correct "Remember"			
Young	.38	.36	.30
Old	.77	.58	.24
False "Remember"			
Young	.01	.04	.04
Old	.03	.13	.43

that, in the Stroop task, reading the irrelevant word sacrifices the opportunity to name that word's color. This capture model provided a good fit to the above recall data, with only the capture parameter differing for young and older adults. That is, the best fits were obtained when the capture parameter was set to zero for the young adults (no capture), consistent with the symmetry in their valid-/invalid-prime data. For the older adults, in contrast, the capture parameter was substantial (.38). This suggests that older adults often "recalled" the false "I told you . . ." prime, accepting it as veridical without even attempting recollection. Such a failure could be described as a form of disinhibition, or goal neglect.

Table 7.2 also shows the subjective-report data. For young adults, the probability of a "remember" response was little affected by presentation of a prime, as would be expected if such responses reflected the probability of recollection, which was unchanged by presentation of a prime. In contrast, older adults were much more likely to claim to "remember" than were young adults, and presentation of a prime had a large effect on their responses. This difference was particularly dramatic for invalid primes (false "remembering"). That is, the probability of falsely recalling an invalid prime and saying "remember" was only .04 for young adults, but was .43 for older adults, a difference that remained when remember responses were conditionalized on reporting an invalid prime (.09 vs. .59).

These subjective-report data were fit using an extended version of the capture model, referred to as the attribution threshold (AT) model (Figure 7.2). For this model, being captured by a prime was assumed to

result in a high-confidence ("remember" or "familiar") response, as does recollection. In contrast, responding on the basis of accessibility bias was assumed to result in a "remember" or " familiar " response only when an attribution "threshold" is exceeded; otherwise, the participant would "guess." This model was able to closely fit the subjective-report data with only two parameters differing for the young and older adults. First, as in the model used to fit the recall data, older adults had a higher capture parameter than the younger adults. Second, the older adults also had a higher AT parameter than the younger adults, indicating a more lenient criterion for saying that their responses were "remembered" or "familiar".

The subjective-report results suggest that, relative to the young, older adults have deficits in monitoring the source and appropriateness of their responses. In a follow-up experiment, Jacoby et al. (2005) showed that they are also more willing than the young to *act* on their subjective experience even when not forced to do so. That is, we compared the performance of young and older adults in the same "I told you . . ." paradigm described above, but under conditions of free versus forced responding (Koriat & Goldsmith, 1994). For the free-responding condition, participants were instructed to not guess. The results replicated many of the findings reported in the previous experiment; older adults were more likely to falsely recall an invalid prime than were young adults when recall was forced. Most interesting, however, was the reduction in false recall that was achieved when participants were allowed to withhold responses. That is, when given the option to pass (free-responding condition), young participants were more likely to do so in the invalid prime condition than were older participants (.28 vs. .11). By not responding, younger adults greatly reduced their probability of falsely recalling invalid primes as compared to when responding was forced (.28 vs. .48). For the older adults, in contrast, false recall of invalid primes was nearly identical in the free- and forced-responding conditions (.59 vs. .62), a finding that agrees with the previous results showing that older adults are much more likely to falsely "remember" invalid primes. Also consistent with the subjective-report results, we were able fit the young and older adults' free- and forced-response data with our attribution threshold model (Figure 7.2) by assuming that "guesses" were equivalent to passes and "remember/familiar" (R/F) judgments were equivalent to emitted responses.

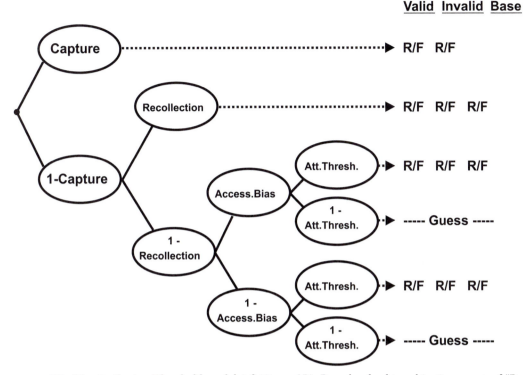

FIGURE 7.2. The Attribution Threshold model (cf. Figure 1B). Branches lead to subjective reports of "Remember" or "Familiar" ("R/F") or "Guess."

The above results thus give reason for worry that older adults are indeed more susceptible to "I told you . . ." scams than are younger adults. More relevant to the present chapter, the results showed older adults to have deficits in two distinct forms of executive control. First, they were more likely to be captured by the prime, suggesting an attentional deficit in maintaining the goal of recollecting studied words. Second, they showed deficits in the ability to monitor the accuracy of their responses. It is worth noting that a third control process—conscious recollection—was also operating in this task. Although older adults generally exhibit deficits in recollection (see PI task above), differential study rates were used in the "I told you . . ." experiments to equate young and older adults on this process. Overall, then, the successful fit of the attribution threshold model suggests that three distinct executive control processes were operating *within the same task* and that appropriate characterization of age-related changes in executive processes requires reference to all three.

PD Estimates as Individual Difference Measures of Executive Control

So far, we have argued that a process-based approach, exemplified by the PD procedure, may hold advantages over task-based approaches for defining and measuring executive functions. However, our case would be stronger if it could be shown that process estimates derived from the procedure are correlated with measures of higher-order cognition, such as fluid intelligence (*gF*) and metacognitive monitoring. This section describes studies relevant to this issue.

An early study by Jennings and Hay (1994, cited in Jacoby et al., 1996) showed that process estimates can be used to predict the frequency of people's everyday memory errors. They examined the relationship between estimates of controlled and automatic processes obtained from a standard recognition task and responses on a questionnaire of everyday memory complaints (Broadbent, Cooper, FitzGerald, & Parkes, 1982; Reason, 1993). The correlation between overall recognition performance and the questionnaire measure was only moderate ($r = .33$). By contrast, memory complaints correlated highly with the estimate of recollection derived from recognition performance ($r = .56$) while the correlation with automatic estimates was near zero ($r = .08$). Thus, isolating control processes afforded greater predictive power.

In a more recent study, Daniels (2003) used the PD procedure to compare estimates of controlled and automatic influences in PI and Stroop tasks as a function of working-memory capacity as indexed by span measures. Most notably in the present context, she found that estimates from both tasks correlated significantly with Raven's Progressive Matrices, a measure of fluid intelligence. That is, recollection estimates were positively related to Raven's (r's of .52 to .67) while word-reading estimates were negatively related to Raven's (r's of -.35 to -.39) as would be expected if word-reading estimates provided an index of inhibitory efficiency. These findings support the notion that PD parameters can provide a valid index of executive control. Indeed, the recollection-based correlations were as large as those produced by the span measures.

Predictive relations between process estimates and measures of cognitive control have also been found in the context of prejudice research. Payne (2001, 2003) used the PD procedure to derive estimates of cognitive control and stereotype accessibility for two tasks. The first was a weapon-identification task where subjects were asked to identify pictures as either guns or tools after being primed with a picture of a black or white face. The second was an evaluative-flanker task that required participants to classify words (e.g., *wonderful, terrific, nasty, horrible*) as either positive or negative when presented simultaneously with a black or white face. Payne found that the control estimates from these tasks correlated significantly with performance on a common measure of attentional control, the antisaccade task (r's were .35 and .19, respectively).

Finally, Salthouse, Toth, Hancock, and Woodard (1997) examined relations between estimates of control and automaticity derived from a cued-recall task and a spatial Stroop task, and performance on a wide range of additional tasks both executive and non-executive. They found good reliability for all of the process estimates ($> .75$), thus confirming that such estimates can be used as individual difference measures. Most notably, however, almost all of the experimental tasks and the control estimates loaded reliably on a common factor that was negatively related to age.

In contrast, automatic estimates from the two tasks showed no (cued recall) or slightly negative (spatial Stroop) loadings on the common factor. We take these results as showing the plausibility of using process estimates in multivariate statistical analyses. They also indicate the need for additional research, examining the relation among process estimates, task-based measures of executive control, and age.

IMPLICATIONS FOR
THE EARLY DEVELOPMENT
OF EXECUTIVE FUNCTIONS

A major goal of the present volume is to encourage greater theoretical cross-talk between researchers studying development and those studying aging. Toward that end, this section describes some of the implications of our research for understanding the early development of executive functions.

One observation that stands out from sampling the developmental literature is that, as with much research with adults, research with children is predominantly task-centered (see Diamond, Chapter 6, this volume). A problem with tasks as the unit of analysis is that performance is often attributed to specific processes, based on qualitative or intuitive assessments of task demands. For example, as noted above, increased proactive interference (PI) as a function of old age or low working-memory capacity has often been attributed to an impairment in the ability to inhibit previously learned information (e.g., Hasher & Zacks, 1988; Engle & Kane, 2004). That explanation has intuitive appeal because (it is reasoned) if only the person could inhibit the previously learned, interfering information (e.g., the A-B pair), the individual would then be able to "get to" the sought-after target information (the A-C pair). An alternative, albeit less intuitive, possibility is that prior learning exerts little or no influence on a person's ability to recollect target information and thus does not need to be inhibited; yet, when recollection is unsuccessful (e.g., when target information is not well learned because of age or divided attention), prior learning will often be expressed because of its influence on accessibility bias (see Jacoby et al., 2001, 2004, experiment 1). The difference between these two explanations is important because recollection deficits and inhibitory deficits implicate distinct cognitive and neural mechanisms, and would likely lead to very different training or rehabilitative strategies.

And, indeed, research using process-dissociation and multinomial-modeling techniques indicates that recollection, rather than inhibition, may often be the primary source of increased PI in older adults (Jacoby et al., 2001) and those working with low working-memory capacity (Daniels, 2003).

Similar analyses may be applicable in the developmental literature. Consider, for example, theory-of-mind tasks that require child A to distinguish between a true state of affairs (e.g., where a recently moved object is currently hidden) and what child B believes (where the object was initially hidden when child B was last in the room). Diamond (Chapter 6, this volume) states that successful performance on such tasks requires "inhibiting the impulse to give the veridical answer" (p. 77). To the extent that there is an impulse to give veridical answers, this explanation may be essentially correct; veridical answers may sometimes capture a child's attention and thus need to be inhibited. An alternative possibility, however, is that success requires the spontaneous (unrequested) recollection of the initial location; when such recollection does not occur, the child simply responds with the most accessible answer (i.e., the object's current location). That is, analogous to PI in older adults and low-span participants, children's performance on theory-of-mind tasks may be akin to the processing structure represented in the RA model rather than the capture model (see Figure 7.1). Note that we are *not* claiming that children's failures on theory-of-mind tasks reflect deficits in recollection rather than inhibition; our point is simply that the two explanations are difficult to untangle at the task (success vs. failure) level.

An encouraging exception to the task-centered approach that typifies developmental research is a recent study by Zelazo, Craik, and Booth (2004; see also Anooshian, 1999). These researchers used the process-dissociation procedure, implemented in the form of a word-stem cued-recall task, to estimate cognitive control across the lifespan (8–10-year-olds vs. young adults vs. older adults). Zelazo and colleagues found that estimates of control (recollection) exhibited a highly symmetrical inverted-U shape across the three age groups while estimates of automatic influences (accessibility bias) were age invariant. Moreover, significant negative correlations were found between control estimates and perseverations on a card-sorting task that required the flexible use of two incompatible rules. In addition to its being generally consistent with the recollection account of theory-of-mind perfor-

mance given above, we see this study as a good example of how formal process models can be used to better understand the "rise and fall" of cognitive control as a function of age. We believe that additional process-oriented studies, especially those directed at multiple forms of control (similar to the "I told you . . ." paradigm) have the potential to tell us a great deal about the development of executive functions.

Developmental studies may also be important, if not indispensable, in understanding the breakdown of executive functions with advancing age. If we are correct in asserting that many tasks require multiple control processes, then a critical issue that can be answered only with developmental research is whether these processes start off as distinct abilities or, instead, emerge out of a single, unified ability. Relevant here is research suggesting that many high-level cognitive abilities are initially undifferentiated in childhood, become more distinct or modular in adulthood, and are then reintegrated (dedifferentiated) during senescence (Li et al., 2004). This possibility raises a number of interesting questions about the developmental trajectory of cognitive control. For example, in what order do executive functions (control processes) become efficacious during development? And does the differentiation of one control process depend on the maturation of others (analogous to sensory systems)? Not only are these issues interesting from a developmental perspective, but they will also likely inform our understanding of age-related declines in cognitive control. That is, although there are certainly qualifications to the idea that old age entails a journey back to childhood (see, e.g., Li et al., 2004), knowing how executive functions initially develop will likely inform our thinking about their later decline in old age. We believe that a focus on processes, coupled with the use of formal process models, can help better integrate studies of development and senescence.

CONCLUSIONS: TOWARD A GREATER UNDERSTANDING OF EXECUTIVE FUNCTIONS AND AGE

Two general approaches have been used to study executive functions, their change with age, and their relation to other cognitive abilities such as general fluid intelligence: a microanalytic approach that employs the methods and goals of experimental psychology and that focuses on the processes operating *within* a task; and a macroanalytic approach that employs latent-factor techniques and that focuses on relations *across* tasks. A number of researchers have called for a greater integration of these two approaches for understanding executive control, a perspective that we fully endorse. At the same time, we believe that the results from our PD experiments suggest important qualifications for how that integration should proceed; and new directions for research on executive functions and their changes with age.

With respect to qualifications, most instructive are the results from the "I told you . . ." experiments. These experiments showed that older adults were more likely than the young to be captured by a prime, thus indicating an age-related deficit in inhibition or goal maintenance. Older adults also showed monitoring deficits both in their memory judgments (false "remember" responses) and in their actions (using the prime as a response even when given the opportunity to pass). Coupled with the success of the capture and attribution threshold models (which included a third control process of recollection), these findings suggest that multiple forms of executive control are required for successful performance in this paradigm.

We believe that the above conclusion is a very general one: that most complex tasks require multiple forms of control. The possibility that task performance can reflect multiple forms of control (multiple executive functions) has a number of important implications. First, it supports the idea that executive control can be fractionated into separable components. Second, it suggests caution in interpreting prior correlations among task-based measures of executive functions including "process-specific" measures of working memory, inhibition, and switching. Third, and perhaps most important, it illustrates the importance of using formal models to estimate relevant processes *prior to* the use of latent-variable techniques for determining how control processes contribute to different tasks.

With regard to future directions, we believe that PD estimates can be fruitfully used as individual-difference measures of executive functions. This is important because, although working-memory span tasks (for example) appear to provide a relatively clean index of executive control, few researchers would claim that such tasks are pure measures of such control. From our perspective, executive control processes are ubiquitous in task performance. Thus, the nature of such processes, their ability to predict performance, their relation to control processes in other tasks, and their change with maturation and advanced aging will require methods that can extract such processes across a variety of tasks, regardless of whether they were explicitly designed to engage working memory or executive processes. We believe that the PD procedure has the potential to provide such a method.

References

Albert, M. S., & Kaplan, E. (1980). Organic implications of neuropsychological deficits in the elderly. In L. W. Poon, J. L., Fozard, L. S. Cermak, D. Arenberg, & L. W. Thompson (Eds.), *New directions in memory and aging* (pp. 403–432). Hillsdale, NJ: Lawrence Erlbaum Associates.

Anooshian, L. J. (1999). Understanding age differences in memory: Disentangling conscious and unconscious processes. *International Journal of Behavioral Development*, 23, 1–17.

Boone, K. B., Miller, B. L., Lesser, I. M., Hill, E., & D'Elia, L. (1990). Performance on frontal tests in healthy, older individuals. *Developmental Neuropsychology*, 6, 215–223.

Braver, T. S., & Barch, D. M. (2002). A theory of cognitive control, aging cognition, and neuromodulation. *Neuroscience & Biobehavioral Reviews*, 26, 809–817.

Brink, J., & McDowd, J. (1999). Aging and selective attention: An issue of complexity or multiple mechanisms? *Journals of Gerontology: Psychological Sciences*, 54B, 30–33.

Broadbent, D. E., Cooper, P. F., FitzGerald, P., & Parkes, K. R. (1982). The Cognitive Failures Questionnaire (CFQ) and its correlates. *British Journal of Clinical Psychology*, 21, 1–16.

Burgess, P. W. (1997). Theory and methodology in executive function research. In P. Rabbitt (Ed.), *Methodology of frontal and executive functions* (pp. 81–116). Hove, UK: Psychology Press.

Burgess, P. W., Alderman, N., Evans, J., Emslie, H., & Wilson, B. A. (1998). The ecological validity of tests of executive function. *Journal of the International Neuropsychological Society*, 4, 547–558.

Cohn, N. B., Dustman, R. E., & Bradford, D. C. (1984). Age-related decrements in Stroop color-word test performance. *Journal of Clinical Psychology*, 40, 1244–1250.

Conway, A. R. A., Kane, M. J., & Engle, R. W. (2003). Working memory capacity and its relation to general intelligence. *Trends in Cognitive Sciences*, 7, 547–552.

Cronin-Golomb, A. (1990). Abstract thought in aging and age-related disease. In F. Boller & J. Grafman

(Eds.), *Handbook of neuropsychology* (Vol. 4, pp. 279–309). Amsterdam: Elsevier.

Damasio, A. (1998). The somatic marker hypothesis and the possible functions of the prefrontal cortex. In A. C. Roberts, T. W., Robbins, & L. Weiskrantz (Eds.), *The prefrontal cortex: Executive and cognitive functions* (pp. 36–50). London: Oxford University Press.

Daniels (2003). *Control, automaticity, and working memory: A dual-process analysis.* Manuscript submitted for publication.

De Jong, R. (2001). Adult age differences in goal activation and goal maintenance. *European Journal of Cognitive Psychology, 13,* 71–89.

Duncan, J., Johnson, R., Swales, M., & Freer, C. (1997). Frontal lobe deficits after head injury: Unity and diversity of function. *Cognitive Neuropsychology, 14,* 713–741.

Duncan, J., & Miller, E. K. (2002). Cognitive focus through adaptive neural coding in the primate prefrontal cortex. In D. T. Stuss & R. T. Knight (Eds.), *Principles of frontal lobe function* (pp. 278–291). London: Oxford University Press.

Dywan, J., Segalowitz, S. J., & Unsal, A. (1992). Speed of processing, health, and cognitive performance in older adults. *Developmental Neuropsychology, 8,* 473–490.

Engle, R. W., & Kane, M. J. (2004). Executive attention, working memory capacity, and a two-factor theory of cognitive control. *The psychology of learning and motivation* (Vol. 44, pp.145–199). Oxford: Academic Press.

Friedman, N. P., & Miyake, A. (2004). The relations among inhibition and interference control functions: A latent variable analysis. *Journal of Experimental Psychology: General, 133,* 101–135.

Fristoe, N., Salthouse, T. A., & Woodard, J. L. (1997). Examination of age-related deficits on the Wisconsin Card Sorting Test. *Neuropsychology, 11,* 428–436.

Fuster, J. (1989). *The prefrontal cortex: Anatomy, physiology, and neuropsychology of the frontal lobe* (2nd ed.). New York: Raven Press.

Garavan, H., Ross, T. J., Murphy, K., Roche, R. A. P., & Stein, E. A. (2002). Dissociable executive functions in the dynamic control of behavior: Inhibition, error detection, and correction. *NeuroImage, 17,* 1820–1829.

Gardiner, J. M., & Richardson-Klavehn, A. (2000). Remembering and knowing. In E. Tulving & F. I. M. Craik (Eds.), *The Oxford handbook of memory* (pp. 229–244). New York: Oxford University Press.

Goldstein, K. (1936). The significance of the frontal lobes to mental performance. *Journal of Neurology & Psychopathology, 17,* 27–40.

Hasher, L., & Zacks, R. T. (1988). Working memory, comprehension, and aging: A review and a new view. In G. H. Bower (Ed.), *The psychology of learning and motivation: Advances in research and theory* (Vol. 22, pp. 193–225). San Diego: Academic Press.

Hasher, L., Zacks, R. T., & May, C. P. (1999). Inhibitory control, circadian arousal, and age. In D. Gopher & A. Koriat (Eds.), *Attention and performance XVII* (pp. 653–675). Cambridge, MA: MIT Press.

Jackson, J. H. (1844). Croonian lectures on evolution and dissolution of the nervous system. *Lancet, 1,* 555–558, 649–652, 739–744.

Jacobsen, C. F., & Nissen, H. W. (1937). Studies of cerebral function in primates: IV. The effects of frontal lobe lesions on the delayed alternation habit in monkeys. *Journal of Comparative Psychology, 23,* 101–112.

Jacoby, L. L. (1991). A process dissociation framework: Separating automatic from intentional uses of memory. *Journal of Memory & Language, 30,* 513–541.

Jacoby, L. L. (1999). Deceiving the elderly: Effects of accessibility bias in cued-recall performance. *Cognitive Neuropsychology, 16,* 417–436.

Jacoby, L. L., Bishara, A. J., Hessels, S., & Toth, J. P. (2005). *Aging, subjective experience, and cognitive control: Dramatic false remembering by older adults. Journal of Experimental Psychology, 134,* 131–148.

Jacoby, L. L., Debner, J. A., & Hay, J. F. (2001). Proactive interference, accessibility bias, and process dissociations: Valid subjective reports of memory. *Journal of Experimental Psychology: Learning, Memory, & Cognition, 27,* 686–700.

Jacoby, L. L., Jennings, J. M., & Hay, J. F. (1996). Dissociating automatic and consciously controlled processes: Implications for diagnosis and rehabilitation of memory deficits. In D. J. Hermann, C. McEvoy, C. Hertzog, P. Hertel, & M. K. Johnson (Eds.), *Basic and applied memory research: Theory in context* (Vol.1, pp. 161–190). Mahwah, NJ: Lawrence Erlbaum Associates.

Jacoby, L. L., McElree, B., & Trainham, T. N. (1999). Automatic influences as accessibility bias in memory and Stroop tasks: Toward a formal model. In D. Gopher & A. Koriat (Eds.), *Attention and performance XVII: Cognitive regulation of performance: Interaction of theory and application* (pp. 461–486). Cambridge, MA: MIT Press.

Jennings, J. M., & Jacoby, L. L. (1997). An opposition procedure for detecting age-related deficits in recollection: Telling effects of repetition. *Psychology and Aging, 12,* 352–361.

Kane, M. J., & Engle, R. W. (2000). Working memory capacity, proactive interference, and divided attention: Limits on long-term memory retrieval. *Journal of Experimental Psychology: Learning, Memory, and Cognition, 26,* 336–358.

Kane, M. J., & Engle, R. W. (2003). Working memory capacity and the control of attention: The contributions of goal neglect, response competition, and task set to Stroop interference. *Journal of Experimental Psychology: General, 132,* 47–70.

Karpel, M. E., Hoyer, W. J., & Toglia, M. P. (2001). Accuracy and qualities of real and suggested memories: Nonspecific age differences. *Journals of Gerontology: Psychological Science & Social Science, 56B,* 103–110.

Koriat, A., & Goldsmith, M. (1994). Memory in naturalistic and laboratory contexts: Distinguishing the accuracy-oriented and quantity-oriented approaches to memory assessment. *Journal of Experimental Psychology: General, 123,* 297–315.

Kramer, A. F, Humphrey, D. G., Larish, J. F., Logan, G. D., & Strayer, D. L. (1994). Aging and inhibition: Beyond a unitary view of inhibitory processing in attention. *Psychology and Aging, 9,* 491–512.

Lehto, J. (1996). Are executive function tests dependent on working memory capacity? *Quarterly Journal of Experimental Psychology, 49A,* 29–50.

Lhermitte, F. (1986). Human autonomy and the frontal lobes. Part II: Patient behavior in complex and social situations: The "environmental dependency syndrome". *Annals of Neurology, 19,* 335–343.

Li, S-C, Lindenberger, U., Hommel, B., Aschersleben, G., Prinz, W., & Baltes, P. B. (2004). Transformations in the couplings among intellectual abilities and constituent cognitive processes across the life span. *Psychological Science, 15,* 155–163.

Lindsay, D. S., & Jacoby, L. L. (1994). Stroop process dissociations: The relationship between facilitation and interference. *Journal of Experimental Psychology: Human Perception and Performance, 20,* 219–234.

Loftus, E. F. (1975). Leading questions and the eyewitness report. *Cognitive Psychology, 7,* 560–572.

Lowe, C., & Rabbitt, P. (1997). Cognitive models of aging and frontal lobe deficits. In P. Rabbitt (Ed.), *Methodology of frontal and executive functions* (pp. 39–59). Hove, UK: Psychology Press.

Luria, A. R. (1966/1980). *Higher cortical functions in man.* New York: Basic Books.

Lyon, G. R., & Krasnegor, N. A. (1996). *Attention, memory, and executive function.* Baltimore, MD: Brookes.

Macmillan, M. B. (1986). A wonderful journey through skull and brains: The travels of Mr. Gage's tamping iron. *Brain & Cognition, 5,* 67–107.

Mesulam, M.-M. (2002). The human frontal lobes: Transcending the default mode through contingent encoding. In D. T. Stuss & R. T. Knight (Eds.), *Principles of frontal lobe function* (pp. 8–30). London: Oxford University Press.

Miyake, A., Friedman, N. P., Emerson, M. J., Witzki, A. H., & Howerter, A. (2000). The unity and diversity of executive functions and their contributions to complex "frontal lobe" tasks: A latent variable analysis. *Cognitive Psychology, 41,* 49–100.

Norman, D. A., & Shallice, T. (1986). Attention to action: Willed and automatic control of behavior. In R. J. Davidson, G. E. Schwartz, & D. Shapiro (Eds.), *Consciousness and self-regulation* (pp. 1–18). New York: Plenum Press.

Park, D. C. (2000). The basic mechanisms accounting for age-related decline in cognitive function. In D.C. Park & N. Schwarz (Eds.), *Cognitive aging: A primer* (pp. 3–21). Philadelphia: Psychology Press.

Parkin, A. J., & Java, R. I. (1999). Deterioration of frontal lobe function in normal aging: Influences of fluid intelligence versus perceptual speed. *Neuropsychology, 13,* 539–545.

Parkin, A. J., & Walter, B. M. (1992). Recollective experience, normal aging, and frontal dysfunction. *Psychology & Aging, 7,* 290–298.

Payne, B. K. (2001). Prejudice and perception: The role of automatic and controlled processes in misperceiving a weapon. *Journal of Personality and Social Psychology, 81,* 181–192.

Payne, B. K. (2003). *Cognitive control in automatic attitude measurement.* Unpublished doctoral dissertation, Washington University in St. Louis.

Pribram, K. H. (1973). The primate frontal cortex: Executive of the brain. In K. H. Pribram & A. R. Luria (Eds.), *Psychophysiology of the frontal lobes* (pp. 293–314). Oxford: Academic Press.

Prull, M. W., Gabrieli, J. D. E., & Bunge, S. A. (2000). Age-related changes in memory: A cognitive neuroscience perspective. In F. I. M. Craik & T. A. Salthouse (Eds.), *The handbook of aging and cognition* (pp. 91–153). Mahwah, NJ: Lawrence Erlbaum Associates.

Rabbitt, P. (1997). Introduction: Methodologies and models in the study of executive function. In P. Rabbitt (Ed.), *Methodology of frontal and executive functions* (pp. 1–38). Hove, UK: Psychology Press.

Rabbitt, P. (2002). Consciousness is slower than you think. *Quarterly Journal of Experimental Psychology: Human Experimental Psychology, 55A,* 1081–1092.

Raz, N. (2000). Aging of the brain and its impact on cognitive performance: Integration of structural and functional findings. In F. I. M. Craik & T. A. Salthouse (Eds.), *The handbook of aging and cognition* (pp. 1–90). Mahwah, NJ: Lawrence Erlbaum Associates.

Reason, J. (1993). Self-report questionnaires in cognitive psychology: Have they delivered the goods? In A. D. Baddeley & L. Weiskrantz (Eds.), *Attention: Selection, awareness, and control: A tribute to Donald Broadbent* (pp. 406–423). Oxford: Clarendon Press.

Robbins, T. W., James, M., Owen, A. M., Sahakian, B. J., Lawrence, L. D., McInnes, L., & Rabbitt, P. M. A. (1998). A study of performance on tests from the CANTAB battery sensitive to frontal lobe dysfunction in a large sample of normal volunteers: Implications for theories of executive functioning and cognitive aging. *Journal of the International Neurological Society, 4,* 474–490.

Ronnlund, M., Lovden, M., & Nilsson, L.-G. (2001). Adult age differences in Tower of Hanoi performance: Influence from demographic and cognitive variables. *Aging, Neuropsychology, & Cognition, 8,* 269–283.

Rosen, V. M., & Engle, R. W. (1998). Working memory capacity and suppression. *Journal of Memory and Language, 39,* 418–436.

Salthouse, T. A., Atkinson, T. M., & Berish, D. E. (2003). Executive functioning as a potential mediator of age-related cognitive decline in normal adults. *Journal of Experimental Psychology: General, 132,* 566–594.

Salthouse, T. A., & Fristoe, N. (1995). Process analysis of adult age effects on a computer-administered trail-making test. *Neuropsychology, 9,* 518–528.

Salthouse, T. A., & Meinz, E. J. (1995). Aging, inhibition, working memory, and speed. *Journals of Gerontology: Psychological Sciences, 50B,* P297–P306.

Salthouse, T. A., Toth, J. P., Hancock, H. E., & Woodard, J. L. (1997). Controlled and automatic forms of memory and attention: Process purity and the uniqueness of age-related influences. *Journals of Gerontology: Psychological Sciences, 52B,* P216–P228.

Schmitter-Edgecombe, M. (1999). Effects of divided attention and time course on automatic and controlled components of memory in older adults. *Psychology and Aging, 14,* 331–345.

Shilling, V. M., Chetwynd, A., & Rabbitt, P. M. A. (2002). Individual inconsistency across measures of inhibition: An investigation of the construct validity of inhibition in older adults. *Neuropsychologia, 40,* 605–619.

Spieler, D. H., Balota, D. A., & Faust, M. E. (1996). Stroop performance in healthy younger and older adults and in individuals with dementia of the Alzheimer's type. *Journal of Experimental Psychology: Human Perception and Performance, 22,* 461–479.

Stuss, D. T., & Benson, D. F. (1986). *The frontal lobes.* New York: Raven Press.

Stuss, D. T., Gow, C. A., & Heatherington, C. R. (1992). "No longer Gage": Frontal lobe dysfunction and emotional changes. *Journal of Consulting and Clinical Psychology, 60,* 349–359.

Teuber, H. L. (1972). Unity and diversity of frontal lobe functions. *Acta Neurobiologiae Experimentalis, 32,* 615–656.

Toth, J. P. (1996). Conceptual automaticity in recognition memory: Levels-of-processing effects on familiarity. *Canadian Journal of Experimental Psychology – Special Issue: Implicit Memory Research in 1996, 50,* 123–138.

Tranel, D., Anderson, S. W., & Benton, A. (1994). Development of the concept of 'executive function' and its relationship to the frontal lobes. In F. Boller & J. Grafman (Eds.), *Handbook of neuropsychology* (Vol. 9, pp. 125–148). Amsterdam: Elsevier.

Verhaeghen, P., Cerella, J., Bopp, K. L., & Chandramallika, B. (in press). Aging and varieties of cognitive control: A review of meta-analyses on resistance to interference, coordination and task switching, and an experimental exploration of age-sensitivity in the newly identified process of focus switching. Chapter to appear in R.W. Engle, G. Sedek, U. von Hecker, & D.N. McIntosh (Eds.), *Cognitive limitations in aging and psychopathology: Attention, working memory, and executive functions.* Cambridge, UK: Cambridge University Press.

Verhaeghen, P., & De Meersman, L. (1998). Aging and the Stroop effect: A meta-analysis. *Psychology & Aging, 13,* 435–444.

Wecker, N. S., Kramer, J. H., Wisniewski, A., Delis, D. C., & Kaplan, E. (2000). Age effects on executive ability. *Neuropsychology, 14,* 409–414.

West, R. L. (1996). An application of prefrontal cortex function theory in cognitive aging. *Psychological Bulletin, 120,* 272–292.

Zacks, R. T., Hasher, L., & Li, K. Z. H. (2000). Human memory. In F. I. M. Craik & T. A. Salthouse (Eds.), *The handbook of aging and cognition* (2nd ed., pp. 293–358). Mahwah, NJ: Lawrence Erlbaum Associates.

Zelazo, P. D., Craik, F. I. M., & Booth, L. (2004). Executive functions across the life span. *Acta Psychologica, 115,* 167–183.

8

Working Memory in Children: A Cognitive Approach

Graham J. Hitch

This chapter discusses the development of working memory as children grow up. We shall argue that working memory is an important resource for acquiring and performing cognitive skills and that its limited capacity places key constraints on children's abilities. The discussion is based on evidence from relatively simple tasks that have been extensively studied in adults, and it is influenced by theoretical ideas about adult working memory. Readers with a background in developmental psychology rather than adult cognition may regard an adult-driven approach as somewhat inappropriate. However, there is much convergence of developmental and adult perspectives in the area of working memory (see, e.g., Kemps, De Rammelaere, & Desmet, 2000; Baddeley & Hitch, 2000). The chapter starts by introducing the concept of working memory as a limited capacity system. We contrast unitary and multicomponent accounts and examine whether working memory is a separate system or part of long-term memory. We then go on to describe some of the tasks that have been used to explore working memory in

adults. We make a key distinction between *simple* span tasks, used to assess the capacity to hold different types of temporary information, and *complex* span tasks that assess the ability to hold and manipulate temporary information. The chapter then moves on to outline the developmental progression of performance in these tasks. We discuss the possible role of speed of information processing as a general factor accounting for developmental change in all aspects of working memory. We also discuss whether the structure of working memory is the same in children and adults, and whether working memory serves similar cognitive functions in children. A final topic concerns the developmental relationship between working memory and knowledge acquisition.

THE CONCEPT OF WORKING MEMORY

Many of our everyday activities involve retaining small amounts of information over short intervals. This happens when we look up and dial an unfamiliar telephone number or use a diagram to locate a control on a new piece of equipment. Tasks such as these involve *short-term memory* for recently perceived information. They can be usefully contrasted with situations where we have not only to maintain current information but also to manipulate it, as in adding a sequence of numbers or relating information on a map to a view of the terrain. Our ability to do this involves *working memory*, loosely defined as a limited-capacity workspace for complex thought (see also Park & Payer, Chapter 9, this volume). Working memory is thought to involve a dynamic interplay between executive processes and currently active stored information, and to be a core component of activities such as reasoning, learning, comprehension, and problem solving (Baddeley & Hitch, 1974)

Baddeley and Hitch (1974) and Daneman and Carpenter (1980) regarded the capacity to combine the storage and manipulation of temporary information as the key characteristic of working memory. Subsequent developments have generated a range of theoretical perspectives (see Andrade, 2001; Shah & Miyake, 1999). For example, there are a number of ways of conceptualizing executive processes. For some investigators, working memory is a source of inhibition for overriding strongly activated automatic response tendencies (Hasher & Zacks, 1988), while for other investigators, working memory is a source of activation for maintaining information in an accessible state (Engle, Tuholski, Laughlin, & Conway, 1999; Cowan, 1995). Yet another view is that executive processes can be fractionated into different subtypes. For example, Baddeley (1996) suggested four kinds of executive process. These are sharing attention among multiple activities, selectively attending to different stimuli, inhibiting strongly primed responses, and activating information in long-term memory. Psychometric evidence provides some support for separating out different executive functions. For example, Miyake et al. (2000) identified three components corresponding to inhibition, mental-set shifting, and information updating. However, separating out and identifying executive functions is problematic given the difficulty of finding tasks that are "pure" measures of its putative components. Thus for many practical purposes, investigators find it useful not to divide up executive processes.

In the present chapter we will need to keep in mind two main points of theoretical debate about working memory that have particular relevance to its development. One concerns whether the working memory system is unitary or differentiated. The unitary approach regards working memory as a central workspace comprising a limited-capacity pool of general-purpose resources for controlled attention (see, e.g., Daneman & Carpenter, 1980, Engle et al., 1999). This approach has the virtue of parsimony. It tends to be associated with the idea of resource sharing, according to which storage and processing compete for available capacity in working memory. Variants of the unitary approach propose separate working memories for different domains of knowledge, such as language and number (Just & Carpenter, 1992), but retain the basic idea of each workspace as an indivisible entity. In contrast, the multicomponent model assumes that working memory consists of a set of buffer stores that are closely connected to, but separate from, a general resource for controlling attention (Baddeley & Hitch, 1974; Baddeley, 1986; Logie, 1995). According to Baddeley (1986), working memory consists of a limited-capacity attentional system (or central executive), and two slave stores for holding temporary information, a speech-based phonological loop and a visuo-spatial sketchpad. The central executive is responsible for control processes that coordinate the operation of working memory and its interactions with other systems such as long-term memory. A subsequent version of the model (Baddeley, 2000) added a fourth component, an episodic buffer that integrates information from the various slave systems and long-term memory. We will argue that the weight of the evidence favors the need to conceptualize the development of working memory as that of a multicomponent system.

The second important point of theoretical debate concerns the relationship between working memory and long-term memory. The multicomponent approach and some unitary accounts assume that working memory is separate from long-term memory systems mediating episodic recollection of past events, semantic knowledge, and procedural learning. However, other investigators suggest that working memory corresponds to the currently activated part of long-term memory and is not an entirely separate system (Cowan, 1995, 1999b; see also Ericsson & Kintsch, 1995). The relationship between working memory and long-term memory assumes a particular importance in a developmental context. As we will see, there is considerable evidence that working memory plays a role in long-term learning and in turn is influenced by acquired knowledge.

WORKING MEMORY TASKS

Generally speaking, a number of tasks used to tap working memory in adults have also proved applicable to children. This has been advantageous for relating data and theory in these two populations. An important distinction can be made between simple and complex span tasks. Simple span assesses an individual's capacity for retaining a particular type of information over a brief interval, whereas complex span tasks assess the ability to retain information in the face of the requirement to perform mental operations that compete for attention. We describe some of the features of adult performance in these tasks before going on to discuss them from the developmental perspective.

Simple Spans

The main simple-span tasks in the verbal domain are digit, letter, and word span, all of which involve presenting a sequence of items for immediate recall in the correct serial order. In the visuo-spatial domain, the principal tasks are Corsi Blocks (Milner, 1971) and visual pattern span (Wilson, Scott, & Power, 1987). In the Corsi procedure a sequence of spatial locations is shown and the task is to point to them in the correct order immediately afterwards. Pattern span involves memory for a briefly presented two-dimensional figure consisting of randomly colored squares. In each task, span is a measure of the upper limit on stimulus complexity permitting accurate recall.

Studies of adults support the idea that verbal and visuo-spatial span tasks tap separate systems, consistent with the multicomponent model. For example, each type of span is reduced more by a concurrent task in the same domain of processing (see Logie, 1995, for a discussion). In addition, neuroimaging studies show left hemispheric lateralization for verbal span tasks and right lateralization for visuo-spatial span tasks (Paulesu, Frith, & Frackowiak, 1993; Smith & Jonides, 1997; see also Henson, 2001), and neuropsychological studies show that damage to roughly corresponding left and right hemisphere regions can selectively impair verbal and visuo-spatial spans (DeRenzi & Nichelli, 1975; Shallice & Warrington, 1970).

There is also evidence for different limits on performance in the varying types of span. For example, verbal span is lower for words that take longer to articulate (Baddeley, Thomson, & Buchanan, 1975), for items that are phonemically similar (Conrad & Hull, 1964), and when subvocal rehearsal is prevented by articulatory suppression, a dual-task procedure involving saying an irrelevant word (Murray, 1967). These three effects interact in a systematic and informative way. Thus, articulatory suppression removes the word-length and phonemic-similarity effects in memory for visually presented items. However, for auditorily presented items, suppression removes the word-length effect and leaves the phonemic-similarity effect intact (Baddeley, Lewis, & Vallar, 1984). These observations suggest a simple model of the phonological loop as a time-based decaying store feeding a rehearsal process that cycles back and refreshes the contents of the store. The phonological-similarity effect is assumed to arise in the store, reflecting the difficulty of discriminating similar traces that have undergone partial decay, whereas the word-length effect is ascribed to rehearsal, with slower rehearsal of long words permitting more time for decay. This interpretation of the word-length effect is strengthened by data showing a linear relationship between the number of words of different lengths that can be recalled and the time it takes to articulate them (Baddeley et al., 1975). The slope of the linear function can be taken as reflecting the decay rate of the phonological store and gives a duration of about 2 seconds of inner speech. The model neatly explains the importance of presentation modality by assuming that spoken stimuli access the phonological store automatically whereas visual stimuli first have to be recoded, a process involving subvocal articulation. Evidence from other experimental paradigms also shows that spoken stimuli activate the corresponding responses automatically, suggesting that the auditory-verbal input-output neural pathway may be hard-wired (McLeod & Posner, 1984).

We know a good deal less about what limits visual and spatial spans, and detailed models of task performance are less well developed (but see Raffone & Wolters, 2001, for an interesting exception). What we do know suggests different types of constraint. For example, Corsi span is not a function of the time taken to make the movements, suggesting it is not limited by a spatial analogue of the word-length effect (Smyth & Scholey, 1992). Similarly, the limit on visual short-term memory for arrays of objects appears to be set by the number of objects rather than the number of visual features they contain (Luck & Vogel, 1997).

Complex Spans

Complex span tasks build on the influential work of Daneman and Carpenter (1980) who devised a novel reading span task that involved reading a short series of unrelated sentences and then immediately attempting to recall the last word in each sentence. Reading span is the maximum number of words that can be recalled while successfully comprehending the sentences. According to Daneman and Carpenter (1980), working memory shares resources for storage and processing, and the limit on reading span reflects the resources left free for storage when others are required for comprehension. They made the interesting observation that reading span was a much better predictor of individual differences in reading ability than was digit span in young adults, suggesting that reading is dependent on the ability to combine storage with ongoing processing rather than simple short-term retention. This observation has been replicated on numerous occasions (Daneman & Merikle, 1996) and nowadays regular use is made of a wide variety of complex span tasks, each devised to assess how much information can be retained in the face of a concurrent demand on processes requiring attention. These working-memory span tasks differ in the types of information retained (typically either verbal or spatial) and the operations involved (such as listening comprehension, numerical calculations, or mental rotations).

Other evidence suggests that individual differences in simple and complex verbal spans can be understood in terms of a statistical model in which both types of task rely on the same short-term memory system but that complex spans also involve executive processes (Engle et al., 1999). Further correlational analysis suggested that the executive component of complex span is related to fluid intelligence. Although they argue for a somewhat different approach, Engle et al.'s data are consistent with the multicomponent model and its distinction between the phonological loop, used in simple span tasks, and the central executive, playing a more important role in complex span (see Baddeley & Logie, 1999). Shah and Miyake (1996) took the analysis further by comparing reading span with a visuo-spatial complex span task. The visuo-spatial task involved judging whether individually presented rotated letters were normal or mirror-reversed while at the same time keeping track of each letter's orientation for subsequent recall. The results sug-

gested a dissociation between the two types of complex span. Thus, individual differences in visuo-spatial complex span correlated with measures of spatial but not verbal ability, whereas reading span showed the converse pattern (see also Daneman & Tardif, 1987). The dissociation was also confirmed experimentally by the observation of different patterns of interference when the storage and processing requirements of the verbal and visuo-spatial complex span tasks were crossed. These findings are evidently difficult to interpret in terms of a unitary account of working memory. However, they are consistent with the multicomponent model (Baddeley & Hitch, 1974) if it is assumed that verbal and spatial complex span tasks differ in terms of the peripheral stores with which the central executive must interact. Shah and Miyake (1996) do not deny the utility of assuming a general-purpose central executive, but propose that domain specificity goes beyond storage and includes resources for processing as well. Thus we can see that complex span is a useful tool for studying individual differences in working memory, but as yet is not a thoroughly well understood task.

DEVELOPMENTAL CHANGES IN WORKING MEMORY

Perhaps the most striking aspect of the development of working memory in childhood is the observation that there are steady improvements in performance in all simple and complex span tasks (see, e.g., Gathercole, 1999). An intriguing general question is whether this improvement reflects a common underlying process or whether we need to entertain a more complex account. Before addressing this we will describe children's performance in more detail.

Simple Span Tasks

Simple span tasks are straightforward to administer to children. Digit span is familiar as a component of the Wechsler Intelligence Scale for Children (WISC), and there have been numerous studies of developmental change in memory span for verbal stimuli (see Dempster, 1981). Visuo-spatial span tasks have been less extensively studied, but there is a growing body of evidence on their development (see Pickering, 2001). In addition, some tasks have been devised especially for use with children. One of special interest involves nonword repetition and assesses the longest such item (e.g., *perplisteronk*) that can be accurately repeated after a single oral presentation (Gathercole & Baddeley, 1996). This task is easy for very young children to grasp, it correlates highly with digit span, and it has been widely used as an alternative measure of the phonological loop.

The dissociation between verbal and visuo-spatial short-term stores seen in adults seems also to apply to children. For example, Pickering, Gathercole, and Peaker (1998) found that individual differences in digit span and Corsi span are uncorrelated with one another at 5 and 8 years of age. However, this is not a consistent finding (Chuah & Mayberry, 1999). More strikingly, verbal span and Corsi span can be differentially impaired by genetic disorders. Thus, children with William's syndrome tend to be impaired on Corsi span and relatively spared on verbal span, whereas children with Down syndrome show the converse pattern (Wang & Bellugi, 1994; Jarrold, Baddeley, & Hewes, 1999).

Verbal Spans

As regards normal development, children ages 4 and upward are sensitive to word length and phonemic similarity of the items in just the same way as are adults, provided stimuli are presented orally (Hulme, Thomson, Muir, & Lawrence, 1984; Hitch, Halliday, & Littler, 1993). A particularly interesting observation is that spans for words of different lengths are a linear function of speech rate in children in just the same way as in adults (Hulme et al., 1984). Moreover, data from different age groups fall along different regions of the line describing young adults' performance. In terms of the phonological loop, these quantitative observations suggest that development is associated with faster subvocal rehearsal while the decay rate of the phonological store remains constant. However, the causal mechanism underlying this developmental change is not clear.

Phonological Recoding

An intriguing aspect of development is evidence for a qualitative change in the way visually presented stimuli are coded in short-term memory tasks. We have already mentioned the idea that spoken stimuli access the phonological loop automatically whereas visual stimuli have to be verbally recoded (Baddeley et al., 1984). In adults, the tendency to recode visual stimuli is pervasive. For example, when presented with a series of nameable drawings to recall, adults show word-length and phonemic-similarity effects of the items' names just as they do for printed or spoken words (Schiano & Watkins, 1981). In contrast, younger children aged 5–6 find the task of recalling nameable drawings more difficult when the items are similar in visual appearance, showing little or no effect of either phonemic similarity or word length of the names of the items (Hitch, Halliday, Schaafstal, & Schraagen, 1988; Hitch, Woodin, & Baker, 1989; Longoni & Scalisi, 1994; Palmer, 2000). Younger children do, however, show word-length and phonemic-similarity effects when items are presented auditorily, consistent with a separate route whereby spoken stimuli gain access to the phonological loop (Hitch, Halliday, Dodd, & Littler, 1989). Visual similarity typically has small effects on memory for visual stimuli in adults and older children, with some evidence that these effects can be enhanced when verbal recoding is disrupted by articulatory suppression (Hitch, Woodin, et al., 1989; see also Logie, Della Sala, Wynn, & Baddeley, 2000; Walker, Hitch, & Duroe, 1993). It appears then that development involves an expansion in the codes available to working memory for visually presented materials rather than simply a switch from visual to phonological codes. This conclusion fits well with Paivio's (1971) dual-coding model, according to which adult memory is typically based on a combination of verbal and visual (imaginal) codes.

Thus, early on in development, children tend to represent visual and spoken stimuli in separate stores that reflect the modality of the stimuli. However, as they develop, verbal coding becomes pervasive. Unfortunately, little is known about the processes behind this substantial developmental change. One suggestion is that verbal recoding is associated with learning to read (Fastenau, Conant, & Lauer, 1998; Palmer, 2000). On this account, the tendency to recode print transfers to nonverbal visual stimuli. This might be because verbal codes are more suitable than visuo-spatial representations for tasks requiring memory for temporal sequence information. Another possibility is that verbal recoding may be useful when it is helpful to lose information about the surface form of visual stimuli (such as contrast) and access more abstract structural descriptions (Hitch, Brandimonte, & Walker, 1995). Alternatively, the ability to recode may result from a general developmental change in executive processing capacity (see, e .g., Luciana & Nelson, 1998). Increased executive capacity may allow more flexibility in strategy use in a range of tasks (see, e.g., Guttentag, 1995) and therefore less dependence on automatic coding routines.

An interesting practical example of recoding may be wayfinding. Thus, Pickering (2001) discusses a study by Fenner, Heathcote, and Jerrams-Smith (2000), who showed children a spatial route and assessed their ability to walk around it. Performance on this task was related to visuo-spatial ability in 5–6-year-olds but not 9–10-year-olds. The authors suggest that older children are able to construct an abstract propositional mental model of the route, whereas younger children, lacking this ability, are forced to rely on visuo-spatial memory.

Functions of the Phonological Loop

It has been suggested that the phonological loop is crucial for vocabulary acquisition (Baddeley, Gathercole, & Papagno, 1998). The basic idea is that in order to learn a new word form, the novel sequence of phonemes must be stored long enough for it to be integrated and recoded as a higher order unit or "chunk" (cf. Miller, 1956). This hypothesis is supported by the observation that phonological storage capacity and measures of vocabulary knowledge tend to be highly correlated in normally developing children. For example, Gathercole, Hitch, Service, and Martin (1997) found that nonword repetition and digit recall were strongly related to vocabulary scores in a large group of 5-year-olds. The phonological loop measures also predicted performance in an experimental word-form learning task but not a control task of learning associations between familiar words. Studies of abnormal development complement these findings. For example, children diagnosed as having a specific language impairment score poorly on vocabulary tests and are typically impaired on tests of phonological short-term storage (Joanisse & Seidenberg, 1998). The question naturally arises whether the role of the phonological loop extends to other language processes. In this case, too, there are strong a priori arguments for supposing the involvement of some kind of backup store. However, empirical studies have not found much support for this hypothesis in the case of language comprehension (see, e.g., Willis & Gathercole, 2001).

Effects of Knowledge and Familiarity

The causal basis of the relationship between short-term phonological storage and vocabulary learning is difficult to unravel. Thus, while there are good grounds for supposing that phonological short-term memory is necessary for learning a new word form, it may equally be the case that phonological short-term memory is supported by long-term lexical knowledge (Snowling, Chiat, & Hulme, 1991; see also Metsala, 1999). For example, children find it easier to repeat nonwords that are more wordlike—that is, closer in form to real words (Gathercole, 1995). Moreover, the evidence that long-term phonological learning relies on short-term phonological storage calls into question whether the phonological loop is best thought of as entirely separate from long-term phonological memory. A more natural way of accounting for this relationship, which it seems is specific to the phonological domain, is to assume that phonological short-term memory corresponds to the currently activated region of phonological long-term memory (consistent with the general theoretical approach taken by Cowan [1995]). Indeed, connectionist modeling of the phonological loop demonstrates the plausibility of assuming a single system in which modifiable connections have both short-term and long-term weights, and the short-term weights decay in about 2 seconds (Burgess & Hitch, 1999). However, an alternative approach is to assume that long-term knowledge is used to clean up (or redintegrate) partially forgotten short-term memory traces at retrieval (Hulme et al., 1997).

From a developmental perspective it is interesting that the effect of long-term knowledge on the recall of nonwords increases with children's age (Roodenrys, Hulme, & Brown, 1993). This fits well with the simple idea that linguistic knowledge increases with exposure to the language and so is able to give a bigger boost to immediate recall. More generally, the influence of verbal knowledge can take many different forms. Thus, letter sequences that can be perceived as familiar units or chunks (e.g., BBC, NATO) are better recalled than unfamiliar sequences (Broadbent & Broadbent, 1981). Given that chunks are learned, it seems likely that the role of chunking will increase with development (though see Huttenlocher & Burke, 1976, for evidence that fails to support this hypothesis).

VISUO-SPATIAL SPANS

Performance on Corsi span and visual pattern span tasks improves steadily as children develop (Isaacs & Vargha-Khadem, 1989; Logie & Pearson, 1997; Wilson et al., 1987). A possible explanation for improvements in visuo-spatial spans is that they reflect older children's tendency to recode information into a verbal/phonological form. If so, older children's performance should be more sensitive when any tendency to use verbal recoding is disrupted by articulatory suppression. However, this is not the case (Pickering, Gathercole, Hall, & Lloyd, 2001).

By analogy with verbal span, rehearsal and knowledge are potential candidates for explaining developmental improvements in visuo-spatial span. Thus rehearsal speed may become faster and rehearsal strategies more elaborate, and greater knowledge may bring about advantages in encoding and retrieval—for example, through chunking. Unfortunately, the role of rehearsal in the nonverbal domain is not very well understood, and its contribution to development is therefore unclear. There are firmer grounds for supposing that changes in knowledge can play an important role in visuo-spatial memory tasks. This is evident in the work of Chi (1978), which built on previous research showing large effects of expertise in adults. Thus chess experts are much better than novices at recalling arrangements of chess pieces taken from actual games, but fare no better when the pieces are randomly arranged (Chase & Simon, 1973). It appears that experts benefit from their ability to encode familiar arrangements in terms of large chunks, an advantage they no longer enjoy when confronted with unfamiliar arrangements. Chi (1978) obtained similar findings for child chess experts, and showed further that they could even outperform adult novices when presented with configurations taken from games. Analogous effects of chunking seem likely to occur in pattern span and Corsi span as children develop, though this has yet to be clearly demonstrated.

The visuo-spatial sketchpad appears to be concerned with visual imagery in problem solving and memorization, and with spatial cognition, as in movement and navigation within an environment (Cornoldi & Vecchi, 2003). Although its functions in children have yet to be fully explored, there are some suggestive findings. For example, Gathercole and Pickering (2000) found a specific association between poor performance on tasks tapping the visuo-spatial sketchpad and poor achievement on national curriculum assessments involving mathematics and English. Relatedly, Dark and Benbow (1990) have shown enhanced visuo-spatial short-term memory performance in children classified as having exceptional mathematical talent.

COMPLEX SPAN

Theoretical Accounts

Case, Kurland, and Goldberg (1982) carried out seminal research on the development of complex span using a task that involved counting the number of targets in a series of arrays while keeping track of all the previous totals. Counting span increased with age and, furthermore, was a linear function of the time taken to perform the counting operations. Case et al. (1982) interpreted this empirical relationship in terms of the unitary view of working memory. Thus as children develop, their counting becomes more practiced and takes up fewer resources in working memory, thereby leaving more resources for storage. By taking counting time as an index of the resources needed for counting, and adding the somewhat counterintuitive assumption that the capacity of working memory does not grow, Case et al. (1982) were able to give a neat explanation for their observations. The plausibility of their account was boosted by further data showing that requiring young adults to count using nonsense syllables not only reduced their counting speed to the level of 6-year-olds but also led to a corresponding reduction in their counting spans.

Hitch, Towse, and Hutton (2001) found that reading span and operation span were also a linear function of the speed of processing operations in each task over development. However, the functions had different slopes for different tasks, suggesting that mapping them onto a single common resource-sharing system is likely to be somewhat complicated. A simple alternative explanation stems from the observation that slower processing lengthens retention intervals for information generated during the span task. Thus, slower processing might be associated with lower spans simply because longer retention intervals allow more forgetting. On this account, different span tasks might well be associated with different rates of forgetting and hence different speed-span functions. Towse and Hitch (1995) investigated the role of forgetting by giving children a counting span task in which the attention demand and duration of counting operations were independently varied. If limited resources are shared between storage and processing, counting span should be lower when counting requires more attention. If, on the other hand, span is limited by rapid forgetting, it should be lower when counting takes longer. The result was that spans were unaffected by the attention demands of counting but were lower when counting took more time. Towse and Hitch proposed a task-switching hypothesis according to which children alternate between processing and storage in complex span tasks and are prone to forget stored information during processing.

In a subsequent study, Towse, Hitch, and Hutton (1998) manipulated the time during which children had to store generated items while holding the total duration of processing and its attention demand constant. This was done for counting span, reading span, and operation span. For all three tasks, spans were lower when the generated items had to be retained over longer delays, as task-switching would predict. Moreover, a similar pattern of results was seen in young adults (Towse, Hitch, & Hutton, 2000). However, the evidence for task switching has been questioned by Saito and Miyake (2004) and Barrouillet and Camos (2001), who suggested that the manipulation of processing duration may also have increased its cognitive cost. In a series of experiments, Barrouillet, Bernardin, and Camos (2004) showed that complex span in young adults depends on both the number of memory retrievals required by the processing task and the time allowed to perform them. They suggested a hybrid model of complex span in which processing and storage compete for attention and memory traces decay when attention is switched away from them. Such a hybrid account raises the possibility that development might involve a shift in the balance between resource sharing and task switching. For example, Hitch et al. (2001) suggested there might be a progression from an early bias in favour of task switching to a greater degree of resource sharing. This could be because younger children have insufficient executive resources to permit sharing, or because they have yet to acquire strategies that involve resource sharing. Although convincing tests of this hypothesis have yet

to be made, it is interesting to note that it may have some relevance to developmental change over the lifespan. Thus, analysis of dual-task performance suggests that any such developmental progression may eventually unwind in aging, with a return to dealing with complex events serially rather than in parallel (Broadbent & Heron, 1962).

Relationship to Cognitive Abilities

Studies of individual differences in children suggest a similar dissociation between simple and complex span to that seen in adults. Thus, listening span is a much better predictor of oral language comprehension than simple word span in 4-year-olds (Daneman & Blennerhassett, 1984). Similarly, listening span and counting span predict variation in reading ability over and above that due to word span in 7-year-olds (Leather & Henry, 1994). Moreover, as well as being able to predict children's abilities at the time of assessment, complex span is a useful predictor of future attainment. Thus, in a longitudinal study, Hitch et al. (2001) assessed children on counting span and reading span on two occasions a year apart. Children were also given standard tests of reading and arithmetic in the second session. Complex spans in the first session predicted children's reading and arithmetic a year later, and this was so even after taking out variance associated with complex spans at the time reading and arithmetic were assessed. This is a potentially important finding as it supports the view that working memory is a key resource not only for the execution of cognitive skills but also for their acquisition (see, e.g., Case, 1995).

Domain Specificity

Data on individual differences in children have also been used to address the issue of domain specificity in working memory. We noted earlier the suggestion that there may be different workspaces for different domains of knowledge, such as language and number (Just & Carpenter, 1992). Studies of children suggest that performance in complex span tasks involves a combination of domain-free and domain-specific processes. For example, Leather and Henry (1994) found that listening span and counting span accounted for both shared and unique variance in children's reading and arithmetic attainment. Similarly, Hitch et al. (2001) reported that children's reading spans and operation spans accounted for both shared and unique variance in performance on a test of reading ability. A heterogeneous pattern is also evident in studies of working memory in children with different types of learning difficulty. Thus, Siegel and Ryan (1989) found that children with reading difficulties were impaired relative to controls on listening span and counting span, whereas children with arithmetical difficulties were significantly impaired only on counting span (see also Hitch & MacAuley, 1991).

These findings form a consistent pattern but are not particularly easy to interpret theoretically. Thus, variance common to different complex span tasks is consistent with the hypothesis that they each involve a domain-free central executive, but does not rule out some other common factor. Furthermore, domain-specific variance is not strong evidence for separate workspaces. For example, domain-specific variance might be explained by assuming that complex span tasks involve a general resource interacting with domain-specific knowledge representations. Ericsson and Kintsch (1995) proposed this type of account to explain why working-memory capacity in adults is much higher in tasks that involve domains of knowledge where they have particular expertise. It seems there is no obvious developmental change here and that for children as in adults, performance in working-memory tasks appears to involve a combination of domain-free and domain-specific factors.

OUTSTANDING ISSUES

Earlier on we raised a number of issues that need to be addressed in any account of the development of working memory during childhood. Some aspects of these have already been dealt with while others require threads to be pulled together from different parts of the discussion. Here we comment briefly on each in turn.

Speed of Processing

How can we explain the ubiquitous improvements in performance on tasks that involve working memory during childhood? By far the most striking and general observation is that performance on all working memory tasks shows steady improvement during childhood. An intriguing question is whether this increase reflects an underlying biological change, and if so,

whether it is unique to working memory. We cannot comment on the biology given that our discussion has been confined to psychological data. However, we can assess one widely entertained version of this account according to which developmental improvements in task performance stem from a general increase in speed of processing (see, e.g., Kail, 1992). We note in particular evidence for persuasively strong associations between developmental improvements in simple word span and speech rate (Hulme et al., 1984; Hitch, Halliday, & Littler, 1989; Hitch et al., 1993) and between complex span and the speed of operations in the complex span task (Case et al., 1982; Hitch et al., 2001). Might these all be examples of a more general relationship involving a common underlying change? It is tempting to think so. Moreover it seems plausible to suppose that developmental change in the speed of neural transmission due to myelinization will have far-reaching ramifications at the cognitive level, to include other abilities besides working memory. However, there are strong arguments for supposing that changes in general information processing speed cannot provide a sufficient account of developmental changes in working memory.

One problem with an explanation in terms of general speed of processing is that empirical relationships between performance in working-memory or short-term memory tasks and processing speed are often specific to a particular type of processing operation. For example, Hitch, Halliday, & Littler (1989, 1993) contrasted speech rate with the speed of perceptually identifying items as predictors of age differences in simple span for verbal materials. As expected, the two speed measures were closely related. However, speech rate was much more closely associated with span, consistent with the idea that subvocal rehearsal is the crucial factor rather than a more general measure of speed of processing (see also Kail & Park, 1994). Other work has suggested that two differentially maturing types of processing speed contribute to the development of digit span (Cowan, 1999a). Turning to complex spans, Towse et al. (1998) found that reading span and operation spans were related to different measures of speed, and Hitch et al. (2001) noted that controlling for processing speed did not eliminate age differences in working memory, implying that developmental change involves additional factors. But perhaps the most destructive argument comes from the effects of expertise in memory for visuo-spatial information, where children with appropriate experience outperform adults (Chi, 1978). This is clearly impossible to explain simply in terms of a developmental change in general processing speed.

A further difficulty for the general speed hypothesis is that it offers no insight into qualitative developmental changes in working memory. Perhaps the most striking of these in the present discussion concerns the development of verbal recoding in tasks involving immediate memory for visual materials (Hitch et al., 1988; Hitch, Woodin, et al., 1989). Early on in development children are clearly reliant on visual codes, but later on there is a distinct shift to using phonological codes.

In conclusion, developmental improvements in processing speed during childhood seem likely to be one general factor contributing to developmental growth in working memory. However, it is also evident that such an account is not going to be sufficient, and that factors associated with specific components of working memory and domain-specific knowledge also need to be taken into account. A continuing challenge for future research is to more clearly separate the role of general processing speed from other factors in the development of working memory.

Structure of the Working Memory System

Does working memory have the same structure in children as in adults? It seems that, to a first approximation, the tripartite model proposed by Baddeley and Hitch (1974) and developed by Baddeley (1986) is applicable to children as well as adults. Thus, we noted earlier evidence for a dissociation between simple spans for visuo-spatial and verbal materials in children, consistent with the notion of separate slave stores. The distinction between the central executive and slave storage systems also seems to apply to children. We also noted earlier that complex spans are more strongly associated with cognitive abilities than simple spans in children, paralleling the general pattern seen in adults.

Some persuasive evidence on the structure of working memory in children comes from an extensive study of individual differences (Gathercole, Pickering, Ambridge, & Wearing, 2004). A large sample of children were give multiple assessments of the phonological loop (digit span, word span, nonword span), the visuo-spatial sketchpad (visual pattern span, a block recall task, a maze memory task), and three (verbal) complex span tasks (listening span, counting span, backwards digit span). Correlations between performance in these tasks showed that a three-factor statistical model corresponding to the multicomponent model of working memory (Baddeley & Hitch, 1974) gave a good fit to the data in different groups from ages 6 to 15. Furthermore, the three-factor model gave a consistently better fit than a simpler two-factor model. It seems on this evidence that the components of the tripartite model of working memory are in place throughout much of childhood development.

A further question is whether more detailed characteristics of working memory undergo developmental change. Where data are available, they speak in the main for developmental continuity in the various subsystems. We saw earlier that this is particularly clear in the case of the phonological loop, where variables such as phonemic similarity and word length have the same effects in children as in adults. The one notable exception was the importance of presentation modality in young children, which we have already discussed at some length. Young children's tendency not to recode visual inputs in simple span tasks suggests that conditions for accessing the phonological loop widen significantly as development proceeds. In the case of the visuo-spatial sketchpad, we noted that both children and adults are sensitive to the similarity of the shapes of stimuli in simple span tasks involving pictured items. Once again, however, there are subtle but potentially important developmental changes. Thus, we noted that visual similarity effects are more likely to be seen in adults when verbal recoding is prevented. We also considered the possibility that executive processes may undergo developmental change. One suggestion was that there is a developmental shift from serial control, as in task-switching accounts of complex span, to parallel processing, as in resource sharing models. However, as yet we do not know enough to draw clear conclusions on this point. A similar conclusion applies to domain specificity. The evidence suggests that complex spans in children typically involve a combination of domain-free and domain-specific resources, as in adults. However, these similarities are clearly somewhat general and may hide differences that would be revealed by more penetrating methods of analysis and investigation.

Functions of Working Memory

Does working memory serve the same functions in childhood? We noted earlier that a major function of the phonological loop in childhood may be to support the acquisition of new vocabulary. Interestingly, this function is by no means limited to learning one's native language. For example Service (1992) found that individual differences in a measure of the phonological loop predicted older children's acquisition of vocabulary in a second language two years later. Moreover, experiments on adults show that learning paired associates containing nonwords is sensitive to manipulations that affect the phonological loop (Papagno, Valentine, & Baddeley, 1991; Papagno & Vallar, 1992). Converging evidence comes from the study of a neuropsychological patient with a selective impairment to the phonological loop and an auditory-verbal span of only about two items (Vallar & Baddeley, 1984). This patient was unable to learn paired associates containing nonwords but performed normally on learning word-word pairs. It seems, then, that the link between the phonological loop and vocabulary acquisition extends from early childhood into adulthood.

Another function of the phonological loop that we have not discussed so far is its role in learning to read. It has been suggested that the phonological loop may be involved when children learn to sound out individual words (Baddeley, 1986). Several studies have shown that children with poor decoding skills do poorly on simple span tasks involving verbal materials (e.g., Shankweiler, Liberman, Mark, Fowler, & Fischer, 1979) while being unimpaired on memory for abstract visual stimuli (Katz, Shankweiler, & Liberman, 1981). However, it seems that there is not a simple relationship between the phonological loop and children's reading. For example, McDougall, Hulme, Ellis, and Monk (1994) found that tasks involving phoneme deletion and rhyme awareness were separate predictors of reading ability along with speech rate, and there was no independent relationship between reading and simple span for words.

Finally we note also that the phonological loop has been associated with a wider range of functions that we do not have space to review here. These include providing a backup store in arithmetic (Furst & Hitch, 2000; Logie, Gilhooly, & Wynn, 1994), in various language skills (Gathercole & Baddeley, 1993) and for keeping track of current goals (Miyake, Emerson, Padilla, & Ahn, 2004).

THE DEVELOPMENTAL RELATIONSHIP BETWEEN WORKING MEMORY AND KNOWLEDGE ACQUISITION

We discussed evidence that working memory is involved in various aspects of knowledge acquisition, and in particular the role of the phonological loop in learning new vocabulary (Baddeley et al., 1998). However, we noted also that the evidence goes beyond knowledge of vocabulary. For example, complex span is a longitudinal predictor of children's reading and arithmetic attainment, consistent with a general role of working memory in learning (Hitch et al., 2001). Another side of the same general picture is that impairments in working memory tend to be associated with learning difficulties (Gathercole & Pickering, 2000; Siegel & Ryan, 1989; Hitch & MacAuley, 1991). Complementary to the role of working memory in learning is evidence that performance on working-memory and short-term memory tasks benefits from learned knowledge, whether low-level phonotactic knowledge (Gathercole, Frankish, Pickering, & Peaker, 1999) or high-level chunks (Broadbent & Broadbent, 1981; Chi, 1978; Ericsson & Kintsch, 1995). Thus, it seems that childhood development involves a fundamental synergy whereby working memory both contributes to the acquisition of knowledge and in turn benefits from its acquisition. The implication is that working memory is not only a workspace for complex thought but also a valuable resource for acquiring knowledge. However, this is not to suggest that working memory is central to all types of learning. For example, it is generally accepted that implicit learning is not dependent on working memory.

The organization of knowledge through chunking seems to be a surprisingly underexplored aspect of developmental change. Baddeley's (2000) proposed episodic buffer seems likely to be relevant here as one of its functions is to integrate new and previously learned information. The observation that chunk size is limited, even for experts (Chase & Ericsson, 1981), certainly seems to fit well with the idea that chunk formation involves a limited capacity system (see also Cowan, 2001). One can speculate that the episodic buffer may be an important part of the mechanism whereby chunks are learned. If so, one might expect a developmental increase in the domain specificity of performance in working-memory tasks as the scope for the episodic buffer to integrate information from different regions of long-term memory expands.

It is interesting to note that the synergy between working memory and knowledge acquisition in childhood may take a different form in aging. Whereas knowledge (or crystallized intelligence) continues to increase over the lifespan, fluid intelligence and measures of working memory decline. How might we explain this? Numerous possibilities have been discussed. However, in terms of the issues raised here, the pattern of aging seems difficult to explain without assuming a fundamental distinction between working memory and long-term memory. Thus, a progressive decline in working memory capacity over the lifespan is perfectly compatible with the steady accumulation of knowledge at the same time. Notice, however, that this argument does not imply that working memory is an entirely separate system from long-term memory. Thus, what declines with age could be the capacity of a separate store, such as the episodic buffer, or the resources available to activate long-term memory. Either possibility is consistent with the total contents of long-term memory continuing to grow at the same time.

CONCLUSION

It should be clear by now that while we know a good deal about working memory and its development in childhood, there is much that we still have to learn. Overall there seems to be a good deal of continuity in the multicomponent structure of working memory from early childhood to young adulthood. However, this is modified by qualitative changes in control processes relating to the use of modality-specific stores and (possibly) the operation of the central executive. Moreover, the general functions of working memory in supporting learning and cognition seem to be the much the same in children and adults, despite evident differences in the content of what is learned and the cognitive tasks that are performed. Finally, we have seen that one of the most intriguing and underexplored sets of theoretical and empirical issues concerns the relationship between working memory and long-term memory. This relationship seems to be important not only for understanding cognitive development in children but also for unravelling the cognitive decline seen in aging.

References

Andrade, J. (2001). The working memory model: Consensus, controversy, and future directions. In J. Andrade (Ed.), *Working memory in perspective* (pp. 281–310). Hove: Psychology Press.

Baddeley, A. D. (1986). *Working memory*. Oxford: Oxford University Press.

Baddeley, A. D. (1996). Exploring the central executive. *Quarterly Journal of Experimental Psychology*, *49A*(1), 5.28.

Baddeley, A. D. (2000). The episodic buffer: A new component of working memory? *Trends in Cognitive Sciences*, *4*(11), 417–423.

Baddeley, A. D., Gathercole, S., & Papagno, C. (1998). The phonological loop as a language learning device. *Psychological Review*, *105*(1), 158–173.

Baddeley, A. D., & Hitch, G. J. (1974). Working memory. In G. A. Bower (Ed.), *Recent advances in learning and motivation* (Vol. 8, pp. 47–90). New York: Academic Press.

Baddeley, A. D., & Hitch, G. (2000). Development of working memory: Should the Pascual-Leone and Baddeley and Hitch models be merged? *Journal of Experimental Child Psychology*, *77*, 128–137.

Baddeley, A. D., Lewis, V. J., & Vallar, G. (1984). Exploring the articulatory loop. *Quarterly Journal of Experimental Psychology*, *36*, 233–252.

Baddeley, A. D., & Logie, R. H. (1999). Working memory: The multiple-component model. In A. Miyake & P. Shah (Eds.), *Models of working memory* (pp. 28–61). New York: Cambridge University Press.

Baddeley, A. D., Thomson, N., & Buchanan, M. (1975). Word length and the structure of short-term memory. *Journal of Verbal Learning and Verbal Behavior*, *14*, 575–589.

Barrouillet, P., Bernardin, S., & Camos, V. (2004). Time constraints and resource sharing in adults' working memory spans. *Journal of Experimental Psychology: General*, *133*,83–100..

Barrouillet, P., & Camos, V. (2001). Developmental increase in working memory span: Resource sharing or temporal decay? *Journal of Memory and Language*, *45*, 1–20.

Broadbent, D. E., & Broadbent, M. H. P. (1981). Articulatory suppression and the grouping of sucessive stimuli. *Psychological Research*, *43*, 57–67.

Broadbent, D. E., & Heron, A. (1962). Effects of a subsidiary task on performance involving immediate memory by younger and older men. *British Journal of Psychology*, *53*, 189–198.

Burgess, N., & Hitch, G. J. (1999). Memory for serial order: A network model of the phonological loop and its timing. *Psychological Review*, *106*, 551–581.

Case, R. D. (1995). Capacity-based explanations of working memory growth: A brief history and reevaluation. In F. E. Weinert & W. Schneider (Eds.),

Memory performance and competencies: Issues in growth and development (pp. 23–44). Mahwah, NJ: Lawrence Erlbaum Associates.

Case, R. D., Kurland, D. M., & Goldberg, J. (1982). Operational efficiency and the growth of short-term memory span. *Journal of Experimental Child Psychology, 33,* 386–404.

Chase, W. G., & Ericsson, K. A. (1981). Skilled memory. In J. R. Anderson (Ed.), *Cognitive skills and their acquisition* (pp. 141–189). Hillsdale, N.J.: Lawrence Erlbaum Associates.

Chase, W. G., & Simon, H. A. (1973). Perception in chess. *Cognitive Psychology, 4,* 55–81.

Chi, M. T. H. (1978). Knowledge structures and memory development. In R. Siegler (Ed.), *Children's thinking: What develops?* (pp. 5–29). Hillsdale, NJ.: Lawrence Erlbaum Associates.

Chuah, Y. M. L., & Maybery, M. T. (1999). Verbal and spatial short-term memory: Common sources of developmental change? *Journal of Experimental Child Psychology, 73,* 7–44.

Conrad, R., & Hull, A. J. (1964). Information, acoustic confusion, and memory span. *British Journal of Developmental Psychology, 55,* 429–432.

Cornoldi, C., & Vecchi, T. (2003). *Visuo-spatial working memory and individual differences.* Hove: Psychology Press.

Cowan, N. (1995). *Attention and memory: An integrated framework.* New York: Oxford University Press.

Cowan, N. (1999a). The differential maturation of two processing rates related to digit span. *Journal of Experimental Child Psychology, 72,* 193–209.

Cowan, N. (1999b). An embedded-processes model of working memory. In A. Miyake & P. Shah (Eds.), *Models of working memory* (pp. 62–101). Cambridge, UK: Cambridge University Press.

Cowan, N. (2001). The magical number 4 in short-term memory: A reconsideration of mental storage capacity. *Behavioral and Brain Sciences, 24,* 87–114.

Daneman, M., & Blennerhassett, A. (1984). How to assess the listening comprehension skills of prereaders. *Journal of Educational Psychology, 76,* 1372–1381.

Daneman, M., & Carpenter, P. A. (1980). Individual differences in working memory and reading. *Journal of Verbal Learning and Verbal Behavior, 19,* 450–466.

Daneman, M., & Merikle, P. M. (1996). Working memory and comprehension: A meta-analysis. *Psychonomic Bulletin & Review, 3,* 422–433.

Daneman, M., & Tardif, T. (1987). Working memory and reading skill re-examined. In M. Coltheart (Ed.), *Attention and performance XII: The psychol-*

ogy of reading (pp. 491–508). Hillsdale, NJ: Lawrence Erlbaum Associates.

Dark, V. J., & Benbow, C. P. (1990). Enhanced problem translation and short-term memory: Components of mathematical talent. *Journal of Educational Psychology, 82,* 420–429.

Dempster, F. N. (1981). Memory span: sources of individual and developmental differences. *Psychological Bulletin, 89,* 63–100.

DeRenzi, E., & Nichelli, P. (1975). Verbal and non-verbal short-term memory impairment following hemishperic damage. *Cortex, 11,* 341–353.

Engle, R. W., Tuholski, S. W., Laughlin, J. E., & Conway, A. R. A. (1999). Working memory, short-term memory, and general fluid intelligence: A latent variable approach. *Journal of Experimental Psychology: General, 128,* 309–331.

Ericsson, K. A., & Kintsch, W. (1995). Long-term working memory. *Psychological Review, 102*(2), 211–245.

Fastenau, P. S., Conant, L. L., & Lauer, R. E. (1998). Working memory in young children: Evidence for modality-specificity and implications for cerebral reorganization in early childhood. *Neuropsychologia, 36,* 643–652.

Fenner, J., Heathcote, D., & Jerrams-Smith, J. (2000). The development of wayfinding competency: Asymmetrical effects of verbal and spatial ability. *Journal of Environmental Psychology, 20*(2), 165–175.

Furst, A., & Hitch, G. J. (2000). Separate roles for executive and phonological components of working memory in mental arithmetic. *Memory & Cognition, 28,* 774–782.

Gathercole, S. E. (1995). Is nonword repetition a test of phonological memory or long-term knowledge? It all depends on the nonwords. *Memory & Cognition, 23,* 83–94.

Gathercole, S. E. (1999). Cognitive approaches to the development of short-term memory. *Trends in Cognitive Sciences, 3,* 410–418.

Gathercole, S. E., & Baddeley, A. D. (1993). *Working memory and language.* Hove, Sussex: Lawrence Erlbaum Associates.

Gathercole, S. E., & Baddeley, A. D. (1996). *The children's test of non-word repetition.* London: Psychological Corporation.

Gathercole, S. E., Frankish, C. R., Pickering, S. J., & Peaker, S. (1999). Phonotactic influences on short-term memory. *Journal of Experimental Psychology: Learning Memory & Cognition, 25,* 84–95.

Gathercole, S. E., Hitch, G. J., Service, E., & Martin, A. (1997). Phonological short-term memory and new word learning in children. *Developmental Psychology, 33,* 966–979.

Gathercole, S. E., & Pickering, S. J. (2000). Working memory deficits in children with low achievements in the national curriculum at 7 years of age. *British Journal of Educational Psychology, 70,* 177–194.

Gathercole, S. E., Pickering, S. J., Ambridge, B., & Wearing, H. (2004). The structure of working memory from 4 to 15 years of age. *Developmental Psychology, 40*(2), 177–190.

Guttentag, R. E. (1995). Mental effort and motivation: Influences on children's memory strategy use. In W. Schneider & F. E. Weinert (Eds.), *Memory performance and competencies: Issues in growth and development* (pp. 207–224). Northvale, NJ: Lawrence Erlbaum Associates.

Hasher, L., & Zacks, R. T. (1988). Working memory, comprehension, and aging: A review and a new view. In G. H. Bower (Ed.), *The psychology of learning and motivation* (pp. 193–225). New York: Academic Press.

Henson, R. (2001). Neural working memory. In J. Andrade (Ed.), *Working memory in perspective* (pp. 151–174.). Hove: Psychology Press.

Hitch, G. J., Brandimonte, M. A., & Walker, P. (1995). Two types of representation in visual memory: Evidence from the effects of stimulus contrast on image combination. *Memory & Cognition, 23,* 147–154.

Hitch, G. J., Halliday, M. S., Dodd, A., & Littler, J. E. (1989). Development of rehearsal in short-term memory: Differences between pictorial and spoken stimuli. *British Journal of Developmental Psychology, 7,* 347–362.

Hitch, G. J., Halliday, M. S., & Littler, J. E. (1989). Item identification time, rehearsal rate and memory span in children. *Quarterly Journal of Experimental Psychology, 41A,* 321–337.

Hitch, G. J., Halliday, M. S., & Littler, J. E. (1993). Development of memory span for spoken words: The role of rehearsal and item identification processes. *British Journal of Developmental Psychology, 11,* 159–169.

Hitch, G. J., Halliday, M. S., Schaafstal, A., & Schraagen, J. M. (1988). Visual working memory in young children. *Memory & Cognition, 16,* 120–132.

Hitch, G. J., & MacAuley, E. (1991). Working memory in children with specific arithmetical learning difficulties. *British Journal of Psychology, 82,* 375–386.

Hitch, G. J., Towse, J. N., & Hutton, U. (2001). What limits children's working memory span? Theoretical accounts and application to scholastic development. *Journal of Experimental Child Psychology, 77,* 128–137.

Hitch, G. J., Woodin, M. E., & Baker, S. (1989). Visual and phonological components of working memory in children. *Memory & Cognition, 17,* 175.

Hulme, C., Roodenrys, S., Schweikert, R., Brown, G. D. A., Martin, A., & Stuart, G. (1997). Word-frequency effects on short-term memory tasks: Evidence for a redintegration process in immediate serial recall. *Journal of Experimental Psychology: Learning, Memory and Cognition, 23,* 1217–1232.

Hulme, C., Thomson, N., Muir, C., & Lawrence, W. A. (1984). Speech rate and the development of short-term memory span. *Journal of Experimental Child Psychology, 38,* 241–253.

Huttenlocher, J., & Burke, D. (1976). Why does memory span increase with age? *Cognitive Psychology, 8,* 1–31.

Isaacs, E. B., & Vargha-Khadem, F. (1989). Differential course of development of spatial and verbal memory span: A normative study. *British Journal of Developmental Psychology, 7*(4), 377–380.

Jarrold, C., Baddeley, A. D., & Hewes, A. K. (1999). Genetically dissociated components of working memory: evidence from Down's and Williams syndrome. *Neuropsychologia, 37,* 637–651.

Joanisse, M., & Seidenberg, M. S. (1998). Specific language impairment: A deficit in grammar or in processing? *Trends in Cognitive Sciences, 2,* 240–246.

Just, M. A., & Carpenter, P. A. (1992). The capacity theory of comprehension: Individual differences in working memory. *Psychological Review, 99,* 122–149.

Kail, R. (1992). Processing speed, speech rate, and memory. *Developmental Psychology, 28,* 899–904.

Kail, R., & Park, Y. (1994). Processing time, articulation time, and memory span. *Journal of Experimental Child Psychology, 57,* 281–291.

Katz, R. B., Shankweiler, D., & Liberman, I. Y. (1981). Memory for item order and phonetic recoding in the beginning reader. *Journal of Experimental Child Psychology, 32,* 474–484.

Kemps, E., De Rammelaere, S., & Desmet, T. (2000). The development of working memory: Exploring the complementarity of two models. *Journal of Experimental Child Psychology, 77,* 89–109.

Leather, C. V., & Henry, L. A. (1994). Working memory span and phonological awareness tasks as predictors of early reading abilily. *Journal of Child Psychology, 58,* 88–111.

Logie, R. H. (1995). *Visuo-spatial working memory.* Hove, UK: Lawrence Erlbaum Associates.

Logie, R. H., Della Sala, S., Wynn, V., & Baddeley, A. D. (2000). Visual similarity effects in immediate serial recall. *Quarterly Journal of Experimental Psychology, 53A*(3), 626–646.

Logie, R. H., Gilhooly, K. J., & Wynn, C. (1994). Counting on working memory in arithmetic problem solving. *Memory & Cognition, 22*(4), 395–410.

Logie, R. H., & Pearson, D. G. (1997). The inner eye and the inner scribe of visuo-spatial working memory: Evidence from developmental fraction-ation. *European Journal of Cognitive Psychology*, 9(3), 241–257.

Longoni, A. M., & Scalisi, T. G. (1994). Developmental aspects of phonemic and visual similarity effects: Further evidence in Italian children. *International Journal Behavioral Development*, 17, 57–71.

Luciana, M., & Nelson, C. A. (1998). The functional emergence of prefrontally-guided working memory systems in four- to eight-year-old children. *Neuropsychologia*, 36(3), 273–293.

Luck, S. J., & Vogel, E. K. (1997). The capacity of visual working memory for features and conjunctions. *Nature*, 390, 279–281.

McDougall, S., Hulme, C., Ellis, A., & Monk, A. (1994). Learning to read: The role of short-term memory and phonological skills. *Journal of Experimental Child Psychology*, 58, 112–133.

McLeod, P., & Posner, M. I. (1984). Privileged loops from percept to act. In H. Bouma & D. G. Bouwhuis (Eds.), *Attention and performance X* (pp. 55–66). London: Lawrence Erlbaum Associates.

Metsala, J. L. (1999). Young children's phonological awareness and nonword repetition as a function of vocabulary development. *Journal of Educational Psychology*, 91, 3–19.

Miller, G. A. (1956). The magical number seven, plus or minus two: Some limits on our capacity for processing information. *Psychological Review*, 63, 81–97.

Milner, B. (1971). Interhemispheric differences in the localization of psychological processes in man. *British Medical Bulletin*, 27, 272–277.

Miyake, A., Emerson, M. J., Padilla, F., & Ahn, J. (2004). Inner speech as a retrieval aid for task goals: The effects of cue type and articulatory suppression in the random task cuing paradigm. *Acta Psychologica*, 115, 123–142.

Miyake, A., Friedman, N. P., Emerson, M. J., Witzki, A. H., Howeter, B. E., & Wager, T. (2000). The unity and diversity of executive functins and their contributions to complex "frontal lobe" tasks: A latent variable analysis. *Cognitive Psychology*, 41, 49–100.

Murray, D. J. (1967). The role of speech responses in short-term memory. *Canadian Journal of Psychology*, 21, 263–276.

Paivio, A. (1971). *Imagery and verbal processes*. New York: Holt, Rinehart & Winston.

Palmer, S. (2000). Working memory: a developmental study of phonological recoding. *Memory*, 8, 179–194.

Papagno, C., Valentine, T., & Baddeley, A. D. (1991). Phonological short-term memory and foreign-language vocabulary learning. *Journal of Memory and Language*, 30, 331–347.

Papagno, C., & Vallar, G. (1992). Phonological short-term memory and the learning of novel words: The effect of phonological similarity and item length. *Quarterly Journal of Experimental Psychology*, 44A, 47–67.

Paulesu, E., Frith, C. D., & Frackowiak, R. S. J. (1993). The neural correlates of the verbal component of working memory. *Nature*, 362, 342–345.

Pickering, S. J. (2001). The development of visuo-spatial working memory. *Memory*, 9, 423–432.

Pickering, S. J., Gathercole, S. E., Hall, M., & Lloyd, S. A. (2001). Development of memory for pattern and path: Further evidence for the fractionation of visual and spatial short-term memory. *Quarterly Journal of Experimental Psychology*, 54A, 397–420.

Pickering, S. J., Gathercole, S. E., & Peaker, S. H. (1998). Verbal and visuo-spatial short-term memory in children: Evidence for common and distinct mechanisms. *Memory & Cognition*, 26, 1117–1130.

Raffone, A., & Wolters, G. (2001). A cortical mechanism for binding in visual working memory. *Journal of Cognitive Neuroscience*, 13(6), 766–785.

Roodenrys, S., Hulme, C., & Brown, G. (1993). The development of short-term memory span: Separable effects of speech rate and long-term memory. *Journal of Experimental Child Psychology*, 56, 431–442.

Saito, S., & Miyake, A. (2004). On the nature of forgetting and the processing-storage relationship in reading span performance. *Journal of Memory and Language*, 50, 425–443.

Schiano, D. J., & Watkins, M. J. (1981). Speech-like coding of pictures in short-term memory. *Memory & Cognition*, 9, 100–114.

Service, E. (1992). Phonology, working memory and foreign-language learning. *Quarterly Journal of Experimental Psychology Section A—Human*, 45(1), 21–50.

Shah, P., & Miyake, A. (1996). The separability of working memory resources for spatial thinking and language processing: An individual differences approach. *Journal of Experimental Psychology: General*, 125, 4–27.

Shah, P., & Miyake, A. (1999). Models of Working Memory: An introduction. In A. Miyake & P. Shah (Eds.), *Models of working memory: Mechanisms of active maintenance and executive control*. New York: Cambridge University Press.

Shallice, T., & Warrington, E. K. (1970). Independent functioning of verbal memory stores: A neuropsychological study. *Quarterly Journal of Experimental Psychology*, 22, 261–273.

Shankweiler, D., Liberman, I. Y., Mark, L. S., Fowler, C. A., & Fischer, F. W. (1979). The speech code and learning to read. *Journal of Experimental Psychology: Human Learning and memory*, 5, 531–545.

Siegel, L. S., & Ryan, E. B. (1989). The development of working memory in normally achieving and subtypes of learning disabled children. *Child Development*, 60, 973–980.

Smith, E. E., & Jonides, J. (1997). Working memory: A view from neuroimaging. *Cognitive Psychology*, 33, 5–42.

Smyth, M. M., & Scholey, K. A. (1992). Determining spatial span: The role of movement time and articulation rate. *Quarterly Journal of Experimental Psychology*, 45A, 479–501.

Snowling, M., Chiat, S., & Hulme, C. (1991). Words, nonwords, and phonological processes: Some comments on Gathercole, Willis, Emslie and Baddeley. *Applied Psycholinguists*, 12(3), 369–373.

Towse, J. N., & Hitch, G. J. (1995). Is there a relationship between task demand and storage space in tests of working memory capacity? *Quarterly Journal of Experimental Psychology*, 48A(1), 108–124.

Towse, J. N., Hitch, G. J., & Hutton, U. (1998). A reevaluation of working memory capacity in children. *Journal of Memory and Language*, 39, 195–217.

Towse, J. N., Hitch, G. J., & Hutton, U. (2000). On the interpretation of working memory span in adults. *Memory & Cognition*, 28(3), 341–348.

Vallar, G., & Baddeley, A. D. (1984). Phonological short-term store, phonological processing and sentence comprehension: A neuropsychological case study. *Cognitive Neuropsychology*, 1, 121–141.

Walker, P., Hitch, G. J., & Duroe, S. (1993). The effect of visual similarity on short-term memory for spatial location: Implication for the capacity of visual short-term memory. *Acta Psychologica*, 83, 203–224.

Wang, P. P., & Bellugi, U. (1994). Evidence from two genetic syndromes for a dissociation between verbal and visual-spatial short-term memory. *Journal of Clinical and Experimental Neuropsychology*, 16, 317–322.

Willis, C. S., & Gathercole, S. E. (2001). Phonological short-term memory contributions to sentence processing in young children. *Memory*, 9(4), 349–363.

Wilson, J. T. L., Scott, J. H., & Power, K. G. (1987). Developmental differences in the span of visual memory for pattern. *Journal of Cognitive Neuroscience*, 13, 766–785.

9

Working Memory Across
the Adult Lifespan

Denise C. Park

Doris Payer

Working memory is a fundamental construct in the study of cognition. It refers to the contents and mental activities associated with conscious awareness. Working memory is a relatively recent newcomer to the lexicon of cognitive psychologists. It is not a term that was used in the classic volume *Cognitive Psychology* authored by Ulrich Neisser in 1967, and was introduced in 1974 by Alan Baddeley and Graham Hitch. Prior to the introduction of the term *working memory*, theorists had distinguished between short-term (primary) and long-term (secondary) memory (Atkinson & Shiffrin, 1968). Both short- and long-term memory were conceptualized as passive stores with short-term memory having limited storage capacity and rapidly decaying traces. Information was hypothesized to flow from short-term memory into a large, more permanent long-term storage because of rehearsal. The unsatisfying aspect of such models was that they were largely structural and did not have a locus for the manipulation, transformation, and processing of information beyond rehearsal. Thus, the distinguishing feature of the working-memory

construct as it is conceptualized today is that it integrates both the storage and the processing aspects of information, better reflecting the experience of consciousness.

As an everyday life example of working memory, consider that you have just gotten off of a plane at the airport and you have a connecting flight in one hour. You are likely holding the information about time and destination in your working memory and rapidly scan the departure sign for your departing gate. You notice that there is a flight leaving for your destination in 20 minutes, and after some rapid computations about how far the gate is, what time it presently is, whether the flight is likely to be full, whether or not you checked luggage, and if you need to stop for some food, you decide to race for the earlier flight. This rapid flow of information requires not just passive storage of facts, but generation of information and manipulation and evaluation of alternatives that are not readily captured by a passive storage model. However, if you conceptualize both generated and available new information as flowing into a passive short-term store that is rapidly examined and transformed by a central executive system, and then either discarded or kept for further maintenance, one's actual experience is more accurately described. This ability to both maintain information in a transient short-term store of limited capacity and simultaneously manipulate and transform the information is the hallmark of working memory. In contrast, short-term memory is typically measured by the number of items that can be passively stored in consciousness without any manipulation of items.

The initial model of working memory proposed by Baddeley and Hitch (1974) and further detailed in Baddeley (1986) is a three-component model. According to this view, working memory consists of a central executive system responsible for manipulating, transforming, deleting, and adding information that gains entrance to two subsystems of the central executive. These subsystems are limited-capacity passive stores constituting a phonological loop that stores verbal information and the visuo-spatial sketch pad that maintains visuo-spatial information. The phonological loop is similar to earlier conceptions of short-term memory (Atkinson & Shiffrin, 1968). An alternative to this model is an independent systems model, where both visuo-spatial and verbal components of working memory are independent of one another with each having its own storage plus processing components (Shah & Miyake, 1996). A third model is one where working memory is a general cognitive resource without clear divisions between storage and processing mechanisms (Engle, Kane, & Tuholski, 1999).

In this chapter we will focus on changes in working memory from young to late adulthood. The construct of working memory has been central in the study of cognitive aging. Even prior to the advent of the formal construct of working memory, cognitive aging researchers had suggested that older adults showed decreased "mental energy," or had decreased "processing resources" available to them. It was common to explain findings on memory tasks where older adults performed more poorly than young adults as being due to decreased processing resources (Craik & Byrd, 1982). The development of the construct of working memory was particularly important to theory development in cognitive aging, as it provided a way to measure the construct of processing resource and to determine whether age-related shrinkage in working-memory capacity was the basis for decreased age-related performance on a range of cognitive tasks. As

a result, the construct of working memory has held a central place in the study of cognitive aging since its introduction into the cognitive lexicon. Although there are other measures of processing resource (e.g., speed of processing, inhibitory function), and other constructs closely related to working memory function (e.g., executive processes such as inhibitory function and task switching proficiency), we will focus almost exclusively on working memory in the present chapter, given its centrality to theorizing in cognitive aging. We will initially review different tasks used to measure working memory in laboratory and clinical settings. Then we will examine data on the lifespan trajectory of working-memory function, followed by central questions about cognitive aging that can be addressed, if not resolved, through the study of working memory and interference effects associated with working memory. Following this, we will consider the neural correlates of working memory, and then compare developments in the study of working memory in children and older adults, and close with promising directions for future research.

MEASURES OF WORKING MEMORY

There are many different tasks to measure working memory, but common to all measures is the requirement that an individual both store and "process"—that is, transform or manipulate information. Thus, simple span measures of how many items can be repeated back in order are measures of short-term memory (or the phonological loop subsystem in working memory), and such simple span measures are not as sensitive to age-related decline as measures of working memory (Craik & Jennings, 1992). Complex span tasks are typically used to measure working memory. Perhaps the simplest of these is the backward digit span from the Wechsler Adult Intelligence Scale (WAIS) (Wechsler, 1997a), where working memory capacity is measured by how many numbers presented auditorily in a string can be reported backwards. The problem with this measure is that on studies that have examined the factor structure of working memory, backward digit span tends to be age insensitive and load more on measures of short-term span than working memory (Park et al., 2002). A better psychometric alternative is the Wechsler Memory Scale Letter-Number Sequencing task (Wechsler, 1997b). In this task, subjects are presented with a string of letters and digits that are interspersed (e.g., "G81BT5"). The task is to repeat the sequence back in alphanumeric order (e.g., "BGT158"), a task that requires substantial mental manipulation and transformation of the information presented. An excellent source of clinical tests used to measure working memory can be found in Spreen and Strauss (1991).

From a laboratory perspective, the best known and most widely used measure of working memory is the reading span task developed by Daneman and Carpenter (1980), which involves presenting subjects with a series of sentences and requiring them to both answer a question about each sentence (processing) and remember the last word in each sentence (maintenance). Working memory is measured by the number of sentences in the series the individual can manage before making an error on either task. Reading span has been used extensively in the study of cognitive aging, as has computational span, a measure developed by Salthouse and Babcock (1991) that involves completing a simple equation while remembering the last number in the equation. A useful visuospatial task is the Self-ordered Pointing Task (Petrides & Milner, 1982) which has a substantial monitoring component that is well described in Shimamura and Jurica (1994). Finally, researchers who have neuroimaged working memory in older adults have often relied on an *n*-back procedure, where subjects are continuously presented with a series of items such as digits, letters, or locations, and they must compare the current item with the item that was presented one, two, or three items earlier, depending on the value assigned by the experimenter (Smith & Jonides, 1999). Good sources of working memory tasks, both verbal and visuospatial, typically used in cognitive aging laboratories can be found in Salthouse (1994), Park and colleagues (2000), and Jenkins, Myerson, Joerding, and Hale (2000).

THE DEVELOPMENTAL TRAJECTORY OF WORKING MEMORY

Studies that have measured working-memory capacity in adult lifespan samples have found that it is greatest in young adulthood and shows a downward trajectory across the lifespan (Park et al., 1996; Park et al., 2002). As Figure 9.1a shows, the decreases begin in the 20s with gradual and regular declines in group performance each decade. These effects are particularly convincing when one considers that the

older adults represented in Figure 9.1 had higher verbal ability scores than younger adults, and that with each decade they represent an increasingly select component of the population owing to the proportionately larger numbers of individuals who are unavailable for testing because of death or illness as age increases. It is when considering this "decline" function that the differentiation between working memory and short-term memory becomes apparent. Note that figure 9.1b, which presents short-term memory function in the same subjects as those in Figure 9.1a, demonstrates much less decline in span measures compared to working memory. The tasks used could be considered measures of Baddeley's (1986) passive subsystems (the phonological loop and visuospatial sketch pad) that feed into the central executive. The verbally based tasks were Backward and Forward Digits (Wechsler, 1997a) and the visuospatial tasks were Backward and Forward Corsi Blocks (Wechsler, 1997b), a task where subjects simply replicate the order in which the experimenter points to a series of blocks. Thus, Figures 9.1a and 9.1b together demonstrate the greater age sensitivity of the central executive relative to the storage-based subsystems. Finally, it is important as well for this discussion to recognize that not all abilities decline with age. Figure 9.1c presents performance on three measures of verbal knowledge, Shipley vocabulary (Shipley, 1986), and a synonyms and antonyms test developed by Salthouse (1993a). Recent work has indicated that older adults rely more on knowledge and verbal skills than young adults do when performing higher order cognitive tasks, conceivably to compensate for declines in working-memory function (Hedden, Lautenschlager, & Park, 2004).

There is some controversy as to whether decline in working-memory function is more pronounced with age for visuo-spatial measures of working memory than for verbal measures. The data from Park et al. (2002) presented in Figure 9.1a suggest that visuo-spatial and verbal memory decline at an equivalent rate in young and old adults, as the functions are identical for the four tasks represented, and two of the tasks presented were visuo-spatial in nature (line span and letter rotation) and two were verbal (computational span and word span). Salthouse, Kausler, & Saults (1988) reached a similar conclusion from a large lifespan sample from which they collected short-term span measures. This conclusion is in stark contrast, however, to the findings of Jenkins, Myerson, Joerding, and Hale (2000), who reported larger differences in work-

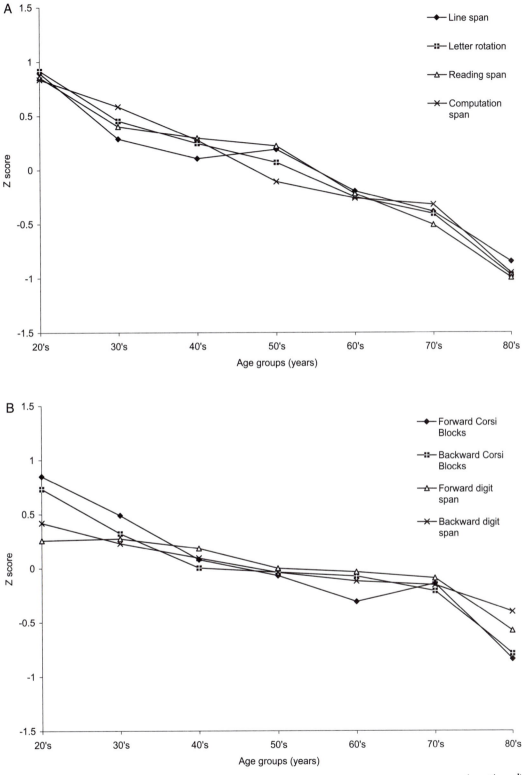

FIGURE 9.1. Lifespan performance on: (A) working memory measures (visuo-spatial and verbal); (B) short-term memory measures (visuo-spatial and verbal); (*continued*)

(*continued*)

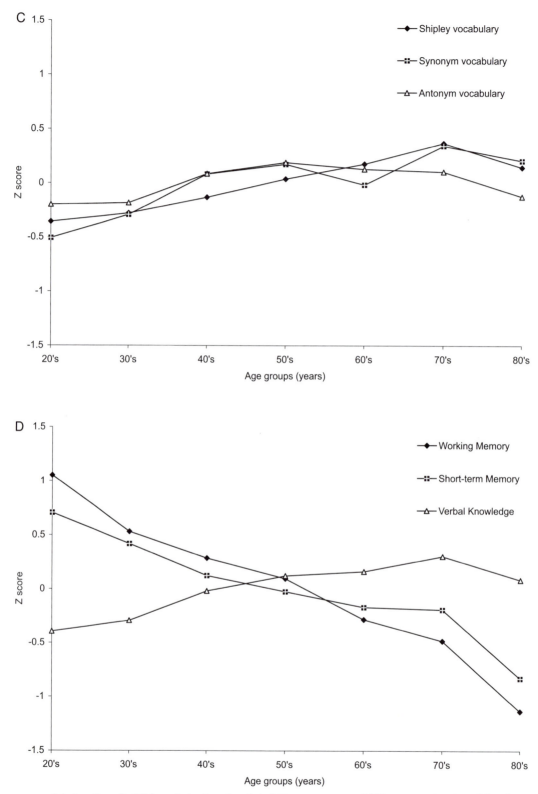

FIGURE 9.1. (*continued*) (C) knowledge-based verbal ability measures; and (D) a composite view of the above measures. Composite scores for each construct represent the z score of the average of all measures for that construct.

ing-memory spans in old adults compared to young for visuo-spatial compared to verbal items, suggesting a greater decline in visuo-spatial working memory than verbal memory with age.

There are some important differences, however, between these studies. The Park et al. (2002) study normalized scores from the different working-memory tasks into Z scores, whereas the Jenkins et al. (2000) study relied on raw scores, using a complex interpolation procedure to calculate span. What this means is that the Park et al. (2002) procedure addressed the question of how span scores were distributed as a function of age in 351 adults across the lifespan. The results from this approach indicated that lower scores on all types of working-memory tasks were increasingly likely with increasing age and that the orderings did not differ as a function of the modality of the task. In contrast, the Jenkins et al. (2000) procedure attempted to equate the demands of the visuo-spatial and verbal working-memory tasks and then examined differences in absolute levels of performance in two groups of subjects (16 young and 16 older adults), leading to the inference that there was greater decline in older adults on visuo-spatial tasks compared to verbal. It is difficult to completely equate task difficulty in different modalities, and it seems likely that the use of Z scores would yield similar findings for the Jenkins et al. (2000) and Park et al. (2002) data.

The neuroscience data also support equivalent decline with age. It is well documented that frontal cortex, an area heavily utilized for the performance of working-memory tasks, shrinks with age (Raz, 2000). Because there is equivalent shrinkage of left and right frontal cortex, with the left hemisphere specialized for verbal processes and the right for visuo-spatial processes, the volumetric data point to equivalent decline. Functional data show that older adults evidence bilateral activation, utilizing both left and right hemispheres to perform a working-memory task (Reuter-Lorenz et al., 2000) that younger adults perform with only one hemisphere, also suggesting equivalence between the two hemispheres. Jenkins et al. (2000) suggest that computational models that assume differential neural connectivity for visuo-spatial and verbal information, which would not be detected by functional or structural imaging, may be a fruitful way to understand the effects they observed. At this point, the question of differential decline in these two domains is open with evidence on both sides, but from our perspective there is more support for equivalent than

differential decline. Nevertheless, more work on this issue remains to be done, particularly since there are so few studies on this important topic.

THEORETICAL ISSUES ASSOCIATED WITH THE STUDY OF WORKING MEMORY

As mentioned earlier, working memory represents a core theoretical construct in cognitive aging, with the presumption that age-related declines in this resource affect performance on many higher order laboratory tasks as well as function on real-world tasks where working memory resources might be important.

Does Working-Memory Capacity Affect Performance on Other Tasks?

There is a rich history in the cognitive aging literature of treating working memory as an individual difference variable and then relating it to performance on higher order cognitive tasks. An initial test of the hypothesis that age-related declines in working memory affect cognitive performance was conducted by Stine and Wingfield (1987), who reported that working-memory capacity mediated age-related variance on a speech recall task. In later work, Salthouse and colleagues reported that working-memory function accounted for age-related variance on laboratory measures of reasoning (Salthouse, 1991, 1992, 1993b; Verhaeghen & Salthouse, 1997). Cherry and Park (1993) examined the relationship of working memory to a complex spatial memory task. Subjects studied the location of small everyday objects that were placed on a two-dimensional black and white map or on a three-dimensional map with colored blocks located on it. They reported that older adults with higher working-memory scores were better able to use the environmental support afforded by the complex three-dimensional array, as working memory mediated 78.9% of the age-related variance for performance on the complex array, but only 42.7% of the variance on the impoverished map condition. Thus, working memory was an important predictor of the ability to use memory cues. In related research, Frieske and Park (1993) found that working memory, measured by computation span, accounted for most of the age-related variance in memory for disorganized, but not organized, scenes. It is likely that older adults relied on familiarity rather than working memory to recognize the organized, complex scenes. However, when the scenes contained an array of objects not related in a coherent way, working memory became more important in explaining differences in performance as a function of age.

Other research has investigated the role of working memory in tasks that more closely approximate real-world behavior, and this work has also found that working memory is important in accounting for age differences. Morrell and Park (1993) asked young and old adults to build complex structures from Lego blocks, providing subjects with building instructions that were exclusively verbal, exclusively pictorial, or a combination of the two. Older adults performed more poorly than young adults with all types of instructions in building the structures. Working-memory function accounted for at least 50% of age-related variance in building performance in all conditions, but accounted for the most variance in the two conditions that included text only or text plus pictures. These data suggest that some other factor, such as visualization ability, along with working memory played an important role in accounting for subjects' ability to follow exclusively pictorial instructions.

Zwahr, Park, and Shifren (1999) examined the quality of women's judgments about a decision to take estrogen replacement therapy (data were collected before findings that ERT was a substantial health risk) and found that age did not predict the decision that was made. However, there were age differences in the number of comparative judgments that women made in reaching a decision and in the overall quality of the rationale underlying the decision made. Using path analysis, Zwahr et al. (1999) demonstrated that although processing resource (as measured by a combined score integrating speed of processing, working memory, and reasoning) was important in predicting the quality of the rationale and number of comparative judgments made, both education and verbal ability also played important roles in predicting women's judgments. These data demonstrate the importance of working memory in making a real-world judgment, but also suggest the impact that other variables have in affecting performance on real-world tasks, including life history (education) and world knowledge (verbal ability).

Is Working Memory the Fundamental Mechanisms That Drives Cognitive Behavior?

The data presented provide convincing evidence that working memory is a critical factor in accounting for age differences on a broad range of cognitive tasks that involve memory, reasoning, judgment, and even following instructions to build an object. One important theoretical debate that has occurred, however, is whether decreased working-memory capacity is the fundamental mechanism driving age-related decline on a multitude of cognitive tasks. Salthouse (1994, 1996) has argued that speed of processing is a more fundamental mechanism than working memory, whereas others have suggested that sensory acuity provides a crude estimate of neural integrity (Baltes & Lindenberger; 1997; Lindenberger & Baltes, 1994) and accounts for age-related variance on a broad range of cognitive tasks. It is certainly plausible that no single mechanism will be able to account for all age-related variance on cognitive tasks and that the best estimate of cognitive resource may be a combined measure of sensory function, speed of processing, and working memory. The best way to determine the role that working memory plays in cognition relative to these other candidate mechanisms is to conduct large lifespan studies that address the interrelationship of different mechanisms to higher order cognitive tasks.

A number of laboratories have produced lifespan studies using such an approach (Anstey, Hofer, & Luszcz, 2003; Baltes & Lindenberger, 1997; Lindenberger & Baltes, 1994; Park et al, 1996, 2002; Salthouse, 1994, 1996 (see the 1994 paper for a review of a corpus of the Salthouse work). Each of these studies involved the collection of data from large lifespan samples across a broad range of cognitive tasks. The Anstey et al. (2003) project, as well as the work of Baltes and Lindenberger (1997) or Lindenberger and Baltes (1994), unfortunately does not include working memory as a measure, so it cannot be compared as a cognitive primitive to other measures. Salthouse (1994), however, has studied speed and working memory jointly, and he presents convincing evidence that speed of processing substantially attenuates the age-related variance in a working-memory measure. Salthouse (1994) suggests that speed is a more fundamental mechanism than working memory in accounting for age-related variance on cognitive tasks, but does not relate performance on either of these measures to higher order cognitive tasks.

In two studies, Park et al. (1996, 2002) investigated the relationship of speed and working memory to higher order memory function, and in Park et al. (2002), measures of sensory function were included as well. In Park et al. (1996) a lifespan sample of 301 subjects completed a complex battery that included multiple measures of speed of processing and working memory, as well as measures of free recall, cued recall, and spatial recall. These higher order memory tasks were hypothesized to vary in their processing resource demands, with free recall having the highest demands and spatial memory, which has been hypothesized to have a component of automaticity (Hasher & Zacks, 1979), requiring the least cognitive resource. Structural equation models demonstrated that all age-related variance operated through speed, in agreement with Salthouse (1994, 1996). However, working memory and speed jointly explained the sample variance in free and cued recall, whereas only speed was important for explaining variance in the less effortful spatial memory. This study makes several important points. First, both speed and working memory are important determinants of higher order cognition; second, tasks on which older adults perform more poorly actually do have higher resource requirements, providing an independent verification of the construct of processing resource. Finally, as Salthouse (1994, 1996) contends, this study suggests that speed of processing is more fundamental in understanding age differences than working memory.

DEDIFFERENTIATION OF COGNITIVE RESOURCES

A central idea regarding cognitive resources that has been advanced by researchers for many years (Balinsky, 1941; Cornelius, Willis, Nesselroade, & Baltes, 1983), and has taken on new vitality with the advent of neuroimaging techniques, is that with age, cognitive and neural resources (e.g., working memory) that are distinct in young adults dedifferentiate into a general pool of resources (Cabeza, 2002; Reuter-Lorenz, 2002; Park et al., 2001). Indeed, the fact that sensory function predicts complex high-order cognition in old but not young is suggestive of such dedifferentiation (Baltes & Lindenberger, 1997; Lindenberger & Baltes, 1994). Baltes and Lindenberger (1997) speculate that centrally mediated decreases in sensory function could be a marker of decreased neural integrity, which is driving decreased function on all higher order cognitive tasks via a "common cause" mechanism. If dedifferentiation occurs, one might expect that distinct visuo-spatial and verbal working-memory systems in young might dedifferentiate into a unitary system

in old. To test this hypothesis, as well as to investigate the relative contributions of sensory function, speed, and working memory to tasks that vary in resource requirements (free recall, cued recall, and recognition), Park et al. (2002) conducted a large lifespan study testing 345 adults ages 20–92. They included both visuo-spatial and verbal measures of working memory and long-term memory to determine if the distinct pools of visuo-spatial and verbal cognitive resources that characterize young adults develop into a single, general resource with age.

The results clearly indicated that the differentiation of visuo-spatial and verbal short-term subsystems that exists in young adults is maintained across the lifespan. The study also indicated that the structure of the central executive does not change across the lifespan, as the same structural model fit the data of old adults and young adults equally well. The model that best described working-memory function in subjects of all ages is displayed in Figure 9.2. In this figure, working memory consists of two highly interrelated visuo-spatial and verbal stores, with short-term visuo-spatial and verbal subsystems associated with each. The interrelationship of the visuo-spatial and verbal working-memory measures is so strong that it can be considered a unitary central executive system, providing general confirmation of the model proposed by Baddeley and Hitch (1974).

The second important finding represented in Figure 9.2 is that although age-related variance operates through speed to mediate working-memory function, working memory makes important independent contributions to long-term verbal and visuo-spatial memory beyond speed. We should also note that the measures of sensory function are not included in the model because they did not form a unitary construct, and including these measures in models did not add to the fit of the overall model. The findings that visuo-spatial and verbal processes remain distinct across the lifespan are not supportive of the notion that aging involves dedifferentiation or a loss of specificity of cognitive function, and are in agreement with the results of another large individual differences study conducted on both longitudinal and cross-sectional data (Anstey, Hofer & Luszcz, 2003).

In summary, the evidence reported in this section suggests that (1) speed is a more fundamental mechanism than working memory in explaining decrements in cognitive performance associated with aging; (2) although working-memory function decreases across

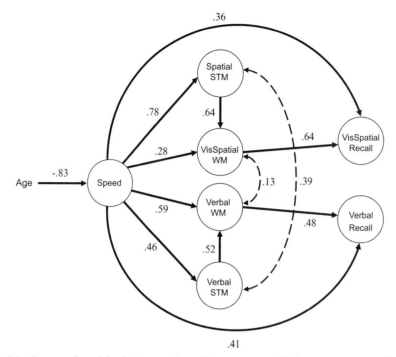

FIGURE 9.2. Structural model relating speed, working memory with short-term stores to long-term memory. For each path in the model, the completely standardized path coefficient is presented. Dashed curved lines represent correlations among residuals. Speed = speed of processing; VisSpatial WM = visuospatial working memory; Verbal WM = verbal working memory; VisSpatial STM = visuospatial short-term memory; Verbal STM = verbal short-term memory; VisSpatial Recall = visuospatial recall.

the lifespan, the cognitive architecture associated with working memory remains unchanged well into late adulthood; (3) individuals high in working-memory function are advantaged in their performance on many cognitive tasks, both in the laboratory and those that are more natural.

SUSCEPTIBILITY TO INTERFERENCE IN WORKING MEMORY WITH AGE

An important aspect of effective working-memory function, given its limited capacity, is the ability to prohibit irrelevant information from entering working memory, as well as the ability to efficiently delete items that are no longer needed for processing from working memory, freeing up space for new, relevant information. Hasher and Zacks (1988) have hypothesized that older adults have difficulties in both gating out irrelevant information from working memory and deleting information that is no longer useful. Accord-

ing to this view, what appear to be limitations in working-memory capacity are actually the result of inefficient inhibitory processes.

The Hasher and Zacks (1988) view predicts that older adults will be more susceptible to both proactive and retroactive interference on working-memory tasks. May, Hasher, and Kane (1999) suggested that, owing to the concurrent demands for processing and storage on laboratory measures of working memory, high-span individuals may be those individuals who are effective at suppressing attention to irrelevant information and attending to focal information required for task performance. To address the role of proactive interference on working-memory tasks, they changed the format for presentation of working-memory trials. Rather than starting with a simple span (e.g., remembering one or two items) and increasing the demands of the task on successive trials by increasing the number of items to be remembered, they began with a trial that included a higher number of elements and presented increasingly lower numbers of elements in successive trials, thus minimizing proactive interference for the most difficult items. May et al. (1999) reported an increased working-memory span when the most difficult items were presented first, suggesting that proactive interference plays a role in span size decrease with age. This result was confirmed by Lustig, May, and Hasher (2001), who also found that by presenting the longest trials first, as well as including distinctive breaks to release individuals from proactive interference (Wickens, 1970), span scores of older adults improved. It is important to note that the increases in working-memory capacity observed in older adults after reducing proactive interference are modest and cannot fully account for the magnitude of the age-related decline in working memory. In an effort to quantify the role of proactive interference in working-memory span scores for older adults, Bowles and Salthouse (2003) used the Rasch psychometric model to account for increased susceptibility to proactive interference with age, and they reported that disproportionate reactivity to proactive interference accounted for approximately half of the age-related variance in working memory performance, suggesting that both inhibitory deficits and capacity limitations play roles in working-memory span decreases with age.

Hedden and Park (2001) studied the role of retroactive interference in working memory of old and young adults by using a variation of the A-B, C-D paradigm (see Kintsch, 1970, for a discussion), presenting subjects with a series of trials where each trial included three paired associates (A-B pairs) for study. These items did not exceed working-memory capacity. Immediately following the presentation of the three study pairs, subjects either rested or read aloud three unrelated pairs (C-D items) or three pairs where the cue was the same as they had received for study (A-C items). Recognition for the three study pairs was tested immediately on each trial following the interfering read items, using the originally presented A-B items as targets, and the "read" items as distractors. The results indicated that older adults were disproportionately slowed when they encountered the A-C read items at recognition and made more errors on deciding whether the A-C items were study items, suggesting increased susceptibility to retroactive interference in working memory in older adults. In later work, Hedden and Park (2003) found that older adults showed large retroactive interference effects in this paradigm when they were required to judge the source of each recognition item they encountered (e.g., study

item, read item, new item), a task that increased source monitoring requirements but decreased inhibitory requirements. Based on a series of experiments, Hedden and Park (2003) demonstrated that poor source monitoring was the basis for the increased interference susceptibility of older adults, rather than inhibitory dysfunction.

In summary, the data on interference effects in working memory indicate that older adults are more susceptible to both proactive and retroactive interference in memory. Studies on proactive interference implicate poor inhibitory function as the source of the deficit, whereas the studies on retroactive interference suggest poor source monitoring as the cause of increased interference in old. Although these findings on proactive and retroactive interference appear to be in conflict, the differences between the retroactive and proactive interference paradigms are substantial. The proactive interference work focuses on the role of increasing versus decreasing complexity of the working-memory span task, where all presented information is relevant, whereas the retroactive work used a paradigm where irrelevant information was presented that was designed to interfere explicitly with working-memory function and source was highly salient to task performance. It may be that the theoretical mechanism that causes interference in working memory will differ with the requirements of the working-memory task. Nevertheless, it seems safe to conclude that older adults are more susceptible to both proactive and retroactive interference in working memory, and that it is likely that multiple mechanisms contribute to decreased working-memory function in older adults.

AGE DIFFERENCES IN NEURAL ACTIVATIONS IN WORKING MEMORY

With the advent of functional neuroimaging techniques, researchers now have the ability to examine the neural activations associated with working-memory performance and to determine whether there are differences in activation patterns between young and old adults. Initial studies in young adults suggested that working-memory function largely resides within the frontal cortex. The ventral regions in the frontal lobes act as passive storage-rehearsal units, whereas dorsal frontal regions serve as sites for the manipulation and monitoring of information (D'Esposito, Postle, Ballard, & Lease, 1999; Owen, 1997; Owen et al., 1998). In a meta-analysis, Smith and Jonides (1999) reported that there appears to be hemispheric specialization of storage in the ventral frontal cortex, with verbal information maintained in the left ventral frontal area and visuo-spatial information in the right ventral frontal cortex. This organization bears a striking resemblance to the working-memory model proposed by Baddeley and Hitch (1974), with a central executive (presumably residing in the dorsolateral prefrontal cortex) and two storage subsystems specialized for content (residing in the left ventral frontal cortex for verbal and right ventral frontal cortex for visuo-spatial information).

There has been a considerable amount of neuroimaging research on cognitive processes and aging. Raz (2000) has conducted careful structural studies of differences in volume of neural structures with age. He reported significant volumetric decreases in frontal cortex with age, with less pronounced shrinkage in mediotemporal structures and relatively preserved visual cortex. Raz, Briggs, Marks, and Acker (1999) related performance on a working-memory task in a lifespan sample to volume of frontal cortex, acquired from structural imaging, and reported that there was a significant relationship between neural resources in frontal areas and cognitive performance.

The shrinkage of frontal cortex with age and the concomitant decline in working-memory function might lead one to expect that older adults would show less neural activity when performing a working-memory task. However, the opposite has consistently been found. That is, older adults show increased neural activation in dorsolateral prefrontal cortex relative to young adults when performing a working memory task. Reuter-Lorenz et al. (2000) used positron emission tomography (PET) to study maintenance of a letter set in young and older adults. They reported that young adults showed focal activation in the left dorsolateral prefrontal cortex, whereas older adults evidenced bilateral activation in these areas. In a follow-up study (Reuter-Lorenz, Marshuetz, Jonides, & Smith, 2001), these findings were replicated. Moreover, there was some evidence that faster older adults (high performers) were more likely to recruit the right hemisphere (an area not activated by young adults for the task) than the slower older adults. Thus, the results suggest that older adults may recruit additional brain regions in compensation for either shrinkage of frontal areas or decreased efficiency of neural circuitry.

A related pattern of findings was reported by Rypma and D'Esposito (2001), who used an event-related functional magnetic resonance imaging (fMRI) design and required young and old adults to maintain a supraspan letter set over a delay interval. They reported that young and old showed equivalent activation of the ventral-lateral cortex (storage areas), but that older showed more bilateral recruitment of dorsolateral prefrontal cortex than young adults. Moreover, they found evidence that faster older adults recruited more right dorsolateral prefrontal cortex, in agreement with Reuter-Lorenz et al. (2001), another finding suggesting the activation is compensatory.

In a more recent study, Park et al. (2003), presented young and old adults with complex pictures that were maintained over a delay interval, using an event-related fMRI paradigm. Picture encoding places high demands on the hippocampus (Cohen et al., 1999) as well as prefrontal areas. Park et al. (2003) found that young adults showed engagement of hippocampus while maintaining the pictures in working memory, but old adults showed markedly less activation. When responding to the probe, however, older adults showed increased activation of left and right inferior prefrontal cortex compared to young adults. Mitchell, Johnson, Ray, and D'Esposito (2000) also reported decreased hippocampal activation in older adults when they were performing an operation that required binding features to a target. These findings suggest that additional frontal activation in older adults occurs in compensation for decreased hippocampal activation, a pattern that appears quite reliably in the long-term memory literature (Park & Gutchess, in press).

Neuroimaging techniques have the potential to reveal a great deal about how cognitive function changes as a function of age. Already, we have learned that the brain has the apparent ability to reorganize in the face of the neural insults of aging in what is an apparently compensatory manner. Future work will reveal more about networks of activations as well as the ability of working-memory circuitry to change and reorganize in response to training.

A LIFESPAN APPROACH TO THE STUDY OF WORKING MEMORY

We now consider the major themes associated with the study of working memory in older adults versus children, addressing commonalities in approaches and particular domains where much could be learned from a "true" lifespan perspective—that is, collecting data on samples from early childhood to old age.

In the cognitive aging literature, the focus has been on documenting declines in working-memory capacity, with evidence that decline is much more pronounced in central executive function than in storage subsystems. Although the pattern is one of working-memory growth in children, the growth is largely due to enhancement of central executive function (rehearsal processes) rather than to increases in the storage subsystems (Hitch, Chapter 8, this volume). Thus, the processing mechanisms that increase in children appear to be most sensitive to decline in late adulthood.

A second theme in the cognitive aging literature has been how the structures of cognitive resources change with age and whether dedifferentiation of cognitive architecture occurs. This has been an important question in understanding cognitive function in young children as well. At present, it appears that there is some limited independence between visuospatial and verbal working memory in both young and old adults, but based on the studies reported by Hitch (Chapter 8, this volume), it appears that the differences between these two subsystems on simple span tasks may be more pronounced in children (Pickering, Gathercole, & Peaker, 1998) than is true for older adults.

A third commonality in the child and aging literature has been a strong focus on determining the most primitive cognitive mechanism that accounts for age-related variance on a task. As noted here, speed of processing is a critical variable underlying function in working memory in the adult lifespan. However, in children, controlling for speed of processing did not eliminate age differences in children's working memory (Hitch, Towse, & Hutton, 2001), suggesting that speed plays a more central role in understanding developmental decline in working memory in late adulthood than it does in early development.

Also of interest has been the relationship of working-memory function to higher order cognition. In both young and older adults there is substantial evidence that working memory mediates considerable variance in higher order cognitive function (Park et al., 1996, 2002 in older adults; Hitch et al., 2001, in children), attesting to the centrality of this construct in understanding cognitive function.

Finally, there is a rich literature emerging on neuroimaging of all basic processes in aging, with a rapidly increasing volume of literature on working memory. This research has invigorated the study of working memory, providing evidence that as people age, they recruit neural resources less selectively (Logan, Sanders, Snyder, Morris, & Buckner, 2002), seemingly in compensation for the decreased volume and efficiency that occur in the brain. Relatively less is known about children owing to the difficulties of neuroimaging them (Hinton, 2002).

Among the most promising directions for future research are lifespan studies that include participants from early childhood to late adulthood, as in the recent work by Li and Baltes (Li et al., 2004), where they reported evidence for dedifferentiation of cognitive function in both children and older adults, relative to young and middle-aged adults. One of the most underexplored areas, noted in both this chapter and the preceding one by Hitch (Chapter 8, this volume), is whether visuo-spatial and verbal working memory decline equally and represent independent systems. This is an important issue where much progress is likely in the immediate future at both the behavioral and neurobiological levels of analyses. Additionally, relatively little is known about neural structures that are universally engaged for working-memory tasks by all ages compared to patterns of neural activation for working memory that are unique to developmental stages. Such studies could yield considerable information about the fundamental architecture of human working memory and will unquestionably be an important area for future working-memory studies.

In sum, it is important to recognize that although there are some behavioral similarities in function at the two endpoints of the lifespan, the neural underpinnings underlying function are likely quite divergent. Understanding the interaction of stages of human development with working-memory structure and function will not only contribute to our understanding of human development but also likely provide important insight into theories of working memory, higher order cognition, and neurobiological function.

ACKNOWLEDGMENT   The preparation of this chapter was supported by the National Institute on Aging Grant R01-AG06265 awarded to Denise Park.

References

Anstey, K. J., Hofer, S. M., & Luszcz, M. A. (2003). Cross-sectional and longitudinal patterns of dedifferentiation in late-life cognitive and sensory function: The effects of age, ability, attrition, and occasion of measurement. *Journal of Experimental Psychology: General, 132*, 470–487.

Atkinson, R. L., & Shiffrin, R. M. (1968). Human memory: A proposed system and its control processes. In K. W. Spence and J. T. Spence (Eds.), *The psychology of learning and motivation* (Vol. 2, pp. 89–195). London: Academic Press.

Baddeley, A. D., & Hitch, G. J., (1974). Working memory. In G. H. Bower (Ed.), *The psychology of learning and motivation* (Vol. 8, pp. 47–89). New York: Academic Press.

Baddeley, A.D. (1986). *Working memory*. Oxford: Clarendon Press.

Balinsky, B. (1941). An analysis of the mental factors of various age groups from nine to sixty. *Genetic Psychology Monographs, 23*, 191–234.

Baltes, P. B., & Lindenberger, U. (1997). Emergence of a powerful connection between sensory and cognitive functions across the adult life span: A new window to the study of cognitive aging? *Psychology & Aging, 12*, 12–21.

Bowles, R. P., & Salthouse, T. A. (2003). Assessing the age-related effects of proactive interference on working memory tasks using the Rasch model. *Psychology & Aging, 18*, 608–615.

Cabeza, R. (2002). Hemispheric asymmetry reduction in old adults: The HAROLD Model. *Psychology and Aging, 17*, 85–100.

Cherry, K. E., & Park, D. C. (1993). Individual difference and contextual variables influence spatial memory in young and older adults. *Psychology & Aging, 8*, 517–525.

Cohen, N. J., Ryan, J., Hunt, C., Romine, L., Wszalek, T., & Nash, C. (1999). Hippocampal system and declarative (relational) memory: Summarizing the data from functional neuroimaging studies. *Hippocampus, 9*, 83–98.

Cornelius, S. W., Willis, S. L., Nesselroade, J. R., & Baltes, P. B. (1983). Convergence between attention variables and factors of psychometric intelligence in older adults. *Intelligence, 7*, 253–269.

Craik F. I. M., & Byrd, M. (1982). Aging and cognitive deficits: The role of attentional resources. In F. I. M. Craik & S. E. Trehub (Eds.), *Advances in the study of communication and affect: Aging and cognitive processes* (pp. 191–211). New York: Plenum Press.

Craik, F. I. M., & Jennings, J. (1992). Human memory. In F. I. M. Craik & T. A. Salthouse (Eds), *The handbook of aging and cognition* (pp 51–110) Hillsdale, NJ: Lawrence Erlbaum Associates.

Daneman, M., & Carpenter, P. (1980). Individual differences in working memory and reading. *Journal of Verbal Learning and Verbal Behavior, 19*, 450–466.

D'Esposito, M., Postle, B. R., Ballard, D., & Lease, J. (1999). Maintenance versus manipulation of information held in working memory: An event-related fMRI study. *Brain & Cognition, 41*, 66–86.

Engle, R. W., Kane, M. J., & Tuholski, S. W. (1999). Individual differences in working memory capacity and what they tell us about controlled attention, general fluid intelligence and functions of the prefrontal cortex. In A. Miyake & P. Shah (Eds.), *Models of working memory: Mechanisms of active maintenance and executive control* (pp. 102–134). New York: Cambridge University Press.

Frieske, D. A., & Park, D. C. (1993). Effects of organization and working memory on age differences in memory for scene information. *Experimental Aging Research, 19*, 321–332.

Hasher, L., & Zacks, R. T. (1979). Automatic and effortful processes in memory. *Journal of Experimental Psychology: General, 108*, 356–388.

Hasher, L., & Zacks, R. T. (1988). Working memory, comprehension, and aging: A review and a new view. In G. H. Bower (Ed.), *The psychology of learning and motivation* (Vol. 22, pp. 193–225). New York: Academic Press.

Hedden, T., Lautenschlager, G., & Park, D. C. (2004). *Contributions of processing ability and knowledge to verbal memory tasks across the adult lifespan*. Unpublished manuscript.

Hedden, T., & Park, D. C. (2001). Aging and interference in verbal working memory. *Psychology and Aging, 16*, 666–681.

Hedden, T., & Park, D. C. (2003). Contributions of source and inhibitory mechanisms to age-related retroactive interference in verbal working memory. *Journal of Experimental Psychology: General, 132*, 93–112.

Hinton, V. J. (2002). Ethics of neuroimaging in pediatric development. *Brain & Cognition, 50*, 455–468.

Hitch, G. J., Towse, J. N., & Hutton, U. (2001). What limits children's working memory span? Theoretical accounts and applications for scholastic development. *Journal of Experimental Psychology: General, 130*, 184–198.

Jenkins, L., Myerson, J., Joerding, J. A., & Hale, S. (2000). Converging evidence that visuospatial cognition is more age-sensitive than verbal cognition. *Psychology & Aging, 15*, 157–175.

Kintsch, W. (1970). *Learning, memory, and conceptual processes*. New York: Wiley.

Li, S. C., Lindenberger, U., Hommel, B., Aschersleben, G., Prinz, W., & Baltes, P. B. (2004). Transformations in the couplings among intellectual abilities and constituent cognitive processes across the life span. *Psychological Science, 15,* 155–163.

Lindenberger, U., & Baltes, P. B. (1994). Sensory functioning and intelligence in old age – a strong connection. *Psychology & Aging, 9,* 339–355.

Logan, J. M., Sanders, A. L., Snyder, A. Z., Morris, J. C., & Buckner, R. L. (2002). Under-recruitment and nonselective recruitment: Dissociable neural mechanisms associated with aging. *Neuron, 33,* 827–840.

Lustig, C., May, C. P., & Hasher, L. (2001). Working memory span and the role of proactive interference. *Journal of Experimental Psychology: General, 130,* 199–207.

May, C. P., Hasher, L., & Kane, M. J. (1999). The role of interference in memory span. *Memory & Cognition, 27,* 759–767.

Mitchell, K. J., Johnson, M. K., Raye, C. L., & D'Esposito, M. (2000). fMRI evidence of age-related hippocampal dysfunction in feature binding in working memory. *Cognitive Brain Research, 10,* 197–206.

Morrell, R. W., & Park, D. C. (1993). Effects of age, illustrations, and task variables on the performance of procedural assembly tasks. *Psychology & Aging, 8,* 389–399.

Neisser, U. (1967). *Cognitive psychology.* New York: Appleton-Century-Crofts.

Owen, A. M. (1997). The functional organization of working memory processes within human lateral frontal cortex: The contribution of functional neuroimaging. *European Journal of Neuroscience, 9,* 1329–1339.

Owen, A. M., Stern, C. E., Look, R. B., Tracey, I., Rosen, B. R., & Petrides, M. (1998). Functional organization of spatial and nonspatial working memory processing within the human lateral frontal cortex. *Proceedings of the National Academy of Sciences of the United States of America, 95,* 7721–7726.

Park, D. C., & Gutchess, A. H. (2005). Long-term memory and aging: A cognitive-neuroscience perspective. In R. Cabeza, L. Nyberg, & D. C. Park (Eds.), *Cognitive neuroscience of aging: Linking cognitive and cerebral aging* (pp. 218–245). New York: Oxford University Press.

Park, D. C., Lautenschlager, G., Hedden, T., Davidson, N. S., Smith, A. D., & Smith, P. K. (2002). Models of visuospatial and verbal memory across the adult life span. *Psychology & Aging, 17,* 299–320.

Park, D. C., Polk, T., Gutchess, A. H., Mikels, J., Taylor, S. F., & Marshuetz, C. (2001). Cerebral Aging: Integration of Neural and Behavioral Findings. *Dialogues in Clinical Neuroscience, 3,*151–165.

Park, D. C. & Schwarz, N. (Eds.) (2000). *Cognitive aging: a primer.* Philadelphia: Psychology Press.

Park, D. C., Smith, A. D., Lautenschlager, G., Earles, J., Frieske, D., Zwahr, M., & Gaines, C. (1996). Mediators of long-term memory performance across the life span. *Psychology & Aging, 11,* 621–637.

Park, D. C., Welsh, R. C., Marshuetz, C., Gutchess, A. H., Mikels, J., Polk, T. A., Noll, D. C., & Taylor, S. F. (2003). Working memory for complex scenes: Age differences in frontal and hippocampal activations. *Journal of Cognitive Neuroscience, 15,* 1–13.

Petrides, M., & Milner, B. (1982). Deficits on subject-ordered tasks after frontal-lobe and temporal-lobe lesions in man. *Neuropsychologia, 20,* 249–262.

Pickering, S. J., Gathercole, S. E., & Peaker, S. M. (1998). Verbal visuospatial short-term memory in children: Evidence for common and distinct mechanisms. *Memory & Cognition, 26,* 1117–1130.

Raz, N. (2000). Aging of the brain and its impact on cognitive performance: integration of structural and functional findings. In: F. I. M. Craik and T. A. Salthouse (Eds.), *The handbook of aging and cognition* (2nd ed., pp. 1–90). Mahwah, NJ: Lawrence Erlbaum Associates.

Raz, N., Briggs, S. D., Marks, W., & Acker, J. D. (1999). Age-related deficits in generation and manipulation of mental images: II. The role of dorsolateral prefrontal cortex. *Psychology & Aging, 14,* 436–444.

Reuter-Lorenz, P. A. (2002). New visions of the aging mind and brain. *Trends in Cognitive Sciences, 6,* 394–400.

Reuter-Lorenz, P. A., Jonides, J., Smith, E., Hartley, A., Miller, A., Marshuetz, C., & Koeppe, R. (2000). Age differences in the frontal lateralization of verbal and spatial working memory revealed by PET. *Journal of Cognitive Neuroscience, 12,* 174–187.

Reuter-Lorenz, P. A., Marshuetz, C., Jonides, J., & Smith, E. E. (2001). Neurocognitive ageing of storage and executive processes. *European Journal of Cognitive Psychology, 13,* 257–278.

Rypma, B., & D'Esposito, M. (2001). Age-related changes in brain-behaviour relationships: Evidence from event-related functional MRI studies. *European Journal of Cognitive Psychology, 13,* 235–256.

Salthouse, T. A. (1985). *A theory of cognitive aging (Advances in psychology, Vol. 28).* Amsterdam: North-Holland.

Salthouse, T. A (1991). Mediation of adult age differences in cognition by reductions in working memory and speed of processing. *Psychological Science, 2,* 179–183.

Salthouse, T. A. (1992). Influence of processing speed on adult age differences in working memoroy. *Acta Psychologica, 79,* 155–170.

Salthouse, T. A. (1993a). Speed and knowledge as determinants of adult age differences in verbal tasks.

Journal of Gerontology: Psychological Sciences, 48, 29–36.

Salthouse, T. A. (1993b). Influence of working memory on adult age differences in matrix reasoning. *British Journal of Psychology, 84,* 171–199.

Salthouse, T. A. (1994). The aging of working memory. *Neuropsychology, 8,* 535–543.

Salthouse, T. A. (1996). The processing speed theory of adult age differences in cognition. *Psychological Review, 103,* 403–428.

Salthouse, T. A., & Babcock, R. L. (1991). Decomposing adult age differences in working memory. *Developmental Psychology, 27,* 763–776.

Salthouse, T. A., Kausler, D. H., & Saults, J. S. (1988). Utilization of path-analytic procedures to investigate the role of processing resources in cognitive aging. *Psychology & Aging, 3,* 158–166.

Shah, P., & Miyake, A. (1996). The separability of working memory resources for spatial thinking and language processing: An individual differences approach. *Journal of Experimental Psychology: General, 125,* 4–27.

Shimamura, A. P., & Jurica, P. J. (1994). Memory interference effects and aging: Findings from a test of frontal lobe function. *Neuropsychology, 8,* 408–412.

Shipley, W. C. (1986). *Shipley Institute of Living Scale.* Los Angeles: Western Psychological Services.

Smith, E. E., & Jonides, J. (1999). Neuroscience—Storage and executive processes in the frontal lobes. *Science, 283,* 1657–1661.

Spreen, O., & Strauss, E. (1991). *A compendium of neuropsychological tests: Administration, norms, and commentary.* New York: Oxford University Press.

Stine, E. L., & Wingfield, A. (1987). Process and strategy in memory for speech among younger and older adults. *Psychology & Aging, 2,* 272–279.

Verhaeghen, P., & Salthouse, T. A. (1997). Meta-analyses of age-cognition relations in adulthood: Estimates of linear and nonlinear age effects and structural models. *Psychological Bulletin, 122,* 231–249.

Wechsler, D. (1997a). *Wechsler Adult Intelligence Scale* (3rd ed.). San Antonio, TX: Psychological Corporation.

Wechsler, D. (1997b). *Wechsler Memory Scale* (3rd ed.). San Antonio, TX: Psychological Corporation.

Wickens, D. (1970). Encoding categories of words: An empirical approach to meaning. *Psychological Review, 77,* 1–15.

Zwahr, M. D., Park, D. C., & Shifren, K. (1999). Judgments about estrogen replacement therapy: The role of age, cognitive abilities, and beliefs. *Psychology & Aging, 14,* 179–191.

10

Children's Memory Development: Remembering the Past and Preparing for the Future

Peter A. Ornstein

Catherine A. Haden

Holger B. Elischberger

Although the first studies of children's memory were published more than 100 years ago (e.g., Binet & Henri, 1894; Jacobs, 1887) and research on this topic was prominent in the early days of the 20th century (e.g., Hunter, 1913), programmatic work on memory development did not begin in earnest until the middle 1960s. Starting with Flavell's seminal studies of early strategy use (e.g., Flavell, Beach, & Chinsky, 1966), the corpus of research on age-related changes in children's mnemonic skills has expanded in an impressive fashion. Two themes now characterize the voluminous literature: (1) the surprising mnemonic competence of infants and young children, at least under some conditions, and (2) the presence of substantial age differences in almost all aspects of memory performance. This assessment of current understanding represents a distillation of evidence that is drawn from research paradigms ranging from elicited imitation (Bauer, Wenner, Dropik & Wewerka, 2000; Meltzoff, 1988) and conditioning (Rovee-Collier, Sullivan, Enright, Lucas, & Fagen, 1980; Rovee-Collier, Schechter, Shyi, &

Shields, 1992) to those involving the production of narrative accounts of previous experiences (Haden, Haine, & Fivush, 1997; McCabe & Peterson, 1991) and verbal measures of both strategy use and remembering (Baker-Ward, Gordon, Ornstein, Larus, & Clubb, 1993; Folds, Footo, Guttentag, & Ornstein, 1990).

Given that a number of fine overviews of various aspects of children's memory have appeared in recent years (e.g., Nelson & Fivush, 2000; Rovee-Collier & Hayne, 2000; Schneider & Bjorklund, 1998), in this chapter, we draw quite selectively from the extant literature. Our aim is to integrate two broad areas of mnemonic competence — children's "event" recall and their skills in using memory strategies — that are not often treated together. We begin with a discussion of children's abilities to remember and report salient events that they have experienced and then progress to an examination of their use of deliberate strategies for encoding information for future memory assessments. Our integration of these two domains is driven by our commitment to a developmental analysis

(Ornstein & Haden, 2001) that requires the use of longitudinal data to make statements regarding changes in mnemonic competence within individual children. To be sure, this orientation is not reflected in the largely cross-sectional literature on children's memory. A review of findings from cross-sectional research, nonetheless, provides a useful vantage point for thinking about children's changing memory skills, even when most statements about development must be inferred on the basis of across-group comparisons.

We take this tack for two reasons. First, although the necessary longitudinal data are not yet available to support the claim, we suspect that skills in talking about the past and in deploying strategies for remembering may lie at different points on a developmental continuum. As we see it, just as early expressions of nonverbal memory give way to later uses of language to make reference to past experiences, it seems likely that growing sophistication in talking about the past may precede later competencies in deliberate planning for future assessments of remembering. Second, we believe that both types of memory performance can be understood in terms of the same underlying processes of encoding, storage, and retrieval. In our view, the encoding of information is driven by the activities in which a child is engaged as an event is experienced or a set of materials is being studied for a subsequent test of memory. Attentional focus—whether achieved by visual examination, physical manipulation, or linguistic means—serves to highlight some of the features of the event/materials being remembered and, accordingly, to facilitate encoding and the establishment of representations in memory. Information from these representations, moreover, must be retrieved and reported when remembering is requested, and these operations are governed by both the deployment of effective search routines and the knowledge of appropriate narrative conventions.

From this perspective, we are particularly interested in factors that govern developmental changes in the encoding, storage, retrieval, and reporting of information. In terms of young children's encoding, we focus on both child and maternal behaviors that regulate understanding of ongoing activities and interaction with to-be-remembered materials, and hence can be expected to influence the establishment of coherent representations. Further, we expect a developmental progression in children's understanding of both events and materials such that, with increases in age,

they may be able to attend to salient features more on their own, with less maternal involvement (Baker-Ward, Ornstein, & Principe, 1997; Haden, Ornstein, Eckerman, & Didow, 2001). Similarly, we see mother-child conversations about events and activities that are to be remembered as potential opportunities for children to gain experience in retrieving information from memory and in using language for reporting the past (Fivush & Haden, 1997). Moreover, over the course of the preschool years, frequent discussions of past events provide a basis for the acquisition of some general principles regarding retrieval and reporting (Fivush & Haden, 1997; Ornstein, Haden, & Hendrick, 2004).

Given the goal of characterizing the development of children's memory, our primary focus is on changes in performance over time. Nevertheless, our discussion would be incomplete without acknowledging that the considerable changes we observe in many aspects of mnemonic competence are complemented by relative invariance across time in a few areas. For example, age-related differences are usually quite attenuated in recognition tasks (e.g., Perlmutter & Lange, 1978), even though contextual factors, such as the similarity between distractors and targets, clearly affect the magnitude of the differences that are observed (Myers et al., 2003). In addition, age-related differences are essentially absent when children's memory is assessed without explicit prompts to remember (e.g., Perrig & Perrig, 1993). That is, the performance of children of different ages is comparable on priming and other implicit memory tasks (see, e.g., Schacter & Buckner, 1998; Zacks & Hasher, Chapter 11, this volume) in which memory for previously presented information affects ongoing information processing in an indirect manner without conscious awareness. The absence of age differences in implicit memory is taken to indicate that the neural substrate underlying performance is maturationally early and different from that presumed to underlie explicit performance (e.g., Rovee-Collier, 1997).

As we present our integration of the event and strategic memory literatures, we will encounter a number of definitional issues concerning intentionality and the operation of deliberate techniques that are under the control of the child (Baker-Ward et al., 1997; Folds et al., 1990; Ornstein, Baker-Ward, & Naus, 1988). From our point of view, event memory can be conceived of as an amalgam of incidental and deliberate memory, with information encoded without intent to remember but with deliberate forces operating at the level of "telling the tale." Similarly, we see strategic memory as being primarily deliberate, but with "automatic" contributions to remembering also reflecting strong inter-item associations in permanent memory. It is noteworthy that this perspective implies an emphasis on matters of "control." Therefore, within our assessment of children's memory for previously experienced events, we will focus on control in the sense of developing (deliberate) skills for searching memory and using the narrative conventions of the culture to report what has been recovered. Moreover, within our assessment of children's planful memory (for the future), we will discuss control in the sense of a growing repertoire of deliberate strategies for remembering (e.g., rehearsal, organization).

For each of these types of memory, we will stress the role of dyadic communication (e.g., parent-child; teacher-child) in the development of control processes. As we see it, social-communicative interaction not only serves to facilitate children's understanding and immediate memory but also provides opportunities for the acquisition of generalized skills for remembering. We thus focus on social interaction as a potential mediator of developmental change, although we recognize that there are certainly other mechanisms that impact the development of memory, including maturational changes in the neural substrate. For example, relatively protracted changes in the reciprocal connections between the association areas and the hippocampus appear to be linked to children's developing memory for temporal order information and long-term recall of the past (Barr, Dowden, & Hayne, 1996; Carver & Bauer, 1999; Carver, Bauer, & Nelson, 2000). This prolonged time course for the development of biological mediators of some aspects of children's changing mnemonic skills contrasts markedly with the relative stability of the other features of memory performance. Thus, for example, the skills that underlie short-term recall are supported by medial temporal lobe components that should be evident relatively early in development (Bauer, 2002). A similar state of affairs exists with regard to maturational changes in frontal lobe functioning that have been implicated in the development of inhibitory control, which is believed to enhance working memory by gating out task-irrelevant information. Although not the focus of this chapter, it should be noted that developmental investigators (e.g., Bjorklund & Harnishfeger, 1990, 1995) have begun to explore inhibitory control with children and that researchers interested in the cognitive function of elderly adults (e.g., Zacks, Hasher, & Li, 2000) have devoted a considerable amount of attention to the loss of such control in aging.

MEMORY FOR EVENTS

Research using nonverbal measures (e.g., elicited imitation, conditioning) suggests that children evidence memory for the events that they experience quite early and that their recall seems to be influenced by reminding, context, prior knowledge, repeated experience, active participation, and enabling relations in ways similar to that observed with older children (see Bauer, 2002). With these nonverbal skills as a foundation, children's memory abilities change markedly once they are able to use language to express what they remember about previously experienced events. Such changes have been observed in a wide range of situations, some of which involve assessing children's memory for specified events (either naturally occurring or laboratory-based), whereas others examine the nature of mother-child conversations about jointly experienced events. We turn now to a treatment of children's memory for salient "target" events, and then move to a discussion of memory as expressed in conversations about the past.

Memory for Salient Experiences

In recent years, a considerable amount has been learned about the abilities of children between 2½ and 8 years of age to provide reports of the details of salient events that they have experienced. In a range of studies, children have been exposed to specially crafted *stimulus* events such as a staged "visiting the pirate" activity (Murachver, Pipe, Gordon, & Owens, 1996) as well as to naturally occurring (mostly medical) events such as routine pediatric checkups and other less familiar and more stressful procedures (Burgwyn-Bailes, Baker-Ward, Gordon, & Ornstein, 2001; Goodman, Quas, Batterman-Faunce, Riddlesberger, & Kuhn, 1997; Peterson & Bell, 1996; Merritt, Ornstein, & Spicker, 1994; Ornstein, Baker-Ward, Gordon, & Merritt, 1997).

To illustrate this approach, consider Baker-Ward et al.'s (1993) exploration of 3-, 5-, and 7-year-olds' retention of the details of a routine visit to the doctor. At each age level, children were interviewed twice, first immediately after their checkups and then again after a delay of 1, 3, or 6 weeks. The interviews made use of a structured protocol that was designed to assess memory for the various component features of the physical examination. Beginning with open-ended probes (e.g., "Tell me what happened during your check-up."), the examiner continued with more specific questions (e.g., "Did the doctor check any parts of your face?"), and then moved on to yes/no questions about features that had not yet been volunteered (e.g., "Did she [he] check your eyes?"). The children were also asked potentially misleading yes/no questions about activities not included in the checkups.

Overall, Baker-Ward et al.'s (1993) data indicated that young children's reports of salient events can be quite impressive, with recall averaging approximately 83% of the component features of the physical examination. Nonetheless, there were striking age-related changes in various aspects of memory performance. In contrast to the older children, the 3-year-olds showed lower levels of overall recall, greater dependency on yes/no types of questions, more forgetting, and a reduced ability to differentiate between activities that had and had not been included in their medical checkups. These basic findings set the stage for a number of questions about age-related changes in the encoding, storage, and retrieval of information in memory. For example, the "problematic" aspects of the performance of the 3-year-olds would seem not to reflect their lower levels of language competence and incomplete mastery of narrative conventions, as they do not benefit from the introduction of alternative methods of assessment that reduce the demands placed on the child to produce a verbal report (e.g., Greenhoot, Ornstein, Gordon, & Baker-Ward, 1999; Myers et al., 2003). Moreover, children's prior knowledge about the events being remembered can both facilitate initial encoding and retention (Ornstein, Shapiro, Clubb, Follmer, & Baker-Ward, 1997) and interfere with subsequent recall as the details of an experience fade over time (Ornstein et al., 1998). We also know that the level of stress experienced as an unpleasant event unfolds can influence the deployment of attention, and thus encoding and subsequent storage (Merritt et al., 1994). In a similar sense, stress experienced during an interview can affect the retrievability of information (Ornstein, Larus, & Clubb, 1991).

Establishing an Event Representation

All in all, we now know a substantial amount about young children's memory for salient, personally experienced events and about age-related differences in performance. However, it is also clear that a complete understanding of the skills of children of different ages requires consideration of how factors such as prior knowledge, stress, and coping style act together to influence the establishment of a representation in memory. Knowledge certainly impacts a child's initial interpretation of a situation and, along with coping style, has implications for how stressful experiences are encoded. It is essential to think about the impact of these variables if we are going to understand what transforms an event (such as a medical procedure) that may be similar across participants from an experimenter's vantage point into something that is unique from the perspective of the individual child. To use the language of the verbal learners (e.g., Underwood, 1963), it is necessary to examine those factors that determine how the *nominal stimulus* that is "presented" by medical personnel is changed into the *functional stimulus* that is attended to by each participant (see Ornstein & Myers, 1996).

This movement from nominal to functional stimulus can be illustrated in Merritt et al.'s (1994) study of children's retention of the details of a stressful and relatively unfamiliar radiological procedure: a voiding cystourethrogram (VCUG) that involves urinary bladder catheterization and subsequent fluoroscopy. There is no doubt that this procedure is a difficult one, and the children in the Merritt et al. study exhibited higher levels of stress than those observed in the studies of memory for the details of routine doctor visits. Indeed, both salivary cortisol assays and behavioral measures during the VCUG indicated that the children were very distressed by the procedure. Interestingly, however, the cortisol and behavioral measures of stress were not correlated with each other, indicating that stress that is measured at the hormonal level is not necessarily reflected in behavioral indicators that can be observed by the medical and research staff. Moreover, Merritt et al. found that the salivary cortisol measure of stress was not related to memory performance, whereas the behavioral measures were negatively linked to recall, such that higher levels of stress were associated with lower levels of recall performance. These findings thus underscore the need to articulate a type of conversion process whereby an "objective" stimulus event (the VCUG in this case) can be transformed and hence encoded in unique ways by different individuals.

As we wrestle with these issues, it is essential to recognize that the encoding process that results in the construction of a representation in memory can be extended in time, as it involves the interpretation of an event on the basis of prior knowledge. Not only does the (often unconscious) activation of knowledge lead to the establishment of event representations that "go beyond the information given," but these interpretative processes can continue long after an experience has ended. Further, when the relevant knowledge is not activated—because of age differences in making knowledge-based inferences (Baker-Ward et al., 1997)—or lacking, the input from parents or other adults can be most important for interpretation and subsequent remembering. Indeed, especially with young children, this "extended encoding" of an event involves the joint involvement of the two members of an adult-child dyad both during and after an experience. These lengthy encoding operations may also continue as some children engage in a considerable amount of post-event reflection and rumination, a process that may lead to self-modification of the representation, as in the case of autosuggestion (Binet & Henri, 1894; Brainerd & Reyna, 1995), thus blurring the line between the normal encoding of information and suggestion (Baker-Ward et al., 1997).

Searching for Mediators of Developmental Change

Although much has been learned about children's memory for salient events, there are patent gaps in our understanding. As suggested in our speculative account of extended encoding, a great deal needs to be learned about the ways in which a variety of factors come together in the construction of representations in memory. In this regard, it seems clear that adults have a great role in facilitating children's understanding and hence the encoding of information in memory. Moreover, as indicated above in our brief discussion of social communication as a potential mediator of change, adults most likely are also involved in helping to "drive" developmental changes in remembering, a topic about which the literature on

memory for salient events is largely silent (Ornstein et al., 2004). Indeed, because research concerning children's memory for salient events is largely cross-sectional in nature, very little can be said about developmental changes within individuals and the factors that serve to bring about these changes. However, these issues are at the core of a series of studies that focus on adult-child conservation as a mediator of developmental changes in remembering (Farrant & Reese, 2000; Haden et al., 1997; Haden et al., 2001; McCabe & Peterson, 1991; Reese, Haden & Fivush, 1993).

Conversational Styles for Talking about the Past

Studies of naturally occurring conversation reveal that between 18 and 24 months of age, children begin to verbally reference the past (e.g., Hudson, 1990; Nelson, 1986). Children's skills for recalling experienced events develop rapidly between 2 and 4 years of age, such that they become able to give coherent, well-organized accounts of routine, everyday activities (e.g., Nelson, 1986), and can also provide information about novel, one-time past experiences. Indeed, by 29–35 months of age, in response to only general "open-ended" prompts (e.g., "Tell me about Disneyland."), children are able to recall in somewhat coherent form events that they experienced only once or twice, such as a visit to a zoo or a museum, more than six months in the past (Fivush, Gray, & Fromhoff, 1987).

These skills notwithstanding, it is also clear that children's early reports of their past experiences are limited both in content and structure (see Fivush & Haden, 1997, for review). For example, when parents and children first begin conversing about past events, the discussions are usually initiated and heavily scaffolded by an adult. To illustrate, consider the following excerpt of a conversation that we recorded between a mother and her 24-month-old about a time they visited an aquarium:

MOTHER: *Do you remember when we went to the aquarium? Remember when we saw fish? (pause) What kind of fish did we see?*

CHILD: *Um.*

MOTHER: *We saw sharks. Do you remember the sharks?*

CHILD: *Um.*

MOTHER: *Was there a man in the water? What was he doing? What was he doing for the fish?*

CHILD: *Eating.*

MOTHER: *Yeah! That's right. They were eating. Do you remember seeing the dolphins?*

CHILD: *Mmhm (= yes).*

MOTHER: *What did they do?*

CHILD: *They be on the water!*

MOTHER: *Yeah! Did they have toys?*

CHILD: *Yeah.*

MOTHER: *What kind of toys did they have?*

CHILD: *Balls.*

MOTHER: *Yeah, (laughs) they had balls. Did they also hear whistles?*

CHILD: *Yeah.*

MOTHER: *Were they very loud?*

CHILD: *Yeah.*

MOTHER: *Did the dolphins do something that went way up high in the air?*

CHILD: *Yeah.*

MOTHER: *What did they do?*

CHILD: *(unintelligible).*

MOTHER: *They jumped?*

CHILD: *Yeah.*

MOTHER: *Who went . . .*

CHILD: *(interrupts) He.*

MOTHER: *Hmm?*

CHILD: *He jumped.*

MOTHER: *Yes, they jumped . . . Who else jumped? . . . Do you remember the penguins? Did they jump and dive in the water?*

CHILD: *Yeah.*

MOTHER: *Did you like them very much?*

CHILD: *Yeah.*

MOTHER: *Was there anything else that you loved? What else?*

Previous research focusing on such mother-child conversations indicates that the nature of mothers' talk with their children about past experiences has an immediate and long-term impact on children's remembering. Consider, for example, two different styles that mothers use to engage their children in conversations about past events. In contrast to *low-elaborative* moth-

ers, *high-elaborative* mothers—such as the one in the above illustration—frequently ask questions and continually add new information to cue memory, even when their children do not provide much in the way of spontaneous recall (Fivush & Fromhoff, 1988; Haden, 1998; Hudson, 1990; McCabe & Peterson, 1991; Reese et al., 1993). Importantly, longitudinal data indicate clearly that differences in maternal style are associated with later differences in children's independent abilities to generate information about past events. To illustrate, Reese et al. (1993) have shown that mothers' elaboration during early conversations with their 40-month-olds was associated positively with children's independent contribution of memory information in conversations at 58 and 70 months of age. Also, other research (e.g., Hudson, 1993; McCabe & Peterson, 1991) demonstrates that the more elaborative mothers of 2-year-olds were, the better their children's independent skills for remembering events with an examiner as much as a year and a half later. In these studies, children with high elaborative mothers were better able to respond to questions posed by an examiner and to produce longer reports concerning their personal experiences, in comparison with children of low-elaborative mothers. As such, mothers who are highly elaborative early in development seem to facilitate their children's abilities to report on their past experiences in a detailed manner. Moreover, it can be argued that as these linguistic skills are mastered, children actually come to understand and represent personally experiences in more elaborated ways (Fivush & Haden, 1997). This scaffolding of children's remembering is interestingly parallel to the positive effects of external environmental support on remembering in older adults (Craik, 1983).

Conversations During Ongoing Events

Just as adult-child conversations about the past can influence the recovery and reporting of information, verbal interactions that occur as events unfold may also have positive mnemonic consequences. As indicated above, it is well known that prior knowledge can affect comprehension, encoding, and subsequent remembering (Bjorklund, 1985; Chi & Ceci, 1987; Ornstein, Shapiro, et al., 1997). However, in the absence of such knowledge, parents and other adults may be able to provide information during an ongoing event that may facilitate children's understanding of the experience, and thus serve to organize the resulting representation in memory. For example, by naming component features of an ongoing event, a mother may focus her child's attention on various aspects of the situation that are particularly salient (Haden et al., 2001). Moreover, if this naming is followed by her verbal elaboration (or better yet, that of the child), a more enriched representation may be established. In this way, mothers and children who are experiencing an event together may come to construct the event in a way that makes it more accessible in the future.

A series of studies that we have carried out supports this notion of linkages between narrative interactions during specified events and children's subsequent memory for these experiences (see also McGuigan & Salmon, 2004; Tessler & Nelson, 1994). In an initial short-term longitudinal investigation, Haden et al. (2001) followed a sample of 21 children from 2.5 to 3.5 years of age, observing mothers and their children as they engaged in unique experiences at three time points across the year. Within the confines of each family's living room, the mother-child dyads took part

in a pretend camping adventure at 30 months, a birdwatching activity at 36 months, and the "opening" of an ice cream store at 42 months. Component features of the events (e.g., the backpack in camping) that were attended to by both members of the mother-child dyad—as judged by physical handling—were considered in analyses examining differences in recall as a function of the type of talk directed toward these features (e.g., joint-verbal, mother-verbal, no-verbal). For each event, Figure 10.1 depicts the percentage of features recalled of those that were jointly handled and jointly discussed, jointly handled and talked about only by the mother, and jointly handled and not discussed. Inspection of this figure indicates a dramatic effect of joint talk as the events unfold on the information the children provided in response to open-ended questions of the interviewers. As can be seen, those features of the activities that were handled and discussed by both the mother and child were better recalled than those that were jointly handled but talked about only by the mother, which, in turn, were

1-Day Delay

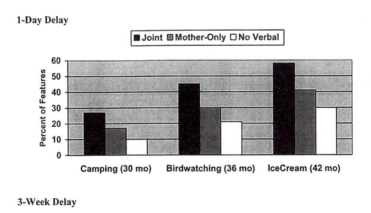

3-Week Delay

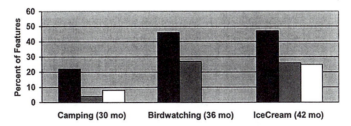

FIGURE 10.1. Proportion of features of the camping, birdwatching, and ice cream store events remembered in response to open-ended questions at the 1-day and 3-week interviews, as a function of the type of talk directed toward jointly handled features. (Adapted from Haden et al., 2001.)

better recalled than those not discussed. This pattern was observed at both memory interviews for each of the activities, with some indication of a drop in recall over the 3-week delay interval for features that had been jointly handled but only discussed by the mother.

The findings from this preliminary study indicate that children as young as 2.5 years of age show mnemonic benefits from conversations about events in the here-and-now. Joint talk between mothers and children about aspects of an ongoing event is associated strongly with children's open-ended recall as much as three weeks later. However, given the basically correlational nature of this finding, Boland, Haden, and Ornstein (2003) designed an experiment in which mothers were trained to use particular conversational techniques that previous work indicated should enhance children's remembering. Trained mothers were asked to use four specific conversational techniques to enhance children's understanding of unfolding events: (1) *wh-questions* to elicit their child's linguistic participation in the activity, (2) *associations* to relate that which was being experienced to what their child already knew, (3) *follow-ins* that encouraged discussion of aspects of the event in which the child was showing interest, and (4) *positive evaluations* to praise their child's verbal and nonverbal contributions to the interaction. When observed engaging with their children in the context of the camping event, trained mothers produced significantly more of all four of the targeted conversational techniques than did untrained mothers. Moreover, the effects of the training did not vary as a function of the children's language skills and did not impact the mothers' use of "untrained" techniques (i.e., *repetitions*, *yes/no questions*, and *statements*). Of even greater interest, the children's recall of information about the camping event was affected by the training that their mothers received. For example, the children of trained mothers ($M = 45.42$) exceeded those whose mothers had not received training ($M = 36.98$) in the production of *event elaborations*, defined in terms of elaborative details about the features (e.g., "Mine was red," when recalling the backpacks) or information that described the event in general (e.g., "We packed up all the food.").

Our exploration of the linkages between mother-child conversational interactions during specified events and children's subsequent remembering continues in an ongoing study of children's memory across the preschool years (see, e.g., Ornstein et al., 2004). As part of this longitudinal investigation, at 36 months of age, children in the sample engaged with their mothers in either the camping or the birdwatching activity. Talk during the event was coded in terms of the number of elaborative questions and statements made by the mothers and the children. Analyses were then conducted to predict the children's average recall across delays of 1 day and 3 weeks from the elaborations that they and their mothers produced during the events. Moreover, levels of maternal elaborativeness as the events unfolded were related to children's subsequent recall of details of the experiences (i.e., their *event elaborations*) beyond simply naming the features. Indeed, taking into account the children's language skills and their own elaborations during the activity, the total amount of maternal elaborative talk during the activity uniquely predicted approximately 5% of the variance in children's recall of embellished information about the events, enabling us to account for a total of 49% of the variance. This work thus adds to a growing body of evidence that shows mnemonic benefits from conversations about events in the here-and-now. The consistency of these findings across delay intervals, events, and different studies reinforces the view that mother-child interaction events contribute substantially to children's understanding and memory.

LEARNING TO BE STRATEGIC

Complementing children's increasing expertise in talking about the past are dramatic age-related changes in the deployment of deliberate strategies for remembering information. In contrast to the more or less incidental nature of event memory, the use of specific mnemonic techniques—such as rehearsal and organization—requires that a child behave intentionally in order to prepare for a future assessment of memory (Folds et al., 1990; Wellman, 1988). From this perspective, young preschoolers can certainly be shown to be "strategic," at least in some situations. For example, when asked to remember the location (e.g., under a pillow, behind a chair) of several familiar stuffed toys (e.g., Big Bird, Snoopy, etc.) so that they could be retrieved later, DeLoache, Cassidy, and Brown (1985) found that even 18-month-olds direct a variety of strategy-like behaviors (e.g., naming, pointing, and "peeking") toward the objects or hiding places. Although the deployment of these behaviors was not unambiguously related to memory performance, their use nonetheless suggests that the children have a rudimentary understanding that they need to do "something" in response to a memory demand. Admittedly, the picture is complicated somewhat by the fact that young children exhibit these same behaviors in a hide-and-seek scenario in which there is no requirement to remember (e.g., Big Bird is "hiding" in plain view on top of a pillow), albeit to a lesser extent (DeLoache et al., 1985, Experiment 3). Moreover, such displays of mnemonic regulation appear to emerge initially in a rather unplanned fashion and as part of ongoing pleasurable activities (e.g., hide-and-seek) in highly salient and meaningful situations. In this sense, they might be more aptly characterized as *proto strategies* that may—or may not—be linked to later expressions of mnemonic skill (see Wellman's [1988] discussion of the concept of intentionality).

These demonstrations are consistent with our view that *intentionality* is only one component of strategic behavior. Indeed, a consideration of two others—*consistency* and *effectiveness*—leads to an understanding of why it is not until the end of the elementary school years that children evidence mastery of a broad set of mnemonic techniques. Although the mature user of deliberate memorization strategies is able to apply them skillfully across a broad range of contexts (Brown, Bransford, Ferrara, & Campione, 1983; Ornstein et al., 1988; Pressley, Borkowski, & Schneider, 1989), young children's use of these techniques is characterized by considerable context specificity. Indeed, the evidence suggests that children may initially evidence strategic "sophistication" only in some highly salient and supportive settings, but not in others (Ornstein et al., 1988). Similarly, young children's initial strategic efforts may not facilitate remembering, and it is with age and experience that strategies come to be increasingly effective (Folds et al., 1990; Ornstein et al., 1988; Wellman, 1988).

Although longitudinal data are not available to chart on a within-individual basis this developmental progression in the use of mnemonic strategies, a rich crosssectional literature documents age-related transitions from relatively passive to active styles of memorization (Ornstein & Naus, 1985; Ornstein et al., 1988). To illustrate the complexities of children's changing skills, consider two seemingly simple classes of strategies— rehearsal and organization—as seen through paradigms that are designed to externalize these techniques. These memory strategies become increasingly effective over the course of the elementary school years and can serve to illustrate the definitional complexities involved in characterizing children's strategic efforts.

Rehearsal and Organization During the School Years

School-age children who are quite sophisticated in terms of reporting the details of salient events that they have experienced are rather limited in their use of deliberate techniques that require studylike behaviors. For example, consider the performance of 9- and 14-year-olds who are given a list of words to be remembered and asked to rehearse aloud as each item is presented. Under these conditions, the two groups of children appear to approach the task of remembering in rather different ways, with 9-year-olds focusing their rehearsal on each item as it is presented and 14-yearolds rehearsing each word along with several previously displayed items (e.g., Ornstein, Naus, & Liberty, 1975; Ornstein & Naus, 1978), as is typically the case with adults (Craik, 1973). A feeling for these differences in rehearsal style can be obtained by inspecting Table 10.1, in which several rehearsal sets for a typical eighth-grade child and a typical third- grader are displayed. By definition, only one item can be present in the first rehearsal set, whereas two can be included in the second set, three in the third, and so on. This protocol indicates that although the older child is mixing a relatively large number of items, the third-grader seems to be rehearsing the currently presented item in a very limited context. These differences in rehearsal style, moreover, are associated with corresponding differences in recall, especially in the recall of the initially presented items (i.e., in the primacy section of the serial position function).

Paralleling these changes in the use of a deliberate rehearsal strategy are comparable differences in the deployment of organizational techniques. For example, when presented with relatively unrelated or low-associated items and told to "form groups that will help you remember," third- and fourth-graders will rarely sort on the basis of semantic relations but rather tend to form fragmented groupings that are not consistent from trial to trial (Bjorklund, Ornstein, & Haig, 1977; Liberty & Ornstein, 1973). In contrast, older children (sixth grade and above) and adults routinely form semantically constrained groups, even though the instructions make reference only to a memory goal and do not prompt semantic grouping. Thus, older individuals readily translate an instruction to form

TABLE 10.1. Typical rehearsal protcols

	Rehearsal Sets	
Word Presented	Eighth Grader	Third Grader
1. Yard	Yard, yard, yard	Yard, yard, yard, yard, yard
2. Cat	Cat, yard, yard, cat	Cat, cat, cat, cat, yard
3. Man	Man, cat, yard, man, yard, cat	Man, man, man, man, man
4. Desk	Desk, man, yard, cat, man desk, cat, yard	Desk, desk, desk, desk

Source: Adapted from Ornstein et al. (1975).

groups that will facilitate remembering into one that involves a search for some form of meaning-based organization (Ornstein, Trabasso, & Johnson-Laird, 1974), whereas children in the middle elementary school grades approach the recall task in a seemingly astrategic manner. These differences in sorting style are associated with corresponding age differences in recall, but it should be noted that the failure of the younger children to group items in a semantically constrained manner does not indicate a lack of understanding of the semantic linkages among the items. Indeed, a number of studies suggest that young children are aware of semantic relations, at least to some extent, both when the items are taxonomically related (Nelson, 1974) and when the organizational structure is less salient (Bjorklund et al., 1977; Liberty & Ornstein, 1973; Worden, 1975). As such, the apparent failure to organize in recall does not stem from a lack of knowledge of organizational structures but, rather, from a failure to apply this knowledge strategically.

Context Specificity in Strategy Development

An extensive literature documents these age-related differences in the use of rehearsal, organization, and other strategies for remembering. With both rehearsal and organizational techniques, training studies have been employed to demonstrate direct links between strategy use and recall. For instance, instructing younger children to rehearse more actively leads to improved recall, and asking older children to rehearse in a passive manner interferes with remembering (see Ornstein & Naus, 1978, for an overview). Moreover, young children's recall can be facilitated by yoking them to the sorting patterns of older children (Bjorklund et al., 1977; Liberty & Ornstein, 1973) by

giving them instructions to sort on the basis of meaning (Bjorklund et al., 1977; Corsale & Ornstein, 1980), or even by providing experience with highly organized materials (Best & Ornstein, 1986). Nevertheless, it must be noted that there are limits to the success of instructional manipulations, and these limits reflect the operation of several key factors that may underlie strategy production. As suggested above, young children benefit from instructions in active rehearsal techniques, but in order to do so they must expend more attentional effort than older children and adults (Guttentag, 1984), and age differences in remembering are typically not eliminated completely (Ornstein, Medlin, Stone, & Naus, 1985). However, by making it easier for young children to carry out the active rehearsal strategy—by combining instructions with a reduction in the information-processing demands of the task—dramatic improvements in strategy use and recall can be obtained. Again, there is a parallel here to work showing that older adults benefit differentially from instructions to employ memory strategies (Craik & Byrd, 1982).

Not only do contextual factors influence the success of training manipulations, they can also affect the likelihood that young children will spontaneously engage in activities that are judged to be strategic, as well as the "sophistication" of their efforts. For example, by permitting third-graders visual access to all previously presented items (thereby reducing the attentional demands of active rehearsal), some typically passive rehearsers will engage spontaneously in a more complex, active rehearsal strategy (Guttentag, Ornstein, & Siemens, 1987). In addition, variations in children's knowledge and understanding of the materials to be remembered can have a profound impact on the strategies that they use when confronted with a memory goal (Ornstein & Naus, 1985). Age-related changes in both the contents of the knowledge base and the ease of access to stored information may influence significantly just what can be done strategically with the to-be-remembered materials. In fact, it is possible that a child will appear to be strategic when trying to remember some types of items and nonstrategic with others, most likely leading to the first expressions of deliberate memorization with highly meaningful materials (Ornstein & Naus, 1985; Ornstein et al., 1988). Further, it is likely that the increasing articulation of the knowledge system may facilitate information retrieval and thus bring about a reduction in the effort required to execute various subcomponents of memory strategies (Ornstein et al., 1988).

The Development of Effective Strategy Use

As implied by this characterization of the context specificity of children's strategic deployment, with increases in age, children extend the range of situations in which their activities can be viewed as strategic. Paralleling this generalization across contexts, there are increments in the effectiveness of children's strategic efforts, as measured by improvements in remembering. This increased effectiveness, moreover, appears to reflect two different patterns. First, as already indicated, there are substantial changes in what children actually do when trying to remember. When asked to remember verbal materials, younger children engage in seemingly passive, rote-type memorization procedures, but with increases in age their strategies appear to be more active and involve a deliberate integration of the to-be-remembered information with existing knowledge. Second, even when the same strategy appears to be used by children of different ages, the procedure routinely has a more facilitative effect on the recall of older, as opposed to younger, children. Both of these types of effectiveness are discussed briefly here, prior to a treatment of some of the factors that may underlie these age-related changes.

With increases in age, not only are children more likely to engage in some form of strategy in response to the challenges of a memory goal, but also what they do to meet this goal changes dramatically. Of course, the nature of the materials to be remembered (and the children's understanding of these materials) can influence the types of strategies that can be deployed,

but in general, over the course of the elementary school years there is a substantial movement to more active and effective memorization techniques (Schneider & Bjorklund, 1998). To some extent, the greater effectiveness of older children's strategic efforts reflects the acquisition of an increasing number of mnemonic techniques and their incorporation into a repertoire from which the most effective strategy can be chosen to meet the demands of any particular task at hand (Folds et al., 1990; Schneider & Bjorklund, 1998). Consistent with these data, there are many instances in which young children select a strategy that is inappropriate for the task, as is the case when preschoolers may choose techniques that do not facilitate performance in any way (see Wellman [1988] for a treatment of "faulty" strategies). However, there also are cases in which young children carry out a strategy that is quite appropriate to the goal of remembering but are not able to implement it so that memory performance is facilitated. For example, although Baker-Ward, Ornstein, and Holden (1984) showed that 4-, 5-, and 6-year-olds prepared for a memory goal in the context of an object-memory task by using quite comparable strategies of naming and visual inspection, they also found that these strategies only facilitated the memory performance of the 6–year-olds. These data—and other demonstrations of utilization deficiencies (Bjorklund & Coyle 1995; Miller 1990)—illustrate that young children may understand the importance of doing "something" in order to respond to a memory demand, but that what they nominate may be quite ineffective.

What Factors Underlie These Changes?

How can we understand these changes in strategy effectiveness? We turn now to a brief treatment of several factors that may influence children's use of strategies and serve as mediators of the observed age-related progression: (1) changes in the knowledge base in permanent memory, (2) reductions in the effort requirements of strategy implementation, (3) increases in metamnemonic understanding, and (4) experiences in school.

Prior Knowledge

As mentioned above, variations in the contents and structure of the knowledge base can have a dramatic effect on memory performance (Chi, 1978; Bjorklund, 1985; Ornstein & Naus, 1985). In recent years, moreover, there has been a growing consensus concerning the importance of both knowledge and strategies for remembering (Muir-Broaddus & Bjorklund, 1990; Ornstein et al., 1988) and recognition that under some conditions the impact of the knowledge base may be mediated by its effects on strategy implementation (Ornstein & Naus, 1985; Rabinowitz & McAuley, 1990). This emerging interactional perspective stresses the extent to which the current state of the child's knowledge system may enable the execution of particular strategies (Folds et al., 1990; Ornstein et al., 1988). There is no doubt that with highly salient and meaningful sets of materials, young children may appear to be quite strategic in their approach to the task of remembering, whereas they may be more tentative when asked to remember less structured items (e.g., Lange, 1978; Bjorklund, 1985). But how should these demonstrations of context specificity be interpreted, and what are their implications for development?

One explanation for the sometimes dramatic performance differences of young children under contrasting task demands is that they may lack knowledge about the study materials that would be necessary to implement a mnemonic strategy. For instance, knowledge of the categorical structure of a set of words is a necessary, albeit not sufficient, prerequisite for implementing a semantically based clustering strategy. A second explanation focuses on the beneficial effects of knowledge on the efficiency of mnemonic processing. With increases in age and experience, the knowledge system becomes more articulated and richly interconnected, thereby contributing to the ease of access that is required for efficient strategy execution (Bjorklund, 1987; Bjorklund, Muir-Broaddus, & Schneider, 1990; Ornstein et al., 1988). Thus, although it is possible that the automatic activation of strong associative links may make young children's strategic efforts not entirely deliberate (Lange, 1978; Bjorklund, 1985), these linkages may increase the efficiency and effectiveness of the strategy use of older children. Moreover, increasing differentiation and integration of the knowledge base is believed to contribute to age-related increases in the likelihood that children will spontaneously *use* their knowledge in the service of a memory goal (e.g., Corsale & Ornstein, 1980).

Effort Requirements of Strategy Use

Age-related changes in the effectiveness of children's strategies may also reflect corresponding differences in the attentional resources required for strategy execution. If we assume a trade-off between the processing and storage operations necessary to carry out any given cognitive task (Case, 1985), then in the early stages of skill acquisition the execution of the strategy alone may require so much capacity that little remains to be allocated to encoding and storage processes (Bjorklund & Harnishfeger, 1987). As a result, even though a child can make use of a particular memory strategy under some conditions, the effort required to do so may be great, and memory performance may not be facilitated. Consistent with this perspective, Guttentag (1984) demonstrated that second-graders are capable of producing an active multi-item rehearsal strategy when so instructed, but that their deployment of this technique is more demanding of their limited capacity than is the case for older children or adults (see also Bjorklund & Harnishfeger, 1987; Kee & Davies, 1988). In addition, Guttentag et al. (1987) found that some children who used a passive strategy under normal presentation conditions switched to the utilization of more active procedures under conditions in which the resource demands of the more active procedures were reduced.

Given that young children may expend more cognitive resources on the processing component of strategy execution than older children, what factors account for age-related improvements in processing efficiency? Several possibilities can be mentioned. First, processing speed (e.g., Kail, 1991) increases across the elementary school years, a change that is believed to be largely maturationally determined. Second, as indicated above, developments in the knowledge base in terms of the greater coherence of the semantic network and increased ease of accessibility may contribute to more efficient processing (Bjorklund, 1987). Third, functional capacity may increase because specific aspects of a task come to require fewer resources, in part as a result of the automatization that usually accompanies repeated practice (Case, 1985; Ornstein et al., 1988, Siegler, 1996). Furthermore, consistent with the view that age-related differences in mental resources play a role in explaining the changing linkage between strategy use and memory performance, Hasher and Zacks (1979) noted that deliberate memory tasks that require the use of strategies typically yield significant age-related differences in levels of performance.

Metamemory

With increases in age, there are corresponding changes in metamemory, or children's understanding of the operation of the memory system and the demands of various tasks that require remembering (Cavanaugh & Perlmutter, 1982; Flavell & Wellman, 1977, Schneider, 1985). However, even though metamemory has often been suggested as being of critical importance for mnemonic growth (e.g., Cavanaugh & Borkowski, 1980; Schneider, 1985), the results of correlational studies have been quite mixed. Examples of some of the difficulties in documenting the presumed linkage between metamemory and strategic deployment and effectiveness include cases in which children verbalize knowledge of a mnemonic technique but fail to actually use it (Sodian, Schneider, & Perlmutter, 1986) and situations in which children use what might be viewed as a deliberate strategy but are unable to demonstrate any corresponding metamnemonic awareness (Bjorklund & Zeman, 1982). On the other hand, early training studies that have included metamnemonic information along with strategy instruction (e.g., Paris, Newman, & McVey, 1982), and more recent studies involving improved methods of assessing young children's understanding (e.g., Schlagmüller & Schneider, 2002; Schneider, Schlagmüller, & Vise, 1998) provide convincing empirical evidence for the metamemory—memory development linkage. For example, in a short-term longitudinal study, Schlagmüller and Schneider (2002) reported that children who acquired an organizational strategy over the course of the project actually showed increases in declarative metamemory well ahead of actually exhibiting the strategy.

Schooling

A number of lines of research point to the potential impact of formal schooling on the development of memory strategies. For example, within the comparative-cultural literature, studies in Morocco (e.g., Wagner, 1978), Liberia (Scribner & Cole, 1978), and Mexico (Rogoff, 1981) reveal that children who attended formal school demonstrated superiority in the types of mnemonic skills that have typically been stud-

ied by Western psychologists and anthropologists. To illustrate, Rogoff reported that that non-schooled children generally do not make use of organizational techniques for remembering unrelated items, and this led her to conclude that school seemed necessary for the acquisition of these skills. In addition, comparisons of same-age children who "just made" the mandated date for entry into first grade (a "young" first-grade group) and those who "just missed" the date (an "old" kindergarten group) document substantial differences in memorization skills, indicating that the first-grade environment may be especially important in shaping children's memory development (Morrison, Smith, & Dow-Ehrensberger, 1995).

Given that the evidence points to formal schooling as a mediator of children's strategy development, we (e.g., Coffman, Ornstein, & McCall, 2003) have carried out a series of studies to characterize memory-relevant behaviors that teachers use that may support children's deliberate memory skills. Some of our findings are consistent with Moely et al.'s (1992) important report that it is quite rare to find explicit instruction in mnemonic techniques by teachers throughout the elementary school grades. But even though mnemonic strategies are not generally taught by teachers in an explicit fashion, we find that first-grade teachers are engaging in a variety of memory-relevant behaviors in the course of whole-class instruction, including indirect requests for deliberate remembering, strategy suggestion, and metacognitive questioning. Moreover, children in first-grade classes taught by teachers who use more of this sort of memory-related language show a greater ability to take advantage of training provided in a specific mnemonic strategy (clustering) than those children with low-mnemonically oriented teachers (Coffman et al., 2003; see Moely et al., 1992, for similar results). As such, this work suggests that just as "parent talk" about events can impact preschoolers' developing abilities to remember (e.g., Boland et al., 2003; Haden et al., 2001; McCabe & Peterson, 1991; Reese et al., 1993), "teacher talk" may also be relevant for the emergence and refinement of mnemonic skills.

Determinants of Performance and Development

Research on the factors considered here indicates clearly the complex and multiply-determined nature of children's strategic memory. Knowledge, effort, metamemory, and schooling each can be viewed as a mediator of the performance of children at any given age. Moreover, three of these mediators—knowledge, effort factors, and metamnemonic understanding—are also relevant to a consideration of the deliberate memory performance of adults of different ages (see Zacks & Hasher, Chapter 11, this volume, for review of factors responsible for changes in memory with aging). These determinants of memory performance may also serve as potential mechanisms underlying developmental changes in strategic deployment and effectiveness. Clearly, changes with age in children's knowledge of the materials being remembered, the cognitive effort they need to exert to carry out tasks that involve remembering, and their understanding of the operation of the memory system all can contribute to developmental increases in strategic effectiveness. However, we attach special status to schooling as a potential mediator of change because the available evidence suggests that school represents a critical context for the emergence and consolidation of children's mnemonic efforts. Further, as suggested above, given the importance of parent-child social communication in the development of early event memory, it seems likely that teacher-child conversation in the classroom is of great relevance for the development of a repertoire of strategies that can be deployed skillfully in the service of goals of remembering.

CONCLUDING REMARKS

The research summarized here indicates clearly that much has been learned in recent years about the complexities of children's memory. However, from our perspective, it is equally clear that much remains to be learned. As we see it, the rich database that has been amassed now sets the stage for the serious exploration of three critical and overlapping issues: (1) an integration of studies of event and deliberate memory performance; (2) a move from the study of children's memory to an understanding of the development of memory; and (3) a blending—at the conceptual level—of the child development and aging literatures. These three broad themes will be treated briefly below.

As indicated at the outset, our decision to treat the development of event and deliberate memory together stems in part from a belief that these seemingly different types of remembering could be understood in terms of the same underlying processes. Memory for events that have been experienced and materials that have been studied both can be analyzed in terms of the factors that affect information encoding, storage, and retrieval, along with subsequent reporting. Event memory and strategic memory also both require the activation of processes that are under the control of the child—as in directed memory searches, skillfully constructed narrative reports, or strategies such as rehearsal—and to a considerable extent it seems to be these control processes that change markedly with age and experience. Further, and somewhat more speculatively, children's skills in talking about salient events and in preparing for subsequent tests of memory both seem to arise in the social contexts of home and classroom. As such, parent- and teacher-child communicative interactions are implicated as mediators of the development of children's repertoire of skills. At a more general level, we feel that the social constructivist approach seems to be an ideal vantage point for the discovery of such mediators, emphasizing as it does the view that many cognitive processes have social origins in interactions between adults and children (Cox, Ornstein, & Valsiner, 1991).

We recognize that children's event and deliberate memory are not typically studied together, but the parallels that we see in the underlying cognitive and social processes lead us to believe that it would be profitable to do so. In addition, a developmental perspective would suggest that tasks that involve event versus deliberate memory performance might be located at different points on a continuum. Indeed, it seems likely that children's abilities to remember their previous experiences and to talk about past events precede their later skills in preparing deliberately for future assessments of remembering. Of course, descriptions of changes in these skills *within* individual children are rare, particularly those that make use of a multitask diagnostic strategy that can yield developmentally changing profiles of mnemonic competence (Guttentag et al., 1987; Ornstein et al., 1988). Moreover, serious exploration of such a presumed developmental continuum requires that researchers commit themselves to move from studying *memory development* to the *development of memory* (Ornstein & Haden, 2001). Longitudinal research in which children are tracked over considerable periods of time—especially work that focuses on potential mediators of change—is central to such a commitment and certainly is not the norm in studies of cognitive development (but see, e.g., Reese et al, 1993; Haden et al., 2001; Schneider & Sodian, 1997). Much can also be learned about developmental change from relatively short-term microgenetic studies (e.g., Siegler, 1996).

Finally, from our point of view, it would be equally important to effect some type of integration of research on the development of children's memory with that of explorations of cognitive aging. Although a comparison of this chapter with that of Zacks and Hasher (Chapter 11) indicates relatively few points of overlap, researchers in these two areas seem to be committed to an exploration of many of the same issues. For example, the memory performance of both young children and the elderly is very much driven by contextual factors, with seemingly minor changes in materials, instructions, conditions of assessment, and so on, having a substantial effect on remembering, and hence on estimates of underlying skill or competence. Similarly, although not the focus of our overview, developmental psychologists are as concerned about issues of accuracy and error in memory as are cognitive psychologists, and they are equally supportive of the application of basic research to issues such as eyewitness testimony (see, e.g., Ceci & Bruck, 1995). Further, researchers in both areas of study are concerned about understanding development, although there are clear differences at present in the potential mediators of change that are being explored. As we see it, these basic similarities might provide the foundation for fruitful collaborations that could lead to a truly integrated lifespan cognitive developmental psychology.

References

Baker-Ward, L., Gordon, B. N., Ornstein, P. A., Larus, D. M., & Clubb, P. (1993). Young children's long-term retention of a pediatric examination. *Child Development, 64,* 1519–1533.

Baker-Ward, L., Ornstein, P. A., & Holden, D. J. (1984). The expression of memorization in early childhood. *Journal of Experimental Child Psychology, 37,* 555–575.

Baker-Ward, L., Ornstein, P. A., & Principe, G. F. (1997). Revealing the representation: Evidence from children's reports of events. In P. W. van den Broek, P. J. Bauer, & T. Bourg (Eds.), *Developmental spans in event comprehension and representation: Bridging fictional and actual events* (pp. 79–107). Mahwah, NJ: Lawrence Erlbaum Associates.

Barr, R., Dowden, A., & Hayne, H. (1996). Developmental changes in deferred imitation by 6- to 24-month-old infants. *Infant Behavior and Development, 19,* 159–170.

Bauer, P. J. (2002). Early memory development. In U. Goswami (Ed.), *Blackwell handbook of childhood cognitive development* (pp. 127–146). Malden, MA: Blackwell.

Bauer, P. J., Wenner, J. A., Dropik, P. L., & Wewerka, S. S. (2000). Parameters of remembering and forgetting in the transition from infancy to early childhood. *Monographs of the Society for Research in Child Development, 65* (4, Serial No. 263).

Best, D. L., & Ornstein, P. A. (1986). Children's generation and communication of mnemonic organizational strategies. *Developmental Psychology, 22,* 845–853.

Binet, A., & Henri, V. (1894). La memoire des mots. *L'Annee Psychologique, 1,* 1–23.

Bjorklund, D. F. (1985). The role of conceptual knowledge in the development of organization in children's memory. In C. J. Brainerd & M. Pressley (Eds.), *Basic processes in memory development* (pp. 103–142). New York: Springer.

Bjorklund, D. F. (1987). How changes in knowledge base contribute to the development of children's memory: An interpretive review. *Developmental Review, 7,* 93–130.

Bjorklund, D. F., & Coyle, T. R. (1995). Utilization deficiencies in the development of memory strategies. In F. E. Weinert & W. Schneider (Eds.), *Memory performance and competencies: Issues in growth and development* (pp. 161–180). Mahwah, NJ: Lawrence Erlbaum Associates.

Bjorklund, D. F., & Harnishfeger, K. K. (1987). Developmental differences in the mental effort requirements for the use of an organizational strategy in free recall. *Journal of Experimental Child Psychology, 44,* 109–125.

Bjorklund, D. F., & Harnishfeger, K. K. (1990). The resources construct in cognitive development: Diverse sources of evidence and a theory of inefficient inhibition. *Developmental Review, 10,* 48–71.

Bjorklund, D. F., & Harnishfeger, K. K. (1995). The evolution of inhibition mechanisms and their role in human cognition and behavior. In F. N. Dempster & C. J. Brainerd (Eds.), *Interference and inhibition in cognition* (pp. 141–173). New York: Academic Press.

Bjorklund, D. F., Muir-Broaddus, J. E., & Schneider, W. (1990). The role of knowledge in the development of children's strategies. In D. F. Bjorklund (Ed.), *Children's strategies: Contemporary views of cognitive development* (pp. 93–128). Hillsdale, NJ: Lawrence Erlbaum Associates.

Bjorklund, D. F., Ornstein, P. A., & Haig, J. R. (1977). Developmental differences in organization and recall: Training in the use of organizational techniques. *Developmental Psychology, 13,* 175–183.

Bjorklund, D. F., & Zeman, B. R. (1982). Children's organization and metamemory awareness in the recall of familiar information. *Child Development, 53,* 799–810.

Boland, A. M., Haden, C. A., & Ornstein, P. A., (2003). Boosting children's memory by training mothers in the use of an elaborative conversational style as an event unfolds. *Journal of Cognition and Development, 4,* 39–65.

Brainerd, C. J., & Reyna, V. F. (1995). Autosuggestibility and memory development. *Cognitive Psychology, 28,* 65–101.

Brown, A. L., Bransford, J. D., Ferrara, R. A., & Campione, J. C. (1983). Learning, remembering, and understanding. In J. H. Flavell & E. M. Markman (Eds.), P. H. Mussen (Series Ed.), *Handbook of child psychology: Vol 3. Cognitive development* (4th ed., pp. 77–166). New York: Wiley.

Burgwyn-Bailes, E., Baker-Ward, L., Gordon, B. N., & Ornstein, P. A. (2001). Children's memory for emergency medical treatment after one year: The impact of individual difference variables on recall and suggestibility. *Applied Cognitive Psychology, 15,* S25–S48.

Carver, L. J., & Bauer, P. J. (1999). When the event is more than the sum of its parts: 9–month-olds' long-term ordered recall. *Memory, 7,*147–174.

Carver, L. J., Bauer, P. J., & Nelson, C. A. (2000). Associations between infant brain activity and recall memory. *Developmental Science, 3,* 234–246.

Case, R. (1985). *Intellectual development: Birth to adulthood.* New York: Academic Press.

Cavanaugh, J. C., & Borkowski, J. G. (1980). Searching for metamemory-memory connections: A developmental study. *Developmental Psychology, 16,* 441–453.

Cavanaugh, J. C., & Perlmutter, M. (1982). Metamemory: A crucial examination. *Child Development, 53,* 11–28.

Ceci, S. J., & Bruck, M. (1995). *Jeopardy in the courtroom: A scientific analysis of children's testimony.* Washington, DC: American Psychological Association.

Chi, M. T. H. (1978). Knowledge structure and memory development. In R. S. Siegler (Ed.), *Children's thinking: What develops?* (pp. 73–96). Hillsdale, NJ: Lawrence Erlbaum Associates.

Chi, M. T. H., & Ceci, S. J. (1987). Content knowledge: Its role, representation, and restructuring in memory development. In H. W. Reese (Ed.), *Advances in child development and behavior* (Vol. 20, pp. 91–142). San Diego, CA: Academic Press.

Coffman, J. L., Ornstein, P. A., & McCall, L. E. (2003, July). *Linking teachers' memory-relevant talk to children's memory performance.* Poster presented at the biennial meeting of the Society for Applied Research in Memory and Cognition, Aberdeen, Scotland.

Corsale, K., & Ornstein, P. A. (1980). Developmental changes in children's use of semantic information in recall. *Journal of Experimental Child Psychology, 30,* 231–245.

Cox, B., Ornstein, P. A., & Valsiner, J. (1991). The role of internalization in the transfer in mnemonic strategies. In L. Oppenheimer & J. Valsiner (Eds.), *The origins of action: International perspectives* (pp. 101–131). New York: Springer-Verlag.

Craik, F. I. M. (1973). A "levels of analysis" view of memory. In P. Pliner, L. Krames, & T. M. Alloway (Eds.), *Communication and affect: Language and thought* (pp. 45–65). New York: Academic Press.

Craik, F. I. M. (1983). On the transfer of information from temporary to permanent memory. *Philosophical Transactions of the Royal Society, Series B, 302,* 341–359.

Craik, F. I. M., & Byrd, M. (1982). Aging and cognitive deficits: The role of attentional resources. In F. I.M. Craik & S. E. Trehub (Eds.), *Aging and cognitive processes* (pp. 191–211). New York: Plenum.

DeLoache, J. S., Cassidy, D. J., & Brown, A. L. (1985). Precursors of mnemonic strategies in very young children's memory. *Child Development, 56,* 125–137.

Farrant, K., & Reese, E., (2000). Maternal style and children's participation in reminiscing: Stepping stones in children's autobiographical memory development. *Journal of Cognition and Development, 1,* 193–225.

Fivush, R., & Fromhoff, F. A. (1988). Style and structure in mother-child conversations about the past. *Discourse Processes, 11,* 337–355.

Fivush, R., Gray, J. T., & Fromhoff, F. A. (1987). Two year olds talk about the past. *Cognitive Development, 2,* 393–410.

Fivush, R., & Haden, C. A. (1997). Narrating and representing experience: Preschooler's developing autobiographical recounts. P. van den Broek, P. J. Bauer, & T. Bourg (Eds.), *Developmental spans in event comprehension and representation: Bridging fictional and actual events* (pp. 169–198). Hillsdale, NJ: Lawrence Erlbaum Associates.

Flavell, J. H., Beach, D. R., & Chinsky, J. M. (1966). Spontaneous verbal rehearsal in a memory task as a function of age. *Child Development, 37,* 283–299.

Flavell, J. H., & Wellman, H. M. (1977). Metamemory. In R. V. Kail & J. W. Hagan (Eds.), *Perspectives on the development of memory and cognition* (pp. 3–33). Hillsdale, NJ: Lawrence Erlbaum Associates.

Folds, T. H., Footo, M. M., Guttentag, R. E., & Ornstein, P. A. (1990). When children mean to remember: Issues of context specificity, strategy effectiveness, and intentionality in the development of memory. In D. F. Bjorklund (Ed.), *Children's strategies: Contemporary views of cognitive development* (pp. 67–91). Hillsdale, NJ: Lawrence Erlbaum Associates.

Goodman, G. S., Quas, J. A., Batterman-Faunce, J. M., Riddlesberger, M. M., & Kuhn, J. (1997). Children's reactions to and memory for a stressful event: Influences of age, anatomical dolls, knowledge, and parental attachment. *Applied Developmental Science, 1,* 54–74.

Greenhoot, A. F., Ornstein, P. A., Gordon, B. N., & Baker-Ward, L. (1999). Acting out the details of a pediatric check-up: The impact of interview condition and behavioral style on children's memory reports. *Child Development, 70,* 363–380.

Guttentag, R. E. (1984). The mental effort requirement of cumulative rehearsal: A developmental study. *Journal of Experimental Child Psychology, 37,* 92–106.

Guttentag, R. E., Ornstein, P. A., & Siemens, L. (1987). Spontaneous rehearsal: Transitions in strategy acquisition. *Cognitive Development, 2,* 307–326.

Haden, C. A. (1998). Reminiscing with different children: Relating maternal stylistic consistency and sibling similarity in talk about the past. *Developmental Psychology, 34,* 99–114.

Haden, C. A., Haine, R. A., & Fivush, R. (1997). Developing narrative structure in parent-child reminiscing across the preschool years. *Developmental Psychology, 33,* 295–307.

Haden, C. A., Ornstein, P.A., Eckerman, C. O., & Didow, S. M. (2001). Mother-child conversational interactions as events unfold: Linkages to subsequent remembering. *Child Development, 72,* 1016–1031.

Hasher, L., & Zacks, R. T. (1979). Automatic and effortful processes in memory. *Journal of Experimental Psychology: General, 108,* 356–388.

Hudson, J. A. (1990). The emergence of autobiographic memory in mother-child conversation. In R. Fivush & J. A. Hudson (Eds.), *Knowing and remembering in young children* (pp. 166–196). New York: Cambridge University Press.

Hudson, J. A. (1993). Reminiscing with mothers and others: Autobiographical memory in young two-year-olds. *Journal of Narrative and Life History, 3,* 1–32.

Hunter, W. S. (1913). The delayed reaction in animals and children. *Animal Behavior Monographs, 2,* 1–86.

Jacobs, J. (1887). Experiments on "Prehension." *Mind, 12,* 75–78.

Kail, R. (1991). Developmental changes in speed of processing during childhood and adolescence. *Psychological Bulletin, 109,* 490–501.

Kee, D. W., & Davies, L. (1988). Mental effort and elaboration: A developmental analysis. *Contemporary Educational Psychology, 13,* 221–228.

Lange, G. (1978). Organization-related processes in children's recall. In P. A. Ornstein (Ed.), *Memory development in children* (pp. 101–128). Hillsdale, NJ: Lawrence Erlbaum Associates.

Liberty, C., & Ornstein, P. A. (1973). Age differences in organization and recall: The effects of training in categorization. *Journal of Experimental Child Psychology, 15,* 169–186.

McCabe, A. & Peterson, C. (1991). Getting the story: A longitudinal study of parental styles in eliciting narratives and developing narrative skill. In A. McCabe & C. Peterson (Eds.), *Developing narrative structure* (pp. 217–253). Hillsdale, NJ: Lawrence Erlbaum Associates.

McGuigan, F. & Salmon, K. (2004). The time to talk: The influences of the timing of adult-child talk on children's event memory. *Child Development, 66,* 669–686.

Meltzoff, A. N. (1988). Infant imitation after a 1–week delay: Long-term memory for novel acts and multiple stimuli. *Developmental Psychology, 24,* 470–476.

Merritt, K. A., Ornstein, P. A., & Spicker, B. (1994). Children's memory of a salient medical procedure: Implications for testimony. *Pediatrics, 94,* 17–23.

Miller, P. H. (1990). The development of strategies of selective attention. In D. F. Bjorklund (Ed.). *Children's strategies: Contemporary views of cognitive development* (pp. 157–184). Hillsdale, NJ: Lawrence Erlbaum Associates.

Moely, B. E., Hart, S. S., Leal, L., Santulli, K. A., Rao, N., Johnson, T., & Hamilton, L. B. (1992). The teacher's role in facilitating memory and study strategy development in the elementary school classroom. *Child Development, 63,* 653–672.

Morrison, F. J., Smith, L., & Dow-Ehrensberger, M. (1995). Education and cognitive development: A natural experiment. *Developmental Psychology, 31,* 789–799.

Muir-Broaddus, J. E., & Bjorklund, D. F. (1990) Developmental and individual differences in children's memory strategies: The role of knowledge. In W. Schneider & F. E. Weinert (Eds.), *Aptitudes, strategies, and knowledge in cognitive performance* (pp. 99–116). New York: Springer-Verlag.

Murachver, T., Pipe, M.-E., Gordon, R., & Owens, J. L.

(1996). Do, show, and tell: Children's event memories acquired through direct experience, observation, and stories. *Child Development, 67,* 3029–3044.

Myers, J., Gramzow, E., Ornstein, P. A., Wagner, L., Gordon, B. N., & Baker-Ward, L. (2003). Children's memory of a physical examination: A comparison of recall and recognition assessment protocols. *International Journal of Behavioural Development, 27,* 66–73.

Nelson, K. (1974). Variations in children's concepts by age and category. *Child Development, 45,* 577–584.

Nelson, K. (1986). *Event knowledge: Structure and function in development.* Hillsdale, NJ: Lawrence Erlbaum Associates.

Nelson, K. & Fivush, R. (2000). Socialization of memory. In E. Tulving & F. I. M. Craik (Eds.), *The Oxford handbook of memory* (pp. 283–295). New York: Oxford University Press.

Ornstein, P. A., Baker-Ward, L., Gordon, B. N., & Merritt, K. A. (1997). Children's memory for medical experiences. *Applied Cognitive Psychology, 11,* S87–S104.

Ornstein, P. A., Baker-Ward, L., & Naus, M. J. (1988). The development of mnemonic skill. In F. E. Weinert & M. Perlmutter (Eds.), *Memory development: Universal changes and individual differences* (pp. 31–50). Hillsdale, NJ: Lawrence Erlbaum Associates.

Ornstein, P. A., & Haden, C. A. (2001). Memory development or the development of memory? *Current Directions in Psychological Science, 6,* 202–205.

Ornstein, P. A., Haden, C. A., & Hedrick, A. M. (2004). Learning to remember: Social-communicative exchanges and the development of children's memory skills. *Developmental Review, 24,* 374–395.

Ornstein, P. A., Larus, D. M., & Clubb, P. A. (1991). Understanding children's testimony: Implications of research on the development of memory. *Annals of Child Development, 8,* 145–176.

Ornstein, P. A., Medlin, R. G., Stone, B. P., & Naus, M. J. (1985). Retrieving for rehearsal: An analysis of active research in children's memory. *Developmental Psychology, 21,* 633–641.

Ornstein, P. A., Merritt, K. A., Baker-Ward, L., Furtado, E., Gordon, B. N., & Principe, G. (1998). Children's knowledge, expectation, and long-term retention. *Applied Cognitive Psychology, 12,* 387–405.

Ornstein, P. A., & Myers, J. T. (1996). Contextual influences on children's remembering. In K. Pezdek & W. P. Banks (Eds.), *The recovered memory/false memory debate* (pp. 211–223). San Diego, CA: Academic Press.

Ornstein, P. A. & Naus, M. J. (1978). Rehearsal processes in children's memory. In P. A. Ornstein (Ed.),

Memory development in children (pp. 69–99). Hillsdale, NJ: Lawrence Erlbaum Associates.

Ornstein, P. A., & Naus, M. J. (1985). Effects of the knowledge base on children's memory strategies. In H. W. Reese (Ed.), *Advances in child development and behavior* (Vol. 19, pp. 113–148). New York: Academic Press.

Ornstein, P. A., Naus, M. J., & Liberty, C. (1975). Rehearsal and organizational processes in children's memory. *Child Development, 26,* 818–830.

Ornstein, P. A., Shapiro, L. R., Clubb, P. A., Follmer, A., & Baker-Ward, L. (1997). The influence of prior knowledge on children's memory for salient medical experiences. In N. Stein, P. A. Ornstein, B. Tversky, & C. J. Brainerd (Eds.), *Memory for everyday and emotional events* (pp. 83–111). Mahwah, NJ: Lawrence Erlbaum Associates.

Ornstein, P. A., Trabasso, T., & Johnson-Laird, P. N. (1974). To organize is to remember: The effects of instructions to organize and to remember. *Journal of Experimental Psychology, 103,* 1014–1018.

Paris, S. G., Newman, R. S., & McVey, K. A. (1982). Learning the functional significance of mnemonic actions: A microgenetic study of strategy acquisition. *Journal of Experimental Child Psychology, 34,* 490–509.

Perlmutter, M., & Lange, G. (1978). A developmental analysis of recall-recognition distinctions. In P. A. Ornstein (Ed.), *Memory development in children* (pp. 243–258). Hillsdale, NJ: Lawrence Erlbaum Associates.

Perrig, W. J., & Perrig, P. (1993). Implizites Gedächtnis: unwillkürlich, entwicklungsresistent und altersunabhängig? [Implicit memory: involuntary, developmentally resistant, and age-independent?] *Zeitschrift für Entwicklungspsychologie und Pädagogische Psychologie, 25,* 29–47.

Peterson, C., & Bell, M. (1996). Children's memory for traumatic injury. *Child Development, 67,* 3045–3070.

Pressley, M., Borkowski, J. G., & Schneider, W. (1989). Good information processing: What is it and what education can do to promote it. *International Journal of Educational Research, 13,* 857–867.

Rabinowitz, M., & McAuley, R. (1990). Conceptual knowledge processing: An oxymoron. In W. Schneider and F. E. Weinert (Eds.), *Interactions among aptitudes, strategies, and knowledge in cognitive performance* (pp. 117–133). New York: Springer-Verlag.

Reese, E., Haden, C. A., & Fivush, R. (1993). Mother-child conversations about the past: Relationships of style and memory over time. *Cognitive Development, 8,* 403–430.

Rogoff, B. (1981). Schooling's influence on memory test performance. *Child Development, 52,* 260–267.

Rovee-Collier, C. (1997). Dissociations in infant memory: Rethinking the development of implicit and explicit memory. *Psychological Review, 104,* 467–498.

Rovee-Collier, C., & Hayne, H. (2000). Memory in infancy and early childhood. In E. Tulving & F. I. M. Craik (Eds.), *The Oxford handbook of memory* (pp. 267–282). New York: Oxford University Press.

Rovee-Collier, C., Schechter, A., Shyi, G. C.-W., & Shields, P. (1992). Perceptual identification of contextual attributes and infant memory retrieval. *Developmental Psychology, 28,* 307–318.

Rovee-Collier, C. K., Sullivan, M. W., Enright, M., Lucas, D., & Fagen, J. (1980). Reactivation of infant memory. *Science, 208,* 1159–1161.

Schacter, D. L., & Buckner, R. L. (1998). Priming and the brain. *Neuron, 20,* 185–195.

Schlagmüller, M., & Schneider, W. (2002). The development of organizational strategies in children: Evidence from a microgenetic longitudinal study. *Journal of Experimental Child Psychology, 81,* 298–319.

Schneider, W. (1985). Developmental trends in the metamemory-memory relationship: An integrative review. In D. L. Forrest-Pressley, G. E. MacKinnon, & T. G. Waller (Eds.), *Metacognition, cognition, and human performance* (Vol. 1, pp. 57–109). Orlando, FL: Academic Press.

Schneider, W., & Bjorklund, D. F. (1998). Memory. In W. Damon (General Ed.), D. Kuhn & R. Siegler (Volume Eds.), *Handbook of child psychology: Cognition, perception, and language* (5th ed., Vol. 2, pp. 467–521). New York: Wiley.

Schneider, W., Schlagmüller, M., & Vise, M. (1998). The impact of metamemory and domain-specific knowledge on memory performance. *European Journal of Psychology of Education, 13,* 91–103.

Schneider, W., & Sodian, B. (1997). Memory strategy development: Lessons from longitudinal research. *Developmental Review, 17,* 442–461.

Scribner, S., & Cole, M. (1978). Literacy without schooling: Testing for intellectual effects. *Harvard Educational Review, 48,* 448–461.

Siegler, R. S. (1996). *Emerging minds: The process of change in children's thinking.* New York: Oxford University Press.

Sodian, B., Schneider, W., & Perlmutter, M. (1986). Recall, clustering, and metamemory in young children. *Journal of Experimental Child Psychology, 41,* 395–410.

Tessler, M., & Nelson, K. (1994). Making memories: The influence of joint encoding on later recall. *Consciousness and Cognition, 3,* 307–326.

Underwood, B. J. (1963). Stimulus selection in verbal learning. In C. N. Cofer & B. S. Musgrave (Eds.), *Verbal behavior and learning: Problems and processes* (pp. 33–48). New York: McGraw-Hill.

Wagner, D. A. (1978). Memories of Morocco: The influence of age, schooling, and environment on memory. *Cognitive Psychology, 10,* 1–28.

Wellman, H. M. (1988). The early development of memory strategies. In F. E. Weinert & M. Perlmutter (Eds.), *Memory development: Universal changes and individual differences* (pp. 3–29). Hillsdale, NJ: Lawrence Erlbaum Associates.

Worden, P. E. (1975). Effects of sorting on subsequent recall of unrelated items: A developmental study. *Child Development, 46,* 687–695.

Zacks, R. T., Hasher, L., & Li, K. Z. H. (2000). Human memory. In F. I. M. Craik & T. A. Salthouse (Eds.), *The handbook of aging and cognition* (pp. 293–357). Mahwah, NJ: Lawrence Erlbaum Associates.

11

Aging and Long-Term Memory: Deficits Are Not Inevitable

Rose T. Zacks

Lynn Hasher

The study of memory encompasses a wide range of phenomena that, together, lie at the center of the individual's cognitive, social, and personal functioning. Indeed, a recent textbook on human memory begins: "If we had no memory, in the broadest sense of the term, we would not be able to function. Memory is essential for all activities" (Neath & Surprenant, 2002, p. 1). The authors note that memory is involved when we ride a bicycle, read, have a conversation, create imagined events, and formulate and update an image of one's self. This diversity was not much acknowledged in the research literature until the onset of the cognitive revolution in the 1960s. However, much of the history of the last 35 to 40 years of research on memory has seen both basic work done on the subdivisions of memory (e.g., working memory, long-term memory, etc.) and an increasing interest in understanding the embeddedness of memory in other cognitive, social, and biological functions. Indeed, we note that very recent work on the roles of social and biological factors is in the process of changing our views about the degree to which we may have overestimated the aspects of memory that really do change with healthy aging. These moderating factors are discussed in the final section of this chapter. We begin, however, with a classic view of aging and memory, a view that suggests that there is variability in the degree to which one can expect to see changes in performance.

Here, we focus on long-term memory, and in this literature, there are replicable findings of age-related decline, stability, and even in some cases, increase in memory performance. Thus, a central fact about memory in the later years of life is the *variability* of age patterns. As well, a number of factors are now known to contribute to this variability, including the cognitive ones that were of initial interest to the field (e.g., type of memory test, familiarity of the materials, concurrent demands), participant characteristics (e.g., verbal ability, education level, domain expertise), biological factors (e.g., circadian synchrony, physical fitness), and social and emotional variables (e.g., activation of negative age stereotypes, remembering in the service of interpersonal goals).

Given this diversity of outcomes and the wide range of factors known to play a role in that diversity, it is hardly surprising that a variety of theoretical accounts of aging and memory have been proposed and that they continue to garner support from at least a subset of the empirical findings on age-related differences in memory. The relevant theoretical frameworks include ones emphasizing age-related declines in speed of mental processing (e.g., Salthouse, 1996), in resources for effortful processing (e.g., Craik, 1986), in the ability to bind or to form associations among elements of an input (e.g., Chalfonte & Johnson, 1996; Naveh-Benjamin, 2000), and in inhibitory processing or executive functions (e.g., Hasher & Zacks, 1988; Hasher, Zacks, & May, 1999; West, 1996; for overviews, see Balota, Dolan, & Duchek, 2000; Park, 2000; Zacks, Hasher, & Li, 2000). In addition, it is increasingly clear that views encompassing social and emotional factors (e.g., Charles, Mather, & Carstensen, 2003; Hess, Auman, Colcombe, & Rahhal, 2003) are also important to our understanding of how memory is impacted by normal aging.

At a global level at least, there are significant parallels between the literatures reviewed in this chapter and in Ornstein, Haden, and Elischberger's chapter (Chapter 10, this volume) on children's memory development. For example, similar to the findings for older adults, the research on children's memory demonstrates variability in age effects across different forms of memory (e.g., conditioning vs. event recall) and also as a function of various contextual and task demand variables (e.g., prior knowledge, retrieval demands of the memory test). Additionally, although the specific issues and perspectives differ, investigators of both children's and older adults' memory have recently shown increased interest in the impact of social and emotional factors. These latter effects may be challenging to all theories of aging and memory, in part because the widely reported age differences on some memory tasks can be overcome by instructions, materials, and other factors that are probably noncognitive in origin.

Our review of the aging and memory literature is selective but tries to give a flavor of the richness of the findings as well as of the diversity of theoretical viewpoints. The chapter is organized into three major parts. The first is a brief summary of major empirical generalizations about aging and memory that will serve as background for the second section, which focuses on episodic memory (or deliberate, intentional memory for particular events) and includes discussions of research on mechanisms of retrieval and on memory errors (source and false memories). These topics are of considerable current interest, are being studied from different theoretical perspectives, and make contact with research on memory development in children. The final section considers noncognitive (social, biological) factors that have important moderating effects on age-related differences in memory. These findings are changing the understanding of memory and aging in the same way as such factors changed our understanding of memory and development.

MAJOR FINDINGS ON AGING AND MEMORY

Spurred on by theoretical considerations as well as striking dissociations in behavioral and neurocognitive findings (e.g., dissociations in the memory effects of localized brain damage), memory researchers have, over the last 30 years, increasingly come to the conclusion that long-term memory, like the memory system as a whole, is not a unitary system. Although the field still lacks consensus on a full-blown model of the architecture of long-term memory, there is fair agreement about the major subdivisions of long-term memory. At the highest level, a distinction is made between *explicit* or *declarative memory* and *implicit* or *nondeclarative memory*. Explicit memory is measured by tests that invoke deliberate, conscious retrieval of information stored in memory. By contrast, implicit memory tests measure the effects of prior experience or learning through performance in the absence of deliberate recollection—for example, by increases in accuracy and/or decreases in reaction time when a response to a particular stimulus is repeated.

Various subdivisions of both explicit and implicit memory have also been proposed. Within explicit memory, the distinction between *semantic* and *episodic* memory (Tulving, 1972) is of particular relevance to aging. Semantic memory includes our vast storehouse of general knowledge of such things as the meanings of words and concepts or facts about the world in which we live. This information is not tied to specific time-space parameters. Episodic memory, on the other hand, includes our memories of information associated with specific events and is defined by the ability to retrieve features of the spatial/temporal context in which the event was experienced.

Distinctions have also been proposed between different subtypes of nondeclarative memory (e.g., procedural memory for highly practiced skills, classical conditioning), but we limit our discussion to the type of implicit memory that has received the most attention in aging research—namely, *repetition priming*. Repetition priming studies involve a two-phase procedure in which the first phase uses an orienting task (e.g., pleasantness ratings) to expose participants to some experimental materials (e.g., pictures, words, etc.). This is followed by a test phase in which the processing of the previously presented items (e.g., on a perceptual identification or fragment completion task) is compared to that of new items to determine the amount of benefit from the prior exposure.

With these distinctions in mind, we turn to findings for age effects on three major components of long-term memory: repetition priming, semantic memory, and episodic memory. Figure 11.1, from Nilsson (2003), presents cross-sectional data that were collected as part of the Betula project, an ongoing longitudinal, prospective study of memory development in adulthood that began in 1988 (see, e.g., Nilsson et al., 1997). Three of the four panels in the figure (all but panel c) display typical results from tests measuring different forms of long-term memory performance. Similar patterns of findings have been obtained in numerous studies that have examined an array of long-term memory functions in older adults (e.g., see Figure 1.1 in Park, 2000, and Figure 1 in Park et al.,

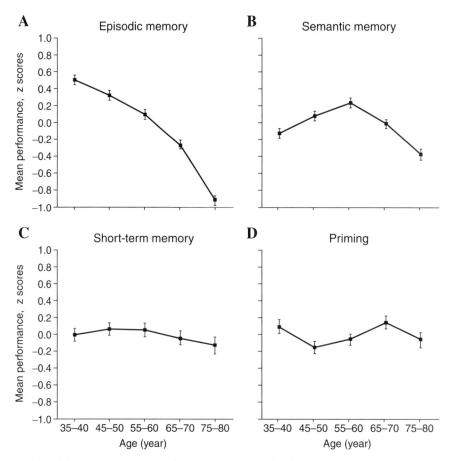

FIGURE 11.1. Mean performance as a function of age in tasks assessing episodic memory, semantic memory, short-term memory and the perceptual representational system. (From Nilsson, 2003, p. 9. Reprinted with the permission of Blackwell Publishing.)

2002). In other words, the age patterns shown in Figure 11.1 are quite robust and the figure provides a good, albeit very global, summary of findings on aging and long-term memory. It is apparent that there is considerable variation in age-related differences across different forms of long-term memory.

Repetition Priming

Analyses of findings on age differences in repetition priming, including formal meta-analyses, have consistently pointed to the conclusion that age differences in this form of implicit memory are quite small relative to age differences in episodic memory, and frequently nonsignificant in individual studies (cf. Fleischman & Gabrieli, 1998; La Voie & Light, 1994; Light, Prull, La Voie, & Healy, 2000). In addition, these analyses suggest that there is minimal variation in age effects across priming tasks that differ considerably in the types of processing involved. In particular, age differences in priming are small and roughly equivalent whether the experimental task is a so-called perceptual priming task (e.g., perceptual identification or picture naming) that relies on the processing of perceptual features or a so-called conceptual priming task (e.g., category instance generation or answering general knowledge questions) that relies on the processing of conceptual or meaning features. (The data in Figure 11.1d are based on a perceptual priming task, stem completion.) Likewise, age effects do not, on average, differ between *item* and *associative* priming, the former referring to priming effects deriving from the repetition of individual familiar items (words, pictures of common objects) and the latter to priming effects deriving from repetition of novel stimuli or novel connections between known items. In view of the findings of large age deficits on explicit measures of memory for new associations (see below), it is somewhat surprising that age deficits are not larger on associative than on item priming measures.

With respect to lifespan patterns, Ornstein et al. (Chapter 10, this volume) mention that performance on implicit memory shows minimal developmental change (p. 144) and, more generally, that children from a very young age show similar patterns of effects on "nonverbal measures" including those such as conditioning that are generally included in the implicit/nondeclarative memory category (pp. 144–145). These findings indicate parallels in the early years to the relative constancy of implicit memory in the later years of life.

Semantic Memory

Semantic memory is another area of relatively preserved performance across the adult lifespan. The data in Figure 11.1b are derived from vocabulary and general knowledge tests, and as is frequently found with similar measures, show an increase in semantic memory performance through the early 60s followed by a gradual decline. However, steeper age deficits do occur on certain semantic memory tests (e.g., Nyberg et al., 2003). These are generally semantic memory tests that put a premium on rapid retrieval of information from memory, as, for example, in fluency tests that measure the number of words beginning with a particular letter or from a particular category that a participant is able to produce in a short time. The greater age deficits on such tasks relative to, for example, a multiple-choice test, are generally assumed to be due to retrieval difficulties rather than to deficits in semantic memory representations themselves. Semantic memory (apart from speed of retrieval) appears to be an area of relatively spared cognitive functioning in old age.

Episodic Memory

As is suggested by the data in Figure 11.1a, age patterns for episodic memory differ significantly from those for repetition priming and semantic memory. Indeed, one of the clearest results to emerge from research on aging and memory is the strong age-related declines in explicit memory for recently experienced events—that is, on episodic memory tests for new information. Such deficits have been consistently demonstrated in both cross-sectional and longitudinal studies, with a wide variety of materials, and with various episodic memory tests (including free recall, cued recall, yes/no and forced-choice recognition, and source memory tests). A closer look at the episodic memory findings from the Betula study (summarized in Figure 11.1a) provides a clear demonstration of the pervasiveness of age-related decline in episodic memory. The eight episodic memory tests administered to Betula study participants include measures of "prospective memory, face recognition, name recognition, action memory, sentence memory, word recall with or without a distractor task, source memory, and memory for activities" (Nilsson et al., 2002, p. 186). Consistent with numerous other studies, the Betula project has demonstrated robust age deficits on each of these measures (e.g., Nilsson et al., 1997, 2002). Indeed, significant negative age trends are seen in normative data on episodic memory measures included in standardized neuropsychological assessments of memory, such as the Logical Memory component of the Wechsler Memory Scale (Wechsler, 1997) and the California Verbal Learning Test (Norman, Evans, Miller, & Heaton, 2000). Given that event recall and use of strategic encoding and retrieval processes are both aspects of episodic memory, it is clear from Ornstein et al.'s review (Chapter 10, this volume) that robust age differences are also true of children's memory development.

Summary

This brief overview of findings on three subtypes of long-term memory clearly demonstrates the theme of variability in age patterns for different memory functions. In the next part of this chapter we delve more deeply into the component of long-term memory that appears to show the largest age deficits, episodic memory.

FURTHER EXPLORATION OF AGE DIFFERENCES IN EPISODIC MEMORY

The overall pattern of poorer episodic memory performance with increasing age as is displayed in Figure 11.1a masks some intriguing complexities. More specifically, an examination of different episodic memory tasks and different testing conditions reveals interesting and seemingly important variations in the precise pattern of age differences. A prominent example of such differential age trajectories within episodic memory is the pattern of age effects typically found for recall versus recognition tests. Early evidence (e.g., Schonfield & Robertson, 1966) indicated that recognition tests show smaller age declines than recall tests, a result that continues to receive confirmation. Among the more recent findings are the results of Nyberg et al.'s (2003) structural equation modeling analyses of the performance of 925 individuals between the ages of 35 and 80 from sample 3 of the Betula study. These data support a division of episodic memory into recall and recognition subcomponents. As well, they find that the recall factor shows greater age deficits than the recognition factor. One account of the differential age trajectory for recall and

recognition (Bäckman, 1989; Craik, 1986; Craik & McDowd, 1987) presumes a reduction in cognitive resources. Because of this, older adults generally engage in less self-initiated processing than do younger adults, including (in the present instance) less of the kind of strategic search processes that are essential for good recall but that are less important for recognition. Similar arguments have been made in the child development literature with respect to the relative age invariance on recognition, as compared to recall tasks (see Ornstein et al., Chapter 10, this volume, pp. 144–145). In any case, the recall-recognition differences in older adults are also consistent with a more general theoretical perspective on the processes underlying episodic memory, the *dual-process* viewpoint, to which we now turn.

Recollection and Familiarity

Although far from new (e.g., Bahrick, 1970), the dual-process approach has received considerable recent attention as a possible basis for integrating a broad range of episodic memory findings, including findings relating to age differences. This theoretical perspective encompasses a body of specific models that propose that episodic retrieval is dependent on the dual processes of *recollection* and *familiarity* (for recent reviews, see Light et al., 2000; Rugg & Yonelinas, 2003; Yonelinas, 2002). Although there is some variation in the specific definitions proposed by different authors, the following from Rugg and Yonelinas (2003) is representative: "recollection depends on a relatively slow process . . . which yields qualitative information about the previous study events (e.g., when or where an item was studied). By contrast, familiarity reflects a purely quantitative 'strength-like' memory signal" (p. 313).

A common claim of dual-process views (Light et al., 2000; Rugg & Yonelinas, 2003) is that recall tasks are more heavily dependent on recollection processes than are recognition tasks. More specifically, it is argued that familiarity alone can support accurate recognition performance, especially on recognition tasks using forced-choice procedures and/or dissimilar distractors (Bastin & Van der Linden, 2003), whereas recollection processes are the primary basis of accurate recall. With respect to aging, it is further argued that, because of the differential impact of aging on the underlying neural mechanisms or other factors (see below), recollection processes show greater age-related declines than familiarity processes.

At least two different procedures have been developed to study the contributions of recollection and familiarity to various tasks and their potential differential rates of decline with aging: the *process-dissociation procedure* and/or the *remember-know procedure*. In a typical instance of the former procedure (first used by Jacoby, 1991), participants study items under two or more conditions or arranged in two or more lists and then are tested in two types of memory tests. In the *inclusion* test participants are told to recall or recognize any studied items, whereas in the *exclusion* condition they are instructed to recall or recognize only a specified subset of studied items (e.g., those that were presented in the second of two lists). According to the analysis of Jacoby and colleagues (e.g., Jacoby, 1991; Jacoby, Yonelinas, & Jennings, 1997), whereas performance on inclusion tests benefits from independent contributions of familiarity and recollection, accurate performance on the exclusion test is dependent on the recollection of qualitative information about how and when the item was initially studied. This analysis serves as the basis for equations that can be applied to inclusion and exclusion test data to provide quantitative estimates of the familiarity and recollection processes for particular conditions and for particular groups of subjects (for details see Jacoby, 1991; Jacoby et al., 1997).

In the remember-know procedure, standard yes/no or forced-choice recognition test conditions are combined with introspective reports about the qualitative characteristics of the memories that resulted in a judgment that a particular test item was "old" (i.e., had been included in the study list). Participants are asked to distinguish between items they judged to be old because they explicitly recall some qualitative information about the study episode (*remember* items) and items they judged to be old because of an acontextual feeling of familiarity (*know* items). These two types of reports map onto recollection and familiarity, respectively (Light et al., 2000; Rugg & Yonelinas, 2003; Yonelinas, 2002).

Regardless of method, age differences are typically larger for recollection than for familiarity (for recent reviews, see Light et al., 2000; Yonelinas, 2002). More specifically, age deficits are uniformly significant on measures of recollection derived from both the process-dissociation (e.g., Jennings & Jacoby, 1993) and remember-know (e.g., Java, 1996) procedures. The pattern of age differences for familiarity estimates is somewhat more variable, with some studies reporting age constancy (e.g., Java, 1996; Jennings & Jacoby, 1993) or even higher familiarity scores (Parkin & Walter, 1992) on the part of older adults and others reporting age deficits (e.g., Mark & Rugg, 1998), albeit smaller than those for recollection. According to Yonelinas (2002), the latter outcome is associated with high levels of overall recognition and thus may reflect distortions relating to ceiling effects. Such qualifications aside, there seems to be a general consensus in the literature that "normal aging disrupts recollection but leaves familiarity largely unaffected" (Yonelinas, 2002, p. 471).

To provide concrete illustrations of this pattern, we briefly review two recent studies using remember-know and process-dissociation procedures. In the first, Bastin and Van der Linden (2003) used the remember-know procedure to investigate age-related differences on two types of recognition tests—yes/no and forced-choice. The comparison of the two types of recognition tests was predicated on findings from prior research (especially with amnesic patients) suggesting that relative to yes/no recognition memory performance, forced-choice recognition performance is more dependent on familiarity and less dependent on recollection. Various predictions that follow from these suggestions were confirmed by Bastian and Van der Linden in a study that used unfamiliar faces as the test materials. In particular, in addition to confirming the suggestions of a greater contribution of familiarity to forced-choice than to yes/no recognition, Bastian and Van der Linden found the expected greater age deficit for a yes/no than for a forced-choice test. These differences as a function of type of recognition test were associated with an overall age decrease in recollection and an increase in familiarity.

Our second example from the recent literature is a study by Davidson and Glisky (2002) that employed the process-dissociation procedure to investigate the contribution of recollection and familiarity to age differences on a yes/no word-recognition test. Study of two lists of words was followed by either an inclusion test (respond "yes" if the item was on either studied list) or an exclusion test (respond "yes" only to items from one of the two study lists). An important aspect of this study was the examination of hypotheses about the brain structures supporting recollection and familiarity. As summarized by Davidson and Glisky, findings from various sources (including studies of patients with localized brain damage as well as ERP and neuroimaging data) suggest that recollection relies on both medial temporal lobe and frontal lobe structures, whereas familiarity is primarily associated with medial temporal lobe structures (see also Rugg & Yonelinas, 2003; Yonelinas, 2002). To pursue these suggestions, the present study employed a neuropsychological test battery that Glisky and colleagues (Glisky, Polster, & Routhieaux, 1995; Glisky, Rubin, & Davidson, 2001) had previously shown reliably distinguishes among older adults who have selective impairments of either frontal lobe or medial temporal lobe function or both. Familiarity and recollection estimates from four groups of older adults, representing all possible combinations of high and low frontal lobe and high and low medial temporal lobe function as measured by the Glisky battery, were compared to estimates from a group of young adults. Relative to the young adults, familiarity estimates were significantly reduced only in the low medial temporal lobe subgroups of older adults, and recollection estimates were significantly reduced in both the low medial temporal lobe and low frontal lobe subgroups. These data thus support, at least in a general way, proposals about the neural substrates of recollection and familiarity, and they suggest that age deficits in both recollection and familiarity vary among older adults in accordance with an individual's functioning of the relevant brain mechanisms.

The assertion that recollection relies on frontal and medial temporal lobe structures is also interesting because structural and neurophysiological data indicate that these structures (and within the medial temporal lobe, particularly the hippocampus) show greater age-related change than other brain regions (Raz, 2000). However, the story is as yet incomplete. For example, it is presumed that the medial temporal lobe structures underlying recollection and familiarity are at least partially nonoverlapping, but the specific details have yet to be worked out. One proposal (Rugg & Yonelinas, 2003; Yonelinas, 2002) is that the hippocampus plays a critical role in recollection and that familiarity depends more on extra-hippocampal/perirhinal structures. If supported by additional research, such proposals may provide at least a partial explanation of why recollection typically shows greater age deficits than does familiarity.

As the above examples suggest, when combined with task analyses, neurocognitive considerations, and the use of various experimental paradigms, dual-process views provide the foundation for integrating a diverse array of findings on age-related differences in episodic memory and, as suggested by the Davidson and Glisky study, potentially also individual differences among older adults.

Items and Associations of Items or Features

Closely related to the dual-process views we have just considered, and also possible candidates for accounts of heterogeneity of age effects in episodic memory, are views that distinguish between episodic memory for the individual elements (features, components, or items) of an input and memory for pairings between items (Naveh-Benjamin, 2000) or between items and contextual features (Chalfonte & Johnson, 1996). A number of studies have demonstrated that age-related deficits are smaller for items than for item-item or item-feature combinations even if the age groups are equated on memory for individual items. For instance, Naveh-Benjamin and colleagues (2000, 2001; Naveh-Benjamin, Hussain, Guez, & Bar-On, 2003; see also Castel & Craik, 2003) have carried out a series of experiments in which study of a list of paired items is followed by independent tests of memory for the items and for the associations between the items. The consistent outcome of these experiments is a greater age deficit in the associative memory tests relative to the item memory tests. This outcome is interpreted by Naveh-Benjamin as a manifestation of a general age-related deficit in association formation, the *associative deficit hypothesis*. A closely related view, the *feature binding deficit view*, has been applied by Johnson and colleagues (e.g., Chalfonte & Johnson, 1996; Mitchell, Johnson, Raye, & D'Esposito, 2000) to findings (from experiments using arrays of differently colored objects) that demonstrate a disproportionate age deficit in memory for combinations of features (e.g., item and color information) relative to memory for individual features (e.g., item or color information).

There is considerable overlap between the associative/binding deficit views and the dual-process recollection-familiarity view. In particular, the definition of recollection as involving retrieval of qualitative information about the earlier study event implies that a recollected memory contains not only the core item of information but also contextual features (e.g., location, temporal order, surface appearance) and perhaps other items experienced in the same context. If so, it is a small step to argue that associative/feature binding deficits in older adults account for their reduced recall of qualitative contextual information about earlier experiences and thus their lower levels of recollection, and also to argue that older adults' relatively intact item/element memory serves as the basis for relatively intact familiarity processes. Despite the possibility of making such connections, it remains to be seen whether the associative deficit and feature binding deficit views can be fully integrated with the more traditional dual-process distinction between recollection and familiarity. For now, it seems to us that research on certain topics draws more heavily on one set of views than the other. Research on recall-recognition differences is heavily based on the familiarity-recollection distinction; in contrast, research on age-related differences in source memory and in memory errors (topics to which we now turn) frequently invokes notions of associative/feature binding deficits.

Source Memory

Source memory refers to the ability to remember the conditions surrounding the encoding of a particular episodic memory. Research on source memory typically employs a broad definition of source that, in addition to information directly specifying the source of the experience (e.g., was the event directly experienced or imagined; did person A or B report the event?), encompasses various aspects of the encoding context, including perceptual, spatio-temporal, affective, and social features (cf. Glisky et al., 2001). Consequently, source memory and context memory are largely interchangeable terms in the relevant literature and will be treated as such in the following discussion.

A meta-analysis by Spencer and Raz (1995) indicated that age deficits in memory of source/contextual features are both large (average age effect size, *d.*, was ~0.9) and fairly uniform across feature type (perceptual qualities, input modality, spatial location, external source vs. self-generation, etc.). For example, visual perceptual features such as spatial location and the color, case, and font of verbal items are less well remembered by older than younger adults (e.g., Chalfonte & Johnson, 1996; Naveh-Benjamin & Craik, 1995). Likewise, relative to younger adults, older individuals show poorer memory for perceptual features of auditory inputs such as the speaker's voice

(e.g., Bayen & Murnane, 1996). Temporal order memory is also reduced in older adults (e.g., Dumas & Hartman, 2003). And finally, age deficits are found for features that would be considered relevant within even a narrow definition of source, including features such as whether particular items were presented visually versus auditorially (e.g., Light, La Voie, Valencia-Laver, Albertson-Owens, & Mead, 1992), or in video versus photo format (Schacter, Koutstaal, Johnson, Gross, & Angell, 1997), or were seen in a video versus mentioned in a questionnaire about the video (Mitchell, Johnson, & Mather, 2003), or were overtly produced by the individual (or read or heard) versus imagined in response to a prompt from the experimenter (e.g., Hashtroudi, Johnson, & Chrosniak, 1990; for more complete reviews of this literature, see Spencer & Raz, 1995; Zacks et al., 2000.)

A central issue in the literature on aging and source memory is whether age deficits in memory for context are *differentially greater* than those in memory for content. Larger age effects for source than for content memory implies that source memory involves age-sensitive mechanisms (e.g., item and context binding) that are relatively unimportant for content memory. By contrast, similar size age effects for source and content memory suggest that similar factors contribute to the age deficits for both types of information. The results of Spencer and Raz's (1995) meta-analysis provided fairly conclusive evidence of greater age effects on memory for context than on memory for content: In contrast to the large average age effect size for context/source memory, the average age effect size for content was only moderate (*d.* ~0.6). Spencer and Raz's findings also suggested that, in contrast to memory for content, age deficits in context memory are unaffected by type of test (recall or recognition), but that older adults have particularly poor memory for general contextual features (e.g., spatio-temporal information) as compared to information that is more directly tied to target content (e.g., target color or size). More recent data add further evidence to these general patterns of results, including the differential impact of aging on memory for source information (e.g., Dywan, Segalowitz, & Arsenault, 2002; Larsson & Bäckman, 1998; Newman, Allen, & Kaszniak, 2001). Because of the considerable overlap in relevant theoretical views, we consider theoretical accounts of age effects in source memory in conjunction with proposals about age differences in memory errors (our next topic).

Memory Errors

Source confusion is an important memory error in its own right, but it is also often invoked in accounts of other types of errors. This is particularly clear in research involving experimental models of eyewitness memory, including research using the Loftus post-event misinformation paradigm (e.g., Loftus, Miller, & Burns, 1978). In typical instances of this paradigm, participants view a live enactment or a video or a series of slides of an event such as a burglary or a car accident, and then are asked to complete a questionnaire on the depicted event. The questionnaire contains misinformation in the form of subtle suggestions about specific objects or actions that conflict with the actual information in the enacted event. When participants are subsequently asked to report, either on recall or recognition tests, what they observed in the original enactment, the suggested misinformation is frequently incorporated into their memory reports. Among others, Johnson and colleagues (e.g., Johnson, Hashtroudi, & Lindsay, 1993; Lindsay, 1994) have argued that these errors, in large part, reflect source-monitoring failures in which the participant confuses suggested information with witnessed information. Such confusion is facilitated by the semantic overlap between the witnessed event and the questionnaire and by the fact that any given piece of information could have been both in the original event and in the questionnaire, so remembering that the information was in the questionnaire does not rule out its also having been in the original event (cf. Mitchell et al., 2003). In other words, the misinformation paradigm entails challenging source-monitoring demands. Indeed, in a recent misinformation paradigm study, Mitchell et al. (2003) found that older adults were more likely than younger adults to misattribute items suggested in a questionnaire to the preceding video of a burglary and also that older adults had greater confidence in those misattributions.

As part of a recent study using an individual differences/structural equation modeling approach to age-related differences in memory errors, Lövdén (2003) included versions of three other procedures that have been frequently used to induce "false" memories—i.e., memories of information or events that were not actually presented. In each case, study materials were presented that elicit associatively or semantically related (nonpresented) items as memory intrusions. The first procedure used by Lövdén was a category-cued recall test in which lists of category members that include most but not all of the strongest items are presented for study. After a filled delay, participants are cued with the category names and asked to recall the presented items. Previous research has demonstrated a significant level of false recall of the omitted category members. Lövdén's second procedure, the Deese-Roediger-McDermott (DRM) procedure (Roediger & McDermott, 1995), also uses lists of associatively semantically related words. In this case, the words in each list are all associates (e.g., *thread, pin, eye, sewing*, etc.) of a critical nonpresented word (*needle*). This critical word is likely to occur as an intrusion—that is, as a false memory—whether memory is tested by recognition or recall. Finally, Lövdén also used a paradigm developed by Koutstaal and Schacter (1997) in which sets of pictures of items from various categories (e.g., shoes, chairs) are used as the study materials. The recognition test includes new pictures from the studied categories (related lures) as well as pictures of unrelated objects. False alarms to the related lures occur at a much higher rate than to the unrelated new pictures.

Although there are some exceptions (Kensinger & Schacter, 1999), the typical outcome with respect to age differences in the above paradigms is an increase in false recall or recognition for older adults in the face of decreased or age-equivalent memory for presented items (e.g., see Balota et al., 1999; Koutstaal & Schacter, 1997). Lövdén's (2003) experiment confirmed these findings with a sample of 146 participants ranging in age from 20 to 80. False memory increased with age on each of the three memory tasks, whereas veridical memory either decreased (category-cued recall, DRM) or remained constant (picture memory task). In addition, false and veridical memory were negatively correlated across individuals, and confirmatory factor analysis of the false memory data, as well as other individual difference variables, indicated that false memory scores from the three tasks all loaded on a common false-memory factor.

The literatures reviewed in this and the previous sections suggest a consistent pattern of age-related increases in the occurrence of memory intrusions and distortions. That is, using a variety of procedures and materials, older adults have been found to be more likely than younger adults to confuse nontarget information with semantically and associatively related target information and to include such nontarget information in their memory reports. In the next section, we attempt to relate the memory error findings to the dual-process viewpoints discussed earlier.

Recollection, Familiarity, and Memory Errors: Possible Commonalities

Although it is far from certain that a common underlying factor accounts for the basic developmental patterns that have been found in studies examining age differences in recollection and familiarity, source memory, and memory errors, there seems to be a common empirical thread. As has been suggested by Craik and others (e.g., Craik, 2002), older adults appear to be more disadvantaged relative to younger adults when the memory test calls for retrieval of detailed, precise information about the encoding event than when the memory test can be performed on the basis of more general information that (in many cases) captures the meaning of the encoded event rather than its perceptual and contextual details. If this is a reasonable, broad summary of the major findings in the areas reviewed above, the question arises: what is (are) the mechanism(s) underlying this general pattern?

A variety of answers have been proposed to this question. One proposal is that reduced cognitive resources in older adults (e.g., Craik, 1986) results in reduced spontaneous use of elaborative strategies such as categorization and organization during encoding. Similar encoding outcomes, as well as reduced strategic processing during retrieval, have also been attributed to decreased frontal lobe functioning in older adults (e.g., Glisky et al., 1995; Moscovitch & Winocur, 1995). As these two examples suggest, despite invoking different causal mechanisms, proposed encoding deficits are a common theme for accounts of the greater age deficits in memory for details than for general meanings of experienced events. That is, it is frequently argued that older adults are less able than younger adults to encode into memory the perceptual and contextual details of inputs and/or to bind such features to target information. This possibility is fully consistent with the associative deficit hypothesis of Naveh-Benjamin (2000) and the binding-deficit view of Chalfonte and Johnson (1996). One further type of supportive evidence comes from the use of instruments such as the Memory Characteristics Questionnaire (MCQ; Johnson, Foley, Suengas, & Raye, 1988) to assess participants' recollections of the perceptual details, spatial and temporal context, affective responses, and so on that accompanied encoding of

remembered items or events. The questionnaire results indicate that, in comparison to younger adults, older adults remember fewer perceptual (e.g., color) and contextual (e.g., list position) details of the encoding event for actually presented items, and they also show less difference in MCQ reports between veridical memories and falsely recalled or recognized items (Hashtroudi et al., 1990; Norman & Schacter, 1997). That is, the MCQ data, like much of the research we surveyed above, suggest that older adults encode fewer distinguishing features of events than do younger adults.

Reduced encoding of distinguishing details would be expected to have a direct impact on the ability to discriminate target from related nontarget memories, but it could also have more strategic effects on post-encoding processing. In particular, if older adults have fewer episodic features to work with, they may well give greater weight to the information they do encode as well as younger adults do—namely, the semantic or gist information. However, in the paradigms under consideration, gist is a poor guide to the source of a piece of information or even whether it actually occurred (for further discussion of these issues, see e.g., Lövdén, 2003; Mitchell et al., 2003).

Thus a reasonable case can be made that encoding deficits contribute to age-related differences in recollection, source memory, and memory errors. Nonetheless, there are other findings that, at the least, complicate conclusions about encoding deficits by suggesting that the supportive evidence may be tied to the use of explicit memory measures that require deliberate, conscious access to information in memory. A clear example of findings that suggest caution comes from the recent study by Koutstaal (2003). The study compared younger and older adults' memory for pictures of common objects (e.g., key, chair, banana) across three different memory tests. Older adults showed the typical increase in false alarms to related lures (different exemplars of studied objects) on a standard old/new recognition test, but they also showed *equal* benefits to younger adults from the repetition of the studied exemplar (versus a new one) on the two other tests—a test requiring recognition judgments on the basis of item type rather than exact repetition (i.e., "old" was the correct response for a new key as well as the original key) and an implicit memory test measuring repetition priming on a size-judgment task. Koutstaal (2003) interprets this pattern of findings as indicating "that older adults do, indeed, encode differentiating perceptual details—possibly even to the same extent as do younger adults, at least for certain types of task-relevant features" (p. 192), but they seem to use such features less effectively in deliberate retrieval situations.

Koutstaal's (2003) results are consistent with findings from the implicit-memory literature (summarized earlier) that demonstrate robust perceptual priming and associative priming effects in older adults. Given the small age effects on these types of memory (e.g., Light et al., 2000), it appears that older adults may encode the perceptual features of individual items (perceptual priming) and novel connections between items (associative priming) nearly as well as younger adults. If so, we need to look at the conditions of deliberate retrieval for a complete explanation of age differences seen on episodic memory tasks. We may also expect to find situations in which older adults do not show age deficits, even on memory tasks that involve deliberate access to perceptual or contextual details (e.g., source information). The next section of this chapter reviews evidence relevant to these possibilities.

FACTORS THAT MODERATE OLDER ADULTS' EPISODIC MEMORY PERFORMANCE

The focus in this section is on recent findings suggesting that, as is the case for research comparing younger and older children (see Ornstein et al., Chapter 10, this volume), a variety of experiential, social, and affective factors can impact the performance of younger and older adults when recalling specific single events or remembering new associations between items or between target items and their contexts. When these factors are taken into account, there is good evidence that older adults can at least occasionally do as well as younger adults.

Consider the following findings from Castel (in press). In one of his experiments, younger and older adults learned paired associate lists of grocery products and prices. In one list, the prices were quite realistic and in the other they were unrealistic, overestimating some and underestimating other prices by wide margins. The memory test required participants to recall the prices that had been paired with each product on the study list. Based on other work in the area, this test should have been a sensitive test of age differences in

binding, but the findings showed an interesting deviation from the pattern expected on that basis. Castel found the usual age differences for lists with unrealistic prices, but no age differences for realistic prices—even though the criterion of correct was stringent: If a product was listed as being sold at $1.79 during learning, only the answer "$1.79" was counted as correct!

Another example of excellent binding on the part of older adults comes from a series of studies in which items of information (e.g., trivia statements or facts about pharmaceuticals) were introduced, in each instance with a covarying perceptual feature. For example, in a study using trivia statements as materials (Rahhal, May, & Hasher, 2002), each statement was read by a male or female speaker, one of whom (according to the scenario provided to participants) always told the truth while the other only spoke falsehoods. In another study people learned the names and uses of pharmaceuticals (May, Rahhal, Berry, & Leighton, 2004). Here, drugs were located on the left or right of a warehouse that had had a flood that damaged all the drugs on one side. After specific facts were presented, older and younger adults were given the target items (trivia statements in one study, drug names in another). One half of the participants in each age group were tested on the perceptual features (who said it, he or she in the trivia study; and where was it, left or right in the warehouse, in the pharmaceuticals study); the other half were tested on the conceptual features (was the statement true or false; can the drug be sold or not). Across four experiments using materials analogous to these, the results were the same: older adults did less well than younger adults on the perceptual details, but did as well as the young adults on the conceptual details. Across the studies, older adults knew whether a statement was true or false, whether a drug could be sold or not, whether food could still be eaten or not, and who was a good or bad person (May et al, 2004; Rahhal et al., 2002). This performance pattern strongly suggests that older adults successfully bind some information (e.g., a statement) to other information (e.g., its truth or falseness) as well as younger adults. Thus, the binding-deficit notion cannot be universally applied to older adults since they clearly do not show it for at least some materials.

A final example of preserved memory comes from a quite different memory task than we have considered so far—that of recalling or retelling a story. In a series of studies, Adams and colleagues (Adams, 1991;

Adams, Labouvie-Vief, Hobart, & Dorosz, 1990; Adams, Smith, Nyquist, & Perlmutter, 1997) have demonstrated that the recollections of older and younger adults are not the same, with young adults being at an advantage when the typical (in this literature as elsewhere) criterion of specific details (or number of propositions) recalled is used. However, older adults recall the gist of the presented stories quite well and their recalls tend to include more integrative and interpretive information than those of younger adults. There is also evidence that when the quality of the retold story is assessed by both younger and older listeners (who are blind with respect to the age of the teller), both age groups rate the stories told by older adults as being better, more interesting tales (James, Burke, Austin, & Hulme, 1998). A particularly interesting study in this area was recently carried out by Adams, Smith, Pasupathi, and Vitolo (2002). Groups of older and younger women were asked to learn a story (a version of either a children's fable or a Sufi folk tale) so that they could retell it either to a 5–6-year-old child or to a young adult experimenter. The usual finding of greater propositional recall by younger participants was replicated when the listener was a young adult but not when the listener was a young child. In addition, both age groups made appropriate adjustments for the comprehension abilities of child listeners, using more elaborations and repetitions and decreasing the complexity of the more complex story when speaking to a child as compared to an adult listener. In fact, the complexity adjustment was greater in the case of the older tellers. Adams et al. (2002) interpret these and related findings in relation to the impact of the social context on remembering. They suggest that older adults do well at story retelling, particularly when the listener is a young child, because this task meshes well with the social cognitive goals of aging, which include transmission of social-cultural knowledge to younger generations. In the present context, a major point of the findings in this area is that older adults can do well (by some criteria better than young adults) in a memory task even when recall is assessed.

What "binds" these findings together and makes them so different from the larger literature on aging and episodic memory? Before offering some speculations, we acknowledge that recent work shows many ways in which older adults' performance in memory tests can be improved relative to typical levels of performance.

For one thing, there are age differences in circadian arousal patterns that impact a number of cognitive functions, including memory (e.g., Hasher, Goldstein, & May, 2005; Hasher et al., 1999; Intons-Peterson, Rocchi, West, McLellan, & Hackney, 1999; West, Murphy, Armilio, Craik, & Stuss, 2002; Yoon, May & Hasher, 1999). A substantial majority of older adults are morning-type people and deliberate memory is best at times that are in synchrony with one's arousal pattern (i.e., in the morning for most older adults; see May, Hasher & Stoltzfus, 1993). In the Intons-Peterson et al. (1999) study, for example, false memories of the sort we discussed earlier were differentially increased for older adults when they were tested at their nonoptimal times (in the afternoon). Such observations are nontrivial because the younger adults against whose performance older adults' memory is typically measured are most decidedly not morning-type people, biasing estimates of age differences whenever time of testing is uncontrolled, allowing a majority of participants (at the preference of typically young experimenters) to be tested in the afternoon (May et al., 1993).

Another aspect of the testing situation may be noted: The identical task instructions delivered to younger and older adults may well have very different impacts on members of the two age groups. Consider first an early study by Zacks, Hasher, and Sanft (1982). Some participants were fully informed about an upcoming free-recall task; these instructions boosted the performance of high-achieving university students relative to other students from the same group who did not know that a memory test was forthcoming. In other words, instructions regarding a deliberate memory task may well boost the performance levels of college students (see also Rahhal, Hasher, & Colcombe, 2001). But what is the impact on older adults of task instructions that emphasize memory? Rahhal et al. (2001) suggest that such instructions may well *lower* the performance of older adults. We assume that university students are challenged by such instructions whereas older adults are to some small degree distressed by them.

One explanation for this reduced performance with memory instructions lies with stereotypes that older adults hold for themselves with respect to memory ability (versus the very different views that younger adults may hold for themselves): if negative stereotypes get triggered in an experimental context and do so differentially for older adults, we can expect (for any number of reasons including motivational and physiological changes) reduced performance (see e.g., Chasteen, Bhattacharyya, Horhota, Tam, & Hasher, in press; Hess, 2000; Hess et al., 2003).

There is also some evidence of the importance of time perspective, particularly of the subjective judgment of time remaining—for example, time to graduation for college students and the time to anticipated mortality and morbidity for older adults. Both younger and older adults make different social choices and prefer different materials (e.g., among advertisements) when time seems limited compared to when time horizons are expanded (e.g., Carstensen, 1993; Fung & Carstensen, 2003). The impact of this factor on memory remains to be seen (but see Charles et al., 2003), but it might ultimately prove to be potent, as it has been shown to be in choice.

If, as Carstensen and her collaborators have argued, older adults have a different set of goals from younger adults (and there is certainly classic evidence on this; see Rokeach, 1973, see also Adams et al., 1997; Labouvie-Vief, 1985), the tasks and materials we have given to older adults may differentially disadvantage them. More so than young adults, older adults may set their own agendas, focusing on information that they see as personally useful or important and satisficing otherwise. To borrow other terms from the decision literature, older adults may be more inclined to engage in shortcuts characteristic of heuristic information-processing styles than are younger adults in experimental settings in which deliberate memory is at stake. That they can engage in more detailed (or analytic) processing styles is clearly seen in studies in which materials are more engaging than is typically the case (e.g., Adams et al, 2002; Castel, in press; Rahhal et al, 2002).

Taken together, these recent findings suggest that we may have seriously underestimated the memory abilities of older adults, as the developmental literature once seriously underestimated the cognitive and memory abilities of younger children. The understanding of greater than anticipated memory abilities in very young children grew slowly in that literature, and we presume an understanding of memory ability in older adults will begin to grow in the aging literature as well.

References

Adams, C. (1991). Qualitative age differences in memory for text: A life-span developmental perspective. *Psychology and Aging, 6,* 323–336.

Adams, C., Labouvie-Vief, G., Hobart, C. J., & Dorosz, M. (1990). Adult age group differences in story recall style. *Journals of Gerontology: Psychological Sciences, 45B,* P17–P27.

Adams, C., Smith, M. C., Nyquist, L., & Perlmutter, M. (1997). Adult age-group differences in recall for the literal and interpretive meanings of narrative text. *Journals of Gerontology: Psychological Sciences, 52B,* P187–P195.

Adams, C., Smith, M.C., Pasupathi, M., & Vitolo, L. (2002). Social context effects on story recall in older and younger women: Does the listener make a difference? *Journals of Gerontology: Psychological Sciences, 57B,* P28–P40.

Bäckman, L. (1989). Varieties of memory compensation by older adults in episodic remembering. In L. W. Poon, D. C. Rubin, & B. A. Wilson (Eds.), *Everyday cognition in adulthood and late life* (pp. 509–544). Cambridge: Cambridge University Press.

Balota, D. A., Cortese, M. J., Duchek, J. M., Adams, D., Roediger, H. L., III, McDermott, K. B., & Yerys, B. E. (1999). Veridical and false memories in healthy older adults and in dementia of the Alzheimer's type. *Cognitive Neuropsychology, 16,* 361–384.

Balota, D. A., Dolan, P. O., & Duchek, J. M. (2000). Memory changes in healthy older adults. In E. Tulving & F. I. M. Craik (Eds.), *The Oxford handbook of memory* (pp. 395–409). New York: Oxford University Press.

Bahrick, H. P. (1970). A two-phase model for prompted recall. *Psychological Review, 77,* 215–222.

Bastin, C., & Van der Linden, M. (2003). The contribution of recollection and familiarity to recognition memory: A study of the effects of test format and aging. *Neuropsychology, 17,* 14–24.

Bayen, U. J., & Murnane, K. (1996). Aging and the use of perceptual and temporal information in source memory tasks. *Psychology and Aging, 11,* 293–303.

Carstensen, L. L. (1993). Motivation for social contact across the life span: A theory of socioemotional selectivity. In J. Jacobs (Ed.), *Nebraska Symposium on Motivation: Vol. 40. Developmental perspectives on motivation* (pp. 209–254). Lincoln, NE: University of Nebraska Press.

Castel, A. D. (in press). Memory for grocery prices in younger and older adults: The role of schematic support. *Psychology and Aging.*

Castel, A. D., & Craik, F. I. M. (2003). The effects of aging and divided attention on memory for item and associative information. *Psychology and Aging, 18,* 873–885.

Chalfonte, B. L., & Johnson, M. K. (1996). Feature memory and binding in young and older adults. *Memory & Cognition, 24,* 403–416.

Charles, S. T., Mather, M., & Carstensen, L. L. (2003). Aging and emotional memory: The forgettable nature of negative images for older adults. *Journal of Experimental Psychology: General, 132,* 310–324.

Chasteen, A. L., Bhattacharyya, S., Horhota, M., Tam, R., & Hasher, L. (2005). How feelings of stereotype threat influence older adults' memory performance. *Experimental Aging Research, 31,* 235–260.

Craik, F. I. M. (1986). A functional account of age differences in memory. In F. Klix & H. Hagendorf (Eds.), *Human memory and cognitive capabilities* (pp. 409–422). New York: North-Holland.

Craik, F. I. M. (2002). Human memory and aging. In L. Bäckman & C. von Hofsten (Eds.), *Psychology at the turn of the millennium* (pp. 262–280). Hove, UK: Psychology Press.

Craik, F. I. M., & McDowd, J. M. (1987). Age differences in recall and recognition. *Journal of Experimental Psychology: Learning, Memory, and Cognition, 13,* 474–479.

Davidson, P. S. R., & Glisky, E. L. (2002). Neuropsychological correlates of recollection and familiarity in normal aging. *Cognitive, Affective, & Behavioral Neuroscience, 2,* 174–186.

Dumas, J. A., & Hartman, M. (2003). Adult age differences in temporal and item memory. *Psychology and Aging, 18,* 573–586.

Dywan, J., Segalowitz, S., & Arsenault, A. (2002). Electrophysiological response during source memory decisions in older and younger adults. *Brain and Cognition, 49,* 322–340.

Fleischman, D. A., & Gabrieli, J. D. E. (1998). Repetition priming in normal aging and Alzheimer's disease: A review of findings and theories. *Psychology and Aging, 13,* 88–119.

Fung, H. H., & Carstensen, L. L. (2003). Sending memorable messages to the old: Age differences in preferences and memory for advertisements. *Journal of Personality and Social Psychology, 85,* 163–178.

Glisky, E. L., Polster, M. R., & Routhieaux, B. C. (1995). Double dissociation between item and source memory. *Neuropsychology, 9,* 229–235.

Glisky, E. L., Rubin, S. R., & Davidson, P. S. R. (2001). Source memory in older adults: An encoding or retrieval problem? *Journal of Experimental Psychology: Learning, Memory, and Cognition, 27,* 1131–1146.

Hasher, L., Goldstein, D., & May, C. P. (2005). It's about time: Circadian rhythms, memory, and aging. In C. Izawa, & N. Ohta (Eds.), *Human learning and memory: Advances in theory and application. The 4th Tsukuba International Conference on Memory* (pp. 199–217). Hillsdale, NJ: Lawrence Erlbaum Associates.

Hasher, L., & Zacks, R. T. (1988). Working memory, comprehension, and aging: A review and a new view. In G. H. Bower (Ed.), *The psychology of learning and motivation: Advances in research and theory* (Vol. 22, pp. 193–225). New York: Academic Press.

Hasher, L., Zacks, R. T., & May, C. P. (1999). Inhibitory control, circadian arousal, and age. In D. Gopher & A. Koriat (Eds.), *Attention and performance XVII. Cognitive regulation of performance: Interaction of theory and application* (pp. 653–675). Cambridge, MA: MIT Press.

Hashtroudi, S., Johnson, M. K., & Chrosniak, L. D. (1990). Aging and qualitative characteristics of memories for perceived and imagined complex events. *Psychology and Aging, 5,* 119–126.

Hess, T. M. (2000). Aging-related constraints and adaptations in social information processing. In U. Von Hecker, S. Dutke, & G. Sedek (Eds.), *Generative mental processes and cognitive resources: Integrative research on adaptation and control* (pp. 129–155). Dordrecht: Kluwer.

Hess, T. M., Auman, C., Colcombe, S. J., & Rahhal, T. A. (2003). The impact of stereotype threat on age differences in memory performance. *Journals of Gerontology: Psychological Sciences, 58B,* P3–P11.

Intons-Peterson, M. J., Rocchi, P., West, T., McLellan, K., & Hackney, A. (1999). Age, testing at preferred or nonpreferred times (testing optimality), and false memory. *Journal of Experimental Psychology: Learning, Memory, and Cognition, 25,* 23–40.

Jacoby, L. L. (1991). A process dissociation framework: Separating automatic from intentional uses of memory. *Journal of Memory and Language, 30,* 513–541.

Jacoby, L. L., Yonelinas, A. P., & Jennings, J. M. (1997). The relation between conscious and unconscious (automatic) influences: A declaration of independence. In J. D. Cohen & J. W. Schooler (Eds.), *Scientific approaches to consciousness* (pp. 13–47). Hillsdale, NJ: Lawrence Erlbaum Associates.

James, L. E., Burke, D. M., Austin, A., & Hulme, E. (1998). Production and perception of "verbosity" in younger and older adults. *Psychology and Aging, 13,* 355–367.

Java, R. I. (1996). Effects of age on state of awareness following implicit and explicit word-association tasks. *Psychology and Aging, 11,* 108–111.

Jennings, J. M., & Jacoby, L. L. (1993). Automatic versus intentional uses of memory: Aging, attention, and control. *Psychology and Aging, 8,* 283–293.

Johnson, M. K., Foley, M. A., Suengas, A. G., & Raye, C. L. (1988). Phenomenal characteristics of memories for perceived and imagined autobiographical events. *Journal of Experimental Psychology: General, 117,* 371–376.

Johnson, M. K., Hashtroudi, S., & Lindsay, D. S. (1993). Source monitoring. *Psychological Bulletin, 114,* 3–28.

Kensinger, E. A., & Schacter, D. L. (1999). When true memories suppress false memories: Effects of aging. *Cognitive Neuropsychology, 16,* 399–415.

Koutstaal, W. (2003). Older adults encode—but do not always use—perceptual details: Intentional versus unintentional effects of detail on memory judgments. *Psychological Science, 14,* 189–193.

Koutstaal, W., & Schacter, D. L. (1997). Gist-based false recognition of pictures in older and younger adults. *Journal of Memory and Language, 37,* 555–583.

Labouvie-Vief, G. (1985). Intelligence and cognition. In J. E. Birren & K. W. Schaie (Eds.), *Handbook of the psychology of aging* (pp. 500–530). New York: Van Nostrand Reinhold.

Larsson, M., & Bäckman, L. (1998). Modality memory across the adult life span: Evidence for selective age-related olfactory deficits. *Experimental Aging Research, 24,* 63–82.

La Voie, D. J., & Light, L. L. (1994). Adult age differences in repetition priming: A meta-analysis. *Psychology and Aging, 9,* 539–553.

Light, L. L., La Voie, D., Valencia-Laver, D., Albertson-Owens, S. A., & Mead, G. (1992). Direct and indirect measures of memory for modality in young and older adults. *Journal of Experimental Psychology: Learning, Memory, and Cognition, 18,* 1284–1297.

Light, L. L., Prull, M. W., La Voie, D. J., & Healy, M. R. (2000). Dual-process theories of memory in old age. In T. J. Perfect & E. A. Maylor (Eds.), *Models of cognitive aging* (pp. 238–300). Oxford: Oxford University Press.

Lindsay, D. S. (1994). Memory source monitoring and eyewitness testimony. In D. F. Ross, J. D. Read, & M. P. Toglia (Eds.), *Adult eyewitness testimony: Current trends and developments* (pp. 27–55). New York: Cambridge University Press.

Loftus, E. F., Miller, D. G., & Burns, H. J. (1978). Semantic integration of verbal information into a visual memory. *Journal of Experimental Psychology: Human Learning and Memory, 4,* 19–31.

Lövdén, M. (2003). The episodic memory and inhibition accounts of age-related increases in false memories: A consistency check. *Journal of Memory and Language, 49,* 268–283.

Mark, R. E., & Rugg, M. D. (1998). Age effects on brain activity associated with episodic memory retrieval: An electrophysiologial study. *Brain, 121,* 861–873.

May, C. P., Hasher, L., & Stoltzfus, E. R. (1993). Optimal time of day and the magnitude of age differences in memory. *Psychological Science, 4,* 326–330.

May, C. P., Rahhal, T., Berry, E., & Leighton, E. (2004). *Aging, source memory, and emotion.* Manuscript in preparation.

Mitchell, K. J., Johnson, M. K., & Mather, M. (2003). Source monitoring and suggestibility to misinformation: Adult age-related differences. *Applied Cognitive Psychology, 17,* 107–119.

Mitchell, K. J., Johnson, M. K., Raye, C. L., & D'Esposito, M. D. (2000). fMRI evidence of age-related hippocampal dysfunction in feature binding in working memory. *Cognitive Brain Research, 10,* 197–206.

Moscovitch, M., & Winocur, G. (1995). Frontal lobes, memory, and aging. In J. Grafman, K. J. Holyoak, & F. Boller (Eds.), *Annals of the New York Academy of Sciences: Vol. 769, Structure and functions of the human prefrontal cortex* (pp. 119–150). New York: New York Academy of Sciences.

Naveh-Benjamin, M. (2000). Adult-age differences in memory performance: Tests of an associative deficit hypothesis. *Journal of Experimental Psychology: Learning, Memory and Cognition, 26,* 1170–1187.

Naveh-Benjamin, M. (2001). The effects of divided attention on encoding processes: Underlying mechanisms. In M. Naveh-Benjamin, M. Moscovitch, & H. L. Roediger, III (Eds.), *Perspectives on human memory and cognitive aging: Essays in honour of Fergus Craik* (pp. 193–207). Philadelphia: Psychology Press.

Naveh-Benjamin, M., & Craik, F.I.M. (1995). Memory for context and its utilization in item memory: Comparisons of young and old. *Psychology and Aging, 10,* 284–293.

Naveh-Benjamin, M., Hussain, Z., Guez, J., & Bar-On, M. (2003). Adult age differences in episodic memory: Further support for an associative-deficit hypothesis. *Journal of Experimental Psychology: Learning, Memory and Cognition, 29,* 826–837.

Neath, I., & Surprenant, A. M. (2002). *Human memory: An introduction to research, data, and theory* (2nd ed.). Belmont, CA: Wadsworth/Thompson Learning.

Newman, M. C., Allen, J. B., & Kaszniak, A. W. (2001). Tasks for assessing memory for temporal order versus memory for items in aging. *Aging, Neuropsychology, and Cognition, 8,* 72–78.

Nilsson, L.-G. (2003). Memory functioning in normal aging. *Acta Neurologica Scandinavia, 107* (Suppl. 179), 7–13.

Nilsson, L.-G., Adolfsson, R., Bäckman, L., Cruts, M., Edvardsson, H., Nyberg, L., & van Broeckhoven, C. (2002). Memory development in adulthood and old age: The Betula prospective-cohort study. In P. Graf & N. Ohta (Eds.), *Lifespan development of human memory* (pp. 185–204). Cambridge, MA: MIT Press.

Nilsson, L.-G., Bäckman, L., Erngrund, K., Nyberg, L., Adolfsson, R., Bucht, G., Karlsson, S., Widing, G., & Wilblad, B. (1997). The Betula prospective cohort study: Memory, health, and aging. *Aging, Neuropsychology, and Cognition, 1,* 1–32.

Norman, K. A., & Schacter, D. L. (1997). False recognition in younger and older adults: Exploring the characteristics of illusory memories. *Memory & Cognition, 25,* 838–848.

Norman, M. A., Evans, J. D., Miller, S. W., & Heaton, R. K. (2000). Demographically corrected norms for the California Verbal Learning Test. *Journal of Clinical and Experimental Neuropsychology, 22,* 80–94.

Nyberg, L., Maitland, S. B., Rönnlund, M., Bäckman, L., Dixon, R. A., Wahlin, Ä., & Nilsson, L.-G. (2003). Selective adult age differences in an age-invariant multifactor model of declarative memory. *Psychology and Aging, 18,* 149–160.

Park, D. C. (2000). The basic mechanisms accounting for age-related decline in cognitive function. In D. C. Park & N. Schwarz (Eds.), *Cognitive aging: A primer* (pp. 3–21). Philadelphia: Psychology Press.

Park, D. C., Lautenschlager, G., Hedden, T., Davidson, N. S., Smith, A. D., & Smith, P. K. (2002). Models of visuospatial and verbal memory across the adult life span. *Psychology and Aging, 17,* 299–320.

Parkin, A. J., & Walter, B. M. (1992). Recollective experience, normal aging, and frontal dysfunction. *Psychology and Aging, 7,* 290–298.

Rahhal, T. A., Hasher, L., & Colcombe, S. J. (2001). Instructional manipulations and age differences in memory: Now you see them, now you don't. *Psychology and Aging, 16,* 697–706.

Rahhal, T. A., May, C. P., & Hasher, L. (2002). Truth and character: Sources that older adults can remember. *Psychological Science, 13,* 101–105.

Raz, N. (2000). Aging of the brain and its impact on cognitive performance: Integration of structural and functional findings. In F. I. M. Craik & T. A. Salthouse (Eds.), *The handbook of aging and cognition* (2nd ed., pp. 1–90). Mahwah, NJ: Lawrence Erlbaum Associates.

Roediger, H. L., III, & McDermott, K. B. (1995). Creating false memories: Remembering words not presented in lists. *Journal of Experimental Psychology: Learning, Memory, and Cognition, 21,* 803–814.

Rokeach, M. (1973). *The nature of human values.* New York: Free Press.

Rugg, M. D., & Yonelinas, A. P. (2003). Human recognition memory: A cognitive neuroscience perspective. *Trends in Cognitive Science, 7,* 313–319.

Salthouse, T. A. (1996). The processing-speed theory of adult age differences in cognition. *Psychological Review, 103,* 403–428.

Schacter, D. L., Koutstaal, W., Johnson, M. K., Gross, M. S., & Angell, K. E. (1997). False recognition induced by photographs: A comparison of older and younger adults. *Psychology and Aging, 12,* 203–215.

Schonfield, D., & Robertson, B. A. (1966). Memory storage and aging. *Canadian Journal of Psychology, 20,* 228–236.

Spencer, W. D., & Raz, N. (1995). Differential effects of aging on memory for content and context: A meta-analysis. *Psychology and Aging, 10,* 527–539.

Tulving, E. (1972). Episodic and semantic memory. In E. Tulving & W. Donaldson (Eds.), *Organization of memory* (pp. 381–403). New York: Academic Press.

Wechsler, D. (1997). *The Wechsler Memory Scale-III manual.* San Antonio, TX: The Psychological Corporation.

West, R. L. (1996). An application of prefrontal cortex function theory to cognitive aging. *Psychological Bulletin, 120,* 272–292.

West, R., Murphy, K. J., Armilio, M. L., Craik, F. I. M., & Stuss, D. T. (2002). Effects of time of day on age differences in working memory. *Journals of Gerontology: Psychological Sciences, 57B,* P3–P10.

Yonelinas, A. P. (2002). The nature of recollection and familiarity: A review of 30 years of research. *Journal of Memory and Language, 46,* 441–517.

Yoon, C., May, C. P., & Hasher, L. (1999). Aging, circadian arousal, and cognition. In N. Schwartz, D. Park, B. Knäuper, & S. Sudman (Eds.), *Aging, cognition, and self-reports* (pp. 117–143). Washington, DC: Psychological Press.

Zacks, R. T., Hasher, L., & Li, K. Z. H. (2000). Human memory. In F. I. M. Craik & T. A. Salthouse (Eds.), *The handbook of aging and cognition* (2nd ed., pp. 293–357). Mahwah, NJ: Lawrence Erlbaum Associates.

Zacks, R. T., Hasher, L., & Sanft, H. (1982). Automatic encoding of event frequency: Further findings. *Journal of Experimental Psychology: Learning, Memory, & Cognition, 8,* 106–116.

12

Development of Representation in Childhood

Katherine Nelson

In this chapter I first present a brief overview of the concepts of representation in cognitive psychology and developmental psychology, together with the issues these raise. I then discuss in more detail theories based on levels of representation and their development in childhood, with the emphasis on what each level provides in an overall cognitive system and how it is constructed through biological, social, and cultural contributions.

Let me begin with the function of representation in human cognition as conceptualized by cognitive psychologist and psycholinguist George Miller:

> Human language is the happy result of bringing together two systems that all higher organisms must have: a representational system and a communication system. A representational system is necessary if an organism is going to move around purposefully in its environment; a communication system is necessary if an organism is going to interact with others of its own kind. . . . Human beings seem to be the only animals in which a single system serves both of these functions. (1990, p. 12)

This statement is interesting in its apparent assumption that language serves the representational function for humans that is otherwise served for nonlanguage creatures. But it leaves open the question of how—if at all—representation is managed by nonhumans or by nonlanguage using humans, such as pre-linguistic infants and very young children. These are questions that have provoked a great deal of theoretical discussion and empirical investigation in developmental psychology, especially in the decades since the cognitive revolution of the 1960s, which placed representation in a central role in cognitive models. These questions also reflect contentious issues in cognitive science based on different computational models of symbolic processing and neural network processing.

If one accepts the premises—language as a representational system and infants as without language—one way around the problem is to suppose that nonlanguage speakers have a language of thought but have not yet mapped it onto their native language. This is the solution proposed by Fodor (1975).

Bickhard (1987, 2002) has argued at length against such a proposal, noting that the assumption of an innate language of thought runs into the logical problem of infinite regress and thus solves nothing. The second way is to deny that language constitutes a representational system different from that previously used by infants and presumably other cognitively endowed animals. From this perspective language is a system for representing cognitive contents in communication, not for representation in cognition. The third solution, outlined here in terms of Donald's (1991) theory but consistent with a number of other cognitive models, is to conceive of representation in terms of developing levels, of which language is a late-comer.

The problem faced by developmental theories of representation is how to reconcile and interconnect early nonsymbolic systems with the symbolic and linguistic systems that are assumed to characterize much of adult cognition. The three alternatives on offer can be reformulated:

1. Assume that all representations are of one form (e.g., neural networks) and that language when acquired is used to express these representations. This is a standard developmental move, common to many current theoretical approaches. From this point of view language expresses concepts but has no independent contribution to them.
2. Assume that there is an underlying analogical representational format (or formats varying by domain) that serves other animals and prelinguistic infants that is overlaid by a digital, symbolic form when language is acquired (Dennett, 1991). This position fits Miller's claim; it assumes that for humans, language takes over representational functions, providing a more flexible and powerful system of thought for carrying out everything but the most low-level routine tasks. When children learn language they become the beneficiaries of this powerful system. Vygotsky's (1986) theory can be read as a developmental version of this position.
3. Assume levels of representation that vary in format and in their potential for abstraction and complexity and that emerge in phases phylogenetically or ontogenetically but continue to operate for different organismic purposes after coming on line, forming in the end a complex or hybrid mind consisting of levels of representation originating through different sources

(Donald, 1991). This assumption has recently been explicated by Sun (2002), who has proposed a dual-system cognitive architecture that utilizes both implicit and explicit learning and memory. His proposal is designed to reconcile the embodied and enculturated claims of many recent critiques of cognitive science (e.g., Clark, 1997), and to bring together the symbolic and neural net computational proposals in the field. This proposal is not specifically designed to work developmentally (although Sun cites Karmiloff-Smith's 1992 work in support), but it seems to be compatible with the levels theories outlined here.

Empirical research and developmental theory both bear on these positions. Piaget (1962) took the position that human infants do not have mental representations, that their knowing is rather constructed in terms of sensori-motor schemas. Representations, he claimed, emerged only during the second year of life signified by the onset of delayed imitation and followed by the development of language. Piaget's account of sensori-motor schemas seems compatible with some recent neuro-cognitive theorizing (Garcia, 1999; this is not surprising because he began as a biologist) and is also in many ways compatible with recent theories of the "duality of mind" (Sun, 2002). However, Piaget denied a major role in cognition to representations, reserving that place for knowledge constructions of universal logic. Mandler (1988, 1992) proposed an explicitly representational theory of infant cognition that relies on "conceptual primitives" for the formation of a conceptual level of representation derived from the analysis of perceptual input, assumed to be in place at least by the middle of the first year. This theory, while differing from Piaget on the issue of representation, nonetheless shares an assumption that language reflects but does not determine underlying cognitive constructions.

Like Mandler's, much of the recent research in infant cognitive development has been explicitly designed to counter Piaget's nonrepresentational account of infancy, demonstrating that young infants maintain perceptual representations of absent objects over delays of several seconds (e.g., Baillargeon, 1993) among other claims. The relation of this kind of domain-specific representation (i.e., specific to objects, space, number, and so on) to later, possibly linguistic levels, has not been systematically spelled out by these infancy researchers, although more recently

Spelke (2003) has proposed that language, when acquired, may integrate knowledge across previously separate domains. This "nativist" position appears to mesh with the second option listed: laying a more powerful and general symbolic representation on a lower level domain-specific representation. The connectionist theory of cognitive development (Elman, et al., 1996), formulated in terms of representations modeled as neural networks, does not distinguish infant cognition from other periods, except in terms of the complexity of the networks formed; it assumes that symbolic processing can be derived from these. This empiricist position also appears to mesh with the second option, although in a different way.

The third option is represented by Karmiloff-Smith's (1992) distinctive developmental model, which proceeds through phases of implicit to explicit representations through a process of representational redescription. This process operates within distinct cognitive domains (such as language or number) rather than across general developmental periods. All infant representations would be implicit by virtue of their limited developmental history. However, beyond infancy this theory does not propose overall cognitive change, or a general role for language, except as a tool in the redescription process (see Perner, 1991, for a related theory).

These brief citations could not do justice to the complexities of the theories or the issues they address, although they do suggest the diversity of views on this topic in the field (see Table 12.1). As is evident from this overview, some developmental theorists appear to take a one-level representational position (e.g., Baillargeon, Spelke, Elman et al., and Mandler), although it is not formulated in language terms as Miller (1990) proposed. Others (e.g., Karmiloff-Smith, Perner) view representation as proceeding through stages from implicit to explicit to meta-representational. Oddly, none of these recent theories of representation addresses the question raised by Miller's presumption that it is language that serves the representation function for humans. Indeed, most developmental theories do not take language into account in discussions of representation at all (the exception being Karmiloff-Smith). Implicit in some views is a symbolic level of conceptual representation; yet how symbols appear and function at this level is not spelled out in any adequate detail, and as Bickhard (1987) has argued vigorously, this is a fatal flaw.

Vygotsky's (1986) proposal may be seen as offering a solution to the developmental dilemma posed by Miller's position. Vygotsky viewed human cognition and communication as each continuous with systems developed in phylogenetically closely related species, such as other primates. These systems were assumed to operate separately in other species, and to continue on separate developmental courses in early human development, eventually coming together into a single system of verbal thought toward the end of the preschool period. In this concept, when children learn to speak they first use language for communication and only later use it for cognitive representation and as a cognitive tool to guide action and thought. In this way Vygotsky prefigured Miller's claim, but with the added proviso that the coming together was a development that took place during human childhood. This theory moves closer to the solution found in theories of levels, discussed next. What is missing from

TABLE 12.1. Representational options (see text for details)

Options	Theorists	Properties
Unified representations— language as expressive only	Piaget Connectionists (Elman) Nativists (Spelke) Theory theorists (Gopnik)	Neural processing model Symbolic systems Modularity systems Information processing
Language as dominant representation	George Miller Dennett Vygotsky	Language takes over from analogical processes in humans Inner speech as mature form
Levels of representation	Donald Karmiloff-Smith Nelson	2 to 4 levels of processes differing in type, emerging in evolution, culture, and development

Vygotsky's account, as from virtually all other cognitive accounts, is explicit recognition of the continuing contribution to mature human cognition of nonlinguistic levels of representation and thought.

LEVELS OF REPRESENTATION IN PHYLOGENY AND ONTOGENY

Merlin Donald (1991) proposed a theory of the evolution of human language and cognition that was explicitly designed to address the symbolic or language representation problem. His solution is captured in the following passage:

> [T]he modern human mind evolved from the primate mind through a series of major adaptations, each of which led to the emergence of a new representational system. Each successive new representational system has remained intact within our current mental architecture, so that the modern mind is a mosaic structure of cognitive vestiges from earlier stages of human emergence. (pp. 2–3)

The symbolic devices of the human mind radically altered its organization from that of previous primate minds (see also Deacon, 1997). Three major transitions were proposed, resulting in four stages in prehuman primate to human mind. This scheme is adopted in its developmental analogues in Nelson (1996).

Level 1. Event Perception

Donald proposed that "the ability to perceive complex, usually moving, clusters and patterns of stimuli as a unit" (1991, p. 153) is the basis for cognitive representation by primates, including the great apes. This concept contrasts with the usual focus in cognitive psychology on the perception of objects, a contrast between dynamic and static patterns, but it is consistent with the assumptions of ecological perception (Gibson, 1979). However, the limitation of this level is its particularity; it is concrete, situation bound, and unreflective. Operating alone, it is characteristic of life lived in the present without temporal parameters. Memory enables the retention of situational information, but its recall depends on environmental conditions; it is not accessible to voluntary recall in the absence of situational cues. From the perspective of memory theory, this level is confined to implicit, nondeclarative, or procedural memory.

In the developmental analogue, basic perceptual representations are dynamic in terms of events and event structures; it is the acquisition of language that stabilizes our conceptions of objects, actions, and people and enables reflective thought (Nelson, 1986, 1996, 2005). From this perspective, an exclusive focus on the perception and conception of objects in infancy or later is misplaced; objects exist naturally in terms of their roles in events and actions.

Level 2. Mimetic Culture and Cognition

Mimesis—a generalized form of imitation—enables reenacting and re-presenting an event or relationship, socially derived through action. Mimesis can be socially used for communication as well as for cognitive purposes, such as deliberate rehearsal and the refinement of a skill (practice). Mimetic acts are characterized by "intentionality, generativity, communicativity, reference, autocueing, and the ability to model an unlimited number of objects" (Donald, 1991, p. 171). Mimesis is both shared—communicative—and individually cognitive, which is the unique characteristic that Miller (1990) attributed to language in the quotation at the beginning of this chapter.

This level enables the first sharing of mental representations with other beings, through action rather than language. In human cognition it enables inventing, transmitting, and maintaining complex social arrangements and technological skills. Donald argues that this level remains basically intact in individual cognition and collective culture today in such practices as athletics, rituals, games, dance, and work routines. Mimesis is vividly apparent in the developments of late infancy and childhood in play, routines, games, and everyday practices not dependent on language.

Level 3. Mythic Cognition and Culture

This level depends on the emergence of language and is expressed also in complex cultural forms of art, artifacts, architecture, and especially in cultural narratives. Through the use of language in narrative, stories, histories, and memories can be shared with others in a group. In particular, mythic narrative characterizes oral cultures, representing an authoritative version of reality filtered through generations of narrative interchange. Language also brings with it mental models or representations distinct from previous forms in that they may be individuated into parts, which may then be independently manipulated and entered into new constructions never experienced in the world. Complex language then moves human minds beyond the present toward new possible worlds.

This model assumes that once language enters the mind, thought and language become closely intertwined. Thus, the mental representations formed through language appear to be thoughts themselves, even as the underlying event perceptions and mimetic representations remain intact. Vygotsky's position is unclear on this point; in some ways it appears to see language as overriding earlier forms of thought, yet it would be wrong to see Vygotsky's position as denying the continuing role of earlier levels of cognition. In alternative cognitive psychology terms, the first two levels remain implicit while the symbolic-language level is explicit. This latter formulation respects Miller's (1990) dictum while at the same time respecting and retaining the levels that have guided pre-human thought and pre-linguistic infant cognition.

Level 4. Theoretic Culture and Cognition

Donald proposed that a final cognitive revolution was achieved in the course of human history through the cultural invention of external representational devices, in particular of written language. Such external representations, pictorial or alphabetic, serve as external memory, as symbolic storage outside the individual human mind. Like oral language and mimesis they are at once individual cognitive devices and communicative shared systems. The human mind of the mythic-oral level is vastly augmented and amplified by these external systems, not only in terms of memory but also of cognitive operations that rely on the accessibility of written forms. This level is then the basis for science, logic, mathematics, and theories. Yet the written forms in turn rely on the interpretation of human biological systems, even as these individual systems are initially "infected" by the collective systems of oral language. Thus, the representations of educated human minds are at once doubly collective but ineluctably individual.

In the whole, the human mind is "hybrid," consisting of distinctive levels of representation, each operative for different, but not exclusive, purposes, separately or simultaneously. Table 12.2 summarizes these levels and projects their development in human infancy and childhood (see Nelson, 1996), considered in more detail in the next section.

DEVELOPING LEVELS OF REPRESENTATION

When we consider the developmental analogy to Donald's levels approach, it seems useful to think of the four levels in Table 12.2 in terms of sources of represented content. At the first level is individual private experience in the world based on perception and action, organized in terms of event representations

TABLE 12.2. Levels of representation

	Hybrid Mind (Donald, 1991)	Developmental Analogue (Nelson, 1996)
Level 1 Episodic mind	Nondeclarative memory for events—no voluntary recall	Event representations and memory—late infancy
Level 2 Mimesis	Representation in action—imitation and practice, recall, cooperative action	Imitation, play, memory for events after delay, early language forms—late infancy to early childhood
Level 3 Narrative	Complex language, mythic cultural representations	Conversations, memory recounting, future plans, emergence of autobiographical memory, theory of mind—preschool
Level 4 Theoretic	External representations—written language, mathematics, science, theory, logic	Reading, writing, learning in school, cultural knowledge systems—school years to adult

(or scripts). The second level is based on social experience, using the actions of others as models for oneself through forms of imitation, learning, replication, and practice. The third level is cultural, adopting the collective linguistic forms of communication for cognitive representations, thus laying a cultural interpretation over one's individual thought. Finally, the fourth level is historical-cultural in that the individual partakes of the historical legacy through written forms. This might also be termed meta-cultural in that it involves external representations accessible to multicultural environments over generations of historical records. Although, as noted previously, Vygotsky's written legacy did not lay out the developing cognitive structure in this way, the account here is in strong agreement with his overall theoretical approach, especially in its claims for the social, cultural, and cultural-historical sources of individual cognition.

In adopting the idea of levels of representation in cognition to the development of representation, it is essential to recognize the distinction between knowledge representation and memory. Memory is concrete and episodic, particularistic; knowledge consists of abstractions derived from generalizations about or inferences from experience and memory. This distinction is roughly equivalent to the distinction between semantic (knowledge) and episodic memory (Tulving, 1983). In cognitive psychology, knowledge representations include such familiar types as concepts, scripts, taxonomies, narratives, and theories, usually assumed to be organizations of linguistically represented knowledge. For example, the concept of "animal" is assumed to relate to a taxonomy of animate types. Nonetheless, when we think of "animal" we may bring to mind not only familiar kinds of animals but also past experiences with animals, involving perceptual characteristics and scripts for animal interactions, as well as episodic content and context.

A major problem for theories of representation in semantics, as well as psychology, has always been to separate the abstract verbal stuff from the episodic experiential stuff (Kintsch, 1974; Nelson, 1985). It is increasingly recognized, however, in both developmental work (e.g., Elman et al., 1996) and cognitive theory (e.g., Clark, 1997), that experiential memory and knowledge representations are inextricably interrelated in the human cognitive system and are kept separate only arbitrarily. One way of doing this is to declare that only one kind of representation is admissible, whether symbolic/linguistic or connectionist, or some other perceptual-based system. As already made clear, I believe the correct view is to admit different levels of interactive systems of representation, based on perception, action, conceptual processes, and cultural constructions.

Representation in Infancy

As previously indicated, the issue of representation in infancy is a contentious one. A moderate stand based on current research can be constructed as follows. Forms of memory exist from experience in utero, as evidenced in the newborn's preference for sounds of the native language over alternative languages (Mehler et al., 1988). The experimental uses of habituation to repeated stimuli and the orienting response to novelty provide solid evidence that prior perceptual experience is retained within the nervous system, presumably through some sort of "tuning" rather than through specific memory. Sensori-motor memory can be observed at least by 4 months and is extended from days to weeks over the course of the first year (Rovee-Collier & Hayne, 2000). Such memory (e.g., kicking to make a mobile move) is activated within specific contexts but is not available to the cognitive system outside of those contexts. These early forms of memory are implicit and are consistent with the first event level of representation, not accessible to active or attentive processing.

Beginning in the second half of the first year there is evidence for more active forms of memory, more accessible both to cognitive organizing processes and to deliberate recall. Two lines of research, one from social development and the other from memory and cognitive development, converge on this evidence. Social development studies have focused on the period from 8 to 9 months during which infants begin to share attention with a caretaker, following her gaze to see what she is attending to, looking to the adult for clues as to what a novel scene or stranger "means" in terms of emotional reactions, and using social signals to communicate wants and needs (Rochat, 2001). Cognitive studies have demonstrated the onset of ready imitation of both vocalizations and actions around the same period, and have used imitation of event sequences to track memory, specifically investigating the capacity for long-term memory. In studies of delayed imitation, infants are first exposed to several mini-events in which the experimenter uses objects in a specific sequence while the infant watches. Infants are brought back to the laboratory after days, weeks, or months, are given the objects to play with, and are encouraged to construct the sequence that they had watched. Delayed imitation indicates the continuing representation of an action sequence; to the extent that the components are reproduced in sequence, it indicates not passive memory but deliberate reconstruction from cognitive representations (Bauer, Hertsgard, & Dow, 1994). Recent work has found delayed recall for sequences by 9-month-olds after one month (Carver & Bauer, 2001).

Bauer's research has clearly demonstrated that children of 1 year or less are capable of remembering the structure of events that they have witnessed, supporting the assumption that experience-based representations in infancy are formulated in terms of events (Bauer & Mandler, 1989; Nelson, 1981, 1986, 1996). Observational research also indicates that very young children easily build up knowledge of familiar routines and rely on them in their everyday lives; and Tomasello (1992) has shown that early language learners are sensitive to the structure of events in acquiring verbs to represent action. In addition, Mandler and McDonough (1993) have provided evidence that 1-year-olds form global categories of objects representing animals and vehicles that are based on the events that these different kinds engage in in the world.

These research findings support the theoretical proposal that basic representations of experience are in the form of dynamic events. This proposal contrasts not only with ancient assumptions that concepts are built up from sensory data in terms of features but also with more contemporary widespread assumptions that objects are the primary focus of initial representations as well as of first words. The theory of event representations is part of a more general theory of "making sense" in terms of relevant functions, of what things and people do rather than (mainly or solely) in terms of what things look like (Nelson, 1974; Nelson & Ware, 2002). The event level also contrasts with a strong domain-specific claim of early cognition. Although in early infancy pre-potent memory processes appear to organize experience along domain-specific lines, as postulated by Greenough, Black, and Wallace (1987) in terms of "experience-expectant" neural development processes, subsequent organizations do not appear to be bounded in the same domain-specific way. Rather, memory and emergent representational

generalizations organize knowledge structures in ways that combine information from different basic domains (e.g., objects, space, action, animates, conspecifics). The developmental conception of domain specificity is semantic rather than structural. The idea that representations are specific within domains (e.g., phonology, syntax, orthography; see Chapter 13, this volume) is quite different, and may have very different developmental implications.

The general claim, then, is that at least one basic level of nonlinguistic representation is in the form of event structures, which may represent unique structures, as in the imitation experiments, or generalized structures, as in the child's knowledge of game and caretaking routines (such as patty-cake or bath). The latter can be considered as scripts for familiar events much like the adult's scripts for riding the subway or going to a restaurant. Donald's theory suggests that these representations would be primarily elicited by environmental cues (there is controversy on this point), as well as that the infant cognitive system is primarily tuned to the present, lacking a specific past or future. In this view infants and toddlers *know* a great deal, based on experiential memory and generalizations and reorganizations of memory, but they use that knowledge primarily within specific contexts and in relation to specific content when the present situation makes such content relevant. Some of this knowledge (e.g., sucking or crawling) is relevant only to the contexts of infancy. Other knowledge is basic to being in the physical and social world at any age (e.g., three-dimensional visual perception and discrimination of voices).

How do general representations arise? Karmiloff-Smith (1992) proposes a process of representational redescription at different levels of explicitness. Bickhard (2002) argues for representational emergence during development, similar to the present view, stating: "Cognition does not have to 'operate on' already-existing representation. Representation can be created and eliminated over and over again in a broader dynamic process" (p. 126). Sun (2002) proposes a dual level of cognition, in which low-level implicit perception-action based distributed memory is reconfigured into localized explicit concepts potentially accessible to verbalization. This general conception appears very compatible with many developmental theories.

Much of the evidence for event knowledge is solidly based in social learning through imitation, which invokes the process of mimesis. In Donald's theory mimesis is an important basis for language development, implying that it is a mode of learning and communicating unique to humans. Tomasello (1999) also believes that deliberate use of imitation for the acquisition of knowledge skills or learning is absent in other primates and is one of the main additions to the human cognitive repertoire from the general primate model. Tomasello emphasizes the considerable difference in social relations between human infants and their mothers and those of our close primate relatives such as the chimpanzee. Human infants share to a much greater degree an intimate communicative and cognitive relationship with caregivers, specifically parents. This is especially notable according to Tomasello and his colleagues at the 9-month transition when infants begin sharing attention with adults and engaging in the deliberate extensive imitation of others that is so commonly observed. Thus the unique convergence of communicative and cognitive functions appears to be an early-appearing characteristic of humans, preceding the acquisition of language.

The sequence of representational forms in human infancy suggests that the progression from event representations to mimesis is subsumed in human infancy into a single basic representational phase that I term *experiential*. In this proposal the idea is that prior to representations there exists a level of memory that simply retains information about encounters in the environment that form the content for the emergent explicitly accessible representations of later infancy. These basic nonlinguistic representations include whole events as well as concepts of objects, actions, and people derived from both individual exploration and social participation and interaction. These representations serve as scaffolds—in addition to social scaffolds—that structure the infant's encounters with the world, constituting the secure base assumed in attachment theory.

This proposal (modified from Nelson 1996) is consistent with Sun's (2002) two-level basic cognitive architecture of implicit distributed and explicit conceptual cognitive architecture. It is consistent as well with Karmiloff-Smith's (1992) first two levels, and with Mandler's (1993) claim of concepts emerging from perceptual analysis. What I emphasize here is that the level of emergent conceptual and event representations derives from social experience, including pre-linguistic forms of communication, establishing the basis for language learning and an emergent form of representation different from those already established in infancy—one equivalent to the linguistic-narrative-mythic level that Donald described. Much recent research in the areas of intentionality and theory of mind supports the proposal that the human infant's experience with close social partners provides a rich basis for the combined communicative and cognitive developments of the first three years. In particular, the role of this experiential base in establishing a level of language representation appears crucial.

Representation Development from 1 to 4 Years

Development of language usually begins toward the end of the first year with increasing attention on the part of the infant to the spoken word and evidence of comprehension of some words and common phrases in terms indicating action, such as "give me," "go night-night" and so on. Toddlers usually also begin to produce a few words between 11 and 15 months, often for actions like those listed or for familiar objects used in activities. Both word types indicate that infants are drawing on their background representations of event knowledge to focus on particular aspects of the events they participate in, as these are labeled in parental talk. This characterization is not conventional. Most authors state that children begin learning first words by naming objects. However, my assessment of the evidence from vocabulary data, diaries, and direct observation (Barrett, 1985; Nelson, 1974), combined with cross-linguistic research (Choi & Gopnik, 1995), is that children learn to reproduce words used in their favorite activities but only gradually come to confine them to specific objects rather than to objects-in-activities and parts thereof. This is similar to the classic hypothesis that children begin with holophrastic speech—utterances that use a single word for a whole sentence. (Space does not permit the elaboration of the various theories of children's word learning, which is not specifically relevant to the current topic.) This beginning allows a child to participate in familiar activities with a new skill—the production of a word-like form (e.g., "da" for dog) appropriate to the context shared with adults. Infants begin to use words and wordlike forms for pragmatic purposes before they use them to achieve cognitive ends, such as categorizing things in the world (Halliday, 1975).

This characterization of the early stages of word learning (up to a vocabulary of about 50 words, at 18 months on average) raises two issues with respect to the topic of representations: (1) What is the representational basis for early (or later) word learning? (2) When, if ever, does language become a cognitive representational level such as assumed by Miller (1990) and elaborated by Donald (1991) and others? The first question addresses the issue of whether first words simply express the pre-linguistic experientially based representations of, for example, events or global categories (Mandler & McDonough, 1993), or whether new representations are constructed to fit words learned. Most researchers assume that the former is the case—that the child's concepts and categories are expressed in their early words, as in their later learning, and that words are, to use the jargon, "mapped onto" concepts and categories. However, as we have seen, the experiential base of infancy is dynamic and holistic, whereas words are stable forms adhering to culturally accepted meanings based on collective cultural experiences that far exceed those of infants and toddlers. The often-observed "over-extensions" of the toddler's early object terms, such as using "dog" to apply to all four-legged animals, or "duck" to indicate any aspect of the bath experience, clearly indicate that such young minds do not share the same category boundaries for language terms that adults adhere to. How the child's dynamic holistic event-based experientially derived representations of things in the world come to be "tamed" by the language's partitioned abstract collective conceptual/semantic base through tuning and shaping over time is a topic badly in need of serious study. At present, the evidence is clear that something like this happens over the second and third years.

Adhering to the levels of representation hypothesis, I assume that to a great extent the dynamic and holistic experiential level is retained during this period, forming the basis for transactions in the world, including those with language. Meanwhile, language itself imposes over time a restructuring to fit the communicative categories of the symbolic system. The word forms that are accessible both to communicative use between people and for cognitive uses within a single mind require this new layer of collective conceptual—that is, semantic—representation. Words can be added to this level in indefinite numbers. At the outset they do not need to have any meaning beyond the context of their use (Levy & Nelson, 1994; Nelson, 1996; Nelson & Shaw, 2002).

Eventually new words take on meanings derived from discourse use and activities where they are used. These derived meanings may expand from their experiential ties to more abstract concepts that fit within a field of related meanings, over time becoming more precise and delimited. With further experience children may also formulate more of their own concepts along the lines that linguistic categories and boundaries define. Then the language may no longer loom as an alien code in which one's ideas fit awkwardly and stumblingly, but a natural mode of both thinking and speaking. This convergence may come about some time in the vicinity of 4 to 6 years, depending on the child's practice and facility with speaking. It is never the case, however, that language forms fit one's ideas perfectly, and it may be that the concept of dedifferentiation in aging (chapter 13, this volume) is related to the imprecise fit between words and their personal representations or meanings.

In brief, as conceptualized here, a major transition in representational development takes place between 1 and 4 years, during which language forms are being acquired and their meanings are shaped into a linguistic level of representation. During this transition the toddler/child continues to rely on experiential representations (based on event participation and mimesis), which provide the background for exploring the potentials of the newly discovered linguistic world. That world consists of conversations that often involve narratives of diverse kinds, such as shared memories of past experiences and projections of future activities, as well as fictional stories, television, and videos. These narratives (and other discourse constructions such as explanations and descriptions) require the child to use the emerging linguistic layer of representation as an interpretive format for understanding the stories that are being told, even the stories that the child constructs with a parent or peer about things they have experienced together. These experiences must be reformulated into linguistic terms in order to be shared with others. And frequently, the reformulation changes the nature of the experience as understood (Nelson, 2005).

Experience with language reconfigures mental life in several ways. To begin, prior to language learning all experience is basically personal, although acquired within a social milieu. When language imports new concepts, new accounts of other people's experiences, emotions, and ideas, these may initially be simply "recorded" in the same self-experiential terms, not distinguished as coming from an outside-of-selfexperience source. Several lines of research support the idea that children of 2 to 3 years do not differentiate others' actions, speech, and minds from their own. For example, Ratner and colleagues (2000) have shown that when children engage in a joint activity with an adult, they tend to appropriate the adult's contributions to themselves when subsequently asked who carried out which part of the activity (Ratner, Foley, & Gimpert, 2000). In source monitoring studies, 3- and 4-year-old children tend not to distinguish whether they thought, heard, or saw what they claim to know (Welch-Ross, 2000). Similarly, in memory studies (Gopnik & Graf, 1988), 3-year-olds have difficulty recalling the source of their knowledge of where an object was hidden, particularly if they have been told the information rather than having seen it placed. Memory studies have also found consistently that children of 3 years or younger are especially susceptible to false suggestions after the fact about what they have seen or done (Ceci & Bruck, 1993). Most strikingly, P. Miller and her colleagues (1990) have observed cases of children's appropriation of other people's stories of their experiences as their own (Miller, Potts, Fund, Hoogstra, & Mintz, 1990). However, over time, evidence incorporated in talk with others highlights the difference between one's own experiential memory and knowledge and another's, implying the need to distinguish in some way one's own conceptions and experience from others' experiences or ideas.

The many different accounts of children's confusions about the source of their information, particularly that something they have been told about becomes incorporated into their own experiential memory, can be understood if language representations are not differentiated from basic experiential knowledge representations. In effect, language initially is transparent; it is not differentiated from the conceptual knowledge, immediate experience, and memory that interpret it or that it expresses. To put this another way, language is not seen as a symbolic or representational system on its own, but rather as a way of "seeing" or "saying" cognitive contents.

This phase of language may be related to another symbolic or representational puzzle of early childhood—namely, the problem that very young children have in using a model (or a picture) as a representation of something else (DeLoache, 1990). Children below the age of 3 years who are shown where a toy is hidden in a small-scale model room cannot use that information to find the similar but larger toy in an adjacent large room furnished in the same way. They do not seem able to differentiate between the model as a place and its potential role as a representation.

Self and Self Memory

With time and experience with language, a new level of specifically linguistic representation becomes established. This statement obviously covers over a great deal of unexplored process. Social-interactive experiences, such as engaging in talk about the past with adults, appear to be particularly important in bringing out a distinction between those experiences that are unique and memorable, by noting the time and place and unique contexts of the novel episode, in contrast to routine happenings. This move leads toward the establishment of autobiographical memory (Nelson & Fivush, 2000). Such talk has the potential to make manifest the differences in knowledge and experience among people, as well as among the child's past, present, and future selves. It may highlight the child's distinctive character and experience, and thereby bring about a new conception of self (Nelson, 2005). Co-construction of narratives of the past with adults, as well as stories that represent the fictional or real experiences of other people, are likely tools for bringing the child into this new awareness and in the process eliminating the confusion of self-knowing and others' knowing as expressed in talk.

The emergence of a level of language representation capable of interpreting and constructing narratives also brings with it a new explicit level of self-awareness. Self-awareness emerges in a new way as the contrast between experiential knowing and knowing conveyed from others' experiences or knowledge becomes evident. Then "knowing" must be differentiated and marked as the child's "own" or not. Knowledge represented in language can then be viewed as true or false, or "unable to tell," known from self-experience or from outside sources. This level has been termed *meta-representational*, involving the ability to reflect on what is represented and to use it in different ways in thought, as well as to differentiate its sources. Ultimately, of course, the utility of such representation may lead to its use in most thinking, planning, and remembering, as George Miller's claim and Vygotsky's theory imply.

The developments that are reflected in the emergence of language as a level of representation are relevant to the emergence of autobiographical memory during the later preschool years, which has been shown to be fostered by parental talk about past experiences with their young children (Nelson & Fivush, 2000). This area of development deserves special attention here because it first becomes established in the later preschool years and then usually remains a significant and enduring part of memory throughout the lifespan. Autobiographical memory studies with adults consistently reveal the phenomenon known as *infantile or childhood amnesia*—the fact that on average adults do not recall episodes from childhood that occurred earlier than 3 years of age (Nelson, 1993). Research has shown that there are large individual differences and cultural variations both in the age of first memory for adults and the practice of memory talk among parents and their children (Nelson & Fivush, 2000). Moreover, the specific characteristics of autobiographical memory—its narrative format, its incorporation of self-experience, temporality, reference to the roles of others, and their motivations, emotions, plans, goals, thoughts, and beliefs—reveal its cognitive complexity. Concepts of time—past and future, social and culturally marked periods of time—and the mental states that underlie behavior—plans, goals—are both linguistically formulated and critical to the narratives of autobiography.

Although autobiographical memory has until recently been neglected by memory researchers, studies of amnesias have brought to the forefront its significance to the cognitive functioning and the very personhood of individuals (Damasio, 1999). It was generally assumed in both the developmental and the adult literature that autobiographical memory is simply an extension of the basic forms of memory existing from infancy, perhaps aided by language cues and a growing self-awareness. Fivush and I argue instead that autobiographical memory is formulated in terms of cultural narrative formats through practice with adults during early childhood, and that it serves specific self and social functions that are irreplaceable in other forms. This kind of memory is quintessentially language based, although experiential in its source. It is only through the medium of language representations that it emerges in memory practices with others (Fivush & Nelson, in press; Nelson & Fivush, 2004).

By the end of the pre-school period, children typically have added significant layers of language representation to their underlying experiential representations and have differentiated between and within these layers based on their social and cultural experiences with language. Thus it is this level that brings the child at the end of the preschool years fully into the human cultural world of persons, personalities, plans, goals, and motivations.

Adding the Literate Meta-Cultural Level

The last transition that Donald (1991) proposed—to external representations through the written word and other graphic forms—was conceived as a move that enabled theoretical thinking, science, and so on, or as I suggested at the outset, the sharing of multicultural realities across time and space. Children begin to embark on this level as they enter school, but its full achievement takes many years of education, reading, and self-instruction. Those of us who write and read professionally, and who partake of the extraordinary advances in cultural knowledge of the past several centuries, take this level for granted. It is now embedded in the Internet, where it is accessible to all who can read, including young children. This level is, even more obviously than the previous one, an interactive cultural level where the individual engages in transactions with diverse sources of knowledge. Obviously it is necessary to learn new symbolic codes in order to be able to engage this level. Some of these codes may themselves take on new mental representational forms, situated within the individual brain. For example, reading and writing clearly become automatic, yet they rely on the same semantic representation level as spoken language, while accessed through different forms.

Mathematics, however, forms a separate meaning or representational level for those proficient in it. "Thinking in physics" or "thinking in economics" may come to be separate modules of representational thought. Indeed, the formation of knowledge domains with their own representational formats appears to be a major consequence of this level of development. Domain specificity, or modularity of knowledge, is evident in studies of lesions and specific amnesias or aphasias of the adult brain and cognitive functioning. As noted previously, domains of representation no doubt develop in domain-specific patterns and also may become dedifferentiated in the aging process. However, the now-widespread assumption in the developmental literature that knowledge accumulates in domain-specific fashion in the early years is, in my opinion, not well supported. Rather, earlier knowledge levels appear situation-bound wherein all information is interrelated within a context and not assorted into specific modules that then need to be recombined when necessary. Evidence for this comes from a variety of research, including word associations, children's definitions, and categories (Nelson, 1996). It seems more useful to think of "domains of practice" in which knowledge is contexted in terms of activities rather than bounded by pre-established categories. In addition, of course, expert knowledge domains such as mathematics are culturally established and formally taught to new generations of learners. How these different kinds of domains may develop and subsequently be affected by the aging process is an area that will repay attention from both ends of the developmental spectrum.

The dependence on external representations, such as note-taking, although a late addition to cognitive operations, may come to be a necessary part of its functioning. It is interesting that Burke (Chapter 13, this volume) reports that the age difference in recall by pilots disappeared when they were allowed to take notes, their usual practice. It is notable that so little of the study of cognition relies on such standard "fourth-level" practices.

A further effect of cultural knowledge acquisition is the widening and deepening of individual awareness. It has been argued (McAdams, 1993) that autobiographical memory becomes formulated in terms of a life story during adolescence, relating the individual to the cultural and social world through new identities. Studies of older adults' autobiographical memory find that memories of late adolescence and early adulthood form a "reminiscence bump" when compared to memories from mid-life, suggesting the importance of this period for further personal as well as educational development (Conway & Pleydell-Pearce, 2000).

SUMMARY AND CONCLUSION

This perspective on representation levels in development implies that earlier levels are not overridden by later ones, but continue to serve functions throughout life, although their organization and processing are transformed as they are integrated with latter symbolic levels, specifically language and external symbol systems and especially written language. The explicit experiential level of representation derived from implicit perceptual-motor learning through mi-

metic processes serves the functions of everyday, routine activities carried out more or less automatically, requiring little explicit thought or attention in adulthood unless or until something interferes (such as losing one's keys or beginning a new job). However, this level is accessible to reflection and may be brought into higher levels for explicitation. Oral linguistic narrative is the level of everyday social relations and theory of mind, and it is derived from experience with language. It necessitates the distinction between personal and social-cultural knowing, and it formulates autobiographical memory. These two representation levels are not domain-specific knowledge systems; they call on knowledge from many different domains for use in linguistic processes.

Specific alleged domains such as space, number, object knowledge, and theory of mind are integrated in the knowledge structures of the early years and serve as background to the pragmatics of everyday life, organized in terms of domains of practice. Cultural-knowledge domains begin to be extracted as taxonomic constructions are highlighted in early educational settings. In adult life all of these levels exist in parallel, forming the flexible, adaptable structures of the hybrid human mind (Donald, 1991). This chapter has emphasized cognition and communication as jointly characterizing the representational systems of human life. We communicate with others and with ourselves, separately or at the same time. This is a hallmark of the social-cultural collective cognitive system mediated through language.

The present perspective raises some important questions for aging theory and research. To what degree do all levels continue to operate effectively or do they lose strength to the same degree? Do the interrelations between them become weaker, or do the boundaries become more or less rigid as suggested by the transmission deficits that Burke (Chapter 13, this volume) refers to? For example, evidence from aphasias and amnesias suggests that even as personal (autobiographical) memory and specific language capabilities may decline or be lost, the capacity for maintaining implicit event memory and everyday routines remains robust. Ample evidence is available to indicate that language is vulnerable to loss of varying kinds and degrees; is narrative processing lost as well? Research in this area might shed light on the question of whether narrative is language dependent or independent of language. For example, can those who, due to brain lesions, have lost some aspect of language follow a nonverbal movie script? If development of autobiographical memory is a function of social-dialogic processes and its maintenance depends on verbalization, does loss of language affect access to autobiographical memory? Why, for older individuals, do memories from early adulthood stand out in comparison to those from later life?

To the extent that either experiential memory or linguistic capacities decline, might older individuals benefit from relying on the last layers of representation, the external symbolic levels? Note-taking, list making, use of computers, and so on might all supplement the less reliable word finding, short-term memory lapses, and other common representational difficulties in communication and cognition found in older adults. Already noted is the positive addition of note-taking to the performance on memory tasks among older individuals. The recognition that language is used (oral and written) for both communicative and cognitive representation may also suggest some ways in which the study of representation in the aging population may be approached. Do both suffer attrition at the same time? Or may one continue to function well while another fails? Comparing audio tape-recording (as in oral histories) with similarly written works might be a fruitful avenue for exploration.

Some specific implications for representation across the lifespan suggest predictions:

1. The experiential level (e.g., routines, skills) as the most basic should be most stable and reliable in aging.
2. Literate adults may rely more on external representations, including written language, as cognitive processing slows.
3. Competing levels of representation (experiential, linguistic) may show deterioration, such as loss of source knowledge similar to that found in early childhood.

References

Baillargeon, R. (1993). The object concept revisited: New directions in the investigation of infants' physical knowledge. In C. E. Granrud (Ed.), *Visual perception and cognition in infancy*. Hillsdale, NJ: Lawrence Erlbaum Associates.

Barrett, M. D. (1985). Early semantic representations and early word-usage. In I. S. A. Kuczaj & M. D. Barrett (Eds.), *The development of word meaning: Progress in cognitive development research* (pp. 39–68). New York: Springer-Verlag.

Bauer, P. J., Hertsgaard, L. A., & Dow, G. A. (1994). After 8 months have passed: Long-term recall of events by 1-to 2-year-old children. *Memory, 2*, 353–382.

Bauer, P. J., & Mandler, J. M. (1989). One thing follows another: effects of temporal structure on one- to two-year-olds' recall of events. *Developmental Psychology, 25*, 197–206.

Bickhard, M. H. (1987). The social nature of the functional nature of language. In M. Hickmann (Ed.), *Social and functional approaches to language and thought* (pp. 39–65). New York: Academic Press.

Bickhard, M. H. (2002). The biological emergence of representation. In T. Brown & L. Smith (Eds.), *Reductionism and the development of knowledge* (pp. 105–132). Mahwah, NJ: Lawrence Erlbaum Associates.

Carver, L. J., & Bauer, P. J. (2001). The dawning of a past: The emergence of long-term explicit memory in infancy. *Journal of Experimental Psychology: General, 130*, 726–745.

Ceci, S. J., & Bruck, M. (1993). Suggestibility of the child witness: A historical review and synthesis. *Psychological Bulletin, 113*, 403–439.

Choi, S., & Gopnik, A. (1995). Early acquisition of verbs in Korean: A cross-linguistic study. *Journal of Child Language, 22*, 497–529.

Clark, A. (1997). *Being there: Putting brain, body, and world together again*. Cambridge MA.: MIT Press.

Conway, M. A., & Pleydell-Pearce, C. W. (2000). The construction of autobiographical memories in the self-memory system. *Psychological Review, 107*, 261–288.

Damasio, A. (1999). *The feeling of what happens: Body and emotion in the making of consciousness*. New York: Harcourt.

Deacon, T. W. (1997). *The symbolic species: The co-evolution of language and the brain*. New York: W. W. Norton.

DeLoache, J. S. (1990). Young children's understanding of models. In R. F. J. Hudson (Ed.), *Knowing and remembering in young children* (pp. 94–126). New York: Cambridge University Press.

Dennett, D. C. (1991). *Consciousness explained*. Boston: Little, Brown.

Donald, M. (1991). *Origins of the modern mind*. Cambridge, MA: Harvard University Press.

Elman, J. L., Bates, E. A., Johnson, M. H., Karmiloff-Smith, A., Parisi, D. & Plunkett, K. (1996). *Rethinking innateness: A connectionist perspective on development*. Cambridge, MA: MIT Press.

Fivush, R., & Nelson, K. (2004). Culture and language in the emergence of autobiographical memory. *Psychological Science, 15*, 573–577.

Fodor, J. A. (1975). *The language of thought*. New York: Crowell.

Garcia, R. (1999). A systemic interpretation of Piaget's theory. In E. K. Scholnick, K. Nelson, S. A. Gelman, & P. H. Miller (Eds.), *Conceptual development: Piaget's legacy* (pp. 165–184). Mahwah, NJ: Lawrence Erlbaum Associates.

Gibson, J. J. (1979). *The ecological approach to visual perception.* Boston: Houghton-Mifflin.

Gibson, J. J. (1986). *The ecological approach to visual perception.* Hillsdale, NJ: Lawrence Erlbaum Associates.

Gopnik, A., & Graf, P. (1988). Knowing how you know: Children's understanding of the sources of their beliefs. *Child Development, 59,* 1366–1371.

Greenough, W. T., Black, J. E., & Wallace, C. S. (1987). Experience and brain development. *Child Development, 58,* 539–559.

Halliday, M. A. K. (1975). *Learning how to mean.* London: Edwin Arnold.

Karmiloff-Smith, A. (1992). *Beyond modularity.* Cambridge, MA: MIT Press.

Kintsch, W. (1974). *The representation of meaning in memory.* New York: Wiley.

Levy, E., & Nelson, K. (1994). Words in discourse: a dialectical approach to the acquisition of meaning and use. *Journal of Child Language, 21,* 367–390.

Mandler, J. M. (1988). How to build a baby: On the development of an accessible representational system. *Cognitive Development, 3,* 113–136.

Mandler, J. M. (1992). How to build a baby II: Conceptual primitives. *Psychological Review, 99,* 587–604.

Mandler, J. M., & McDonough, L. (1993). Concept formation in infancy. *Cognitive Development, 8,* 291–319.

McAdams, D. P. (1993). *The stories we live by: Personal myths and the making of the self.* New York: Guilford Press.

Mehler, J., Jusczyk, P. W., Lambertz, G., Halsted, N., Bertoncini, J., & Amiel-Tison, C. (1988). A precursor of language acquisition in young infants. *Cognition, 29,* 144–178.

Miller, G. A. (1990). The place of language in a scientific psychology. *Psychological Science, 1,* 7–14.

Miller, P. J., Potts, R., Fung, H., Hoogstra, L., & Mintz, J. (1990). Narrative practices and the social construction of self in childhood. *American Ethnologist, 17,* 292–311.

Nelson, K. (1974). Concept, word, and sentence: Interrelations in acquisition and development. *Psychological Review, 81,* 267–285.

Nelson, K. (1981). Social cognition in a script framework. In J. Flavell & L. Ross (Eds.), *Social cognitive development.* New York: Cambridge University Press.

Nelson, K. (1985). *Making sense: The acquisition of shared meaning.* New York: Academic Press.

Nelson, K. (1986). *Event knowledge: Structure and function in development.* Hillsdale, NJ: Lawrence Erlbaum Associates.

Nelson, K. (1993). The psychological and social origins of autobiographical memory. *Psychological Science, 4,* 1–8.

Nelson, K. (1996). *Language in cognitive development: The emergence of the mediated mind.* New York: Cambridge University Press.

Nelson, K. (2005). Language pathways to the community of minds. In J. W. Astington & J. Baird (Eds.), *Why language matters to theory of mind* (pp. 26–39). New York: Oxford University Press.

Nelson, K., & Fivush, R. (2000). Socialization of memory. In E. Tulving & F. I. M. Craik (Eds.), *The Oxford handbook of memory.* (pp. 283–295). New York: Oxford University Press.

Nelson, K., & Fivush, R. (2004). Emergence of autobiographical memory: A social developmental theory. *Psychological Review, 111,* 486–511..

Nelson, K., & Shaw, L. K. (2002). Developing a socially shared symbolic system. In E. Amsel & J. Byrnes (Eds.), *Language, literacy and cognitive development* (pp. 27–58). Mahwah, NJ: Lawrence Erlbaum Associates.

Nelson, K., & Ware, A. (2002). The re-emergence of function. In N. Stein, P. Bauer, & M. Rabinowitz (Eds.), *Essays in honor of Jean Mandler* (pp. 161–184). Mahwah, NJ: Lawrence Erlbaum Associates.

Perner, J. (1991). *Understanding the representational mind.* Cambridge, MA: MIT Press.

Piaget, J. (1962). *Play, dreams, and imitation in childhood.* New York: W. W. Norton.

Ratner, H. H., Foley, M. A., & Gimpert, N. (2000). Person perspectives on children's memory and learning: What do source-monitoring failures reveal? In K. P. Roberts & M. Blades (Eds.), *Children's source monitoring* (pp. 85–114). Mahwah, NJ: Lawrence Erlbaum Associates.

Rochat, P. (2001). *The infant's world.* Cambridge, MA: Harvard University Press.

Rovee-Collier, C., & Hayne, H. (2000). Memory in infancy and early childhood. In E. Tulving & F. I. M. Craik (Eds.), *The Oxford handbook of memory* (pp. 267–279). New York: Oxford University Press.

Spelke, E. S. (2003). What makes us smart? Core knowledge and natural language. In D. Gentner & S. Goldin-Meadow (Eds.), *Language in mind: Advances in the study of language and thought* (pp. 277–312). Cambridge, MA: MIT Press.

Sun, R. (2002). *Duality of the mind: A bottom up approach toward cognition.* Mahwah, NJ: Lawrence Erlbaum Associates.

Tomasello, M. (1992). *First verbs: A case study of early grammatical development.* New York: Cambridge University Press.

Tomasello, M. (1999). *The cultural origins of human cognitions.* Cambridge, MA: Harvard University Press.

Tulving, E. (1983). *Elements of episodic memory.* New York: Oxford University Press.

Vygotsky, L. (1986). *Thought and language.* Cambridge MA: MIT Press.

Welch-Ross, M. K. (2000). A mental-state reasoning model of suggestibility and memory source monitoring. In K. P. Roberts & M. Blades (Eds.), *Children's source monitoring* (pp. 227–256). Mahwah, NJ: Lawrence Erlbaum Associates.

13

Representation and Aging

Deborah M. Burke

The nature of mental representation is a central issue for understanding cognitive development from birth through old age. The question of how infants develop mental representation—in particular, how they advance from sensori-motor experience to symbolic representation, especially language—has animated developmental theory (see Chapter 12, this volume). One theoretical approach, most notably Piaget's (1969), postulates innate and immutable mental processes (e.g., assimilation, accommodation) that interact with the environment to modify or create mental representations so as to produce new and fundamentally different knowledge. The problem of aging and mental representation is approached somewhat differently, no doubt because representation of knowledge is widely believed to be stable in form and organization during adulthood. Older adults do, however, show declines in the ability to create new representations (see, e.g., Light, 1991; MacKay & Burke, 1990). This aging pattern provides the foundation for theories of adult development that postulate two distinct

components of cognition: fluid versus crystallized intelligence (Horn & Catell, 1967; Horn & Hofer, 1992) or the related dichotomy of mechanics versus pragmatics of intelligence (Baltes, Staudinger, & Lindenberger, 1999). At the heart of this two-component approach is the belief that existing knowledge representations—the basis for crystallized intelligence/cognitive pragmatics—are insensitive to aging, whereas cognitive mechanics—that is, cognitive processes that underlie new learning—for example, decline with aging. This theoretical approach is the developmental inverse of Piaget's theory because it postulates stability of representations and age-related modification of processes that act on these representations. This chapter is concerned with the state of mental representations during adulthood, and in particular, with the interaction of mental processes with representations and the effect of this on representational structure in old age.

Developmental research on children and adults has demonstrated that experience and neurocognitive factors affect the content, organization, and integrity of existing mental representations (e.g., Stern & Carstensen, 2000). Inasmuch as old age is associated with changes in neural structures and with changes in people's social and cognitive experience in everyday life, we would expect aging to affect mental representations. These changes in representation, however, are likely to be specific to certain types of knowledge rather than general changes affecting all knowledge. This expectation is based on developmental evidence that many changes in representations during childhood are specific to a domain, or subdomain, of knowledge (Karmiloff-Smith, 1992) and on neuropsychological evidence that cognitive impairments produced by many types of brain damage are also specific to a domain. Domains organize mental representations of different types of knowledge; for example, language, concepts, sensory information, and emotions, with finer divisions creating subdomains within a domain—for example, representations of proper names or of lexical versus phonological information within the language domain. The representational segregation of domains is supported by neuropsychological disorders that affect highly specific representations—for example, lexical representations in some forms of aphasia (Goodglass & Wingfield, 1997) or proper names in some specific language impairments (Semenza, 1997) . Developmental changes during childhood also are specific to some representations, most notably changes associated with language acquisition. For example, infants are sensitive to clause boundaries in spoken language long before they are able to embed objects in their sensory-motor behavior (Hirsh-Pasek et al., 1987).

Consistent with evidence for domain specificity in the neuropsychological and development literature, we review evidence that stability in representations in old age is found for some domains of knowledge and not others. Thus, while older adults experience both neural changes and social-cultural changes that lead us to expect changes in representation in old age, we do not expect changes to be homogeneous across different types of representations. We present a model that attempts to explain how domain-specific effects on behavior can emanate from neurocognitive changes that occur across domains.

To summarize, our goal in this chapter is to identify shifts in cognitive performance during adulthood that suggest changes in mental representation, and to identify the cognitive mechanisms that are responsible for these changes, especially when they are domain specific. We also consider the relevance of these cognitive mechanisms for the development of mental representation during childhood. Our search for cognitive mechanisms is guided by consideration of both social-cultural factors and neural-cognitive factors that influence mental representation, and we are mindful that these factors are not independent but rather interactive in their effects. This interaction highlights the difficulty of isolating experiential versus neural factors that are responsible for developmental change in mental representation. This is demonstrated nicely in research by Farah, Polk, and their colleagues (Polk & Farah, 1998; Polk et al., 2002). Letters and numbers are symbol systems that share the same visual properties and sometimes the same underlying concepts (e.g., *ten* vs. 10), but they are distinguished by cultural practice and constitute different domains. Studies of the visual recognition of letters and numbers show that numbers "pop out" from a sequence of letters, providing behavioral evidence that their mental representations are segregated at least at a cognitive level. Moreover, functional neuroimaging shows that recognition of letters and numbers activates separate regions of the brain. These effects seem to be a consequence of the co-occurrence of letters with letters and numbers with numbers in common cultural experiences. People exposed to an environment of co-occurring rather than separate letters and digits—namely, Canadian postal workers working with Canadian postal codes—show less behavioral evidence of segregation of letters and numbers (Polk & Farah, 1998; Polk et al., 2002). Thus, aspects of mental representations that appear to be stable in old age—for example, the organization of semantic representations—may owe their stability either to continuity of cultural practice during adulthood or to the resilience of the neural organization.

SEMANTIC REPRESENTATION DURING ADULTHOOD

Reviews of empirical studies of adult development of conceptual knowledge, including word meanings and world knowledge, have consistently concluded that there is no evidence that the representational structures for this knowledge, or access to them, decline with aging (e.g., Light, 1991; Wingfield & Stine-Morrow, 2000). A number of studies have reported that adults ages 65 years and older perform as well as or better than 20-year-olds on tests of vocabulary and general knowledge (e.g., Beier & Ackerman, 2001; Schaie, 1994). Indeed, Verhaeghen (2003) recently reported that a meta-analysis of vocabulary test scores for 324 samples of young and older adults showed a substantial effect size (0.80 SD) in favor of older adults having greater knowledge of word meaning. In very old adults, however, vocabulary declined from age 70 to 103 (Lindenberger & Baltes, 1997). Measures such as word association (Burke & Peters, 1986), script generation (Light & Anderson, 1983), and category generation (Howard, 1980) that reflect the content, structure, and organization of semantic representations are highly consistent across adulthood.

Another index of the integrity of semantic representations is language comprehension because it requires the retrieval of lexical and semantic information to construct a meaning of the discourse. On-line measures of sentence comprehension show no evidence for deficits in old age (for a review, see Burke, MacKay & James, 2000; Wingfield & Stine-Morrow, 2000). Semantic priming effects during language processing, which are attributed to the automatic spread of activation through a semantically organized network of conceptual representations, are often greater for older than for young adults (e.g., Madden, 1988; Pichora-Fuller, Schneider, & Daneman, 1995), an age difference confirmed in meta-analyses (e.g., Laver & Burke, 1993). It has been suggested that older adults show larger semantic priming effects because their greater accumulation of knowledge produces a more elaborated semantic network with more connections between semantically related concepts, increasing the transmission of excitation (Laver & Burke, 1993; Taylor & Burke, 2002).

Conceptual knowledge is both general and situated in specific situations. That is, language comprehension requires the ability to construct word meaning that is situated in the particular context of the sentence by activating aspects of word meaning that are relevant and by suppressing those that are irrelevant. Does aging reduce this flexibility in instantiating word meaning? Apparently not. After reading a sentence biasing a specific aspect of meaning for a target word (e.g., "The oranges rolled off the uneven table"), young and older adults showed comparable facilitation in a property-verification task involving the relevant compared to the irrelevant property of the target ("Oranges-Round"? faster than "Oranges-Juicy"?;

Burke & Harrold, 1988). Thus there is no evidence that aging causes language processes to become more rigid—that is, less influenced by the relevant context. There is also evidence that during the processing of discourse, older adults are at least as proficient as young adults in constructing a model of the specific situation described in the discourse, drawing heavily on existing world knowledge that is instantiated in the discourse context (e.g., Radvansky, Zwaan, Curiel, & Copeland, 2001). In sum, there is strong and consistent evidence that representations of conceptual knowledge relevant to single words or texts are intact in old age and enable a high level of language comprehension.

Although representation of conceptual semantics seems to be intact in old age, older adults' language production suggests that some linguistic knowledge—specifically word phonology and orthography—is not intact. Older adults report that one of their most annoying cognitive problems is the inability to produce a well-known word (e.g., Rabbitt, Maylor, McInnes, Bent, & Moore, 1995). While people of all ages suffer such word-finding failures, this type of error becomes more frequent in old age. For example, older adults make more errors in naming pictures than do young adults (for a meta-analysis confirming this aging effect, see Feyereisen, 1997). In spoken discourse, older adults produce more errors of a type that suggests retrieval failures—for example, filled pauses and substitution of a related but incorrect word (e.g., Kemper, 1992; Schmitter-Edgecombe, Vesneski, & Jones, 2000).

The clearest evidence that older adults' production problems reflect the condition of phonological representations comes from studies of the tip-of-the-tongue phenomenon (TOT). The TOT state is a dramatic instance of word-finding difficulty in which a person is temporarily unable to produce a word that is very familiar and that the individual is certain he or she knows. Both naturally occurring and experimentally induced TOTs increase with aging (e.g., Burke, MacKay, Worthley & Wade, 1991; Brown & Nix, 1996). TOT targets are rated as highly familiar, although they tend to be words that have low frequency of occurrence in the language or that are proper names that have not been used recently (e.g., Burke et al., 1991).

What is the evidence that TOTs are caused by deficits in phonological representations and not semantic representations? During a TOT state, people report that semantic information is available to them but the word form is not (Brown, 1991). Moreover, production of words sharing only the sound of a target word reduces TOTs for the target word. For example, James and Burke (2000) presented TOT-inducing questions ("What is the name of the nylon fabric which has two pieces which stick to each other and is used as a fastener?") and when participants responded "TOT" or "don't know," they were presented 10 words to pronounce. On some trials, half of these words shared some phonemes with the answer to the question (e.g., *decreed*, *pellet* for target *Velcro*). When the question was re-presented, TOTs were more likely to be resolved following production of phonologically related rather than unrelated words. Further research has shown that the production of the initial phonological component increases resolution more than production of middle or final phonemes (White & Abrams, 2002). A similar phonological effect on TOTs was shown for prior production of homophones of the target word: production of *pit* as in "cherry pit" increased successful naming and decreased TOTs in naming a picture of a famous person whose name is a homophone of the prior word—for example, Brad Pitt (Burke, Locantore, Austin, & Chae, 2004).

An account of why phonological representations are more vulnerable to aging or infrequent use than semantic representations has been proposed within the context of a connectionist model of knowledge representations. Node Structure Theory (NST) is a general interactive activation model of perception and action that describes the representations underlying sequential behavior, including language (MacKay, 1987; MacKay & Abrams, 1998). NST postulates hierarchical representations underlying skilled behavior in a vast network of nodes, which are the processing units for representations. Like other models of language, NST postulates a *semantic system* (subdomain) representing conceptual knowledge and a *phonological system* (subdomain) representing word sounds. Figure 13.1 shows a partial representation of the word *Velcro* within this model that we will use to illustrate how the model accounts for production and failures of production.

Word production starts with activation of representations in the semantic system corresponding to the thought that is to be expressed; let us say in this case the intention of naming the plastic-like fastening tape on walking shoes. Activation of the semantic information corresponding to "Velcro" transmits priming to lexical representations for words whose meaning share

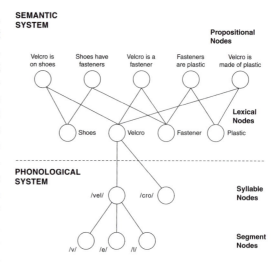

FIGURE 13.1. Representation of some semantic and phonological components of the word *Velcro* in node structure theory (e.g., Burke et al, 1991; MacKay, 1987). All phonological nodes must be activated for spoken production. Many nodes and connections have been omitted to simplify the figure.

components of the semantic information. Priming is a form of subthreshold excitation that is transmitted across connections linking nodes and that prepares a node for activation, the basis for retrieval of its information. The lexical representation is activated whose meaning corresponds most closely to the activated semantic information—in this case, the lexical representation for *Velcro*—and this transmits priming to corresponding nodes in the phonological system. Spoken production of this word requires activation of corresponding phonological representations to the lowest level.

A TOT for *Velcro* occurs when its semantic and lexical representations are activated, causing a strong feeling of knowing the word, but activation of phonological information about the sounds of the word is incomplete. According to the transmission-deficit principle (Burke et al., 1991), activation of phonology fails because connections to phonological representations have become weak, reducing the transmission of priming. What causes weak connections among nodes? Frequent or recent activation of nodes strengthens connections, increasing priming transmission. Aging weakens connections, reducing transmission of priming. Weak connections caused by aging or infrequent practice can prevent a node from reaching a threshold of priming necessary for activation, resulting in retrieval failure (e.g., MacKay & Burke, 1990). For example, a TOT occurs for *Velcro* in Figure 13.1 when weak connections transmit insufficient excitation from its lexical node to its phonological nodes. This explains why words that are produced infrequently are more likely to be involved in TOTs than frequently used words and why TOTs increase with aging.

Why does decreased connection strength—a general, age-related change distributed across different domains and levels of knowledge—cause retrieval failures for information in one subdomain (phonological system) but not another (semantic domain)? Within NST, the architecture of the phonological representational system renders its top-down connections more vulnerable to transmission deficits than top-down or bottom-up connections in the semantic system. This is because the functional effect of transmission deficits is more severe when one-to-one connections are involved. As can be seen in Figure 13.1, representations of semantic components of a word are highly interconnected and thus a transmission deficit in any one connection will be offset by other connections to the same feature. For example, consider what would occur if there were an especially weak connection between the lexical node for *Velcro* and the node representing the semantic information that Velcro is a fastener. The reduced transmission of priming caused by this weak connection would be compensated by additional sources of priming from nodes connected to "Velcro" and indirectly to "Velcro is a fastener" (e.g., "Velcro is on shoes," "Velcro is made of plastic"). The node representing the knowledge that Velcro is a fastener would be likely to receive sufficient priming to be activated through connections from "Velcro is on shoes" and "shoes have fasteners."

In retrieval of phonology for production of speech, however, transmission of priming diverges from lexical nodes along single connections to associated phonological nodes. A transmission deficit in a single connection will prevent retrieval of the phonology represented by that node because there is no source of compensatory priming (see Figure 13.1). The nature of conceptual and phonological knowledge is fundamentally different, and this is reflected in the architecture of the respective representations. This fundamental difference in representational structure explains within NST why failures of language production increase in old age, even though, as demonstrated in the research reviewed above, conceptual retrieval during receptive language shows little change.

The differential effect of weak connections on phonological compared to semantic representations also explains why tests of semantic knowledge that require production rather than recognition may impair performance for older compared to young adults. Verhaeghen's (2003) meta-analysis of age differences in performance on vocabulary tests showed a greater effect size in favor of older adults for multiple-choice tests than for vocabulary tests like the Wechsler Adult Intelligence Scale (WAIS) that require production of the meaning of test words. As Verhaeghen points out, multiple-choice tests require recognition, not word production, and these would not handicap older adults who, even though they know more words, have difficulty producing them.

In addition to explaining deficits in production of spoken language in old age, the transmission deficit principle also predicts deficits in orthographic production because orthographic representations like phonological representations depend on single connections to lexical nodes. A growing number of studies have demonstrated this aging-related decline in the ability to produce correct spelling. Older adults make more errors than younger adults in spelling spoken words that are hard to spell—for example, *colonel, spontaneous* (MacKay & Abrams, 1998; MacKay, Abrams, & Pedroza, 1999). Cortese, Balota, Sergent-Marshall, and Buckner (2003) presented spoken homophones that had different spellings for their different meanings *vein, capitol*. Older adults not only made more spelling errors than did young adults, but they were more likely than young adults to produce a spelling that corresponded to the dominant meaning but that was a nondominant spelling for that sound (*vein*); young adults were more likely to produce a spelling that corresponded to a nondominant meaning and was a dominant spelling for that sound (e.g., *vane*). This suggests that semantics has a stronger effect on lexical selection for older than for young adults.

Experiential factors are critically important for maintaining language production. Indeed, under NST, lack of practice—that is, infrequent production of language—is one cause of the transmission deficits that produce word-retrieval failures in adults of any age. We evaluate below the role of experiential and neural factors in the cognitive mechanisms responsible for aging effects. It is important to point out, however, that even if aging-related word-production failures were linked to neural changes in old age, cultural factors such as the frequency of language use affect performance. Moreover, the effect of age-related neural change seems to depend on another cultural factor: the nature of the language in a culture. Neurocognitive deficits have been shown to have language-specific effects. For example, the prevalence of dyslexia varied in countries whose languages differed in the consistency of sound-letter mappings (Landerl, 2003; Paulesu et al., 2001). Although developmental dyslexics appear to have the same underlying neurocognitive deficit regardless of the language spoken, the prevalence of dyslexia in a country depends on the transparency of the orthography of its language. English is a notoriously inconsistent language in terms of sound-letter mappings, with multiple and sometimes unpredictable pronunciations for graphemes. Countries such as Italy, whose language involves highly consistent grapheme-phoneme mappings, report lower rates of dyslexia than the United States (Paulesu et al., 2001).

Although, there has been little cross-cultural comparison of language-production deficits in old age, there is evidence that age-related declines in spelling in Spanish, a highly transparent language, occur primarily for words that have sounds that are spelled differently in different words (Burke, Ruz, Christidis, & Santiago, 2004). Because most words in Spanish have sounds that can be spelled in only one way, transmission deficits would have little impact on everyday spelling, regardless of whether they are caused by experiential or neural factors. Indeed, with languages featuring regular phoneme-grapheme mappings with no exceptions, such as Finnish or Serbo-Croatian, the age deficit in spelling that was observed for English is predicted to disappear.

THE REPRESENTATION OF SKILL

Language is a highly practiced skill, and some components of language—namely, conceptual knowledge—appear to be stable in old age. Is this stability unique to language or is it also found for representations underlying other domains of expertise? The fate of representations underlying various types of expertise has obvious practical significance—for example, its relevance to the evaluation of the competence of

aging pilots (e.g., Morrow et al., 2003). It is also theoretically significant inasmuch as it reveals whether or not expert knowledge compensates for age-sensitive mental processes like forming new representations (e.g., Baltes et al., 1999). In particular, the study of expertise is relevant to the "use it or lose it" adage: Does continued practice in an area of expertise preserve the skill and is there a more general beneficial effect of the practice on basic cognitive processes involved in the skill?

When experts are asked to perform their skill, the relevant knowledge appears to be well preserved in old age. There are no aging deficits in expert performance in such skills as chess (Charness, 1981) and bridge (Charness, 1979), piano playing (Krampe & Ericsson, 1996), and transcription typing (Bosman, 1993; Salthouse, 1984). This age constancy, however, depends on the continued practice of the skill. The best predictor of the level of skilled performance for young and old pianists, both amateur and expert, was the amount of daily practice during the last 10 years (Krampe & Ericsson, 1996). This is consistent with the transmission-deficit principle because practice counteracts age-linked transmission deficits by strengthening connections. Morrow et al. (2003) tested pilots and nonpilots on knowledge of aviation navigation and air traffic control communication. Test performance declined with age, but older pilots had far fewer recent flying hours and a longer interval since studying for licensing exams. Thus, the research suggests that high levels of continued practice are essential, and with such practice older experts' knowledge representations that underlie their expert performance are well preserved. This includes performance involving declarative knowledge such as bidding a bridge hand and procedural knowledge such as finger movements in piano playing. Stable expert performance, however, appears to be highly domain specific to the area of expertise: older experts show declines relative to young experts on performance that extends outside the domain of expertise and requires the creation of representations that are not part of the existing representation of the skill. For example, Krampe and Ericsson (1996) found little age-related decline for expert pianists in the speed of *music-related* finger movements, but there were the usual age declines in speed of *nonmusic related* finger movements requiring new representations.

Within the framework of NST, production of a new behavior requires new connections to form an appropriate representation of the behavior. Older adults' difficulty in forming new links between representations in memory has been labeled a binding deficit (Chalfonte & Johnson, 1996; MacKay & Burke, 1990). Under NST, binding deficits are caused by transmission deficits that impede the sustained activation of representations required under NST for the formation of new connections between the representations. When memory for new information related to the area of expertise is tested, old and young experts typically show comparable advantage over amateurs, indicating that both age groups use their expert knowledge in an equivalent way to organize the to-be-remembered material. But age differences between young and old experts are commonly found on these tasks, showing the typical age-related decline in memory for new information. For example, older musicians recalled fewer unfamiliar melodies than did younger musicians (Mcinz & Salthouse, 1998). Pilots recalled more air traffic control instructions than nonpilots, but older pilots recalled fewer instructions than young pilots. The age difference for pilots disappeared when they were allowed to take notes, a common procedure when actually flying (Morrow et al., 2003).

In sum, when evaluating aging effects on representation of expert knowledge, it is critical to distinguish between tasks that involve activation of existing knowledge structures—for example, performing the highly practiced skill—and tasks that involve formation of new representations of material related to but not the same as existing representations. This distinction holds even for expert language-processing skills. For example, processing written text is similar across ages when measurement involves on-line techniques such as allocation of reading time (Kemtes & Kemper, 1997; Stine, 1990) and semantic priming effects for relevant information (e.g., Paul, 1996). However, memory for the new information in written text, measured off-line, is consistently reduced in older compared to young adults even though linguistic processing is comparable (e.g., Kemtes & Kemper, 1997; Wingfield, Tun, & Rosen, 1995).

Our focus on representations is helpful in understanding how experience—in this case expert practice—affects cognitive aging. The "use it or lose it" adage correctly describes the maintenance of existing representations that are relevant to the skill, but the benefit is highly specific to the domain of expertise. Although existing expert performance can be well maintained, it requires practice for both young and older adults. Even in language performance, words that have not been used recently are likely to show production failures, especially for older adults. The "use it or lose it" adage does not, however, apply to the processes involved in encoding *new* representations, even new representations related to the skill. The evidence so far suggests that using the mental processes involved in forming new representations will not protect these processes from aging effects (e.g., Kliegl, Smith, & Baltes, 1989).

DOMAINS OF REPRESENTATIONS

Aging effects on existing representations are visible in only some specific domains or subdomains (e.g., phonological representations), but aging effects on the formation of new representations are general, applying across domains. With respect to semantic representations, we have seen that vocabulary and world knowledge are usually superior in older than in young adults. This knowledge, however, does not continue to increase during late middle age and old age; the level of acquired knowledge levels off in middle age (e.g., Ackerman & Rolfhus, 1999; Schaie, 1994). A likely cause is a decline in the ability to form new semantic representations in old age, impeding the accumulation of new knowledge and causing a leveling off of performance. There is empirical evidence for aging-related declines in learning new factual semantic information (e.g., McIntyre & Craik, 1987; Schacter, Osowiecki, Kaszniak, Kihlstrom, & Valdiserri, 1994). Moreover, older adults in their 60s and 70s were more accurate in factual knowledge about current events that occurred when they were 11–30 years old compared to when they were 40 years or older (Rubin, Rahhal, & Poon, 1998). Thus, semantic representations, like other types of representation, are vulnerable to the age-linked decline in forming new representations. In contrast, activation of existing knowledge representations during reading, speaking, and thinking strengthens connections in these representations, thereby maintaining the integrity of this previous knowledge.

Neural factors contribute to the decline in forming new semantic representations in old age, at least as indicated by parallel but more severe effects for patients with brain damage causing anterograde amnesia. The learning deficit in amnesia affects the acquisition of semantic knowledge. HM is a famous amnesic who suffered virtually a complete loss of the ability to form new representations after surgery removing his hippocampus. HM had no recognition of the lexical status or meaning of words and proper names that he had encountered for the first time after his surgery, indicating that his learning deficit includes semantic knowledge (Gabrieli, Cohen, & Corkin, 1988). Moreover, from age 57 to age 71, HM has shown a marked deterioration in his knowledge of low-frequency words that he knew from before his surgery. This decline does not occur for high-frequency words. Because low-frequency words are used infrequently, their representations may have become dysfunctional from disuse. HM, unlike normal adults, is unable to form new representations to replace the dysfunctional ones when he encounters these words again (James & MacKay, 2001). Because older adults have a reduced ability to form new semantic representations, they may show a similar, albeit much smaller effect. This suggests another mechanism that contributes to the leveling off of acquired knowledge in old age. Both young and older adults may lose representations of infrequently used words, but older adults may be less able than young adults to replace those representations when the word is encountered again.

An explanation for why the level of semantic knowledge does not continue to increase in old age must also include factors unrelated to cognitive decrements in old age. There is compelling evidence that social values shift in old age so that there is greater emphasis on feelings and less emphasis on the accumulation of knowledge. Carstensen and her colleagues (e.g., Carstensen, Isaacowitz, & Charles, 1999) have developed the socioemotional selectivity theory that claims that perception of time influences goals and motivation. When time is perceived as running out, a greater emphasis is placed on the present rather than the future. This produces a shift in goals away from the accumulation of knowledge because of the uncertainty of the future when this knowledge would be put to use and a shift to emotional goals of bringing immediate emotional satisfaction. Carstensen has demonstrated that when the end of life is approached, healthy older adults and terminally ill patients are guided in their choices by emotional goals rather than goals related to learning new information (Carstensen & Fredrickson, 1998). Socioemotional selectivity theory presents an important alternative to the decremental approach that dominates cognitive aging research. We return to it shortly in considering predictions for changes in autobiographical representations in old age.

Episodic memory refers to a person's ability to remember specific events experienced at a specific time (Tulving, 1983). Older adults exhibit major declines in laboratory tests of episodic memory, performing more poorly on episodic recall or recognition of virtually any stimuli—for example, single words or prose passages, spatial locations, pictures, faces, and activities (Craik & Jennings, 1992). Meta-analyses of episodic memory performance show large effect sizes in favor of young adults (e.g., Verhaeghen, Marcoen, & Goossens, 1993). Does this suggest that the domain of episodic representations is more vulnerable to aging effects than the domain of semantic representations? There is a fundamental difference between standard semantic and episodic tests in that episodic tests invariably require formation of new representations whereas semantic tests require retrieval of existing representations. Even when an episodic recall test involves well-known material—for example, familiar single words or proverbs—new connections must be made between the representations for to-be-remembered items—for example, words—and the temporal or spatial context in which they appeared. Older adults are less able to form these new connections. The claim that episodic memory is more sensitive to aging than semantic memory is based on tests showing age constancy in retrieval of existing semantic representations and age declines in retrieval of new episodic connections (e.g., Nyberg, Bäckman, Erngrund, Olofsson, & Nilsson, 1996). As we demonstrated earlier, however, aging impairs formation of new representations regardless of whether they involve semantic or episodic information.

AUTOBIOGRAPHICAL MEMORIES

Autobiographical memory is a subdomain of episodic memory that represents personally experienced events that chronicle one's life. It has been argued that autobiographical representations are organized into narratives that integrate disparate experiences and provide a sense of continuity of self (Nelson, 2003). The organization of autobiographical memory is influenced by a perspective in the narrative that emphasizes goals and causal events, and functions to explain the individual's past and to define the future. Thus autobiographical representations are the basis for self-identity and for communicating this identity to others. This highlights the important social function of autobiographical memory because it is the basis for expressing significant personal experiences to family and acquaintances (Nelson, 2003).

Older adults' goals in remembering autobiographical memories would be expected to differ from young adults' within the framework of socioemotional selectivity theory because aging increases the emphasis on the experience of positive feelings (Carstensen et al., 1999). Toward the end of life, the autobiographical narrative is predicted to focus on the significance and positive emotional value of remembered events. This prediction is supported by studies showing that aging was associated with increased positive emotion during recall of specific autobiographical experiences (Pasupathi & Carstensen, 2003).

An alternative approach, however, postulates decrements in older adults' autobiographical memory that are caused by neural-based changes in "mechanics." Arbuckle and Gold and their colleagues (e.g., Gold, Andres, Arbuckle, & Schwartzman, 1988) reported that older adults' responses to questions about their life history became increasingly prolonged and irrelevant to the question asked as their age increased from 60 years to over 90 years. Arbuckle and Gold (1993) argued that older adults' autobiographical descriptions wander off-topic because they have a deficit in the ability to inhibit irrelevant information so that extraneous personal observations clutter their descriptions of their lives (Zacks & Hasher, 1994; Chapter 11, this volume). The argument is not that the representation of autobiographical information changes but rather the mechanics (i.e., inhibitory processes) acting on these representations are affected by aging.

If older adults produce more verbose autobiographical descriptions because of a cognitive decrement that increases irrelevant and tangential speech, it is surprising that ratings of the quality of autobiographical or fictional narratives are higher for older than for younger speakers (Kemper, Rash, Kynette, & Norman, 1990; Pratt & Robins, 1991). Older adults' autobiographical narratives were also rated as more interesting and informative than were young adults' narratives (James, Burke, Austin, & Hulme, 1998). James et al. (1998) reported that older adults produced more off-topic speech than did young adults, but only on autobiographical topics, not descriptions of pictures. This is inconsistent with a general inhibition deficit.

It has also been suggested that age differences in autobiographical descriptions reflect the preservation of semantic representations and the selective decline of episodic representations with aging. Levine, Svoboda, Hay, Winocur, and Moscovitch (2002) measured the number of episodic details and semantic details in young and older adults' description of autobiographical events. Episodic details were specific descriptions of an event including time and place, whereas semantic details were factual details not situated in time and space or events unrelated to the target event. The semantic details seem likely to have been candidates for off-topic speech in other studies. In general, older adults produced more semantic details than did young adults and fewer episodic details.

These age differences in autobiographical descriptions are consistent with a shift in perspective to emphasize the *significance* of life events rather than present a simple delineation of life events. Consistent with socioemotional selectivity theory, age differences in autobiographical descriptions appear to reflect the different communicative goals of young and older adults (James et al., 1998). Older adults organize and retrieve their life events motivated by a goal to communicate the significance of their life experiences rather than a goal of imparting information concisely. Such an age-related change in communicative goals explains both the more favorable evaluative ratings that older adults receive for their autobiographical descriptions and the finding that age differences in off-topic speech are specific to autobiographical descriptions. This change in autobiographical description seems to reflect a change in pragmatic aspects of discourse, and there is no evidence to suggest that the representational structure of autobiographical information is involved.

COGNITIVE MECHANISMS FOR DEVELOPMENT IN CHILDHOOD AND OLD AGE

We have identified several cases where the state of underlying representations caused increased cognitive failures in old age. Contrary to the view that existing knowledge is intact in old age, aspects of crystallized intelligence do show age-related decline. This decline is specific to certain domains and subdomains. We have attributed older adults' decline in producing the spoken or written form of words to changes in phonological and orthographic representations. The formation of new representations also declines in old age, and here the decline is across domains. Within the NST model, existing phonological and orthographic representations in semantic memory are vulnerable to weak connections because of the nature of their architecture, and the formation of new representations across domains is undermined by deficits in creating new connections. We turn now to two issues: Do these cognitive mechanisms play a role in development during childhood? Do these changes in cognitive mechanisms originate in experience or in neural changes?

It has been argued that the state of underlying representations is critical to cognitive development during childhood. Munakata, McClelland, Johnson, and Siegler (1997) investigated the paradoxical findings that infants as young as 3.5 months will look longer at an impossible event involving an occluded object, suggesting a concept of object permanence, and yet infants younger than 8 months fail to retrieve hidden objects, suggesting an absence of object permanence. They account for this pattern by postulating a gradual strengthening of connections in the representations of occluded objects based on experience with objects during an infant's first year. Early representations are adequate for infants to form expectations about occluded objects and thus react to impossible events, but are not adequate to guide reaching responses for occluded objects. Munakata et al. argue against the view that object permanence is an all-or-none concept that depends on ancillary processes such as memory or processing resources—that is, mechanics, for its expression. Rather, they argue that the representation of occluded objects evolves with experience and the current state of a representation determines behavior.

The importance of experience on children's development has been demonstrated even for domains that are heavily influenced by innate factors. While it is not surprising that experience influences some aspects of language acquisition, the large effect of environment on the acquisition of complex syntax is more unexpected. Huttenlocher, Vasilyeva, Cymerman, and Levine (2002) reported that preschoolers' improvement in language comprehension during the school year was positively related to the production of multi-clause utterances by their teacher. Children in classrooms with teachers who produced more complex syntactic structures showed greater improvement in their understanding of syntax than children in classrooms with teachers who used simpler syntax. This relation was independent of the child's initial level of comprehension and no such relation was found for improvement in nonverbal math performance. Variation in language experience influences the development of complex syntactic structures.

In adult development, we have argued that the state of a representation is critical in explaining certain aspects of cognitive performance—namely, word retrieval failures. Do these changes in representations during adulthood reflect the experiences of older adults? Within the NST framework, the state of the representation depends on experience. For example, recent production of a rare word reduces the probability of a TOT for that word and in some cases eliminates the age difference in TOTs (Rastle & Burke, 1996; Burke et al., 2004). The impact of production/ repetition within NST and other connectionist models (Dell, 1986; Munakata et al, 1997) is the strengthening of connections within and between representations. Within this framework, older adults would have more word-production failures if they produced language less than young adults. It is difficult to evaluate this possibility because little is known about the quantity of everyday language use in old age. In self-reports of hours spent reading and writing, there was no difference between young and older adults in either activity in one study (MacKay et al., 1999) and young adults reported more time writing in the other study (MacKay & Abrams, 1998)—hardly surprising since they were college students. Older adults do not typically differ from young adults in the quantity of speech in laboratory studies analyzing descriptions of pictures (e.g., James et al., 1998) or videos (Heller & Dobbs, 1993), but older adults spoke more in describing autobiographical events such as their education or their family (James et al., 1998). However, it is difficult to extrapolate from the talkativeness in the laboratory to speech production in daily life. For older adults who live in the community, there is no obvious reason to suspect that they produce language less than young adults. Moreover, 35–45-year-old adults experience more TOTs than young adults age 20 years, and since most of the 35–45-year-old adults were employed full time, it is unlikely that they had reduced levels of speech production compared to young adults (Burke et al., 1991). Thus, there is no obvious basis for suspecting that increased word-finding failures in old age are a consequence of changes in daily experience, but more specific research is needed on the relation between language use and language failures in old age.

There is more direct evidence that older adults' deficits in forming new representations are not related to experiential factors. A number of studies have attempted to increase the ability to learn new information by teaching young and older adults mnemonic techniques that improve learning. If older adults' decline in new-connection formation was related to inadequate practice of memory skills in everyday life, then they would benefit even more than young adults from the extensive practice that is typical in these studies. The results emerging from these studies are that the training benefits older adults' ability to learn new information, but that age differences are even greater after training (e.g., Kleigl et al., 1989)

In conclusion, experience in the form of practice will maintain many existing skills in old age, but not the ability to learn new information or to produce infrequently used words. While experience has been shown to play an important role in children's cognitive development, it does not seem to be the critical factor in cognitive changes in normal old age. Similar cognitive mechanisms have been used to account for age-related changes at both ends of the lifespan—namely, changes in connection strength within a network of representations. The role of experience and neural factors in producing these changes in mechanism may differ for children and adults.

References

Ackerman, P. L., & Rolfhus, E. L. (1999). The locus of adult intelligence: Knowledge, abilities and nonability traits. *Psychology & Aging. 14*, 314–330.

Arbuckle, T. Y., & Gold, D. P. (1993). Aging, inhibition, and verbosity. *Journal of Gerontology: Psychological Sciences, 48*, P225–P232

Baltes, P. B, Staudinger, U. M., & Lindenberger, U. (1999). Lifespan psychology: Theory and application to intellectual functioning. *Annual Review of Psychology, 50*, 471–50.

Beier, M. E., & Ackerman, P. L. (2001) Current-events knowledge in adults: An investigation of age, intelligence, and nonability determinants. *Psychology & Aging. 16 ,* 615–628.

Bosman, E. A. (1993). Age-related differences in motoric aspects of transcription typing skill. *Psychology and Aging, 8*, 87–102.

Brown, A. S. (1991). A review of the tip-of-the-tongue experience. *Psychological Bulletin, 109*, 204–223.

Brown, A. S., & Nix, L. A. (1996). Age-related changes in the tip-of-the-tongue experience. *American Journal of Psychology, 109*, 79–91.

Burke, D., & Harrold, R. M. (1988). Automatic and effortful semantic processes in old age: Experimental and naturalistic approaches. In L. Light, & D. Burke, (Eds.), *Language, memory and aging* (pp.100–116). New York: Cambridge University Press.

Burke, D. M., Locantore, J., Austin, A., & Chae, B. (2004). Cherry pit primes Brad Pitt: Homophone priming effects on young and older adults' production of proper names. *Psychological Science, 15*, 164–170.

Burke, D. M., MacKay, D. G., & James, L. E. (2000). Theoretical approaches to language and aging. In T. Perfect & E. Maylor (Eds.), *Models of cognitive aging* (pp. 204–237). Oxford, UK: Oxford University Press.

Burke, D. M., MacKay, D. G., Worthley, J. S., & Wade, E. (1991). On the tip of the tongue: What causes word finding failures in young and older adults. *Journal of Memory and Language, 30*, 542–579.

Burke, D., & Peters, L. (1986). Word associations in old age: Evidence for consistency in semantic encoding during adulthood. *Psychology and Aging, 4*, 283–292.

Burke, D. M., Ruz, M. L., Christidis, P., & Santiago, J. (2004). *Orthographic retrieval in Spanish: Spelling regularity reduces aging deficits.* Manuscript submitted for publication.

Carstensen, L. L., Isaacowitz, D. M., & Charles, S. T. (1999). Taking time seriously. *American Psychologist, 54*, 165–181.

Carstensen, L. L., & Fredrickson, B. F. (1998). Socioemotional selectivity in healthy older people and younger people living with the human immunodeficiency virus: The centrality of emotion when the future is constrained. *Health Psychology, 17*, 1–10.

Chalfonte, B. L., & Johnson, M. K. (1996). Feature memory and binding in young and older adults. *Memory and Cognition, 24*, 403–416.

Charness, N. (1979). Components of skill in bridge. *Canadian Journal of Psychology, 33*, 1–16.

Charness, N. (1981). Aging and skilled problem solving. *Journal of Experimental Psychology, 110*, 21–38.

Cortese, M. J., Balota, D. A., Sergent-Marshall, S. D., & Buckner, R. L. (2003). Spelling via semantics and phonology: exploring the effects of age, Alzheimer's disease, and primary semantic impairment. *Neuropsychologia, 41*, 952–967.

Craik, F. I. M., & Jennings, J. (1992). Human memory. In F. I. M. Craik & T. A. Salthouse (Eds.), *The *handbook of aging and cognition* (pp.51–110). Hillsdale, NJ: Lawrence Erlbaum Associates.

Dell, G. S. (1986). A spreading-activation theory of retrieval in sentence production. *Psychological Review, 93,* 283–321.

Feyereisen, P. (1997) A meta-analytic procedure shows an age-related decline in picture naming: Comments on Goulet, Ska, and Kahn. *Journal of Speech and Hearing Research, 40,* 1328–1333.

Gabrieli, J. D., Cohen, N. J., & Corkin, S. (1988). The impaired learning of semantic knowledge following bilateral medial temporal-lobe resection. *Brain & Cognition. 7,* 157–177.

Gold, D., Andres, D., Arbuckle, T., & Schwartzman, A. (1988). Measurements and correlates of verbosity in elderly people. *Journal of Gerontology: Psychological Sciences, 43,* P27–P33.

Goodglass, H., & Wingfield, A. (1997). Word-finding deficits in aphasia: Brain-behavior relations and clinical symptomatology. In H. Goodglass & A. Wingfield (Eds.), *Anomia: Neuroanatomical and cognitive correlates* (pp.3–27). San Diego: Academic Press.

Heller, R. B., & Dobbs, A. R. (1993). Age differences in word finding in discourse and nondiscourse situations. *Psychology and Aging , 8,* 443–450.

Hirsh-Pasek, K., Kemler-Nelson, D. G., Jusczyk, P. W., Wright Cassidy, K., Druss, B., & Kennedy, L. (1987). Clauses are perceptual units for young infants. *Cognition, 26,* 269–286.

Howard, D. V. (1980). Category norms: A comparison of the Battig and Montague (1960) norms with the responses of adults between the ages of 20 and 80. *Journal of Gerontology, 35,* 225–231.

Horn, J. L., & Cattell, R. B. (1967). Age differences in fluid and crystallized intelligence. *Acta Psychologica. 26*(2), 107–129

Horn, J. L., & Hofer, S. M. (1992). Major abilities and development in the adult period. In R. J. Sternberg & C. A. Berg (Eds.), *Intellectual development* (pp.44–99). Cambridge, UK: Cambridge University Press.

Huttenlocher, J, Vasilyeva, M., Cymerman, E., & Levine, S. (2002). Language input and child syntax. *Cognitive Psychology, 45,* 337–374.

James, L. E. & Burke, D. M. (2000). Phonological priming effects on word retrieval and tip-of-the-tongue experiences in young and older adults. *Journal of Experimental Psychology: Learning, Memory and Cognition, 26,* 1378–1391.

James, L. E., Burke, D. M., Austin, A., & Hulme, E, (1998). Production and perception of verbosity in young and older adults. *Psychology and Aging, 13,* 355–367.

James, L. E. & MacKay, D.G. (2001). H.M., word knowledge, and aging: Support for a new theory of long-term retrograde amnesia. *Psychological Science, 12,* 485–492.

Karmiloff-Smith, A. (1992). *Beyond modularity: A developmental perspective on cognitive science.* Cambridge, MA: MIT Press.

Kemper, S. (1992). Adults' sentence fragments: Who, what, when, where, and why. *Communication Research, 19,* 444–458.

Kemper, S., Rash, S., Kynette, D., & Norman, S. (1990). Telling stories: The structure of adults' narratives. *European Journal of Cognitive Psychology, 2,* 205–228.

Kemtes, K., & Kemper, S. (1997). Younger and older adults' on-line processing of syntactically ambiguous sentences. *Psychology & Aging, 12,* 362–371.

Kliegl, R., Smith, J., & Baltes, P. B. (1989). Testing-the-limits and the study of adult age differences in cognitive plasticity of a mnemonic skill. *Developmental Psychology. 25,* 247–256.

Krampe, R. T. & Ericsson, K. A.. (1996). Maintaining excellence: Deliberate practice and elite performance in young and older pianists. *Journal of Experimental Psychology: General, 125,* 331–359.

Landerl, K. (2003). Dyslexia in German-speaking children. In N. Goulandris (Ed.), *Dyslexia in different languages: Cross-linguistic comparisons* (pp. 15–32). London, UK: Whurr Publishers.

Laver, G. D., & Burke, D. M. (1993). Why do semantic priming effects increase in old age? A meta-analysis. *Psychology and Aging, 8,* 34–43.

Levelt, W. J., Roelofs, A., & Meyer, A. S. (1999). A theory of lexical access in speech production. *Behavioral & Brain Sciences, 22,* 1–75.

Levine, B., Svoboda, E., Hay, J. F., Wincour, G., & Moscovitch, M. (2002). Aging and autobiographical memory: Dissociating episodic from semantic retrieval. *Psychology and Aging, 17,* 677–689.

Light, L. L. (1991). Memory and aging: Four hypotheses in search of data. *Annual Review of Psychology, 42,* 333–376.

Light, L. L., & Anderson, P. A. (1983). Memory for scripts in young and older adults. *Memory and Cognition, 11,* 435–444.

Lindenberger, U. & bates, P. B. (1997). Intellectual functioning in old and very old age: cCross-sectional results from the Berlin Aging Study. *Psychology & Aging, 12,* 410–432.

MacKay, D. G. (1987). *The organization of perception and action: A theory for language and other cognitive skills.* New York: Springer-Verlag.

MacKay, D. G., & Abrams, L. (1998). Age-linked declines in retrieving orthographic knowledge: Empirical, practical, and theoretical implications. *Psychology and Aging, 13*, 647–662.

MacKay, D. G., Abrams, L., & Pedroza, M. J. (1999). Aging on the input versus output side: Theoretical implications of age-linked asymmetries between detecting versus retrieving orthographic knowledge: Empirical, practical, and theoretical implications. *Psychology and Aging, 13*, 647–662..

MacKay, D. G., & Burke, D. M. (1990). Cognition and aging: New learning and the use of old connections. In T. M. Hess (Ed.), *Aging and cognition: Knowledge organization and utilization* (pp. 213–263). Amsterdam: North Holland.

Madden, D. J. (1988). Adult age differences in the effects of sentence context and stimulus degradation during visual word recognition. *Psychology and Aging, 3*, 167–172.

McIntyre, J. S. & Craik, F. I. M. (1987). Age differences in memory for item and source information. *Canadian Journal of Psychology, 45*, 175–192.

Meinz, E. J., & Salthouse, T. A. (1998). The effects of age and experience on memory for visually presented music. *Journals of Gerontology: Series B: Psychological Sciences & Social Sciences, 53B*, P60–P69.

Morrow, D. G., Ridolfo, H. E., Menard, W. E., Sanborn, A., Stine-Morrow, E. A. L., Magnor, C., Herman, L., Teller, T., & Bryant, D. (2003). Environmental support promotes expertise-based mitigation of age differences on pilot communication tasks. *Psychology and Aging, 18*, 268–284.

Munakata, Y., McClelland, J. L., Johnson, M. H., & Siegler, R. S. (1997). Rethinking infant knowledge: Toward an adaptive process account of successes and failures in object permanence tasks. *Psychological Review, 104*, 686–713

Nelson, K. (2003). Self and social functions: Individual autobiographical memory and collective narrative. *Memory, 11*, 125–136.

Nyberg, L., Bäckman, L., Erngrund, K., Olofsson, U., & Nilsson, L. (1996) Age differences in episodic memory, semantic memory, and priming: Relationships to demographic, intellectual, and biological factors. *Journal of Gerontology, 51B*, 234–240.

Pasupathi, M., & Carstensen, L. L. (2003). Age and emotional experience during mutual reminiscing. *Psychology & Aging, 18*, 430–442.

Paul, S. T. (1996). Search for semantic inhibition failure during sentence comprehension by younger and older adults. *Psychology and Aging, 11*, 10–20.

Paulesu, E., Demonet, J.-F., Fazio, F., McCrory, E., Chanoine, V., Brunswick, N., Cappa, S. F., Cossu, G., Habib, M., Frith, C. D., & Frith, U. (2001). Dyslexia: Cultural diversity and biological unity. *Science, 291*, 2165–2167.

Piaget, J. (1969). *The psychology of intelligence.* Totowa, NJ: Littlefield, Adams.

Pichora-Fuller, M. K., Schneider, B. A., & Daneman, M. (1995). How young and old adults listen to and remember speech in noise. *Journal of the Acoustical Society of America, 97*, 593–608.

Polk, T. A., & Farah, M. J. (1998). The neural development and organization of letter recognition: Evidence from functional neuroimaging, computational modeling and behavioral studies. *Proceedings of the National Academy of Sciences, 95*, 847–852.

Polk, T. A, Stallcup, M., Aguirre, G. K, Alsop, D. C, D'Esposito, M., Detre, J. A., & Farah, M. J. (2002). Neural specialization for letter recognition. *Journal of Cognitive Neuroscience. 14*, 145–159.

Pratt, M. W., & Robins, S. L. (1991). That's the way it was: Age differences in the structure and quality of adults' personal narratives. *Discourse Processes, 14*, 73–85.

Rabbitt, P., Maylor, E., McInnes, L., Bent, N., & Moore, B. (1995). What goods can self-assessment questionnaires deliver for cognitive gerontology? *Applied Cognitive Psychology, 9*, S127–S152.

Radvansky, G. A., Zwaan, R. A., Curiel, J. M., & Copeland, D. E. (2001). Situation models and aging. *Psychology and aging, 16*, 145–160.

Rastle, K. G. & Burke, D. M. (1996). Priming the tip of the tongue: Effects of prior processing on word retrieval in young and older adults. *Journal of Memory and Language, 35*, 586–605.

Rubin, D. C., Rahhal, T. A., & Poon, L. W. (1998). Things learned in early adulthood are remembered best. *Memory & Cognition. 26*, 3–19.

Salthouse, T. A. (1984). Effects of age and skill in typing. *Journal of Experimental Psychology: General, 113*, 345–371.

Schacter, D. L., Osowiecki, D., Kaszniak, A. W., Kihlstrom, J. F., & Valdiserri, M. (1994). Source memory: Extending the boundaries of age-related deficits. *Psychology and Aging, 9*, 81–89.

Schaie, K. W. (1994). The course of adult intellectual development. *American Psychologist, 49*(4), 304–313.

Schmitter-Edgecombe, M., Vesneski, M., & Jones, D. (2000). Aging and word finding: A comparison of discourse and nondiscourse tests. *Archives of Clinical Neuropsychology, 15*, 479–493.

Semenza, C. (1997). Proper-name-specific aphasias. In H. Goodglass & A. Wingfield (Eds.), *Anomia: Neuroanatomical and cognitive correlates* (pp.115–134). San Diego: Academic Press.

Stern, P., & Carstensen, L. (2000). *The aging mind: Opportunities in cognitive research.* Washington, DC: National Academy Press.

Stine, E. L. (1990). On-line processing of written text by younger and older adults. *Psychology & Aging. 5,* 68–78.

Taylor, J. K., & Burke, D. M. (2002). Asymmetric aging effects on semantic and phonological processes: Naming in the picture-word interference task. *Psychology and Aging, 17,* 662–676.

Tulving, E. (1983). *Elements of episodic memory.* New York: Oxford University Press.

Verhaeghen, P. (2003). Aging and vocabulary score: A meta-analysis. *Psychology & Aging, 18,* 332–339.

Verhaeghen, P., Marcoen, A., & Goossens, L (1993). Improving memory performance in the aged through mnemonic training: A meta-analytic study. *Psychology & Aging, 7,* 242–251.

White, K. K., & Abrams, L. (2002). Does priming specific syllables during tip-of-the-tongue states facilitate word retrieval in older adults? *Psychology and Aging, 17,* 226–235.

Wingfield, A., & Stine-Morrow, E.A.L. (2000). Language and speech. In F. I. M. Craik & T. A. Salthouse (Eds), *The handbook of aging and cognition* (2nd ed., pp. 359–416). Mahwah, NJ: Lawrence Erlbaum Associates.

Wingfield, A., Tun, P. A., & Rosen, M. J. (1995). Age differences in veridical and reconstructive recall of syntactically and randomly segmented speech. *Journal of Gerontology: Psychological Sciences, 50B,* P257–P266.

Zacks, R. T., & Hasher, L. (1994). Directed ignoring: Inhibitory regulation of working memory. In D. Dagenbach & T. H. Carr (Eds.), *Inhibitory processes in attention, memory, and language* (pp. 241–264). San Diego: Academic Press.

14

The Emergentist Coalition Model of Word Learning in Children Has Implications for Language in Aging

Roberta Michnick Golinkoff

Kathy Hirsh-Pasek

[T]here are no single effective pushes to the developing system, but rather a combination of influences that lead to observable change. (Nelson 1996, p. 85)

In this quotation, Katherine Nelson (1996) captured the spirit of this volume and of this chapter. We live in a multifactorial world. If we are to understand the complex behaviors characteristic of humans, we will have to embrace systems-based models that offer a more comprehensive and integrative account of development than single-factor explanations. As Bronfenbrenner and Morris (1998) argued, systems operate at many levels, from the multiple proximal inputs that directly affect the child to the more distal effects including the time and context in which these inputs are encountered and evaluated by the child. Much of the current research in language development that does not rely on language production suffers from a more limited perspective on development, from what Bronfenbrenner (1974) suggested is the "science of the behavior of children in strange situations with strange adults" (p. 3). Indeed, much of our research is also conducted at a single point in time as opposed to longitudinally and on a single variable as opposed to multiple variables. Thus, we rarely ask how a child might coordinate various strands of input toward the goal of constructing language nor do we ask how these strands might begin to pull apart with aging.

In this chapter, we begin to ask empirically how a combination of influences can lead to observable changes in language comprehension. We speculate about how such an integrated model could help us see atypical development as part of the continuum of typical development and how aging might affect the more normative processes of language learning. Throughout, we use one aspect of language development, word learning, as our test case. Words are the bedrock of language, the building blocks around which sentences are formed.

The chapter is organized in four sections. First, we review the families of theories that have been posited to account for word learning. We then describe a theoretical alternative that incorporates the best of the theories in an integrative framework and allows for testable hypotheses about word learning. Third, we examine the impact of an integrated theory for approaching questions in language development for both normal and atypical children. Such a study forces us not only to consider how the combination of influences might interact but also how they are interpreted by children with different cognitive starting points. Finally, we ask how attention to a broader proximal system that includes person characteristics as well as proximal influences from the perceptual, social, and linguistic contexts might explain breakdowns in language with age. Empirically testable theories of development that embrace more complex and overarching models of word learning might allow us to find alternative pathways to development. The same is true for the study of degradation; parsimonious single-factor explanations may miss the necessity for complex accounts .

THREE THEORIES OF WORD LEARNING

The Problem Space

On its face, word learning seems like a simple problem. The child need only attach the word to an object in plain view. On closer inspection, however, word learning proves to be a difficult task. To learn a word, infants must first segment the sound stream, finding the carving joints in the continuous stream of speech around them. Second, they must discover a world of objects, actions, and events, and figure out how those are divided into meaningful units. Finally, they must map words they have uncovered from the sound stream (or visual stream in sign languages) onto some referent in the world. Quine's (1960) often-cited story highlights the inherent difficulty of this so-called mapping problem: a linguist in a foreign land sees a rabbit scurrying by while hearing a native exclaim "gavagai!" Among an enormous number of other possibilities, the word *gavagai* could refer to the whole rabbit, the rabbit's ears, or to the rabbit's hopping. The world allows an infinite number of possible word-to-world mappings. This leads many to ask how the child ever learns how a word maps onto a referent.

Theories of word learning can be distinguished on the basis of whether they embrace the Quinean conundrum as a foundational assumption or whether they reject it. Theories that posit constraints or principles adopt Quine's view of the problem space. Theories that emphasize social input or associative learning

consider Quine's example largely irrelevant to the problem of word learning. These theories form the landscape for the debate about the nature of early word learning.

Constraints or principles theories take Quine seriously. Because word-to-world mapping is underdetermined, human minds must be equipped with constraints or principles that narrow the search space. Under this theory, children approach the word-learning task biased to make certain assumptions over others for what a word might mean. Domain-specific constraints theories have been posited for a number of cognitive development domains. As Gelman and Greeno (1989) wrote with respect to theories of number development:

> If we grant learners some domain-specific principles, we provide them with a way to define the range of relevant inputs, the ones that support learning about that domain. Because principles embody constraints on the kinds of input that can be processed as data that are relevant to that domain, they therefore can direct attention to those aspects of the environment that need to be selected and attended to. (p. 130)

Similar statements have appeared in the literature on spatial development (Newcombe & Huttenlocher, 2000) and object perception (Spelke, 1990). The general thrust of the constraints or principles position is to make a daunting task manageable by restricting the number of hypotheses the learner need entertain to arrive at a representation of a domain.

A substantial body of evidence has accumulated to support the constraints position in word learning. Markman's (1989) principle of mutual exclusivity, for example, states that children assume that an object can have only one name. The consequence of this principle is that a novel name will not label an already named object but rather will label an unfamiliar object. Others have shown that 28-month-olds will assume that a novel label maps to an unnamed object when presented with a set of familiar and unfamiliar objects (Evey & Merriman, 1998; Golinkoff, Hirsh-Pasek, Bailey, & Wenger, 1992; Mervis & Bertrand, 1994). These findings support not only Markman's mutual exclusivity principle but also a more flexible principle (novel name-nameless category, or N3C) posited by Golinkoff, Mervis, and Hirsh-Pasek (1994). Similarly, Clark (1983) suggested that children operate with a principle called *conventionality*: use the word that your linguistic community uses or you won't be understood. Mervis (see Golinkoff et al., 1994) provided numerous diary entries that showed that children abandon their idiosyncratic terms in favor of the standard terms (e.g., over time *pops* becomes *pacifier*).

The principles/constraints theories have flourished. Indeed, over the last 15 years, there has been a proliferation of principles including Waxman and Kosowski's (1990) *noun-category bias*, Markman's (1989) *mutual exclusivity*, Markman and Hutchinson's (1984) *taxonomic assumption*, and Clark's (1983) pragmatic constraint of *contrast*. These principles were reviewed and placed in a developmental framework by Golinkoff et al. (1994), who posited a set of six principles (some new and some in the literature) that were necessary and sufficient to account both for how children get word learning "off the ground" and how they become "vacuum cleaners for words" (Pinker, 1994) at around 19 months of age.

The Golinkoff et al. framework offered a developmental model in which the principles of word learning were organized on two tiers that captured the changing character of word learning (see Figure 14.1). On the first tier, and appearing at around 12 months of age, were the principles of reference (that words map to objects, actions, and events), extendibility (that words do not uniquely refer to the original referent but rather to a category of objects, actions, and events), and object scope (that words refer to whole objects rather than to object parts and to objects over actions). On the second tier, the principles of N3C (that novel names label novel categories), categorical scope (that words label taxonomic categories), and conventionality (use socially agreed-upon names for things; Clark,

1983) are born from the first-tier principles and help children catapult into the mature word learning characterized by the vocabulary spurt. Fundamental to the principles framework is the idea that the *principles themselves undergo change with development and are an emergent product of the combination of word-learning experience and some inborn biases.* Nested in the Golinkoff et al. (1994) framework is a powerful developmental solution to the Quinean dilemma.

Social-pragmatic theorists stand in stark contrast to those holding the constraints position. Children, embedded in a social nexus, are guided by expert word learners as they embark upon the word-learning task. As Nelson (1988) has written, Quine's problem becomes irrelevant:

> The typical way children acquire words . . . is almost completely opposite of the Quinean paradigm. Children do not try and guess what it is that the adult intends to refer to; rather . . . it is the adult who guesses what the child is focused on and then supplies the appropriate word. (pp. 240–241)

Bloom (1993, 2000) similarly concludes that adults talk about objects, actions, and events that are *relevant* to children. Children don't have to wade through alternative interpretations for a word; the correct interpretation is already the focus of their attention.

There is considerable evidence that children are capable of utilizing social cues in the service of word learning. For example, various researchers have shown that 18- and 24-month-olds can use the intention of the experimenter to attach a label to a novel object or action (Akhtar & Tomasello, 2000; Baldwin &

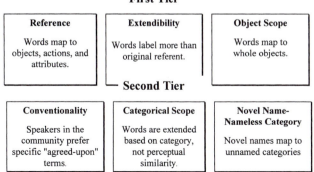

FIGURE 14.1. The principles of word learning proposed by Golinkoff, Mervis, and Hirsh-Pasek (1994).

Tomasello, 1999; Carpenter, Nagell, & Tomasello, 1999; Disendruck & Markson, 2001; Tomasello & Barton, 1994; Tomasello, Strosberg, & Akhtar, 1996). If the experimenter indicates that she erred in using a label, children will not attach a novel label to the first object or action they see but to the second object. Akhtar and Tomasello (1996) showed that 24-month-old children mine the social context to attach a novel label to a hidden object instead of to novel objects that they are shown. Furthermore, Baldwin, Markman et al. (1996) showed that 18-month-olds can evaluate whether an adult uttering a label in great excitement ("It's a toma!") while on the telephone is intending to label the child's object or something else. Young children are not fooled into forming a link between a label uttered by a woman who is not addressing them at the same moment they are focused on a novel toy. Nor do 12-month-olds form mismappings between names and potential referents (Hollich, Hirsh-Pasek, & Golinkoff, 2000).

Under the social-pragmatic view, children are seen as skilled apprentices to expert word learners participating in a structured social world. Children are also seen as able to read the social intent of their mentors (Bloom, 1999) in this world. By virtue of being a social animal, language comes for free. Under this interpretation, Quine's linguist differs from real children because children are immersed in rich social contexts that naturally delimit the possible mappings between words and their referents.

The constraints/principles and the social-pragmatic theories of word learning represent the most common positions in the literature. Recently, however, Smith (1995, 1999, 2000), Samuelson and Smith (1998), and Plunkett (1997) have offered a third perspective on the word-learning problem. The domain-general view of word learning rejects Quine's conundrum, suggesting that word learning can be best accounted for through "dumb attentional mechanisms" like perceptual saliency, association, and frequency. In comparing the differences in constraints theories and her own systems-theory view, Smith (1995) wrote:

> The empirical focus [of constraints theories] becomes not the processes that enable children to interpret words in context, but whether children's biased learning has the properties needed to "solve the induction problem." The present thesis is that the induction problem is irrelevant to developmentalists. Learning is not necessarily hypothesis testing. Development is not induction. (p. 4)

Children do not need constraints or principles to forge word-to-world mappings. The process of mapping a word onto an object is straightforward. Children notice objects, actions, and events that are the most salient in their environment. They associate the most frequently used label with the most salient candidate (Smith, Jones, Landau, Gershkoff-Stowe, & Samuelson, 2002). In this way, ambiguity in the word-learning situation is removed. General cognitive mechanisms are sufficient not only to account for how young children first map words onto referents but also to account for the complexity of more sophisticated word learning (Smith, 2000).

This synopsis of the theoretical debate in the area of word learning parallels that in the developmental literature. For any given developmental problem space, theories arise that represent the constraints, domain-specific alternative, or a social-pragmatic, cultural alternative, and an associationistic alternative. As in the area of word learning, there is mounting data to support each of the positions. There are also reasons to reject each theory. By way of example, one could argue that despite many attempts to sweep away the Quinean problem in word learning, it refuses to disappear. Any single object, action, or event presents an array of possible referents to be named. Even something as simple as a "sippy cup" has a lid, an elevated portion on the lid (mouthpiece), and possibly pink flowers on its blue plastic base. All of the parts move together when the cup is lifted and some of these parts—such as the mouthpiece—may prove more salient than the whole object. Which of these parts is graced with the name *cup*? Neither perceptually based nor socially based theories assist the child in reaching the final determination of what makes word-to-world mapping possible. Only the constraints or principles theories solve the Quinean problem. Yet, they do so by default. Either they assume that principles come in full-blown and are nondevelopmental (Markman, 1989) or they offer a developmental perspective with little emphasis on the mechanisms of change.

The debate presses on (Golinkoff et al., 2000) as scientists try to determine which theory best accounts for the data. Yet science's steadfast and historically rooted view that parsimony demands a *choice* of one theoretical explanation over the other might lie at the root of the problem. Perhaps the issue should not be cast as *which* of the particular theories is right. Perhaps the issue should be recast as which components of which theories seem to govern children's word learning at different points in the course of development. This reframing of the question requires the creation of a hybrid approach with clear hypotheses that make the theory empirically testable. The idea that we need to consider multiple perspectives to solve complex problems is not new (Bloom, 1978, 1993, 2000). It was from this idea that the emergentist coalition model was born.

THE EMERGENTIST COALITION MODEL OF WORD LEARNING

The emergentist coalition model (ECM) of word learning is a hybrid that builds on the developmental lexical principles framework (Golinkoff et al., 1994). This model (Hollich, Hirsh-Pasek, & Golinkoff, 1998; Golinkoff, Hirsh-Pasek, & Hollich, 1999; Hollich et al., 2000) incorporates the impact of diverse factors on word learning because, as in the real world, it is likely that children avail themselves of social, attentional, cognitive, *and* linguistic cues to learn new words. The ECM embraces this complexity. It allows for the full range of cues that contribute to word learning rather than forcing artificial choices among them. Thus, the first defining tenet of the model is that children mine a coalition of cues on their way to word learning. Figure 14.2 graphically depicts the multiple inputs that are available for word learning.

Although a range of cues is always *available*, not all cues for word learning are equally *used* in the service of word learning. Younger children, just beginning to learn words, rely on only a subset of the cues in the coalition. Older, more experienced word learners rely on a wider subset of cues and on some cues more heavily than others. The model posits that so-cial cues such as eye gaze, which are subtle and may demand at least a primitive theory of mind, will be less utilized than perceptual cues such as the salience of objects. Given a choice between attaching a novel name to a boring object that an adult is looking at and a colorful, exciting object, the child just beginning to learn words should rely on perceptual salience (consistent with the associationist) before relying on the subtle social cue of eye gaze (consistent with the social-pragmatic perspective). Thus, the second major tenet of the theory is that the cues for word learning change their weights over developmental time.

Because children make differential use of the available cues with development, this model holds that principles for word learning are emergent. They develop over the course of the second year of life as children gain word-learning experience. Unlike other constraints posited in the literature, the ECM states that not all of the principles are available from the start of word learning. Lexical principles are the products and not the engines of lexical development. Children do not start word learning, for example, with the novel name-novel category principle (N3C). Mervis and Bertrand (1994) have shown that the N3C principle is not in place until after the vocabulary spurt. The third tenet of this model, then, is that the principles for word learning are emergent and not given a priori.

The developmental cast of this model makes it imperative to study the origins of word learning as well as the transformation that takes place in the second year of life when the child becomes an expert word learner. Data need to be collected that demonstrate that children detect and use multiple cues for word learning; that their reliance on these cues changes over the course of development; and that principles for word learning emerge from word-learning experience.

Our research has assessed these claims within the context of the first-tier principles of reference (that words map onto the child's representation of objects, actions, and events) and extendibility (that words map onto more than one exemplar). First, we hypothesized that children learning their first words (at 10 or 12 months of age) would be informed by multiple cues of an attentional, social, and linguistic nature. Second, we hypothesized that perceptual salience would be more heavily weighted than social cues for the novice than for the expert word learner. Third, we hypothesized that the word-learning principles themselves develop along a continuum from immature to mature such that children are first attracted by what is most

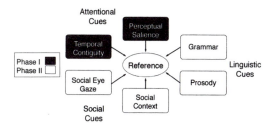

FIGURE 14.2. The multiple inputs available for word learning.

salient to them and only later note what is important to the speaker. As they break through the language barrier, children are guided (though not completely) by associationist laws. As they mature into veteran word learners, they are guided (though not completely) by social-pragmatic strategies. Both views are united under one theory.

Evidence for the Emergentist Coalition Model

Investigation of this hybrid ECM model demanded experiments that could trace development of the principles of reference and extendibility from their immature to their mature states. To assess the principle of reference, we examined whether infants would attach a label to both interesting and boring objects. We reasoned that a child with an immature principle of reference might attach a novel label to the interesting object regardless of which object an adult was labeling. The child with a mature principle, on the other hand, should overcome the salience of the object in favor of relying on the speaker's social cues to what is being labeled. To assess the principle of extendibility, we first asked whether infants would extend a label for a given object to one that differed only in color from the original exemplar. We then put infants in a very difficult task and asked whether they would use social information to extend that label to an object that bore no resemblance to the original object. After all, bean bag chairs and dining room chairs bear little resemblance to one another and yet they are both called chairs. Children who fail to extend a label or who will only extend the label to close perceptual relatives possess an immature principle of extendibility. Alternatively, children who trust a social mentor extending a label in the face of contrasting perceptual cues are operating with a mature principle of extendibility (Maguire, Hennon, Hirsh-Pasek, & Golinkoff, 2003).

Examination of the emergentist coalition theory required a method that could be used equally effectively with children in the age range of interest (10–24 months) and one that would enable researchers to manipulate multiple cues (attentional, social, and linguistic) and their interactions. The Interactive Intermodal Preferential Looking Paradigm (IIPLP) provided this new method (e.g., Hollich et al., 2000). Based on the IIPLP (Golinkoff, Hirsh-Pasek, Cauley, & Gordon, 1987; Hirsh-Pasek & Golinkoff, 1996) used to study lexical and syntactic comprehension, Bald-

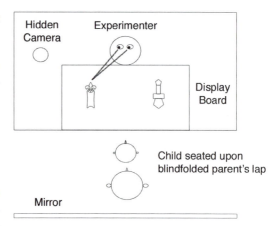

FIGURE 14.3. The Interactive Intermodal Preferential Looking paradigm.

win's (1991, 1993) bucket task, and Fagan's (1971; Fagan, Singer, Montic, & Shepard, 1986) infant intelligence test, allows for the study of multiple cues to word learning in the first two years of life. The physical set up is depicted in Figure 14.3.

Infants are seated on their blindfolded mother's lap facing the experimenter and our testing apparatus. After pre-exposure to the toys—familiar toys on some trials and novel toys on others—the toys are fixed with Velcro onto one side of a two-sided black board that can be rotated so that the toys can go in and out of view for a specified period of time. The experimenter hides behind the board while children inspect the toys during test trials. Coding is done off-line from videotaped records.

Using this apparatus, it is possible to examine word learning in a controlled setting. Familiar object trials allow us to ask whether the child can "play our game." The use of unfamiliar, novel objects permits exploration of the cues and *combinations* of cues that children use to guide word learning across development. The logic of the design (Golinkoff et al., 1987; Hirsh-Pasek & Golinkoff, 1996) is that children should look more at an object that "matches" the linguistic stimulus than at an object that does not match. Thus, the dependent variable is visual fixation time to the target (named) object versus to the unnamed object.

Validation of the method comes from the familiar trials. Children at three ages were tested: 12–13-month-olds just at the beginning of word learning; 19–20-month-olds who may or may not have yet experienced a vocabulary spurt; and 24–25-month-olds who typically have sizable production vocabularies. In over 23 experiments children demonstrated the potency of the method by looking significantly more at the target item than at the nontarget item in the familiar condition when an item was requested (Hollich et al., 2000). Evaluation of the hypotheses comes from children's responses to *novel* stimuli. Using this method, we were able to explore how infants move from immature to mature principles of reference and extendibility and to examine the hypotheses that form the foundation for the emergentist coalition model.

Evidence from the Studies on the Principle of Reference

Reference, or the assumption that words refer, is the most basic of the word-learning principles. Do infants assume that a word refers to an object, action, or event? How do they decide which object, action, or event should receive a label when one is offered? To investigate these questions, we created conditions in which multiple cues were available to children but were sometimes placed in conflict. In what we called the *coincident* condition, we labeled the novel toy that coincided with children's preferences—the interesting toy. In the *conflict* condition, we labeled the novel toy that did not coincide with the children's preferences—the boring toy. We reasoned that learning the word in the coincident case should be easy for children because all of the cues—attentional, social, and linguistic—were in alignment. In contrast, learning a novel word in the conflict condition should be more difficult because the coalition of cues is not acting in concert.

The experiment was conducted in four phases. First, children were given the opportunity to explore both the interesting and the boring toys. Second, children participated in a salience trial in which they saw both the interesting and the boring toys mounted side by side on the black board. Third, in the labeling phase, the experimenter captured children's attention, displayed both toys, and labeled the target five times with a novel word (e.g., *danu*). In the coincident condition, the experimenter looked at and labeled the interesting toy; in the conflict condition, she looked at and labeled the boring toy. Finally in the test trials, the experimenter, now hiding behind the board, asked for the object that was labeled during training, once again getting the child's attention first. For example, she might say, "Eve, where's the danu?" If children

learned the name of the correct toy, they should look more at the target than at the nontarget (see Hollich et al., 2000, for details).

Do children understand that words refer? What cues do they use to determine the referent of a word? The participants in this study were 32 children at each of 12, 19, and 24 months of age. At all three ages, there is evidence that children detected the range of cues available. For example, even the 12-month-olds detected the social cue of eye gaze, although they could not use it when it was in conflict with perceptual salience. They learned the name of the object only in the coincident condition, as several further studies indicated (Hollich et al., 2000). The 19-month-olds learned the names of the objects in both conditions, but were still influenced heavily by perceptual salience. Even the oldest group that learned the names of the novel objects in both the conflict and the coincident conditions showed the effects of perceptual salience by looking much longer at the target object in the coincident condition than in the conflict condition. This suggests that children were lured by the perceptual salience of the interesting toy, but were able to overcome it when the boring toy was the focus of the experimenter's attention. In short, these data suggest that infants with an immature principle of reference are more dominated by perceptual salience than are their counterparts with a more mature principle of reference. Nineteen- and 24-month-old children recruit the speaker's social intent when mapping word to object. In light of these data, we conducted studies with 10-month-old infants to see whether children who were just beginning to acquire a comprehension vocabulary operated like the 12-month-olds who were starting to produce language. Results from this age group suggest that 10-month-olds are even more bound to perceptual salience than the 12-month-olds. They demonstrated a clear preference for the interesting toy even in the conflict condition, suggesting that these children ignore the presence of conflicting social cues. They apparently assume that labels "go with" interesting rather than boring objects, regardless of what the speaker is labeling (Hirsh-Pasek, Hennon, & Golinkoff, 2003)!

What we see in the data is a clear pattern that changes over time such that infants become less dependent on perceptual cues and more dependent on social cues to determine reference. Such data speak to both the associationist and the social-pragmatic theorist. The associationist position would predict that children *would* form a mismapping between the *interesting* object and the label in the conflict condition. If the 10-month-old data stand, then these data fit this prediction—but only for the very youngest children. Yet, by as early as 12 months of age, children with only three words in their productive vocabularies are already demonstrating some sensitivity to social information in a word-learning task. These children, at the cusp of word learning, learned the novel labels only in the coincident condition. In the coincident condition, the experimenter labeled the object that the babies were most interested in. For these babies, learning took place when the cues coincided. However, when multiple cues failed to coincide in the conflict condition, infants showed little evidence of word learning. They wanted to look at the interesting object despite the fact that the experimenter persisted in labeling the boring object. Though they looked at the interesting object much more than the boring object in the conflict condition, they did not falsely conclude that the novel label was attached to the interesting object. Even 12-month-olds were sensitive to the fact that the experimenter was looking elsewhere and *not* labeling the interesting object. Even 12-month-olds are able to use multiple cues for word learning, but for learning to occur, the cues had to *overlap*. While the 12-month-olds are not social pragmatists yet, they also defy the predictions made by the associationistic camp. Only a hybrid theory that talks about attention to multiple cues and differential attention to these cues over time can account for these data.

IMPLICATIONS OF THE EMERGENTIST COALITION MODEL

If there are data to suggest that studies of word learning offer only incomplete snapshots of behavior, and if it is the case that we can find testable hypotheses in an integrated view, then it should be possible to apply the theory broadly and to gain new insights into language development. Two areas that might prove particularly fruitful are the study of language disabilities and the study of elder speech. In each area, questions that could be profitably explored are (1) whether the three systems of input (perceptual/attentional, social, and linguistic) are all accessible to older adults; (2) whether the systems have differential weighting both within certain populations and across time; and (3) whether children and adults can

coordinate the cues in ways that optimize learning and processing.

Atypical Language Development

One of the breakthroughs afforded by a systems-based approach like the emergentist coalition model is that atypical development is considered to have the same sources as typical development (Hennon, 2002). In fact, researchers like Bates (personal communication, 2000) have argued that atypical development is but the extreme end of the normal continuum and that when stressed, even a normally developing adult will show the same language patterns found in atypical populations. If we take the systems model seriously, it would mean that all atypical development should emerge by tweaking the weightings and the developmental timing of the available cues that children might use to learn language.

Traditionally, researchers who examine atypical development have not adopted a unified and integrated view of language development. This leads researchers to adopt a pet theory that helps to explain a particular aspect of atypical language but fails to provide an integrated view of what goes wrong. Constraint theories with a strong linguistic focus, for example, appeal to those who study disorders having known biological etiology (Levy, 1994; Pinker, 1994) like specific language impairment (SLI). What is impaired here is thought to be some fundamental aspects of the innate grammar (Rice, 1996). While such accounts do a reasonable job of explaining SLI, they have difficulties interpreting evidence of language disorder with no known neurological abnormalities. In stark contrast, socio-pragmatic theories offer excellent starting points for explaining language disorders like autism that are associated with impairments in social relationships (Hertzig & Shapiro, 1990; Howlin & Yule, 1990).

The ECM offers a more comprehensive theory that might allow the problems observed in various disordered populations to be explained within a single framework. Imagine, for example, that language impairment comes from a dampening of one of the input cues or from a delay in the accessibility of that cue. Is there any evidence in the literature that might support this speculation? Autism offers one test case. Autism has often been described as a primary impairment in interpreting the social intent of others. If we assume that social pragmatic cues are primary for language development, and that the autistic child has little access to these cues, we are presented with a paradox: How can we explain the relative success of language development in some autistic children? If, however, we understand that their social impairment influences a language *system* that also includes perceptual, attentional, and grammatical elements, interventions may be developed that strengthen the contribution of each of these other aspects (e.g., perception or grammar) as a means of compensating for the "missing" social component. In the framework of the ECM model, children with autism might differentially rely on the perceptual and linguistic components of early word learning with relatively little sensitivity to the socio-pragmatic component. They might continue to use perceptual strategies for learning well into the second year when most children come to rely on the socio-pragmatic cues. If our theory is right, these children might never experience the naming explosion that characterizes normal development and sets the stage for later syntactic advances (Berko Gleason, 1997). Notice that the very foundation for grammar might be compromised here as the vocabulary fails to reach a sufficient size to support the later acquisition of specific grammatical skills. If this is the case, then even successful autistic word learners should be acquiring vocabulary in a way that compensates for the dampening of the socio-pragmatic information.

Research by Hennon, Hirsh-Pasek, & Golinkoff (2003) suggests that this is exactly what happens. Three-year-old autistic children were shown *not* to have the ability to use cues to social intent in word learning even though they had amassed some words in their productive vocabulary. They tended to learn their words through increased attention to perceptual salience, responding more like typical 1-year-olds in their language processing. With a more comprehensive theory of language acquisition, then, we can ask not just what is wrong or "broken" but how children might find some compensatory mechanisms to partially repair the system. If the theory of language development were socio-pragmatic, for example, without looking at the co-development of perceptual and linguistic information, these compensatory mechanisms would not be as apparent.

A similar example comes from the study of populations that have atypical perceptual abilities. Word learning in Williams syndrome, for instance, may be partially explained by the visuo-spatial deficits associated with the disorder. Visual processing in Williams syndrome is compromised to the extent that they draw a picture not with lines but with words. Thus, while they are not technically blind, individuals with Williams syndrome may not "see" the world in the same manner as normally developing children do (Mervis, 1999; Wang, Doherty, Rourke, & Bellugi, 1995). This distortion of the visual domain would be predicted to result in delay in early word learning, akin to that found in the blind child. As the exceptional social abilities of individuals with Williams syndrome begin to be utilized for word learning, they may provide a source of compensation for the perceptual difficulties. This would predict that early word learning would be exceptionally slow, when perceptual information is dominant. Moreover, even once the social information has gained in importance, the specific words learned by individuals with Williams syndrome may be "odd," as the perceptual component that is critical to early normal development is distorted or lacking in Williams syndrome. This is precisely the pattern of vocabulary development that has been found in individuals with Williams syndrome (Karmiloff-Smith, et al., 1997; Mervis, 1999'). If this explanation is true, then a spurt in vocabulary growth in Williams syndrome should be correlated with an advance in their use of social information in a nonword learning task.

A systems-based language theory that posits the interaction of multiple cues over time permits the study of alternative pathways to learning. It also makes clear predictions. First, early word learning should be facilitated when children have access to multiple cues and when these cues are redundant. That is, if the adult demonstrates the intention to label the most interesting object in the environment (coincident information), that label should be easier to learn than if she intends to label the more boring object in the environment (conflict information). Data from both typical and autistic children confirm this prediction. Second, children should learn even better when all three of the cues are available, as opposed to when only two cues are available for word learning. Evidence comparing the word development of typical and atypical development from our lab confirms these hypotheses (Hennon, 2002). Evidence of this sort is also available for how adults identify the verb being uttered in a silent, videotaped scene of a mother interacting with her child (Gillette, Gleitman, Gleitman, & Lederer, 1999). Adults were able to identify the videotaped actions only when perceptual and social cues were available along with the frames the verbs appeared in. All three sources of information were necessary for correct verb identification. Third, the model predicts a developmental sequence in which the cues for word learning are differentially weighted such that perceptual information is the most potent early on, to be followed by social cues to word comprehension and later linguistic comprehension. Work in our lab (Hollich et al., 2000) and in others (Hoff & Naigles, 2002) lead to the same conclusion. Indeed, Hoff and Naigles argue that differences in early word learning are a result of children's ability to mine the social cues speakers offer. However, by 2 ½ years, it is no longer the social cues that account for the variance in language learning but the diverse linguistic cues children receive.

The ECM is thus a quintessentially integrative and developmental model. It should be as applicable to the study of aging as it is to the study of atypical development. If language development is about the development of, use of, and coordination of multiple cues across time, then any disruption in the processing of those cues should impair the acquisition and processing of language in both comprehension and production. How might this translate into an explanatory model for how the elderly process language?

LANGUAGE IN ELDERLY POPULATIONS

To date, the ECM has been applied only to contexts of language learning with no attention to potential language degradation in the elderly. Yet we can speculate about how the model might apply and ask whether there is any supporting evidence for these speculations. Kemper and her colleagues (Chapter 15, this volume; Kemper, Thompson, & Marquis, 2001; Kemper, Greiner, Marquis, Prenovost, & Mitzner, 2001) and Schneider, Daneman, and Pichora-Fuller (2002; see also Hamilton-Wentworth District Health Council, 1988) report that elderly people, particularly in their mid-70s, have more trouble processing and understanding language than younger people. As Schneider et al. note:

The difficulties could be in higher-level cognitive processes such as language comprehension, memory, attention, and cognitive slowing, or they could be in lower-level sensory and perceptual processes. A complicating factor in determining how these sources might contribute to age-related declines in speech understanding is that they are highly correlated. (p. 139)

At least one researcher (Kemper et al., 2001) argues that the core of the problem might come in the form of a decline in the ability to process more complex grammatical input.

The ECM model could offer a way to disentangle the multiple sources of information that might contribute to the decline in language learning and to offer corroborating evidence for the decline in grammatical processing. Elderly people's ability to learn novel words could be a test case. We could make a series of predictions that parallel what we know in the study of early language development and in the study of atypical development. First, given the data from Kemper et al. and Schneider et al., we might find that the weightings of the three types of input cues shift in a direction opposite to that from the language-learning child. By way of example, the elderly should have access to all three types of input information (perceptual, social, and linguistic) during conversation, but the ability to use the linguistic information should be less heavily weighted over time. In the absence of a social context in which language is accompanied by gesture and other nonlinguistic nuances, elderly adults might be expected to be less capable of deriving meanings from texts. Thus, when elderly adults are placed in a "fast-mapping" (single-trial) word-learning situation, they should be less able to pick up correct denotations and connotations for novel words.

Work by McGinnis and Zelinski (2000) comes closest to a fast-mapping situation, since novel words are presented once in paragraph contexts. They found that older adults do indeed produce more general and less precise definitions of novel words when they are encountered in written text. In a second experiment, they asked adults to select (instead of produce) from among one of four choices for what a novel word presented in a paragraph context meant. Adults over 75 years old selected fewer precise definitions, suggesting that the limitations observed in the first experiment were not a function of requiring production and the concomitant retrieval demands. Instead, older adults were more likely to take the meaning of a new word to be a less precise, higher order meaning than were young adults. For example, for the new word *dippoldism*, an exact definition was the "whipping of children." A generalization that was much less precise ("getting fired for inappropriate behavior") was more often selected by elderly adults than the exact definition. This suggests that, as the ECM predicts, elderly adults are indeed less accomplished at fast-mapping tasks.

Second, we should find that language-compromised elderly people should learn words best when the novel word labels an object or an action that is *redundantly signaled* by perceptual salience (something in the here and now), clear social intent, and overlapping and varied linguistic frames so that the novel words are repeated in contexts. This is for several reasons. One reason, as Schneider et al.'s (2002) results suggested, may be auditory declines. Sensory problems, therefore, may be responsible for a significant portion of elder adults' comprehension problems. Redundant presentations—whether from providing repeated linguistic data and/ or having (when possible) some visual instantiation of what is being discussed—may assist comprehension. In our research, we found that 12-month-olds learned words best when all the cues were in alignment (Hollich et al., 2000). This may be paradoxically true for elder adults as well.

The second reason redundancy may help comes from Schneider et al. (2002), who suggest that using multiple frames for presentation of new information may more likely trigger elderly adults' world knowledge. On the assumption that world knowledge is greater for older than for younger listeners, older adults may be more skilled at using context-based knowledge to derive word and sentence meaning. This prediction also flows from our work with young children and children with atypical development. New words used in coincident contexts are more interpretable than new words used in conflict situations in which the speaker labels an object that is not in the listener's focus of attention. If elderly adults understand the surrounding context, it becomes a coincident situation for them. Note that the words in the McGinnis and Zelinski study (2000) described above were presented in written text. The ECM predicts that if the passage were presented with an accompanying video representation of the meaning—to provide redundant cues—elderly adults would do better abstracting more precise definitions of the novel words.

Third, we might posit a developmental progression such that elderly adults first have trouble "reading" language input cues (both from a perceptual standpoint because of auditory decline and from a grammatical standpoint) and later on, trouble understanding speaker social intent. If true, this order of loss would mirror in reverse the order in which these cues come online in children, with sensitivity to social cues coming in last. Among adults, a speaker's social intent is signaled as it is for children—with eye gaze, body posture, gesture, and other paralinguistic devices. However, among adults and far less so among children, speaker intent is often signaled with irony. People sometimes say just the opposite of what they mean, utilizing irony and sarcasm to make their point. For example, a speaker might say how awful it is that someone needs to travel to Paris on business, meaning the exact opposite. Do elderly adults have difficulty computing the meaning of ironic statements in discourse? Here, to our knowledge, there is only anecdotal evidence. It is often reported by neurologists (Fink, 2003, personal communication) that understanding of irony declines with age, sometimes the apparent result of mini-strokes that leave the individual otherwise unimpaired. In any event, it would be interesting to see if part of the problem elderly adults experience in language comprehension is attributable to a declining ability to interpret social cues.

Fourth, we could investigate the facility that listeners have in *coordinating* the various sources of information available in learning new words or in comprehending language. If there are new words, and they are presented in complicated grammatical constructions, and they are presented in writing instead of about witnessed events, elderly adults' information-processing system may be especially taxed. This would suggest that working memory per se is not a fundamental problem (Daneman & Green, 1996), but rather the coordination and assembly of the relevant cues for language comprehension is the problem. What exactly elderly adults rely on in such situations, and whether one could tease out which cues hold precedence, would be important to find out. Such knowledge would enable us to play to the strengths of the elderly, to borrow a metaphor. Here, too, there is little research. The ECM could guide researchers in formulating hypotheses about how the elderly coordinate the language-comprehension process and which cues they rely on more heavily. If we could pinpoint the source of difficulties using novel word learning as a kind of diagnostic, we might be able to use the model to suggest ways to facilitate processing. Perhaps those who work with the elderly could enhance comprehension, for example, by making sure that their talk is about things in the here and now and shows strong cues for social intent. That is, alternative pathways for understanding language are suggested in a more integrative model like the ECM. Talking about the here and now and providing strong cues for social intent are exactly what is done in infant-directed (ID) speech or baby talk. Interestingly, there is a parallel register used in talk to the elderly. Much research in recent years has been directed at understanding the factors that trigger elderspeech and whether it facilitates the language comprehension of older adults (e.g., Kemper et al., 2001). Next we turn to an examination of elderspeech in the context of the emergentist coalition model.

The Case of Elderspeak

What is *elderspeak*? It is a "simplified speech register with exaggerated pitch and intonation, simplified grammar, limited vocabulary, and slow rate of delivery" (Kemper, Ferrell, Harden, Finter-Urczyk, & Billington, 1998, p.43). This definition is virtually identical to the way that ID speech is described. Golinkoff, Hirsh-Pasek, and Alioto (2002), for example, defined ID speech as having "a slower rate, an extended frequency range, higher overall fundamental frequency, repeated pitch contours, marked intensity shifts, longer pauses between utterances, word lengthening, and simplified vocabulary" (p.1;e.g., for related definitions see Morgan & Demuth, 1996; Snow, 1995). Interestingly, however, the functions of ID speech seem to be different from the functions of elderspeak, and we can analyze these differences in the context of the ECM.

Clark (2003) argued that ID speech has three functions when used with infants. First, it seems to be designed to get the baby's attention. Whether it is high-pitched or a whisper, it is designed to be differentiated from speech ordinarily addressed to adults. It is as if the ID speaker says, "Hey baby, this talk is for you!" Second, it is apparently used by speakers to maintain infants' attention—not an easy thing to do. High pitch and exaggerated intonation contribute to that goal. Finally, to communicate with a listener who has much less knowledge than the speaker, the speaker must carefully choose appropriate words and make them stand out in the stream of speech. ID speech sounds almost tailored to the child's linguistic level.

What are the functions of elderspeak? Why do we observe this confluence of speech registers at opposite points of the life cycle? Before answering these questions we must distinguish between elderspeak

used to communicate with elderly adults with verifiable neurological impairments (e.g., Alzheimer's disease) and elderspeak used with healthy elder adults. When it is used by spouses to their partners suffering from dementia and possible Alzheimer's, elderspeak has been shown to improve performance in a picture description task (Kemper, Anagnopoulos, Lyons, & Heberlein, 1994). Spouses who used a simplified speech register that presumably reduced processing demands had partners who were better at selecting the correct picture from among a set of choices. Thus, one function of elderspeak with a population with a true disability is to improve comprehension.

What function, if any, does elderspeak serve when used with a population of elderly adults with no diagnosis of impairment? Here the results are mixed and depend on the aspect of speech that is focused on. For prosodic aspects, the use of elderspeak can cause adults to do *worse* on comprehension tasks (Kemper & Harden, 1999; Kemper et al., 1998). Why should that be? When adults are spoken to with the prosodic, high-pitched, sing-song speech characteristic of baby talk, they apparently feel patronized, demeaned, and insulted. What function do the attention-grabbing features of ID speech serve for infants? Presumably the exaggerated prosody grabs and maintains infant attention. Babies prefer to listen to ID over adult-directed (AD) speech as early as at birth (Cooper & Aslin, 1990). The pitch fluctuations characteristic of baby talk are probably what is responsible for this preference (e.g., Fernald, 1991). Elderly adults do not need to be induced to listen to and maintain their attention to language! They know that speech is directed to them. Therefore, this aspect of elderspeak serves little function for them and yet young adults seem to have difficulty in inhibiting it in a simulation with nonimpaired older adults (Kemper et al., 1998).

The aspect of elderspeak that does seem to make a difference for comprehension in a referential communication task is an increase in semantic elaborations and a reduction in the number of subordinate and embedded clauses. Such modifications are parallel to the modifications that probably assist toddlers' comprehension of ID speech, although this is but a speculation. All we know is that ID speech facilitates various phonological (Karzon, 1985) and perceptual processes (Kemler Nelson, Hirsh-Pasek, Jusczyk, & Wright Cassidy, 1989). We do not know if hearing sentences in ID speech as opposed to AD speech is a boon to understanding language, although preliminary research by Golinkoff et al. (2002) suggests that ID speech facilitates children's word learning. However, this is just what parents do when they repeat themselves and paraphrase what they have just said in another way. Exposure to this sort of input presents a word or expression in a variety of contexts, thereby providing more information about how it can be used.

For elderly adults, hearing semantic elaborations may serve two possible functions. First, it may help them compensate for auditory declines. Using a new word in another context narrows the degrees of freedom for identifying what that word might have been. Second, it may provide more time to process the syntactic elements they are hearing and allow them to build a more complete representation (McGinnis & Zelinski, 2000). Recall that adults gave overly broad definitions of new words heard in a single context. Semantic elaborations provide additional information about how a word is used and what it means. Therefore, this aspect of elderspeak serves a similar function as the role of ID speech: to help the listener understand the speaker.

Reducing syntactic complexity allows, too, for easier retrieval of sentence meaning. The fact that this aspect of elderspeak facilitates comprehension in older adults suggests that the syntactic part of language skill may well have declined—for whatever underlying reason. The ECM predicts that the addition of perceptual, attentional, or semantic information should boost comprehension. This could come in the form of real-life or video accompaniment or by adding additional information of a semantic nature, as elderspeak does. In short, there may well be ways to accommodate elderly adults' constrained rapid word learning and sentence comprehension. These accommodations would flow out of predictions from the ECM framework.

CONCLUSIONS

We have presented a new theory of lexical acquisition in the emergentist coalition model (e.g., Hollich et al., 2000). It is a system-based view of language that combines the best of the available theories of lexical acquisition and results in an empirically testable model of the process. Because it takes the complexity into account, it provides us with a richer picture of the factors necessary for language acquisition, and in particular lexical acquisition, to occur. It also spurs us to

consider a variety of factors when disability occurs, as when children have autistic disorder. Without the emergentist coalition model, it is impossible to explain how it is that autistic children still are capable of learning new words. The emergentist model predicts, however, that of the various cues available for word learning, an absence of sensitivity to one sort of cue (in this case, social cues) may be compensated for by sensitivity to other cues (in this case, perceptual and linguistic). Thus, the emergentist coalition model helps us to think in new ways about the variety of factors that can play a role in possible remediation.

At the same time, the ECM helps us take a new perspective on what might go wrong in the elderly when language starts to suffer. Ironically, it appears that a theory that was developed to help account for word learning in children gives us a new way to think about the problems elderly adults can have in language comprehension. It also helps us to understand why a register parallel to infant-directed speech— elderspeak—might have arisen. Most important, the ECM may offer us a new way to think about how to *compensate* for changes that might have occurred in comprehension in the elderly. An approach like the ECM moves us beyond searching for a single-factor, "smoking gun" explanation for language degradation in elderly adults. Instead, it encourages us to take multiple, interacting factors into account. Progress in understanding complex processes in both acquisition and decline can occur only if our theories match those processes in their complexity, despite the fact that single-factor theories have intrinsically greater appeal.

ACKNOWLEDGMENTS   The research reported here and the writing of the chapter were supported by NSF grants #SBR9601306 and SBR9615391 to both authors and by NICHD grant #3U10HD25455-0552 to Hirsh-Pasek. We thank our laboratory coordinators, Dede Addy and Meredith Meyer, whose good work allowed us to concentrate on this project.

References

Akhtar, N., & Tomasello, M. (1996). Twenty-four-month-old children learn words for absent objects and actions. *British Journal of Developmental Psychology*, 14, 79–93.

Akhtar, N., & Tomasello, M. (2000). The social nature of words and word learning. In R. M. Golinkoff, K. Hirsh-Pasek, L. Bloom, L. Smith, A. Woodward,

N. Akhtar, M. Tomaselloello, & G. Hollich (Eds.), *Becoming a word learner: A debate on lexical acquisition* (pp. 115–135). New York: Oxford University Press.

Baldwin, D. A. (1993). Early referential understanding: Infants' ability to recognize referential acts for what they are. *Developmental Psychology, 29*, 832–843.

Baldwin, D. A., Markman, E. M., Bill, B., Desjardins, N., Irwin, J. M., & Tidball, G. (1996). Infants' reliance on a social criterion for establishing word-object relations. *Child Development, 67*, 3135–3153.

Baldwin, D. A., & Tomasello, M. (1999). Word learning: A window on early pragmatic understanding. In E. V. Clark (Ed.), *Proceedings of the Stanford Child Language Research Forum* (pp. 3–23). Stanford, CA: Center for the Study of Language and Information.

Berko Gleason, J. (1997). *The development of language.* Boston: Allyn & Bacon.

Bloom, L. (1978). *The semantics of verbs in child language.* Paper presented at the Eastern Psychological Association, New York, NY.

Bloom, L. (1993). *The transition from infancy to language: Acquiring the power of expression.* New York: Cambridge University Press.

Bloom, L. (2000). The intentionality model of word learning: How to learn a word, any word. In R. M. Golinkoff, K. Hirsh-Pasek, L. Bloom, L. Smith, A. Woodward, N., Akhtar, M. Tomasello, & G. Hollich (Eds.), *Becoming a word learner: A debate on lexical acquisition* (pp. 19–50). New York: Oxford University Press.

Bloom, P. (2000). *How children learn the meaning of words.* Cambridge, MA: MIT Press.

Bronfenbrenner, U. (1974). *Is early intervention effective? A report on longitudinal evaluations of preschool programs (Vol. 2).* Washington DC: Department of HEW, Office of Child Development.

Bronfenbrenner, U., & Morris, P. A. (1998). The ecology of developmental processes. In R. M. Lerner (Ed.), *Handbook of child psychology: Theoretical models of human development* (5th ed., Vol 1, pp. 993–1028). New York: Wiley.

Carpenter, M., Nagell, K., & Tomasello, T. (1999). Social cognition, joint attention, and communicative competence from 9 to 15 months of age. *Monographs of the Society for Research in Child Development* (Serial No. 255).

Clark, E. V. (1983). Meanings and concepts. In J. H. Flavell & E. M. Markman (Eds.), *Handbook of child psychology, Vol. III, Cognitive development* (pp. 787–840). New York: Wiley.

Clark, E. (2003). *First language acquisition.* Cambridge, UK: Cambridge University Press.

Cooper, R. D., & Aslin, R. N. (1990). Preference for infant-directed speech in the first month after birth. *Child Development, 61*, 1584–1595.

Daneman, M., & Green, I. (1986). Individual differences in comprehending and producing words in context. *Journal of Memory and Language, 25*, 1–18.

Diesendruck, G., & Markson, L. (2001). Children's avoidance of lexical overlap: A pragmatic account. *Developmental Psychology, 37*, 630–642.

Evey, J. A., & Merriman, W. E. (1998). The prevalence and the weakness of an early naming mapping preference. *Journal of Child Language, 25*, 121–148.

Fernald, A. (1991). Prosody in speech to children: Prelinguistic and injuistic functions, In R. Vasta (Ed.), *Annals of child development, Vol. 8* (pp. 43–80). Philadelphia, PA: Jessica Kingsley Publishers.

Fagan, J. (1971). Infant recognition memory for a series of visual stimuli. *Journal of Experimenta; Child Psychology, 11*, 244–250.

Fagan, J., Singer, L., Montie, J., & Shephard, D. (1986). Selective screening device for the early detection of normal or delayed cognitive development in infants at risk for later mental retardation. *Pediatrics, 78*, 1021–1026.

Fink, A. (2003). *Personal communication*, July 6, 2003.

Gelman, R., & Greeno, J. G. (1989). On the nature of competence: Principles for understanding in a domain. In L. B. Resnick (Ed.), *Knowing and learning: Essays in honor of Robert Glaser* (pp. 125–186). Hillsdale, NJ: Lawrence Erlbaum Associates.

Gernsbacher, M. A. (1990). *Language comprehension as structure building.* Hillsdale, NJ: Lawrence Erlbaum Associates.

Gillette, J., Gleitman, H., Gleitman, L., & Lederer, A. (1999). Human simulations of vocabulary learning. *Cognition, 73*, 135–176.

Golinkoff, R. M., Hirsh-Pasek, K., & Alioto, A. (2002). *Lexical items are learned better in infant-directed than in adult-directed speech.* Unpublished manuscript, University of Delaware, Newark, DE.

Golinkoff, R., M., Hirsh-Pasek, K., Bailey, L., & Wenger, N. (1992). Young children and adults use lexical principles to learn new nouns. *Developmental Psychology, 28*, 99–108.

Golinkoff, R. M., Hirsh-Pasek, K., Bloom, L., Smith, L., Woodward, A., Akhtar, N., Tomasello, M., & Hollich, G. (2000). *Becoming a word learner: A debate on lexical acquisition.* New York: Oxford University Press.

Golinkoff, R. M., Hirsh-Pasek, K., Cauley, K. M., & Gordon, L. (1987). The eyes have it: Lexical and syntactic comprehension in a new paradigm. *Journal of Child Language, 14*, 23–46.

Golinkoff, R. M., Hirsh-Pasek, K., & Hollich, G. (1999).

Emergent cues for early word learning. In B. MacWhinney (Ed.), *The emergence of language* (pp. 305–331). Mahwah, NJ: Lawrence Erlbaum Associates.

Golinkoff, R. M., Mervis, C., & Hirsh-Pasek, K. (1994). Early object labels: The case for a developmental lexical principles framework. *Journal of Child Language, 21,* 125–155.

Hamilton-Wentworth District Health Council. (1998). *Services for seniors study: Report of findings and recommendations.* Hamiltion, ON: Regional Municipality of Hamilton-Wentworth & Hamilton-Wentworth District Health Council.

Hennon, E. (2002). *How children with austic disorder use attentional and intentional social information for word learning.* Unpublished doctoral dissertation, Temple University, Philadelphia, PA.

Hennon, E., Hirsh-Pasek, K., & Golinkoff, R. M. (2003, April). *Speaker intention?: Autistic children may learn words without it.* Society for Research in Child Development.

Hertzij, M.E., & Shapiro, T. (1990). Autism and pervasive developmental disorders. In M. lewis & S. M. Miller (eds.). *Handbook of developmental psychopathology* (pp. 385–395). New York: Plenum Press.

Hirsh-Pasek, K., & Golinkoff, R. M. (1996). *The origins of grammar: Evidence from early language comprehension.* Cambridge, MA: MIT Press.

Hirsh-Pasek, K., Hennon, E., & Golinkoff, R. M. (2003). *Birth of words.* Manuscript submitted for publication.

Hoff, E., & Naigles, L. (2002). How children use input to acquire a lexicon. *Child Development, 73,* 418–433.

Hollich, G., Hirsh-Pasek, K., & Golinkoff, R. M. (1998). Introducing the 3–D intermodal preferential looking paradigm: A new method to answer an age-old question. In C. Rovee-Collier (Ed.), *Advances in infancy research* (Vol. 12, pp. 355–373). Norwood, NJ: Ablex.

Hollich, G., Hirsh-Pasek, K., & Golinkoff, R. M. (2000). *Breaking the language barrier: An ECM for the origins of word learning.* Society for Research in Child Development Monograph Series. Chicago: University of Chicago Press.

Howlin, D., & Yule, W. (1990). Taxonomy of major disorders in childhood. In M. Lewis & S. M. Miller (Eds.), *Handbook of developmental psychopathology* (pp. 371–383). New York: Plenum Press.

Karmiloff-Smith, A., Grant, J., Berthaud, I., Davies, M., Howlin, P., & Udwin, O. (1997). Language and Williams syndrome: How intact is "intact"? *Child Development, 68,* 246–262.

Karzon, R. G. (1985). Discrimination of polysyllabic sequences by one- to four-month-old infants. *Journal of Experimental Child Psychology, 39,* 326–342.

Kemler Nelson, D. G., Hirsh-Pasek, K., Jusczyk, P. W. & Cassidy, K. W. (1989). How the prosodic cues in might assist language learning. *Journal of Child language, 16,* 55–68.

Kemper, S., Anagnopoulos, C., Lyons, K., & Heberlein, W. (1994). Speech accommodations to dementia. *Journal of Gerontology, 49,* P223–P229

Kemper, S. Ferrell, P, Harden, T., Finter-Urczyk, A., & Billington, C. (1998). Use of elderspeak by young and older adults to impaired and unimpaired listeners. *Aging, Neuropsychology, and Cognition, 5,* 43–55.

Kemper, S., Greiner, L., Marquis, J. G., Prenovost, K., & Mitzner, T. L. (2001). Language decline across the life span: Findings from the nun study. *Psychology and Aging 16,* 227–239.

Kemper, S., & Harden, T. (1999). Experimentally disentangling what's beneficial about elderspeak from what's not. *Psychology and Aging, 14,* 656–670.

Kemper, S., Thompson, M., & Marquis, J. (2001). Longitudinal change in language production: Effects of aging and dementia on grammatical complexity and propositional content. *Psychology and Aging, 16,* 600–614.

Levy, Y. (Ed.). (1994). *Other children, other languages: Issues in the theory of language acquisition.* Hillsdale, NJ: Lawrence Erlbaum Associates.

Maguire, M., Hennon, E., Hirsh-Pasek, K., & Golinkoff, R. M. (2003). *When does mother know best? Linguistic cues to lexical category formation in infants.* Unpublished manuscript, Temple University, PA.

Markman, E. M. (1989). *Categorization and naming in children: Problems of induction.* Cambridge, MA: MIT Press.

Markman, E. M., & Hutchinson, J. E. (1984). Children's sensitivity to constraints on word meaning: Taxonomic versus thematic relations. *Cognitive Psychology, 16,* 1–27.

McGinnis, D., & Zelinski, E. M. (2000). Understanding unfamiliar words: The influence of processing resources, vocabulary knowledge, and age. *Psychology and Aging, 15,* 335–350.

Mervis, C. B. (1999). The Williams syndrome cognitive profile: Strengths, weaknesses, and interreations among auditory short-term memory, language, and visuospatial constructive cognition. In E. Winograd & R. Fivush (Eds.), *Ecological approaches to cognition: Essays in honor of Ulric Neisser. Emory Symposium in Cognition* (pp. 193–227). Mahwah, NJ: Lawrence Erlbaum Associates.

Mervis, C. B., & Bertrand, J. (1994). Acquisition of the novel name-nameless category (N3C) principle. *Child Development, 65,* 1646–1663.

Merriman, W. E., & Bowman, L. L. (1989). The mutual exclusivity bias in children's word learning. *Mono-*

graphs of the Society for Research in Child Development, 54 (3–4, Serial No. 220).

Morgan, J., & Demuth, K. (1996). *Signal to syntax: Bootstrapping from speech to grammar in early acquisition.* Hillsdale, NJ: Lawrence Erlbaum Associates.

Nelson, K. (1988). Constraints on word learning? *Cognitive Development, 3,* 221–246.

Nelson, K. (1996). *Language in cognitive development.* New York: Cambridge University Press.

Newcombe, N. S., & Huttenlocher, J. (2000). *Making space: The development of spatial representation and reasoning.* Cambridge, MA: MIT Press.

Pichora-Fuller, M. K., Schneider, B. A., & Daneman, M. (1995). How young and old adults listen to and remember speech in noise. *Journal of the Acoustical Society of American, 97,* 593–608.

Pinker, S. (1994). *The language instinct: How the mind creates language.* New York: William Morrow.

Plunkett, K. (1997). Theories of early language acquisition. *Trends in Cognitive Sciences, 1,* 146–153.

Quine, W. V. O. (1960). *Word and object.* Cambridge, UK: Cambridge University Press.

Rice, M. L. (Ed.). (1996). *Toward a genetics of language.* Mahwah, NJ: Lawrence Erlbaum Associates.

Samuelson, L. K., & Smith, L. B. (1998). Memory and attention make smart word learning: An alternative account of Akhtar, Carpenter, and Tomasello. *Child Development, 69,* 94–104.

Schneider, B. A., Daneman, M., & Pichora-Fuller, M. (2002). Listening in aging adults: From discourse comprehension to psychoacoustics. *Canadian Journal of Experimental Psychology, 56,* 139–152.

Smith, L. B. (1995). Self-organizing processes in learning to learn words: Development is not induction. In C. A. Nelson (Ed.), *Basic and applied perspectives on learning, cognition, and development: The Minnesota Symposia on Child Psychology* (Vol. 28, pp. 1–32). Mahwah, NJ: Lawrence Erlbaum Associates.

Smith, L. B. (1999). Children's noun learning: How general learning processes make specialized learning mechanisms. In B. MacWhinney (Ed.), *The emergence of language* (pp. 227–305). Mahwah, NJ: Lawrence Erlbaum Associates.

Smith, L. B. (2000). Learning how to learn words: An associative crane. In R. M. Golinkoff, K. Hirsh-Pasek, L. Bloom, L. Smith, A. Woodward, N. Akhtar, M. Tomasello, & G. Hollich (Eds.), *Becoming a word learner: A debate on lexical acquisition* (pp. 51–80). New York: Oxford University Press.

Smith, L. B., Jones, S. S., Landau, B., Gershkoff-Stowe, L., & Samuelson, L. (2002). Object name learning provides on-the-job training for attention. *Psychological Science, 13,* 13–20.

Snow, C. E. (1995). Issues in the study of input: Finetuning, universality, individual and developmental differences, and necessary causes. In P. Fletcher & B. MacWhinney (Eds.), *The handbook of child language* (pp. 180–193). Cambridge, MA: Cambridge University Press.

Spelke, E. S. (1990). Principles of object perception. *Cognitive Science, 14,* 29–56.

Tomasello, M., & Barton, M. (1994). Learning words in non-ostensive context. *Developmental Psychology, 30,* 639–650.

Tomasello, M., Strosberg, R., & Akhtar, N. (1996). Eighteen-month-old children learn words in non-ostensive contexts. *Journal of Child Language, 23,* 157–176.

Wang, P. P., Doherty, S., Rourke, S. B., & Bellugi, U. (1995). Inique profile of visuo-perceptual skills in genetic syndrome, *Brain and Cognition, 29,* 54–65.

Waxman, S. R., & Kosowski, T. D. (1990). Nouns mark category relations: Toddlers' and preschoolers' word-learning biases. *Child Development, 1,* 139–156.

15

Language in Adulthood

Susan Kemper

It is tempting to postulate that language development across the lifespan is U-shaped such that language "regression" mirrors language acquisition (Jackson, 1958; Jakobson, 1941/1968). Typically, this regression hypothesis is put forth to account for aphasic disorders (Grodzinsky, 1990); it has also been applied to language loss with regard to the discontinued use of a first language (Hyltenstam & Obler, 1989) and the decline of language in dementia (Emery, 1985, 1986). Both strong and weak forms of the regression hypothesis have been proposed: The strong form holds that language regression is the mirror image of language acquisition at all levels of analysis; the weak form suggests parallels while acknowledging different mechanisms or principles. There is little empirical support for the strong hypothesis (see Kemper, 1992a, for a discussion). This chapter and the corresponding chapter on acquisition (Golinkoff & Hirsh-Pasek, Chapter 14, this volume) explore the weak hypothesis.

Within the cognitive-aging framework, there has been an emphasis on four contrasting accounts of age-related changes to language: cognitive slowing, inhibitory deficits, the effects of working-memory limitations, and language-specific effects on word retrieval. This chapter considers each account with regard to a salient phenomenon: older adults' use of a simplified speech register resulting from an age-related decline in the syntactic complexity of oral and written language.

Older adults appear to use to simplified speech register (Benjamin, 1988; Cooper, 1990; Davis, 1984; Kemper, Kynette, Rash, Sprott, & O'Brien, 1989; Kynette & Kemper, 1986; Shewan & Henderson, 1988), and this simplification appears to be progressive with age. Kemper, Thompson, and Marquis (2001) have traced this age-related simplification of language by tracking two aspects of the linguistic structure of spontaneous speech: developmental level (D-level) and propositional density (P-density).

D-level is computed by assigning points to sentences based on their complexity and order of emergence in children's language. D-level is sensitive to the amount of embedding and the type of embedding used to create complex sentences. Simple, one-clause sentences earn zero points. Sentences containing infinitives, gerunds, relative clauses, and other forms of embedding earn 1 to 6 points. Sentences with multiple forms of embedding and subordination earn 7 points. The second measure, propositional density (P-density), assesses how much information is packed into a sentence relative to the number of words. Each utterance is decomposed into its constituent proposi-

tions, which represent propositional elements and relations between them. The P-density for each speaker is defined as the average number of propositions per 100 words.

The oral language samples were elicited from a panel of older adults, and mixed modeling was used to examine longitudinal change in D-level and P-density (see Figures 15.1 and 15.2). The fixed effects describe two aspects of the linguistic measures: the initial level (or intercept) and the pattern of change with age

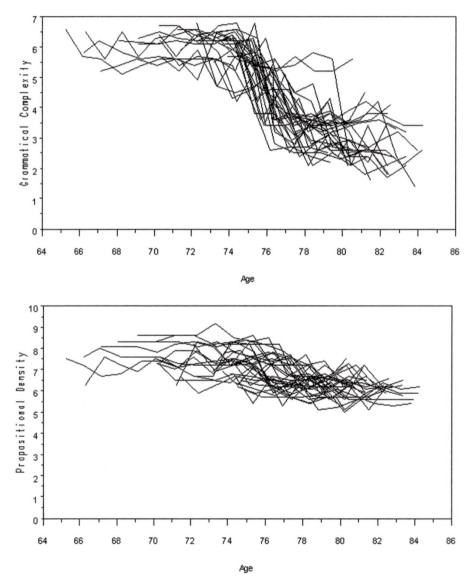

FIGURE 15–1. Longitudinal change in grammatical complexity (D-level) (top panel) and in propositional content (P-density) (bottom panel) for healthy older adults. (From Kemper, Thompson, & Marquis, 2001. Reprinted with permission of the American Psychological Association.)

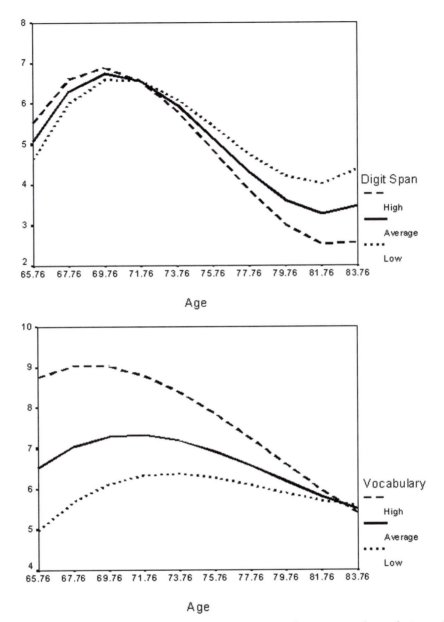

FIGURE 15–2. Illustration of digit span as a covariate in the age by grammatical complexity model for the healthy older adults (top panel) and vocabulary as a covariate in the age by propositional content model for the healthy older adults (bottom panel). (From Kemper, Thompson, & Marquis, 2001. Reprinted with the permission of the American Psychological Association)

(coefficient for the linear slope for age, and, potentially, coefficients for higher order age terms—e.g., age^2 and age^3). Random effects indicate that there is individual variation in the intercepts or pattern of change. This analysis indicated that the syntactic complexity of healthy adults' speech declines in late adult-

hood. Both the grammatical complexity and the propositional content of older adults' spontaneous speech decline between ages 74 and 78. In both cases, the pattern of decline was a cubic function of age, such that a period of relative stability was followed by a period of accelerated decline and by a third period of more gradual decline. The mixed modeling also indicated that there was considerable individual variation in older adults' initial level of grammatical complexity and propositional content, as well as individual variation in their rate of decline. The initial level of grammatical complexity was predicted in part by the participant's composite score on the Digits Forward and Digits Backwards test from the Wechsler Adult Intelligence Scales–Revised (WAIS) (Wechsler, 1958); further, the grammatical complexity of those with higher initial scores also declined somewhat more rapidly with advancing age. In contrast, the initial level of propositional content was predicted in part by the participant's score on the Vocabulary test from the WAIS, and those with higher initial scores declined somewhat more rapidly with advancing age.

The age-related decline in grammatical complexity and propositional content may have its onset in young adulthood. Snowdon et al. (1996) analyzed language samples from a group of nuns, members of the School Sisters of Notre Dame. The nuns produced autobiographical writing samples at the time they took their final religious vows, between 18 and 32 years of age. When the nuns were 75 to 93 years of age, they were given a battery of tests of cognition and memory designed to assess probable Alzheimer's dementia. Low linguistic ability in young adulthood, indicated by low D-level (termed *grammatical complexity* by Snowdon et al., 1996) and/or low P-density (or *idea density*) in these language samples, was associated with increased risk for poor performance on the cognitive and memory tests in late adulthood. Low P-density in young adulthood was also associated with increased neuropathology characteristic of Alzheimer's disease for a small number of nuns who had died. In a follow-up study, Snowdon, Greiner, Kemper, Nanayakkara, and Mortimer (1999) linked low linguistic ability, measured by P-density in young adulthood, to increased all-cause mortality among the nuns.

Kemper, Greiner, Marquis, Prenovost, and Mitzner (2001) have traced these measures of linguistic ability over the lifespan, comparing the initial samples collected from the nuns to those elicited when they were in their 40s, 70s, and 80s. Further, they investigated how education and adult experiences affected initial linguistic ability and its decline. P-density appears to be a general measure of cognitive and neurological development that is not related to grades in high school English or mathematics nor is it affected by adult experiences including obtained advanced educational degrees. Low P-density in young adulthood may reflect poor neurocognitive development, which in turn may increase susceptibility to age-related decline due to Alzheimer's or other diseases.

The simplified speech register used by older adults differs from three other simplified speech registers (restricted codes, pidgin languages, and elderspeak). Bernstein (1968) characterized the speech of individuals from lower socioeconomic levels as involving "short, grammatically simple, often unfinished, sentences with a poor syntactical construction; simple and repetitive use of conjunctions . . . thus modifications, qualifications, and logical stress tend to be indicated by non-verbal means; frequent use of short commands and questions; rigid and limited use of adjectives and adverbs; infrequent use of the impersonal pronoun (it, one) as subject of a conditional sentence; statements formulated as questions. . . . a statement of fact is often used as both a reason and a conclusion . . . traditional phrases . . . symbolism of a low order of generality . . . implicit meaning" (1968, p. 228). While the speech of older adults and young adults under dual-task conditions shares many of these properties, it differs from this "restricted" register in a number of ways, most significantly in terms of its varied vocabulary and expressive content, as reflected in the P-density measure. Sentence length exceeds that reported by Bernstein and a wide range of grammatical constructions are used, although complex forms with relative clauses, embedded infinitives, that-clauses, and so on are infrequent.

This simplified speech register of older adults also differs from another form of simplified speech, pidgin language. Pidgins are simplified languages formed when speakers of two or more languages come in contact in trade or maritime situations. Pidgins are typically lacking many features, including "consistent marking of tense, aspect, and modality; relative clauses; movement rules; embedded complements, in particular infinitival constructions; articles, especially indefinite" (Bickerton, 1981). Older adults' speech resembles pidgin language only that complex, embedded constructions are rarely produced, reflecting the demands placed on working memory by these constructions.

Another form of simplified speech is elderspeak. Elderspeak is a special speech register directed to older adults; it is evoked by negative stereotypes of older adults but it is also used somewhat indiscriminately (Caporael, 1981; Caporael & Culbertson, 1986; Kemper, 1994; Ryan, Giles, Bartolucci, & Henwood, 1986). Many of the characteristics of elderspeak, such as its slow rate, exaggerated prosody, and simplified syntax and vocabulary, resemble the characteristics of other speech registers such as those directed at young children, foreigners, and household pets (see Golinkoff & Hirsh-Pasek, Chapter 14, this volume).

Kemper and her collaborators (Kemper, Vandeputte, Rice, Cheung, & Gubarchuk, 1995; Kemper, Othick, Warren, Gubarchuk, & Gerhing, 1996) have examined this claim experimentally. They have shown that young adults spontaneously adopt a simplified speech register when addressing older listeners during a referential communication task. Young adults provide more information in terms of words, utterances, instructions, and location checks on the listener's progress and they also "package" this information differently. The young adults pause more often, use shorter sentences, use few complex syntactic constructions, and reduce the informational content of individual utterances by lowering the propositional density. These speech adjustments appeared to benefit the older listeners, who were able to reproduce the maps more accurately than when they were paired with older speakers.

The use of elderspeak in these studies did enhance the performance of the older adults, but the older adults reported experiencing more expressive and receptive communication problems when they were paired with young partners who used elderspeak. The use of elderspeak appeared to trigger older adults' perceptions of themselves as communicatively impaired and led to increased self-report of expressive and receptive problems. Harwood, Giles, and Ryan (1995) argue that the use of elderspeak, as well as other age-based behavioral modifications, contributes to development of an "old" identity, reinforcing negative stereotypes of older adults and lowering older adults' self-esteem.

Kemper and Harden (1999) tried to disentangle those parameters of elderspeak that actually benefit older adults' performance from those that trigger older adults' negative self-assessments. They concluded, after a series of experimental studies evaluating different variants of elderspeak, that semantic elaborations and syntactic simplifications improve the performance of young and older adults, whereas reducing sentence length and using exaggerated prosody have no effect on performance. They also found that older adults experience more negative self-assessments when their partners address them in modified "babytalk"—with high pitch, exaggerated prosody, slow speaking rate, and short sentences.

Older adults do not appear to adopt different speech registers for different partners (Kemper et al., 1995, 1996). In these studies, the older adults used a consistent speech register for young versus older partners. They may do so for a variety of reasons: they may not be sensitive to the same situational or interpersonal cues that elicit code-switching by young adults, or they may be unwilling to adopt a form of babytalk when addressing peers because they are sensitive to its negative connotations. Older adults may use elderspeak with other older adults whom they perceive to be cognitive impaired, but will not use elderspeak with healthy, active older adults in order to avoid giving offense or being patronizing.

FOUR ACCOUNTS OF AGE-RELATED CHANGES TO LANGUAGE

Effects of Cognitive Slowing

General slowing has been implicated in a variety of models of the effects of aging on cognition (Salthouse, 1992), including language and text processing. Wingfield and his colleagues have investigated how cognitive slowing may constrain older adults' language processing using a variety of auditory listening paradigms. Stine, Wingfield, and Poon (1986), for example, tested whether increased propositional density of text and increased presentation rates disrupt older adults' recall of auditorily presented text. Stine and colleagues found that older adults were not differentially affected by propositionally dense text, though their recall performance was differentially poorer for speeded text presentation. In a related study, Wingfield, Tun, and Rosen (1995) examined younger and older adults' recall of speech segments that varied in terms of rate of presentation, length, and syntactic well-formedness (i.e., whether or not the segment started or concluded at a syntactic boundary). Older adults' recall, like that of young adults,' was best at normal rates of speech and for segments that occurred at syntactic boundaries. These findings suggest that older adults encounter a processing bottleneck in parsing rapidly presented speech, particularly when its segmentation is random. Recall was poorest for segments presented at fast rates and that occurred at random intervals. Cognitive slowing has also been implicated in a series of studies using a self-paced listening procedure in which participants are able to control the auditory presentation of texts segment by segment. Older adults tend to select slower speech rates and smaller segments (Wingfield & Ducharme, 1999; Wingfield, Lahar, & Stine, 1989).

Cognitive slowing may also affect how young and older adults allocate processing time during reading. Studies by Stine-Morrow and her colleagues (Stine, 1990; Stine, Cheung, & Henderson, 1995; Stine-Morrow & Hindman, 1994; Stine-Morrow, Milinder, Pullara, & Herman, 2001) examined word-by-word reading times, regressing young and older adults' reading times on a variety of word-level, sentence-level, and text-level features. In general, young and older adults have been found to allocate time very similarly; however, age differences in reading-time allocation have been reported for specific aspects of syntactic and semantic processing. For example, Stine (1990) found that both young and older adults allocate reading time to word-level and constituent-level processing. However, they found qualitative differences in how time was allocated at clause and sentence boundaries. Young adults spent extra time reading words that occurred at sentence boundaries, minor clause boundaries, and major clause boundaries. While older adults also allocated extra time to major and minor clause boundaries, they did not spend extra time at sentence boundaries.

Stine-Morrow, Ryan, and Leonard (2000) confirmed this finding in a study of sentence processing, comparing subject-relative ("The noise that terrified the baby was very loud") and object-relative ("The noise that the man made was very loud") clause constructions. They found that young adults allocated additional processing time to the object-relative constructions whereas older adults did not. As a result, young adults had good comprehension of these constructions whereas older adults often interpreted these constructions incorrectly.

Stine-Morrow, Loveless, and Soderberg (1996) let young and older adults read syntactically coherent text at their own pace. Both young and older adults who achieved good recall allocated extra reading time to syntactically complex sentences. However, some age differences were found with regard to other time-allocation strategies used to achieve good recall. For young adults, good recall was related to the allocation of additional reading time to infrequent words and to new concepts first mentioned in the text. However, for older adults, good recall was related to allocation of additional reading time as they progressed serially through the text. These findings indicate that older adults use a different strategy than do young adults to achieve good recall. Whereas young adults rely on recalling key words and concepts, older adults may rely on recalling a global text structure that is built up serially.

If so, context may be particularly beneficial to older adults, as it is for children. Soederberg Miller and Stine-Morrow (1998) explored the effects of background knowledge on reading strategies. In one condition, a passage title established a meaningful context. The titles did facilitate conceptual integration at sentence boundaries, particularly for older adults. When no titles were provided, the readers spent more time accessing low-frequency words and read more slowly as the text progressed serially, suggesting that they were spending additional time building up a context in which to interpret individual words and sentences. The latter effect was exacerbated for older readers, again suggesting that older readers rely on a global or situational model in order to interpret what they read. Successful older readers may be those who are best able to differentially allocate reading time and other cognitive resources (see also Morrow, Stine-Morrow, Leirer, Andrassy, & Kahn, 1997).

Critique

It is plausible that an overall decline in processing speed might account for older adults' use of a simplified speech register. Two assumptions are necessary: (1) Speech production is constrained by implicit or explicit time pressures in many tasks and situations; and (2) older adults' slower rate of speaking reflects general slowing of all component linguistic processes. Hence, older adults may adopt a simplified speech register in order to maintain acceptable speech-production rates by avoiding costly production rate increases associated with complex constructions. However, this account would also imply that older adults' complexity should vary with their speech rate and perception of time pressures; this does not appear to be the case. Kemper et al. (1995, 1996) examined older adults' speech rates with different partners and found that speech rates with young partners were equivalent to those with older partners who might be expected to be more tolerant of slow production rates.

Effects of Inhibitory Deficits

A different account of older adults' language has been put forth by Hasher and Zacks (1988). They proposed that inhibitory mechanisms weaken with age and permit the intrusion of irrelevant thoughts, personal preoccupations, and idiosyncratic associations during text encoding and retrieval. These irrelevant thoughts compete for processing resources and impair older adults' comprehension and recall. Hence, older adults' comprehension may be affected by distractions or intrusive thoughts. For example, when a text contains distracting words printed in a different typeface, young adults are able to ignore the distracting material, even when it is related to the text, whereas older adults are not able to ignore the distracting material, which slows their reading, impairs their comprehension, and renders them subject to memory distortions (Connelly, Hasher, & Zacks, 1991; Zacks & Hasher, 1997).

Hasher, Zacks, and May (1999) postulate three functions of inhibition: preventing irrelevant information from entering working memory, deleting irrelevant information from working memory, and restraining probable responses until their appropriateness can be assessed. They argue that older adults suffer from a variety of processing impairments that can be attributed to decreased inhibitory mechanisms. Hence, older adults' language processing may mirror that of young adults whenever the task requires the active application of processing strategies, since excitatory mechanisms are spared, whereas older adults' language processing may be impaired relative to young adults' whenever inhibitory mechanisms are required to block out distractions, clear away irrelevancies, or switch between activities. Individuals with poor inhibitory mechanisms may not only be more susceptible to distraction but also be less able to switch rapidly from one task to another and rely on well-learned "stereotypes, heuristics, and schemas" (Yoon, May, & Hasher, 1998, p. 123).

This hypothesis received support in a study by Kwong See and Ryan (1996). Kwong See and Ryan examined individual differences in text processing attributable to working-memory capacity, processing speed, and efficiency of inhibitory processes, estimated by backward digit span, color naming speed, and Stroop interference, respectively. Their analysis suggested that older adults' text-processing difficulties can be attributed to slower processing and less efficient inhibition, rather than to working-memory limitations

Two studies by Connelly et al. (1991) compared young and older adults' reading to provide key support for inhibitory deficit theory. In the first study, the investigators compared passage reading times and answers to probe-comprehension questions for young and older adults for texts that did or did not have distracting material interspersed amid target texts. In the distracting version, irrelevant words and phrases were inserted every three to four words. The distractors were presented in a different typeface. The distractors consisted of words or phrases conceptually related to the content of the target text (in experiment 1) and recurred repeatedly throughout the target text. Connelly et al. reported that young adults not only read the texts containing the distracting material more rapidly than older adults but also showed greater comprehension of the target material. This simple finding has provided the clearest support for inhibitory-deficit theory. Older adults are more distractible than young adults because they are less able to suppress or inhibit reading-task-irrelevant words and phrases.

In their second experiment Connelly et al. (1991) compared three types of distractors: words related in meaning to the passage, words unrelated in meaning, and meaningless strings of Xs. They found that related distractors slowed older adults' reading times more than unrelated ones and that the Xs slowed older adults' reading times relative to a baseline condition. They also found that young adults' reading times were slowed by the Xs as well as by distractor words, but that related versus unrelated distractors did not differentially affect the young adults. They suggested that the related distractor words "produce what might be a greater breadth of spontaneous activation" (p. 539) for older adults who may also expend "greater effort to understand" (p. 539) the related distractors and text passage. Despite their efforts to understand the text, older adults are ultimately less successful than young adults in terms of performance on the comprehension probes.

Connelly et al.'s (1991) conclusion has been challenged by Dywan and Murphy (1996), who modified the procedure to include a surprise word-recognition test for the interposed material. They found that the young adults had superior recognition memory for the distractor words, a result that is difficult to explain if the young adults are assumed to have been successful at inhibiting processing of the distractors. Burke (1997) also argues that research on semantic priming, the activation of word meanings, and the detection of ambiguity provides "no support" for claims that "older adults are deficient in suppressing contextually irrelevant meaning or that they activate more irrelevant semantic information than young adults or that they retrieve more high frequency, dominant, or typical information than young adults" (p. P257).

However, inhibitory deficits may contribute to a variety of difficulties reported for older adults in dual- and multi-tasking situations. For example, Stine, Wingfield, and Myers (1990) examined younger and older adults' recall of information from a television newscast that was presented in auditory format, auditory supplemented with a written transcript, or the original auditory and visual recording. Although the written transcript and visual presentation aided younger adults' recall of the information, older adults did not benefit from a written transcript.

Tun, O'Kane, & Wingfield (2002) asked young and older adults to listen to lists of words while ignoring competing speech. They varied whether the competing speech was meaningful (read in English) or meaningless (read in Dutch by the same speaker). Whereas young adults were capable of ignoring the competing speech, the older adults' recall of the target words was severely impaired by the competing speech. This competing speech effect was greater for older adults when the competing speech was in English than when it was in Dutch (a language that closely resembles English phonology and prosody), suggesting that the effect is due to attentional factors (see also Tun & Wingfield, 1999). Indeed, controlling for hearing acuity did not eliminate this effect. They concluded that young adults are able to filter out competing speech whereas older adults are less able to do so.

Critique

Is inhibitory deficit theory a good candidate for explaining the simplified speech of older adults? Inhibitory deficit theory predicts that older adults should be more distracted as they speak; thus, older adults' speech should resemble that of young adults' under divided attention conditions. There does not appear to be a significant research literature on the effects of distraction on speech, apart from a few studies of the effects of distraction on speech organization and fluency. These studies suggest that hesitations, false starts, filled and unfilled pauses, and vague, disorganized "scattered" speech result (Hassol, Margaret, & Cameron,

1952; Jou & Harris, 1992; Southwood & Dagenais, 2001).

Some support for inhibitory deficit theory comes from a recent study by Kemper, Herman, and Lian (2003) that suggests that the speech of young adults is sensitive to dual-task demands and can shift to a speech register resembling that of older adults under demanding conditions. Hence, speech production may compete for critical processing resources with other tasks, affecting grammatical complexity at the cost of maintaining secondary task performance.

Hasher and Zacks (1988; Zacks & Hasher, 1997) have suggested that off-target verbosity (Arbuckle & Gold, 1993) is a characteristic of older adults resulting from the breakdown of inhibitions, but this claim is highly controversial. Even if off-target verbosity is proved to be an age-related phenomenon, it is inconsistent with the observed simplification of older adults' speech. While off-target speech does tend to have reduced propositional density, as it is often vague, redundant, and repetitious, it can be syntactically complex as well as rapid and fluent. Hence, inhibitory deficit theory does not seem to provide a viable account of older adults' use of a simplified speech register.

Effects of Working Memory

Working-memory limitations do appear to affect older adults' language. Most of the support for this hypothesis is correlational. For example, Kemper et al. (1989) reported that the mean number of clauses per utterance, a general measure of the complexity of adults' language, is positively correlated with the adults' backward digit span using the WAIS subtest (Wechsler, 1958). Further, Kemper and Rash (1988) calculated Yngve depth (Yngve, 1960), a measure of the working memory demands of sentence production, and found that it was positively correlated with WAIS digit span as well as with mean clauses per utterance.

The working-memory explanation for age-related changes to language is supported by findings from a few studies of sentence comprehension. For example, Zurif, Swinney, Prather, Wingfield, and Brownell (1995) examined younger and older adults' online processing of object- and subject-relative sentences using a cross-modal priming task. In object-relative sentences, the object "moves" from the object position of the subordinate clause and leaves a "gap" or trace (e.g., "The tailor hemmed the cloak$_i$ that the actor from the studio needed (t_i) for the performance"). In subject–relative sentences, the gap is indexed by the object of the matrix clause (e.g., "The gymnast loved the professor$_i$ from the Northwestern city who (t_i) complained about the bad coffee"). The focus of their analysis was to determine whether reactivation of the antecedent occurs at the gap during sentence processing. Zurif et al. (1995) found that older adults evidenced priming for the subject- but not object-relative sentences (experiment 1). In a second experiment, Zurif et al. (1995) reduced the distance between gap and antecedent in object-relative sentences from seven or eight intervening words to five and found a significant priming effect at the gap position. The authors conclude that older adults reactivate the antecedent when the distance between antecedent and gap is short. Zurif et al. do not report a direct comparison of young and old, but interpret their results as showing that older adults' immediate syntactic analysis of a sentence is affected by working-memory limitations.

This study and other studies attempting to link sentence-processing problems to working-memory limitations have been severely criticized on a number of methodological and procedural grounds (see Caplan & Waters, 1999, and subsequent responses). Caplan and Waters (1999, 2002) have argued that syntactic parsing and other interpretive processes—including lexical access, assignment of thematic roles, and the determination of topic, focus, and co-reference—rely on a specialized processing system with a separate sentence-interpretation resource unrelated to traditional span measures of working memory. The Caplan and Waters's theory (1999) predicts similar patterns of online processing for all readers since interpretive processes are buffered from working-memory limitations. All readers should show increased processing delays at points of maximal syntactic complexity.

Caplan and Waters (1999) point to a study by Kemtes and Kemper (1997) as support for their theory. Kemtes and Kemper examined the relationship between younger and older adults' working memory and online syntactic processing. They used a word-by-word reading paradigm to assess younger and older adults' online comprehension of temporarily ambiguous sentences (e.g., "Several angry workers warned about low wages . . .") that were resolved with either a main verb *interpretation* ("Several angry workers warned about low wages during the holiday season"), or a reduced relative clause interpretation ("Several angry workers

warned about low wages decided to file complaints"). Kemtes and Kemper also assessed adults' off-line comprehension of the sentences by presenting a comprehension question immediately after each sentence had been read. The primary finding was that while older adults' online reading times were slower than those of younger adults, the syntactic complexity did not differentially impair older adults' online comprehension of the sentences. In contrast, older adults' off-line question comprehension was influenced by the syntactic ambiguity manipulation in that question comprehension was reliably poorer, relative to young, for the syntactically ambiguous sentences.

Waters and Caplan (1996a, 1996b, 2001), in a series of studies, have directly examined the hypothesis that working-memory limitations affect older adults' ability to process complex sentences. These studies have used the auditory moving windows paradigm. This technique allows the listener to start and stop the presentation of sentence and permits the analysis of phrase-by-phrase listening times, analogous to visual moving windows paradigms that permit the analysis of word-by-word or phrase-by-phrase reading times. The studies by Caplan and Waters typically examine the processing of subject- and object-relative clause constructions, such as those below:

Subject Relative Clause: The cabin$_{i,j}$ that (t_i) *warmed* the scout (t_j) contained the firewood.

Object Relative Clause: The cabin$_{i,j}$ that the scout warmed (t_j) (t_i) contained the firewood.

The subject-relative clause construction imposes few processing demands on the reader or the listener: In the relative-clause construction, the subject of the main clause, (t_i), is also the subject of the embedded relative clause, (t_i). The object-relative clause construction challenges the reader or listener to assign the correct syntactic relations. In the relative clause construction, the subject of the main clause, (t_j), must also be interpreted as the object of the embedded clause, (t_i).

Waters and Caplan (2001) compared how young and older readers allocate listening time to critical phrases of relative clause sentences. Despite differences in working memory, listening times were distributed similarly by young and older listeners. All paused longer when they heard the embedded verb in the complex relative-clause sentences than when they heard the corresponding verb in the simple version; this additional time is attributable to the extra processing required to recover its direct object. They found no evidence that differences in age or working memory led to different processing strategies, supporting their theory.

Critique

Although few of the studies reviewed by Caplan and Waters hold up under their scrutiny, their own experiments are not without flaw. The central issue is their choice of the auditory moving window paradigm over other, more widely accepted techniques such as word-by-word reading paradigms or eye-tracking paradigms. They defend the auditory moving window paradigm as "not obviously less natural" (Waters & Caplan, 2001) than other techniques. However, it may clash with the findings of Wingfield and his colleagues (discussed above) who compared young and older adults' segmentation strategies, preferred presentation times, and allocation of processing time during listening and reading tasks. Wingfield et al. (1989, 1999) showed that older adults prefer slower speech rates but also smaller segments than young adults. Stine et al. (1995) showed that older adults ignore clause, phrase, and sentence boundaries. Waters and Caplan segment the sentences so that they can compare listening times for words or phrases used in different constructions. Some segments are single words, some noun phrases, some a complementizer plus a noun phrase. Hence, participants do not control the length of segments or the location of segment boundaries, only the interval between the presentation of one segment and the next. It may be that this imposed segmentation conflicts with older adults' natural segmentation strategies, obscuring any differences in the remaining processing parameter—time—owing to age or working memory. A task that permits participants to control both segmentation and presentation may be more sensitive to individual differences in syntactic processing than the auditory moving window paradigm.

A recent study by Kemper, Crow, and Kemtes (2004) using eye-tracking methodology re-examined these issues. Eye-tracking is a more naturalistic task that imposes few restrictions on readers; they are free to skip words or phrases, read ahead and glance backwards, and reread entire segments. Using this technology, Kemper and colleagues examined three aspects

of reading: first fixations to key phrases, regressions to earlier phrases, and the total time key phrases were fixated. They examined reduced relative clause sentences such as those below:

> Reduced Relative Clause Sentence: Several angry workers warned about the low wages decided to file complaints.

> Main Clause Sentence: Several angry workers warned about the low wages during the holiday season.

> Focused Reduced Relative Clause Sentence: Only angry workers warned about the low wages decided to file complaints.

Kemper and colleagues (2004) found partial support for Waters and Caplan's theory: young and older adults' first pass fixations were alike and both groups showed a clear "garden path" effect: a peak in fixation time at the second verb in reduced relative-clause sentences but not main-clause sentences. This garden path effect suggests that all readers initially interpret the first verb as the main verb and must reanalyze it when they encounter the second verb in the reduced relative-clause sentence. However, Kemper and colleagues also observed an increase in regressions and in total fixation times for older readers for the reduced relative-clause sentences, suggesting that older adults were unable to correctly process these sentences. Further, low-span readers, identified by their scores on a battery of working-memory tests, also produced more regressions and an increase in total fixation times for reduced relative-clause sentences, suggesting that they were unable to correctly parse the sentences. The results from the eye-tracking analysis of the focused reduced relative-clause sentences also posed problems for Caplan and Waters' theory: high-span readers initially allocated additional processing time to the first noun phrase and then were able to avoid the "garden path" because the focus operator "only" led them to correctly interpret the first verb phrase as a reduced relative clause.

Thus, this eye-tracking study poses some challenges to Waters and Caplan's theory by revealing age-group and span-group differences in reading. Eye-tracking may be more sensitive to individual differences in language processing that the auditory moving window paradigm and may reveal subtle differences in processing strategies that other techniques miss. Caplan and

Waters may be able to accommodate these findings by carefully specifying the range of interpretative versus post-interpretative processes.

Language-Specific Deficits

Word-finding problems are among the most frequent complaints of older adults. Pauses, circumlocutions, "empty speech" such as pronouns lacking clear referents, and substitution errors during spontaneous speech may all reflect age-related impairments in accessing and retrieving lexical information (Cohen, 1979; Obler, 1980). It appears that older adults have difficulty accessing lexical information, especially the phonological form of words (Burke, MacKay, Worthley, & Wade, 1991). Consequently, tip-of-the-tongue experiences, in which familiar words are temporarily irretrievable, are more common for older adults than for young adults and less often resolved by retrieval of the intended word.

Burke and her colleagues (Burke & Laver, 1990; Burke et al., 1991) have offered an explanation of word retrieval failures: the transmission deficit hypothesis. This theory holds that aging affects the strength of mental connections linking an idea to the pronunciation of a specific word—or in more formal terms, a network linking conceptual representations to phonological specifications. If one or more links between the idea and pronunciation is broken, a speaker will be able to retrieve the idea but be unable to translate that idea into an actual spoken word. The transmission deficit hypothesis pinpoints the locus of the broken connection as the link between the idea and the pronunciation of the word because speakers will often have partial phonological information about the target word as well as detailed information about the target idea. Older adults are more vulnerable to word retrieval failures because all network connections weaken with age; words are more vulnerable than ideas because words must be precisely articulated from a unique sequence of phonological features (pronouncing "cat" partially correctly might get you a "hat" instead), whereas ideas are redundantly specified by many converging associations and linkages (instead of thinking of a "cat" you might think of a "lion" or a "tiger" or Garfield).

In a clever experiment, James and Burke (2000) asked young and older adults general-knowledge questions designed to promote word retrieval failures.

The questions were embedded in a list of words. Sometimes, these words shared phonological features with the target, sometimes they were unrelated to the target word. James and Burke reported that fewer retrieval failures occurred when the target was preceded by phonologically related words than when it wasn't. For example, participants were more likely to correctly answer the question "What word means to formally renounce a throne?" [*abdicate*] when they had just read "abstract" than when they had read "reread." White and Abrams (2002) report that words sharing the first syllable with the target—for example, *abacus, abrogate*, are most effective at reducing word retrieval failures, whereas words sharing other phonologically features with the target, such as *indigent, handicap, educate*, and *duplicate* are ineffective.

Critique

The transmission deficit hypothesis implies that older adults' speech should become increasingly fragmented as a result of increasing common word-finding problems. When word retrieval fails, sentence production should be disrupted. However, older adults' speech does not appear to become fragmented but simplified, and when fragments do occur, they seem to reflect syntactic planning problems rather than word finding problems (Kemper, 1992b). It may be that older adults who are prone to word-finding problems have developed skilled metalinguistic strategies to cover up or compensate for these disruptions.

CONCLUSION

Many aspects of the language of older adults are unafflect by cognitive slowing, processing limitations, inhibitory deficits, or word-retrieval problems. Basic verbal abilities, as measured by vocabulary tests, have been traditionally studied by testing older adults' abilities to produce definitions (Wechsler, 1958), select synonyms (Shipley, 1940), pronounce phonologically irregular words (Grober & Sliwinski, 1991), or name pictures or drawings (Dunn & Dunn, 1997). Across a wide range of tests both longitudinally and cross-sectionally, vocabulary has been shown to increase throughout the middle adult years but to decline in late adulthood (Albert, Heller, & Milberg, 1988; Botwinick & Siegler, 1980; Eisdorfer & Wilkie, 1973; Hultsch,

Hertzog, Dixon, & Small, 1998; Schaie, 1996). Basic syntactic and morphological processes appear unaffected by aging: on metalinguistic judgment tasks, older adults typically do well except when challenged by complex constructions imposing temporary processing demands on working memory (Kemper, 1997; Pye, Cheung, & Kemper, 1992); older adults are no more prone than young adults to produce agreement errors ("he *run* fast"), case errors ("*me* got it"), overgeneralizations ("he *sitted* down on chair"), or other types of morphological errors such as those characteristic of children with language impairments. Healthy older adults do not regress to fragmented or formulaic speech, two- and three-word utterances, or vague empty non sequiturs, even when dual-task demands are high (Kemper, Herman, & Nartowitz, 2003); rather, they slow down both their actions and their words, and may use fillers, such as "you know" and "well" to segment their speech into smaller production units.

Although allocation of attention seems to be relevant for language development in children (see Golinkoff & Hirsh-Pasek, Chapter 14, this volume), few aspects of the language development of children have been linked to developmental changes in the speed of processing, reductions in processing limitations, gains in inhibition, or improvements in lexical access. There are some exceptions:

1. Speed of processing, particularly of rapid auditory information, has been implicated in delays and disorders of language development (Benasich & Leevers, 2003; Benasich & Tallal, 2002; Tallal, 2003).

2. Working memory limitations have been implicated in a variety of syntactic processing problems associated with intermediate stages of language development (Adams & Willis, 2001; Crain & Shankweiler, 1988, 1990) and may characterize poor readers (Daneman & Blennerhassett, 1984; Engel, Carullo, & Collins, 1991; Shankweiler & Smith, 1984). Working memory limitations have also been implicated in developmental language disorders (Conti-Ramsden & Botting, 2001; Dollaghan & Campbell, 1998; Gathercole & Baddeley, 1990a, 1990b; Montgomery, 1995).

3. Inhibitory deficits have been linked to a variety of developmental disorders including dyslexia (Chiappe, Hasher & Siegal, 2000; Chiappe, Siegal, & Hasher, 2002; Gernsbacher & Robertson, 1995; Gioia, Isquith, Kenworthy,

& Barton, 2002; McNamara & McDaniel, 2004).

4. Word-finding deficits have been associated with dyslexia as well as other language-disorders (Faust, Dimtrovsky, & Davidi, 1997; Faust, Dimtrovsky, & Shacht, 2003; Wiig & Becker-Caplan, 1984).

It is important to know that these linkages are intended to explain significant delays and disorders of language development, rather than normal variation in the rate of acquisition or pattern in the acquisition of specific forms.

References

Adams, A., & Willis, C. (2001). Language processing and working memory: A developmental perspective. In J. Andrade (Ed.), *Working memory in perspective* (pp. 79–100). East Sussex, UK: Psychology Press.

Albert, M. S., Heller, H. S., & Milberg, W. (1988). Changes in naming ability with age. *Psychology and Aging, 3,* 173–178.

Arbuckle, T., & Gold, D. P. (1993). Aging, inhibition, and verbosity. *Journal of Gerontology: Psychological Sciences, 48,* P225–P232.

Benasich, A. A., & Leevers, H. J. (2003). Processing of rapidly presented auditory cues in infancy: Implications for later language development. In H. Hayne & J. W. Fagen (Eds.), *Progress in infancy research* (Vol. 3, pp. 245–288). Mahwah, NJ: Lawrence Erlbaum Associates.

Benasich, A. A., & Tallal, P. (2002). Infant discrimination of rapid auditory cues predicts later language impairment. *Behavioral Brain Research, 136,* 31–49.

Benjamin, B. J. (1988). Changes in speech production and linguistic behavior with aging. In B. Shadden (Ed.), *Communication behavior and aging* (pp. 163–181). Boston: Williams & Wilkins.

Bernstein, B. (1968). Some sociological determinants of perception: An inquiry into sub-cultural differences. In J. A. Fishman (Ed.), *Readings in the sociology of language* (pp. 223–239). The Hague: Mouton.

Bickerton, D. (1981). *Roots of language.* Ann Arbor, MI: Karoma.

Botwinick, J., &. Siegler, I. C. (1980). Intellectual ability among the elderly: Simultaneous cross-sectional and longitudinal comparisons. *Developmental Psychology, 16,* 49–53.

Burke, D. (1997). Language, aging, and inhibitory deficits: Evaluation of a theory. *Journal of Gerontology: Psychological Sciences, 52B,* P254–P264.

Burke, D. M., & Laver, G. D. (1990). Aging and word retrieval: Selective age deficits in language. In E. A. Lovelace (Ed.), *Aging and cognition: Mental processes, self-awareness, and interventions* (pp. 281–300). New York: Elsevier-North Holland.

Burke, D. M., MacKay, D. G., Worthley, J. S., & Wade, E. (1991). On the tip of the tongue: What causes word finding failures in young and older adults. *Journal of Memory and Language, 30,* 542–579.

Caplan, D., & Waters, G. (1999). Verbal working memory and sentence comprehension. *Behavioral and Brain Sciences, 22,* 114–126.

Caplan, D., & Waters, G. (2002). Working memory and connectionist models of memory: A reply to MacDonald and Christiansen (2002). *Psychology Review, 109,* 66–74.

Caporael, L. (1981). The paralanguage of caregiving: Baby talk to the institutionalized aged. *Journal of Personality and Social Psychology, 40,* 876–884.

Caporael, L. R., & Culbertson, G. H. (1986). Verbal response modes of baby talk and other speech at institutions for the aged. *Language and Communication, 6,* 99–112.

Chiappe, P., Hasher, L., & Siegel, L. S. (2000). Working memory, inhibitory control, and reading disability. *Memory and Cognition, 28,* 8–17.

Chiappe, P., Siegel, L. S., & Hasher, L. (2002). Working memory, inhibition and reading skill. In S. P. Shohov (Ed.), *Advances in psychology research* (Vol. 9, pp. 30–51). Huntington, NY: Nova Science Publishers.

Cohen, G. (1979). Language comprehension in old age. *Cognitive Psychology, 11,* 412–429.

Connelly, S. L., Hasher, L., & Zacks, R. T. (1991). Age and reading: The impact of distraction. *Psychology and Aging, 6,* 533–541.

Conti-Ramsden, G., & Botting, N. (2001). Psycholinguistic markers for specific language impairment (SLI). *Journal of Child Psychology and Psychiatry, 42,* 741–748.

Cooper, P. V. (1990). Discourse production and normal aging: Performance on oral picture description tasks. *Journal of Gerontology: Psychological Sciences, 45,* P210–P214.

Crain, S., & Shankweiler, D. (1988). Syntactic complexity and reading acquisition. In A. Davison & G. Green (Eds.), *Critical approaches to readability* (pp. 167–192). Hillsdale, NJ: Lawrence Erlbaum Associates.

Crain, S., & Shankweiler, D. (1990). Explaining failures in spoken language comprehension by children with reading disability. In D. A. Balota, G. B. Flores d'Arcais, & K. Rayner (Eds.), *Comprehension processes in reading* (pp. 529–556). Hillsdale, NJ: Lawrence Erlbaum Associates.

Daneman, M., & Blennerhassett, A. (1984). How to assess the listening comprehension skills of pre-readers. *Journal of Educational Psychology, 76,* 1372–1381.

Davis, G. A. (1984). Effects of aging on normal language. In A. Holland (Ed.), *Language disorders in adults.* San Diego, CA: College-Hill Press.

Dollaghan, C., & Campbell, T. (1998). Nonword repetition and child language impairment. *Journal of Speech, Language, and Hearing Research, 41,* 1136–1146.

Dunn, L. M., & Dunn, L. M. (1997). *Peabody Picture Vocabulary Test—Revised.* Circle Pines, MN, American Guidance Service.

Dywan, J., & Murphy, W. E. (1996). Aging and inhibitory control in text comprehension. *Psychology and Aging, 11,* 199–206.

Eisdorfer, C., & Wilkie, F. (1973). Intellectual changes with advancing age. In L. F. Jarvik, C. Eisdorfer, & J. Blum (Eds.), *Intellectual functioning in adults* (pp. 102–111). New York, Springer.

Emery, O. (1985). Language and aging. *Experimental Aging Research, 11,* 3–60.

Emery, O. (1986). Linguistic decrement in normal aging. *Language and Communication, 6,* 47–64.

Engle, R. W., Carullo, J. J., & Collins, K. W. (1991). Individual differences in working memory for comprehending and following directions. *Journal of Educational Psychology, 84,* 253–262.

Faust, M., Dimitrovsky, L., & Davidi, S. (1997). Naming difficulties in language-disabled children: Preliminary findings with the application of the tip-of-the-tongue paradigm. *Journal of Speech, Language, and Hearing Research, 40,* 1026–1036.

Faust, M., Dimitrovsky, L., & Shacht, T. (2003). Naming difficulties in children with dyslexia: Application of the tip-of-the-tongue paradigm. *Journal of Learning Disabilities, 36,* 203–215.

Gathercole, S. E., & Baddeley, A. (1990a). The role of phonological memory in vocabulary acquisition: A study of young children learning arbitrary names of toys. *British Journal of Psychology, 81,* 439–454.

Gathercole, S. E., & Baddeley, A. D. (1990b). Phonological memory deficits in language disordered children: Is there a causal connection? *Journal of Memory and Language, 29,* 336–360.

Gernsbacher, M. A., & Robertson, R. R. W. (1995). Reading skill and suppression revisited. *Psychological Science, 6,* 165–169.

Gioia, G. A., Isquith, P. K., Kenworthy, L., & Barton, R. M. (2002). Profiles of everyday executive function in acquired and developmental disorders. *Child Neuropsychology, 8,* 121–137.

Grober, E., & Sliwinski, M. (1991). Development and

validation of a model for estimating premorbid verbal intelligence in the elderly. *Journal of Clinical and Experimental Neuropsychology, 13,* 933–949.

Grodzinsky, Y. (1990). *Theoretical perspectives on language deficits.* Cambridge, MA: MIT Press.

Harwood, J., Giles, H., & Ryan, E. B. (1995). Aging, communication, and intergroup theory: Social identity and intergenerational communication. In J. F. Nussbaum & J. Coupland, (Eds.), *Handbook of communication and aging research* (pp. 133–159). Hove, UK: Lawrence Erlbaum Associates.

Hasher, L., & Zacks, R. T. (1988). Working memory, comprehension, and aging: A review and a new view. In G. H. Bower (Ed.), *The psychology of learning and motivation* (Vol. 22, pp. 193–226). New York: Academic Press.

Hasher, L., Zacks, R. T., & May, C. P. (1999). Inhibitory control, circadian arousal, and age. In D. Gopher & A. Koriat (Eds.), *Attention and performance XVII: Cognitive regulation of performance: Interaction of theory and application* (pp. 653–675). Cambridge, MA: MIT Press.

Hassol, L., Margaret, A., & Cameron, N. (1952). The production of language disorganization through personalized distraction. *Journal of Psychology, 33,* 289–299.

Hultsch, D. F., Hertzog, C., Dixon, R. A., & Small, B. J. (1998). *Memory change in the aged.* Cambridge: Cambridge University Press.

Hyltenstam, K., & Obler, L. K. (1989). Introduction. In K. Hyltenstam & L. K. Obler (Eds.), *Bilingualism across the lifespan* (pp. 1–12). Cambridge: Cambridge University Press.

Jackson, J. H. (1958). Evolution and dissolution of the nervous system. In J. Taylor (Ed.), *Selected writings of John Hughlings Jackson* (pp. 191–212). New York: Basic Books.

Jakobson, R. (1941/1968). *Child language, aphasia, and phonological universals.* The Hague: Mouton.

James, L. E., & Burke, D. M. (2000). Phonological priming effects on word retrieval and tip-of-the-tongue experiences in young and older adults. *Journal of Experimental Psychology: Learning, Memory, and Cognition, 26,* 1378–1391.

Jou, J., & Harris, R. J. (1992). The effect of divided attention on speech production. *Bulletin of the Psychonomic Society, 30,* 301–304.

Kemper, S. (1992a). Adults' sentence fragments: Who, what, when, where, and why. *Communication Research, 19,* 332–346.

Kemper, S. (1992b). Language and aging. In F. I. M. Craik & T. A. Salthouse (Eds.), *Handbook of aging and cognition* (pp. 213–270). Hillsdale, NJ: Lawrence Erlbaum Associates.

Kemper, S. (1994). Elderspeak: Speech accommodations to older adults. *Aging and Cognition, 1,* 17–28.

Kemper, S. (1997). Metalinguistic judgments in normal aging and Alzheimer's disease. *Journal of Gerontology: Psychological Sciences, 52B,* P147–P155.

Kemper, S., Crow, A., & Kemtes, K. (2004). Eye fixation patterns of high and low span young and older adults: Down the garden path and back again. *Psychology and Aging, 19,* 157–170.

Kemper, S., Greiner, L. H., Marquis, J., Prenovost, K., & Mitzner, T. (2001). Language decline across the life span: Findings from the Nun Study. *Psychology and Aging, 16,* 227–239.

Kemper, S., & Harden, T. (1999). Disentangling what is beneficial about elderspeak from what is not. *Psychology and Aging, 14,* 656–670.

Kemper, S., Herman, R. E., & Lian, C. H. T. (2003). The costs of doing two things at once for young and older adults: Talking while walking, finger tapping, and ignoring speech or noise. *Psychology and Aging, 18,* 181–192.

Kemper, S., Herman, R.E., & Nartowitz, J. (2003). The costs of doing two things at once for young and older adults: Talking while walking, finger tapping, and ignoring speech or noise. *Psychology and Aging, 18,* 181–192.

Kemper, S., Kynette, D., Rash, S., Sprott, R., & O'Brien, K. (1989). Life-span changes to adults' language: Effects of memory and genre. *Applied Psycholinguistics, 10,* 49–66.

Kemper, S., Othick, M., Warren, J., Gubarchuk, J., & Gerhing, H. (1996). Facilitating older adults' performance on a referential communication task through speech accommodations. *Aging, Neuropsychology, and Cognition, 3,* 37–55.

Kemper, S., & Rash, S. (1988). Speech and writing across the life-span. In M. M. Gruneberg, P. E. Morris, & R. N. Sykes (Eds.), *Practical aspects of memory: Current research and issues* (pp. 107–112). Chichester, UK: Wiley.

Kemper, S., Thompson, M., & Marquis, J. (2001). Longitudinal change in language production: Effects of aging and dementia on grammatical complexity and propositional density. *Psychology and Aging, 16,* 600–614.

Kemper, S., Vandeputte, D., Rice, K., Cheung, H., & Gubarchuk, J. (1995). Speech adjustments to aging during a referential communication task. *Journal of Language and Social Psychology, 14,* 40–59.

Kemtes, K. A., & Kemper, S. (1997). Younger and older adults' on-line processing of syntactic ambiguities. *Psychology and Aging, 12,* 362–371.

Kynette, D., & Kemper, S. (1986). Aging and the loss of grammatical forms: A cross-sectional study of language performance. *Language and Communication, 6,* 43–49.

Kwong See, S. T., & Ryan, E. B. (1996). Cognitive mediation of discourse processing in later life. *Journal of Speech Language Pathology and Audiology, 20,* 109–117.

McNamara, D. S., & McDaniel, M. A. (2004). Suppressing irrelevant information: Knowledge activation or inhibition? *Journal of Experimental Psychology: Learning, Memory, and Cognition, 30,* 465–482.

Montgomery, J. (1995). Sentence comprehension in children with specific language impairment: The role of phonological working memory. *Journal of Speech and Hearing Research, 38,* 187–199.

Morrow, D. G., Stine-Morrow, E. A. L., Leirer, V. O., Andrassy, J. M., & Kahn, J. (1997). The role of reader age and focus of attention in creating situation models from narratives. *Journal of Gerontology. Series B: Psychological Sciences and Social Sciences, 52B,* P73–P80.

Obler, L. K. (1980). Narrative discourse style in the elderly. In L. K. Obler & M. L. Albert (Eds.), *Language and communication in the elderly* (pp. 75–90). Lexington, MA: Heath.

Pye, C., Cheung, H., & Kemper, S. (1992). Islands at eighty. In H. Goodluck & M. Rochemont (Eds.), *Island constraints: Theory, acquisition, and processing.* Dordrecht: Reidel.

Ryan, E. B., Giles, H., Bartolucci, G., & Henwood, K. (1986). Psycholinguistic and social psychological components of communication by and with the elderly. *Language and Communication, 6,* 1–24.

Salthouse, T. A. (1992). *Mechanisms of aging-cognition relations in adulthood.* Hillsdale, NJ: Lawrence Erlbaum Associates.

Schaie, K. W. (1996). *Intellectual development in adulthood: The Seattle Longitudinal Study.* New York: Cambridge University Press.

Shankweiler, D., & Smith, S. A. (1984). Repetition and comprehension of spoken sentences by reading-disabled children. *Brain and Language, 23,* 241–257.

Shewan, C. M., & Henderson, V. L. (1988). Analysis of spontaneous language in the older normal population. *Journal of Communication Disorders, 21,* 139–154.

Shipley, W. C. (1940). A self-administered scale for measuring intellectual impairment and deterioration. *Journal of Psychology, 9,* 371–377.

Snowdon, D. A., Greiner, L. A., Kemper, S., Nanayakkara, N., & Mortimer, J. A. (1999). Linguistic ability in early life and longevity: Findings from the Nun Study. In J. M. Robine, B. Forette, C. Franschesci & M. Allard (Eds.), *The paradoxes of longevity* (pp. 103–113). Amsterdam: Springer.

Snowdon, D. A., Kemper, S. J., Mortimer, J. A., Greiner, L. H., Wekstein, D. R., & Markesbery, W. R. (1996). Cognitive ability in early life and cognitive function and Alzheimer's disease in late life: Findings from the Nun study. *Journal of the American Medical Association, 275,* 528–532.

Soederberg Miller, L. M., & Stine-Morrow, E. A. L. (1998). Aging and the effects of knowledge on on-line reading strategies. *Journal of Gerontology: Psychological Sciences, 53B,* P223–P233.

Southwood, M. H., & Dagenais, P. (2001). The role of attention in apraxic errors. *Clinical Linguistics and Phonetics, 15,* 113–116.

Stine, E. A. L. (1990). On-line processing of written text by younger and older adults. *Psychology and Aging, 5,* 68–78.

Stine, E. A. L., Cheung, H., & Henderson, D. (1995). Adult age differences in the on-line processing of new concepts in discourse. *Aging and Cognition, 2,* 1–18.

Stine, E. A. L., & Hindman, J. (1994). Age differences in reading time allocation for propositionally dense sentences. *Aging and Cognition, 1,* 2–16.

Stine, E. L., Wingfield, A., & Myers, S. D. (1990). Age differences in processing information from television news: The effects of bisensory augmentation. *Journal of Gerontology, 45,* P1–P8.

Stine, E. L. A., Wingfield, A., & Poon, L. W. (1986). How much and how fast: Rapid processing of spoken language in later adulthood. *Psychology and Aging, 1,* 303–311.

Stine-Morrow, E. A. L., Loveless, M. K., & Soederberg, L. M. (1996). Resource allocation in on-line reading by younger and older adults. *Psychology and Aging, 11,* 475–486.

Stine Morrow, E. A. L., Milinder, L. A., Pullara, O., & Herman, B. (2001). Patterns of resource allocation are reliable among younger and older readers. *Psychology and Aging, 16,* 69–84.

Stine-Morrow, E. A. L., Ryan, S., & Leonard, J. S. (2000). Age differences in on-line syntactic processing. *Experimental Aging Research, 26,* 315–322.

Tallal, P. (2003). Language learning disabilities: Integrating research approaches. *Current Directions in Psychological Science, 12,* 206–211.

Tun, P. A., O'Kane, G., & Wingfield, A. (2002). Distraction by competing speech in young and older adult listeners. *Psychology and Aging, 17,* 453–467.

Tun, P. A., & Wingfield, A. (1999). One voice too many: Adult age differences in language processing with different types of distracting sounds. *Journals of Gerontology. Series B: Psychological Sciences and Social Sciences, 54B,* P317–P327.

Waters, G. S., & Caplan, D. (1996a). The capacity theory

of sentence comprehension: Critique of Just and Carpenter (1992). *Psychological Review, 103,* 761–772.

Waters, G. S., & Caplan, D. (1996b). The measurement of verbal working memory capacity and its relation to reading comprehension. *Quarterly Journal of Experimental Psychology, 49A,* 51–79.

Waters, G., & Caplan, D. (2001). Age, working memory, and on-line syntactic processing in sentence comprehension. *Psychology and Aging, 16,* 128–144.

Waters, G. S., & Caplan, D. (1997). Working memory and on-line sentence comprehension in patients with Alzheimer's disease. *Journal of Psycholinguistic Research, 26,* 337–400.

Wechsler, D. (1958). *The measurement and appraisal of adult intelligence.* Baltimore: Williams & Wilkins.

White, K. K., & Abrams, L. (2002). Does priming specific syllables during tip-of-the-tongue states facilitate word retrieval in older adults? *Psychology and Aging, 17,* 226–235.

Wiig, E. H., & Becker-Caplan, L. (1984). Linguistic retrieval strategies and word-finding difficulties among children with language disabilities. *Topics in Language Disorders, 4,* 1–18.

Wingfield, A., & Ducharme, J. L. (1999). Effects of age and passage difficulty on listening-rate preferences for time-altered speech. *Journals of Gerontology. Series B: Psychological Sciences and Social Sciences, 54B,* 199–202.

Wingfield, A., Lahar, C. J., & Stine, E. L. (1989). Age and decision strategies in running memory for speech: Effects of prosody and linguistic structure. *Journal of Gerontology: Psychological Sciences, 44,* P106–P113.

Wingfield, A., Tun, P. A., & Rosen, M. J. (1995). Age differences in veridical and reconstructive recall of syntactically and randomly segmented speech. *Journal of Gerontology: Psychological Sciences, 50B,* P257–P266.

Yngve, V. (1960). A model and a hypothesis for language structure. *Proceedings of the American Philosophical Society, 10,* 444–466.

Yoon, C., May, C. P., & Hasher, L. (1998). *Aging, circadian arousal patterns, and cognition.* Philadelphia, PA: Psychology Press.

Zacks, R., & Hasher, L. (1997). Cognitive gerontology and attentional inhibition: A reply to Burke and McDowd. *Journal of Gerontology: Psychological Sciences, 52B,* P274–P283.

Zurif, E., Swinney, D., Prather, P., Wingfield, A., & Brownell, H. (1995). The allocation of memory resources during sentence comprehension: Evidence from the elderly. *Journal of Psycholinguistic Research, 24,* 165–182.

16

Language Meaning and Form Disorders

Maureen Dennis

Language can be affected by injury to the immature brain, including congenital malformations originating at various points during prenatal brain development (Fletcher, Barnes, & Dennis, 2002) and acquired brain disorders caused by stroke, neoplasm, or trauma (Dennis, 2003). Unlike adults, children may be born with significant compromise of the brain mechanisms important for language. Like adults, children may exhibit language disorders from injury to the central nervous system after a period of normal development. Childhood-acquired language disorder, or childhood-acquired aphasia, refers to language impairment evident after a period of normal language acquisition that is precipitated by, or associated with, an identified form of brain insult.

Children with brain injury exhibit a range of language disorders. Some of these are different from those of adults with aphasia and language disturbances; others are similar to those in adults, albeit with different base frequencies. Studies of language disorders following congenital and acquired brain injury in children have provided not only descriptive information about language but also grist for theoretical discussions about whether meaning and form are separable, the nature of semantic representations, and the place of language in the functional architecture of cognition. This paper is concerned with three questions: What is the range of meaning and form disorders in children with brain injury? How do patterns of meaning and form breakdown bear on some general theoretical questions about the derivation of meaning? Are similar or different processes involved in the breakdown of meaning after brain injury in childhood and in normal or aberrant aging?

DISORDERS OF MEANING AFTER BRAIN INJURY IN CHILDREN

Disorders of meaning in children with brain injury are diverse. They range from severe verbal auditory agnosia for common sounds, such as a dog barking, or a doorbell ringing (Cooper & Ferry, 1978) to problems deriving the meaning of words (Dennis, 1992) and deficits in the production of extended oral or written texts (Barnes & Dennis, 1998).

Symptoms of fluent adult aphasia have provided clues to how word meanings are generated. Logorrhea, verbal stereotypies, perseverations, neologisms (sequences of sounds that do not form words), jargon, circumlocutions, phonemic paraphasias (omissions and/ or misordering of phonemes), and semantic paraphasias (words semantically related to the target) were once thought to be rare in children (Alajouanine & Lhermitte, 1965), but aphasic symptoms in children are actually quite varied (Van Hout, 1991), with many adult aphasic syndromes having been described in children, albeit with different base frequencies (Rapin, 1995).

Lexical Meaning

According to standard models of speech production (Levelt, 1989), producing semantically appropriate words requires accessing word forms as well as word-sound planning in order for the representation of a word sound to be converted into a form suitable for production.

Impairments in *accessing word forms* from concepts are exhibited by failure to produce a word in response to a picture, definition, or context, despite intact semantic and phonological processing (evidenced by preserved ability to describe, categorize, or repeat the target word). Several forms of childhood brain injury are associated with word-finding difficulties whereby a word can be produced in response to a picture but not to semantic cues, such as "What lives in the jungle, has big floppy ears and a trunk?" (Dennis, 1992).

Indications of a disorder in accessing word forms include pauses, neologisms, semantic paraphasias, and circumlocutions. The fluent form of childhood aphasia, associated with lesions to the posterior left hemisphere cortical language areas (Klein, Masur, Farber, Shinnar, & Rapin, 1992), results in anomia, word-finding deficits, semantic paraphasias, and circumlocutions (Dennis, 1980b; Hynd, Leathem, Semrud-Clikeman, Hern, & Wenner, 1995). Children with aphasia from head injury exhibit a variety of language symptoms in the acute stage that resolve over time (with anomia and reduced verbal fluency being consistent long-term deficits).

Impairments in word-sound planning are demonstrated by substitutions involving phones with dissimi-lar distinctive features, and/or phonemic paraphasias. Brain-injured children's word-finding errors include phonemic paraphasias, phonemic jargon, and neologisms (Dennis, 1980b; Van Dongen & Paquier, 1991).

Modality-specific anomia has been described in children. Reading and spelling, as well as tactile object identification, may be relatively preserved with cortical lesions in the left-hemispheric posterior language areas in children with anomia (Dennis, 1980b; Hynd et al., 1995), suggesting a problem activating auditory word forms from modality-specific semantic systems.

The adult aphasia literature includes a series of *category-specific semantic disorders*, with reports of selective semantic impairment of particular concepts, such as those related to animate things and food compared to man-made objects (e.g., Sartori & Job, 1988). The data from children are limited (one case report suggested relative loss of body part naming relative to other forms of naming and to body part identification; Dennis, 1976). Interpretations of the data on category specificity are evolving (see Martin & Caramazza, 2003). Earlier views of category-specific deficits suggested that conceptual knowledge is structured by content; a more recent interpretation is that semantic structure concerns, not the manner in which semantic concepts are represented, but the kind of processing required (Tyler & Moss, 2003).

Figurative Meaning

Idioms are nonliteral phrases (e.g., "kick the bucket") whose figurative meanings ("to die") cannot be derived from the literal meanings of their individual words (*kick* and *bucket*). Idioms are ubiquitous, and about four figures of speech, most of them idioms, occur in each minute of conversation (Brinton, Fujiki, & Mackey, 1985; Pollio, Barlow, Fine, & Pollio, 1977). Idioms are an important part of conversational and instructional language (Hoffman & Honeck, 1980; Lazar, Warr-Leeper, Nicholson, & Johnson, 1989; Pollio et al., 1977). Idiom comprehension is impaired in children with spina bifida meningomyelocele (Huber-Okrainec, Blaser, & Dennis, 2005) who are able to understand the individual words in the idiom, but not its figurative meaning.

Textual Meaning

The derivation of meaning in texts and narrative requires multi-layered comprehension (van Dijk &

Kintsch, 1983). The flow of topics, narrative script, and the plotline form the schematic structure. The text macrostructure concerns the relations among sentences sharing a topic, and deficits in macrostructure are usually manifest as failures of text coherence. Text microstructure concerns local sentential relations, and these are usually manifest as failure of text cohesion. A variety of brain insults in children are associated with problems in the derivation of meaning in texts and narratives.

Problems in *schematic structure* are common in children with brain injury. Both children with head injury and children with hydrocephalus, most with spina bifida meningomyelocele, have deficits in producing and understanding social scripts (Chapman et al., 1992; Dennis & Barnes, 1990).

Problems in *text macrostructure* are also common in children with brain injury. Children with head injury have difficulty establishing coherence among the topics in a narrative (Chapman et al., 2004). Children with hydrocephalus, most with spina bifida meningomyelocele, produce ambiguous and off-topic material and a more limited number of core propositions than controls, which makes their narratives poorly incoherent, off-topic, and lacking in ease of processing, clarity, and economy (Barnes & Dennis, 1998; Dennis, Jacennik, & Barnes, 1994).

Off-topic speech occurs in both children with spina bifida meningomyelocele and normally aging adults (Arbuckle & Gold, 1993). The functional effect of off-topic narration seems to be different: in aging adults, it increases the communicative value of the narrative and expresses distinctive communicative goals (James, Burke, Austin, & Hulme, 1998); in children with spina bifida meningomyelocele, it decreases textual coherence and increases comprehension demands for the listener.

Problems in *text microstructure* are also common in children with brain injury. Children with left hemidecortication for congenital left hemisphere damage have impaired referential cohesion in texts: they state the referent name rather than pronominalizing it, produce free-floating pronouns not tied to a referent, and fail to sustain a chain of anaphoric reference (Lovett, Dennis, & Newman, 1986). Children with early focal brain injury also show impairments in referential cohesion (Reilly, Bates, & Marchman, 1998). Compared to controls, the narratives of children with hydrocephalus, most with spina bifida meningomyelocele, include referentially ambiguous material (Dennis et al., 1994).

DISORDERS OF LANGUAGE FORM AFTER BRAIN INJURY IN CHILDREN

Role Disorders

Syntactic structures are representations that assign important aspects of sentence meaning (Caplan & Hildebrandt, 1988), especially of functional roles (who is acting, who is being acted on). The adult left hemisphere has a strong association with syntax; functionally, it constructs syntactically licensed dependencies in real time (Swinney, Zurif, Prather, & Love, 1996) and assigns syntactic structure during language comprehension (Caplan, 1992; Caplan & Hildebrandt, 1988; Stromswold, Caplan, Alpert, & Rausch, 1996).

Individuals who are unable to assign and interpret syntactic structure have a syntactic comprehension disorder, the hallmark of which is inability to assign aspects of sentence meaning correctly in sentences that are logically and pragmatically semantically reversible when interpreted solely by a lexical-pragmatic route (e.g., Caramazza & Zurif, 1976). Some patients with syntactic comprehension deficits are able to construct relevant syntactic structures even when they fail to map the products of these constructions to establish meaning (e.g., Linebarger, 1990).

As with the adult left hemisphere, the immature left hemisphere has a strong association with syntax. Compared to those with early right hemisphere damage and hemispherectomy, individuals with congenital damage to, and removal of, the left hemisphere are slower and less accurate in understanding sentences with noncanonical word orders (e.g., reversible passive sentences such as "the dog is chased by the cat") in which meaning is provided by syntactic structure but not semantic plausibility, whether comparisons are made between hemidecorticate groups with early lateralized hemispheric damage from varying pathologies (Dennis & Kohn, 1975) or from a single pathology (Dennis & Whitaker, 1976). The syntactic comprehension deficit after left hemisphere damage is evident whether comparisons are made to chronological age (Aram, Ekelman, Rose, & Whitaker, 1985; Dennis, 1980a; Dennis & Kohn, 1975; Dennis & Whitaker, 1976; Paquier & Van Dongen, 1993), mental age (Stark, Bleile, Brandt, Freeman, & Vining, 1995), or brain-intact co-twins (Feldman, Holland, & Keefe, 1989; Hetherington & Dennis, 2004). Syntactic comprehension deficits for noncanonical word orders are also evident when only part of the left hemisphere is removed but speech control has shifted to the right hemisphere (Kohn, 1980).

Syntactic comprehension disorders in adults arise from at least two separable impairments (Caplan & Hildebrandt, 1988). The first is a specific disturbance with parsing processes and/or linguistic representations, including problems with functional argument structure and difficulties with noncanonical orders of sentence constituents (possibly because of defective representations or procedures for handling the traces of moved semantic roles in sentences like passives and object relatives with noncanonical word orders; Berndt, Mitchum, & Wayland, 1997). The second is a reduction in the computational resources available for syntactic comprehension. For one linguistic construction, the restricted relative clause, the computational resource account seems to provide a better explanation for the difficulties of agrammatic aphasics (Crain, Ni, & Shankweiler, 2001).

Individuals with hemispherectomy for early left hemisphere injury appear to have a combined impairment. They are insensitive to the role of function words that cue syntactic structure, even on metacognitive tasks with no time constraints (Dennis, 1980a), which suggests that they have trouble constructing functional argument structures. In addition, they make fewer errors on noncanonical sentences when they respond slowly (Dennis & Kohn, 1975), which suggests a limitation in processing resources whereby performance deficits become attenuated when more resources are allocated to the task of comprehension.

Morphology Disorders

Components of the language production system are important for producing freestanding function words and inflectional morphemes in sentences. These morphological components are different from, say, vocabulary words because they do not bear nonemphatic stress in derived words or sentence structures and they fail to follow regular word formation processes. The speech of adult aphasic patients with anterior lesions is often agrammatic, with a breakdown of sentence structure and the omission or misuse of grammatical morphemes, even while access to content words, such as verbs and nouns, remains relatively unimpaired. In adults, a disturbance affecting the production of inflections and derivational morphemes has been termed *agrammatism* or *paragrammatism*,

and the characteristic is the omission or substitution of function words and affixes (Menn, Obler, & Goodglass, 1990).

The language of children with hemispherectomy has been analyzed with respect to functional morphology. One focus has been the capacity of each remaining hemisphere to acquire the inflectional (I) system and its subcategories: tense, subject agreement, and object agreement. Compared to those with right hemispherectomy, children with left hemispherectomy use a restricted range and number of I-system morphemes, and have particular problem with auxiliaries, despite intact syntactic and morphological structures of other types (Curtiss & Schaeffer, 1997). Of interest, almost all of the children did exhibit some I-system structures in their speech, so that the deficit is a relative one. Children with left hemispherectomy also have problems producing tag questions (such as "Isn't it?"), which involve inflectional morphology (Dennis & Whitaker, 1976), a deficit that also occurs in some adults with paragrammatism. In agreement with data highlighting the selective vulnerability of particular aspects of syntactic structure to various kinds of language pathology (Platzak, 2001), the data on tense, subject agreement, and object agreement suggest a high level of vulnerability of the inflectional system to developmental and adult acquired language pathology.

MEANING DISORDERS AND DISSOCIATIONS WITHIN LANGUAGE

The data on meaning disorders, described above, bear on some theoretical dissociations within the language system.

Literal and Figurative Lexicons

Studies of figurative language have identified two types of idioms, one processed like literal language, the other requiring semantic decomposition. Nondecomposable idioms (e.g., "kick the bucket") are learned and represented in the mental lexicon as units; being syntactically and lexically inflexible, they depend on context for interpretation (Gibbs, 1991; Huber-Okrainec & Dennis, 2005). Children acquire decomposable idioms, in which the individual lexical items contribute to the figurative meaning (e.g., the words in "talk a mile a minute" suggest a fast speech rate), in a relatively context-independent manner (Huber-Okrainec & Dennis, 2005).

Nondecomposable and decomposable idioms are at least partly distinct, with semantically decomposable idioms, but not semantically nondecomposable idioms, sharing some of the processing characteristics of literal language. The idea of two forms of figurative language, one sharing more features of literal language than the other, is supported by studies of idiom comprehension in congenital brain injury. Compared to age peers, children with spina bifida meningomyelocele can understand decomposable idioms, but not nondecomposable idioms (Huber-Okrainec et al., 2005).

Inferencing and Text Representation

Inferencing is a series of processes that, collectively, effect the derivation of text meaning. Knowledge-based or coherence inferencing occurs when semantic knowledge is integrated with lexical content to interpret the text. Elaborative inferencing (which is not required for text coherence) creates a richer mental model of the situation described by the text (Morrow, Bower, & Greenspan, 1990; Whitney, 1987).

Inferencing problems can arise from limitations in semantic knowledge. For instance, lower IQ children knowledgeable about soccer make more inferences about soccer stories than do higher IQ children with less soccer knowledge (Yekovich, Walker, Ogle, & Thompson, 1990). To equalize semantic knowledge, children have been required to make coherent and elaborative inferences using novel knowledge about an invented world (Barnes, Dennis, & Haefele-Kalvaitis, 1996) whose objects have counterfactual properties (flower petals are hot, leaves on trees are pink). Children with hydrocephalus, most with spina bifida meningomyelocele, can learn new knowledge about the invented world, but they do not use their knowledge to make coherence and elaborative text inferences (Barnes & Dennis, 1998). Although semantic memory and text comprehension deficits often co-exist (e.g., in Alzheimer's Disease; Rochon, Kavé, Cupit, Jopel, & Winocur, 2004), inferencing failures can occur in individuals who possess the requisite semantic knowledge.

Text inferences enhance both the creation of a propositional text representation, through coherence inferences, and the creation of a mental model of the situation described by the text, through elaborative inferences (Zwann, Langston, & Graesser, 1995). Compared to controls, children with closed head injury make coherence but not elaborative inferences (Barnes & Dennis, 2001; Dennis & Barnes, 2001), which suggests that brain damage can separately affect these two forms of text representation.

HOW DO DATA FROM CHILDHOOD LANGUAGE DISORDERS BEAR ON THEORIES ABOUT COGNITION AND LANGUAGE?

The data on meaning and form disorders bear on some theoretical issues concerning the interface between language and cognition.

Word Decoding, Processing Speed, and Reading Comprehension

In the course of normal development, word decoding and reading comprehension are yoked: typically, good decoders understand the meaning of texts while poor decoders do not (Adams, 1990; Perfetti, 1985; Shankweiler, 1989); accordingly, the most common cause of poor reading comprehension is poor word decoding (Carr & Levy, 1990). The *reading bottleneck* hypothesis suggests a less direct link between reading decoding and reading comprehension; in this view, slow word reading interferes with comprehension because inefficient decoding pre-empts processing resources for understanding and integrating text (LaBerge & Samuels, 1974; Perfetti, 1985).

Children with closed head injury are rate-disabled readers, being slow but accurate in word decoding; importantly, their decoding speed directly predicts their level of reading comprehension (Barnes, Dennis, & Wilkinson, 1999). In contrast, children with hydrocephalus, most with spina bifida meningomyelocele, decode words as rapidly as controls (although they do not demonstrate a spelling-sound regularity effect); for them, decoding speed contributes little to reading comprehension beyond word decoding accuracy (Barnes, Faulkner, & Dennis, 2001). These data show two distinct decoding accuracy-decoding fluency-reading comprehension patterns: in one, fluency directly determines the level of reading comprehension; in the other, reading comprehension is not related to early-stage processing deficits in word recognition speed, but rather to broader inferencing and discourse deficits.

The Lexicon and Declarative Memory, Syntax, and Procedural Memory

Studies of adult aphasia and studies of normal adults using behavioral and electrophysiological measures suggest that the processing of language form (e.g., sentence structure) differs from the processing of meaning. Damage to perisylvian areas of the left hemisphere disrupts syntax; conversely, left hemisphere damage that spares this region and disrupts lexical-semantic function is associated with preserved sensitivity to obligatory syntactic dependencies (Dogil, Haider, Schaner-Wolles, & Husmann, 1995). A recent functional magnetic resonance imaging study showed that form errors (e.g., "Trees can grew") trigger increased activation in the left inferior frontal area (Broca's area), whereas meaning anomalies (e.g., "Trees can eat") result in superior temporal and middle and superior frontal activation (Ni et al., 2000).

Cutting across the division of the brain into language and other cognitive systems is a division into two major types of memory system (Squire, Knowlton, & Musen, 1993), one a declarative system underlying the learning and storage of information about facts and events that is subserved by a medial temporal circuit connected with the temporal and parietal neocortex, the other one a procedural system for the learning and processing of motor, perceptual, and cognitive skills, subserved by basal ganglia circuits connected largely with frontal cortex.

The declarative-procedural distinction in adult human memory has been related to the two major components of language: form and meaning (Ullman et al., 1997). The argument is that, given that word forms are like facts in being arbitrary, the declarative memory system may subserve words as well as facts and events, and given that rules are like skills in requiring the coordination of procedures in real time, the procedural memory system may process grammatical rules as well as motor and perceptual skills Although there are different views about whether regular and irregular past tense forms of verbs are both computed by rules (Chomsky & Halle, 1968) or by connectionist associative memory (MacWhinney & Leinbach, 1991), the study hypothesized that irregular past-tense verb forms are memorized, while regular forms (verb stem + *ed*) are generated by a rule that comprises two operations: copying the stem and adding a suffix. Patients with relative damage to temporal or parietal neocortex, and with impairments of declarative memory (Alzheimer's disease) or lexical memory (posterior aphasia), overgeneralized the past-tense suffix and had more difficulty converting irregular verbs to past-tense forms than they did converting regular or novel verbs. Patients with damage to the frontal-basal ganglia system, and with general impairments of procedures (Parkinson's disease) or with agrammatism (anterior aphasia), showed the opposite pattern.

The broad dissociation between form and procedural memory, on the one hand, and meaning and semantic memory, on the other, is evident in children with brain injury. Despite a range of cognitive and language problems in the semantic and pragmatic domains (Fletcher et al., 2002), children with spina bifida meningomyelocele have intact procedural learning and memory (Edelstein et al., 2004), as well as relatively intact ability to assign thematic roles in syntactic comprehension tasks (Dennis, Hendrick, Hoffman, & Humphreys, 1987). The opposite dissociation is also demonstrable after childhood acquired brain injury. A recent study compared recovery of lost language skills and development of new language in 13-year-old identical twins, one of which had sustained an arteritic stroke to the left hemisphere language areas at age 7 (Hetherington & Dennis, 2004). Compared to his co-twin, the twin with the stroke showed full recovery of semantic memory and word production, although he had persisting impairments in tag-question production and the ability to assign thematic roles in syntactic comprehension tasks. Taken together, these data suggest an association between the procedural system and grammar, and a dissociation between the procedural system and semantics, within a form of congenital brain injury, and, further, an association between recovery of semantic memory and word finding and a dissociation between recovery of semantic memory and the persistence of syntactic impairments in childhood acquired stroke. This issue merits further exploration in children with brain injury, especially with material such as regular and irregular verb tense forms.

ACQUISITION AND DISSOLUTION: THE BREAKDOWN OF LANGUAGE AFTER BRAIN INJURY IN CHILDREN COMPARED TO NORMAL AND ABERRANT AGING

Interest in the relation between language development and language dissolution is long standing. In his

Croonian lectures to the Royal College of Physicians in March 1884, John Hughlings Jackson (1884/1958) proposed that the language of adults with aphasia represented a relapse to an early stage of normal language development. The linguist Roman Jacobson (1968) subsequently argued that the order in which speech sounds were eliminated in aphasia is the mirror image of the order of normal acquisition, and also that the order in which speech sounds are restored during recovery from aphasia corresponds to the sequence of their development. These regression hypotheses, however, have found only limited support from an analysis of language development (Dennis & Wiegel-Crump, 1979) and language breakdown in Broca's aphasia (Grodzinsky, 2000).

The Meaning versus Form Dissociation

Perhaps more interesting than whether pathological language loss and normal language acquisition are mirror images is whether child and adult language disorders fractionate along the lines of meaning and form.

Because of differences in the pathologies that produce language impairment in children and adults (Dennis, 2003), the clearest comparisons are those between similar pathologies, such as that between children and adults who have both sustained arteritic strokes. Language disorders in child and adult stroke with similar pathology, generally from arteritis, are strikingly similar, suggesting that, as Caplan and Waters (Chapter 17, this volume) put it, focal pathology trumps age as the determinant of language outcome.

Many forms of acquired brain injury in children (from stroke, tumor, or trauma) occur after a period of normal language development; in those instances, the dissolution of language occurs along many of the same fault lines as in adults. Several of the acquired brain injury conditions that affect the derivation and expression of meaning leave morphology and syntactic comprehension relatively unaffected (Dennis, 2003). In semantic dementia, the severe and continual degradation in semantic knowledge occurs in the context of preserved syntactic comprehension (Rochon et al., 2004). In the final novel of Iris Murdoch, an individual of exceptional language expertise, Alzheimer's disease disrupted semantics (e.g., lexical diversity) but not syntax (Garrard, Maloney, Hodges, & Patterson, 2005). To be sure, the lexicon and grammar interact in normal adults, and selective language vulnerabili-

ties (e.g., in the function words of grammar) can be exhibited by normal individuals under conditions of perceptual degradation or cognitive overload; all of these results have been used to argue against a strictly modular distinction between lexicon and grammar (Bates & Goodman, 1997). The broad distinction between meaning and form, however, does seem robustly evident in childhood acquired aphasia, adult aphasia, and dementia.

Meaning in Early Brain Damage, Aging, and Dementia

Congenital perturbations of brain development find no easy parallel in adults with acquired, focal brain lesions. For example, the issue of how phonemic paraphasias reveal phonological structure in individuals with stroke and pre-stroke normal language function is not a meaningful question in children who have had no such history. Proto-declarative pointing in adults with lobar strokes, which has not been reported, would be a meaningful comparison for the children.

For children with congenital brain damage, a more theoretically interesting comparison is the one between the acquisition and the dissolution of meaning in individuals with diffuse or multi-focal brain injury—that is, between some forms of congenital brain injuries and dementia. The question of semantic representation in texts provides the basis for a comparison between development and aging, with respect to both capacity constraints and comprehension mechanisms.

Capacity Constraints on Meaning: Working Memory

Understanding sentences and texts is subject to capacity constraints, and text comprehension requires active memory for meaning construction (Clifton & Duffy, 2001; van den Broek, Young, Tzeng, & Linderholm, 1999). Because texts extend over time, with semantic representations being iteratively modified by reactivating old information and linking it with incoming information, working memory is a capacity-limited component of many comprehension models (e.g., Kintsch, 1988; van den Broek et al., 1999).

Capacity constraints limit comprehension over the lifespan: in normal and abnormal development, and in normal and aberrant aging. Sentence and text comprehension is impaired in both spina bifida meningomyelocele (e.g., Dennis & Barnes, 1993) and

Alzheimer's disease (Rochon, Waters, & Caplan, 1994), with comprehension deficits being driven, at least in part, by capacity limitations. Children with hydrocephalus, most with spina bifida meningomyelo-cele, are more disadvantaged than controls by greater textual distance between sentences to be integrated, indicating problems in holding semantic information in working memory (Barnes, Faulkner, Wilkinson, & Dennis, 2004). Individuals with Alzheimer's disease have working-memory impairments that are related to the ability to map the meanings of sentences on to depictions of events in the world (Rochon, Waters, & Caplan, 2000). Working memory, it appears, helps to link semantic information and its source, and to inte-grate distant information across text segments. Work-ing-memory limitations are therefore associated with poor text comprehension performance.

Comprehension Mechanisms: Semantic Activation and Suppression

In general, aging is associated with considerable con-stancy in activating semantic knowledge (e.g., Burke, 1997; MacKay & Abrams, 1998). Semantic priming effects (and also mediated semantic priming effects) are as large in older as in younger adults (Myerson, Ferraro, Hale, & Lima, 1992; Bennett & McEvoy, 1999). Certainly, several forms of semantic knowledge seem to be preserved in abnormal aging. Individuals with Alzheimer's disease, who have problems in se-mantic memory, are able to understand idioms, both absolutely, compared to controls, and relatively, com-pared to their own literal language skills. Also, idiom comprehension does not worsen at a later stage of the disease (Papagno, 2001). These individuals can also explain idioms correctly (Papagno, Lucchelli, Muggia, & Rizzo, 2003), although they are inconsis-tent at identifying idioms in all testing paradigms (Papagno et al., 2003; Kempler, Van Lancker, & Read, 1988).

Inhibitory control emerges during development (Harnishfeger, 1995) and declines with normal aging (May, Zacks, Hasher, & Multhaup, 1999). On the other hand, some automatic inhibitory processes, such as inhibition of return, are evident early in life and are spared in normal aging, and some forms of response suppression show age constancy.

Suppression is that aspect of inhibitory control preventing no-longer-relevant information from re-maining activated. Suppression is an active process, not simply a passive decay, and one that is driven by top-down semantic representations (Gernsbacher, Keysar, Robertson, & Werner, 2001). Suppression uses mental resources; for example, the inhibition of in-appropriate lexical interpretations puts demands on cognitive processes (Tompkins, Lehman Blake, Baumgaertner, & Fassbinder, 2002).

The processes involved in understanding meaning have been studied in online paradigms that separate activation and suppression processes. Unfolding over time, an initial meaning construction phase involves passive activation of word meaning without respect to the context; typically, more semantic information is activated than will be required to represent the text (Schmalhofer, McDaniel, & Keefe, 2002). In a later, integration phase, contextually irrelevant meanings are suppressed or their activation is not sustained, and appropriate meanings are enhanced (Gernsbacher, 1990).

Studies using an online lexical ambiguity paradigm have explored semantic representations in children with hydrocephalus, most with spina bifida meningo-myelocele, and typically developing age peers. The meaning of ambiguous words (e.g., *spade*) was mea-sured in different sentence contexts and at different time points during online processing (Barnes et al., 2004). For each group, both meanings (*shovel* and *playing card*) were activated immediately after read-ing the word, and each group used context to enhance activation of context-appropriate meaning. Unlike the control group, however, the hydrocephalus group continued to show interference from the contextually inappropriate meaning. Failure to suppress contex-tually irrelevant meaning was associated with poor text comprehension, in agreement with the find-ings in adults that active suppression is important for both literal and figurative language comprehen-sion (Gernsbacher & Faust, 1991; Gernsbacher & Robertson, 1999).

Deficient suppression may not only preempt other comprehension processing resources but also provide incomplete input to mental computations that gener-ate a well-specific semantic representation (Tompkins, Lehman Blake, Baumgartner, & Fassbinder, 2001). Children with spina bifida meningomyelocele have poorly specified semantic representations that contain extraneous, contextually irrelevant information. This might explain the longstanding observation (Taylor, 1961) that their conversational language is referentially underspecified and tangential. The consequences of impaired semantic representation are considerable. Semantic representations may be well specified or underspecified, the latter form of shallow parsing being sufficient for some tasks, such as generating an index or chatting at a cocktail party, although not for others, such as providing or understanding specific instructions, communicating referentially detailed information, or academic learning (Sanford & Sturt, 2002).

Suppression Deficits in Congenital Brain Injury, Normal Aging, and Dementia: Common Mechanisms or Phenocopies?

Semantic activation seems resistant, not only to brain injury at various points in the life span but also to the processes of normal and abnormal aging. Language disorders in normal aging have been argued to represent deficits in retrieving phonological and orthographic forms rather than impairments of semantic representations per se (e.g., Burke, MacKay, & James, 2000).

Suppression of contextually irrelevant information, in contrast, is disrupted by congenital brain injury (Barnes et al., 2004), focal right hemisphere adult lesions (Tomkins, et al., 2001), aging (May et al., 1999), and dementia (Papagno et al., 2003). Some parts of the language system, including not only semantic suppression but also some domains of syntax (Platzack, 2001), appear to be more vulnerable than others, being impaired after a variety of forms of brain insult or cognitive compromise.

Although suppression seems more vulnerable than activation to a range of disorders, it is not clear that defective suppression arises from the same brain mechanism, or has the same functional effect, in the various conditions in which it has been reported. Deficits in suppression of contextually irrelevant information are related to the integrity of the corpus callosum in children with spina bifida (Huber-Okrainec et al., 2005) and to right hemisphere lesions in adults with stroke (Tomkins et al., 2002). While the brain insult is different, the common effect is to impair interhemispheric integration of lexical and contextual information. That idiom comprehension is impaired in relation to corpus callosum agenesis and hypoplasia suggests that interhemispheric integration is important for figurative language comprehension in children, just as in adults (Faust & Weisper, 2000).

The brain mechanisms of poor inhibition and suppression in aging are not fully understood, but they appear to be different in younger and older adults; during the act of successful inhibition, older adults activate the same brain areas as younger adults, but they also activate additional areas (Nielson, Langenecker, & Garavan, 2002).

The functional effect of impaired suppression affects some core semantic representations more in children with spina bifida meningomyelocele than in individuals with dementia. The evidence for impaired inhibition in dementia comes from correlations between Stroop performance and idiom comprehension (Papagno et al., 2003), rather than from online studies of lexical suppression; nevertheless, representation of frozen semantic idiomatic information seems relatively better preserved in dementia. The more frozen the semantic information, the more it resists semantic dementia and the less children with congenital brain injury are able to understand it.

Why core semantic representations are somewhat robust in the face of dementia is unclear, although the data seem less obviously explained by modular views of semantic organization (whereby conceptual knowledge is structured by content) than by recent theories proposing that concepts in the adult brain are represented as patterns of activation over multiple semantic properties within a unitary but redundant semantic system (Tyler et al., 2003). Why semantic representations are poor after early brain damage is also unclear. Perhaps early brain damage prevents the establishment of redundant patterns of semantic activation, or perhaps inefficient suppression prevents semantically redundant information from being effectively exploited. The comparison of semantic representations in congenital brain disorder and normal and aberrant aging remains to be better understood through the use of online language-comprehension models, such as the lexical ambiguity model described above.

CONCLUSION

Children exhibit a range of language disorders after acquired or congenital brain injury. Each disorder helps to delineate the cognitive morbidity associated with the various conditions. Some childhood disorders are of additional interest because of how they map, or fail to map, on to some of the patterns of language meaning and form breakdown in adults with aphasia or dementia. A few disorders, of particular interest, provide information relevant to some lifespan questions about the functional architecture of meaning in words, sentences, and texts.

References

Adams, M. J. (1990). *Beginning to read: Thinking and learning about print*. Cambridge, MA: MIT Press.

Alajouanine, T. H., & Lhermitte, F. (1965). Acquired aphasia in children. *Brain, 88*, 653–662.

Aram, D. M., Ekelman, B. L., Rose, D. F., & Whitaker, H. A. (1985). Verbal and cognitive sequelae following unilateral lesions acquired in early childhood. *Journal of Clinical and Experimental Neuropsychology, 7*, 55–78.

Arbuckle, T. Y., & Gold, D. P. (1993). Aging, inhibition, and verbosity. *Journal of Gerontology: Psychological Sciences, 48*, 225–232.

Barnes, M. A., & Dennis, M. (1998). Discourse after early-onset hydrocephalus: core deficits in children of average intelligence. *Brain and Language, 61*, 309–334.

Barnes, M. A., & Dennis, M. (2001). Knowledge-based inferencing after childhood head injury. *Brain and Language, 76*, 253–265.

Barnes, M. A., Dennis, M., & Haefele-Kalvaitis, J. (1996). The effects of knowledge availability and knowledge accessibility on coherence and elaborative inferencing in children from six to fifteen years of age. *Journal of Experimental Child Psychology, 61*, 216–241.

Barnes, M. A., Dennis, M., & Wilkinson, M. (1999). Reading after closed head injury in childhood: Effects on accuracy, fluency, and comprehension. *Developmental Neuropsychology, 15*, 1–24.

Barnes, M. A., Faulkner, H., & Dennis, M. (2001). Poor reading comprehension despite fast word decoding in children with hydrocephalus. *Brain and Language, 76*, 35–44.

Barnes, M. A., Faulkner, H., Wilkinson, M., & Dennis, M. (2004). Meaning construction and integration in children with hydrocephalus. *Brain and Language, 89*, 47–56.

Bates, E., & Goodman, J. C. (1997). On the inseparability of grammar and the lexicon: Evidence from acquisition, aphasia and real-time processing. *Language and Cognitive Processes, 12*, 507–584.

Bennett, D. J., & McEvoy, C. L. (1999). Mediated priming in younger and older adults. *Experimental Aging Research, 25*, 141–159.

Berndt, R. S., Mitchum, C. C., & Wayland, S. (1997). Patterns of sentence comprehension in aphasia: A consideration of three hypotheses. *Brain and Language, 60*, 197–221.

Brinton, B., Fujiki, M., & Mackey, T. (1985). Elementary school-age children's comprehension of specific idiomatic expressions. *Journal of Communication Disorders 18*, 245–257.

Burke, D. M. (1997). Language, aging and inhibitory deficits: Evaluation of a theory. *Journal of Gerontology: Psychological Sciences, 52B*, 254–264.

Burke, D. M., MacKay, D. G., & James, L. E. (2000). Theoretical approaches to language and aging. In T. J. Perfect & E. A. Maylor (Eds.), *Models of cognitive aging* (pp. 204–237). Oxford, UK: Oxford University Press.

Caplan, D. (1992). *Language. Structure, processing, and disorders*. Cambridge, MA: Bradford/MIT Press.

Caplan, D., & Hildebrandt, N. (1988). *Disorders of syntactic comprehension*. Cambridge, MA: Bradford/MIT Press.

Caramazza, A., & Zurif, E. B. (1976). Dissociation of algorithmic and heuristic processes in language comprehension: Evidence from aphasia. *Brain, 119*, 993–949.

Carr, T., & Levy, B. A. (1990). *Reading and its development: Component skills approaches*. San Diego: Academic Press.

Chapman, S. B., Culhane, K. A., Levin, H. S., Harward, H., Mendelsohn, D., Ewing-Cobbs, L., Fletcher, J. M., & Bruce, D. (1992). Narrative discourse after closed head injury in children and adolescents. *Brain and Language, 43*, 42–65.

Chapman, S. B., Sparks, G., Levin, H. S., Dennis, M., Roncadin, C., Zhang, L., & Song, J. (2004). Discourse macrolevel processing after severe pediatric traumatic brain injury. *Developmental Neuropsychology, 25*, 37–60.

Clifton, C., & Duffy, S. A. (2001). Sentence and text comprehension: Roles of linguistic structure. *Annual Review of Psychology, 52*, 167–196.

Chomsky, N., & Halle, M. (1968). *The sound pattern of English*. New York: Harper and Row.

Cooper, J. A., & Ferry, P. C. (1978). Acquired auditory verbal agnosia and seizures in childhood. *Journal of Speech and Hearing Disorders, 43*, 176–184.

Crain, S., Ni, W., & Shankweiler, D. (2001). Grammatism. *Brain and Language, 77*, 294–304.

Curtiss, S., & Schaeffer, J. (1997). Syntactic development in children with hemispherectomy: The Infl-System. In E. Hughes (Ed.), *Boston University Conference on Language Development Proceedings, 21*, 103–114.

Dennis, M. (1976). Dissociated naming and locating of body parts after left anterior temporal lobe resection: An experimental case study. *Brain and Language, 3*, 147–163.

Dennis, M. (1980a). Capacity and strategy for syntactic

comprehension after left or right hemidecortication. *Brain and Language, 10,* 287–317.

Dennis, M. (1980b). Strokes in childhood I: Communicative intent, expression, and comprehension after left hemisphere arteriopathy in a right-handed nine-year-old. In R. Rieber (Ed.), *Language development and aphasia in children* (pp. 45–67). New York: Academic Press.

Dennis, M. (1992). Word finding after brain-injury in children and adolescents. *Topics in Language Disorders, 13,* 66–82.

Dennis, M. (2003). Acquired disorders of language in children. In T. E. Feinberg & M. J. Farah (Eds.), *Behavioural neurology and neuropsychology* (pp. 783–799). New York: McGraw-Hill.

Dennis, M., & Barnes, M. A. (1990). Knowing the meaning, getting the point, bridging the gap, and carrying the message: Aspects of discourse following closed head injury in childhood and adolescence. *Brain and Language, 3,* 203–229.

Dennis, M., & Barnes, M. A. (1993). Oral discourse after early-onset hydrocephalus: Linguistic ambiguity, figurative language, speech acts, and script-based inferences. *Journal of Pediatric Psychology, 18,* 639–652.

Dennis, M., & Barnes, M. A. (2001). Comparison of literal, inferential, and intentional text comprehension in children with mild or severe closed head injury. *Journal of Head Trauma Rehabilitation, 16,* 456–468.

Dennis, M., Hendrick, E. B., Hoffman, H. J., & Humphreys, R. P. (1987). The language of hydrocephalic children and adolescents. *Journal of Clinical and Experimental Neuropsychology, 9,* 593–621.

Dennis, M., Jacennik, B., & Barnes, M. (1994). The content of narrative discourse in children and adolescents after early-onset hydrocephalus and in normally-developing age peers. *Brain and Language, 46,* 129–165.

Dennis, M., & Kohn, B. (1975). Comprehension of syntax in infantile hemiplegics after cerebral hemidecortication: Left hemisphere superiority. *Brain and Language, 2,* 472–482.

Dennis, M., & Whitaker, H. A. (1976). Language acquisition following hemidecortication: Linguistic superiority of the left over the right hemisphere. *Brain and Language, 3,* 404–433.

Dennis, M., & Wiegel-Crump, C. A. (1979). Aphasic dissolution and language acquisition. In H. Avakian-Whitaker & H. A. Whitaker (Eds.) *Studies in neurolinguistics* (pp. 211–224). New York: Academic Press.

Dogil, G., Haider, H., Schaner-Wolles, C., & Husmann, R. (1995). Radical autonomy of syntax: Evidence

from transcortical sensory aphasia. *Aphasiology, 9,* 577–602.

Edelstein, K., Dennis, M., Copeland, K., Frederick, J., Francis, D., Hetherington, R., Brandt, M. E., & Fletcher, J. (2004). Motor learning in children with spina bifida: Dissociation between performance level and acquisition rate. *Journal of the International Neuropsychological Society, 10,* 877–887.

Faust, M., & Weisper, S. (2000). Understanding metaphoric sentences in the two cerebral hemispheres. *Brain & Cognition, 43,* 186–191.

Feldman, H., Holland, A., & Keefe, K. (1989). Language abilities after left hemisphere brain injury: A case study of twins. *Topics in Early Childhood Special Education, 9,* 32–47.

Fletcher, J. M., Barnes, M., & Dennis, M. (2002). Language development in children with spina bifida. *Seminars in Pediatric Neurology, 9,* 201–208.

Garrard, P., Maloney, L. M., Hodges, J. R., & Patterson, K. (2005). The effects of very early Alzheimer's disease on the characteristics of writing by a renowned author. International Neuropsychological Society Joint Mid-Year Meeting, Dublin, Ireland, July 6–9, 2005. program and Abstract Book (p. 82).

Gernsbacher, M.A. (1990). *Language comprehension as structure building.* Hillsdale, NJ: Lawrence Erlbaum Associates.

Gernsbacher, M. A., & Faust, M. (1991). The role of suppression in sentence comprehension. In G. B. Simpson (Ed.), *Understanding word and sentence* (pp. 97–128). Amsterdam: North Holland.

Gernsbacher, M. A., & Robertson, R. R. W. (1999). The role of suppression in figurative language comprehension. *Journal of Pragmatics, 31,* 1619–1630.

Gernsbacher, M. A., Keysar, B., Robertson, R. R. W., & Werner, N. K. (2001). The role of suppression and enhancement in understanding metaphors. *Journal of memory and Language, 45,* 433–450.

Gibbs, R. W. (1991). Semantic analyzability in children's understanding of idioms. *Journal of Speech and Hearing Research, 34,* 613–620.

Grodzinsky, Y. (2000). The neurology of syntax: Language use without Broca's area. *Behavioral and Brain Sciences, 23,* 1–71.

Harnishfeger, K. K. (1995). The development of cognitive inhibition: Theories, definitions, and research evidence. In .N. Dempster & C. J, Brainerd (Eds.), *Interference and inhibition in cognition* (pp. 175–204). San Diego: Academic Press.

Hetherington, R., & Dennis, M. (2004). Plasticity for recovery, plasticity for development: Cognitive outcome in twins discordant for mid-childhood ischemic stroke. *Child Neuropsychology, 10,* 117–128.

Hoffman, R. R., & Honeck, R. P. (1980). A peacock looks at its legs: Cognitive science and figurative language. In R. P. Honeck & R. R. Hoffman (Eds.), *Cognition and figurative language* (pp. 3–24). Hillsdale, NJ: Lawrence Erlbaum Associates.

Huber-Okrainec, J., Blaser, S. E., & Dennis, M. (2005). Idiom comprehension deficits in relation to corpus callosum agenesis and hypoplasia in children with spina bifida myelomeningocele. *Brain and Language, 93,* 349–368.

Huber-Okrainec, J., & Dennis, M. (2005). *Idiom comprehension in typically developing 6 to 17 year old children: Effects of literality, compositionality, and contextual support.* Manuscript submitted for publication.

Hynd, G. W., Leathem, J., Semrud-Clikeman, M., Hern, K. L., & Wenner, M. (1995). Anomic aphasia in childhood. *Journal of Child Neurology, 10,* 189–293.

Jackson, J. H. (1884/1958). On some implications of dissolution of the nervous system. In J. Taylor (Ed.), *Selected writings of John Hughlings Jackson* (pp. 29–44). New York: Basic Books.

Jacobson, R. (1968). *Child language aphasia and phonological universals* (Janua Linguarum Series Minor No. 72). The Hague: Mouton.

James, L. E., Burke, D. M., Austin, A., & Hulme, E. (1998). Production and perception of verbosity in young and older adults. *Psychology and Aging, 13,* 355–367.

Kempler, D., Van Lancker, D., & Read, S. (1988). Proverb and idiom comprehension in Alzheimer disease. *Alzheimer Disease and Associated Disorders, 2,* 38–49.

Kintsch, W. (1988). The role of knowledge in discourse comprehension: a construction-integration model. *Psychological Review, 95,* 163–182.

Klein, S. K., Masur, D., Farber, K., Shinnar, S., & Rapin, I. (1992). Fluent aphasia in children: Definition and natural history. *Child Neurology, 7,* 50–59.

Kohn, B. (1980). Right-hemisphere speech representation and comprehension of syntax after left cerebral injury. *Brain and Language, 9,* 350–361.

LaBerge, D., & Samuels, J. (1974). Toward a theory of automatic information processing in reading. *Cognitive Psychology, 6,* 293–323.

Lazar, R. T., Warr-Leeper, G. A., Nicholson, C. B., & Johnson, S. (1989). Elementary school teachers' use of multiple meaning expressions. *Language, Speech, and Hearing Services in Schools, 20,* 420–430.

Levelt, W. J. M. (1989). *Speaking: From intention to articulation.* Cambridge, MA: MIT Press.

Linebarger, M. C. (1990). Neuropsychology of sentence parsing. In A. Caramazza (Ed.), *Cognitive neuropsychology and neurolinguistics: Advances in models of cognitive function and impairment* (pp. 55–122). Hillsdale, NJ: Lawrence Erlbaum Associates.

Lovett, M. W., Dennis, M., & Newman, J. (1986). Making reference: The cohesive use of pronouns in the narrative discourse of hemidecorticate adolescents. *Brain and Language, 29,* 224–251.

MacKay, D. G., & Abrams, L. (1998). Age-linked declines in retrieving orthographic knowledge: Empirical, practical and theoretical implications. *Psychology and Aging, 13,* 647–662.

MacWhinney, B., & Leinbach, J. (1991). Implementations are not conceptualizations: Revising the verb learning model. *Cognition, 40,* 121–157.

Martin, A., & Caramazza, A. (2003). Neuropsychological and neuroimaging perspectives on conceptual knowledge: an introduction. *Cognitive Neuropsychology, 20.* 195–212

May, C. P., Zacks, R. T., Hasher, L., & Multhaup, K. S. (1999). Inhibition in the processing of garden-path sentences. *Psychology and Aging, 14,* 304–313.

Menn, L., Obler L., & Goodglass, H. (1990). *A cross-language study of agrammatism.* PA: John Benjamins.

Morrow, D. G., Bower, G. H., & Greenspan, S. L. (1990). Situation-based inferences during narrative comprehension. In A. C. Graesser & G. H. Bower (Eds.), *Inferences and text comprehension* (pp. 123–135). San Diego: Academic Press.

Myerson, J. Ferraro, F. R., Hale, S., & Lima, S. D. (1992). General slowing in semantic priming and word recognition. *Psychology and Aging, 7,* 257–270.

Ni, W., Constable, R. T., Mencl, W. E., Pugh, K. R., Fulbright, R. K., Shaywitz, S. E., Shaywitz, B. A., Gore, J. C., & Shankweiler, D. (2000). An event-related neuroimaging study distinguishing form and content in sentence processing. *Journal of Cognitive Neuroscience, 12,* 120–133.

Nielson, K. A., Langenecker, S. A., & Garavan, H. (2002). Differences in the functional neuroanatomy of inhibitory control across the adult life span. *Psychology and Aging, 17,* 56–71.

Papagno, C. (2001). Comprehension of metaphors and idioms in patients with Alzheimer's disease. A longitudinal study. *Brain, 124,* 1450–1460.

Papagno, C., Lucchelli, F., Muggia, S., & Rizzo, S. (2003). Idiom comprehension in Alzheimer's disease: The role of the central executive. *Brain, 126,* 2419–2430.

Paquier, P., & Van Dongen, H. R. (1993). Current trends

in acquired childhood aphasia: An introduction. *Aphasiology, 7*, 421–440.

Perfetti, C. A. (1985). *Reading ability.* New York: Oxford University Press.

Platzak, C. (2001). The vulnerable C-domain. *Brain and Language, 77*, 364–377.

Pollio, H. R., Barlow, J. M., Fine, H. J., & Pollio, M. R. (1977). *Psychology and the poetics of growth: Figurative language in psychology, psychotherapy, and education.* Hillsdale, NJ: Lawrence Erlbaum Associates.

Rapin, I. (1995). Acquired aphasia in children. *Journal of Child Neurology, 10*, 267–270.

Reilly, J. S., Bates, E. A., & Marchman, V. A. (1998). Narrative discourse in children with early focal brain injury. *Brain and Language, 61*, 335–375.

Rochon, E., Kavé, G., Cupit, J., Jokel, R., & Winocur, G. (2004). Sentence comprehension in semantic dementia: A longitudinal case study. *Cognitive Neuropsychology, 21*, 317–330.

Rochon, E., Waters, G. S., & Caplan, D. (1994). Sentence comprehension in patients with Alzheimer's disease. *Brain and Language, 46*, 329–349.

Rochon, E., Waters, G. S., & Caplan, D. (2000). The relationship between measures of working memory and sentence comprehension in patients with Alzheimer's disease. *Journal of Speech, Language, and Hearing Research, 43*, 395–413.

Sanford, A. J., & Sturt, P. (2002). Depth of processing in language comprehension: Not noticing the evidence. *Trends in Cognitive Science, 6*, 382–386.

Sartori, G., & Job, R. (1988). The oyster with four legs: A neuropsychological study on the interaction of visual and semantic information. *Cognitive Neuropsychology, 5*, 105–132.

Schmalhofer, F., McDaniel, M. A., & Keefe, D. (2002). A unified model for predictive and bridging inferences. *Discourse Processes, 33*, 105–132.

Shankweiler, D. (1989). How problems of comprehension are related to difficulties in decoding. In D. Shankweiler & Y. Liberman (Eds.), *Phonology and reading disability: Solving the reading puzzle. International Academy for Research in Learning Disabilities Monograph Series* (No. 6. p. 35–68). Ann Arbor, MI: University of Michigan Press.

Squire, L. R., Knowlton, B., & Musen, G. (1993). The structure and organization of memory. *Annual Review of Psychology, 44*, 453–495.

Stark, R. E., Bleile, K., Brandt, J., Freeman, J., & Vining, E. P. (1995). Speech-language outcomes of hemispherectomy in children and young adults. *Brain and Language 51*, 406–421.

Stromswold, K., Caplan, D., Alpert, N., & Rausch, S. (1996). Localization of syntactic comprehension by positron emission tomography. *Brain and Language, 52*, 452–473

Swinney, D., Zurif, E., Prather, P. & Love, T. (1996). Neurological distribution of processing resources underlying language comprehension. *Journal of Cognitive Neuroscience, 8*, 174–184.

Taylor, E. M. (1961). *Psychological appraisal of children with cerebral defects.* Cambridge, MA: Harvard University Press.

Tompkins, C. A., Lehman Blake, M., Baumgaertner, A., & Fassbinder, W. (2001). Mechanisms of discourse comprehension impairment after right hemisphere brain damage: Suppression in inferential ambiguity resolution. *Journal of Speech, Language, & Hearing Research, 44*, 400–415.

Tompkins, C. A., Lehman Blake, Baumgaertner, A., & Fassbinder, W. (2002). Characterising comprehension difficulties after right brain damage: attentional demands of suppression function. *Aphasiology, 16*, 559–572.

Tyler, L. K. Bright, P., Dick, E., Tavares, P., Pilgrim, L., Fletcher, P., Greer, M., & Moss, H. (2003). Do semantic categories activate distinct cortical regions? Evidence for a distributed neural semantic system. *Cognitive Neuropsychology, 20*, 541–559.

Tyler, L. K., & Moss, H. E. (2003). The conceptual structure of cabbages and things. *Brain and Language, 87*, 84–85.

Ullman, M. T., Corkin, S., Coppola, M., Hickok, G., Growdon, J. H., Koroshetz, W. J., & Pinker, S. (1997). A neural dissociation within language: evidence that the mental dictionary is part of declarative memory, and that grammatical rules are processed by the procedural system. *Journal of Cognitive Neuroscience, 9*, 266–276.

van den Broek, P., Young, M., Tzeng, Y., & Linderholm, T. (1999). The landscape model of reading: Inferences and the online construction of a memory representation. In H. van Oostendorp & S. R. Goldman (Eds.), *The construction of mental representation during reading* (pp. 71–98). Mahwah, NJ: Lawrence Erlbaum Associates.

van Dijk, T. A., & Kintsch, W. (1983). *Strategies of discourse comprehension.* New York: Academic Press.

Van Dongen, H. R., & Paquier, P. (1991). Fluent aphasia in children. In I. P. Martins, A. Castro-Caldas, H. R. Van Dongen, & A. Van Hout (Eds.), *Acquired aphasia in children* (pp. 125–141). Dordrecht, Netherlands: Kluwer Academic.

Van Hout, A. (1991). Characteristics of language in acquired aphasia in children. In I. P. Martins, A. Castro-Caldas, H. R. Van Dongen, & A. Van Hout (Eds.), *Acquired aphasia in children* (pp.117–124). Dordrecht, Netherlands: Kluwer Academic.

Whitney, P. (1987). Psychological theories of elaborative inferences: Implications for schema-theoretic views of comprehension. *Reading Research Quarterly, 22,* 299–310.

Yekovich, F. R., Walker, C. H., Ogle, L. T., & Thompson, M. A. (1990). The influence of domain knowledge on inferencing in low-aptitude individuals. *Psychology of Learning and Motivation, 25,* 259–278.

Zwann, R., A., Langston, M.C., & Graesser, A.C. (1995). The construction of situation models in narrative comprehension: An event-indexing model. *Psychological Science, 6,* 292–297.

17

Language Disorders in Aging

David Caplan

Gloria Waters

This chapter reviews language disorders that follow strokes—focal vascular disease of the cerebral hemispheres. Collectively, these disorders are known as *aphasias*. This subject was chosen for discussion here because stroke is a leading cause of language impairment in older age. For reasons of space, other common neurological diseases that affect language, such as Alzheimer's disease, cannot be discussed here. For a review of such conditions, see Mesulam (2003) and work by Snowdon and colleagues (Snowdon et al., 1996; Snowdon, Greiner, & Markesbery, 2000).

A few introductory comments may help set a framework for the descriptions of language disorders that follow. While stroke has its own particular features, the language disorders seen after stroke can be very similar to those seen after other types of neurological disease. What seems to matter most to the generation of language symptoms is whether the disease is focal or broadly distributed and how fast it develops. Focal, rapidly developing diseases such as abscesses, contusions, or certain tumors can produce

language symptoms that are clinically indistinguishable from those seen in stroke and that differ from those seen in slowly developing diseases in the same brain regions. Indeed, the language symptoms that occur after lesions in a given area can change abruptly with changes in a disease. A biopsy that removes a tiny portion of a diffuse, slow-growing infiltrative tumor can change a mild word-finding problem into a florid jargon replete with nonwords and grammatical errors, showing the sensitivity of language symptoms to acute damage of a small part of a brain area that is barely compensating for a diffuse disease it harbors.

We have said that whether a lesion is focal or distributed has an important effect on what language symptoms it creates. This would seem to suggest that where a lesion occurs also has a great impact on what symptoms are associated with it. That is true to some extent, but there are important limitations on this relationship. Lesions have to occur in "language areas" to produce language symptoms; these areas surround the sylvian fissure and are lateralized to the left hemisphere in almost all right-handed and the majority of left-handed and ambidextrous individuals. They may also include some subcortical structures, the anterior inferior temporal lobe, and the cerebellum. Certain language functions, such as computing aspects of discourse and prosody, appear to be commonly bilateral or lateralized to the opposite hemisphere. Within the core language area, however, the effect of a lesion of language is highly variable. Many patients have lesions in this region without much, if anything, in the way of aphasia. Despite studies that purport to localize specific aspects of language in highly restricted parts of the language area, it is almost impossible to predict the exact language process that will be damaged after a lesion in a particular part of the language area. One exception to this is that lesions in the anterior part of this area are associated with speech-production deficits. This is probably because the anterior region of this zone is part of the motor-planning area of the brain. However, if we look at the nature of the language processes that are affected, not the ability to produce speech itself, lesion-deficit correlations are not very robust. This may be due to different degrees to which language is lateralized to one hemisphere, to different degrees to which adaptation can occur, and/or to individual differences in localization of language-processing components. For one discussion of the organization of language in the brain, see Caplan and Gould (2002).

With respect to the effect of age on language impairments after stroke, though stroke itself is a disease mainly of older individuals, the language disorders seen after stroke occur at any age after the language system is mature (probably in the mid-to-late teens). Individuals unfortunate enough to suffer strokes in their late teens and twenties (often due to ruptured blood vessels, drug use, or other causes) have the same range of symptoms as adults in middle age or elderly patients. Clinical neurological wisdom holds that aphasia in childhood differs from aphasia in adults. However, Dennis's survey of language disorders in childhood (see Chapter 16, this volume) indicates a considerable degree of similarity of these disorders to the disorders that are listed in this chapter. Language disorders due to neurological disease appear to affect isolated language-processing components in both childhood and adulthood. Differences in the effects of these lesions may be due to differences in how developed these components are, and also to the ubiq-

uity of nonfluency in children with stroke. Again, this indicates that disorders of speech production need to be distinguished from disorders of processing language itself.

Where age matters is in the area of recovery. Recovery of language after stroke is much faster and more compete in children than in adults and decreases with advancing age. However, there are numerous exceptions: young people who have long-lasting, even lifelong, language disorders after stroke and older individuals who recover very well. The biological factors that determine outcome in an individual are far from completely understood.

We have said several times that we think it is important to distinguish disorders of speech from those of language, without saying what we think language is. Since what follows briefly outlines disorders of what we take to be language processing, we end this introduction with this topic.

We think it is most useful to view human language as a code that links linguistic representations to aspects of meaning. The basic levels of language are simple words, morphologically complex words, sentences, and discourse. Studies to date have demonstrated disorders affecting all of these levels of language. In many patients, a large number of operations and language structures are affected, and in some, the effects of stroke are highly restricted. We shall concentrate on the second type of impairment in our descriptions because these shed light on the language system itself, sometimes illuminating its components in ways that are not easily visible when the system is intact. Our description of language impairments will focus on disturbances of language operations at the word and sentence levels.

We close by pointing out that, although what follows might strike the reader as an arid list of arcane disorders, disturbances of these language operations have important functional consequences. The relationship between impairments of language operations and problems in functional communication is complex because patients adapt to their language impairments in many ways. Nonetheless, without the ability to use the language code quickly and accurately, functional communicative powers are limited, and most patients who have disturbances of elements of the language code or psycholinguistic operations experience limitations in their functional communicative abilities. These, in turn, have consequences in many spheres of their lives.

LANGUAGE IN FOCAL VASCULAR DISEASE

The prototype of vascular disease is lobar stroke due to arterial occlusion and cerebral hemorrhages. Lobar strokes disrupt functions carried out in the region they damage. Because different parts of the brain support different language operations and strokes are highly variable in their size and location, strokes are associated with a very broad range of disruptions of language. Patients can present with impairments ranging from relatively isolated disturbances of specific types of language operations to massive interference with virtually all language functions. We will briefly present some of the impairments that have been described and then describe one impairment—disorders affecting the use of syntactic structure to determine sentence meaning—in more detail.

Beginning with perception, some stroke patients have difficulties recognizing spoken words. These disturbances may be related to impairments of acoustic-phonetic processing (Blumstein, Baker, & Goodglass, 1977), though it is unclear what type and severity of these disturbances lead to problems in recognizing or understanding spoken words (see Caramazza, Berndt, & Basili, 1983; Saffran, Marin, & Yeni-Komshian, 1976, for cases with both impairments. and Basso, Casati, & Vignolo, 1977; Blumstein, Baker, et al., 1977; Miceli, Gainotti, Caltagirone, & Masullo, 1980, for cases with only phonemic impairments). An interesting fact is that, as far as we know, there is no case of a patient who has had an impairment in recognizing spoken words without a concurrent disorder of acoustic-phonetic processing. This type of deficit was attributed to a patient by Karl Wernicke (1874/1974) in a paper that has greatly influenced neurological thinking about how the brain is organized to support language (see, e.g., Geschwind, 1965), but there is no evidence that the patient had this functional impairment. The fact that such patients do not seem to exist is one of many reasons to question neurolinguistic models that are based on his work.

Moving further along the processing chain, we find disturbances of word meanings have been described in patients with stroke. These disturbances have shown dissocations of affected and spared features along a number of interesting dimensions.

One dimension along which disorders of word meanings dissociate is semantic category. Several authors have reported a selective semantic impairment of concepts related to living things and foods compared to man-made objects (Sartori & Job, 1988; Silveri & Gainotti, 1988; Warrington & Shallice, 1984). The opposite pattern has also been found (Warrington & McCarthy, 1983, 1987). Selective preservation and disruption of abstract versus concrete concepts, and of nominal versus verbal concepts, have also been reported (Miceli, Silveri, Villa, & Caramazza, 1984; Schwartz, Marin, & Saffran, 1979; Warrington, 1981; Zingeser & Berndt, 1988). A great deal of work has gone into trying to understand what determines category-specific semantic disturbances. Many researchers are uncomfortable with the idea that the brain organizes items into categories such as those that have been alleged to be individually disrupted, and they have tried to reduce these apparent category-specific effects to perceptual or functional features of objects in particular domains. For instance, foods differ more in terms of their physical features than their functional uses, whereas tools show the opposite pattern; some researchers have suggested that selective impairment of one or another of these categories is due to disorders affecting the representation of physical properties or functional uses, which seems (to these researchers) to be a more plausible type of deficit. Other researchers have argued that these accounts do not work and that category-specific semantic deficits exist. Martin and Caramazza (2003) have edited a recent set of papers on this topic that present these positions.

Turning to speech production, most models of speech production postulate that the sound of a word is produced in several steps (see Levelt, 1989, Chap. 9, for discussion). Though details vary, these models tend to share the assumption that speakers first access a semantic and syntactic representation, then access a partial phonological representation of a word, and then perform a number of operations on the phonological representation to turn it into a form that is suitable for programming the articulators. Disturbances affecting each of these processes have been described.

A disturbance in activating word forms from concepts is manifest by an inability to produce a word from a semantic stimulus (a picture or a definition), coupled with intact processing at the semantic and phonological levels (determined by answering questions about pictures, picture categorization tests, and repetition). This is a problem commonly seen in aging (see Burke, Chapter 13, this volume). A useful test of the ability to access the form of a word is picture-homophone matching, in which a subject must say if the words corresponding to two pictures are the same or not (e.g., reading glasses and drinking glasses). This test does not require speech but can be performed only if a person can activate word forms. Disturbances in accessing word forms may appear in a variety of ways, including pauses, neologisms (complex sequences of sounds that do not form words), semantic paraphasias (words related to the meaning of the target item), and the use of vague terms. Rarely, patients show an inability to name objects presented in one modality only, even though they demonstrate understanding of the concept associated with that object when it is presented in that modality (*optic aphasia*—Beauvois, 1982; *auditory aphasia*—Denes & Semenza, 1975). These modality-specific naming disorders have been taken to reflect a failure to transmit information from modality-specific semantic systems to the processor responsible for activating the forms of words.

A small number of patients show disturbances largely restricted to the production of one grammatical class of words. We shall review the performance of patients with agrammatism below; these patients have a disturbance affecting the production of grammatical words (pronouns, articles, certain prepositions, etc.). Some of them also show dissociations within the content word vocabulary, with much greater problems producing verbs than nouns (McCarthy & Warrington, 1985). Caramazza and his colleagues (e.g., Rapp & Caramazza, 1997) have described even more selective problems of this sort, documenting patients who could produce nouns but not verbs in one output modality (e.g., writing) and the opposite patterns in another modality (speech). This suggests that very peripheral parts of the language-output system are organized in terms of grammatical categories, a conclusion that is at least as difficult to accept as the conclusion that the brain is organized in terms of semantic categories.

Disturbances of a patient's ability to convert the representation of the sound of a word into a form appropriate for articulatory production—often called *planning* articulation—are usually manifest as phonemic paraphasias (substitutions involving phonemes with highly dissimilar distinctive features, omissions, and misorderings of phonemes). Three features of a patient's performance suggest a disturbance in word-sound planning. First, some phonemic paraphasias are closely related to target words (e.g., *befenit* for *benefit*; Lecours & Lhermitte, 1969). Second, some patients make multiple attempts that come closer and closer

to the correct form of a word (Joanette, Keller, & Lecours, 1980). Third, some patients make similar phonological errors in word repetition, word reading, and picture naming. Because the form of a word is presented to the output system in very different ways in these three tasks, the errors in such patients most likely arise in the process of planning the form of the word that is suitable for articulation (Caplan, Vanier, & Baker, 1986). These characteristics of errors can also be found in some lower level speech-production disorders (McNeill, Levy, & Pedelty, 1990).

There have been fewer surprises about the patterns of planning errors than semantic and grammatical production disturbances. Patients with sound-planning problems tend to be more affected on longer words and on words with consonant clusters (Kohn, 1984; Nespoulous, Joanette, Beland, Caplan, & Lecours, 1984). The frequency of occurrence of a word in the language has a variable effect upon the occurrence of these types of errors (Garrett, 1982; Pate, Saffran, & Martin, 1987). Planning disturbances only rarely affect function words compared to nouns, verbs, and adjectives (Buckingham, 1979). Perhaps the most surprising finding has been that some patients have trouble planning the sounds of words only when words are inserted into sentences, making phonemic paraphasias in sentence production but not in naming or repetition tasks (Kohn, 1989). However, this is relatively easily explicable: in these cases, the errors probably arise when words are inserted into syntactic structures.

Patients often have disturbances of articulation itself, as shown by abnormalities in the acoustic waveform produced by a patient (Blumstein, Alexander, Ryalls, Katz, & Dworetzky, 1987; Blumstein, Cooper, Zurif, & Caramazza, 1977) and in the movement of the articulators in speech (Itoh, Sasanuma, Hirose, Yoshioka, & Ushijima, 1980). Investigators have identified two major disturbances of articulation: dysarthria and apraxia of speech. *Dysarthria* is marked by hoarseness, excessive nasality, and imprecise articulation, and is said to be largely uninfluenced by the type of linguistic material that the speaker produces or by the speech task (Darley, 1983). *Apraxia* of speech is marked by difficulty in initiating speech, searching for a pronunciation, better articulation for automatized speech (e.g., counting) than volitional speech, abnormal prosody, omissions of syllables in multisyllabic words, and simplification of consonant clusters (often by adding a short neutral vowel sound between consonants; Bowman, Hodson, & Simpson, 1980; Kent

& Rosenbek, 1982). Both dysarthria and apraxia of speech result in sounds that are perceived as distorted (Odell, McNeil, Rosenbek, & Hunter, 1990, 1991). Apraxia of speech often co-occurs with dysarthria or with the production of phonemic paraphasias, and the relations between these disorders and the empirical basis for distinguishing one from another are the subject of active research.

Disturbances affecting morphological processing mostly appear in sentence production, but can also occur in single-word production tasks. Goodglass and Berko (1960) described patients with difficulties in producing plural, possessive, and third-person singular forms of nonwords. The fact that this disorder arose with nonwords that the patients were given by the experimenters suggests that the impairment affected the ability to produce morphological forms. Miceli and Caramazza (1988) described a patient with a disturbance affecting the production of morphologically complex words, and Badecker, Hillis, and Caramazza (1990) have shown that such disturbances can arise in patients who perform well on tasks that require recognition and comprehension of written morphologically complex words.

Disturbances affecting the production of morphologically complex words are most commonly seen in sentence production, where they are known as *agrammatism* and *paragrammatism*. The most noticeable deficit in agrammatism is the widespread omission of function words and affixes, accompanied by good production of common nouns (Menn, Obler, & Goodglass, 1990). This disparity is always seen in the spontaneous speech of patients termed agrammatic, and often occurs in their repetition and writing as well. Patients in whom substitutions of these function words predominate, and whose speech is fluent, are called *paragrammatic* (Goodglass & Geschwind, 1976). Recent observations have emphasized the fact that these two patterns co-occur in many patients (Goodglass & Menn, 1985; Heeschen, 1985; Menn et al., 1990). They may result from a single underlying deficit that has different surface manifestations (Caplan, 1986; Grodzinsky, 1984).

Agrammatism and paragrammatism vary considerably, with different sets of function words and bound morphemes being affected or spared in different cases (Menn et al., 1990; Miceli, Silveri, Romani, & Caramazza, 1989). In some patients, there seems to be some systematicity to the pattern of errors. For instance, English agrammatic patients frequently produce infinitives (e.g., *to walk*) and gerunds (e.g., *walking*) because these are the basic forms in the verbal system (Lapointe, 1983). In other cases, substitutions are closely related to the correct target (Miceli et al., 1989). Agrammatics' errors also tend to follow the tendencies seen in normal subjects with respect to errors that "strand" affixes (e.g., "I am going to school"→ "I am schooling to go"), and the *sonorance hierarchy* that establishes syllabic forms as easier to produce than simple consonants (Goodglass & Berko, 1960; Kean, 1977; see also Lapointe, 1983; Menn et al., 1990; and Nespoulous et al., 1988, for additional discussion). Agrammatics generally produce real words, which makes for different patterns of errors in different languages that differ with respect to whether or not they require inflections to appear on a word (Grodzinsky, 1984; Miceli et al, 1989). The fact that, in almost all cases, errors do not violate the word-formation processes of the language suggests that most agrammatic and paragrammatic patients retain some knowledge of the rules of word formation.

Agrammatic patients usually produce only very simple syntactic structures. Goodglass, Gleason, Bernholtz, and Hyde (1972) found virtually no syntactically well-formed utterances in the syntactic constructions produced by one agrammatic patient. All the agrammatic patients studied in a large contemporary cross-language study showed some impoverishment of syntactic structure in spontaneous speech (Menn et al., 1990). The failure to produce complex noun phrases and embedded verbs with normal frequency was the most striking feature of the syntactic simplification shown by these patients. Ostrin and Schwartz (1986) described four patients who could produce either a determiner and a noun (*the man*) or an adjective and a noun (*old man*), but not both (*the old man*) in a picture description task. Since the patients produced either phrase on different attempts, Ostrin and Schwartz concluded that they could not produce adequately complex syntactic structures for the thoughts they had in mind. In a second study of the repetition abilities of six agrammatic subjects, Ostrin and Schwartz found that the patients tended to reproduce the order of nouns and verbs in the presented sentence, but made many syntactic errors, such as producing "The bicycle is riding by the boy" for "The bicycle is being ridden by the boy." They argued that these performances resulted from an incomplete memory trace of the thematic roles of the noun phrases in the presented sentence.

Several studies suggest that syntactic errors in sentence production differ in paragrammatic and agrammatic patients (e.g., Butterworth & Howard, 1987). Butterworth and Howard (1987) described five paragrammatic patients who each produced many "long and complex sentences, with multiple interdependencies of constituents" (p. 23). Patients with primarily paragrammatic errors tend to produce many types of syntactic errors, including errors in tag questions (e.g., "The boy will come later, won't he?"), illegal noun phrases in relative clauses, and illegal use of pronouns to head relative clauses (Butterworth & Howard, 1987). A type of error that has often been commented on in paragrammatism is a "blend," in which the output seems to reflect a conflation of two different ways of saying the same thing (e.g., "They are not prepared to be of helpful," a combination of "They are not prepared to be helpful" and "They are not prepared to be of help";[Butterworth & Howard, 1987). Because of the evidence that paragrammatic patients retain some ability to use syntactic structures, Butterworth (1982, 1985; Butterworth and Howard, 1987) has argued that the syntactic and morphological errors in paragrammatism result from the failure of these patients to monitor their speech-production processes and their output.

The various disturbances that affect sentence production usually co-occur. A complex disturbance that results from the combination of the deficits in producing syntactic forms, disturbances in accessing and planning word forms, and impairments in producing morphologically complex words, is known as *jargonaphasia* (Buckingham & Kertesz, 1976; Lecours & Rouillon, 1976).

Our research has mostly dealt with comprehension of sentences. Understanding a sentence requires relating the meanings of the words to extract information about who is undertaking an action, who is receiving an action, what features are attributed to which items, and so on—collectively called propositional content. The relationships between words that determine propositional content are based on the syntactic structure of the sentence. For instance, the sentence "The boy who saw the girl left the room" means that the boy left the room, not the girl, despite the sequence of words *the girl left the room*, because *the boy*, not *the girl*, is the subject of the sentence. Normally, listeners use many cues to determine what a sentence means, including pragmatic expectations, information about the frequency with which construc-

tions and words follow one another, and so on, but finally almost always rely on the syntactic structure of the sentence for its meaning. (Exceptions arise when a listener cannot construct a structure, as in some "tricky" sentences such as "The daughter of the king's son shaved himself," which is perfectly acceptable but hard to figure out.) Aphasic patients tend to rely more on these other cues because their ability to construct syntactic representations is affected.

Caramazza and Zurif (1976) were the first researchers to show that some patients have selective impairments of this ability. These researchers described patients who could match "semantically reversible" sentences such as "The apple the boy is eating is red" to one of two pictures but not "semantically irreversible" sentences such as "The girl the boy is chasing is tall." The difference between the two types of sentences resides in the fact that a listener can understand a sentence such as "The apple the boy is eating is red" via the lexico-pragmatic route, whereas understanding "The girl the boy is chasing is tall" requires assigning its syntactic structure since both boys and girls are capable of chasing one another.

Some patients can assign and interpret syntactic structures unconsciously but not use these structures in a conscious, controlled fashion. For instance, Tyler (1985) reported a patient whose online word-monitoring performances indicated that he was sensitive to certain syntactic anomalies, but who could not make judgments regarding these same anomalies at the end of a sentence. Linebarger and her colleagues (Linebarger, Schwartz, & Saffran, 1983; Linebarger, 1990) have reported that some patients who have syntactic comprehension problems (who cannot match reversible sentences to pictures, for instance) can make judgments as to whether or not a sentence is grammatical. For instance, some patients can indicate that the utterance "The woman was watched the man" is ill-formed and the utterance "The woman was watched by the man" is acceptable, despite not being able to match sentences such as "The woman was watched by the man" to one of two pictures. These researchers have interpreted these results as an indication that some patients can construct syntactic structures but not use them to determine propositional meaning (a so-called mapping problem; Schwartz, Linebarger, & Saffran, 1985). As with other areas of language functioning, it appears that patients may retain unconscious, online sentence comprehension processes but lose the ability to use the products of these processes in a controlled, conscious fashion in some tasks.

Our own research suggests that disorders of syntactic comprehension can be described within a general framework that may apply to other aphasic impairments. These disorders seem to vary along two lines. The first is a dimension that we may call overall severity. When analyzed as a group, patients show two important features (Caplan, Baker & Dehaut, 1985; Caplan, Hildebrandt & Makris, 1996). As a group, they perform more poorly on sentences that are more complex, and patients whose performances are overall worse show the effects of sentence complexity earlier—that is, they fail on simpler sentences. These features are suggestive of patients' running out of computational abilities to assign syntactic structure at earlier points than normal subjects. This can be seen as a form of resource, or working-memory limitation. There is also evidence for a pathologically limited working memory in individual patients in the form of a pattern of performance that is very similar to that described by Ostrin and her colleagues in sentence production. Some patients show the ability to understand sentences that contain either of two syntactic structures, but not sentences in which both structures co-occur. These features of group and individual case performance suggest that one dimension along which an aphasic deficit in syntactic processing can be characterized is the degree to which the patient's working memory for syntactic processing is reduced.

Simultaneously, we believe there is a second dimension that defines the impairment, consisting of disturbances of specific syntactic operations (Hildebrandt, Caplan, & Evans, 1987; Linebarger et al., 1983). For instance, two patients we studied showed a double dissociation in their abilities to understand sentences with reflexive elements (*himself*) and pronouns (*him*) (Caplan & Hildebrandt, 1988). Another set of patients showed isolated disturbances of specific sentence types that required relating noun phrases to distant syntactic positions, with different patients retaining or losing the ability to understand sentences with relative clauses, passive forms, and certain relationships between the subject of a sentence and an embedded infinitive (as in "John promised Bill to leave" vs. "John seemed to Bill to leave"). These selective impairments, which are the hallmark of aphasic disturbances in other areas, are thus also seen in relationship to syntactic comprehension. We believe they co-occur with reductions in working-memory capacity related to language operations in this domain as well as in other types of language processing.

In the area of syntactic comprehension, patients' interpretations of a sentence depends on the structure they assign and how they take that structure to determine the sentence's meaning. Patients who do not assign normal structures can still often assign some structure and use heuristics to determine meaning, and therefore can understand very simple syntactic forms, such as active sentences ("The man hugged the woman"), but not more complex forms, such as passive sentences ("The woman was hugged by the man"; Caplan et al., 1985). Many of these patients use strategies such as assigning the thematic role of agent (doer of the action) to a noun immediately before a verb to understand semantically reversible sentences, leading to systematic errors in comprehension of sentences such as "The boy who pushed the girl kissed the baby." Other patients have virtually no ability to use syntactic structure at all. Most of these patients appear to use the lexico-pragmatic route at least in part, and to rely on inferences based on their knowledge of the real world and their ability to understand some words in a sentence (Schwartz, Saffran, & Marin, 1980).

Many researchers and clinicians believe limitations in verbal short-term memory can cause sentence comprehension disturbances. Some researchers maintain the view that short-term memory is used in comprehending more complex sentences and have pointed out a variety of sentence comprehension disturbances in patients with short-term memory limitations (Vallar & Baddeley, 1987). Sentence length has been shown to affect certain comprehension tasks in some patients who do not show disturbances of syntactic comprehension (Schwartz, Linebarger, Saffran, & Pate, 1987; Martin & Fener, 1990). However, in an analysis of the comprehension abilities of all the short-term memory patients in the recent neuropsychological literature, Caplan and Waters (1990) argued that the comprehension deficits found in these patients do not prove that short-term memory limitations lead to syntactic comprehension deficits. In fact, case studies show that patients with short-term memory impairments can have excellent syntactic comprehension abilities (McCarthy & Warrington, 1987; Waters, Caplan, & Hildebrandt, 1991). Though many short-term memory patients have trouble in comprehension tasks, the relationship of these short-term memory disorders to sentence-comprehension impairments remains unclear (see Caplan & Waters, 1990, for a review). Our own work suggests that the working memory needed to assign syntactic structure has somehow become a specialized subsystem, perhaps through extensive use or perhaps because language is inherently a special cognitive domain. Our work suggests that people rely on a second, more consciously controlled short-term memory only to review sentences they did not understand sufficiently well in the first place (see Caplan & Waters, 1999, for discussion). Since this is likely to happen more often in children, who are less proficient language users, short-term memory as measured in standard psychological tests may be more relevant to language comprehension in children than it is in adults.

In summary, stroke produces an extremely wide variety of impairments of language processors. Though the emphasis has been on relatively isolated disorders in research papers, this focus reflects researchers' interests in how the language system is structured (which can be revealed by identifying very specific deficits in the system), not the dominant clinical picture. Most stroke patients have many language impairments when these impairments are defined at the level of detail we have been describing here. We note in passing that traditional neurological thinking about aphasia identifies some 10 or so combinations of deficits as having particular importance to models of language-brain relationships. These classic aphasic syndromes (Broca's aphasia, Wernicke's aphasia, conduction aphasia, etc.) are, however, no more important than any other arbitrary combination of deficits that is seen and serve only as gross descriptors of patients' disorders. Therapy cannot be directed toward "Broca's aphasia," but must be directed toward a difficulty in accessing certain types of function words, a certain type of articulatory disorder, and so on.

SUMMARY AND CONCLUSIONS

We have reviewed the effects of stroke, a common neurological disease seen in aging, on language. The main conclusion we take away from this review is that language can be affected in very selective and even unexpected ways by neurological disease. From a clinical point of view, the presence of seemingly odd language deficits should not be dismissed but should prompt consideration of small strokes. On the other hand, certain general findings still apply to the effects of stroke on language. Taken as a group, stroke victims with language disorders tend to be more affected by more complex language operations and to use simple ways of structuring language as compensatory strategies to understand and probably to produce language. From a research point of view, the language deficits seen after neurological disease provide a window into the components of the language-processing system and their relationship to other cognitive functions such as short-term and working memory.

We close on a note about language disorders seen in stroke and aging. Language abilities seen after stroke are necessarily affected by an individual's premorbid language functioning and therefore are affected by age. Disease does not improve people's language (although logically it could), so language abilities after stroke or any other disease are, so to speak, capped by the language capacities that are seen in individuals of a certain age. We would expect different effects of stroke or other diseases on language in 5-year-olds and 80–year-olds because 5-year-olds and 80-year-olds have different language abilities before diseases strike. With this in mind, we may ask how much language changes over the adult lifespan. In our view, it is quite remarkable how little this happens. While detailed psychological studies do show changes in language abilities, some of which (such as word-finding problems) are great enough to be noticed by many people, a very striking feature of language processing is that it remains very efficient from about late adolescence through very old age; certainly, most people age with few macroscopically noticeable changes in their language. As far as we know, language changes less than, say, the speed of processing in other cognitive tasks, the ability to encode and retrieve information in episodic memory, or many motor and sensory functions. If this is true, it may explain why the effects of stroke on language are not very different in younger and older adults. Though there are differences in the effects of stroke in the adult population as a function of age (see, e.g., Joanette et al., 1983), the big divide in the effects of focal neurological disease as a function of age seems to occur between childhood, when the language system is developing, and adulthood. Pathological focal disruption to the neural substrate of language, when it occurs, basically trumps aging as the factor that determines the nature of language abilities.

ACKNOWLEDGMENTS This work was supported by grants from NIDCD to David Caplan (DC04608) and from NIA to Gloria Waters (AG09661).

References

Badecker, W., Hillis, A., & Caramazza, A. (1990). Lexical morphological and its role in the writing process: Evidence from a case of acquired dysgraphia. *Cognition*, *35*, 205–234.

Basso, A., Casati, G., & Vignolo, L. A. (1977). Phonemic identification defect in aphasia. *Cortex*, *13*, 85–95.

Beauvois, M. -F. (1982). Optic aphasia: A process of interaction between vision and language. Philosophical Transactions of the Royal Society of London, B298, 35–47.

Blumstein, S., Alexander, M. P., Ryalls, J. H., Katz, W., & Dworetzky, B. (1987). On the nature of the foreign accent syndrome: A case study. *Brain and Language*, *31*, 215–244.

Blumstein, S., Baker, E., & Goodglass, H. (1977). Phonological factors in auditory comprehension in aphasia. *Neuropsychologia*, *15*, 19–30.

Blumstein, S., Cooper, W. E., Zurif, E. B., & Caramazza, A. (1977). The perception and production of Voice-Onset Time in aphasia. *Neuropsychologia*, *15*, 371–383.

Bowman, C. A., Hodson, B. W., & Simpson, R. K. (1980). Oral apraxia and aphasic misarticulation. In R. H. Brookshire (Ed.), *Clinical aphasiology* (pp. 89–95). Minneapolis: B. R. K. Publishers.

Buckingham, H. W. (1979). Linguistic aspects of lexical retrieval disturbances in the posterior fluent aphasias. In H. Whitaker & H. Whitaker (Eds.), *Studies in neurolinguistics* (Vol. 4, pp. 269–292). New York: Academic Press.

Buckingham, H. W., & Kertesz, A. (1976). *Neologistic jargon aphasia*. Amsterdam: Swets & Zeitlinger.

Butterworth, B. (1982). Speech errors: Old data in search of new theories. In A. Cutler (Ed.), *Slips of the tongue in language production* (pp. 73–108). The Hague: Mouton.

Butterworth, B. (1985). Jargon aphasia: Processes and strategies. In S. Newman & R. Epstein (Eds.), *Current perspectives in dysphasia* (pp. 61–97). Edinburgh: Churchill Livingstone.

Butterworth, B., & Howard, D. (1987). Paragrammatisms. *Cognition*, *26*, 1–37.

Caplan, D. (1986). In defense of agrammatism. *Cognition*, *24*, 263–276.

Caplan, D., Baker, C., & Dehaut, F. (1985). Syntactic determinants of sentence comprehension in aphasia. *Cognition*, *21*, 117–175.

Caplan D., Carr, T., Gould, J., Martin, R. (1999). Language and speech. In M. Zigmond, F. E. Bloom, S. C Landis, J. L. Roberts, & L. R. Squire (Eds), *Fundamental neuroscience* (pp. 1487–1519). New York: Academic Press.

Caplan, D., & Gould, J. (2002). Language and communication. In M. Zigmond, F. E. Bloom, S. C. Landis, J. L. Roberts, & L. R. Squire (Eds.), *Fundamental neuroscience*, (2nd ed., pp. 1329–1352). New York: Academic Press.

Caplan, D., & Hildebrandt, H. (1988). *Disorders of syntactic comprehension*. Cambridge, MA: Bradford Books.

Caplan, D., Hildebrandt, H., & Makris, N. (1996). Location of lesions in stroke patients with deficits in syntactic processing in sentence comprehension. *Brain*, *119*, 993–949.

Caplan, D., Vanier, M., & Baker, C. (1986). A case study of reproduction conduction aphasia I: Word production. *Cognitive Neuropsychology*, *3*, 99–128.

Caplan, D., & Waters, G. S. (1990). Short-term memory and language comprehension: A critical review of the neuropsychological literature. In G. Vallar & T. Shallice (Ed.), *Neuropsychological impairments of short-term memory* (pp. 337–389). Cambridge, UK: Cambridge University Press.

Caplan, D., & Waters, G. S. (1999).Issues regarding general and domain specific resources. *Behavioral and Brain Sciences*, *22*, 114–126.

Caramazza, A., Berndt, R., & Basili, A. (1983). The selective impairment of phonological processing: A case study. *Brain & Language*, *18*, 128–174.

Caramazza, A., & Zurif, E. B. (1976). Dissociation of algorithmic and heuristic processes in language comprehension: Evidence from aphasia. *Brain and Language*, *3*, 572–582.

Darley, F. L. (1983). Foreword. In W. R. Berry (Ed.), *Clinical dysarthria* (pp. xii–xv). San Diego: College Hill Press.

Denes, G., & Semenza, C. (1975). Auditory modality-specific anomia: Evidence from a case of pure word deafness. *Cortex*, *11*, 401–411.

Garrett, M. F. (1982). Production of speech: Observations from normal and pathological language use. In A. W. Ellis (Ed.), *Normality and pathology in cognitive functions* (pp. 19–75). London: Academic Press.

Geschwind, N. (1965). Disconnection syndromes in animals and man. *Brain*, *88*, 237–294, 585–644.

Goodglass, H., & Berko, J. (1960). Agrammatism and inflectional morphology in English. *Journal of Speech and Hearing Research*, *3*, 257–267.

Goodglass, H., & Geschwind, N. (1976). Language disorders (aphasia). In E. C. Carterette & M. P. Friedman (Eds.), *Handbook of perception. Vol. 7: Language* (pp. 389–428). New York: Academic Press.

Goodglass, H., Gleason, J. B., Bernholtz, N., & Hyde, M. R. (1972). Some linguistic structures in the speech of a Broca's aphasic. *Cortex*, *8*, 191–212.

Goodglass, H., & Menn, L. (1985). Is agrammatism a unitary phenomenon? In M. L. Kean (Ed.), *Agrammatism* (pp. 1–26). London: Academic Press.

Grodzinsky, Y. (1984). The syntactic characterization of agrammatism. *Cognition, 16,* 99–120.

Heeschen, C. (1985). Agrammatism versusparagrammatism: A fictitious opposition. In M. -L. Kean (Ed.), *Agrammatism* (pp. 207–248). London: Academic Press.

Hildebrandt, N., Caplan, D., & Evans, K. (1987). The mani left ti without a trace: A case study of aphasic processing of empty categories. *Cognitive Neuropsychology, 4,* 257–302.

Itoh, M., Sasanuma, S., Hirose, H., Yoshioka H., & Ushijima, T. (1980). Abnormal articulatory dynamics in a patient with apraxia of speech: X-ray microbeam observation. *Brain and Language, 11,* 66–75.

Joanette, Y., Ali-Cherif, A., Delpuech, F., Habib, M., Pellissier, J., & Poncet, M. (1983). Evolution de la semeiologie aphasique avec l'age. *Revue Neurologique, 11,* 567–664.

Joanette, Y., Keller, E., & Lecours, A. -R. (1980). Sequence of phonemic approximations in aphasia. *Brain and Language, 11,* 30–44.

Kean, M. -L. (1977). The linguistic interpretation of aphasic syndromes: Agrammatism in Broca's aphasia, an example. *Cognition, 5,* 9–46.

Kent, R., & Rosenbek, J. (1982). Prosodic disturbance and neurological lesion. *Brain and Language, 15,* 259–291.

Kohn, S. E. (1984). The nature of the phonological disorder in conduction aphasia. *Brain and Language, 23,* 97–115.

Kohn, S. E. (1989). The nature of the phonemic string deficit in conduction aphasia. *Aphasiology, 3,* 209–239.

Lapointe, S. (1983). Some issues in the linguistic description of agrammatism. *Cognition, 14,* 1–39.

Lecours, A. R., & Lhermitte, F. (1969). Phonemic paraphasias: Linguistic structures and tentative hypotheses. *Cortex, 5,* 193–228.

Lecours, A. R., & Rouillon, F. (1976). Neurolinguistic analysis of jargon aphasia and jargon agraphia. In H. Whitaker & H. Whitaker (Eds.), *Studies in neurolinguistics: Vol. 2.* (pp. 95–144. New York: Academic Press.

Levelt, W. J. M. (1989). *Speaking: From intention to articulation.* Cambridge, MA: MIT Press.

Linebarger, M. C. (1990). Neuropsychology of sentence parsing. In A. Caramazza (Ed.), *Cognitive neuropsychology and neurolinguistics: Advances in models of cognitive function and impairment* (pp. 55–122). Hillsdale, NJ: Lawrence Erlbaum Associates.

Linebarger, M. C., Schwartz, M. F., & Saffran, E. M. (1983). Sensitivity to grammatical structure in so-called agrammatic aphasics. *Cognition, 13,* 361–392.

Martin, A., & Caramazza, A. (Eds.) (2003). The organization of conceptual knowledge in the brain: Neuropsychological and neuroimaging perspectives [Special Issue]. *Cognitive Neuropsychology, 20*(3–6), 195–212.

Martin, R. & fener, E. (1990). The consequences of reduced memory span for the comprehension of semantic versus syntactic information. *Brain and Language, 38,* 1–20.

McCarthy, R., & Warrington, E. K. (1985). Category specificity in an agrammatic patient: The relative impairment of verb retrieval and comprehension. *Neuropsychologia, 23,* 709–727.

McCarthy, R., & Warrington, E. K. (1987). Understanding: A function of short-term memory? *Brain, 110,* 1565–1578.

McNeill, D., Levy, E. T., & Pedelty, L. L. (1990). Speech and gesture. In G. E. Hammond (Ed.), *Cerebral control of speech and limb movements* (pp. 203–256). Amsterdam: Elsevier.

Menn, L., Obler, L., & Goodglass, H. (1990). *A cross-language study of agrammatism.* Philadelphia: John Benjamins.

Mesulam, M. -M. (2003). Current concepts—Primary progressive aphasia—A language-based dementia. *New England Journal of Medicine, 349,* 1535–1542.

Miceli, G., & Caramazza, A. (1988). Dissociation of inflectional and derivational morphology. *Brain and Language, 35,* 24–65.

Miceli, G., Gainotti, G., Caltagirone, C., & Masullo, C. (1980). Some aspects of phonological impairment in aphasia. *Brain and Language, 11,* 159–169.

Miceli, G., Silveri, M., Villa, G., & Caramazza, A. (1984). On the basis for the agrammatic's difficulty in producing main verbs. *Cortex, 20,* 207–220.

Miceli, G., Silveri, M. C., Romani, C., & Caramazza, A. (1989). Variation in the pattern of omissions and substitutions of grammatical morphemes in the spontaneous speech of so-called agrammatic patients. *Brain and Language, 36,* 447–492.

Nespoulous, J. L., Joanette, Y., Beland, R., Caplan, D., & Lecours, A. R. (1984). Phonological disturbances in aphasia: Is there a "markedness" effect in aphasic phonemic errors? In F. C. Rose (Ed.), *Progress in aphasiology: Advances in neurology* (pp. 203–214). New York: Raven Press.

Nespoulous, J. -L., Dordain, M., Perron, C., Ska, B., Bub, D., Caplan, D., Mehler, J., & Lecours, A. R. (1988). Agrammatism in sentence production without comprehension deficits: Reduced availability of syntactic structures and/or of grammatical morphemes? A case study. *Brain and Language, 33,* 273–295.

Odell, K., McNeil, M. R., Rosenbek, J. C., & Hunter, L. (1990). Perceptual characteristics of consonant production by apraxic speakers. *Journal of Speech and Hearing Disorders, 55,* 345–359.

Odell, K., McNeil, M. R., Rosenbek, J. C., & Hunter, L. (1991). Perceptual characteristics of vowel and prosody production in apraxic, aphasic, and dysarthric speakers. *Journal of Speech and Hearing Research, 34,* 67–80.

Ostrin, R., & Schwartz, M. F. (1986). Reconstructing from a degraded trace: A study of sentence repetition in agrammatism. *Brain and Language, 28,* 328–345.

Pate, D. S., Saffran, E. M., & Martin, N. (1987). Specifying the nature of the production impairment in a conduction aphasic: A case study. *Language and Cognitive Processes, 2,* 43–84.

Rapp, B., & Caramazza, A. (1997). The modality-specific organization of grammatical categories: Evidence from impaired spoken and written sentence production. *Brain and Language, 56,* 248–286.

Saffran, E. M., Marin, O., & Yeni-Komshian, G. (1976). An analysis of speech perception in word deafness. *Brain and Language, 3,* 209–228.

Sartori, G., & Job, R. (1988). The oyster with four legs: A neuropsychological study on the interaction of visual and semantic information. *Cognitive Neuropsychology, 5,* 105–132.

Schwartz, M. F., Linebarger, M. C., & Saffran, E. M. (1985). The status of the syntactic deficit theory of agrammatism. In M.-L. Kean (Ed.), *Agrammatism* (pp. 83–124). New York: Academic Press.

Schwartz, M. F., Linebarger, M. C., Saffran, E. M., & Pate, D. S. (1987). Syntactic transparency and sentence interpretation in aphasia. *Language and Cognitive Processes, 2,* 85–113.

Schwartz, M. F., Marin, O., & Saffran, E. (1979). Dissociation of language functions in dementia: A case study. *Brain and Language, 7,* 277–306.

Schwartz, M. F., Saffran, E., & Marin, O. (1980). The word order problem in agrammatism. I: Comprehension. *Brain and Language, 10,* 249–262.

Silveri, M. C., & Gainotti, G. B. (1988). Interaction between vision and language in category-specific semantic impairment for living things. *Cognitive Neuropsychology, 5,* 677–709.

Snowdon, D., Greiner, L., & Markesbery, W. (2000). Linguistic ability in early life and the neuropathology of Alzheimer's disease and cerebrovascular disease: Findings from the Nun Study. In R. N. Kalaria & P. Ince (Eds.), *Vascular factors in Alzheimer's disease* (Vol. 903, pp. 34–38). New York: New York Academy of Sciences.

Snowdon, D. A., Kemper, S., Mortimer, J. A., Greiner, L. H., Wekstein, D. R., & Markesbery, W. R. (1996). Linguistic ability in early life and cognitive function and Alzheimer's disease in late life: Findings from the Nun Study. *Journal of the American Medical Association, 275,* 528–532.

Tyler, L. K. (1985). Real-time comprehension processes in agrammatism: A case study. *Brain and Language, 26,* 259–275.

Vallar, G., & Baddeley, A. D. (1987). Phonological short-term store and sentence processing. *Cognitive Neuropsychology, 4,* 417–438.

Warrington, E. K. (1981). Neuropsychological studies of verbal semantic systems. *Philosophical Transactions of the Royal Society of London, B295,* 411–423.

Warrington, E. K., & McCarthy, R. (1983). Category specific access dysphasia. *Brain, 106,* 859–878.

Warrington, E. K., & McCarthy, R. (1987). Categories of knowledge: Further fractionations and an attempted integration. *Brain, 110,* 1273–1296.

Warrington, E. K., & Shallice, T. (1984). Category-specific semantic impairments. *Brain, 107,* 829–854.

Waters, G. S., Caplan, D., & Hildebrandt, N. (1991). On the structure of the verbal short-term memory and its functional role in language comprehension: Evidence from neuropsychology. *Cognitive Neuropsychology, 8,* 81–126.

Wernicke, K. (1874/1974). *The aphasic symptom complex: A psychological study on a neurological basis.* In R. S. Cohen & M. W. Wartofsky (Eds.), *Boston studies in the philosophy of science* (Vol. 4, pp. 34–97). Boston: Reidel.

Zingeser, L. B., & Berndt, R. S. (1988). Grammatical class and context effects in a case of pure anomia: Implications for models of lexical processing. *Cognitive Neuropsychology, 5,* 473–516.

18

Patterns of Knowledge Growth and Decline

Frank Keil

The last two decades of cognitive science have revealed a number of new patterns of cognitive development—patterns that have changed dramatically how scholars think about the growth of knowledge and of cognitive competencies. In this chapter I consider some of these patterns and the possible implications for what might happen when knowledge and ability change in old age. The general message is that many of the patterns that have come to figure prominently in recent explanations of knowledge acquisition are likely to be involved in explanations of decline as well. At the same time, however, it is equally clear that the story for aging will not simply be that of development in reverse. I know of no physical biological system for which the development-in-reverse model is remotely plausible for explaining what happens as an organism ages. Thus, the decline in kidney function or heart function in the elderly does not resemble at all the functioning of the infant kidney or heart.

There is, of course, the common thread that as one moves both younger and older beyond some optimal age of maturity, there are declines in function; beyond that very global pattern of change the specifics vary greatly. This chapter, therefore, seeks to establish a middle level of analysis, that while rejecting the aging as development-in-reverse argument, it embraces the more general principle that many of the same factors that have proved to be essential to understanding developmental change are also ones that may be critical in understanding aging, albeit in different ways. Although I am certainly an aging researcher, I am not a researcher of aging, so my focus will primarily be on developmental patterns with a more speculative eye toward aging, assuming that others in this volume will look at development in the same manner from an aging perspective. In particular, Chapter 19 (this volume) by Salthouse on the aging of thought illustrates in detail the different aging patterns related to processing efficiency and knowledge. While the focus here is more on knowledge, as Salthouse points out, there is a clear need to understand how processing strategies and knowledge interact.

This chapter considers four topics that have been especially prominent in changing views of cognitive development and seem to have a special relevance for cognition in the elderly: claims of abstract and concrete thought shifts, influences of intuitive theories at both implicit and explicit levels, domain specificity, and the need for hybrid models of cognition. In each case, the topics have been fertile areas for the study of cognitive development. I will also argue that their particular influences on cognitive development suggest that they are especially relevant to the study of changes in cognition in the elderly.

ABSTRACT-TO-CONCRETE PROGRESSIONS IN DEVELOPMENT

Children's behaviors sometimes seem to suggest that they are immersed in a cognitively concrete world. Researchers with otherwise dramatic theoretical differences, ranging from Vygotsky to Piaget, and from Werner to Bruner, all have in one sense or another suggested that younger children are more concrete than older children in terms of how they understand, represent, and think about the world (Inhelder & Piaget, 1958; Vygostky, 1962; Werner & Kaplan, 1963). This eclectic set of scholars sees preschoolers and often young elementary schoolchildren as reasoning in the here and now and being unable to abstract away from perceptually salient aspects of displays. Failures to conserve quantities, for example, have been explained in this manner as having difficulties in zeroing in on one critical dimension while ignoring other salient but irrelevant ones. Failures to apprehend some metaphors have been attributed to a tendency on the part of young children to have difficulty grasping the sorts of abstract relations that link two domains that are dissimilar at a perceptual level.

There is clearly something that these diverse theorists have identified as changing in childhood, but it may have little to do with a cognitive ability to grasp and use abstract relational information and much more to do with a constellation of other problems that may mistakenly suggest a problem with abstraction. Clarifying the real pattern here is essential because it offers a different way of thinking about some changes in aging. Part of the problem is that unambiguous specifications of what is meant by abstract and concrete thought are not usually apparent. For purposes of discussion, we can describe abstract thought as that

which is more removed from direct perceptual experience and that often involves properties that take several arguments. We will, therefore, assume that abstract relations are those that operate above the level of immediate perception. Thus, a car can be red, but it can also be rare or expensive, with the latter properties being more abstract. Note that both of those abstract properties are also relational in nature since they require some reference to other cars. Other relational sorts of properties include "is convenient," "is portable," and "is well suited for its niche."

The contrast between concrete and abstract thought is never easy to specify, but a final resolution is not needed to make the point here, which is simply that, however the distinction is made, there is no straightforward developmental pattern going from concrete to abstract thought. Why, then, is such a pattern so often claimed? One major source of confusion may center on the difference between being able to explicitly talk about abstract relations and being able to use abstract relations in information more implicitly in various tasks. Based on their early vocabularies, it is certainly the case that many relations and nonphysical properties are not in the normal vocabularies of young children. Few 5-year-olds can correctly deploy or understand a phrase such as "well suited for its niche." For that reason, if the ability to have abstract thought is equated with the ability to verbalize abstract properties and relations, then a major developmental change could be seen as occurring. But such an equation of thought with verbalization in language is suspect if we can show other ways in which young children are sensitive to abstract relations and use them in cognitive tasks. Developmental psychology in the past 20 years or so has repeatedly demonstrated rich sensitivities to such abstract relations in quite young children. Indeed, in many cases the developmental shift seems not be from the concrete to abstract but the other way around.

Consider several examples of shifts that seem to go from the abstract to the concrete. One venerable case involves the acquisition of language. It has been argued repeatedly that younger children often seem to grasp highly abstract properties of a grammar long before they have acquired concrete details. Thus, they start ordering abstract syntactic elements such as noun phrase, verb phrase, and prepositional phrase before they have mastered all the details of the syntax of their language (Crain & Lillo-Martin, 1999). Similarly, they honor abstract constraints on movement rules even as the details of those movement rules remain to be addressed (Pinker, 1994). They clearly know (at least implicitly) many of the abstract properties and relations of a language even as they, and for that matter most adults, are completely unable to verbalize them. Language, therefore, illustrates in an especially striking manner how implicit knowledge can precede explicit knowledge. Metalinguistic awareness—that is, conscious knowledge about language structures and relations—emerges quite late (Bialystok, 1982; Bialystok & Ryan, 1985). Moreover, it hardly emerges to a full extent in normal adults, as can be seen in the surprise that beginning linguistics students show when first exposed to rulelike regularities in areas such as syntax and phonology. It does seem to be the case that in situations where there is an abstract-to-concrete shift in development, the earlier abstract form is usually implicit while the later concrete form may be explicit to varying degrees.

A second example is seen in the naïve biologies of young children (Inagaki & Hatano, 2002). Preschoolers sense a great deal about the living world at an abstract level. They know that living kinds are embedded in rich and unique hierarchies. They know that living kinds have "vital forces" inside them that are responsible for growth and movement and that need food to replenish those forces. They also know that living kinds have properties that serve purposes even as the organism as a whole is rarely considered to have a purpose (Keil, 1992). They may make mistakes in extending teleological interpretations too broadly to nonliving kinds (Keleman, 1999), but they nonetheless have a rich variety of expectations about the causal properties of living kinds. They also clearly have a sense of organisms having properties that make them adapted to their niches (Keil & Richardson, 1999). Even as they have those expectations, however, they can be woefully inadequate on the details of physiology, reproduction, and disease (Inagaki & Hatano, 2002). The mechanistic details of animals and plants continue to be learned over most of one's lifetime but always within a constant backdrop of skeletal abstract expectations about the special causal character of living kinds. Again, however, while this knowledge can be revealed as guiding judgments in many tasks, it is invariably not of the sort that either children or adults find easy to verbalize.

A third example involves naïve essentialism—the attribution of essences to natural kinds and to intentional beings (Gelman, 2002). Children in the pre-school years assume the presence of hidden microstructures that are causally responsible for surface appearances. They do so for properties of living things, for elements like gold and silver, and for personality traits. They are usually completely ignorant as to how essence is causally linked to surface phenomena, but strongly believe in the essence nonetheless and make judgments reflecting this assumption of essence.

More broadly, young children often seem to sense the broad-brush causal patterns associated with various domains while lacking virtually all the mechanistic details. In this manner, they sense the abstract before they know the concrete. Even in tasks as simple as classification of objects or induction of new properties, very young children can be shown to sometimes generalize over very high-level and abstract categories such as vehicles and animals despite not having those high-level labels in their lexicons (Mandler, 2004). Children also founder in tasks that use arbitrary or nonsensical stimulus patterns as opposed to ones that are more familiar or involve real-world cases. This pattern of failure can again be confused with a difficulty with abstract thought, when in fact it seems more to involve motivational issues and difficulties in understanding the pragmatics of tasks with meaningless components. Adults in other cultures also often find such tasks bizarre and do poorly on them, leading to erroneous claims that they are cognitively immature, like children (Cole & Means, 1981).

In the later years of life, this same sense of causal patterns may be preserved, and often expanded on, even as myriad details about the workings of the world are lost. Indeed, much of what we think of as wisdom may be a gradually expanding sense of broad causal patterns without being swamped by the details. It frequently seems that an elderly person has a sense that a new plan will or will not work or that a particular approach is not feasible. When asked to say why, the individual is often at a loss for specific supporting arguments; he or she simply senses that something is missing. This global sense of a good experiment, a good political decision, or a good marketing strategy may arise from a well-elaborated skeletal sense of abstract causal patterns in a domain and of how well a proposal fits with those patterns. This idea of losing the concrete while preserving the abstract resonates closely with other proposals about the elderly; for example, Craik (2002) has suggested that older adults lose access to specific (episodic) representations of events while retaining access to generalities abstracted from these specifics. In other cases, the elderly may continue to acquire and use detailed patterns such as those that facilitate solving of crossword puzzles (see Chapter 19, this volume). How are we to characterize the sort of knowledge that enables people to improve their ability to solve *New York Times* crossword puzzles well into their 80s while at the same time they fail to learn new details of a novel task? It may be that a lifetime of accumulating knowledge structures provides a richly structured framework for words and their relations that enables easy retrieval of crossword puzzle facts while not enabling performance on novel tasks that depend more on declining processing efficiency.

The interaction between different formats of knowledge and declines in processing efficiency in the elderly may shed considerable light on the way those forms of knowledge are represented at all ages.

THE ROLE OF INTUITIVE THEORIES

Much has been made of the importance of intuitive theories in guiding the development of concepts and categories (Barrett, Abdi, Murphy, & Gallagher, 1993; Gelman, 1996; Keil, 1989). Theories tell us which correlations are important, what features to weight among equally frequent ones, and which properties are more likely to be inductively projectible (Murphy & Medin, 1985). Yet, a closer look at the structure of the intuitive theories that adults and children actually use suggests that they are far more skeletal than they seem. Indeed, intuitive theories seem to be often little more than gists of how things work in a domain. It is often not obvious just how sparse our intuitive theories are because we are all under the sway of an "illusion of explanatory depth," in which we think we know the world in much more detail than we really do (Rozenblit & Keil, 2002). These new views of theories are in fact suggesting far more continuity to development. If our theories are much coarser in grain than they seem, then we carry about in our heads not blueprints of how the world works but only the crudest sketches. These sketches are accessible not only to adults but also to young children and are often represented implicitly.

The coarseness of intuitive theories does not in any way diminish their importance as influences on cognitive development. Beliefs about why and how do have dramatic influences on all aspects of cognitive development and make clear the folly of attempting

to model all of cognitive development solely in terms of associative models (Gelman, 2002). In addition, children are often eager to flesh out their skeletal theories on the fly in a particular task. Thus, they seem primed to use situational cues to fill in as many gaps as they can, often coming up with highly unusual ad hoc explanations of the world around them. For example, their intuitive cosmologies, often elaborated in the course of questioning, reveal novel, but conceptually coherent, accounts of how heavenly bodies move and interact (Vosniadu & Brewer, 1992). One of the major challenges for the future is to understand better the constraints on theory elaboration that guide children in certain ways and not others when situations ask for more detailed explanations.

A related issue concerns patterns of inquiry. What drives children to ask why? How do they recognize the limits of their own understanding and thereby appreciate the need to gather more information from others, and how do they know who to ask? Young children are in the curious position of thinking they understand the world in far more detail than they do, while at the same time being willing to ask far more questions about how the world works than older children and adults. At some level, they seem to know where the largest explanatory gaps are and guide the questions accordingly, while at the same time often claiming to understand things that they do not. It may be that these patterns of behavior are related to an irrational optimism that is much more common in younger children (Lockhart, Story, & Chang, 2002). Young children in general think that the future is likely to be much more positive than the present and that negative aspects of people and situations are likely to improve for the better (Lockhart et al., 2002). For example, they judge that other children who are below average in physical or psychological abilities are likely to end up well above average when they grow up. This notion of an improving world with better and better future outcomes may be related to a feeling that even if they know a great deal, they can know much more and should expand their knowledge through questions.

Aging populations may be quite different from young children in terms of their intuitive theories and their views about rosy futures. There may be much less optimism about everything improving and thus fewer feelings of confidence about what one knows and what one can know with further inquiry. Inquisitiveness may seem less promising in its own right and the elderly may be less prone to feelings of ever-expanding understandings. The elderly may also be less under the sway of the illusion of explanatory depth, having a much better sense of the limits of their understanding.

In a manner that may link with the abstract/concrete contrast, older adults, like younger children, may have intuitive theories that are relatively skeletal and abstract and less rich in mechanistic details. In addition, these intuitive theories, like those in younger children, may be largely implicit and more difficult to articulate explicitly with increasing age. If one thinks back to the details that one learned in various science and engineering classes in college and of the traces that exist some 30 or 40 years later, it is clear that while one retains some sense of what one studied, most of the details are lost. It is that sense of a domain that seems to have great resiliency across ages.

If we consider what changes from early childhood to adulthood in terms of the structure and use of intuitive theories, several factors come into play that may also be involved in aging. Knowledge structures get larger and more differentiated, and processing capacity and efficiency also increase, especially in tasks that use those knowledge structures. In the elderly, knowledge structures may stay relatively differentiated and thus help offset declining processing capacity as long as the tasks involved rely on those forms of knowledge. To the extent that they depart from familiar knowledge, the raw power to consider several novel relations in mind at the same time is revealed as declining quite dramatically with age (see Chapter 19, this volume). Thus, intuitive theories may lose some details with increasing age, but enough remains to compensate for processing-efficiency declines in tasks that rely on those theories.

DOMAIN SPECIFICITY

One clear message of developmental research in the past two decades has been that domains of knowledge matter greatly to accounts of how knowledge is acquired. The pattern of cognitive growth in folk biology may have little in common with that found in theory of mind or spatial understanding. This is a major departure from earlier views of development in which a central capacity underwent developmental changes that then had sweeping consequences across all domains of thought. Whether the theorist was Piaget, Vygotsky, Bruner, or any number of other clas-

sic developmental scholars, development was considered to reflect primarily a domain-general ability that often underwent dramatic and qualitative changes. Thus, in the classic accounts, when a child changed from preoperational thought to the stage of concrete operations, that change could then be seen in moral thought, conservation of quantities, causal reasoning, patterns of language use, among many other domains. But those sweeping across-the-board changes in cognition are in fact difficult to find. Instead, knowledge in each domain seems to take its own distinctive developmental journey that is mostly unrelated to development in other domains.

Domain specificity still allows for quite different accounts of development. Some accounts are couched in the perspective of evolutionary psychology and build on the idea that the child's mind is a collection of cognitive adaptations, each tailored to different classes of information. Just as the body has different organs serving different functions, the mind has mental organs that have been selected for serving distinct cognitive functional roles (Cosmides & Tooby, 1994; Pinker, 1997). By this perspective, there are powerful boundary conditions on the structure of knowledge in each domain that result in universal domain-specific constraints on knowledge. Moreover, from the earliest points in development, the child's learning and knowledge follow these domain-specific principles. Thus, the path of knowledge acquisition for number, space, morality, and many other domains is, from the start, highly constrained in ways unique to that domain.

An alternative view of domain-specific development sees the structure of the world as causing an ever-increasing diverse set of knowledge structures, which initially start out as similar if not the same in manner of representation and computation. Such a view might be decidedly empiricist in nature but holds that as the child learns more and more about specific domains, the special properties of each domain take on a life of their own. The unique causal and informational patterns of each domain guide learning along a path specific to that domain. This approach assumes that the world itself is not a homogeneously distributed network of information and causal patterns but rather that the statistical and causal patternings in the living world are different from that of the inanimate world, as well as from the world of artifacts. This assumption seems well justified and can be seen from research on the physics of natural vs. artificial scenes (Olshausen &

Field, 2000), as well as the causal patterns that govern property clusters for living kinds vs. artifacts (Keil, 1989; Kitcher, 1989; Salmon, 1984, 1989).

Domain specificity may have important implications for how we view changes in cognitive capacities in the elderly. Rather than trying to explain declines in function only in global terms, it may well be that different patterns of decline are observed in different domains. Thus, for example, if a domain such as spatial memory is less dependent on working memory and conscious heuristics than memory for lists of numbers, it might stay intact longer. The elderly may experience loss of source-monitoring abilities and some executive functions, but the consequences of these losses may be radically different across domains, as might be the potential for compensatory mechanisms and strategies for dealing with some forms of decline.

Domain specificity may also help explain how performance in some domains can show virtually no decline with age and often show continuous improvement. A good deal of rapid performance depends more on the richness of precompiled knowledge structures than on any basic processing speeds. Thus, in a domain where rich background knowledge can be exploited to guide real-time decisions, even the very elderly may be able to perform more rapidly than younger adults because of the richer array of long-term knowledge that they can access. I know a number of elderly racers of sailboats who often sense wind shifts earlier than anyone else. They may not be asked to steer a boat, where quicker reflexes are needed, but they may be the most rapid authority on changing large-scale configurational patterns on the race course. Thus, even as the age-related components of task performance may all slow down, larger-scale aspects of performance that are heavily dependent on pre-compiled knowledge may show little or no decrement and may actually continue to improve in fairly old populations.

The study of aging should, therefore, benefit substantially from domain-specific considerations and not just of domain-general patterns of decline. In addition, questions about the scope and rigidity of domains in both children and adults need further exploration. Consider, for example, how the domain of folk biology might change from early preschool to young adulthood. One prominent proposal is that preschoolers don't really have a domain of biology at all and can understand things only as if they were in the domains of psychology and folk mechanics (Carey, 1985). By this view, the domain of folk biology expands greatly when the child undergoes a form of conceptual revolution in which living entities are understood as such, perhaps first in a way that includes animals and then later in a manner that includes plants. The view of children undergoing such dramatic conceptual revolutions that generate whole new conceptual domains is controversial, and indeed biological thought may cover a broad domain from a much earlier age and may not show a dramatic shift in terms of what sorts of entities are considered living things (Inagaki & Hatano, 2002), but if any such dramatic cases of conceptual change do occur in children, they may not have close parallels in changes in the elderly. It seems far less plausible that patterns of conceptual change in the elderly have the flavor of radical paradigm shifts of the sort that have been proposed for children. This is presumably because there is a richness to the conceptual structures in the elderly that makes them relatively immune from such radical shifts.

More broadly, it appears that there are several distinct forms of conceptual change ranging from dramatic conceptual revolutions to gradual incremental accretion of knowledge (Keil, 1999). Most of these forms can be found in young children, but some may be much less likely in the elderly. A fascinating question arises as to how the distributions of these different kinds of conceptual change might differ across age groups, especially between young children and elderly.

A related topic is to consider how the interplay between domain-specific and domain-general processes changes over time. For example, one model of change in childhood argues that as domain-specific knowledge gets more and more elaborated, the associative component is relied on less and less, as previous elements that were linked associatively are linked in terms of more structured relations (Keil, 1989). The interplay with associative relations is considered in the next section.

THE INFLUENCE OF
FREQUENCY-BASED INFORMATION

From many perspectives there seems to be a need for hybrid models of knowledge and learning. Such models not only need a component that tracks frequency information and is largely associative but also another part that is more rule-like in nature. That contrast has had an important effect on theories of cognitive development. Consider, for example, the now extensive literature on the acquisition of language. In a variety of subareas of language there is a need for models that incorporate both an ability to monitor how frequently various linguistic structures occur and an ability to represent rule-like structures. One extensively studied case involves the past-tense inflections on English verbs. Most verbs have past-tense forms that are governed by simple rules, such as adding *ed*, hence past tenses such as *kicked, liked, helped,* and so on. At the same time, for some verbs that are the most frequent in the language, the past-tense forms are idiosyncratic and seem to require memorization of their frequencies of occurrence, for example, *went, had, was.* Although there have been repeated attempts to model this contrast in terms of one form of representational system, most notably pure frequency-based systems associated with connectionist models (Plunkett & Marchman, 1993; Rumelhart & McClelland, 1986), it appears that hybrid systems may be a much more effective way of capturing the range of relevant data (Pinker & Ullman, 2002). Behavior genetics studies, patterns of brain damage, and recent neuroimaging studies all point to two distinct systems, one which monitors basic frequencies and one which represents lexical rules (Pinker & Ullman, 2002).

The need for hybrid models recurs throughout cognition. Models of concept formation (Murphy, 2002), pattern recognition, and errors in reasoning all involve blends of these two aspects of mind (Sloman, 1996). Developmentally, the central question arising from such work has been whether one form of representation is privileged early on in development. It has been often proposed, for example, that younger children are more purely associative creatures, tabulating up all correlations in their environments and only later in development do rule-like representations arise out of the networks of associations (Quine, 1969). But that doctrine of "original sim" (or *original associative similarity*) does not seem to comport with the facts. Study after study of young children, and even infants, suggests that they are mixes of rule-like representational capacities and frequency-based ones (Gelman, 2003; Keil, Smith, Simons, & Levin, 1998). Some still argue that very young infants in the first month or two of life are pure bottom-up tabulators of perceptually salient patterns of co-occurrence (e.g., Johnson, 2003); but even if such controversial accounts turn out to be correct, it is clear that well before the first half year of life, infants are forming representations of the world that appear to include mixtures of rules and associa-

tions. From my perspective, these two aspects of representation are intrinsically interdependent and cannot exist without each other throughout the entire course of development (Keil et al., 1998).

What develops are increasingly differentiated sets of rule-like representations and increasing access to explicit rules that then can be used in more novel domains (Rozin, 1976). Associative tabulations are also obviously being modified throughout the course of development as they reflect new experiences gained by the child. Rules, however, also favor some sorts of associative tabulations over others by directing attention to some relations as much more relevant than others (Keil, 1981; Murphy & Medin, 1985).

In the elderly, the interplay between these two aspects of mind remains a critical area of inquiry. It does appear that an elderly individual may retain a highly intact ability to monitor frequencies of instances but lose an explicit sense of their occurrences and perhaps also of explicit rules governing those instances (e.g., Jacoby, Hessels, & Bopp, 2001). Repetitions of a name or a concept will be absorbed implicitly in lawful ways related to their frequency while explicit aspects of their message may be lost. It is unlikely that even the most elderly and debilitated individuals have become largely associative minds any more than that account seems to be true for infants. There may, however, be more subtle but nonetheless significant shifts in the interplay between frequency-based representations and more rule-like ones, especially those that are explicit. Older adults, for example, may use rule-like representations more generally in a manner that is less context dependent and tuned to particular situations. A basic ability to implicitly register frequencies may be robustly present at all points in development; but it is never the only mechanism of cognition and indeed is quite impotent without interactions with higher level cognition.

CONCLUSIONS

Over the past two decades, a revolution has occurred in the study of cognitive development. That revolution has endorsed the importance of domain-specific patterns of cognitive development, of reconsideration of the primacy of concrete over abstract thought in early development, and of the role of intuitive theories while at the same time recognizing the continued importance of more associative models of mind. These patterns are only some of the major shifts in how cognitive development is being understood, but they do seem to have intriguing implications for the study of aging.

More generally, several themes concerning comparisons of aging and cognitive development have been suggested as well:

1. Aging should not be considered as merely development in reverse. This is obviously not the case for the body's physiology and is no more likely to be the case for the mind. It is tempting to tell such stories since there are diminished abilities at both ends of the age spectrum, but there is no reason patterns of decline of function in old age should mirror those of the rise of function in childhood. If, for example, patterns of conceptual change tend to be quite different in the young and the old, it follows that domains of knowledge and the processes that operate on them will change in different ways as well.

2. Both development and aging provide cases of change, which in turn provides a way to look for invariant constraints on cognition. One of the most revealing new directions of developmental research in recent years has been to determine what aspects of knowledge seem to be structurally preserved across otherwise dramatic change. For example, while the child's grammar may become much more elaborated between the ages of 3 and 13, the basic universal constraints on grammar remain the same. Patterns of change, therefore, provide a way of highlighting overarching constraints on cognition that hold in all situations. In the same manner, aging provides yet another case of change that illuminates those constraints.

3. While aging is not development in reverse, the diminished levels of performance at both ends of the age spectrum may provide some insight into core as opposed to less essential cognitive functions. As the cognitive system becomes more taxed and limited in what it can do, resources may be devoted more to core cognitive functions that must remain robust both in young children and in the elderly. Thus, looking at what aspects of mind are most preserved in the very young and the very old may tell us something about those aspects that have the most functional value. This strategy may break down in some cases, however, because even if there are adaptive reasons for certain core functions being preserved in infancy and early childhood, it is far less likely that there were any

evolutionary pressures on preserving core functions in the elderly. For that reason, a related question of interest will be about what core functions are *not* in common between the very old and the very young. Thus, some functions may be lost or greatly diminished in old age that are present in young children. These might include the abilities to learn a new grammar, and perhaps some complex motor patterns such as those involved in learning to play musical instruments.

4. Cognitive strategies may be far more domain-specific than they seem. Thus, in children, the early work showing the emergence of meta-cognitive strategies for memory and attention suggested a general increase in such strategies across the board. In fact, however, meta-cognitive awareness seems to be linked to domain expertise as well, such that children are more aware of their own mental abilities in domains where they are more expert. It seems likely that in the elderly as well, the burgeoning literature on compensatory strategies used by the elderly to deal with some deficits will need to be considered relative to the amount of expertise a person has in a particular area. Thus, an aging expert accountant might have developed a number of strategies for dealing with failing memory processes, but not use those same strategies in less familiar domains where that accountant has less experience. As seen in Chapter 19 (this volume), when relevant domains of knowledge can be exploited heavily, performance can continue to improve well into the 80s even if, in tasks with more novel materials, there is a clear pattern of decline.

Just as cross-cultural research and developmental research have richly cross-fertilized each other in recent years by looking at patterns of variation and constancy across different ages and cultures, comparisons of changing aspects of cognition in development and aging should be highly fruitful as well. There will be no simple mirroring of effects, but a deeper comparison of patterns of change should be highly informative.

ACKNOWLEDGMENTS   Preparation of this chapter and some of the research described therein was supported by NIH grant R-37-HD023922 to Frank Keil. Thanks to Ellen Bialystok, Gus Craik, and Tim Salthouse for comments on earlier drafts of this chapter.

References

Barrett, S. E., Abdi, H., Murphy, G. L., & Gallagher, J. M. (1993). Theory-based correlations and their role in children's concepts. *Child Development, 64,* 1595–1616.

Bialystok, E. (1982). On the relationship between knowing and using linguistic forms. *Applied Linguistics, 3,* 181–206.

Bialystok, E., & Ryan, E. B. (1985). Toward a definition of metalinguistic skill. *Merrill Palmer Quarterly, 31,* 229–251.

Carey, S. (1985). *Conceptual change in childhood.* Cambridge, MA: MIT Press.

Cole, M., & Means, B. (1981). *Comparative studies of how people think: An introduction.* Cambridge, MA: Harvard University Press.

Cosmides, L., & Tooby, J. (1994). Origins of domain-specificity: The evolution of functional organization. In L. Hirschfeld & S. Gelman (Eds.), *Mapping the mind: Domain-specificity in cognition and culture* (pp. 85–116). New York: Cambridge University Press.

Craik, F. I. M. (2002). Human memory and aging. In L. Bäckman & C. von Hofsten (Eds.), *Psychology at the turn of the millennium* (pp. 261–280). Hove, UK: Psychology Press.

Crain, S., & Lillo-Martin, D. (1999). *An introduction to linguistic theory and language acquisition.* Oxford: Blackwell Publishers.

Gelman, S. A. (1996). Concepts and theories. In R. Gelman & T. K. Au (Eds.), *Perceptual and cognitive development* (pp. 117–150). New York: Academic Press.

Gelman, R. (2002). Cognitive development. In D. Medin & H. Pashler (Eds.), *Steven's handbook of experimental psychology* (3rd ed., Vol. 2, pp. 533–559).

Gelman, S. (2003). *The essential child.* New York: Oxford University Press.

Inagaki, K., & Hatano, G. (2002). *Young children's naïve thinking about the biological world.* Brighton, UK: Psychology Press.

Inhelder, B., & Piaget, J. (1958). *The growth of logical thinking from childhood to adolescence.* New York: Basic Books.

Jacoby, L. L., Hessels, S., & Bopp, K. (2001). Proactive and retroactive effects in memory performance: Dissociating recollection and accessibility bias. In H. L. Roediger III, J. S. Nairne, I. Neath, & A. M. Surprenant (Eds.), *The nature of remembering: Essays in honor of Robert G. Crowder* (pp. 35–54). Washington, DC: American Psychological Association.

Johnson, S. P. (2003). The nature of cognitive development. *Trends in Cognitive Sciences, 7,* 102–104.

Keil, F. C. (1981). Constraints on knowledge and cognitive development. *Psychological Review, 88,* 197–227.

Keil, F. C. (1989). *Concepts, kinds and cognitive development.* Cambridge, MA: MIT Press.

Keil, F. C. (1992). The origins of an autonomous biology. In M. R. Gunnar & M. Maratos (Eds.), *Modularity and constraints in language and cognition: The Minnesota symposia on child psychology* (Vol. 25, pp. 103–137). Hillsdale, NJ: Lawrence Erlbaum Associates.

Keil, F. C. (1999). Conceptual change. In R. Wilson & F. Keil (Eds.), *The MIT encyclopedia of cognitive sciences* (pp. 179–182). Cambridge: MIT Press.

Keil, F. C., Smith, C. S., Simons, D., & Levin, D. (1998). Two dogmas of conceptual empiricism. *Cognition, 65,* 103–135.

Keil, F. C., & Richardson, D. (1999). Species, stuff, and patterns of causation. In R. A. Wilson (Ed.), *Species: New interdisciplinary essays* (pp. 263–282). Cambridge, MA: MIT Press.

Keleman, D. (1999). Function, goals, and intention: Children's teleological reasoning about objects. *Trends in Cognitive Sciences, 3,* 461–468.

Kitcher, P. S. (1989). Explanatory unification and the causal structure of the world. In P. S. Kitcher & W. Salmon (Eds.), *Scientific explanation: Minnesota studies in the philosophy of science* (Vol. 13, pp. 336–373). Minneapolis: University of Minnesota Press.

Lockhart, K. L., Story, T., & Chang, B. (2002). Young children's beliefs about the stability of traits: Protective optimism? *Child Development, 75,* 1408–1430.

Mandler, J. M. (2004). *The foundations of mind: Origins of conceptual thought.* Oxford: Oxford University Press.

Murphy, G. (2002). *The big book of concepts.* Cambridge, MA: MIT Press.

Murphy, G., & Medin, D. (1985). The role of theories in conceptual coherence. *Psychological Review, 92,* 289–316.

Olshausen, B. A., & Field, D. J. (2000). Vision and the coding of natural images. *American Scientist, 88,* 238–245.

Pinker, S. (1994). *The language instinct.* New York: HarperCollins.

Pinker, S. (1997). *How the mind works.* New York: W. W. Norton.

Pinker, S., & Ullman, M. (2002). The past and future of the past tense. *Trends in Cognitive Science, 6,* 456–463.

Plunkett, K., & Marchman, V. (1993). From rote learning to system building: Acquiring verb morphology in children and connectionist nets. *Cognition, 48*, 21–69.

Quine, W. V. O. (1969). Natural kinds. In *Ontological relativity and other essays* (pp. 114–138). New York: Columbia University Press.

Rozenblit, L., & Keil, F. C. (2002). An illusion of explanatory depth. *Cognitive Science, 26*, 521–562.

Rozin, P. (1976). The evolution of intelligence and access to the cognitive unconscious. In J. N. Sprague & A. N. Epstein (Eds.), *Progress in psychobiology and physiological psychology* (Vol. 6, pp. 245–280). New York: Academic Press.

Rumelhart, D. E., & McClelland, J. L. (1986). *On learning the past tenses of English verbs*. Cambridge, MA: MIT Press.

Salmon, W. C. (1984). *Scientific explanation and the causal structure of the world*. Princeton: Princeton University Press.

Salmon, W. C. (1989). *Four decades of scientific explanation*. Minneapolis: University of Minnesota Press.

Sloman, S. A. (1996). The empirical case for two systems of reasoning. *Psychological Bulletin, 119*, 3–22.

Vosniadou, S., & Brewer, W. F. (1992). Mental models of the earth: A study of conceptual change in childhood. *Cognitive Psychology, 24*, 535–585.

Vygotsky, L. S. (1962). *Thought and language*. Cambridge, MA: MIT Press.

Werner, H., & Kaplan, B. (1963). *Symbol formation: An organismic developmental approach to language and the expression of thought*. New York: Wiley.

19

Aging of Thought

Timothy A. Salthouse

Thinking can be defined as the application of reasoning and other cognitive processes to one's available knowledge to achieve some goal. It is therefore useful to begin this chapter by considering the relations between adult age and performance on two activities that involve thinking from this definition. One task is based on the analytical reasoning test formerly used in the Graduate Record Examination to supplement assessments of quantitative and verbal abilities. In this test the examinee reads several statements that establish various constraints, and then evaluates a set of assertions to determine which of them best satisfies those constraints. A very simple problem in this test might consist of the following statements:

Judy and Elaine want to get together for dinner this week. Judy has to work late on Monday and Tuesday, and is going out with her boyfriend on Friday. Elaine will be out of town on Tuesday and Wednesday. Which days are possible for their

dinner—Monday, Tuesday, Wednesday, Thursday, or Friday?

A second activity that can be considered to involve thinking, because it also combines reasoning and knowledge, consists of solving difficult crossword puzzles such as those found in weekend editions of the *New York Times* newspaper. Like the analytical reasoning test, solution of crossword puzzles can be hypothesized to involve reasoning from constraints, although in this case the constraints are the clue: the number of letters in the word, and the identity of any letters that have already been determined from intersecting words.

Because the variables are in different units, in order to allow them to be directly compared they have been converted into standard scores by subtracting the mean from each value and dividing the difference by the standard deviation. The relations of age on the standard scores in these two tasks from four different samples of approximately 200 adults each (i.e., three studies in Hambrick, Salthouse, & Meinz, 1999, and one in Salthouse, 2001) are illustrated in Figure 19.1. It can be seen that the age trends in the two tasks are quite different, with a nearly linear decline across the adult years in analytical reasoning performance, but with older adults achieving the highest average level of performance in the crossword puzzle measure. Because the age trends on these tasks are so different, it is reasonable to ask whether it is meaningful to refer to them both as illustrations of the same phenomenon. In fact, some researchers have argued that the existence of different developmental trends is evidence that the variables represent distinct theoretical constructs (e.g., Horn, 1989; McArdle, Ferrer-Caja, Hamagami, & Woodcock, 2002). However, an alternative perspective, which will be adopted here, is that variables with different age trends could represent a common construct but may differ with respect to the impact of relevant knowledge.

The possibility that at least two different types of age-related influences contribute to performance in cognitive activities has been mentioned since the earliest studies on this topic (e.g., Foster & Taylor, 1920; Jones & Conrad, 1933). Welford (1958) provided a particularly eloquent discussion of the two types of age trends when he referred to one function, which he designated A, as representing organic capacities, and a second function, which he designated B, as representing effects of cumulative experience. He described their developmental trajectories as follows:

> Curve (A) for the organic factors rises to a peak in early adulthood and then declines. Curve (B) for experience rises throughout life.... The curve (B) is the integral of (A) on the assumption that it should depend upon cumulative exposure to environmental stimulation, and upon the level of (A) in the sense that this will determine the extent to which environmental stimulation is converted into experience. (p. 13)

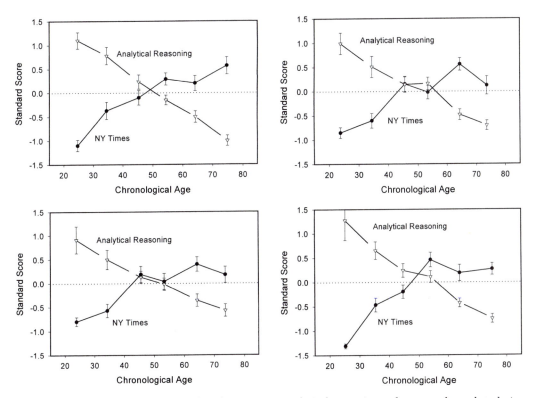

FIGURE 19.1. Relations between age and performance on analytical reasoning and crossword puzzle tasks in studies by Hambrick, Salthouse & Meinz (1999) and Salthouse (2001). Each study involved at least 200 adults with nearly equal numbers at each age between 18 and 80. Bars above and below each point are standard errors.

He went on to suggest that:

> Tasks which make their chief demands upon organic capacities will tend to follow curve (A), those demanding knowledge and experience curve (B). In most cases both types of demand would be made and the result would be intermediate between (A) and (B) according to the balance of demands and the extent to which compensation for deficiencies of organic origin could be made by knowledge gained in the course of experience. (p. 14)

Welford's characterization would probably be readily accepted by most contemporary researchers, but it is surprising how little research is relevant to what he referred to as curve B, or to his hypothesis of knowledge-based compensation. Considerable evidence does exist for the first type of age trajectory mentioned by Welford. Perhaps the most convincing data are those from samples used to establish the norms for standardized cognitive test batteries, such as the Wechsler Abbreviated Scale of Intelligence (WASI, 1999). The matrix reasoning test in this battery involves the examinee inspecting a matrix of geometric figures and patterns, and then attempting to determine the best completion of a section missing from the matrix. In the block design test, the examinee manipulates blocks to produce patterns that will match a target design. Lifespan age trends on these two tasks, with the scores expressed in proportions of the maximum across all ages, are portrayed in Figure 19.2A. It is apparent that these measures of processing efficiency or effectiveness increase dramatically from early childhood until about age 18, after which they decline in a nearly linear manner.

Much less research is consistent with Welford's hypothesized curve B, in which the variable increases continuously from childhood and across most of the adult years. Instead, the majority of the results resemble the patterns illustrated in Figure 19.2B, which are based on the normative data for the WASI Vocabulary and Similarity tests. The Vocabulary test requires the examinee to provide definitions of words, and the Similarities test requires the examinee to state how two words are similar to one another. Inspection of Figure 19.2B reveals that performance in these variables increases dramatically up to about age 50, followed by a gradual decline. Other variables reflecting word knowledge or general information have also revealed a similar curvilinear pattern in adulthood (e.g., Salthouse, 1998, 2003). Furthermore, although there have been many speculations about the role of compensation in adult development (e.g., see Dixon & Backman, 1995), there is still very little empirical evidence documenting the existence of age-related compensation in cognitive activities.

In certain respects, the current chapter can be viewed as an update and extension of Welford's (1958) speculations. The remainder of the chapter is organized as follows. First is a brief summary of the research literature on adult age differences in processing efficiency, or what Welford termed "organic capacities." Next is a discussion of attempts to investigate the relation between processing efficiency and experience-based knowledge in the performance of specific

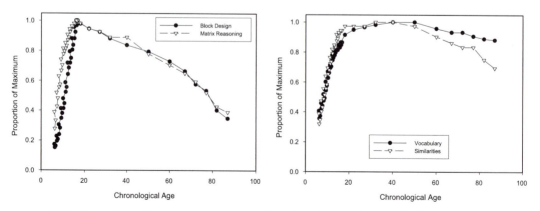

FIGURE 19.2. Proportion of the maximum score as a function of age in four standardized tests. The tests in panel A were designed to have minimal involvement of knowledge while those in panel B primarily reflect acquired knowledge. (Data from Table A.1 in WASI, 1999.)

cognitive activities. The final section of the chapter consists of speculations about change mechanisms that might account for age differences in measures of thinking and other aspects of higher order cognition in both the last 75%, and the first 25%, of the human lifespan.

EFFECTS OF AGING ON EFFICIENCY OF BASIC COGNITIVE PROCESSES

A wide variety of tests and tasks have been used to assess efficiency or effectiveness in what Welford (1958, p. 12) referred to as "mental gymnastic" exercises. A key feature of these tests is that they have been designed to minimize the influence of prior experience in an attempt to assess basic abilities or capacities. Many tests included in standardized cognitive test batteries share this characteristic, and because the

normative samples are moderately large and selected to be representative of the population, age trends in "organic capacities" can be illustrated with the normative data from these test batteries.

Tests included in four recent cognitive test batteries that can be considered to assess various aspects of thinking are briefly described in Table 19.1. Sixteen different tests are included in the table, with each test involving somewhat different requirements, materials, and procedures (e.g., some had time limits and others did not). In order to express all of the variables in a common scale, the scores have been converted into standard deviation units of a reference group of young adults.

Age trends in these 16 tests are illustrated in the four panels of Figure 19.3. In each case there is a monotonic decline with increased age, such that the average at age 65 is about one standard deviation below the average of the reference group. There is some

TABLE 19.1. Descriptions of tests from standardized cognitive test batteries

Source	Variable	Description
WAIS III (N = 2,150)	Digit symbol	Substitute symbols for digits according to a code table as rapidly as possible.
	Block design	Arrange colored blocks to match a design
	Matrix reasoning	Select the alternative that provides the best completion of a missing section of a matrix
	Letter-number sequencing	Listen to an intermixed sequence of letters and numbers and then repeat them back with letters first in alphabetical order and numbers second in numerical order
Woodcock-Johnson III (N = 2,505)	Visual auditory learning	Learn associations between words and drawings
	Spatial relations	Identify pieces that form a target shape
	Concept formation	Determine the rule that can be used to categorize items
	Visual matching	Speeded identification of matching numbers
Kaufman Adolescent and Adult Intelligence Test (N = 1,350)	Logical steps	Use logical premises to reach deductions
	Mystery codes	Determine the code (concept) associated with a new pattern
	Memory for block designs	Immediate reproduction of design by manipulation of blocks
	Rebus learning	Learn associations between drawings and words
Delis-Kaplan Executive Function System (N = 875)	Tower of Hanoi	Move disks among three towers to convert a starting configuration into a target configuration
	20 questions	Determine the target item from among a set of 30 items with the fewest number of questions
	Card sorting	Identify the basis of cards sorted by the examiner
	Figural fluency	Create as many different line pattern figures as possible in 60 seconds

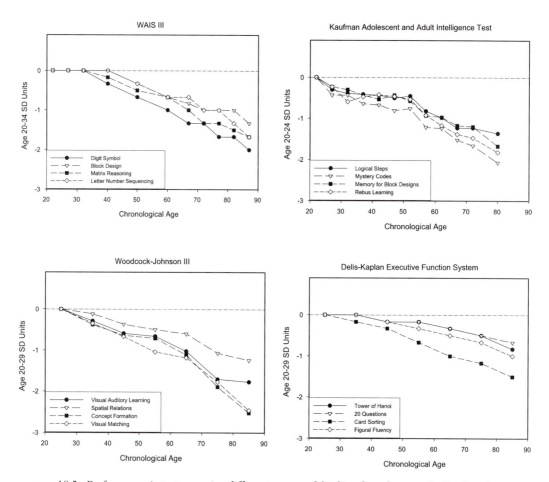

FIGURE 19.3. Performance in tests assessing different aspects of thinking from four standardized test batteries, expressed in units of young adult standard deviation units. Sample sizes are reported in Table 19.1. (Data for this table taken from Table A.1 in Wechsler, 1997; Table A.1 in McGrew & Woodcock, 2001; Table 8.5 in Kaufman & Kaufman, 1993; and Tables H.1, F.1, E.1, and Table C.1 in Delis, Kaplan, & Kramer, 2001.)

variability in the functions, as they appear to be shallower for the four variables in the D-KEFS battery than for the variables in the other batteries. Unfortunately, because different samples of individuals performed the tests in each battery, it is not possible to determine the relative contribution of the tests and of the samples to the apparent differences in age trends.

The data in Figure 19.3 indicate that linear age-related decreases have been observed in a variety of tests that can be postulated to involve thinking. Moreover, it is noteworthy that the pattern was similar across test batteries involving different samples of adults and in variables involving different combinations of materials and procedures. This is an important finding because psychometric tests are often criticized as in-

volving unknown mixtures of theoretical processes, which makes it difficult to determine which particular processes are contributing to any age differences that might be observed. However, when similar age trends are found across a variety of tests involving different combinations of processes it is unlikely that the age-related effects are attributable to one or two critical processes.

Somewhat different patterns of results are occasionally found in studies involving small convenience samples of young and old adults, and with variables of unknown reliability. However, the results most often resemble the patterns in Figure 19.2A and Figure 19.3 when moderately large samples of adults across the entire age range are examined with variables established to have at least moderately high reliability. Results such as these leave little doubt that the average older adult is less nimble than the average young adult in a variety of mental gymnastic exercises.

However, it is important to recognize that all of the tests represented in Table 19.1 and Figure 19.3 were explicitly designed to assess cognitive abilities in the abstract, independent of experience and of any particular context. In fact, abilities assessed by these types of tests have been characterized as determining the level of performance that can be achieved when one doesn't know what to do and has no relevant experience. Because this is seldom the case in situations outside the laboratory, assessments such as those represented in Figure 19.3 reflect only a limited perspective on adult thinking.

INVESTIGATING RELATIONS BETWEEN PROCESSING EFFICIENCY AND KNOWLEDGE

In part because many leadership positions in business and government are occupied by older adults, it is often assumed that increased age confers advantages in activities requiring complex thought and decision making. Factors related to seniority may play a role in the high prevalence of older adults in many leadership positions, but it is also possible that increased age is associated with higher levels of knowledge or skills that have been difficult to document in the laboratory. In fact, there have been many suggestions that compared to young adults, older adults rely more on wisdom or accumulated knowledge to compensate for any deficiencies that may be evident in basic abilities. An early statement of this position was the claim by Jones and Conrad (1933) that "much of the effective power of the adult . . . is evidently derived from accumulated stocks of information" (p. 254).

Although seemingly obvious and probably widely accepted, the idea that increased age is associated with greater knowledge and experience that may serve to compensate for age-related declines in basic cognitive abilities has been difficult to investigate for at least three reasons. First, almost by definition, people with very high levels of experience and knowledge are rare, and it is possible that results based on small samples of elite individuals might not be typical of what would be found in the general population. Second, many cognitive activities that are dependent upon knowl-

edge, such as making decisions about finances, medical treatments, or consumer purchases, are quite complex, and sometimes it is not even possible to specify the optimum level of performance in these activities because it depends on characteristics of the individual such as his or her personality (e.g., preference for risk-taking, tolerance for uncertainty), values, and goals. And third, the influence of knowledge on performance has not been rigorously examined because of the difficulty of assessing the quality and quantity of an individual's relevant knowledge.

How can the relative contributions of processing efficiency and knowledge be investigated in the face of these difficulties? One strategy is to begin with relatively simple tasks in which: (1) there are large populations of potential participants; (2) the tasks have objectively correct solutions or answers; and (3) it is possible to assess the quantity of potentially relevant knowledge in each individual. The primary prediction under these conditions is that to the extent that both processing efficiency and knowledge contribute to successful performance, then statistical control of a measure of knowledge should increase the relative influence of processing efficiency and result in more negative relations between age and task performance. Data from studies reported in Hambrick et al. (1999) can be used to examine this prediction because the participants in these studies performed a variety of simple verbal tasks and also completed tests of vocabulary that assessed relevant knowledge. Among the tasks in these studies were anagrams, make words, and word switch. In the anagrams task the examinee was to identify specific target words that could be created by rearranging a set of letters, and in the make words task the goal was to create as many different words as possible from a specified set of letters. The word switch task required the participant to identify the fewest number of intermediate words needed to convert one word into another, with each intermediate word involving a change of only one letter from the previous word. As an example, if the initial word was *foot* and the final word was *head*, then one possible solution would involve the following sequence of words: *foot-food-hood-hold-held-head*.

Each of these tasks can be considered to require thinking because successful performance requires the application of cognitive operations to one's knowledge. However, with none of these variables was the correlations with age significantly different from zero. That is, the age correlations were -.02 ($N = 402$) with anagram performance, .03 (N = 202) with make words performance, and -.03 (N = 202) with word switch performance. As expected, each variable was positively correlated with an index of relevant knowledge in the form of scores on tests of vocabulary (i.e., correlations ranging from .36 to .58), and increased age was associated with higher vocabulary scores (i.e., correlations ranging from .15 to .39). Moreover, when the variance in the vocabulary variable was statistically controlled with a partial correlation procedure, all of the age correlations became significantly negative (i.e., $p <$ .01). Specifically, after partialling the vocabulary score the age correlations for anagrams, make words, and word switch were, respectively, -.17, -.22, and -.25.

This pattern of results suggests that, at least in these samples and with these particular tasks, greater knowledge on the part of older adults appears to offset the negative age relations in processing efficiency such that there was no relation of age to overall performance. That is, these statistical control results imply that increased age would have been associated with substantially lower levels of performance if relevant knowledge had not been positively related to age. A further implication of these findings is that under the right circumstances greater knowledge may not only eliminate age differences but could even reverse them. The combination of adults recruited on the basis of experience working crossword puzzles and a measure of the number of words answered correctly in solving difficult crossword puzzles may be one such combination of circumstances because the results in Figure 19.1 indicate that there were positive relations between age and crossword puzzle performance (i.e., the age correlations in the four studies ranged from .31 to .46).

The results just described suggest that when knowledge is relevant to the task, and when the amount is greater with increased age, age differences in measures of thinking performance are either reduced, eliminated, or reversed. However, the possession of a larger amount of knowledge does not necessarily mean that it is relied upon to a greater extent in the performance of cognitive activities. A key question regarding the role of knowledge in thinking is, therefore, whether increased age is merely associated with a greater quantity of knowledge or whether it is also associated with a greater dependence on that knowledge.

Salthouse (1993; also see 2003) attempted to investigate this question by computing regression equations relating performance on several target tasks to measures of speed (perceptual comparison scores) and knowledge (vocabulary scores). For the purpose of these analyses, speed was viewed as an indicator of processing efficiency, or what Welford (1958) termed "organic capacities," and vocabulary was viewed as an indicator of the effects of cumulative experience. The target tasks in this project were simple verbal tasks such as letter fluency, anagrams, make words, and so on.

The analytical method involved constructing separate regression equations for the samples of young and old adults of the form:

$$\text{Performance} = b1(\text{Processing Efficiency}) + b2(\text{Knowledge}).$$

The major issue was whether, in addition to differences in the level of the predictors, there were age differences in the b parameters representing the weighting of the predictors on performance. That is, based on earlier research, young adults were expected to have a higher average level of processing efficiency and older adults were expected to have a higher level of relevant knowledge. Of particular interest, however, was whether the groups also differed in their regression weights, with older adults having smaller values of the $b1$ parameter and larger values of the $b2$ parameter than young adults. A finding of this type could be interpreted as evidence of compensation in the sense that increased age was associated with greater reliance on one's strengths and reduced reliance on one's weaknesses.

The same analytical method was applied in two studies, with each study consisting of separate samples of young and old adults and involving somewhat different criterion tasks. The results in both studies indicated that the two groups differed in the expected directions with respect to the level of the processing efficiency and knowledge variables and that both processing efficiency and knowledge were important in predicting performance in the criterion tasks (i.e., the $b1$ and $b2$ parameters were both significantly different from 0 with each task in each sample). However, the magnitudes of those influences were nearly the same for young and old adults (i.e., there were no age differences in the values of the $b1$ or $b2$ parameters). This pattern of results indicates that although young adults had a higher average level of processing efficiency, and old adults had a higher average level of knowledge, the regression weights, representing the degree to which performance in the criterion task varied with a given amount of change in each predictor variable, were similar in the two groups. It therefore appears that young and old adults achieved similar performance in these simple verbal tasks because of differences in the levels of the relevant factors, and not because of a different pattern of reliance on those factors.

This regression-based analytical approach is promising because it has the potential to provide quantitative estimates of the contributions of different factors to level of performance in adults of different ages, and it also allows investigation of the possibility that reliance upon those factors differs as a function of age. However, a limitation of the analyses reported by Salthouse (1993) is that only one value of processing efficiency and one value of relevant knowledge were available for each person, and thus the analyses had to be conducted at the level of groups instead of the level of individuals. It would be desirable to extend this type of analysis to allow estimates of the level and the weighting of predictors for each individual, and to apply the analyses to more complex tasks involving different types of relevant knowledge and other measures of processing efficiency.

AN ANALOGY TO ATHLETICS?

From the current perspective the effects of aging on thinking can be considered somewhat analogous to the effects of aging on the proficiency of a professional athlete. That is, beginning in their 20s most athletes probably experience a gradual decline in many physical abilities, but there may be increases in aspects of their relevant knowledge (e.g., declarative, or *what* information; procedural, or *how* information; and conditional, or *when* information). Furthermore, it is possible that the relation between knowledge and physical ability changes with age, perhaps in the direction of better awareness of when and how particular actions should be performed. However, at some point the increased level of knowledge may no longer offset the decreased level of physical ability, at which time the athlete probably ceases to be competitive at the highest level.

The thinking/athlete analogy is also meaningful because it may help explain why predictions from measures of performance on abstract tests to competence in activities outside the laboratory have frequently been low. That is, there may be only a modest relation between performance in one's sport and the level of physical abilities assessed by speed of running a fixed distance, amount of weight that can be lifted, distance a ball can be thrown or kicked, and so on, because the latter do not reflect the knowledge one has acquired about his or her sport. For the same reasons, a weak relation might also be expected between performance on cognitive exercises in the laboratory and level of functioning in daily activities because of the failure to take relevant knowledge into consideration.

Although there are some intriguing parallels, the analogy between thinking and the skills of an elite athlete should not be carried too far because knowledge is likely to be much more important in most mental activities than in physical activities. At the very least this could mean that the point at which greater knowledge no longer offsets declines in "organic capacities" occurs later in life, and it may also mean that level of performance could continue to increase throughout adulthood in activities that are highly dependent on knowledge.

CHANGE MECHANISMS

How can the effects of aging in adulthood (or of development in childhood) on thinking be explained from the perspective described above? The preceding discussion implies that two, and possibly three, distinct types of change mechanisms will be needed. Although the discussion focused on research in aging, it seems likely that similar change mechanisms will be required to account for phenomena in cognitive development. First, there is a need to explain what is responsible for age-related decreases (or increases in childhood) in the efficiency of many cognitive processes. Second, there is a need to explain what is responsible for age-related increases in the accumulation and maintenance of knowledge. And third, depending on the outcome of relevant research, there may also be a need to explain what is responsible for any changes found in how processing efficiency and knowledge are combined in the performance of specific cognitive activities.

Because the age trends apparent in Figures 19.2A and 19.3 can be presumed to be attributable to changes in the efficiency of processing, explanations are needed to account for improvements and declines in the effectiveness of these mental gymnastics exercises. However, before evaluating particular proposals, three meta-issues concerned with possible mechanisms and the manner in which they might be most productively investigated should be considered. The issues are meta in nature because they are likely to affect the nature and scope of any specific hypotheses that might be proposed.

One of these issues is whether the focus of the explanation is on a single variable or on multiple variables. Most cognitive variables are positively correlated with one another, and thus it is important to determine the extent to which the age-related influences on a particular variable are unique to that variable and statistically independent of age-related influences on other variables. When only one variable is considered in isolation, it is impossible to investigate relations of that variable to other variables or to examine age-related effects on that variable in the context of age-related effects on other variables. Furthermore, a multivariate focus is necessary to determine the most meaningful grouping or organization of variables for the interpretation of age-related influences, which is the kind of information that would be relevant to the question of the degree to which the cognitive system is modular with respect to age-related influences (see Chapter 18, this volume).

A second meta issue is whether the proposed change mechanisms are hypothesized to operate at the same level as the phenomena to be explained, or whether they are postulated to operate at a lower, more reductionistic level. Many of the currently popular interpretations of individual differences in cognitive functioning are based on the assumption that certain cognitive constructs are more fundamental or primitive than others in the sense that changes in these constructs precipitate changes in other constructs. Among the constructs that have been hypothesized to possess this privileged status are aspects of attention such as inhibitory efficiency, executive functioning, working memory, and processing speed. An advantage of explanatory constructs at the same level of analysis as the to-be-explained phenomena is that it is possible to identify plausible mechanisms, such as how the amount of information that can be maintained in working memory could affect performance on many different types of cognitive tasks. However, two limitations of interpretations at the same level of analysis are that an explanation would still be needed to account for changes in the hypothesized primitive construct (e.g., why are there age-related changes in working memory?), and it is difficult to establish causal priority when both the cause and effect constructs are operationalized in terms of similar types of observable behavioral variables.

Interpretations in which the hypothesized causal construct is at a different level of analysis than the to-be-explained construct, such as when it is operationalized with a measure of neurobiological structure or function, have a different pattern of strengths and weaknesses. For example, it may be more difficult to specify the mechanism by which a neurobiological characteristic such as synaptic density, quantity of a particular type of neurotransmitter, or intactness of myelin contributes to different levels of performance on a cognitive test, but because these types of neurobiological characteristics are unlikely to be affected by level of cognitive performance, there may be less ambiguity about the causal direction between the constructs.

The third meta issue relevant to evaluating possible interpretations of age-related changes in processing efficiency is whether the relevant comparisons are based on static or dynamic information. Many of the speculations about change mechanisms in both aging and child development are based on relatively static cross-sectional information, but strong conclusions about mechanisms of change will require longitudinal information. Moreover, because information on concurrent or correlated change in two or more variables is ambiguous about causal priority, the most informative patterns for investigating change mechanisms will likely be lead-lag relations in which changes in the hypothesized causal construct precede changes in the hypothesized consequence construct.

A large number of specific hypotheses have been proposed, and many more could be proposed, to account for changes in processing efficiency in the period of child development and across the adult years. However, the meta issues just discussed appear so fundamental that they need to be considered before attempting to evaluate the plausibility, or even the applicability, of any specific hypotheses.

Knowledge

As noted earlier, most of the results from large representative samples indicate that performance on various tests of knowledge increases only to about age 50, after which it either remains stable or declines. An initial question concerned with age-related change in knowledge, therefore, is why knowledge does not continue to increase with increased age. Several hypotheses were discussed by Salthouse (2003), including the possibilities that exposure to new sources of information may decrease with age and that forgetting of old information might offset the acquisition of new information. Perhaps the most plausible interpretation of the failure to find continuous increases in knowledge across adulthood is that most standardized tests have been designed to assess general, culturally shared knowledge, and not the personal idiosyncratic knowledge that is acquired as an individual develops his or her unique vocational and avocational interests. Unfortunately, because assessments of idiosyncratic knowledge are not yet available, there is currently little evidence relevant to this interpretation.

Another issue with respect to change in knowledge is whether experience is merely necessary, or is also sufficient, for the acquisition of knowledge. That is, when other factors are equal, is mere exposure (which throughout life will tend to be positively correlated with age) sufficient to account for increased knowledge, or are deliberate or conscious efforts at acquisition (which might increase in efficiency across the period of child development and decrease in efficiency across the adult years) necessary? Other questions that will need to be answered before one can claim to understand age-related changes in knowledge are the role of quantity and quality of existing knowledge, frequency and variety of exposure to new information, and level of processing efficiency on the acquisition and maintenance of knowledge.

Dependence on Knowledge

If future research reveals evidence of age-related differences in the reliance on knowledge during the performance of cognitive activities, then an explanation will also be needed to account for those changes. However, because very little research has been reported on this topic, it is still an open question whether change mechanisms are needed to account for differences of this type.

Five models for the role of knowledge on cognitive performance across adulthood were recently described by Salthouse (2003). Four of the models assume additive effects of knowledge and age, and differ with respect to the direction of the relations between age and knowledge, and between age and ability. Because the two sets of relations were assumed to combine in an additive fashion, from the perspective of these models explanations would only be needed to account for age-related effects on basic abilities and on knowledge. However, the fifth model discussed by Salthouse (2003) was a moderation model that postulates that knowledge alters the relations between age and cognitive performance in the direction of greater positive effects of knowledge at older ages. Only if the data were found to be consistent with this type of model would an explanation necessarily be required to account for age-related changes in the relation between knowledge and cognitive performance.

Given the paucity of relevant information at the current time, a high priority for research in both the child and adult portions of the lifespan is information on how knowledge contributes to cognitive functioning and whether the relation between knowledge and cognitive performance varies as a function of age. However, rather than relying exclusively on speculation as has largely been the case in the past, analytical methods should be used that allow rigorous empirical investigation. This will likely require explicit operational definitions of key constructs and articulating the hypothesized relations in enough detail to allow sensitive evaluations of their plausibility.

SUMMARY

Adult age differences, and developmental differences in childhood, have been clearly documented in measures of what are often assumed to reflect the efficiency of basic cognitive processing. There is also considerable evidence of (nonlinear) positive relations between age and amount of general, culturally shared, knowledge, although little is known about the relation of age to one's total knowledge, which includes the difficult-to-measure knowledge that is idiosyncratic to a particular individual. Unfortunately because there have been few investigations of the role of knowledge in specific activities that require thinking, it is difficult to reach strong conclusions at the current time concerning effects of development or aging on quality or effectiveness of thinking. Some research has indicated how greater knowledge might allow high levels of functioning to be achieved by older adults despite lower levels of processing efficiency, but it has thus far been limited to a few, very simple, tasks, and there is apparently no comparable research with children.

With respect to change mechanisms, at least two distinct age-related influences need to be explained:

negative effects on processing efficiency (positive across the childhood years) and positive effects on knowledge. However, a third age-related influence may also need to be explained if future research were to indicate that the relation between task performance and either processing efficiency or knowledge differs as a function of age.

Finally, it is important to note that a major weakness of the contemporary literature in aging and cognition, and likely also in the literature on cognitive development, is very limited understanding of the relations between age and knowledge, and of the impact of relevant knowledge on functioning in cognitively demanding activities inside and outside of the psychological laboratory. Because most of our cognitive activities are based at least in part on what we know and what we have done in the past, any conclusions about the effects of development or aging on the efficiency or effectiveness of thinking must remain tentative until more is known about the role of knowledge in the cognitive functioning of adults (and children).

References

Delis, D. C., Kaplan, E., & Kramer, J. H. (2001). *Delis-Kaplan Executive Function System*. New York: Psychological Corporation.

Dixon, R. A., & Backman, L. (1995). *Psychological compensation: Managing losses and promoting gains*. Hillsdale, NJ: Lawrence Erlbaum Associates.

Foster, J. C., & Taylor, G. A. (1920). The applicability of mental tests to persons over 50. *Journal of Applied Psychology, 4*, 39–58.

Hambrick, D. Z., Salthouse, T. A., & Meinz, E. J. (1999). Predictors of crossword puzzle proficiency and moderators of age-cognition relations. *Journal of Experimental Psychology: General, 128*, 131–164.

Horn, J. L. (1989). Models of intelligence. In R. L. Linn (Ed.), *Intelligence: Measurement, theory, and public policy* (pp. 28–73). Urbana: University of Illinois Press.

Jones, H. E., & Conrad, H. (1933). The growth and decline of intelligence: A study of a homogeneous group between the ages of ten and sixty. *Genetic Psychological Monographs, 13*, 223–298.

Kaufman, A. S., & Kaufman, N. L. (1993). *Kaufman Adolescent and Adult Intelligence Test (KAIT)*. Circle Pines, MN: American Guidance Service.

McArdle, J. J., Ferrer-Caja, E., Hamagami, F., & Woodcock, R. W. (2002). Comparative longitudinal structural analyses of growth and decline of multiple intellectual abilities over the life span. *Developmental Psychology, 38*, 115–142.

McGrew, K. S., & Woodcock, R. W. (2001). *Woodcock-Johnson III technical manual*. Itasca, IL: Riverside Publishing Company.

Salthouse, T. A. (1993). Speed and knowledge as determinants of adult age differences in verbal tasks. *Journal of Gerontology: Psychological Sciences, 48*, P29–P36.

Salthouse, T. A. (1998). Independence of age-related influences on cognitive abilities across the life span. *Developmental Psychology, 34*, 851–864.

Salthouse, T. A. (2001). Structural models of the relations between age and measures of cognitive functioning. *Intelligence, 29*, 93–115.

Salthouse, T. A. (2003). Interrelations of aging, knowledge, and cognitive performance. In U. Staudinger & U. Lindenberger (Eds.), *Understanding human development: Dialogues with lifespan psychology* (pp. 265–287). Dordrecht, Netherlands: Kluwer Academic Publishers.

WASI: Wechsler Abbreviated Scale of Intelligence. (1999). San Antonio, TX: Psychological Corporation.

Wechsler, D. (1997). *Wechsler Adult Intelligence Scale – Third Edition*. San Antonio, TX: Psychological Corporation.

Welford, A. T. (1958). *Ageing and human skill*. London: Oxford University Press.

20

Inter- and Intra-individual Differences in Problem Solving Across the Lifespan

Robert S. Siegler

Among the most striking characteristics of human cognition is its variability. This variability is present both between people—inter-individual variability—and within a given person—intra-individual variability. Although inter-individual variability has received far more attention, identifying the sources and functions of intra-individual variability may prove to be at least as important for understanding development.

The study of individual differences—inter-individual variability—has a long and distinguished history within psychology; indeed, such efforts go back to the earliest days of psychology as a formal discipline. For example, Galton (1879) and Spearman (1904) hypothesized that individual differences in intelligence were due to differences in sensory functioning: people whose sensory functioning was exceptional would also be intellectually exceptional. The formulation of psychometric instruments, such as tests of intelligence (e.g., Binet & Simon, 1905), personality (e.g., Allport, 1928), and musical ability (e.g., Seashore, 1938) also reflects the early and continuing interest in inter-individual differences.

Contemporary individual differences research is used to address at least five main goals:

1. *Identification of quantitative dimensions along which people vary and that are hypothesized to underlie a broad range of behaviors.* The "Big 5" dimensional analysis of personality (Tellegen, Watson, & Clark, 1999) is an example.
2. *Identification of qualitative differences among people.* Different patterns of attachment between infants and mothers (Thompson, 1998), different styles of learning (Ferrari & Sternberg, 1998), and different problem solving strategies (Hunt, 1987) are three examples.
3. *Identification of differences among demographic groups.* Many studies are aimed at examining whether quantitative and qualitative variables that differentiate among individuals also differentiate among demographically defined groups, such as men and women, African-Americans and Euro-Americans, or children from families of higher and lower socioeconomic status (Ruble & Martin, 1998).

4. *Examination of longitudinal stability.* Considerable research is conducted to examine whether quantitative and qualitative differences among individuals are maintained over time—for example, whether temperament in early childhood predicts later personality (Caspi & Silva, 1995).

5. *Examination of predictive validity.* Another prominent research question regarding inter-individual differences is whether performance on one measure can be used to predict performance on other measures, both at the same time and over time. Thus, IQ test performance of adults is used to predict differences in income among adults, and IQ test performance of children is used to predict future differences in income when they become adults (Brody, 1992).

All of these are core issues for any science of development; they have been central from the past to the present and in all likelihood will continue to be central in the future. Along with such variation between individuals, however, recent research has documented substantial variation within individuals. On a wide range of tasks individual children know and use multiple rules, strategies, theories, and concepts. For example, individual children know and use multiple strategies for solving arithmetic problems, for spelling words, for generating verb tenses, for reasoning about moral dilemmas, for conceptualizing natural phenomena, and for remembering information (Siegler, 1996). Such intra-individual variability is present even on tasks that are used as classic illustrations of stage theories, despite such theories positing that at a given level of development, a child will reason consistently in a given way. For example, on number conservation, a task that Piaget (1952) used to illustrate his stage theory, most 5-year-olds use different strategies on different problems (Siegler, 1995). Most often, they do what Piaget said they do—rely on the relative lengths of the rows to judge which row has more objects. However, most children use other approaches as well. Sometimes, they count the objects and choose the row with more; sometimes they reason that simply spreading a row does not change the number of objects; and sometimes they guess or say that they do not know. Siegler (1995) found that on average, 5-year-olds used three different number-conservation strategies, rather than uniformly relying on a single approach at a single age, as depicted in stage theories.

Similar variation within individuals has been found on children's and adults' reasoning on the moral dilemmas central to Kohlberg's (e.g., 1969) theory (Colby, Kohlberg, Gibbs, & Lieberman, 1983).

This intra-individual variability is not just a curio, a phenomenon that is prevalent but without further ramification. Rather, it seems to influence both performance and learning. In many domains, the ideal strategy or way of thinking varies with the particular problem. For example, when preschoolers are asked to add 2+2, retrieval from memory is the optimal strategy, whereas when they are asked to add 2+22, counting from the larger addend is the optimal strategy of which they are capable (because almost no preschoolers can retrieve the answer to 2+22). The optimal strategy also varies with task circumstances. Sometimes, accuracy is the main consideration; other times, speed is equally or even more important. Knowing several alternative approaches allows children and adults to adapt their strategies to the particular problem and task circumstances.

Of course, knowing a variety of strategies does not guarantee that people will choose adaptively among them. People might choose arbitrarily among the strategies that they know or might be biased in ways that lead them to use certain strategies even though others would be more effective. Indeed, there is a substantial literature on ways in which children's strategy choices are less than optimal. For example, children who have been taught new strategies often do not use them after the initial instruction, even though using them improved their performance (Fabricius & Hagen, 1984; Ghatala, Levin, Pressley, & Goodwin, 1986). Similarly, several studies of aging have shown that whereas elderly adults can learn and use mnemonic systems, and that their memory performance is then boosted in a laboratory study, the participants typically fail to use these techniques in their everyday lives (Auschutz, Camp, Markley, & Kramer, 1987; Neely & Bäckman, 1993). In other situations, children use new strategies, even though doing so brings them no benefit over previously mastered approaches, a phenomenon that Miller and Seier (1994) labeled "utilization deficiency." Such findings have led some reviewers to conclude that children tend to choose unwisely among strategies. For example, Flavell, Miller, and Miller (1993) wrote:

Certainly one of the lessons from research across many areas of cognition is that children do not use their available knowledge. . . . A child might know that rehearsal is a good strategy for remembering a list of chores that need to be done but not rehearse because he or she lacks time, energy, capacity, or motivation to exert the effort. (p. 261)

In analyzing this conclusion, it seems crucial to distinguish between the optimality of the process and the optimality of the product. If a child does not know a strategy that is optimal for solving a problem, it is not a failure of the strategy-choice process when the child does not choose it; rather, it is a failing of the child's knowledge of the available strategies. Similarly, if a child knows an excellent strategy but does not have the cognitive resources to execute it effectively, it is not a failure of the strategy-choice process if the child chooses not to use it. Indeed, choosing not to use a strategy that cannot be executed effectively is exactly what an optimal choice process should do. In the same way, if a child lacks the time to execute a superior strategy that the child could execute given more time, and instead chooses a less good approach that is the most effective approach that the child can execute in the available time, the child once again would be choosing optimally. Cognitive activity is inherently subject to constraints of capacity, knowledge, motivation, and circumstances. The adaptive quality of choice processes can be evaluated only relative to a standard of what is possible within these constraints.

An important implication of this perspective is that improvements in the strategies that are chosen do not necessarily imply a change in the strategy-choice process. Children might choose better strategies than in the past owing to acquisition of strategies, either through discovery or through instruction, that they did not know previously. They also might increase their reliance on the better strategies from among those they know because of improvements in ability to execute the strategies. This could occur through practicing the strategies or through increases in cognitive resources.

The same issue of process versus product in strategy choices arises at the other end of the lifespan. Baltes's S.O.C. theory (selection, optimization, and compensation), a theory that focuses on strategy choices in older adulthood, is based on a perspective very similar to the present one. The central idea of S.O.C. theory is that people further their development by maximizing their opportunities and minimizing their losses (Baltes, 1997; Li, Lindenberger, Freund, & Baltes, 2001). The process involves selecting attain-

able goals, optimizing the means for pursuing the goals, and compensating for any declines in abilities by adjusting both goals and means to ongoing biological changes. This may mean, for example, focusing cognitive resources on the more important goal in a dual-task situation because biological declines interfere with ability to simultaneously pursue both goals at a high level. The older adults' choice would lead to lower performance on the secondary task than younger adults would generate, but might still reflect an optimal choice process.

An increasing body of evidence indicates that children's strategy choices tend to be highly adaptive, in the sense of responding in reasonable ways both to inherent characteristics of problems and to fluctuating situational demands. This is especially true when the focus is on the adaptive quality of the process rather than on the outcome. For example, if a child cannot execute a strategy within the available time, an entirely rational decision process may lead him or her to choose a less accurate but faster approach. Similarly, if a child does not know an effective strategy, no choice process, no matter how rational, will lead the child to choose it. Thus, it only makes sense to evaluate the adaptive quality of strategy choices within the set of strategies that children know and are able to execute under the experimental conditions. Within these constraints, children's choices tend to be extremely adaptive.

This chapter is devoted to examining two main hypotheses. The first is that substantial variability in higher level cognition is present throughout the lifespan. The second is that people of all ages generally choose adaptively among alternative approaches, subject to constraints of capacity, knowledge, and task conditions. To examine these hypotheses, we consider findings on strategy use and strategy choice in infancy, childhood, and younger and older adulthood. The findings will be organized into three sections: one on intra-individual variability, one on inter-individual variability, and one on relations between the two.

INTRA-INDIVIDUAL VARIABILITY

Strategy Use and Choice During Infancy

From the first year of life, infants' problem solving shows considerable variability. A number of clear examples of this variability come from studies of infants' reaching and locomotor activity—tasks that are not problematic for older children and adults but that do constitute real problems for infants. For example, infants often reach for a toy with one hand on one trial yet reach with both hands on the next trial (Thelen, Corbetta, & Spencer, 1996). Similarly, babies often use multiple patterns of inter-limb coordination even while crawling a few feet along a flat path (Veriejken et al., 1995).

One of the clearest demonstrations of the variability of infants' problem solving comes from Karen Adolph's (e.g., 1997) studies of 7- to 15-month-olds' efforts to locomote up and down ramps of varying slopes. Locomoting down a ramp constitutes a novel problem for these very young infants. As long as the slope is relatively shallow, they can use their usual locomotor approach (crawling or walking in most cases), but as the slope becomes steep relative to their skill at coordination, they must consider other approaches or risk falling, particularly on the descending ramps.

Faced with such problems, babies use a variety of strategies: walking, crawling on all fours, sliding prone, sliding while sitting, backing down, or refusing to descend (Adolph, Eppler, & Gibson, 1993; Adolph, 1997). In both studies, more than 90% of the babies used at least one strategy other than their usual approach of walking, and roughly half used two or more approaches other than walking.

The toddlers' choices among these locomotor approaches were adaptive in a number of ways. Babies were far more likely to use approaches other than walking or crawling on the more dangerous descending ramps than on the safer ascending ones. Within the group of descending ramps, and within the group of ascending ramps, individual children were much more likely to use approaches other than walking for slopes that were beyond the steepness they could successfully navigate than for ones less steep than that cutoff. Their choices were impressively consistent; if they refused to walk down a ramp of a given slope, they usually either slid down or refused to attempt all steeper slopes. Moreover, the babies looked for a longer time, hesitated, and tested alternative sliding positions to a greater extent when descending down steep slopes than when ascending comparable slopes.

Infants do not seem to be born with this ability to judge the difficulty of slopes relative to their locomotor ability and to use their judgments to guide their choice of strategy. Rather, general experience with crawling and walking seems to be essential for the

choice process to operate adaptively. Adolph (1997) examined babies microgenetically, on a week-by-week basis, after they began to crawl and also when they were just beginning to walk. She found that when infants began to crawl, around 7 months of age, their initial choices were quite risky, leading many to tumble headlong on the relatively risky descending slopes. Over the next weeks, their choices became increasingly adaptive. However, when they began to walk, around 13 months, most attempted to walk down hills that were well beyond their ability. Again, several weeks of experience with the new form of locomotion led to adaptive choices among alternative strategies. Thus, although strategy choices are often somewhat adaptive from early in learning, task-relevant experience is essential for the strategies to become adaptive.

Chen and Siegler's (2000) study of toddlers' tool use yielded comparable patterns of choice and change in a very different type of problem-solving situation. Younger toddlers (18–26-month-olds) and older toddlers (27–35-month-olds) were presented an attractive toy on a table; the toy was roughly a foot beyond their reach. Six potential tools, such as short and long straight sticks, a toy rake, and the head of a rake, were on the table between the child and the toy. To obtain the toy, the child needed to use the one tool that had a sufficiently long shaft and a head at the right angle to the shaft to pull in the toy (in the above example, the toy rake). Children first were encouraged to obtain the toy without any help; then, some of them saw a model pull in the toy using the appropriate tool and were given opportunity to solve the same problem for themselves. Then, they were presented a parallel problem but with numerous superficial differences: tools of different colors, shapes, and sizes; a different toy, a different posture (standing rather than sitting), and so on. Thus, if the optimal tool on the first problem was rake with a solid red shaft, the second problem might have as an optimal tool a cane with a striped blue shaft, with distractor tools having solid red shafts or rake heads. Children also received a third problem with a third optimal tool and a third set of superficially different distractors.

As when facing the problem of how to descend a steep ramp, the toddlers generated a variety of strategies. These strategies included reaching for the toy, asking their mother for help (which was not forthcoming), using a tool, and just sitting and looking at the toy, perhaps in the hope that the experimenter would help. The large majority of toddlers (74%) used at least three of these four strategies. Even after first using a tool, most children in the control group, and some in the instructed group, continued to use other strategies as well.

The toddlers also chose among the tools in adaptive ways. This was true to a degree from the first trial onward. Even then, the toddlers were more likely than chance to choose the target tool, and even when they did not, they generally chose a tool with a shaft long enough to reach the toy. However, as in the Adolph studies of locomotion, experience influenced the degree of adaptiveness of the choices. Children in the modeling condition increased the percentage of trials on which they chose the target tool on each successive problem. This reflected both greater use of tools in general and increasingly high percentages of choice of the target tool relative to other tools. The rate of improvement both in target tool use and in adaptiveness of the choices among tools was faster for the older toddlers than for the younger ones, but by the third problem, strategy choices were nearly optimal for both younger and older toddlers.

Strategy Use and Choice During Childhood

Strategic variability in preschoolers and school-age children has been well documented in many domains. Perhaps the most extensive documentation comes from children's arithmetic (e.g., Geary & Burlingham-Dubree, 1989; Geary, Fan, & Bow-Thomas, 1992; Hopkins & Lawson, 2002; Siegler, 1987, 1988). Between ages 4 and 10 years, children use a wide variety of strategies to solve single-digit addition, subtraction, and multiplication problems. For example, to solve single-digit addition problems such as 3+6, 4–7-year-olds sometimes use the sum strategy, in which they count from one; sometimes use the min strategy, in which they count "6, 7, 8, 9"; sometimes use decomposition, which involves translating the problem into easier form, for example by thinking "3+7 = 10, so 3+6 must be 9"; sometimes retrieve the answer from memory; and sometimes guess.

When presented a set of 45 simple addition problems, the majority of kindergartners, first-graders, and second-graders used at least three of these strategies; a substantial minority used four or all five (Siegler, 1987). Similar amounts of intra-individual variability have been observed in both other simple arithmetic

tasks, such as single-digit subtraction (Siegler, 1989) and multiplication (Miller & Paredes, 1990); in the arithmetic used in game-playing contexts (Bjorklund & Rosenblum, 2001); and in more complex arithmetic, such as that used in problems that require understanding of mathematical equality (Alibali, 1999; Goldin-Meadow, 2001) and decimal fractions (Rittle-Johnson, Siegler, & Alibali, 2001).

Children show substantial strategic variability on nonmathematical tasks as well. Among the tasks on which such variability has been documented are causal reasoning (Shultz, Fisher, Pratt, & Rulf, 1986), scientific reasoning (Kuhn, Garcia-Mila, Zohar, & Anderson, 1995; Schauble, 1996), drawing (Rosengren, 2002), and judgments of grammaticality (Kuczaj, 1977).

The multiple-strategy use is present within classes of similar problems and even within the same problem presented to the same child by the same experimenter in the same room on two days within the same week. In two studies, one on addition (Siegler & Shrager, 1984) and one on time telling (Siegler & McGilly, 1989), one-third of children used different strategies on the identical problem. This day-to-day variability could not be explained by learning; in both experiments; children were almost as likely to use the more advanced strategy the first day and the less advanced strategy the second as to show the opposite pattern.

Like infants and toddlers, older children's strategy choices shift progressively toward reliance on the more effective approaches (Siegler, 1996). In some cases this means moving toward more accurate strategies; for example, on a variety of Piagetian tasks, including conservation, matrix completion, and balance scale problems, children move from less accurate to more accurate approaches (Siegler & Svetina, 2002). In other cases, the trend is toward greater speed; in arithmetic, for example, reliance on retrieving answers from memory increases with age and experience, whereas reliance on slower (and sometimes less accurate) counting approaches decreases. It is striking, however, that even when children know and sometimes use faster and more accurate approaches, they continue also to use slower and less accurate approaches. This is especially the case in arithmetic, where slower and less accurate strategies continue to be used for many years after children sometimes retrieve answers from memory on the same problems. Thus, contrary to traditional characterizations of cognitive development, in which children are described as first using strategy X, then strategy Y, and then strategy Z, strategic variability, as well as changes in strategy use, are typical in cognitive development (Siegler, 1996).

Children's strategy choices are adaptive in the same way as infants' and toddlers'. They are sensitive to problem characteristics. For example, in basic arithmetic, the easier the problem (measured by problem size, solution times, or error rates in contexts where children must retrieve the answers to all problems), the more likely 4–8-year-olds are to retrieve the answer from memory. The more difficult the problem, the more likely they are to use more time-consuming backup strategies, such as counting from the larger addend (Siegler, 1987). This approach is adaptive because it allows children to answer quickly as well as accurately on easy problems and accurately though more slowly when problem difficulty precludes accurate retrieval.

Children's strategy choices also are sensitive to experimental outcomes. When a nonoptimal but easy-to-execute memory strategy yields incorrect recall, 5–9-year-olds are more likely to switch to a more effortful strategy on the next trial than if the strategy yielded a correct answer. In contrast, when an optimal strategy yields an incorrect answer, 5–9-year-olds are no more likely to switch to a different approach than if the strategy yielded correct recall (McGilly & Siegler, 1990).

Children's responses to experimental instructions are similarly adaptive. Thus, 7- and 9-year-olds who were told that only speed is important answered faster but less accurately than a control group of peers who were told that both were important. Conversely, peers who were told that only accuracy was important answered more accurately but also more slowly than the control group (Siegler, 1996).

Younger and Older Adults

Variable strategy use and adaptive choices among strategies are characteristic of younger and older adults, just as they are of children. This was illustrated in Siegler and Lemaire's (1997) study of college students' and senior citizens' arithmetic strategies. In one experiment, people of mean ages 20 and 66 years were asked to solve arithmetic problems either (1) through use of mental arithmetic, (2) on a calculator, or (3) using either mental arithmetic or the calculator. In another experiment, people of mean ages 20 and 75

years were asked to solve similar problems using either mental arithmetic, the calculator, or pencil and paper, or to choose among the three strategies. This method, labeled the choice/no-choice design, allowed a test of a theoretical prediction regarding strategy choices. Computer simulations of strategy choice (Shrager & Siegler, 1998; Siegler and Shipley, 1995) predict that frequency of choice of a given strategy should be a function of the difference between the strengths of the strategies, which in turn reflects the differences in accuracy and solution times that the strategies generate. However, assessments of the effectiveness of strategies in situations in which people can use multiple approaches is inevitably biased because people use some strategies more often on more difficult problems, and because people who are more skilled in a domain almost always use a different distribution of strategies than people who are less skilled. To illustrate the problem, Siegler and Lemaire (1997) found that on two-digit by two-digit multiplication problems, both younger and older adults solve problems in less than half the time when required to use a calculator than when required to use mental arithmetic. However, when they could choose which approach to use, mean solution times were actually faster when they used mental arithmetic. The reason was that mental arithmetic was used primarily on the easiest problems and was used more often by the people who were generally best at mental arithmetic.

The choice/no-choice design was developed to circumvent this problem. Requiring people to always use a given strategy on a given set of problems, then to use a different strategy on a comparable set of problems, provided unbiased estimates of each strategy's effectiveness on each problem. For example, it allowed unbiased estimates of the difference in time required to solve a given problem via a given strategy. The computer simulation models predicted that the greater the difference in effectiveness of the strategies on a given problem, the more often the more effective strategy would be chosen. The extent to which this prediction was accurate could be tested by correlating the difference in effectiveness of the strategies with percent use of the more effective approach.

It turned out that both older and younger adults chose strategies in a very adaptive way, and that the degree of adaptiveness was equal. Difference in solution times yielded by each strategy in the no-choice conditions accounted for about 70% of the variance in how often both older and younger adults chose each strategy on each problem in the choice condition.

The choice/no-choice method also yielded measures of bias in strategy choices. One such measure is the difference in solution times generated by use of each strategy on problems on which people use each strategy on about 50% of trials. Both younger and older adults proved to have a slight but consistent bias toward using mental arithmetic: 1.5 seconds for college students and 1.6 seconds for older adults. Seen another way, on problems on which solution times in the no-choice condition were within 1 second, college students used mental arithmetic on 58% of trials and senior citizens on 59%. Thus, the direction and magnitude of the bias, as well as the adaptive quality of strategy choice, was comparable for college students and senior citizens.

This does not mean that all aspects of strategy choice are comparable for different age groups. When given a choice of using pencil and paper as well as the calculator and mental arithmetic, senior citizens used pencil and paper as often as the calculator. In contrast, no college student given this choice ever used pencil and paper. It seems likely that this reflects historical change rather than age-related change per se; if the same experiment is run 50 years from now, when today's college students are senior citizens, it seems likely that they will also choose calculators (or their successor) over pencil and paper.

Older adults show adaptive strategy-choice patterns on other tasks and domains as well. This sometimes entails older adults' making different strategy choices than younger adults but ones that make sense in the context of their capabilities. For example, Li et al. (2001) found that when presented a task that required walking along a narrow track while memorizing unrelated words, older adults' strategy for responding to increases in difficulty differed from that of younger adults. In particular, older adults did not differ from younger ones in the effects of increased task difficulty on their walking speed, but their memory performance did decline to a greater extent with greater difficulty of either the memory or the walking task. The older adults' greater allocation of resources to the walking task made sense, given the greater cost to older people of losing their balance and falling. Thus, their resource allocation strategy allowed them to maintain a high level of performance on the task that mattered most to them—walking—and to funnel the costs of the greater difficulty to the less important task.

Inter-Individual Differences

The same studies that have revealed substantial intra-individual differences also have revealed substantial inter-individual differences. The differences again are present in infancy, childhood, and early and late adulthood.

Individual Differences in Infancy

The studies of infants' locomotion revealed substantial differences in the approaches of individual children to the challenge they faced. Of the 31 14-month-olds in the Adolph (1995) study, for example, slightly more than half walked down all ramps with slopes that they could navigate without falling and on almost none of those where falling was reasonably likely. The precision of these children's strategy choices was impressive. They walked down 90% of slopes that were just within their capabilities, but only 10% that were just beyond their capabilities (2 to 8 degrees beyond the slope they could usually navigate without falling). A second group, roughly one-quarter of the sample, took greater risks. They generally tried to walk down hills until they became impossibly steep, so that attempting to walk down them would almost certainly lead to falling (18 degrees or more beyond their boundary). A third group, roughly one-eighth of the sample, attempted to walk down virtually all slopes, no matter how steep and no matter how certain that they would fall. Adolph suggested that these children were either absolutely fearless, confident that they would be rescued before any serious mishap could occur, or deficient in perceptual-motor skills.

Individual Differences in Childhood

Individual differences in children's strategy choices reflect variation in both knowledge and cognitive styles. This is evident in elementary school children's use of arithmetic and reading strategies. Three characteristic patterns of individual performance have emerged from research on strategy choices in addition, subtraction, and word identification: the good student, not-so-good student, and perfectionist patterns (Siegler, 1988). Good students usually rely on retrieval and generally answer problems both quickly and accurately. Not-so-good students use retrieval fairly often, but are considerably slower and less accurate.

Perfectionists present an interesting mix of patterns; they are as accurate as good students and use each strategy as quickly. However, they state retrieved answers even less often than not-so-good students. Because retrieval is much faster than alternative approaches such as counting and sounding out, they therefore are considerably slower than good students when all trials are considered, even though they are as quick in using each individual strategy.

These three individual difference groups have emerged in parallel experiments of predominantly high-SES, Euro-American, suburban populations and predominantly low-SES, African-American, urban populations (Kerkman & Siegler, 1993; 1997). The individual difference classifications predict standardized test scores and future placement in programs for children with learning disabilities. They also are stable, at least over a one-year period.

These individual differences have a straightforward interpretation within the Siegler and Shipley (1995) and the Shrager and Siegler (1998) computer simulations of strategy choice. They reflect variations in two parameters of the models. One involves the way in which knowledge is created—in particular, the creation of associations between problems and answers. When a problem is presented and an answer stated, correct or incorrect, the association between problem and answer increases. The increase is greater for correct answers, reflecting the intuition that reinforcement and feedback lead to greater strengthening of correct than incorrect answers. Therefore, one dimension of individual differences within the simulation models is the ratio of strengthening when a correct answer is stated to that when an incorrect answer is stated; a higher ratio leads to faster learning.

This knowledge-creation parameter was sufficient to separate the not-so-good students from the good students and perfectionists. However, a second parameter, the confidence criterion, appeared to distinguish the latter two groups. This parameter indicates how strongly an answer or strategy needed to be associated with the problem for that answer or strategy to be stated. The intuition is that some children are cautious and will state an answer or use a strategy only when the association is strong, whereas others, like the risk-takers among Adolph's toddlers, will try an approach even if they are less sure it will work.

In terms of these two parameters, perfectionists have a high rate of knowledge creation and set high confidence criteria; good students have equally high rate of knowledge creation but set somewhat lower confidence criteria; and not-so-good students have a lower rate of knowledge creation and set yet lower confidence criteria. Simulation results indicated that varying the two parameters in this way led to data patterns that closely matched those of the three individual difference groups (Siegler & Shipley, 1995).

Individual Differences in Adulthood

Prior to the experiment in which older adults had a choice of solving multiplication problems via mental arithmetic, pencil and paper, or use of a calculator, Siegler and Lemaire (1997) presented them with a questionnaire regarding their prior use of calculators. Roughly one-third of the older adults had never used calculators, one-third used them less than once per month during both their working days and since, and one-third used them more than once per month at some point in their lives. Not surprisingly, the amount of prior experience with calculators proved to be related to the amount of use in the experiment. Percentage of calculator use on nonretrieval trials (trials on which either the calculator or pencil and pen were used) increased from 40% to 52% to 67% with increasing experience. More surprising were the large individual differences within the subgroup of older adults (mean age = 75 years) who had never used a calculator before the experiment. The experimenter provided these adults with five minutes of instruction in how to use the calculator, and then told them that it was equally good from the experimenter's perspective to solve the problems via mental arithmetic, pencil and paper, or the calculator. Almost half of the older adults chose the calculator on all or almost all trials on which they did not use mental arithmetic; another group of equal size never used the calculator. Thus, it turns out that it is possible to teach at least some old dogs new tricks.

INTRA-INDIVIDUAL DIFFERENCES CONTRIBUTE TO INTER-INDIVIDUAL DIFFERENCES

Although intra- and inter-individual differences are conceptually distinct, they also are interrelated. One dimension on which individuals differ is in their variability. One child may use many strategies to perform a given task, another child only one or two; one child may express different strategies in gesture and speech on a given trial, another child may use the same strategy in both modalities; and so on. Complementarily, intra-individual variability also contributes to other dimensions of inter-individual variability. In particular, on a variety of measures of variability, the more variable a child's initial performance, the more likely the child is to learn from relevant experience.

On all tasks on which the issue has been examined, different children use different numbers of strategies. For example, in Siegler (1987), 1% of children used a single strategy to solve all of the addition problems that were presented, 37% used two strategies, and 62% used three or more strategies. Similarly, on the number conservation problems presented in Siegler (1995), 15% of children used two strategies and 85% used three or more.

Just as greater variability often makes possible adaptation to situational and task demands and to limited processing resources, it also facilitates learning. In many studies of children's cognitive development, the greater the initial variability, the more likely that children will generate useful problem-solving strategies and abandon ineffective older ones (Alibali & Goldin-Meadow, 1993; Graham & Perry, 1993; Siegler, 1995). Several specific forms of initial cognitive variability have been found to be positively related to subsequent learning: number of strategies used over a set of problems, frequency of use of multiple strategies on a single trial, frequency of self-corrections in verbal descriptions of strategies, and frequency of gesture-speech mismatches. For example, Perry and Lewis (1999) found that children who subsequently learned to solve gear problems were more likely than children who subsequently failed to learn from the same experience to begin a trial using one strategy and then switch to another strategy on the same trial. Similarly, Siegler (1995) found that two measures of pretest variability—number of different strategies used and whether more than one strategy was ever used on a given trial—accounted for 55% of the variance in subsequent learning on conservation problems. This result was not attributable to children who generated more pre-test strategies being more likely to generate correct approaches; half of the children did generate optimal approaches on at least one pre-test trial, but whether they did so was unrelated to learning.

Not all types of variability are equally related to learning. For example, Church (1999) examined three types of variability as predictors of conservation learning: gesture-speech mismatches, number of different verbal justifications across the three tasks, and number of trials on which children advanced multiple verbal justifications. Each of the three types of variability was a significant predictor of learning. However, number of gesture-speech mismatches proved to be more strongly predictive than the other two types of variability.

In addition to these variations in the potency of positive predictors of learning, some types of variability are negatively related to subsequent learning. For example, Coyle and Bjorklund (1997) found that frequency of shifts in strategy use on successive trials was negatively related to learning on serial recall problems. This may have reflected adoption of a win-stay-lose-shift approach, in which incorrect recall would increase the likelihood of shifting strategies on the next trial. Consistent with this interpretation, McGilly and Siegler (1990) found that strategy shifts on serial recall problems were more likely following incorrect recall than after correct recall.

In contrast to these results with children, Lindenberger and von Oertzen (Chapter 21, this volume) describe a number of studies of older adults in which inter-individual differences in variability are negatively related to performance and discuss several mechanisms that may underlie these negative relations. One mechanism that appears to operate at both the ontogenetic and microgenetic levels is processing fluctuation, a form of unreliability of processing that produces deviations from optimal performance on some trials and thus heightens variability. This mechanism has been studied primarily in adult populations, but it seems likely that the same mechanism operates in childhood—in the opposite direction. That is, it seems likely that in childhood, processing fluctuation decreases with age, leading to enhanced performance on many tasks. One good example is everyday motor activities, such as drawing. Variability of reproducing geometric shapes decreases with age, due both to greater biomechanical control and to learning of cultural conventions for drawing; the decreased variability is associated with more accurate reproduction (Braswell & Rosengren, 2000). Studying more systematically the influence of processing fluctuations on childhood cognitive development seems likely both to enrich understanding in that domain and to contribute to understanding of development across the lifespan.

As these examples suggest, types of variability vary in their relation to learning. An important goal for future research is to identify principles that indicate when variability is likely to be positively related to learning and when it is not. Church (1999) suggested one such principle: variability based on the simultaneous activation of different representations in different modalities is likely to be a positive predictor of learning. Bertenthal (1999) suggested another: variability that reflects structural variation in the situation is likely to be positively related to learning. Coyle (2001) suggested a third principle: early in development, using a greater variety of strategies is predictive of learning because the more varied strategies allow adaptation to a wide range of circumstances, but later in development, consistently using the best strategies is predictive of learning. Lindenberger and von Oertzen (Chapter 21, this volume) suggest a fourth principle, one related to Coyle's (2001) hypothesis: at points in learning when strategic diversity is an important part of overall variability, the relation between variability and learning will be positive, but at points when strategic diversity is low and processing fluctuation is the primary source of variability, the relation between variability and learning will be negative. Expansion and refinement of such principles seems likely to produce a better understanding of the reciprocal influence of intra-individual and inter-individual variability.

References

Adolph, K. E. (1995). A psychophysical assessment of toddlers' ability to cope with slopes. *Journal of Experimental Psychology: Human Perception and Performance, 21,* 734–750.

Adolph, K. E. (1997). Learning in the development of infant locomotion. *Monographs of the Society for Research in Child Development, 62*(3, Serial No. 251), 1–140.

Adolph, K. E., Eppler, M. A., & Gibson, E. J. (1993). Crawling versus walking infants' perception of affordances for locomotion over sloping surfaces. *Child Development, 64,* 1158–1174.

Alibali, M. W. (1999). How children change their minds: Strategy change can be gradual or abrupt. *Developmental Psychology, 35,* 127–145.

Alibali, M. W., & Goldin-Meadow, S. (1993). Gesture-speech mismatch and mechanisms of learning: What the hands reveal about a child's state of mind. *Cognitive Psychology, 25,* 468–523.

Allport, G. W. (1928). A test for ascendance-submission. *Journal of Abnormal and Social Psychology, 23,* 118–136.

Auschutz, L., Camp, C. J., Markley, R. P., & Kramer, J. J. (1987). Remembering mnemonics: A three-year follow-up on the effects of mnemonics training in elderly adults. *Experimental Aging Research, 13,* 141–143.

Baltes, P. B. (1997). On the incomplete architecture of human ontogeny: Selection, optimization, and compensation as foundation of developmental theory. *American Psychologist, 52,* 366–380.

Bertenthal, B. (1999). Variation and selection in the development of perception and action. In G. Savelsbergh, H. van der Maas, & P. van Geert (Eds.), *Non-linear developmental processes* (Vol. 175, pp. 105–121). Amsterdam: Royal Netherlands Academy of Arts and Sciences.

Binet, A., & Simon, T. (1905). Methodes nouvelles pour le diagnostic du niveau intellectual des anormaux. *L'Année Psychologique, 11,* 191–244.

Bjorklund, D. F., & Rosenblum, K. E. (2001). Children's use of multiple and variable addition strategies in a game context. *Developmental Science, 4,* 184–194.

Braswell, G. S., & Rosengren, K. K. (2000). Decreasing variability in the development of graphic production. *International Journal of Behavioral Development, 24,* 153–166.

Brody, N. (1992). *Intelligence* (2nd ed.). San Diego: Academic Press.

Caspi, A., & Silva, P. A. (1995). Temperamental qualities at age 3 predict personality traits in adulthood: Longitudinal evidence from a birth cohort. *Child Development, 66,* 486–498.

Chen, Z., & Siegler, R. S. (2000). Across the great divide: Bridging the gap between understanding of toddlers' and older children's thinking. *Monographs of the Society for Research in Child Development, 65*(2, Whole No. 261), 1–96.

Church, R. B. (1999). Using gesture and speech to capture transitions in learning. *Cognitive Development, 14,* 313–342.

Colby, A., Kohlberg, L., Gibbs, J., & Lieberman, M. (1983). A longitudinal study of moral judgment. *Monographs of the Society for Research in Child Development, 48,* (Serial No. 200, 1–124), 1–96.

Coyle, T. R. (2001). Factor analysis of variability measures in eight independent samples of children and adults. *Journal of Experimental Child Psychology, 78,* 330–358.

Coyle, T. R., & Bjorklund, D. F. (1997). Age differences in, and consequences of, multiple- and variable-strategy use on a multiple sort-recall task. *Developmental Psychology, 33,* 372–380.

Fabricius, W. V., & Hagen, J. W. (1984). Use of causal attributions about recall performance to assess metamemory and predict strategic memory behavior in young children. *Developmental Psychology,* 20, 975–987.

Ferrari, M., & Sternberg, R. J. (1998). The development of mental abilities and styles. In W. Damon (Series Ed.) & D. Kuhn & R. S. Siegler (Vol. Eds.), *Handbook of child psychology: Vol. 2: Cognition, perception & language* (5th ed., pp. 899–946). New York: Wiley.

Flavell, J. H., Miller, P. H., & Miller, S. A. (Eds.). (1993). *Cognitive development* (3rd ed.). Englewood Cliffs, NJ: Prentice-Hall.

Galton, F. (1879). Psychometric experiments. *Brain, 2,* 149–162.

Geary, D. C., & Burlingham-Dubree, M. (1989). External validation of the strategy choice model for addition. *Journal of Experimental Child Psychology, 47,* 175–192.

Geary, D. C., Fan, L., and Bow-Thomas, C. C. (1992). Numerical cognition: Loci of ability differences comparing children from China and the United States. *Psychological Science, 3,* 180–185.

Ghatala, E. S., Levin, J. R., Pressley, M., & Goodwin, D. (1986). A componential analysis of the effects of derived and supplied strategy-utility information on children's strategy selection. *Journal of Experimental Child Psychology, 41,* 76–92.

Goldin-Meadow, S. (2001). Giving the mind a hand: The role of gesture in cognitive change. In J. L McClelland, & R. S. Siegler, (Eds.), *Mechanisms of cognitive development: Behavioral and neural perspectives* (pp. 5–31). Mahwah, NJ: Lawrence Erlbaum Associates.

Graham, T., & Perry, M. (1993). Indexing transitional knowledge. *Developmental Psychology, 29,* 779–788.

Hopkins, S. L., & Lawson, M. J. (2002). Explaining the acquisition of a complex skill: Methodological and theoretical considerations uncovered in the study of simple addition and the moving-on process. *Educational Psychology Review, 14,* 121–154.

Hunt, E. (1987). The next word on verbal ability. In P. A. Vernon (Ed.), *Speed of information processing and intelligence.* Norwood, NJ: Ablex.

Kerkman, D. D., & Siegler, R. S. (1993). Individual differences and adaptive flexibility in lower-income children's strategy choices. *Learning and Individual Differences, 5,* 113–136.

Kerkman, D. D., & Siegler, R. S. (1997). Measuring individual differences in children's addition strategy choices. *Learning and Individual Differences, 9,* 1–18.

Kohlberg, L. (1969). Stage and sequence: The cognitive-developmental approach to socialization. In D. A. Goslin (Ed.), *Handbook of socialization theory and research* (pp. 347–480). Chicago: Rand McNally.

Kuczaj, S. A. (1977). The acquisition of regular and irregular past tense forms. *Journal of Verbal Learning and Verbal Behavior, 16,* 589–600.

Kuhn, D., Garcia-Mila, M., Zohar, A., & Anderson, C. (1995). Strategies of knowledge acquisition. *Monographs of the Society for Research in Child Development* (Serial No. 245), 1–128.

Li, K. Z. H., Lindenberger, U., Freund, A. M., & Baltes, P. B. (2001). Walking while memorizing: Age-related differences in compensatory behavior. *Psychological Science, 12,* 230–237.

McGilly, K., & Siegler, R. S. (1990). The influence of encoding and strategic knowledge on children's choices among serial recall strategies. *Developmental Psychology, 26,* 931–941.

Miller, K. F., & Paredes, D. R. (1990). Starting to add worse: Effects of learning to multiply on children's addition. *Cognition, 37,* 213–242.

Miller, P. H., & Seier, W. L. (1994). Strategy utilization deficiencies in children: When, where, and why. In H. W. Reese (Ed.), *Advances in child development and behavior* (Vol. 25, pp. 108–156). New York: Academic Press.

Neely, A. S., & Bäckman, L. (1993). Maintenance of gains following multifactorial and unifactorial memory training in late adulthood. *Educational Gerontology, 19,* 105–117.

Perry, M., & Lewis, J. L. (1999). Verbal imprecision as an index of knowledge in transition. *Developmental Psychology, 25,* 749–759.

Piaget, J. (1952). *The child's concept of number.* New York: W.W. Norton.

Rittle-Johnson, B., Siegler, R. S., & Alibali, M. W. (2001). Developing conceptual understanding and procedural skill in mathematics: An iterative process. *Journal of Educational Psychology, 93,* 346–362.

Rosengren, K. S. (2002). Thinking of variability during infancy and beyond. *Infant Behavior and Development, 25,* 337–339.

Ruble, D. N., & Martin, C. L. (1998). Gender development. In W. Damon (Series Ed.) & N. Eisenberg (Vol. Ed.), *Handbook of child psychology: Vol. 3: Social, emotional, and personality development* (5th ed., pp. 933–1016). New York: Wiley.

Schauble, L. (1996). The development of scientific reasoning in knowledge-rich contexts. *Developmental Psychology, 32,* 102–119.

Seashore, C. E. (1938). *Psychology of music.* New York: McGraw-Hill.

Shrager, J., & Siegler, R. S. (1998). SCADS: A model of children's strategy choices and strategy discoveries. *Psychological Science, 9,* 405–410.

Shultz, T. R., Fisher, G. W., Pratt, C. C., & Rulf, S. (1986). Selection of causal rules. *Child Development, 57,* 143–152.

Siegler, R. S. (1987). The perils of averaging data over strategies: An example from children's addition. *Journal of Experimental Psychology: General, 116,* 250–264.

Siegler, R. S. (1988). Individual differences in strategy choices: Good students, not-so-good students, and perfectionists. *Child Development, 59,* 833–851.

Siegler, R. S. (1989). Hazards of mental chronometry: An example from children's subtraction. *Journal of Educational Psychology, 81,* 497–506.

Siegler, R. S. (1995). How does change occur: A microgenetic study of number conservation. *Cognitive Psychology, 25,* 225–273.

Siegler, R. S. (1996). *Emerging minds: The process of change in children's thinking.* New York: Oxford University Press.

Siegler, R. S., & Lemaire, P. (1997). Older and younger adults' strategy choices in multiplication: Testing predictions of ASCM via the choice/no-choice method. *Journal of Experimental Psychology: General, 126,* 71–92.

Siegler, R. S., & McGilly, K. (1989). Strategy choices in children's time-telling. In I. Levin & D. Zakay (Eds.), *Time and human cognition: A life span perspective* (pp. 185–218). Amsterdam: North-Holland.

Siegler, R. S., & Shipley, C. (1995). Variation, selection, and cognitive change. In T. Simon and G. Halford (Eds.), *Developing cognitive competence: New approaches to process modeling.* Hillsdale, NJ: Lawrence Erlbaum Associates.

Siegler, R. S., & Shrager, J. (1984). Strategy choices in addition and subtraction: How do children know what to do? In C. Sophian (Ed.), *The origins of cognitive skills* (pp. 229–293). Hillsdale, NJ: Erlbaum.

Siegler, R. S., & Svetina, M. (2002). A microgenetic/ cross-sectional study of matrix completion: Comparing short-term and long-term change. *Child Development, 73,* 793–809.

Spearman, C. (1904). "General Intelligence" objectively determined and measured. *American Journal of Psychology, 15,* 201–293.

Tellegen, A., Watson, D., & Clark, L. A. (1999). Further support for a hierarchical model of affect: Reply to Green and Salovey. *Psychological Science, 10,* 307–309.

Thelen, E., Corbetta, D., & Spencer, J. P. (1996). The development of reaching during the first year: The role of movement speed. *Journal of Experimental Psychology: Human Perception and Performance, 22,* 1059–1076.

Thompson, R. A. (1998). Early sociopersonality development. In W. Damon (Series Ed.) & N. Eisenberg (Vol. Ed.), *Handbook of child psychology: Vol. 3: Social, emotional, and personality development* (5th ed., pp. 23–104). New York: Wiley.

Veriejken, B., Adolph, K. E., Denny, M. A., Fadl, Y., Gill, S. V., & Lucero, A. A. (1995). Development of infant crawling: Balance constraints on interlimb coordination. In G. Bardy, R. J. Bootsma, & Y. Guiard (Eds.), *Studies in perception and action III* (pp. 255–258). Hillsdale, NJ: Lawrence Erlbaum Associates.

21

Variability in Cognitive Aging: From Taxonomy to Theory

Ulman Lindenberger

Timo von Oertzen

Variability pervades cognitive aging. Shining examples of older individuals who preserved outstanding intellectual abilities well into very old age, such as Johann Wolfgang von Goethe or Sophocles, stand in contrast to individuals whose intellectual capacities are depleted by the time they reach later adulthood. Similar contrasts exist between different intellectual abilities. For example, if one looks at perceptual speed, one is likely to find monotonic decline after late adolescence and early adulthood. But if one looks at vocabulary, one will find age stability or positive change into very old age (Singer, Verhaeghen, Ghisletta, Lindenberger, & Baltes, 2003).

Despite its prominence, the conceptual significance of variability in cognitive aging is difficult to evaluate. On the one hand, variability in old age is often portrayed as the late-life culmination of interacting developmental causes that affect different individuals and different task domains to varying degrees. Here, variability in intellectual functioning is seen as a dependent variable, or outcome (for an

example, see Figure 7 in Lindenberger & Baltes, 1997). On the other hand, variability can also be conceived as an agent, or mechanism, of senescent changes in cognition (Hultsch & MacDonald, 2004; Li, Lindenberger, & Sikström, 2001; Thaler, 2002). According to this complementary position, certain forms of variability index basic properties of senescing cognitive systems at neural or behavioral levels of analysis, and may help to explain ontogenetic changes in cognition from early adulthood to old age.

Thus, the conceptual status of variability is ambiguous, as it denotes both consequences and causes of development. The same kind of ambiguity holds for other central phenomena of cognitive aging. For instance, the ubiquitous slowing of information processing with advancing age is conceived both as an antecedent (e.g., Salthouse, 1996) and as a consequence (e.g., Ratcliff, Spieler, & McKoon, 2000) of other senescent changes in behavior.

The general objective of the present chapter is to help in categorizing and clarifying the conceptual status of variability in cognitive aging. We first introduce a taxonomy of intra-individual variability. Then, we evaluate the common practice of measuring variability between persons to test propositions about within-person variability. Third, we focus on two variability phenomena in cognitive aging: high processing fluctuation (i.e., low processing robustness), and intellectual ability dedifferentiation. Fourth and finally, we report a neurocomputational model that integrates evidence about variability in cognitive aging across neural and behavioral levels of analysis and across microgenetic and ontogenetic timescales. We show how this neurocomputational model links ability dedifferentiation to low processing robustness, and may further guide the investigation of variability in cognitive aging.

A TAXONOMY OF WITHIN-PERSON VARIABILITY

Following Cattell's (1966) data box of individuals, variables, and occasions, Buss (1974) presented a schema of inter-individual differences and intra-individual changes that constituted 15 different data-gathering strategies for studying variability. Recently, S.-C. Li, Huxhold, and Schmiedek (2004) modified this picture by focusing on intra-individual variability and by adding substantive assumptions about its timescale and scope. A modified version of this scheme is presented in Table 21.1.

The taxonomy shown in Table 21.1 coordinates two dichotomous dimensions, timescale and scope. On the timescale dimension, we follow the distinction between microgenetic variations and ontogenetic change (e.g., Lindenberger & Baltes, 1995; Siegler, 1989). Microgenetic variations are short term and often reversible, whereas ontogenetic changes are long term and often cumulative, progressive, and permanent. Both microgenetic and ontogenetic changes can be adaptive, maladaptive, or both (i.e., adaptive with respect to one developmental goal but maladaptive with respect to another; cf. Baltes, 1987). On the scope dimension, alterations in a single function are set apart from transformations in functional organization involving more than one function. Alterations in a single function are often assumed to be local in character— that is, confined to the function under study. However, both microgenetic variations and ontogenetic change may co-involve more than one function and entail

global reorganization (structural modification). Such system-general transformations necessitate a multivariate approach.

A further dimension not explicitly represented in Table 21.1 is the distinction between neural and behavioral levels of analysis. Most forms of within-person variability can be studied at both neural and behavioral levels. For instance, age-associated decline in episodic memory performance during adulthood and old age can be studied from a neural perspective— what are its anatomical, neurochemical, and neurofunctional correlates?—but it also can be studied from a behavioral perspective: what are its behavioral antecedents, correlates, and consequences?

For illustration, we may apply this classificatory scheme to one specific cognitive function such as episodic memory. At the microgenetic timescale, trial-to-trial variability in the ability to represent contextual information at encoding would qualify as univariate microgenetic variability (i.e., the upper left cell of Table 21.1). Shifts in resource allocation between an episodic memory task and a simultaneously performed perceptual-motor task are instances of functional reorganization (upper right cell). At the ontogenetic timescale, longitudinal age changes in episodic memory ability from young adulthood to old age, when viewed in isolation, fall into the univariate, local category (lower left cell). In contrast, ontogenetic changes in the functional relation between episodic and semantic memory represent an instance of global functional reorganization (lower right cell).

In our view, a major challenge for cognitive aging research is to identify neural and behavioral mechanisms that link local to global variations and microgenetic variations to ontogenetic change. Specifically, developmental researchers need to specify how microgenetic variations are affected by and result in ontogenetic change, and how local variability is affected by and results in global organization, both neurally and behaviorally. In other words, if we wish to move from taxonomy to theory, we need to explicate mechanisms that link developmental phenomena across the cells of our classificatory scheme. Based on the criteria of parsimony and explanatory power, mechanisms that link local microgenetic variations to global ontogenetic transformations seem especially attractive. One such hypothetical mechanism, the stochastic gain parameter of connectionist networks, will be described in the last section of this chapter.

TABLE 21.1. Taxonomy of within-person variability in cognitive functioning across the lifespan

Time scale	Scope	
	Variations in a Single Function (e.g., *local, univariate*)	Transformations in Functional Organization (e.g., *global, multivariate*)
Microgenetic (e.g., usually across trials, sessions, or weeks)	Relatively reversible variations in one function Examples: • *processing fluctuation (processing liability or lack of processing robustness)* • neural and behavioral plasticity (short-term learning potential) • within-task strategic diversity (richness of within-task behavioral repertoire) • adaptability/resilience to environmental perturbations • cyclic (e.g., state) variations in any specific function	Relatively reversible variations in functional organization Examples: • shifts in resource allocation, coordination and compensatory behavior during multitasking • context-driven variations in mental set and functional organization (e.g., posture control with eyes open or closed) • situational choice and preference behavior
Ontogenetic (e.g., usually across months, years, or decades)	Relatively permanent (e.g., cumulative, progressive) changes in one function Examples: • physical growth • progressive (e.g., trait) changes in any specific cognitive function (e.g., mechanics of cognition / broad Gf, episodic memory) • long-term learning and skill acquisition (e.g., pragmatics of cognition / broad Gc, semantic memory)	Relatively permanent (e.g., cumulative, progressive) alterations in functional organization Examples: • *ability dedifferentiation from adulthood to old age* • ability differentiation from childhood to early adulthood • corticogenesis and functional specification of brain areas during maturation and learning • functional reintegration of brain circuitry in old age • shrinkage of brain volume and loss of receptor density during senescence • cortical reorganization after brain damage or trauma

Note: This taxonomy is not meant to be exhaustive. For instance, societal sources of variability are not systematically considered. All listed forms of variability can be studied at neuronal and behavioral levels of analysis. Examples are drawn from both levels. Examples printed in italics are discussed in more detail in this chapter. A major challenge for lifespan psychology is to identify mechanisms that link local to global variations, microgenetic variations to ontogenetic change, and neuronal mechanisms to behavior. Theories that link neuronal mechanisms in a single function acting at a microgenetic timescale to global ontogenetic transformations in behavior are high in parsimony and explanatory power. (Modified after S.-C. Li, Huxhold, & Schmiedek, 2004.)

MEASURING VARIABILITY WITHIN AND BETWEEN INDIVIDUALS

Whereas developmental theories about variability generally refer to ontogenetic changes and microgenetic variations *within* individuals, most of the data used to evaluate such theories refer to variability *between* individuals. This habitual mismatch between theory and data has been noted for a long time in lifespan psychology (e.g., Baltes, Reese, & Nesselroade, 1977/1988), child development (e.g., Reuchlin, 1978), dynamic systems approaches (e.g., Smith & Thelen, 2003), and proponents of an idiographic approach (e.g., Magnusson & Stattin, 1998).

Though many researchers are aware of the mismatch, its consequences are often overlooked or belittled. The study of univariate ontogenetic changes forms a notable positive exception to this rule. Here, the difference between intra- and inter-individual variation generally refers to the distinction between cross-sectional age differences and longitudinal age changes. The benefits and costs of both data-analytic schemes, and the issue of extrapolating average age changes on the basis of cross-sectional age differences and observed longitudinal changes, are fairly well understood (e.g., Baltes, 1968; Lindenberger & Baltes, 1994; Lövdén, Ghisletta, & Lindenberger, 2004; Salthouse, 1991; Schaie, Maitland, Willis, & Intieri, 1998). For instance, cross-sectional age differences are confounded with stable differences between birth cohorts, whereas longitudinal observations contain retest effects and are often conditioned by selective attrition (e.g., Lindenberger, Singer, & Baltes, 2002).

In contrast, much less is known about the relationship between intra- and inter-individual variability with respect to global ontogenetic changes in functional organization, univariate microgenetic variations, and multivariate microgenetic variations (i.e., the remaining three cells of the cross-classification of timescale and scope of variability presented in Table 21.1). Cognitive aging researchers often ignore the relation between intra-individual and inter-individual variability, and simply substitute intra-individual with inter-individual observations, primarily because the latter are more easily available than the former. The methodological assumptions underlying this strategy are discussed in the next section.

Extrapolating Intra-Individual Variability Based on Inter-Individual Variability

The generalizability of inter-individual to intra-individual variability hinges on two interrelated criteria: variation equivalence and sample homogeneity (Lövdén & Lindenberger, 2005). We use the term *variation equivalence* to designate an empirical situation in which intra-individual and inter-individual variability do not differ in important ways with respect to the variables under study. Variation equivalence holds when the processes that generate variability between and within individuals are identical, but it may also hold for other reasons (e.g., by coincidence). Formal criteria that need to be met to *guarantee* variation equivalence depend on statistical context (e.g., Markov chains, Bayesian nets) and have been discussed under the heading of *ergodicity* (e.g., Molenaar, Huizenga, & Nesselroade, 2003). A formal treatment of these criteria is beyond the scope of the present chapter.

Equivalance of inter-individual and intra-individual variability is often assumed but rarely tested. Imagine, for instance, a correlation of $r = .50$ between episodic memory and semantic memory that was ob-

tained by administering indicators of the two abilities to different individuals at a given point in time. In the absence of intra-individual information, such a between-person correlation is often meant to suggest a moderately positive correlation *within individuals*, perhaps reflecting the existence of two separate but overlapping memory systems. One way to test this interpretation empirically would actually be to obtain extensive observations on measures of episodic and semantic memory within individuals. Even for the same sample of individuals, the correlation based on between-person variability does not have to approximate the mean of the distribution of the within-person correlations, nor does it prescribe its range. For instance, in the case of an $r = .50$ between-person correlation between episodic and semantic memory, within-person correlations may be $r = -.30$ in some individuals and $r = .80$ in others.

Sample homogeneity refers to the assumption that structural relations among variables of interest do not differ significantly from person to person. In the present case, sample homogeneity requires that the correlations between episodic and semantic memory be of similar magnitude within all individuals (e.g., a sufficiently narrow normal distribution around the same mean). Sample homogeneity is a necessary but not a sufficient condition for variation equivalence. In our previous example, the intra-individual correlations between episodic and semantic memory may be homogeneously distributed around $r = .30$, but the inter-individual correlation may still be $r = .50$.

The assumption of sample homogeneity is at odds with the more general notion that individuals differ in the way they change over time. According to lifespan theory (e.g., Baltes et al., 1977/1988; cf. Lindenberger & Baltes, 1999; Tetens, 1777), the developmental path of each individual corresponds to a multivariate pattern of intra-individual change. Description and explanation of these intra-person patterns is a prerequisite for arriving at unbiased descriptions and explanations of the differences and commonalities among them. Premature aggregation across individuals can mask both differences and commonalities in change (e.g., Estes, 1956; Wohlwill, 1973). In the extreme case, certain laws and regularities may be specific to aggregate data and not apply to any of the individuals on which the aggregate data were based.

To conclude, the quid pro quo approach to variability, in which inter-individual variability is taken as a valid proxy for intra-individual variability, mandates equivalence between inter-individual and intra-individual variation, and presupposes homogeneity of change. Except for univariate ontogenetic changes we know exceedingly little about the degree to which these assumptions are met.

Illustrating the Difference Between Inter- and Intra-Individual Variability

The following illustration further specifies the difference between inter-individual and intra-individual variability. It uses the metaphor of leaves falling down to earth (see Figure 21.1). The movements of any given leaf falling down to earth will differ from the movements of all other leaves as a function of shape, weight, air pressure, initial conditions, and so on. Physicists may want to arrive at general laws of leaf falling that generalize across all possible constellations of variables (e.g., apply to all possible leaves). Such general laws would accommodate both the differences and commonalities in movement among various types of leaves. Probably, gravity and turbulence will play prominent roles in formulating such laws. For instance, all leaves eventually reach the ground because of gravity but each leaf moves down to earth in a slightly different manner because of turbulence.

To arrive at such laws, physicists probably would refrain, except for special cases, from using averages over different leaves as their primary database. In fact, the trajectory of the "average leaf" would be more similar to a stone falling down to earth in slow motion than to the falling patterns of any existing leaf because movements due to turbulence would cancel each

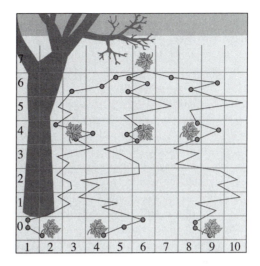

FIGURE 21.1. Illustrating the difference between intra-individual and inter-individual variability. The picture shows the path of three leaves falling from a tree to the ground. The dots correspond to observations, and are summarized in Table 21.2.

other out. Thus, the movements of the average leaf would not provide a good empirical basis for arriving at adequate models of leaf falling.

Figure 21.1 depicts the positions of three individual leaves on their way down to earth. The three leaves start falling at a vertical position (i.e. height) of 8 meters and a horizontal position of 6 meters, and their horizontal positions are repeatedly measured as a function of height as they are falling down to earth. Table 21.2 reports the means and variances in hori-

TABLE 21.2. Means and standard deviations in horizontal position of three individual leaves and the "average leaf": Illustrating the difference between intra-individual and inter-individual variability

	Horizontal Position (meters)											
	left leaf			middle leaf			right leaf			all leaves		
Vertical Position (range in meters)	scores	mean	SD	scores	mean	SD	scores	mean	SD	mean	SD	mean of intra-SDs
6-7	5,4,3	4.00	0.82	5,6,5	5.33	0.47	7,8,8	7.67	0.47	5.67	1.81	0.59
4-5	2,4,3	3.00	0.82	6,5,6	5.67	0.47	8,9,8	8.67	0.47	5.67	2.26	0.59
0-1	1,1,2	1.33	0.47	6,5,4	5.00	0.82	8,8,9	8.33	0.47	4.89	2.92	0.59

Note: Date are illustrated in Figure 21.2.

zontal position for these leaves 6–7, 4–5, and 0–1 meters above the ground. Intra-individual standard deviations indicate that the leaves' intra-individual variability in movement stays relatively constant over time; in fact, the average intra-individual standard deviation (i.e., mean of SDs) stays constant. In contrast, inter-individual standard deviations (i.e., the overall SD) increase over time, reflecting the fact that the three leaves diverge in horizontal position over time. The corresponding comparisons of central tendency yield opposite results. Here, the intra-individual means show greater divergence over time than the inter-individual average (i.e., the overall mean).

This illustration demonstrates that empirical results based on inter-individual variability may not always be appropriate to test propositions about intra-person mechanisms. It also suggests that endorsing individuals as privileged units of analysis does not mandate a withdrawal from the search for laws of behavioral development that generalize across collections of individuals. Instead, chances of arriving at such laws may increase, rather than decrease, when intra-individual variability is brought to the fore.

EMPIRICAL FINDINGS ABOUT VARIABILITY IN COGNITIVE AGING

The empirical investigation of variability in cognitive aging has intensified in recent years. In the following, we concentrate our discussion on two central phenomena: processing fluctuation and ability dedifferentiation. Whereas processing fluctuation (i.e., processing lability or lack of processing robustness) operates at the microgenetic timescale, ability dedifferentiation is operating at an ontogenetic timescale (see also Table 21.1). After a selective review of empirical findings, we report a neurocomputational model, originally introduced by S.-C. Li and Lindenberger (1999), that links ability dedifferentiation to lack of processing robustness by means of a hypothetical neuronal mechanism.

Processing Fluctuation

Processing fluctuation, or lack of processing robustness, refers to a predominantly maladaptive form of microgenetic variability. For instance, in the context of a choice-reaction time task, processing fluctuation would correspond behaviorally to response time variability within a given experimental condition. Here, greater variability indicates that individuals are less able to reproduce their behavior over time. Little is known about adult age changes in processing fluctuation, and about the relative magnitude of such fluctuations in comparison to ontogenetic age trends in mean levels of functioning. Based on the general notion that senescence produces an increasingly labile, less efficiently regulated internal milieu (Thaler, 2002), and for more specific reasons outlined in the next section, we expect that processing fluctuation is increasing with advancing adult age.

Nesselroade and Salthouse (2004) investigated cross-sectional adult age differences in processing fluctuation in adults ranging from 20 to 91 years of age. Research participants were asked to perform three perceptual-motor tasks on three different occasions administered within a two-week period. For each task, three types of variability (i.e., standard deviations) were computed: (1) standard between-person variability; (2) within-person, within-session variability, computed as a person's average within-session standard deviation over three repeated administrations of each task; (3) within-person, between-session variability, computed as the standard deviation of each person's mean session scores.

Nesselroade and Salthouse (2004) made several important observations. First, the two indices of processing fluctuation showed substantial positive correlations within and across tasks, indicating that people differed reliably and consistently in variability of perceptual-motor performance. Second, when computing ratios of within-person over between-person variability, Nesselroade and Salthouse (2004) discovered that the magnitude of both types of within-person variability amounted to about half the magnitude of the standard measures of inter-individual variability. The corresponding ratios ranged from 0.31 to 0.85, with the majority being in the 0.40–0.55 range. In fact, the average fluctuation of a single individual within a single session, if projected onto average age trends, corresponded to an age range of 21–44 years! In other words, depending upon whether a given 32-year-old individual performed more or less variably (e.g., "had a good or a bad day"), he or she would look like an average 21-year-old or an average 44-year-old individual. Third, intra-individual fluctuation was negatively related to performance level, confirming its dysfunctional character. Fourth, intra-individual fluctuations increased with age, supporting the hypothesis that the cognitive system functions less reliably with advancing age.

The consistency, magnitude, external validity, and age association of within-person variability observed by Nesselroade and Salthouse (2004) have profound implications for cognitive aging research. Methodologically, they demonstrate that measures of central tendency fail to represent the performance characteristics of a given individual. A major portion of variability commonly attributed to between-person differences or measurement error appears to be due to within-person fluctuations. As noted by Nesselroade and Salthouse (2004), these findings challenge "the value of even a 'working' notion of the classical test theory conception of true score"(p. 53). As a consequence, attempts to resolve methodological problems associated with developmental sample heterogeneity by relying on so-called narrow age-cohort designs; that is, the comparative study of strictly age-homogeneous samples (Hofer & Sliwinski, 2001) do not appear to be particularly promising. If within-person microgenetic variability corresponds to several decades of average ontogenetic age gradients, and if within-person variability increases with age, then matching individuals with respect to chronological age does not effectively control for developmental status.

Instead, it seems more promising to incorporate intensive within-person observations, or measurement bursts (Nesselroade, 1991), into the design of longitudinal studies to explicitly study interactions among microgenetic and ontogenetic forms of variability such as processing fluctuation, plasticity (short-term learning potential), and long-term development (cf. Lindenberger & Baltes, 1995; Siegler, Chapter 20, this volume; for recent empirical examples, see MacDonald, Hultsch, & Dixon, 2003; Singer, Lindenberger, & Baltes, 2003). Given that empirical associations between perceptual-motor performance of the kind measured by Nesselroade and Salthouse (2004) and other aspects of intellectual and sensorimotor performance are substantial, especially in aging samples (Baltes & Lindenberger, 1997; Li & Lindenberger, 2002; Lindenberger & Baltes, 1997), this conclusion is likely to generalize to many behavioral domains.

Of course, not all forms of microgenetic variability are maladaptive. Contradictory findings about the functional meaning of microgenetic variability can be reconciled by separating mechanisms supporting skill acquisition and resilience to environmental perturbations from mechanisms permitting stable performance at asymptotic levels of learning. According to this view,

a variety of mechanisms contribute to observed microgenetic variability. For instance, during early phases of learning and with difficult reasoning tasks, microgenetic variability may be dominated by strategic diversity—that is, by an individual's capacity to approach the task in many different ways (Chapter 20, this volume). The contribution of strategic diversity to variability may fade out late in learning when optimal behavioral repertoires have been selected, trained, and automatized. Furthermore, its contribution may be small from the very start whenever tasks are sufficiently simple or constrained to effectively prevent strategic diversity. Processing fluctuation is likely to be present throughout learning, but its relative contribution to overall microgenetic variability may increase as the contribution of strategic diversity decreases. In addition, processing fluctuation may also increase in absolute magnitude with learning because the production of asymptotic performance may tax the system's capacity limits, thereby rendering its behavior more susceptible to minor external and internal perturbations.

Based on these considerations, we expect that interindividual differences in within-person variability early in learning should be positively related to interindividual differences in performance level, reflecting differences in strategic diversity. In contrast, variability late in learning should be negatively related to performance level, primarily reflecting differences in processing fluctuations. Thus, the association between variability and performance should switch signs in the course of learning. The results of a recent study (Allaire & Marsiske, 2002) exactly followed this pattern.

In sum, processing fluctuation, a maladaptive form of microgenetic variability, can be conceptually and empirically dissociated from other, more beneficial forms of microgenetic variability such as strategic diversity and short-term learning. Moreover, recent evidence (Nesselroade & Salthouse, 2004) suggests that processing fluctuation in perceptual-motor cognitive tasks is of considerable magnitude in relation to ontogenetic age trends in mean levels of performance, and increases significantly from adulthood to old age.

Ability Dedifferentiation in Old Age

Within the psychometric research tradition, the differentiation/dedifferentiation hypothesis is arguably the most comprehensive proposition about lifespan changes in variability (cf. Lindenberger, 2001). The hypothesis asserts that the functional organization of intellectual abilities is relatively compressed in childhood, unfolds (differentiates) during maturation (e.g., Garrett, 1946), and contracts (dedifferentiates) again in old age (e.g., Baltes, Cornelius, Spiro, Nesselroade, & Willis, 1980; Reinert, 1970). During childhood and old age, operation and expression of intellectual abilities are assumed to depend strongly on system-general constraints, reflecting the age-graded developmental status of relevant biological substrates. With maturation and during adulthood, these system-general ensembles of constraints are relaxed, and other factors, such as interest, motivation, and occupational/educational opportunities, determine intellectual development to a relatively greater degree, leading to greater diversity in levels of functioning across different intellectual abilities. As such, the hypothesis conveys a dynamic view of the structure of intellectual abilities (cf. Krampe & Baltes, 2003). The hypothesis is specified further by two-component theories of intellectual development that distinguish between biological and cultural dimensions of cognition (Baltes, 1987; Cattell, 1971; Horn, 1989; Tetens, 1777; for comparison, see Baltes, Lindenberger, & Staudinger, 1998; Lindenberger, 2001). The general constraints assumed to operate more strongly early and late in ontogeny are assumed to be biological in kind.

Clearly, the differentiation/dedifferentiation hypothesis of lifespan intelligence refers to the organization of intellectual abilities within individuals. However, almost all of the empirical evidence brought to bear on this hypothesis consists in comparing the structure of inter-individual differences (i.e., between-person variability) in different age groups, such as decreasing correlations among intellectual tests sampled across persons from childhood to adolescence, and increasing correlations among intellectual tests sampled across persons from adulthood to old age. Thus, just as described in the previous section, evidence obtained by structuring variability between individuals has been used routinely to test a hypothesis that refers to age changes in functional organization within individuals.

Most of the evidence based on inter-individual differences seems to favor the existence of ability dedifferentiation in advanced old age (e.g., Baltes & Lindenberger, 1997; Hultsch, Hertzog, Dixon, & Small, 1998; Li, Lindenberger, et al., 2004; Schaie et al., 1998; but see Park et al., 2002). Discrepancies in findings may relate to sample composition, differ-

ences in age groups, and restriction of range (e.g., Deary et al., 1996; Nesselroade & Thompson, 1995). Only a few studies have examined the dedifferentiation hypothesis at the intra-person level, by assessing age differences in ability covariance structures within young and older adults (for a review on the relation between sensorimotor and intellectual domains, see Li & Lindenberger, 2002). Here, the evidence generally appears to be supportive as well (e.g., Li, Aggen, Nesselroade, & Baltes, 2001).

Links Between Dedifferentiation and Processing Fluctuation

Recently, S.-C. Li, Lindenberger, et al. (2004) empirically linked inter-individual differences in microgenetic processing fluctuation to the differentiation/dedifferentiation hypothesis of lifespan intelligence. The authors administered a psychometric battery comprising 15 tests assessing three marker abilities of fluid mechanics (perceptual speed, reasoning, and fluency) and two marker abilities of crystallized pragmatics (verbal knowledge and fluency) to a sample of 291 individuals ages 6–89 years. Participants were classified into six age groups, childhood (6–11 years), adolescence (12–17 years), early adulthood (18–35 years), middle adulthood (26–54 years), late adulthood (55–69 years), and old age (70–89 years). In addition, Li, Lindenberger, et al. (2004) also administered five basic experimental cognitive tasks (i.e., visual search, response competition, memory search, and choice reactions). Based on performance on these tasks, the authors computed two overall indicators of information processing: processing speed (i.e., a person's average speed of responding across the five tasks) and processing robustness (i.e., the inverse of a person's average within-task reaction-time fluctuation).

Two sets of findings are relevant in the present context (see Figure 21.2). First, within the limitations of the inter-individual variability approach, results provided support for the differentiation/dedifferentiation hypothesis. Across the lifespan, fluid intelligence, crystallized intelligence, processing speed, and processing robustness all followed the expected inverted U-shape pattern. Fluid intelligence showed the earliest increase during early and the earliest decrease in late life, whereas crystallized intelligence showed a later increase and a later decrease. Principal component analyses of the 15 psychometric tests were performed separately in each group. In childhood, late

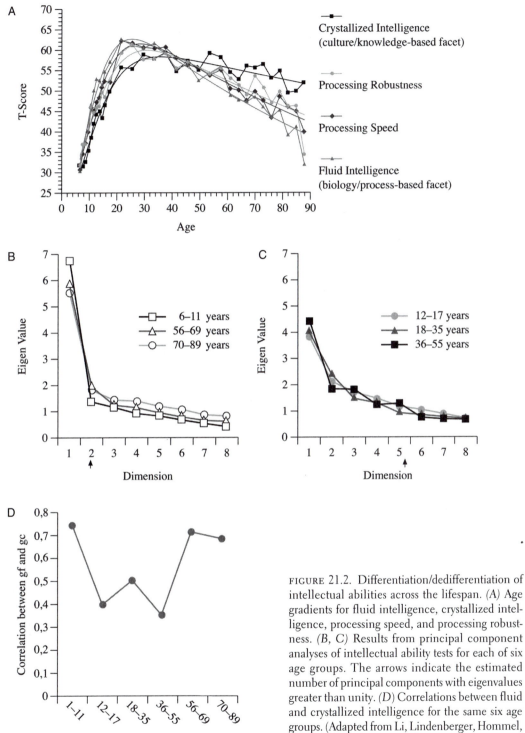

FIGURE 21.2. Differentiation/dedifferentiation of intellectual abilities across the lifespan. (A) Age gradients for fluid intelligence, crystallized intelligence, processing speed, and processing robustness. (B, C) Results from principal component analyses of intellectual ability tests for each of six age groups. The arrows indicate the estimated number of principal components with eigenvalues greater than unity. (D) Correlations between fluid and crystallized intelligence for the same six age groups. (Adapted from Li, Lindenberger, Hommel, Aschersleben, Prinz, & Baltes, 2004.)

adulthood, and old age, only two components with eigenvalues greater than 1 were extracted. In adolescence, young, and middle adulthood, five components displayed eigenvalues greater than unity. Also, fluid and crystallized intelligence were more highly correlated in childhood, late adulthood, and old age than in adolescence, young, and middle adulthood.

Second, processing speed was a strong predictor of intellectual performance in all age groups, and especially in childhood and old age. In contrast, the unique predictive validity of processing robustness was restricted to late adulthood and old age (see Table 21.3). Thus, in late adulthood and old age, higher processing fluctuation was uniquely associated with lower performance on psychometric measures of intelligence. This empirical association between high processing fluctuation, low average performance, and compressed ability structure will be taken up again in the next section.

Dedifferentiation at the Neuronal Level

The behavioral neuroscience of aging has been remarkably successful in promoting variability as a key concept in research on aging. Regional covariation methods suggest that functional interconnections found in younger adults are typically weaker in older adults (e.g., Schreurs, Bahro, Molchan, Sunderland, & McIntosh, 2001). With respect to activated brain areas, both under- and overactivation relative to young adults have been observed. Possibly, some of the observed age changes in activation patterns reflect a loss of distinctiveness (or dedifferentiation) of mental representations (Park, Polk, Park, Minear, Savage, & Smith, 2004). In addition, some increments in the bilaterality of prefrontal activation may represent adaptive (compensatory) changes in functional circuitry (Cabeza, 2002).

Recently, strong evidence in favor of dedifferentiation at the intra-person, neuronal level of analysis has been found (Park et al., 2004). Park et al. examined whether neural structures become less functionally differentiated and specialized with age, as predicted by the differentiation/dedifferentiation hypothesis. Whereas much of the earlier work has focused on frontal cortex, this study investigated age differences in specificity of regions in ventral visual cortex. Compared to frontal areas, ventral visual cortex shows considerably less neurodegenerative change (Raz, 2000). Also, in young adults, this area is known to respond

TABLE 21.3. Commonality analyses of processing robustness and processing speed as predictors of fluid and crystallized intelligence in late adulthood and old age (55–89 years)

	Dependent variables	
Predictors	Fluid Intelligence	Crystallized Intelligence
Unique processing robustness	4.7	0.1
Unique processing speed	4.1	4.4
Shared	28.7	13.3
Total	37.5	13.5

Note: Components different from zero are reprinted in boldface ($p < .01$). (Adapted from Li, Lindenberger, Hommel, Aschersleben, Prinz, & Baltes, 2004.)

differentially to different visual categories. Park et al. (2004) administered stimuli from four different visual categories—faces, houses, pseudowords (plausible non-words), and chairs—to young and old adults, and assessed neural activity during stimulus perception using functional magnetic resonance imaging. Within the ventral visual cortex, the authors isolated, separately for each participant, the most active regions for each of the stimulus categories relative to phase-scrambled control stimuli. Note that this person-based procedure takes care of inter-individual differences in brain activation patterns, thereby avoiding some of the problems commonly associated with averaging brain activity across individuals.

Young adults showed clear peaks in activation profiles. For instance, when processing faces, the voxels selected because of their activation peak during face perception were much more active than the voxels selected because of activation peaks for houses, pseudowords, or chairs. In contrast, old adults showed considerably flatter performance profiles, though the overall amount of activation relative to control stimuli was about the same. For instance, when processing faces, the activation differences between voxels selected because of their activation peak for faces and voxels selected because of corresponding activation peaks for the other three categories were small. These findings demonstrate that visual processing in the neocortex becomes less functionally specialized with advancing age, perhaps reducing the distinctiveness of cortical representations (cf. Li & Sikström, 2002).

A FORMAL MODEL OF VARIABILITY
IN COGNITIVE AGING

Formalization of theoretical assumptions is a particularly powerful tool in science. When applied to cognitive aging, such models enable researchers to map differences observed at neural and behavioral levels of analysis onto model parameters that express theoretical assumptions about the ontogeny of human information processing. In the following, we will present one such model (e.g., Li & Lindenberger, 1999), which has been inspired by the neural noise hypothesis of cognitive aging. According to this model, age-based decrements in the modulation of neuronal signals negatively affect the distinctiveness of cortical representations, with widespread consequences for performance level, variance, and covariation. Most important, this model attempts to link microgenesis to ontogeny, univariate variation to global change, and neuronal mechanisms to behavior (Li , Lindenberger, et al., 2001).

About 40 years ago, Welford (1965) hypothesized that senescing brains are marked by an increase in neural noise. At a more cognitive level of analysis, Craik (1983) noted that older adults encode events in a less distinctive manner than young adults because of reduced attentional resources. Relatedly, Kinsbourne and Hicks (1978) proposed the notion of functional cerebral space to better understand attention regulation, interference, and individual differences in performance. Here, the metaphor of declining processing resources was reframed as an aging-induced compression of functional cerebral space. In all three cases, behavioral aging was linked to some form of *representational dedifferentiation*, or a decrease in the distinctiveness of brain states, well in line with the differentiation/dedifferentiation hypothesis pursued independently in psychometrics and foreshadowing the results of current-day brain-imaging studies.

Still another line of recent research has linked behavioral aging to continuous age-associated shifts in neurochemical functioning. Specifically, the dopaminergic system has been identified as a promising neurochemical correlate of behavioral aging (Bäckman & Farde, 2004). First, dopamine transmitter content and binding mechanisms show an almost universal and highly consistent pattern of age-associated decline in various brain regions during normal aging. Second, much of behavioral aging has been attributed to prefrontal cortex dysfunction (Raz, 2000), where dopam-

inergic pathways serve to activate and maintain representations in the absence of environmental cues, and to direct attention to goal-relevant stimuli, actions, and action effects (Miller & Cohen, 2001). Third, more direct experimental evidence based on animal models points to the functional significance of dopamine receptor density. Taken together, age-associated differences in dopaminergic neuromodulation appear to be related to negative age differences in behavior.

The theory of representational dedifferentiation proposed by S.-C. Li and colleagues simulates the effects of aging-related changes in neuromodulation on behavior through a series of neurocomputational simulations. It combines earlier theoretical propositions regarding representational dedifferentiation with recent neurochemical evidence about adult age differences in neuromodulation. Variations in the gain parameter (G) of connectionist models are used to simulate the effects of age differences in neuromodulation on neural network signal processing and behavior. G regulates the input sensitivity of the network's processing units. When G is at its lower boundary, units become completely insensitive to input variations. With high values of G, processing units produce very little output with signals below a certain threshold, and close to maximum output for signals above threshold (see Figure 21.3, top panel). Thus, reductions in G flatten the sigmoidal activation function, thereby reducing a unit's capacity to discriminate between different levels of input signals.

In all neurocomputational simulations used to implement the theory, the only difference between "young" and "old" networks concerns mean levels of G; in all other respects, the two groups of networks are identical. In contrast to earlier work (Servan-Schreiber, Printz, & Cohen, 1990), empirical evidence about natural fluctuations in transmitter availability is considered by randomly sampling G from a given distribution at each processing step. Thus, the difference between "old" and "young" networks concerns the mean of the range from which G is sampled; for instance, the Gs of "young" networks are sampled from a range of 0.6 to 1.0, whereas the Gs of "old" networks are sampled from a range of 0.1 to 0.5 (see Figure 21.3, top panel). To reiterate, both the range and the distribution of the gain parameters and all other aspects of the network do not differ between "young" and "old" networks; the only difference by design concerns the mean level at which the gain parameter is varied.

The most basic consequence of the difference in stochastic gain between "young" and "old" networks is seen in the middle panel of Figure 21.3. This figure displays the output activation of two units with high versus low mean gain in response to the same signal. In the unit with the lower mean gain, output activation is less extreme and more variable. The units' increase in stochastic output variability fundamentally alters the network's state space. As illustrated in the bottom panel of Figure 21.3, networks with a greater proportion of stochastic output variation to a given signal are less capable of mapping different patterns of input signals onto discriminable activation patterns, or network states. The panel displays the internal activation patterns across five different units to four different stimuli in an episodic memory task. The activation patterns, or internal representations, of the four stimuli are much less discriminable in the "old" than in the "young" network.

Decrements in stochastic gain have been used to simulate aging phenomena at both neural and behavioral levels of analysis. Table 21.4 provides a listing of phenomena simulated thus far. As noted already, decrements in gain lead to increments in stochastic variability and to decrements in the distinctiveness of

activation patterns. In addition, decrements in gain also can account for less distinct cortical representations (Li, Lindenberger, et al., 2001; Li, Naveh-Benjamin, & Lindenberger, 2005) and neural-network dedifferentiation at the level of processing modules (Li & Sikström, 2002). Thus, at the neural simulation level, the gain manipulation successfully simulates the "contraction of functional cerebral space" envisioned by Kinsbourne and Hicks (1978) and observed by Park et al. (2004) in the domain of visual perception.

At the behavioral level, comparisons between groups of high-gain networks (young networks) and groups of low-gain networks (old networks) reveal striking similarities to comparisons between groups of young and old individuals (see Figure 21.4). First, *mean level* of performance is lower among old networks than among young networks. Second, *inter-individual differences* are larger among old networks than among young networks. Third, *intercorrelations between tasks* are higher among old networks than among young networks. Figure 21.4 illustrates all of these findings with respect to two different word lists learned by 20 "young", 20 "middle-aged," and 20 "old networks" (Li & Lindenberger, 1999; Li, Lindenberger, & Frensch, 2000).

TABLE 21.4. Relating neuromodulation to cognitive aging by reducing the mean of distribution of the gain parameter (G) of neural networks: List of simulated phenomena at neural and behavioral levels of analysis

Neural Aging

- *Increase in stochastic, stimulus-unrelated fluctuation of neuronal output activation* (reduced processing robustness)
- Less distinct internal representations (e.g., dedifferentiation of neural activation patterns)
- Less distinct processing pathways (e.g., dedifferentiation of functional connectivity)[a]

Behavioral Aging

- *Increase in performance fluctuation* (within-network variability)
- *Decrease in mean levels of performance* (e.g., list learning, category discrimination)
- *Increase in interindividual differences in performance*
- *Increase in covariation between tasks across individuals*
- Greater age deficits with more difficult tasks (e.g., ordinal interactions between task difficulty and age in 5-item vs. 8-item list learning)
- Greater proactive interference (e.g., greater age differences in A-B, A-C relative to A-B, C-D list learning)
- Lower maximum levels of performance (e.g., age differences in asymptotes of list learning performance)
- Conjunctive binding deficit in associative learning (e.g., simulating empirical results reported by Naveh-Benjamin (2000)[b]

Note: Reductions in the gain parameter G of neural networks flatten the sigmoidal shape of a unit's activation function, thereby leading to decrements in the total amount as well as increments in the stochastic, stimulus-unrelated component of output activation (see Figure 21.3, top panel). (Unless noted otherwise, the list refers to simulations reported in Li, 2002; Li and Lindenberger, (1999); Li, Lindenberger, & Frensch, (2000); and Li, Lindenberger, and Sikström, 2001. Phenomena printed in italics are discussed in more detail in the present chapter.)

[a]Based on Li & Sikström (2002).

[b]Based on Li & Lindenberger (in press).

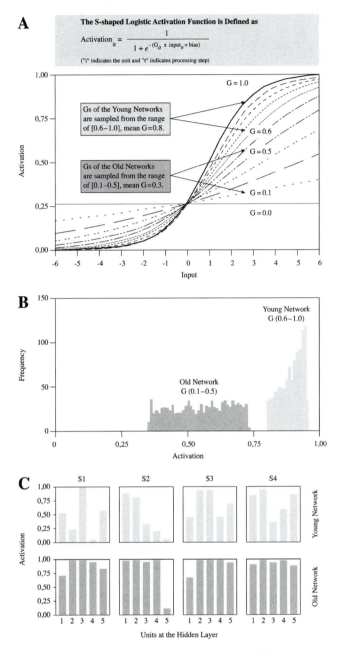

FIGURE 21.3. *(A)* The S-shaped logistic activation function at different values of the gain parameter (G). Physiological evidence suggests that a logistic function with a negative bias captures the function relating the strength of an input signal to a neuron's firing rate, with the slope being steepest around baseline. Reducing mean G flattens the activation function so that a unit becomes less responsive. *(B)* G and the variability of activation across processing steps. Reducing mean G increases the temporal variability of a unit's response to an identical input signal. *(C)* Activation patterns across five hidden units of one "young" and one "old" network in response to four different stimuli (S_1 to S_4). The internal representations of the four stimuli are much less differentiable in the "old" than in the "young" network. (Panels *(A)* to *(C)* are adapted from Li et al., 2000.)

To conclude, these simulations show that increments in stochastic (i.e., stimulus-unrelated) variability induced by lowering the gain parameter of connectionist networks may lead to decrements in means as well as increments in variance and correlations at the population level. Age differences in the structure of inter-individual differences were solely brought about by increased stochastic variability at the intra-individual (i.e., intra-network) level (for more details, e.g., Li & Lindenberger, 1999); no additional assumptions about differences in life histories or antecedent conditions were needed. Hence, the present model specifies reductions in the mean of stochastic gain as a mechanism that links univariate microgenetic variability to ontogenetic changes in functional organization, tracing a path from the upper left to the lower right cell of the taxonomy presented in Table 21.1.

OUTLOOK

Interest in variability as an agent of development during adulthood and old age has increased during the last decade. Researchers increasingly recognize the need to assess and articulate various forms and functions of variability, and to identify relevant mechanisms (Hultsch & MacDonald, 2004; Lövdén & Lindenberger, 2005; Rabbitt, Osman, Moore, & Stollery, 2001). General theories of cognitive aging that emphasize central tendency such as average response latency (e.g., Salthouse, 1996) have been augmented by formal theories that emphasize stochastic variability at various levels of analysis (e.g., Li & Lindenberger, 1999; Ratcliff et al., 2000). For instance, recent empirical findings (e.g., Li, Lindenberger, et al., 2004; Nesselroade & Salthouse, 2004) suggest that inter-individual differences in processing fluctuation may functions as traits that change with age and predict mean levels of performance.

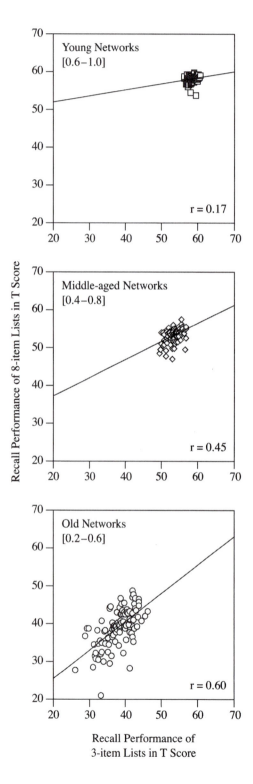

FIGURE 21.4. Scatterplots of between-network (i.e., inter-individual) correlations between memory performance for a 3-item list and memory performance for an 8-item list in groups of networks with high, medium, and low mean values of stochastic gain (G). (Modified after Li and Lindenberger, 1999.)

We agree with Nesselroade and Salthouse (2004) that classical test-theory interpretations of observed between-person variability need to be abandoned once and for all (cf. Hertzog, 1985). The contributions of intra-person fluctuations to observed between-person variability are simply too large and too systematic to be accommodated by a theory that makes no principled reference to variability at the within-person level. Researchers' increasing reliance on statistical procedures capable of representing inter-individual differences in intra-individual change (e.g., Baltes et al., 1977/1988) indicates a change for the better (e.g., Lindenberger & Ghisletta, 2004; Wilson et al., 2002).

There continues to be a dearth of data on age differences in various forms of microgenetic variability—trial-by-trial, session-to-session, and day-to-day (but see Li, Aggen, et al., 2001; MacDonald et al., 2003; Nesselroade & Salthouse, 2004; Rabbitt et al., 2001). Extensive multivariate time series of carefully selected collections of individuals, young and old, are needed to investigate the functional status and multiple meanings of variability (e.g., Jones & Nesselroade, 1990). Ideally, behavioral and neural variables should be assessed conjointly to examine links between variability at both levels of analysis. To provide more direct tests of the differentiation/dedifferentiation hypothesis, intra-person structures of intellectual abilities need to be assessed at different ages and stages of learning. The ensuing comparisons between intra-person and inter-person structures will help to quantify sample heterogeneity and departure from variation equivalence. The phenomenon of strategic diversity and other forms of adaptive microgenetic variability also awaits further study, including the difficult issue of how different strategies emerge in the first place (e.g., Lautrey, 2003; chapter 20, this volume). The selection, optimization, and compensation (SOC) model of successful development offers a productive theoretical context for examining this issue (e.g., Baltes & Baltes, 1990; Krampe & Baltes, 2003).

Finally, the role of noise in aging systems needs further exploration. Generally, noise is assumed to degrade information processing in physical and biological systems. However, under certain conditions, noise actually enhances rather than hinders the detection of weak signals. The simplest possible system showing this property consists of a threshold, a sub-threshold signal, and added noise. Whenever the noise plus the signal crosses the threshold in one direction, it triggers a response in the output. As a detector of weak signals, this system is optimally sensitive at some non-zero level of input noise. Recently, researchers have begun to examine this phenomenon, called *stochastic resonance* (Wiesenfeld & Moss, 1995), in aging individuals (e.g., Collins et al., 2003). Future work needs to examine the fate of stochastic resonance in networks with low stochastic gain in order to specify optimal levels of external noise for signal processing in old age (Li, Oertzen, & Lindenberger, in press).

ACKNOWLEDGMENTS   We thank Paul Baltes, Ellen Bialystok, and Gus Craik for comments on an earlier version of the present chapter, and Shu-Chen Li for many helpful and stimulating discussions.

References

Allaire, J. C., & Marsiske, M. (2002, April). *Intra-individual variability in cognitive functioning: Is inconsistency an index of vulnerability?* Paper presented at the Cognitive Aging Conference, Atlanta, Georgia.

Bäckman, L., & Farde, L. (2004). The role of dopamine systems in cognitive aging. In R. Cabeza, L. Nyberg, & D. C. Park (Eds.), *Cognitive neuroscience of aging: Linking cognitive and cerebral aging* (pp. 58–84). New York: Oxford University Press.

Baltes, P. B. (1968). Longtitudinal and cross-sectional sequences in the study of age and generation effects. *Human Development, 11*, 145–171.

Baltes, P. B. (1987). Theoretical propositions of life-span developmental psychology: On the dynamics between growth and decline. *Developmental Psychology, 23*, 611–626.

Baltes, P. B., & Baltes, M. M. (1990). Psychological perspectives on successful aging: The model of selective optimization with compensation. In P. B. Baltes & M. M. Baltes (Eds.), *Successful aging: Perspectives from the behavioral sciences* (pp. 1–34). New York: Cambridge University Press.

Baltes, P. B., Cornelius, S. W., Spiro, A., Nesselroade, J. R., & Willis, S. L. (1980). Integration vs. differentiation of fluid-crystallized intelligence in old age. *Developmental Psychology, 16*, 625–635.

Baltes, P. B., & Lindenberger, U. (1997). Emergence of a powerful connection between sensory and cognitive functions across the adult life span: A new window at the study of cognitive aging? *Psychology and Aging, 12*, 12–21.

Baltes, P. B., Lindenberger, U., & Staudinger, U. M. (1998). Life-span theory in developmental psychology. In R. M. Lerner (Ed.), *Handbook of child psychology: Vol. 1. Theoretical models of human development* (5th ed., pp. 1029–1143). New York: Wiley.

Baltes, P. B., Reese, H. W., & Nesselroade, J. R. (1977/ 1988). *Life-span developmental psychology: Introduction to research methods*. Hillsdale, NJ: Lawrence Erlbaum Associates. Buss, A. R. (1974). A general developmental model for interindividual differences, intraindividual differences, and intraindividual changes. *Developmental Psychology, 10*, 70–78.

Cabeza, R. (2002). Hemispheric asymmetry reduction in older adults: The HAROLD model. *Psychology and Aging, 17*, 85–100.

Cattell, R. B. (1966). The data box: Its ordering of total resources in terms of possible relational systems. In R. B. Cattell (Ed.), *Handbook of multivariate experimental psychology* (pp. 67–128). Chicago: Rand McNally.

Cattell, R. B. (1971). *Abilities: Their structure, growth, and action*. Boston, MA: Houghton Mifflin.

Collins, J. J., Priplata, A. A., Gravelle, D. C., Niemi, J., Harry, J., & Lipsitz, L. A. (2003). Noise-enhanced human sensorimotor function. *IEEE Engineering in Medicine and Biology Magazine, March/April*, 76–83.

Craik, F. I. M. (1983). On the transfer of information from temporary to permanent memory. *Philosophical Transactions of the Royal Society of London*, B302, 341–359.

Deary, I. J., Egan, V., Gibson, G. J., Austin, E. J., Brand, C. R., & Kellaghan, T. (1996). Intelligence and the differentiation hypothesis. *Intelligence, 23*, 105–132.

Estes, W. K. (1956). The problem of inference from curves based on group data. *Psychological Bulletin, 53*, 134–140.

Garrett, H. E. (1946). A developmental theory of intelligence. *American Psychologist, 1*, 372–378.

Hertzog, C. (1985). An individual differences perspective: Implications for cognitive research in gerontology. *Research on Aging, 7*, 7–45.

Hofer, S. M., & Sliwinski, M. J. (2001). Understanding aging: An evaluation of research designs for assessing the interdependence of ageing-related changes. *Gerontology, 47*, 341–352.

Horn, J. L. (1989). Models of intelligence. In R. L. Linn (Ed.), *Intelligence: Measurement, theory, and public policy* (pp. 29–73). Urbana, IL: University of Illinois Press.

Hultsch, D. F., Hertzog, C., Dixon, R. A., & Small, B. J. (1998). *Memory change in the aged*. Cambridge, UK: Cambridge University Press.

Hultsch, D. F., & MacDonald, S. W. S. (2004). Intraindividual variability in performance as a theoretical window onto cognitive aging. In R. A. Dixon,

L. Bäckman & L.-G. Nilsson (Eds.), *New frontiers in cognitive aging* (pp. 65–88). New York: Oxford University Press.

Jones, C. J., & Nesselroade, J. R. (1990). Multivariate, replicated, single-subject, repeated measures designs and P-technique factor analysis: A review of intraindividual change studies. *Experimental Aging Research, 16*, 171–183.

Kinsbourne, M., & Hicks, R. E. (1978). Functional cerebral space: A model for overflow, transfer and interference effects in human performance: A tutorial review. In J. Requin (Ed.), *Attention and performance VII*, (pp. 345–362). Hillsdale, NJ: Lawrence Erlbaum Associates.

Krampe, R. T., & Baltes, P. B. (2003). Intelligence as adaptive resource development and resource allocation: A new look through the lenses of SOC and expertise. In R. J. Sternberg & E. L. Grigorenko (Eds.), *Perspectives on the psychology of abilities, competencies, and expertise* (pp. 31–69). New York: Cambridge University Press.

Lautrey, J. (2003). A pluralistic approach to cognitive differentiation and development. In R. J. Sternberg, J. Lautrey & T. Lubart (Eds.), *Models of intelligence: International perspectives* (pp. 117–131). Washington, DC: American Psychological Association.

Li, K. Z. H., & Lindenberger, U. (2002). Relations between aging sensory/sensorimotor and cognitive functions. *Neuroscience and Biobehavioral Reviews, 26*, 777–783.

Li, S.-C. (2002). Connecting the many levels and facets of cognitive aging. *Current Directions in Psychological Science, 11*, 38–43.

Li, S.-C., Aggen, S., Nesselroade, J. R., & Baltes, P. B. (2001). Short-term fluctuations in elderly people's sensorimotor functioning predict text and spatial memory performance. *Gerontology, 47*, 100–116.

Li, S.-C., Huxhold, O., & Schmiedek, F. (2004). Aging and attenuated processing robustness. *Gerontology, 50*, 28–34.

Li, S.-C., Lindenberger, L., & Sikström, S. (2001). Aging cognition: From neuromodulation to representation. *Trends in Cognitive Science, 5*, 479–486.

Li, S.-C., & Lindenberger, U. (1999). Cross-level unification: A computational exploration of the link between deterioration of neurotransmitter systems and dedifferentiation of cognitive abilities in old age. In L.-G. Nilsson & H. Markowitsch (Eds.), *Cognitive neuroscience of memory* (pp. 104–146). Toronto: Hogrefe & Huber.

Li, S.-C., & Lindenberger, U. (in press). Aging deficits in neuromodulation of representational distinctiveness and conjunctive binding: Computational explorations of possible links. In H. D. Zimmer, A.

Mecklinger & U. Lindenberger (Eds.), *Binding in human memory: A neurocognitive approach*. New York: Oxford University Press.

Li, S.-C., Lindenberger, U., & Frensch, P. A. (2000). Unifying cognitive aging: From neuromodulation to representation to cognition. *Neurocomputing, 32–33*, 879–890.

Li, S.-C., Lindenberger, U., Hommel, B., Aschersleben, G., Prinz, W., & Baltes, P. B. (2004). Lifespan transformations in the couplings among intellectual abilities and constituent cognitive processes. *Psychological Science, 15*, 155–163.

Li, S.-C., Naveh-Benjamin, M., & Lindenberger, U. (2005). Aging neuromodulation impairs associative binding: A neurocomputational account. *Psychological Science, 16*, 445–450.

Li, S.-C., Oertzen, T. V., & Lindenberger , U. (in press). A neurocomputational model of stochastic resonance and aging. *Neurocomputing*.

Li, S.-C., & Sikström, S. (2002). Integrative neurocomputational perspectives on cognitive aging, neuromodulation, and representation. *Neuroscience and Biobehavioral Reviews, 26*, 795–808.

Lindenberger, U. (2001). Lifespan theories of cognitive development. In N. J. Smelser & P. B. Baltes (Eds.), *International encyclopedia of the social & behavioral sciences* (Vol. 13, pp. 8848–8854). Amsterdam: Elsevier Science.

Lindenberger, U., & Baltes, P. B. (1994). Aging and intelligence. In R. J. Sternberg (Ed.), *Encyclopedia of human intelligence* (Vol. 1, pp. 52–66). New York: Macmillan.

Lindenberger, U., & Baltes, P. B. (1995). Testing-the-limits and experimental simulation: Two methods to explicate the role of learning in development. *Human Development, 38*, 349–360.

Lindenberger, U., & Baltes, P. B. (1997). Intellectual functioning in old and very old age: Cross-sectional results from the Berlin Aging Study. *Psychology and Aging, 12*, 410–432.

Lindenberger, U., & Baltes, P. B. (1999). Die Entwicklungspsychologie der Lebensspanne (Lifespan-Psychologie): Johann Nicolaus Tetens zu Ehren (1736–1807). *Zeitschrift für Psychologie, 207*, 299–323.

Lindenberger , U., & Ghisletta, P. (2004). Modeling longitudinal changes in old age: From covariance structures to dynamic systems. In R. A. Dixon, L. Bäckman & L.-G. Nilsson (Eds.), *New frontiers in cognitive aging* (pp. 199–216). New York: Oxford University Press.

Lindenberger, U., Singer, T., & Baltes, P. B. (2002). Longitudinal selectivity in aging populations: Separating mortality-associated versus experimental

components in the Berlin Aging Study (BASE). *Journal of Gerontology: Psychological Sciences, 57B(6)*, 474–482.

Lövdén, M., Ghisletta, P., & Lindenberger, U. (2004) Cognition in the Berlin Aging Study (BASE): The first ten years. *Aging, Neuropsychology, and Cognition, 11*, 104–133..

Lövdén, M., & Lindenberger, U. (2005). Development of intellectual abilities in old age: From age gradients to individuals. In O. Wilhelm & R. W. Engle (Eds.), *Understanding and measuring intelligence* (pp. 203–221). Thousand Oaks, CA: Sage.

MacDonald, S. W. S., Hultsch, D. F., & Dixon, R. A. (2003). Performance variability is related to change in cognition: Evidence from the Victoria Longitudinal Study. *Psychology and Aging, 18*, 510–523.

Magnusson, D., & Stattin, H. (1998). Person-context interaction theories. In R. M. Lerner (Ed.), *Theoretical models of human development. Volume 1: Handbook of child psychology* (5th ed.) (pp. 685–759). New York: Wiley.

Miller, E. K., & Cohen, J. D. (2001). An integrative theory of prefontal cortex function. *Annual Review of Neuroscience, 24*, 167–202.

Molenaar, P. C. M., Huizenga, H. M., & Nesselroade, J. R. (2003). The relationship between the structure of inter-individual and intra-individual variability: A theoretical and empirical vindication of developmental systems theory. In U. M. Staudinger & U. Lindenberger (Eds.), *Understanding human development: Lifespan psychology in exchange with other disciplines* (pp. 339–360). Dordrecht, Netherlands: Kluwer Academic Publishers.

Nesselroade, J. R. (1991). The warp and the woof of the developmental fabric. In R. M. Downs, L. S. Liben & D. S. Palermo (Eds.), *Visions of aesthetics, the environment and development: The legacy of Joachim Wohlwill* (pp. 213–240). Hillsdale, NJ: Lawrence Erlbaum Associates.

Nesselroade, J. R., & Salthouse, T. A. (2004). Methodological and theoretical implications of intraindividual variability in perceptual motor performance. *Journal of Gerontology: Psychological Sciences, 59B*, P49–P55.

Nesselroade, J. R., & Thompson, W. W. (1995). Selection and related threats to group comparisions: An example comparing factorial structures of higher and lower ability groups of adult twins. *Psychological Bulletin, 117*, 271–284.

Park, D. C., Lautenschlager, G., Hedden, T., Davidson, N. S., Smith, A. D., & Smith, P. K. (2002). Models of visuospatial and verbal memory across the adult lifespan. *Psychology and Aging, 17*, 299–320.

Park, D. C., Polk, T. A., Park, R., Minear, M., Savage,

A., & Smith, M. R. (2004). *Aging reduces neural specialization in ventral visual cortex. PNAS, 101,* 13091–13095.

Rabbitt, P., Osman, P., Moore, B., & Stollery, B. (2001). There are stable individual differences in performance variability, both from moment to moment and from day to day. *The Quarterly Journal of Experimental Psychology, 54A,* 981–1003.

Ratcliff, R., Spieler, D. H., & McKoon, G. (2000). Explicitly modeling the effects of aging on response time. *Psychonomic Bulletin and Review, 7,* 1–25.

Raz, N. (2000). Aging of the brain and its impact on cognitive performance: Integration of structural and functional findings. In F. I. M. Craik & T. A. Salthouse (Eds.), *The handbook of aging and cognition* (2 ed., pp. 1–90). Mahwah, NJ: Lawrence Erlbaum Associates.

Reinert, G. (1970). Comparative factor analytic studies of intelligence throughout the human life span. In L. R. Goulet & P. B. Baltes (Eds.), *Life-span developmental psychology: Research and theory* (pp. 476–484). New York: Academic Press.

Reuchlin, M. (1978). Processus vicariants et différences individuelles. *Journal de Psychologie, 2,* 133–145.

Salthouse, T. A. (1991). *Theoretical perspectives on cognitive aging.* Hillsdale, NJ: Lawrence Erlbaum Associates.

Salthouse, T. A. (1996). The processing-speed theory of adult age differences in cognition. *Psychological Review, 103,* 403–428.

Schaie, K. W., Maitland, S. B., Willis, S. L., & Intieri, R. C. (1998). Longitudinal invariance of adult psychometric ability factor structures across 7 years. *Psychology and Aging, 13,* 8–20.

Schreurs, B. G., Bahro, M., Molchan, S. E., Sunderland, T., & McIntosh, A. R. (2001). Interactions of prefrontal cortex during eyeblink conditioning as a function of age. *Neurobiology of Aging, 22,* 237–246.

Servan-Schreiber, D., Printz, H., & Cohen, J. D. (1990). A network model of catecholamine effects: Gain, signal-to-noise ratio, and behavior. *Science, 249,* 892–894.

Siegler, R. S. (1989). Mechanisms of cognitive development. *Annual Review of Psychology, 40,* 353–379.

Singer, T., Lindenberger, U., & Baltes, P. B. (2003). Plasticity of memory for new learning in very old age: A story of major loss? *Psychology and Aging, 18,* 306–317.

Singer, T., Verhaeghen, P., Ghisletta, P., Lindenberger, U., & Baltes, P. B. (2003). The fate of cognition in very old age: Six-year longitudinal findings in the Berlin Aging Study. *Psychology and Aging, 18,* 318–331.

Smith, L. B., & Thelen, E. (2003). Development as a dynamic system. *Trends in Cognitive Science, 7,* 343–348.

Tetens, J. N. (1777). *Philosophische Versuche über die menschliche Natur und ihre Entwicklung.* Leipzig, Germany: Weidmanns Erben und Reich.

Thaler, D. S. (2002). Design of an aging brain. *Neurobiology of Aging, 23,* 13–15.

Welford, A. T. (1965). Perfomance, biological mechanisms, and age: A theoretical sketch. In A. T. Welford & J. E. Birren (Eds.), *Behavior, aging, and the nervous system* (pp. 3–20). Springfield, IL: Thomas.

Wiesenfeld, K., & Moss, F. (1995). Stochastic resonance and the benefits of noise: From ice ages to crayfish and SQUIDs. *Nature, 373,* 33–36.

Wilson, R. S., Beckett, L. A., Barnes, L. L., Schneider, J. A., Bach, J., Evans, D. A., & Bennett, D. A. (2002). Individual differences in rates of change in cognitive abilities in older persons. *Psychology & Aging, 17,* 179–193.

Wohlwill, J. F. (1973). *The study of behavioral development.* New York: Academic Press.

22

Intelligence and Cognitive Abilities as Competencies in Development

Damian P. Birney

Robert J. Sternberg

Cronbach's (1957) presidential address to the American Psychological Association presented the strongest argument of the time for what he perceived to be a rupture in psychology. He warned against considering individual-differences (differential) psychology and experimental psychology as two distinct scientific disciplines, and announced that "Psychology continues to this day to be limited by the dedication of its investigators to one or the other method of inquiry rather than to scientific psychology as a whole." (p. 671). Almost 50 years on, the resistance to combining differential and experimental paradigms within the field of intelligence is still apparent (Deary, 2001; Lohman & Ippel, 1993). Cronbach classified psychological theories as a function of the methods used to develop and test them: the differential paradigm is dominated by correlational methods; the experimental paradigm is dominated by "comparison-of-means" methods. If one considers the metaphors that theorists use to think about how the mind works, a finer taxonomy emerges. Our aim in this chapter is to consider four theoretical approaches and the associated methodologies that are used to understand intelligence and intellectual development. We then reflect on a relatively new theory that, following from the triarchic theory of intelligence (Sternberg, 1984, 1985, 1997), conceptualizes abilities as *competencies in development* (Sternberg, 1998, 1999). This multifaceted account of intelligence has been proposed to integrate what are often considered to be disparate paradigms.

THEORIES OF THE DEVELOPING MIND

Sternberg (1990) suggested that theorizing about intellectual functioning could be classified by the metaphors that theorists use to frame their research. A geographic metaphor as a map of the mind underlies *psychometric* theories, whereas a metaphor of intelligence as a computational device underlies *information-processing* theories. An *epistemological* metaphor of intelligence as an ongoing process of cognitive development and knowledge acquisition characterizes Piagetian and neo-Piagetian theories. *Contextualist* theories are characterized by metaphors that focus on the external world of the individual (e.g., sociological and anthropological metaphors). There are a number of other metaphors that have been proposed (e.g., biological and systems approaches), but we limit the current discussion to these four because they continue to take on the lion's share of intelligence research. Psychometric theories have drawn on the correlational methods of the differential paradigm; epistemological and information-processing theories have used mostly experimental methods; and contextualist theories have arguably drawn on both methodological paradigms. In the following sections we consider how each conceives of intelligence and identify key findings, assumptions, and limitations.

Intellectual Development from the Perspective of the Psychometric Tradition

The conventional notion of intelligence is built around a loosely consensual definition of intelligence in terms of generalized adaptation to the environment (see, e.g., Intelligence and its measurement: A symposium, 1921; Sternberg & Detterman, 1986). Many of the psychometric theories most widely accepted today hierarchically nest a variety of mental abilities under a general (g) factor at successively greater levels of specificity (e.g., Carroll, 1993; Gustafsson, 1994; Horn, 1994; Jensen, 1998). For example, Carroll has suggested that three levels (narrow, broad, and general) can nicely capture the hierarchy of abilities, whereas Cattell (1971) suggested two levels were especially important. In the case of Cattell, nested under general ability are fluid abilities (Gf) and crystallized abilities (Gc). Fluid abilities are of the kind considered to represent measurable outcomes of the influence of biological factors on intellectual development, and are enlisted to solve abstract-reasoning problems such as figural matrices or series completions. Crystallized abilities are of the kind considered to be the main manifestation of education, experience, and acculturation. These theories and others like them, described in more detail elsewhere (e.g., Brody, 2000; Carroll, 1993; Embretson & McCollam, 2000; Herrnstein & Murray, 1994; Jensen, 1998), use evidence from correlational research to support their view.

The constructs under psychometric investigation typically are based on two important premises that have significant implications for the conceptualization of development. Neither premise actually holds in its entirety. First, mental abilities are conceptualized to be fixed relatively early in development—we refer to this fixedness as the *stability assumption*. Second, mental abilities are assumed to necessarily precede achievement—we refer to this precedence as the *priority assumption*. However, there is no a priori psychological reason why either of these assumptions must hold. In fact, there is substantial evidence that the relationship between cognitive abilities and achievement is much more interactive (Cahan & Cohen, 1989; Flynn, 1987). Indeed, mental abilities to some extent reflect achievements.

The Stability Assumption: Intelligence as a Stable Construct

The finding that intelligence becomes fixed relatively early in life, after which it remains stable, is seen by some as an epiphenomenon (Cattell, 1987; McArdle, Ferrer-Caja, Hamagami, & Woodcock, 2002). Cattell (1987), for instance, argued that the apparent stability of intelligence is the necessary outcome of aggregating across multiple abilities that have different developmental trajectories. That is, Cattell argued that while both Gf and Gc were conceptualized as rising through youth until early adulthood, Gf reaches its peak relatively early (15–20 years), and later declines at a relatively rapid rate. On the other hand, Gc functions tend to continue increasing well into the 60s and 70s. This research has been extended more recently by McArdle and colleagues (2002) to consider the developmental trajectories of the cognitive abilities and academic knowledge assessed by the Woodcock-Johnson tests (WJ-R; Woodcock & Johnson, 1989). In addition to Gf and Gc, long-term retrieval, short-term memory, processing speed, auditory and visual processing, and a composite of all these, broad cognitive ability (BCA), were assessed. The forms of academic knowledge assessed were broad quantitative ability, broad academic knowledge, and broad reading and writing skills.

Using sophisticated statistical modeling techniques, McArdle and colleagues (2002) assessed change in cognitive abilities of about 1,200 people ranging in age from about 2 to 95 years, measured on two occasions. Consistent with Cattell (1987) and

Horn (1988), the growth function of all abilities tended to follow the curve represented in Figure 22.1. Similar growth patterns were observed for all abilities during the first few years of life. The trajectories of the abilities then started to diverge, particularly at the point of asymptote and in their rate of decline. With BCA as the comparison, differences in growth trajectories were observed for all cognitive abilities and the various forms of academic knowledge. McArdle and colleagues interpreted these significant deviations from the BCA trajectory to suggest that a description of the cognitive system with only a single *g* factor is overly simplistic. According to Rabbitt and Anderson (Chapter 23, this volume), the rate of decline and the variation in performance during old age (in at least some abilities) is likely to be underestimated owing to a number of factors, including self-selection on entry, differences in the effects due to practice, and selective dropout of the most frail and least able.

Psychometric test scores after about 5 years of age tend to be reasonably predictive of later abilities and achievement (Bjorklund, 1995). At younger ages, the stability and predictive utility of ability estimates is substantially weaker, particularly for individuals in the average or superior levels (Chen & Siegler, 2000; Sattler, 1992). For infants, sensory-oriented measures such as rapidity of habituation-dishabituation and encoding are better predictors of future abilities than are reasoning measures, although the correlations are typically modest (McCall & Carriger, 1993; Rose & Feldman, 1997). One explanation for the lack of predictive power of early performance on psychometric tests is that cognitive abilities become increasingly differentiated with age (Carroll, 1993; Halford, 1993).

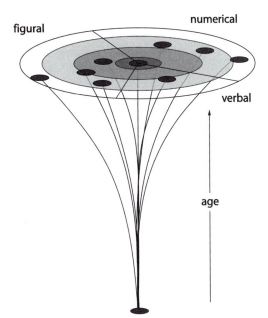

FIGURE 22.2. Differentiation of cognitive abilities over time from the psychometric perspective. (Adaptated from Carroll, 1993, and Marshalek et al., 1983.)

Differentiation, therefore, is arguably the key factor or process in cognitive development as it is conceived in psychometric theories. Figure 22.2 presents a schematic representation of what the differentiation process might look like. It incorporates aspects of differentiation as proposed by Carroll (1993, Figure 5.1, p. 147) and aspects of Guttman's (1954) RADical EXpansion of complexity (RADEX) model as described by Marshalek, Lohman, and Snow (1983).

The series of concentric circles at the top of Figure 22.2 represents a canvas on which distinct abilities (dark discs) are mapped. The closer the discs are to each other, the higher the correlation between abilities (Marshalek et al., 1983). The series of concentric circles is a significant part of the RADEX model and represents the proposition that complexity defines the intellectual landscape. At the center are abilities tapped by complex reasoning tasks (e.g., progressive matrices). As we move away from the center toward the outer circles, tasks tend to be represented that are less complex and more content specific. Differentiation as it occurs over age is represented in Figure 22.2 by the branching of abilities over time. The extent that this branching is a function of biological

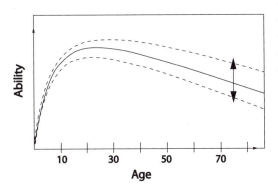

FIGURE 22.1. Typical shape of the ability-age relationship observed in psychometric studies.

maturation, education, or both, is difficult to disassociate using correlational methods (Carroll, 1993). It is interesting to note that this differentiation may not necessarily continue indefinitely. Rabbitt and Anderson (Chapter 23, this volume) argue that the differentiation processes eventually begin to change direction, leading to a dedifferentiation of abilities in old age.

The Priority Assumption: Abilities Precede Achievement

The second common assumption of psychometric theories—that abilities precede achievement—propagates an almost arbitrary dichotomy between performances on what are essentially similar tasks. Both intelligence tests and achievement tests sample aptitude, learning, and achievement to some degree. Achievement tests tend to be more content specific, assessing a narrow range of skills acquired through formal learning at school or home. Ability tests have a broader scope and tend to be targeted at the measurement of the outcomes of less formal experiences, although some ability tests are clearly more focused on achievement than others (e.g., crystallized ability tests as described earlier).

While these are valid differences, they do not provide much insight into why ability is assumed to precede achievement. Yet, this is an assumption that has important developmental implications, not simply because it suggests that one cannot learn (or achieve) without first possessing some underlying ability but also that one's achievements do not feed back to modify one's abilities. Recent research in mathematical abilities, for instance, has shown that, on the contrary, skill acquisition can entail nonlinear and recursive development of different abilities and skills over time (Rittle-Johnson, Siegler, & Alibali, 2001). There are also methodological reasons for why it is convenient to make a distinction between ability and achievement. Achievement is assumed to be the direct product of learning—there is no controversy here. However, cognitive abilities are assumed by psychometric theories to be largely immune to learning—that is, they exhibit the stability assumption we just described. The capacity to learn is assumed to be just another stable ability that is distinct from other abilities. With this assumption, it would seem appropriate to assess capacity to learn using *static* tests. For instance, crystallized ability is the capacity to profit from *past* experience and is often measured by vocabulary tests (e.g., providing synonyms; Carroll, 1993). Furthermore, it follows from the stability assumption that abilities also remain constant *during* assessment. In fact, to the extent that individual differences in *within-task* learning exist and operate in ways that change the nature of the primary ability being assessed, a nonrandom source of variance will be added to the measurement. If one considers the test-development process, these types of measurement "error" are reflected in lower reliability estimates because, rather than measuring one construct, such a test will measure at least two reliable but imperfectly correlated effects: (1) individual differences in the primary ability of interest, and (2) individual differences in *within-task* learning that feeds back to modify the primary ability. If the effect of the latter is strong, then the test will appear unreliable—our confidence in the test will be shaken and we will look for more stable items. With repeated iterations, the end result is a test that captures a narrowly defined and *static* component of intelligence. One of the greatest disappointments of psychology, we believe, is that this approach has led to the popular view that what these tests measure is all there is to intelligence. The charade is perpetuated because new tasks are validated against tests that have also been specifically engineered to be immune to learning. While Edwin Boring's (1923) definition of intelligence as "what the tests test" has been widely ridiculed by psychologists, in reality we may not have moved so far away from it. Sternberg has argued repeatedly that a much broader conceptualization of intelligence is needed (e.g., Sternberg, 1985, 1997).

In general, it should be clear that psychometric theories and the methods used to test them provide few clues to understanding either the processes of learning, or what a process underlying an identified ability might look like (Deary, 2001; Lohman & Ippel, 1993). There is a caveat to this statement related to speed of processing (SOP). SOP has been suggested to describe a more process-oriented account of individual differences in abilities from within the psychometric tradition (e.g., Jensen, 1987; Roberts & Stankov, 1999). The general concept is also linked to development across the lifespan (Chapter 23, this volume; Salthouse, 1996). Yet, there is still some controversy over what the nature of SOP is and how it relates to (1) other abilities where speed is not involved (or at least, not directly assessed), and (2) speed of response. For instance, speed at the biological level (e.g., activation speed / rate of neural transmission) seems less (or inconsistently) important to ecological performance (Sternberg, 2003). As the nature of the task becomes more complex, speed of *response* (cf. speed of processing) seems to have a greater impact on performance (or accuracy). The relationship between speed of response and accuracy of response is also nontrivial and to some extent under the strategic control of the individual. The investigation of the speed-accuracy trade-off is associated with various methodological problems (Dennis & Evans, 1996), and has been shown to differ as a function of task characteristics, ability, and personality factors (Birney, 2002). In any case, information-processing theories, to which we now turn, tend to have addressed the issue of component processes much more directly than psychometric theories.

INTELLECTUAL DEVELOPMENT FROM THE PERSPECTIVE OF THE INFORMATION-PROCESSING TRADITION

Compared to psychometric theories, *information-processing theories* have tended to focus on more theoretically based information-processing tasks, on specific task characteristics or components, and on person characteristics with respect to learning that lead to performance differences (e.g., novices versus expertise; Chi, Glaser, & Rees, 1982). These theories are characterized by computational models of constructs, such as cognitive components (Sternberg, 1977), relational processes (Halford, Wilson, & Phillips, 1998), psycho-logic/deduction rules (Braine, 1990; Rips, 1983, 1994), and mental-models (Halford, 1993; Johnson-Laird & Byrne, 1991; Johnson-Laird, Byrne, & Schaeken, 1992). More recent information-processing research is beginning to incorporate a role for individual differences (e.g., Schroyens, Schaeken, & d'Ydewalle, 1999; Schunn & Reder, 2001), in part to deal with the criticism that the theories are too reductionistic (e.g., Roberts, 1993).

A variety of theories can be aligned with the information-processing perspective. Common to each is an attempt to model the effect of task characteristics on problem solving while taking into consideration psychological limitations, such as working-memory capacity using rule-based (e.g., Braine, 1990; Rips, 1989) or mental-model based approaches (Johnson-Laird,

2001; e.g., Johnson-Laird et al., 1992). Although there are important distinctions between theories (Braine, 1993; Johnson-Laird, Byrne, & Schaeken, 1994), information-processing models are probably best epitomized by the early work of Newell and Simon (1972) in their conceptualization of a rule-based *production system*. Braine (1993) argued that mental models are actually premised on a rule-based account of reasoning. Anderson's Adaptive Control of Thought (ACT) framework is arguably the most well known production–system-based theory currently available (Anderson, 1983, 1990; Anderson & Lebiere, 1998). It is *adaptive* in that it attempts to model both learning and problem-solving processes in the same network. In the ACT framework, learning entails the assimilation of new information into the network as a series of declarative facts or productions (Anderson, 1982; Anderson & Milson, 1989; Anderson & Neves, 1981; Anderson & Schunn, 2000). With each successful application of this information, links between appropriate nodes are strengthened and procedures (i.e., collection of productions) become automatized to further facilitate subsequent knowledge acquisition and problem solving. Individual differences in intelligent behavior from this perspective are considered to be the result of variations in system efficiency and flexibility in selecting and applying appropriate knowledge to problem solving (Just & Carpenter, 1992).

Not all information-processing models are based on production systems (e.g., see Humphreys, Wiles, & Dennis, 1994; McClelland, Rumelhart, & Hinton, 1986; Rumelhart, 1990; Simon & Halford, 1995, for descriptions of connectionist models) and not all have a sophisticated computational architecture of knowledge acquisition as their basis (e.g., Sternberg's componential analyses; Sternberg, 1977). Relational complexity theory (Halford, 1993; Halford et al., 1998), for instance, models both processing capacity limitations and cognitive development. In this theory, cognitive components, or processes, are conceptualized as n-dimensional relations between the n pieces of information that need to be represented simultaneously to problem-solve—for example, making a comparison of size requires a binary dimensional relation that has two arguments, such as: LARGER-THAN (elephant, mouse), "elephant is larger than mouse." Ternary relations have three arguments and are of the type required—for instance, to make transitive inferences, such as: "A is taller than B, B is taller than C, Who is tallest?" The more arguments that are required to instantiate a relation, the greater the cognitive complexity of the task and the greater the demand placed on working memory (Andrews & Halford, 2002; Birney & Halford, 2002). Halford and colleagues (1998) argued that most adults are capable of instantiating four arguments simultaneously, although many everyday tasks can be segmented and chunked into less demanding, lower order relations.

From an information-processing perspective, intellectual development occurs as the network of informational nodes becomes differentiated and more efficient over time. Some researchers place biological maturation at the center of this process. For example, Halford and his associates propose that cognitive resources become differentiated with age and that this leads to an increased capacity to deal with more complex relations. Evidence cited for this view is that similar ages of attainment exist on tasks of similar relational complexity (Andrews & Halford, 2002; Halford, 1993; Halford, Andrews, Dalton, Boag, & Zielinski, 2002). If we consider adaptive production systems such as ACT, an equally plausible explanation may be that intellectual development is a function of an increasing knowledge base and the subsequent availability of increasingly efficient automatized procedures and schemas (e.g., Just & Carpenter, 1992). Although Andrews and Halford (2002, p. 158) argue that "the growth of processing capacity is an enabling factor that interacts with learning, induction, and other knowledge acquisition processes in cognitive development," discriminating between capacity effects and knowledge is more difficult in practice (Gentner & Rattermann, 1998). Epistemological theories attempt to describe the developmental relationship between knowledge and cognitive capacity explicitly. In the next section we reflect on these theories in more detail.

Intellectual Development from the Perspective of the Epistemological Tradition

Piaget's Theory

Epistemological theories are characterized by accounts of cognitive development that emphasize the acquisition of special types of knowledge and processes. Piaget (1896–1980) was arguably the most influential researcher within the epistemological approach (Bidell & Fischer, 1992). He conceived of intelligence

as a form of biological adaptation to the environment. Development of knowledge and abilities were, according to the Piagetian account, the result of the individual's constantly interacting with the environment in an attempt to maintain a balance between his or her current needs and understandings and the demands of the environment. The interactions of the individual with the environment were thought to be governed by the process of *organization*—a tendency toward generalization—and by the two subprocesses of *adaptation*: assimilation and accommodation. *Assimilation* is the process of fitting information from new experiences into existing concepts. *Accommodation* is the process of changing existing knowledge structures to take account of new information. Cognitive structures and hence abilities are seen as a result of the child's (and later adult's) attempts to organize experience in a coherent way (for detailed discussion, see Lutz & Sternberg, 1999).

In terms of intellectual development, the Piagetian theory proposes four periods through which the child progresses. These are the (1) sensorimotor period, (2) preoperational period, (3) concrete-operations period, and (4) formal-operations period. The stages reflect the gradual reorganization of basic cognitive processes and operations that facilitate (or at least coincide with) important developmental milestones. Although substantial biological maturation occurs at each of these stages, maturation is seen primarily as a necessary but not sufficient condition for the development of many cognitive skills. Learning experiences derived from optimal interactions with the environment help to determine the full extent of the development of cognitive abilities (Bidell & Fischer, 1992; Halford, 1999; Piaget, 1950). In fact, learning experiences, particularly those in which the complexity of the environment is mediated by a "teacher," are considered by many to be not only advantageous, but crucial to cognitive development (e.g., Feuerstein, 1979; Lidz, 2000; Vygotsky, 1962).

Neo-Piagetian Perspective

Limitations of Piaget's theory (as described, for example, in Lutz & Sternberg, 1999) led to subsequent extensions and advances on many of the theory's original conceptualizations (e.g., Carey, 1985; Case, 1985, 1992; Halford, 1993; Pascual-Leone, 1970). In general, neo-Piagetian researchers acknowledge the existence of stagelike maturation but focus more within a framework of working-memory development (Case, 1992). For instance, as mentioned previously, Halford and his associates (Andrews & Halford, 2002; Halford, 1993; Halford et al., 1998) view cognitive development as the result of a differentiation of working memory that facilitates the capacity to deal with tasks of increasing complexity. While Halford et al. (1998) argue that relational-complexity theory is not a stage theory in the way other neo-Piagetian theories might be considered (Case, 1985; Pascual-Leone, 1970), attainment of levels of relational processing has been aligned with ages of attainment that are similar to Piagetian stages (Halford, 1993).

It is instructive to consider with an example how epistemological theories conceive of the interplay between knowledge and cognitive capacity. An algorithmic approach to determining whether a beam with various weights at certain distances on each side of a fulcrum will balance is to calculate the product of weight and distance on one side of the beam and to compare this with the product of weight and distance on the other side (Halford et al., 2002; Siegler & Chen, 2002). Such a strategy is demanding of working-memory resources. Young children typically resort to considering fewer dimensions (e.g., only distance). Halford et al. (2002) argue that more complex relationships between weight, distance, and balance can be represented as age increases consistent with the predictions of relational complexity theory (Halford, 1993). However, adults have also been observed to have difficulty with the balance-beam task (even though capacity is presumably less of an issue) and this difficulty tends to indicate that knowledge and experience are also important factors.

Epistemological theories have provided many insights into the sequential development of children's long-term understanding of basic logical reasoning (e.g., Carey, 1985; Case, 1985, 1992; Halford, 1993; Pascual-Leone, 1970; Schliemann & Carraher, 2002). However, it is not always clear that development is as regular and sequential as epistemological theories might imply. Recent research in mathematical abilities, for instance, has shown that skill development can, in fact, be quite chaotic and nonlinear (Rittle-Johnson et al., 2001). Whereas epistemological theories have tended to focus on the individual's interaction with the environment, individual differences in performance per se are typically not modeled empirically.

Methodological limitations partly contribute to the reluctance to model individual differences. First, there are difficulties associated with collecting sufficient samples of young children for correlational studies of these types of tasks. Second, comparison-of-means methods typically used to test these theories are not ideal for exploring individual differences. And third, the types of tasks explored by these researchers tend to have poor psychometric properties (see our discussion above on the role of within-task learning and reliability in psychometric theories).

In the next section we consider variability not as a function of the person but rather of the context.

Intellectual Development from the Perspective of the Contextualist Tradition

Contextualist theories have tended to focus on the impact of different contexts on learning and the assessment of abilities in different contexts (Ceci, Ramey, & Ramey, 1990; Roberts & Stevenson, 1996). These theories place an increasing emphasis on problem-solving strategies that take advantage of previous experiences and acquired knowledge. Probably the most famous line of research on the effect of context within experimental psychology has been on the Wason Selection Task (Wason & Johnson-Laird, 1972), which requires turning cards to validate a rule (e.g., "If a card has a vowel on one side, then it has an even number on the other"). Performance is invariably better when the task is presented using familiar content than when the task is presented in its original abstract form (Johnson-Laird, 2001).

This type of context effect has also been generalized into everyday reasoning. Carraher, Carraher, and Schliemann (1985) studied Brazilian children who, for economic reasons, often worked as street vendors (Nuñes, 1994). Most of these children had very little formal schooling. Carraher and colleagues compared the performance of these children on mathematical problems that were embedded in real-life situations (i.e., vending) with their performance on problems presented in an academic context (e.g., 2 + 2 = ?). The children correctly solved significantly more questions that related to vending than mathematical problems that were academic in nature.

The same principle that applies to children also appears to apply to adults. Ceci and Liker (1986, 1988; Ceci & Ruiz, 1991) attempted to relate performance of expert handicappers at the racetrack to performance in a less familiar context in which the same algorithm was involved—making stock-market predictions. The handicappers performed no better than chance on the stock market (after 611 trials) and there was no significant difference in performance as a function of IQ. Possible reasons for the facilitating effect of practical content are that (1) there is a relatively greater opportunity for strengthening of the activation of necessary solution algorithms within a personally relevant context, and (2) there is an increased level of motivation to perform. Knowledge-acquisition skills and experience are therefore central to the developmental process in this account.

Although above examples are illuminating, for most people, schooling is a substantial source of experience in the first 10–15 years of life that tends to homogenize performance—at least for the dominant culture. In a rather ingenious study conducted by Cahan and Cohen (1989), the influence on intelligence-test scores of formal education, as opposed to chronological age, was investigated. Cahan and Cohen took advantage of the natural experiment created by the fact that in many school systems, children tend to start school at a fixed time during the school year. First, the authors compared the youngest and oldest children in the same school class who differed by up to 12 months in age. Second, they compared the adjacent lower and higher school classes that differed by 12 months in their duration of education (but whose chronological age was similar). The former 12-month span reflects biological maturation plus the effects of other experiences not related to schooling, and the latter, the additional effects of school experiences (Morrison, Griffith, & Alberts, 1997). Raw scores on established conventional tests of intelligence were compared. The results showed (1) that schooling was a major factor underlying the increase of intelligence-test scores as a function of age, and (2) that the relative importance of schooling over age varied as a function of the type of skill being assessed—schooling appeared to have a larger impact on verbal tests than on nonverbal tests. Similar mediating effects of schooling and experience on cognitive-ability test scores (distinct from age) have also been reported elsewhere (e.g., Morrison et al., 1997; Rutter, Pickles, Murray, & Eaves, 2001).

Summary

So far in this chapter, we have identified two related taxonomies. The first makes a rather broad paradigmatic distinction between differential and experimental research. We have aimed to demonstrate that important theoretical implications for conceptualizing development follow from the methods employed. The second, finer categorization makes a distinction between various approaches based on metaphors for conceptualizing intelligence (Sternberg, 1990)—we reviewed the psychometric, information-processing, epistemological, and contextualist theories. Although methodological limitations in one theoretical approach tend to be partly compensated for by strengths of others, multifaceted approaches that combine strengths across traditions are still not common. In the remainder of this chapter, we reflect on how conceptualizing abilities as competencies in development within the triarchic theory can integrate these approaches. First, we describe Sternberg's (1998; 1999) theory of developing expertise as it is framed within the broader triarchic theory of intelligence (Sternberg, 1985). We then finish by considering how such a conceptualization advances our understanding of intelligence.

THE TRIARCHIC THEORY OF INTELLIGENCE: A MULTIFACETED APPROACH

The triarchic theory of intelligence comprises three subtheories: a componential subtheory dealing with the (universal) components of intelligence; a contextual subtheory dealing with processes of adaptation, shaping, and selection; and an experiential subtheory dealing with the importance of coping with novelty and automatization.

Subtheories

Componential Subtheory

According to the triarchic theory (Sternberg, 1980, 1984, 1985, 1997), a common set of processes underlies all aspects of intelligence. These processes are hypothesized to be universal. For example, although the solutions to problems that are considered intelligent in one culture may be different from the solutions considered to be intelligent in another culture, the need to define problems and translate strategies to solve these problems exists in any culture. The componential subtheory is closely linked to traditional conceptualization of g and has three distinct aspects:

metacomponents, performance components, and knowledge-acquisition components.

Metacomponents, or executive processes, plan what to do, monitor things as they are being done, and evaluate things after they are done. *Performance components* execute the instructions of the metacomponents. For example, *inference* is used to decide how two stimuli are related and *application* is used to apply what one has inferred (Sternberg, 1977). *Knowledge-acquisition components* are used to learn how to solve problems or simply to acquire declarative knowledge in the first place (Sternberg, 1985).

The Contextual Subtheory

The contextual subtheory involves the practical application of the metacomponents, performance components, and knowledge-acquisition components to real-world contexts (Sternberg, 1985). These components can be brought to bear on the environment in one or more of three ways: (1) to help the individual *adapt* to the environment; (2) to *change* (shape) the environment to fit the individual; or (3) to help in *selecting* a new environment. Intelligence from this perspective entails a more practical set of abilities than those typically assessed by g based tests. Knowing when to apply these strategies is central to the conceptualization of *practical intelligence*.

The Experiential Subtheory

The experiential aspect of intelligence involves the ability to capitalize on one's experiences to solve novel problems and develop automatized procedures. Intelligence from this subtheory entails use of the knowledge-acquisition components of selective encoding, selective combination, and selective comparison to extract and apply relevant information from the novel task—that is, to see connections between apparently unrelated experiences to solve novel tasks and generate novel solutions to traditional problems. Because of the ability to either cope with novelty or to produce a novel solution, the experiential subtheory has often been linked with theories of creativity (e.g., Sternberg, 1985).

Dealing with novelty has also been related to traditional conceptions of fluid intelligence (Gf). The experiential subtheory extends the conceptualization of Gf in a number of important ways. First, it helps account for the fact that although many people who

are quite skillful at insightful processing of new information typically have high fluid abilities, some people with high fluid abilities are not at all skilled at insightful reasoning (Sternberg & Davidson, 1982). Second, it incorporates automatization abilities more directly into the theory of intelligence. Automatization reflects the move from effortful, controlled, and deliberate processing of task components to more subconscious, automatic processing (Schneider & Shiffrin, 1977; Shiffrin & Schneider, 1984). This conceptualization is consistent with Anderson's ACT theory, which we described above (e.g., Anderson & Neves, 1981). Automatization frees limited resources for other activities, such as the acquisition of new knowledge or further problem solving. The speed of automatization can also be viewed as an indicator of intelligence in that those individual who are better able to deal with novelty are likely to proceduralize tasks more quickly.

Abilities as Competencies in Development: The Theory of Developing Expertise

The theory of developing expertise draws on many of the features of the triarchic theory. It conceptualize abilities as a set of cognitive competencies in varying stages of development (Sternberg, 1998, 1999). There are five important sets of skills. The first are *metacognitive skills* that, as we described above, are related to skills required for recognizing, defining, and representing the problem; for formulating strategies and resource allocation; and for planning, monitoring, and evaluating success of a chosen strategy. Second are *learning skills* or knowledge-acquisition skills. These are the skills that are necessary to know which information in a problem to attend to; to know which existing information to select for comparison with the new information; and to know how to combine new and old understandings to solve the problem at hand. Third are *thinking skills* that are related to the performance component of the triarchic theory. A context-appropriate balance of analytical, creative, and practical thinking skills is necessary to optimize success (Sternberg, 1997). Fourth is *knowledge* in both declarative and procedural forms. The fifth and determining element is having sufficient *motivation* to bring these skills to bear on problem solving.

Without sufficient motivation, abilities remain inert. Hence motivation is the driving force behind the developing-expertise model (Sternberg, 1998,

1999). Past experiences and differences in personality will influence levels of motivation in any given context. Parents and teachers are significant determinants of the experiences of young children (Ceci et al., 1990). They are also likely to have some impact on the whether the child perceives these experiences as successful or not, and this perception is likely to influence future levels of motivation. Over time, the developing child has increasingly more choice in the types of experiences he or she engages in and a more complex array of factors start to play on levels of motivation (e.g., developing interests, peer pressure, financial and romantic rewards). The five components of the developing-expertise theory all interact fully in context as the novice works toward expertise through deliberate practice. For instance, motivation drives the application of meta-cognitive skills. These skills in turn facilitate learning, which enables not only one's level of expertise to increase, but also the efficiency with which these skills will be implemented in the future.

Evidence for Conceiving of Abilities as Competencies in Development

Sternberg (1998; 1999) has summarized a number of previous research findings that are consistent with the theory of developing expertise. A particularly interesting line of research reviewed is work that explores "cognitive modifiability" using the dynamic-assessment paradigm. Sternberg, Grigorenko, and their colleagues administered tests that measured the kinds of skills required on conventional tests of intelligence (see Sternberg & Grigorenko, 1997; Sternberg et al., 2002). However, the researchers administered the tests dynamically rather than statically (Feuerstein, 1979; Grigorenko & Sternberg, 1998; Lidz, 1987, 1991). Dynamic testing is like conventional static testing in that individuals are tested and inferences about their abilities are made. But dynamic tests differ from static ones in that children are given some kind of feedback in order to help them improve their scores. Vygotsky (1978) suggested that children's ability to profit from guided instruction could serve as a measure of children's zone of proximal development, or the difference between their developed abilities and their latent capacities. In other words, testing and instruction are treated as of one piece rather than as distinct processes. This integration makes sense in terms of traditional definitions of intelligence as the ability to learn (Intelligence and its measurement: A symposium, 1921; Sternberg & Detterman, 1986), but as we have argued above, this conceptualization has not always made its way into common assessment tools.

SYNTHESIZING THEORIES

When one considers the investigation of intelligence and intellectual development across the four approaches that we have reviewed, at least two key sets of questions arise that impact current and future understandings of intellectual development. The first set of questions relates to the stability of cognitive abilities. Is intelligence really stable as a constellation of cognitive abilities? The history of psychometric research using the individual-differences paradigm would suggest that they probably are (Carroll, 1993). At the same time, epistemological theories and, to some extent, information-processing theories, model explicit cognitive change more flexibly in terms of strategy development and knowledge acquisition using the experimental paradigm. It would seem that there is some tension between the individual-difference and experimental paradigms in defining the extent of cognitive modifiability.

The second set of questions relates to how experience and context (including education) interact with cognitive capacity over time to determine an individual's unique set of abilities. This has implications for lifespan development. Epistemological theories tend to focus on the development of cognitive capacity in the first few years of life. Although context and experience are acknowledged, the common methods employed are not adequate for linking capacity with experience. Information-processing theories model the effects of experience on task performance, but typically do not model the development of capacity. Psychometric theories have trouble with modeling the processes of differentiation (and dedifferentiation; Chapter 23, this volume) although it is acknowledged as a key factor in development. In the remainder of this chapter, we reflect on how conceptualizing abilities as competencies in development within the triarchic theory views these questions.

Stability of Intelligence as a Constellation of Abilities versus Developing Competencies

We argued earlier that the methodological assumptions of psychometric theories may have served to perpetuate the common assumption that cognitive abilities are fixed. Although conceptualizing abilities as competencies in development precludes the notion that intelligence is fixed and that ability is separate from achievement, it is of course possible that some competencies are more susceptible to development than others. Is it possible to reconcile these differences?

We believe the answer is yes—if a broader conceptualization of intelligence is permitted. The triarchic theory postulates that there are three aspects or sets of processes involved in intelligence: componential processes, contextual processes, and experiential processes. One view of conventional (psychometric) tests of intelligence is that they have been developed primarily to target the componential aspects of intelligence as if it were part of a closed system that is (1) devoid of context, (2) separated from personality, and (3) accompanied by maximal levels of motivation to succeed on the tests that exist (Most & Zeidner, 1995). Although the processes of the componential subtheory are universal (Sternberg, 1985) and are therefore likely to have a relatively larger biological (hereditary) element, it is important to keep in mind that they constitute only one part of the triarchic conceptualization of intelligence. As such, developing tests to assess only componential processes in isolation from other skills produces a rather static view of intellectual functioning. The contextual and experiential subtheories provide mechanisms that allow for strategic knowledge and experience to mediate the development and appropriate application of the meta-cognitive and knowledge-acquisition components in different contexts. Furthermore, these experiences facilitate more efficient recall and use of these skills in the future. Research using the dynamic-assessment paradigm has corroborated these predictions and has demonstrated that intelligence is more than what is typically assessed on conventional tests of intelligence (Guthke & Beckmann, 2000; Sternberg & Grigorenko, 1997; Sternberg et al., 2002).

Experience and Cognitive Capacity as Determinants of Intellectual Development

Attempts to clarify the relation between cognitive capacity and experience have caused considerable debate in psychology. For instance, as we described above, age-of-acquisition effects in Piagetian tasks have

been explained by some researchers as primarily the result of age-related differentiation of capacity, with experience providing a facilitating role (e.g., Halford et al., 1998). Others argue more explicitly that changes in knowledge that occur with experience provide a more parsimonious account of age-of-acquisition effects (e.g., Gentner & Rattermann, 1998). An interesting question is whether the developing-expertise model within the broader triarchic theory is able to address this issue. Again, we argue that it can because it allows for a broad view of intellectual development that incorporates a role for motivational factors directly. First we consider how the competencies-in-development account might conceptualize development in practice—first for older children and adults, for younger children. We then conclude by reflecting on the concept of dedifferentiation as proposed by Rabbitt and Anderson (Chapter 23, this volume) in relation to what we have presented here.

Older Children and Adults

Initial performance on a new task will be driven primarily by basic componential processes because there are relatively few experiences that can be drawn upon to facilitate problem solving. The componential processes are the universal meta-cognitive skills required for selective encoding, comparison, and combination; for implementing chosen strategies; and for monitoring the success of these strategies. Unfortunately, utilization of these types of processes is resource intensive (Anderson, 1990; Anderson & Neves, 1981; Rumelhart & Norman, 1981). It makes sense to shortcut the effortful componential processes with automatized routines whenever possible. As experience in a domain develops, links between a given context and clusters of declarative facts and procedures are strengthened. Componential skills become less predictive of success because problem solving starts to draw more heavily on the contextual and experiential aspects of intelligence and on motivation to perform.

Young Children and Infants

This argument also applies to early cognitive development. For infants, rudimentary forms of selective encoding and comparison are likely to be the main part of a rather small collection of intellectual tools and strategies. As we described earlier, McCall and Carriger (1993; see also, Rose & Feldman, 1997) have demonstrated that for infants, individual differences in encoding and habituation-dishabituation are the best predictors of future success. Theory of mind research following the epistemological tradition suggests that meta-cognitive skills like planning, monitoring, and entertaining multiple perspectives are immature early and develop gradually over the first few years of life (e.g., Frye, Zelazo, & Palfai, 1995; Halford, 1993). This research is entirely consistent with the competencies-in-development account. Until a certain level of expertise develops, it is necessary to have generalizable skills at the front line. These skills will be used to deal with the everyday challenges the child faces in navigating new features in his or her environment. In concert with biological maturation, sufficient motivation, and the opportunity to interact with the environment, each success and failure is incorporated into the cognitive system. Knowledge is refined, abilities are honed, and interests are broadened. Learning is seen as an ongoing process that occurs at all levels of the triarchic model. Learning is not only a function of ability; it determines future abilities as well and is a crucial aspect of intellectual functioning. We believe that it is the interaction of these factors that results in the differentiation effect observed in both psychometric and information processing accounts of cognitive development. Furthermore, the competencies-in-development view would suggest that, to some extent, the degree of differentiation is under individual control.

Developing Expertise in Old Age: A Comment on Rabbitt and Anderson

In our scheme, the theory proposed by Rabbitt and Anderson (Chapter 23, this volume) would be classified as belonging to the psychometric approach. As we indicated above, the conceptualization of psychometric intelligence has been somewhat agnostic regarding the processes that underlie the constellation of abilities that have been proposed, except in regard to speed of processing (SOP). Rabbit and Anderson argue three points that are ultimately related to SOP. First, they suggest that age-related decline observed on measures of cognitive abilities is attenuated, due to methodological limitations. We concur with this point and have reported other similar methodological limitations in the various approaches we have reviewed. Second, they propose that the differentiation in cognitive abilities that occurs as children become older (which we also report), is in fact reversed as old adults grow even older. This is labeled dedifferentiation (see also Lindenberger and von Oertzen, Chapters 21 this volume and Li and Baltes, Chapter 24 this volume). That is, with old age, problem solving comes to rely more on domain-general abilities than on specific abilities, and therefore an increase in inter-task correlations is expected with age. This is an interesting hypothesis and one to which we will return in a moment. Third, Rabbitt and Anderson argue that the cause of differentiation as children grow older and dedifferentiation as adults grow older is related to changes in a single Global Functional Performance Characteristic (GPC) and that the GPC is SOP. We prefer to conceptualize these last two points somewhat differently.

To begin, while we are theoretically open to dedifferentiation, the evidence cited for it by Rabbitt and Anderson is not yet convincing. While we acknowledge that an increase in the size of the correlation between the 11 specific tasks (reported in their Table 23.3) and a general ability measure in favor of the very old group could be interpreted as evidence for de-differentiation with age, the data presented in their Table 23.3 suggest only marginal support for this hypothesis. The average increase in correlations between the two groups (49–69 years and 70–90 years) on the 11 tasks is less than .02 correlational points. The largest difference between the older and younger age groups is for the Cumulative Learning task, and this difference is also small (i.e., -0.061)!

We are also not closed theoretically or empirically to a GPC model driven by biological changes in a SOP- or Gf-type factor. However, consistent with what we have presented, we do question the *practical* significance and importance of this change in relation to general development (and aging) and the ability to adapt to the needs of one's environment—the consensual definition of intelligence reported above. Individual differences in knowledge, strategies, motivation, and personality, as well as the ability to compensate for declines during old age in one or more systems of abilities (e.g., analytical abilities) using relative strengths in other areas (e.g., knowledge, or practical and creative abilities), are more likely to influence everyday successes. Many individuals do exceedingly well in their old age regardless of biological declines. Conceptualizing abilities as competencies-in-development does not preclude the possibility that some abilities may decline in old age, and that the overall process of developing expertise may be slowed. The extent to which practical and creative abilities also decline, or decline at relatively slower rates, is still open to empirical investigation.

CONCLUSION

There have been many significant advances in psychological methods in the last 50 years. We have described the limits of some of these methods that we feel have constrained further attempts at a unified theory of intellectual functioning. It would seem that the challenge of psychology remains the same now as it did for Cronbach in 1957 — to disengage ourselves from theoretical assumptions that are entrenched in inadequate methods and to continue searching for new ways to understand the human condition. A broader application of the triarchic theory that conceptualizes abilities as competencies in development is one way to proceed toward a natural, unified, and ecologically more plausible view intelligence.

References

Anderson, J. R. (1982). Acquisition of cognitive skill. *Psychological Review, 89*, 369–406.

Anderson, J. R. (1983). *The architecture of cognition.* Cambridge, MA: Harvard University Press.

Anderson, J. R. (1990). *The adaptive character of thought* (Vol. 1). Hillsdale, NJ: Lawrence Erlbaum Associates.

Anderson, J. R., & Lebiere, C. (1998). *The atomic components of thought.* Mahwah, NJ: Lawrence Erlbaum Associates.

Anderson, J. R., & Milson, R. (1989). Human memory: An adaptive perspective. *Psychological Review, 96*, 703–719.

Anderson, J. R., & Neves, D. M. (1981). Knowledge compilation: Mechanisms for the automatization of cognitive skills. In J. R. Anderson (Ed.), *Cognitive skills and their acquisition* (pp. 57–84). Hillsdale, NJ: Lawrence Erlbaum Associates.

Anderson, J. R., & Schunn, C. D. (2000). Implications of the ACT-R learning theory: No magic bullets. In R. Glaser (Ed.), *Advances in instructional psychology* (Vol. 5, pp. 1–33). Mahwah, NJ: Lawrence Erlbaum Associates.

Andrews, G., & Halford, G. S. (2002). A cognitive complexity metric applied to cognitive development. *Cognitive Psychology, 45*, 153–219.

Bidell, T. R., & Fischer, K. W. (1992). Beyond the stage debate: Action, structure, and variability in Piagetian theory and research. In R. J. Sternberg & C. A. Berg (Eds.), *Intellectual development* (pp. 100–140). New York: Cambridge University Press.

Birney, D. P. (2002). *The Measurement of Task Complexity and Cognitive Ability: Relational Complexity in Adult Reasoning.* Unpublished PhD Dissertation, University of Queensland, St Lucia, Brisbane.

Birney, D. P., & Halford, G. S. (2002). Cognitive complexity of suppositional reasoning: An application of the relational complexity metric to the knight-knave task. *Thinking and Reasoning, 8*, 109–134.

Bjorklund, D. F. (1995). *Children's thinking: Developmental function and individual difference.* Pacific Grove, CA: Brooks/Cole Publishing Company.

Boring, E. G. (1923). Intelligence as the tests test it. *New Republic, 35*, 35–37.

Braine, M. D. S. (1990). The "Natural Logic" approach to reasoning. In W. F. Overton (Ed.), *Reasoning, necessity, and logic: Developmental perspectives* (pp. 133–157). Hillsdale, NJ: Lawrence Erlbaum Associates.

Braine, M. D. S. (1993). Mental models cannot exclude mental logic and make little sense with out it. *Behavioral and Brain Sciences, 16*, 338–339.

Brody, N. (2000). History of theories and measurements of intelligence. In R. J. Sternberg (Ed.), *Handbook of intelligence* (pp. 16–33). New York: Cambridge University Press.

Cahan, S., & Cohen, N. (1989). Age versus schooling effects on intelligence development. *Child Development, 60*, 1239–1249.

Carey, S. (1985). *Conceptual change in childhood.* Cambridge, MA: MIT Press.

Carraher, T. N., Carraher, D., & Schliemann, A. D. (1985). Mathematics in the streets and in schools. *British Journal of Developmental Psychology, 3*, 21–29.

Carroll, J. B. (1993). *Human cognitive abilities: A survey of factor-analytic studies.* New York: Cambridge University Press.

Case, R. (1985). *Intellectual development: Birth to adulthood.* New York: Academic Press.

Case, R. (1992). Neo-Piagetian theories of child development. In R. J. Sternberg & C. A. Berg (Eds.), *Intellectual development* (pp. 161–196). New York: Cambridge University Press.

Cattell, R. B. (1971). *Abilities: Their structure, growth, and action.* Boston: Houghton Mifflin.

Cattell, R. B. (1987). *Intelligence: Its structure, growth and action.* Amsterdam: Elsevier Science Publishers.

Ceci, S. J., & Liker, J. (1986). Academic and nonacademic intelligence: An experimental separation. In R. J. Sternberg & R. K. Wagner (Eds.), *Practical intelligence: Nature and origins of competence in the everyday world* (pp. 119–142). New York: Cambridge University Press.

Ceci, S. J., & Liker, J. (1988). Stalking the IQ-expertise relationship: When the critics go fishing. *Journal of Experimental Psychology: General, 117,* 96–100.

Ceci, S. J., Ramey, S. L., & Ramey, C. T. (1990). Framing intellectual assessment in terms of person-process-context model. *Educational Psychologist, 25,* 269–291.

Ceci, S. J., & Ruiz, A. (1991). Cognitive complexity and generality: A case study. In R. Hoffman (Ed.), *The psychology of expertise.* New York: Springer-Verlag.

Chen, Z., & Siegler, R. S. (2000). Intellectual development in childhood. In R. J. Sternberg (Ed.), *Handbook of intelligence* (pp. 92–116). New York: Cambridge University Press.

Chi, M. T., Glaser, R., & Rees, E. (1982). Expertise in problem solving. In R. J. Sternberg (Ed.), *Advances in the psychology of human intelligence* (Vol. 1, pp. 7–75). Hillsdale, NJ: Lawrence Erlbaum Associates.

Cronbach, L. J. (1957). The two disciplines of scientific psychology. *American Psychologist, 12,* 671–684.

Deary, I. J. (2001). Human intelligence differences: Towards a combined experimental-differential approach. *Trends in Cognitive Sciences, 5,* 164–170.

Dennis, I., & Evans, J. S. T. (1996). The speed-error trade-off problem in psychometric testing. *British Journal of Psychology, 87,* 105–129.

Embretson, S. E., & McCollam, K. (2000). Psychometric approaches to the understanding and measurement of intelligence. In R. J. Sternberg (Ed.), *Handbook of intelligence* (pp. 423–444). New York: Cambridge University Press.

Feuerstein, R. (1979). *The dynamic assessment of retarded performers: The learning potential assessment device theory, instruments, and techniques.* Baltimore, MD: University Park Press.

Flynn, J. R. (1987). Massive IQ gains in 14 nations: What IQ tests really measure. *Psychological Bulletin, 101,* 171–191.

Frye, D., Zelazo, P. D., & Palfai, T. (1995). Theory of mind and rule-based reasoning. *Cognitive Development, 10,* 483–527.

Gentner, D., & Rattermann, M. J. (1998). Deep thinking in children: The case for knowledge change in analogical development. *Behavioral and Brain Science, 24,* 837–838.

Grigorenko, E. L., & Sternberg, R. J. (1998). Dynamic testing. *Psychological Bulletin, 124,* 75–111.

Gustafson, J. E. (1994). Hierarchical models of intelligence and educational achievement. In A. Demetriou & A. Efklides (Eds.), *Intelligence, mind, and reasoning: Structure and developments. Ad-*

vances in psychology (pp. 45–73). Amsterdam, Netherlands: North-Holland/Elsevier Science Publishers.

Guthke, J., & Beckmann, J. (2000). The learning test concept and its application in practice. In C. S. Lidz & J. Elliot (Eds.), *Dynamic assessment: Prevailing models and applications (Advances in cognition and educational practice)* (Vol. 6, pp. 17–69). New York: Elsevier Science.

Guttman, L. (1954). A new approach to factor analysis: The radex. In P. F. Lazarsfeld (Ed.), *Mathematical thinking in the social sciences* (pp. 258–348). Glencoe, IL: Free Press.

Halford, G. S. (1993). *Children's understanding: The development of mental models.* Hillsdale, NJ: Lawrence Erlbaum Associates.

Halford, G. S. (1999). The development of intelligence includes capacity to process relations of greater complexity. In M. Anderson (Ed.), *The development of intelligence* (pp. 193–213). Hove, East Sussex: Psychology Press.

Halford, G. S., Andrews, G., Dalton, C., Boag, C. C., & Zielinski, T. (2002). Young children's performance on the balance scale: The influence of relational complexity. *Journal of Experimental Child Psychology, 81,* 383–416.

Halford, G. S., Wilson, W. H., & Phillips, S. (1998). Processing capacity defined by relational complexity: Implications for comparative, developmental, and cognitive psychology. *Behavioral and Brain Sciences, 21,* 803–831.

Herrnstein, R. J., & Murray, C. (1994). *The bell curve.* New York: Free Press.

Horn, J. L. (1988). Thinking about human abilities. In J. R. Nesselroade (Ed.), *Handbook of multivariate psychology* (2nd ed., pp. 645–685). New York: Plenum Press.

Horn, J. L. (1994). Theory of fluid and crystallized intelligence. In R. J. Sternberg (Ed.), *The encyclopedia of human intelligence* (Vol. 1, pp. 443–451). New York: Macmillan.

Humphreys, M. S., Wiles, J., & Dennis, S. (1994). Toward a theory of human memory: Data structures and access processes. *Behavioral and Brain Sciences, 17,* 655–692.

Intelligence and its measurement: A symposium. (1921). *Journal of Educational Psychology, 12,* 123–147, 195–216, 271–275.

Jensen, A. (1987). The g beyond factor analysis. In R. R. Ronning & J. A. Glover & J. C. Conoley & J. C. Witt (Eds.), *The influence of cognitive psychology on testing* (Vol. 3, pp. 87–142). Hillsdale, NJ: Lawrence Erlbaum Associates.

Jensen, A. (1998). *The g factor: The science of mental ability.* Westport, CT: Praeger/Greenwood.

Johnson-Laird, P. N. (2001). Mental models and deduction. *Trends in Cognitive Sciences, 5,* 434–442.

Johnson-Laird, P. N., & Byrne, R. M. (1991). *Deduction.* Hove: Lawrence Erlbaum Associates.

Johnson-Laird, P. N., Byrne, R. M., & Schaeken, W. (1992). Propositional reasoning by model. *Psychological Review, 99,* 418–439.

Johnson-Laird, P. N., Byrne, R. M., & Schaeken, W. (1994). Why models rather than rules give a better account of propositional reasoning: A reply to Bonatti and to O'Brien, Braine, and Yang. *Psychological Review, 101,* 734–739.

Just, M. A., & Carpenter, P. A. (1992). A capacity theory of comprehension: Individual differences in working memory. *Psychological Review, 99,* 122–149.

Lidz, C. S. (Ed.). (1987). *Dynamic assessment.* New York: Guilford Press.

Lidz, C. S. (1991). *Practitioner's guide to dynamic assessment.* New York: Guilford Press.

Lidz, C. S. (2000). Theme and some variations on the concepts of mediated learning experience and dynamic assessment. In A. Kozulin & Y. Rand (Eds.), *Experience of mediated learning: An impact of Feuerstein's theory in education and psychology* (pp. 166–174). Oxford, UK: Elsevier Science Ltd.

Lohman, D. F., & Ippel, M. J. (1993). Cognitive diagnosis: From statistically based assessment toward theory-based assessment. In N. Frederiksen, R. J. Mislevy, & I. I. Bejar (Eds.), *Test theory for a new generation of tests* (pp. 41–70). Hillsdale, NJ: Lawrence Erlbaum Associates.

Lutz, D. J., & Sternberg, R. J. (1999). Cognitive development. In M. H. Bornstein & M. E. Lamb (Eds.), *Developmental psychology: An advanced textbook* (4th ed.). Mahwah, NJ: Lawrence Erlbaum Associates.

Marshalek, B., Lohman, D. F., & Snow, R. E. (1983). The complexity continuum in the radex and hierarchical models of intelligence. *Intelligence, 7,* 107–127.

McArdle, J. J., Ferrer-Caja, E., Hamagami, F., & Woodcock, R. W. (2002). Comparative longitudinal structural analyses of the growth and decline of multiple intellectual abilities over the life span. *Developmental Psychology, 38,* 115–142.

McCall, R. B., & Carriger, M. S. (1993). A meta-analysis of infant habituation and recognition memory performance as predictors of later IQ. *Child Development, 64,* 57–79.

McClelland, J. L., Rumelhart, D. E., & Hinton, G. E. (1986). The appeal of parallel distributed processing. In D. E. Rumelhart & J. L. McClelland (Eds.), *Parallel distributed processing* (Vol. 1, pp. 3–44). Cambridge, MA: MIT Press.

Morrison, F. J., Griffith, E. M., & Alberts, D. M. (1997). Nature-nurture in the classroom: Entrance age, school readiness, and learning in children. *Developmental Psychology, 33,* 254–262.

Most, R. B., & Zeidner, M. (1995). Constructing personality and intelligence instruments. In D. H. Saklofske & M. Zeidner (Eds.), *International handbook of personality and intelligence* (pp. 475–503). New York: Plenum.

Newell, A., & Simon, H. A. (1972). *Human problem solving.* Englewood Cliffs, NJ: Prentice-Hall.

Nuñes, T. (1994). Street intelligence. In R. J. Sternberg (Ed.), *Encyclopedia of human intelligence* (Vol. 2, pp. 1045–1049). New York: Macmillan.

Pascual-Leone, J. (1970). A mathematical model for the transition rule in Piaget's developmental stages. *Acta Psychologica, 32,* 301–345.

Piaget, J. (1950). *The psychology of intelligence* (M. Piercy & D. E. Berlyne., Trans.). Oxford, UK: Harcourt.

Rips, L. (1983). Cognitive processes in propositional reasoning. *Psychological Review, 90,* 38–71.

Rips, L. (1989). The psychology of knights and knaves. *Cognition, 31,* 85–116.

Rips, L. (1994). *The psychology of proof: Deductive reasoning in human thinking.* Cambridge, MA: MIT Press.

Rittle-Johnson, B., Siegler, R. S., & Alibali, M. W. (2001). Developing conceptual understanding and procedural skill in mathematics: An iterative process. *Journal of Educational Psychology, 93,* 346–362.

Roberts, M. J. (1993). Human reasoning: Deduction rules or mental models, or both? *Quarterly Journal of Experimental Psychology, 46A,* 569–589.

Roberts, M. J., & Stevenson, N. J. (1996). Reasoning with Raven—with and without help. *British Journal of Educational Psychology, 66,* 519–532.

Roberts, R. D., & Stankov, L. (1999). Individual differences in speed of mental processing and human cognitive abilities: Toward a taxonomic model. *Learning and Individual Differences, 11,* 1–120.

Rose, A. S., & Feldman, J. F. (1997). Memory and speed: Their role in the relation of information-processing to later IQ. *Child Development, 68,* 630–641.

Rumelhart, D. E. (1990). Brain style computation: Learning and generalisation. In S. F. Zornetzer, J. L. Davis, & C. Lau (Eds.), *An introduction to neural and electronic networks* (pp. 405–420). Cambridge, MA: MIT Press.

Rumelhart, D. E., & Norman, D. A. (1981). Analogical processes in learning. In J. R. Anderson (Ed.), *Cognitive skills and their acquisition* (pp. 335–359). Hillsdale, NJ: Lawrence Erlbaum Associates.

Rutter, M., Pickles, A., Murray, R., & Eaves, L. (2001). Testing hypotheses on specific environmental causal effects on behavior. *Psychological Bulletin, 127,* 291–324.

Salthouse, T. A. (1996). The processing-speed theory of adult age differences in cognition. *Psychological Review, 103*, 403–428.

Sattler, J. M. (1992). *Assessment of children* (rev. and updated 3rd ed.). San Diego: Jerome M. Sattler, Publisher.

Schliemann, A. D., & Carraher, D. W. (2002). The evolution of mathematical reasoning: Everyday versus idealized understandings. *Developmental Review, 22*, 242–266.

Schneider, W., & Shiffrin, R. M. (1977). Controlled and automatic human information processing: I. Detection, search, and attention. *Psychological Review, 84*, 1–66.

Schroyens, W., Schaeken, W., & d'Ydewalle, G. (1999). Error and bias in meta-propositional reasoning: A case of the mental model theory. *Thinking and Reasoning, 5*, 29–65.

Schunn, C. D., & Reder, L. M. (2001). Another source of individual differences: Strategy adaptivity to changing rates of success. *Journal of Experimental Psychology: General, 130*, 59–76.

Shiffrin, R. M., & Schneider, W. (1984). Automatic and controlled processing revisited. *Psychological Review, 91*, 269–276.

Siegler, R. S., & Chen, Z. (2002). Development of rules and strategies: Balancing the old and the new. *Journal of Experimental Child Psychology, 81*, 446–457.

Simon, T., & Halford, G. S. (Eds.). (1995). *Developing cognitive competence: New approaches to cognitive modelling.* Hillsdale, NJ: Lawrence Erlbaum Associates.

Sternberg, R. J. (1977). *Intelligence, information processing, and analogical reasoning: The componential analysis of human abilities.* Hillsdale, NJ: Lawrence Erlbaum Associates.

Sternberg, R. J. (1980). Sketch of a componential subtheory of human intelligence. *Behavioral and Brain Science, 3*, 573–584.

Sternberg, R. J. (1984). *Mechanisms of cognitive development.* San Francisco: Freeman.

Sternberg, R. J. (1985). *Beyond IQ: A triarchic theory of human intelligence.* New York: Cambridge University Press.

Sternberg, R. J. (1990). *Metaphors of mind: Conceptions of the nature of intelligence.* New York: Cambridge University Press.

Sternberg, R. J. (1997). *Successful intelligence.* New York: Plume.

Sternberg, R. J. (1998). Abilities are forms of developing expertise. *Educational Researcher, 27*, 11–20.

Sternberg, R. J. (1999). Intelligence as developing expertise. *Contemporary Educational Psychology, 24*, 359–375.

Sternberg, R. J. (2003). Biological intelligence. In R. J. Sternberg & E. L. Grigorenko (Eds.), *The psychology of abilities, competencies, and expertise* (pp. 240–262). Cambridge, UK: Cambridge University Press.

Sternberg, R. J., & Davidson, J. E. (1982). The mind of the puzzler. *Psychology Today, 16*, 37–44.

Sternberg, R. J., & Detterman, D. K. (1986). *What is intelligence?* Norwood, NJ: Ablex Publishing.

Sternberg, R. J., & Grigorenko, E. L. (Eds.). (1997). *Intelligence, heredity, and environment.* New York: Cambridge University Press.

Sternberg, R. J., Grigorenko, E. L., Ngrosho, D., Tantufuye, E., Mbise, A., Nokes, C., Jukes, M., & Bundy, D. A. (2002). Assessing intellectual potential in rural Tanzanian school children. *Intelligence, 30*, 141–162.

Vygotsky, L. (1934/1962). *Thought and language.* Cambridge, MA: MIT Press.

Vygotsky, L. (1978). *Mind in society: The development of higher psychological processes.* Cambridge, MA: Harvard University Press.

Wason, P., & Johnson-Laird, P. (1972). *Psychology of reasoning: Structure and content.* Cambridge, MA: Harvard University Press.

Woodcock, R. W., & Johnson, M. B. (1989). *Woodcock-Johnson psycho-educational battery—revised.* Allen, TX: DLM Teaching Resources.

23

The Lacunae of Loss?
Aging and the Differentiation
of Cognitive Abilities

Patrick Rabbitt

Mike Anderson

A scientific approach usually starts with a question to be answered. The central question that we ask in this chapter has two main parts. The first is very general: What is the effect of aging on cognitive abilities? A crude answer might be that they almost all decline. This brings us to the second part of our question: Do all cognitive abilities show evidence of a similar decline or are some abilities relatively spared? To use a now-hackneyed phrase "Does it all go when it goes ?" Declines in specific abilities would be lacunae of loss sparing the archipelagos of surviving abilities. Evidence for unevenness in decline would be decreased correlations between tests of specific abilities as some declined while others did not. This chapter will present the case for looking at the data from the perspective of maintenance or loss of consistency of relationships between mental abilities as age advances and attempt to draw conclusions from such comparisons as are available.

Scientific questions can seem deceptively simple, and we should admit at the outset that our apparently straightforward questions bypass many conceptual and methodological problems. We aim to point out many of the methodological complexities in the course of this chapter, but for want of space we will only briefly touch on conceptual problems and this mainly in response to the views of our colleagues Damian Birney and Robert Sternberg (see Chapter 22, this volume).

It is hard to disagree with Birney and Sternberg's propositions that in research there is more than one way to skin a cat and that this is particularly the case for processes that are as multidetermined as changes in cognitive abilities with age. Birney and Sternberg suggest four different approaches to studying developmental changes. In this chapter we pursue only one of them, the psychometric approach, though there is a heavy undercurrent of an implicit information-processing view. While it is arguable that this narrows the scope of our chapter, in our view there are also costs associated with a much broader approach, the main one being a loss of focus on the question at hand. Let us use an analogy here. No one could sensibly disagree that many phenomena in psychology can be viewed from a number of different perspectives or dealt with at different levels of description. However, since complete pictures of developmental or involutional change are still a long way off, it currently seems more useful to deal with a narrow but tractable set of phenomena than to capitulate to vague acknowledgments of the complexity of dealing simultaneously with all possible points of view and levels of description.

As people grow old, they perform less well on most cognitive tasks, including tests of general fluid intelligence (*gf*) and speed of processing (SOP). Significant declines in average age-unadjusted scores on tests of *gf* and SOP are measurable before the age of 40 and thereafter steadily accelerate. The absolute amounts of these declines have been underestimated because older participants in cross-sectional comparisons are usually self-selected, and so are atypically healthy and able (e.g., Lachman, Lachman, & Taylor, 1982). Longitudinal comparisons are also compromised by participant self-selection on entry and probably even more substantially by selective dropout of frailer and less able individuals as studies continue (e.g. Rabbitt, Watson, Donlan, Bent, & McInnes, 1994; Rabbitt, Diggle, Holland, McInnes et al, 2004; Schaie, Labouvie, & Barrett, 1973). Longitudinal studies have also underestimated rates because of improvements due to repeated experience of the same tests over many years. Such practice gains are marked, and even when inter-test intervals are as long as 7+ years, are large enough to cancel out losses associated with up to 5 years' increase in age (Rabbitt, Diggle, Smith, Holland, & McInnes, 2001; Rabbitt, Diggle, Holland, & McInnes, 2004). Moreover, older and less able individuals experience greater practice improvements (Rabbitt, 1993; Rabbitt et al., 2004). After the effects of both practice and dropout have been identified and taken into account, age-related declines in unadjusted intelligence-test scores are seen to be substantial and accelerated (Rabbittt et al., 2001, 2004).

Figure 23.1 plots mean scores on the Heim (1970) AH4-1 and -2 group tests of intelligence, and on the Catell and Catell (1960) Culture Fair intelligence test obtained from successive decade samples within a group of 2,193 members of the University of Manchester longitudinal research panel who, when first assessed, were aged between 49 and 92 years (for description of the panel, see Rabbitt Donlan, Bent, McInnes & Abson, 1993). The apparent linearity of declines across successive age-decades in these single-

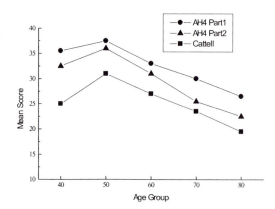

FIGURE 23.1. Means of unadjusted scores for AH4-1, AH4-2 and Cattell Culture Fair tests for successive decade samples between 49 and 89 years.

time-point cross-sectional comparisons is misleading. When data from subsequent successive longitudinal screenings of these same individuals over periods up to 17 years are analyzed to take account of the effects of practice and selective dropout, declines in average test scores are seen to markedly accelerate as age increases (Rabbitt et al., 2001, 2004). This difference between corrected longitudinal and unadjusted cross-sectional data reflects strong attrition by selective dropout.

It is easy to acquire evidence for age-related declines in average scores on tests of *gf* but such data are uninformative unless they give insights into the practical difficulties that people experience as they grow older or into the relationships between age-related changes in cognition and physiological changes in the brain. Longitudinal data, showing that rates of age-related decline are steeper for some tests than for others, might suggest that age has earlier and more severe effects on distinct functional neurophysiological systems that support different qualitative test demands. However, differences in the sizes of the effects of age on different test scores may reflect differences in task difficulty rather than in task demands. Differences in longitudinal rates of change in performance on different tasks may also reflect differences in the sizes of practice effects on different tasks during longitudinal studies (Rabbitt et al., 2004).

The questions whether some mental abilities decline earlier than others or whether all abilities decline at the same rates are basic to our understanding of the functional basis of cognitive aging but cannot be properly answered by comparing average test scores obtained at single time-points. They require computations of associations between rates of decline on different tests after the effects of practice and dropout have been taken into consideration. Such results are not yet available.

A different limitation of cross-sectional data is that comparisons between average test scores of different age groups at a single time-point cannot reveal whether or not individuals age at very different rates. In contrast, longitudinal studies show that because people experience markedly different trajectories of change, differences in performance between members of a sample correspondingly increase with the ages at which they are compared. Unadjusted data from longitudinal studies also do not immediately reveal this increase in variance between individuals because this is progressively curtailed by selective dropout of the most frail and least able. When practice and dropout effects have been taken into consideration, it becomes clear that variance in ability between individuals, and also the average differences in ability between the most and least able persons in a sample, increases with age (Rabbitt et al., 2001, 2004).

Differences between individual trajectories of change are theoretically informative because they reflect the joint and interactive effects of the enormous diversity of different factors that prolong life and maintain competence. These include both heritable factors like immune system robustness, biological factors such as health and gender (Voitenko & Tokar, 1983) and other genetic factors (Pendleton et al., 2002; Payton et al., 2003; Yaffe, Cauley, Sands, & Browner, 1997). They also include factors that may derive from maternal advantage, such as differences in birth weight and thriving in infancy (Sorensenson, 1997), and also demographic and socioeconomic factors (Arbuckle, Gold & Andres, 1986), level of education (e.g., Evans et al., 1993; White et al., 1994), lifetime nutrition and health care (e.g., Rabbitt, Bent & McInnes, 1997), general health in old age and incidence of specific illnesses (Bent, Rabbitt, & Metcalf, 2000; Hertzog, Schaie, & Gribbin, 1978; Holland & Rabbitt, 1991), less exposure to toxicity and environmental hazards (Dirken, 1972), competence in everyday self-care (McInnes & Rabbitt, 1997), and incidence of depression and dysphoria in later life (e.g., Beekman, Deeg, van Tilburg, Smith & van Tilburg, 1995; McBride & Abeles, 2000; Rabbitt, Donlan, Watson, McInnes, & Bent, 1996). The identification and statistical control

of factors that promote diversity in longevity, and so maintenance of cognitive ability in later life is often problematic because each may be a proxy for several others. For example, because factors that promote longevity tend also to be associated with greater mental competence throughout the lifespan, we might expect that individuals who show higher ability as young adults will also live longer and so experience relatively slower cognitive declines. Thus the identification of factors that promote maintenance of intelligence in old age is even more complicated than is the identification of factors that determine rates of improvement and levels of asymptotic performance during infancy and childhood. For example, associations between particular genes and levels of mental ability in elderly populations are as likely to reflect indirect influences through prolongation of life as to signal any direct genetic determination of intellectual ability. Among other difficulties, this complicates attempts to answer apparently simple questions such as whether rates of decline in old age are affected by levels of youthful ability independently of the protective factors such as the socioeconomic advantages and better self-care that higher ability usually entails. For example, a unique population of nuns whose lifestyles were very similar after they joined their order as novices allowed an exceptionally well-controlled epidemiological study. Older nuns' levels of young adult intelligence were estimated from the semantic and syntactic complexity of personal statements that they had written just before taking their vows. This meant that the status in old age of more and less able nuns could be compared in relation to their youthful ability. It emerged that nuns who had higher levels of ability as young adults subsequently lived longer and experienced slower cognitive decline and lower incidence of dementias (Snowden et. al., 1994). While they are statistically convincing, these relationships between youthful intelligence and sustained competence in later life are hard to interpret. Nuns' lifespan levels of intellectual competence, health, and longevity were probably determined long before they wrote the essays on which their levels of ability were assessed, including their birth weights, infant and childhood nutrition, levels of socioeconomic advantage in healthcare and education, and many other factors.

Horn and his associates have made an important distinction between "crystallized" mental abilities involving acquired information and learned cognitive skills, such as vocabulary and use of language, and "fluid mental abilities" involving the ability to learn new information and unfamiliar tasks (Horn, 1982, 1987; Horn, Donaldson, & Engstrom, 1981). This excellent body of work has shown that crystallized abilities acquired early in life and maintained by continual practice into old age are relatively age-robust, but fluid abilities show marked declines. Levels of crystallized abilities in old age must, of course, depend to a considerable extent on levels of fluid abilities that will determine the speed and ease with which information and skills are acquired earlier in the lifespan. However, evidence that vocabulary remains stable or even improves into the eighth decade (Birren, Butler, Greenhouse, Sokoloff, & Yarrow, 1963; Rabbitt, 1993) means that elderly individuals' scores on vocabulary tests are good proxy measures for their young adult scores on tests of fluid intelligence. This suggests an alternative way to answer the question whether people's levels of gf when young affect their subsequent rates of loss of gf in old age. Comparisons of elderly persons' estimated youthful gf with their currently observed gf scores indicates that rates of decline in unadjusted intelligence test scores (UITSs) appear the same at all baseline levels of gf (Rabbitt, Chetwynd, & McInnis, 2003). More direct evidence from longitudinal studies also suggests that rates of decline in UITSs do not differ between individuals with different levels of ability (Rabbitt et al., 2004). These findings are strikingly similar to a common observation of child development: IQ scores, which are age-standardized, show a marked stability over a number of years of child development despite very large changes in absolute scores (e.g., Hindley & Owen, 1978). However, these correlations are not perfect (being around 0.6 from age 5 to 15). A much higher correlation would be expected if the cause of the initial individual differences drove the developmental change itself. Indeed, Bartels et al. (2002) have shown in a study of twins that the stability of IQ scores is largely due to the same genetic factors that contribute at all ages of testing, whereas nonshared environment contributes to any observed change. Interestingly, while shared environment contributes some variance to stability, it also contributes variance to change, and the authors speculate that this may be due to common effects of changing teachers each year in the Dutch school system. This pattern is consistent with the view of Anderson (1992) that the factors that cause individual differences and those that cause developmental change may be independent of each other.

Exploration of this consistency in rates of both developmental gain and age-related decline in intelligence is a central issue for this chapter.

VARIANCE ASSOCIATED WITH AGE IS A SMALL PROPORTION OF THE VARIANCE IN ABILITIES

It is important to recognize the distinction between the total variance in cognitive abilities between individuals that is associated with all of the multifarious factors that have made them different from each other and the relatively small proportion of this total variance that is associated with differences in their ages. This latter proportion of age-related variance can be estimated from simple correlations between individuals' calendar ages and their scores on cognitive tasks. Table 23.1 shows correlations between age and performance on 14 different cognitive tests obtained from over 2,000 members of the University of Manchester volunteer sample, ages 49 and 92 years. Correlations between age and scores on three different intelligence tests, six different memory tests, and two different tests of speed of information processing are all negative, and statistically reliable, but are also very modest, accounting for only between 3.8% and 20.5% of all the variance between individuals that is associated with all of the biological and demographic factors that have made them different from each other. That is to say, compared to individual differences in intrinsic, lifelong ability and the the effects of biological and other events experienced during their lifetimes, differences in individuals' calendar ages account for very modest proportions of the total variance in mental abilities between them. As we have seen, the contributions of age to variance in scores on three different vocabulary tests—the Mill Hill A and B and the Wechsler Adult Intelligence Scales (WAIS)—are relatively minor and consistent with many previous findings.

We have seen that competencies that depend on learned information show much smaller effects of age than do fluid mental abilities. A different question is whether age affects some fluid abilities earlier and more severely than others. Speculations that the process of aging may be "modular" or "differentiated" between functional neurophysiological systems, and so between the mental abilities that they support, have been encouraged by neurophysiological and neuroanatomical evidence that the processes of biological aging affect different areas of the brain at different times and rates. Postmortem studies and more recent imaging studies agree that age-related changes generally occur earlier in the prefrontal cortex and hippocampus than in other parts of the brain (e.g., Albert, 1993; Haugh & Egers, 1991; Scheibel & Scheibel, 1975; Raz, 2000). This evidence for local or differentiated brain aging has prompted many behavioral comparisons between older and younger people on executive tasks that are putatively diagnostic of damage to frontal and prefrontal systems in young and middle-aged adults (Hasher, Quig, & May, 1997; Hasher, Stoltzfus, Zacks, & Rypma, 1991; Lamar, Zonderman, & Resnick, 2002; Parkin & Lawrence, 1994). While on balance there does seem to be evidence that prefrontal functions may be especially sensitive to age, results have been mixed. One reason for failures of replication is methodological problems with the tasks on which older and younger individuals have been compared. Many tasks that have been considered good clinical diagnostic tests of prefrontal damage have poor test/retest reliability, making longitudinal comparisons problematic (Lowe & Rabbitt, 1998). There are also problems of test construct validity (Burgess, 1997). Scores on tests that have been assumed to assess the same cognitive functions correlate only weakly (Lowe and Rabbitt,1998). Finally, and most important, both the shared variance between test scores and the shared variance between test scores and calendar age are usually completely accounted for when UITS are entered as additional predictors into regression equations (Lowe and Rabbitt, 1998; Phillips, 1998). Similar meta-analyses suggest that the effects of age between 20 and 80 years on particular tasks, such as the Stroop test, can be more parsimoniously explained as consequences of simple scaling effects of decision times rather than of selective impairment of a particular frontal function such as inhibition (e.g., Verhaeghen & Cerella, 2002; Verhaeghen & De Meersman, 1998a, 1998b). The implication of this is that the greater age sensitivity of particular frontal and executive tasks is only apparent and disappears when differences in gf or SOP are taken into consideration.

A more general theoretical difficulty has emerged from computer simulations showing that apparently very disparate task demands can be supported by the same system architecture. This difficulty has brought into question the functional specificity of particular tasks such as indices of frontal and executive impairments (e.g., Kimberg & Farah, 1993). Such demonstrations imply that if levels of ability on different categories of tasks do, indeed, become increasingly decoupled by age, this process may be evident only between extremely broad categories of task demands.

This view of the broad range of frontal or executive abilities is supported by compelling behavioral and neuroimaging studies that suggest that well-validated intelligence tests such as the Cattell and Cattell (1960) Culture Fair test are the most efficient tests we have of the executive functions associated with frontal and prefrontal systems (Duncan, Burgess, & Emslie, 1995; Duncan, Emslie, Williams, Johnson, & Freer, 1996; Duncan & Owen, 2000). The inference drawn from such findings is that age-related variance in performance of all cognitive tasks, including those that make demands on frontal and executive systems, can be mainly or entirely accounted for by reduction of gf indexed by declines in intelligence test scores.

The methodological problems in evaluating the frontal aging hypothesis leave open the alternative idea that the most parsimonious description of age-related declines in fluid mental abilities is that they are driven by corresponding declines in some single Global Functional Performance Characteristic (GPC). It is, of course, assumed that the GPC must have some identifiable neurophysiological basis, but perhaps pending further investigations along the lines initiated by Duncan and his colleagues, none has yet been specified. At present, GPC models rest entirely on behavioral evidence that all or most age-related declines in mental abilities can be parsimoniously accounted for in terms of changes in some single master-performance characteristic of the functional cognitive system. The two candidates proposed have been speed of processing (SOP), indexed by decision speed in simple laboratory tasks (Salthouse, 1985, 1991, 1996), and gf indexed by age-unadjusted scores on intelligence tests (Deary, 2001). In the view of some investigators, such as Anderson (1992) and Deary (2001), these two measures of performance are functionally closely associated because SOP reflects performance parameters of the neurophysiological system that form the biological basis of intelligence (see also Eysenck, 1988; Jensen, 1982).

The common prediction from GPC models is that age affects performance on all or most cognitive tasks in proportion to the extent that they make demands on a single, easily measurable task performance index, SOP or UITS. A corollary prediction is that scores on tests of speed or *gf* should mainly, or entirely, account for that small proportion of variance between individuals on all or most other cognitive tasks that is associated with differences in their ages.

Lindenberger and Potter (1998) have developed a useful extension of multivariate regression analysis to estimate the precise proportion of age-related variance in performance on one task that can be accounted for by scores on another task or by some other biological marker. Note that in the present context, this method allows us to compute the amount of variance between individuals in performance of a cognitive task that is associated with differences in their ages (i.e., R^2 for age) and then compute the proportion of this age-associated variance that is associated with some other variable. We applied this *t*-method to the same test scores for which age-related variance is shown in Table 23.1 to compute the proportions of age-related variance between individuals that is associated with unadjusted scores and with scores on a test of *gf*, the Cattell & Cattell (1960) Culture Fair test, and on two measures of information processing speed: a letter/letter coding task (see Savage, 1984) and a simple visual search task in which participants scanned printed pages of capital letters of the alphabet to locate and mark all occurrences of the targets *O* and *I*.

Scores on the Culture Fair test account for between 86% and 100% of that part of the variance in

scores on each of the other tests that is associated with differences in participants' ages between 49 and 92 years. Letter/letter coding speed does just as well, accounting for between 85% and 100% of variance. Visual search speed does rather less well, but still accounts for between 65% and 100% of age-related variance in all other tasks. It should be noted that while the visual search task is very simple and involves virtually no memory load, performance on the letter/letter coding task has been shown to strongly depend on more complex factors, principally the number of elements of the letter/letter transformation code that can be learned while carrying out the task (Piccinin & Rabbitt, 1999).

Note that while the proportions of age-related variance in test scores that can be accounted for by tests of *gf* and SOP seem impressively large, Table 23.1 reminds us that in absolute terms they are small because they refer to the very modest amounts of variance that are associated with age. That is, they are proportions of only between 6% and 21 % of the total variance between individuals that is brought about by all of the many factors that make their test scores different from each other. Nevertheless, consistently with GPC theory, it seems that almost all of this small absolute amount of age-related variance can be accounted for by differences in scores on a well-designed and standardized intelligence test or by scores on either of two simple measures of SOP.

Table 23.2 also makes the point that in contrast to their strong predictions of age-related variance in tasks involving learning and memory, tests of *gf* or of SOP account for much smaller amounts of age-related variance in vocabulary tests. This is, of course, entirely consistent with the findings on which Horn and his associates have based their important distinction between age-sensitive fluid abilities and age-robust crystallized abilities (Horn, 1982, 1987; Horn et al., 1981). It seems that long practice of a skill, and perhaps especially its acquisition in early childhood, brings about changes in the neurophysiological structures that support it that make it less vulnerable to age-related changes and possibly also to trauma such as closed head injury. Indeed, there is some evidence from functional imaging that very intensive and extended practice at acquiring particular databases is associated with local increase in volume of the neural structures involved in the representation of specific, delimited bodies of information, such as the "knowledge" of routes acquired by London taxi-cab drivers (Maguire,

TABLE 23.1. Correlations between age (42–96 years) and scores on cognitive tasks; also percentages of total variance between individuals accounted for by age

Task	Correlation	Variance
AH4-1 intelligence test	−.366**	13.4%
AH4-2 intelligence test	−.453**	20.5%
Cattell ingelligence test	−.436**	19.0%
Mill Hill A vocabulary test	−.026	0.01%
Mill Hill B vocabulary test	−.048*	0.02%
WAIS vocabulary test	−.169**	2.6%
Letter/Letter Coding Speed	−.431**	18.5%
Visual Search Speed	−.347**	12.0%
Digit Span	−.194**	3.8%
Free recall of 10 words	−.297**	8.8%
Free recall of 30 words	−.323**	10.4%
Recall 12 object names	−.377**	14.2%
Recall people information	−.293**	8.6%
Picture recognition memory	−.247**	6.1%

Note: **Significant at *p* < .01; *Significant at *p* < .05

TABLE 23.2. Percentages of age-related variance in task scores predicted by scores on the Cattell Culture Fair Test, letter/letter coding speed, and visual search speed

Task	Cattell	Letter/ Letter	Visual Search
AH4-1 intelligence test	100%	100%	93%
AH4-2 intelligence test	98%	96%	88%
Cattell ingelligence test	—	99%	81%
Letter/Letter Coding Speed	99%	—	92%
Visual Search Speed	93%	99%	—
Digit Span	94%	98%	100%
Free recall of 10 words	86%	88%	73%
Free recall of 30 words	91%	93%	80%
Recall 12 object names	86%	88%	76%
Recall people information	88%	85%	65%
Picture recognition memory	95%	96%	83%
Cumulative learning of 15 nouns	92%	93%	81%

Frackowiak & Frith, 1997). The important topic of the neurological basis of knowledge acquisition and maintenance falls beyond the scope of this chapter, which is concerned with the much more limited issue as to how well GPC theory accounts for age-related changes only in those mental abilities that Horn and his associates would classify as being fluid rather than crystallized.

It is important to note that while these findings are consistent with GPC models, they do not resolve the related, but conceptually different, question whether age affects some fluid abilities earlier or more severely than others. Even if changes in single-performance characteristics such as *gf* or SOP are responsible for most of the age-related variance in all or most cognitive tasks, it might still be the case that some tasks make substantially greater demands on SOP and *gf* than do others. These tasks might well be earliest affected by initial, slight declines in *gf* or SOP and would show correspondingly larger decrements as these declines proceed. The most satisfactory approach to this question would be to compare rates of change in performance on different tasks within large samples of people who are longitudinally tested over considerable periods of time. Pending availability of such data we are reduced to the weaker approach of analyzing cross-sectional data to discover whether correlations between scores on different tasks change as sample ages increase. Declines in the size of these correlations with

increasing sample age would be consistent with the idea that age impairs performance on some of them more than on others so that scores appear increasingly decoupled or differentiated as older samples are assessed. Findings that correlations between test scores remain constant would suggest that age affects all of them to a similar extent. A finding that correlations between test scores increase with sample age would be more difficult to interpret. Such dedifferentiation between levels of performance on different tasks would, at least, be consistent with the hypothesis that all abilities depend on a common functional system performance parameter and that because this dependency increases with age, correlations between scores on tests of different abilities become correspondingly stronger. In the next section we will be using evidence about age effects on differentiation as another way of approaching the question of what cognitive functions decline with age. Finally, we will examine a simple simulation of the differentiation of abilities in developing children and how this might apply to two contrasting models of the effect of aging on cognition: (1) that aging reflects a global decline in all cognitive functions (GPC model), or (2) that age affects some abilities more than others (specific abilities model, or SAM).

DOES PERFORMANCE ON TESTS OF FLUID ABILITIES BECOME MORE OR LESS DIFFERENTIATED AS AGE INCREASES?

Table 23.3 shows correlations between scores on the AH4-1 intelligence test and on 11 other tasks involving fluid mental abilities obtained in samples aged from 49 to 69 and from 70 to 92 years.

Correlations between AH4-1 test scores and scores on other tests are higher in the older groups in 8 out of 11 cases. This serves as an illustration of a general trend apparent in the correlations between scores on all tests. While these findings are uncongenial for the hypothesis that different fluid mental abilities decline at different rates, it is important to note that they do not yet provide clear evidence that all fluid abilities are driven by a common decline in a single functional performance characteristic. GPC models might equally well predict that correlations between test scores should remain constant across age groups because declines in the common performance characteristic affect all tests to a similar extent or that correlations should decline because some tests make

TABLE 23.3. Correlations between scores on the AH4-1 intelligence test and scores on other cognitive tasks. Correlations are shown separately for participants aged 49–69 years and 70–92 years

Task	49–69 years	70–92 years
AH4-1 intelligence test	.792	.813
Cattell ingelligence test	.694	.715
Letter/Letter Coding Speed	.630	.662
Visual Search Speed	.479	.414
Digit Span	.293	.410
Free recall of 10 words	.311	.319
Free recall of 30 words	.425	.417
Recall 12 object names	.291	.324
Recall people information	.391	.267
Picture recognition memory	.260	.377
Cumulative learning of 15 nouns	.468	.529

greater demands on the "master" performance characteristic than others do. Clearly we need a formalism for specifying these predictions. But first let us return to the data.

At first sight, the trend for higher correlations between different abilities in the older groups seems evidence for dedifferentiation of mental abilities and is consistent with the idea that as age increases, declines in all abilities are driven by declines in some basic common resource or functional characteristic of the cognitive system. However, while this idea may be straightforward enough, there are methodological problems that need to be addressed. Psychometric measures of abilities seem to be more differentiated at higher IQs (Detterman & Daniel, 1989; Deary & Pagliari, 1991; Deary et al., 1996)—that is, the general ability factor, g, accounts for less of the individual differences variance. In addition, measures of basic processes have lower inter-correlations at above average IQ levels (Detterman & Daniel, 1989). Since old age markedly reduces scores on most cognitive tests, apparent dedifferentiation in older samples may be another example of this "Detterman effect." The Detterman effect may not reflect differences in the functional characteristics of the cognitive systems of more and less able young people and of young and elderly adults but only the nonlinearity of relationships between scores on the different tests on which they are assessed. That is, apparent dedifferentiation might be regarded as a simple scaling artifact with no functional consequence. However, in at least one exemplar of a GPC model this nonlinearity is not an artifact

but reflects underlying functional relationships (Anderson, 1992). Anderson (1999) has attempted to formalize the possible relationships between age and differentiation in child development. We will explore the properties of this particular model for children and attempt to draw implications for our interpretation of dedifferentiation in elderly adults.

MODELS THAT MAP HYPOTHETICAL COGNITIVE ABILITIES ONTO PSYCHOMETRIC PERFORMANCE

Anderson's (1992) theory of the minimal cognitive architecture underlying intelligence and development describes two routes to knowledge acquisition. One of those routes (thought) is subject to the large individual differences that are typically measured by IQ-type tests of intelligence. The other route in the theory (knowledge acquisition via dedicated information-processing modules) need not concern us here as this route does not contribute to IQ-related individual differences in ability. Knowledge is acquired through thought by the implementation of knowledge-acquisition algorithms that are written in a code (a kind of language of thought) that comes in two basic varieties, generated by two alternative specific processors (SP1 and SP2). One specific processor generates knowledge-acquisition algorithms in a code that is best described as visual-spatial, the other in a code best described as verbal-propositional. It might be helpful to think of the specific processors as being akin to two different kinds of computer programming languages, each better suited to different classes of problems, but like all computer programs, problems solvable using one code are in principle solvable using the other. The theory states that the latent "power" (or ability) of these two processors varies between individuals and moreover is uncorrelated in the population as a whole. This means that if they were the only mechanisms that contributed to individual differences in intelligence, then there would be two independent intelligences (verbal and spatial). However, they are not the only mechanisms. The knowledge-acquisition algorithm from each specific processor is implemented on a basic processing mechanism (BPM). The BPM varies in its speed and this constrains the complexity of the algorithms that can be implemented. Simply put, faster speeds allow more complex (powerful) algorithms to be implemented. The consequence of this architecture is that the manifest abilities in the visual-spatial and verbal-propositional domains will become correlated. So it is the constraint that the SOP of the BPM imposes on specific processor algorithms that is the fount of general intelligence.

The Detterman effect is a natural consequence of this architecture. If we consider individual differences between children of the same age, or within samples of older and younger adults, SOP constrains the expression of specific abilities such that at faster processing speed the latent differences between the specific processors become more manifest and correlations between tasks measuring these abilities should decrease. Simply put the basic model states:

$$SA = \ln(BPMspeed) \times \ln(SPl)$$

The manifest specific ability (SA) is a function of the natural logarithm of the latent power of the specific processor (SPl) multiplied by the natural logarithm of the speed of the basic processing mechanism (BPM). This equation captures the requisite property of the theory—namely, that the constraint of speed of processing on the manifest power of a specific processor decreases as speed increases. This should lead to more differentiated specific abilities in higher IQ groups of children of the same age, although in the population of children as a whole there will be a large g-factor (i.e., differences in IQ will largely reflect differences in SOP). There is of course a shift in level between hypothetical cognitive processes underlying abilities and measurement of those abilities themselves by psychometric tests. So we need a further stage to simulate the consequences of differences in underlying cognitive functions on hypothetical test scores.

MODELING PSYCHOMETRIC MEASURES OF ABILITY IN DEVELOPING CHILDREN

In the theory of the minimal cognitive architecture, specific processors underlie specific abilities, but only combinations of specific abilities themselves can be directly measured by any psychometric test. The global or g-factor comes about because the hypothetical process underlying this (SOP) operates on the expression of those specific processors. In other words, in psychometric tests, speed of processing is never directly measured but its influence on test performance

is felt through the manifest specific abilities. Let us suppose that the intelligence test battery consists of heterogeneous tasks that rely on different loadings of each specific ability. For example, let us assume that the manifest specific ability one (SA_1) is largely spatial and the manifest specific ability two (SA_2) is largely verbal ability. Given 9 different subtests in a test battery, graded on their loading on each specific ability, the subtests could range from $(0.9 \times SA_1) + (0.1 \times SA_2)$—a highly spatial test—through to $(0.1 \times SA_1) + (0.9 \times SA_2)$—a highly verbal test. We can then take our estimate of IQ as the simple sum of the subtest scores. The resulting psychometric battery can then be factor-analyzed, and when we do this what we find is a smaller percentage of the variance of the resulting scores being due to the g factor in higher IQ groups. In short, this model predicts psychometric differentiation of specific abilities with increasing IQ, as it was designed to do.

MODELS THAT CONTRAST GLOBAL DEVELOPMENTAL CHANGE WITH THE DEVELOPMENT OF SPECIFIC ABILITIES IN CHILDREN

We can now extend this individual differences model to determine the consequences of alternative models for the development of abilities in children. Anderson (1999) contrasted two models, and while there are many other variants possible, we will stick to this simple contrast to make our point about what the current data from differentiation can tell us about alternative underlying functional models.

In the global model (GPC), speed of processing increases with developmental age. In the specific abilities model (SAM), the power of each of the specific processors changes with age but SOP does not. Comparing the psychometric consequences of each model is interesting. It might be thought that the development of specific abilities might lead to more differentiation between abilities in older children. However, simulated data show that the development of SAM leads to dedifferentiation, while increasing SOP with age in children but no developmental change in the underlying specific abilities (GPC) leads to increasing differentiation with age. So, if we took increasing differentiation with developmental age (lower intercorrelations between tests) to be the product of the development of specific abilities in children we would be wrong—in these models it is the consequence of increasing SOP.

APPLICATION TO COGNITIVE CHANGE IN THE ELDERLY

The relationship between general and specific abilities in the developmental model might illuminate our original proposition: that changes in patterns of correlation between abilities and, in particular, the possible dedifferentiation of abilities with age, might tell us something about the specificity of age effects on cognitive abilities in the elderly. To the extent that a similar model might apply to the elderly, the modeling suggests strongly that the increased correlation between cognitive abilities in older samples could be due to a general decline in a global performance characteristic . However, there are at least two important caveats to this hypothesis.

First, the developmental model presented here applies to those abilities that normally underlie the variance in IQ. So if our battery of hypothetical tests were to be factor-analyzed it would reveal the commonly found hierarchical structure with a large g factor at the apex and two smaller group factors (verbal and spatial) sitting underneath. The specific abilities underlying group factors may be different in kind from those that are commonly contrasted with GPCs in the gerontological literature—in particular, executive functions. Anderson (2001) has argued that the cluster of processes that might constitute executive functions contributes to a developmental g-factor in children. The developmental model presented here does not consider the effect that such modular abilities could have on differentiation. It might be that those abilities would act just like other GPCs (for example, SOP in the minimal cognitive architecture) on the differentiation of abilities. However, testing this possibility would require further modeling.

Second, the particular version of differentiation discussed here is in the sense proposed by Detterman (1987; Detterman & Daniel, 1989). Here the question is what the relationship between elemental components of cognitive processing is and whether these change with level of IQ and/or age. Another usage is to distinguish between the mechanics and pragmatics of cognition (e.g., Baltes, Lindenberger, & Staudinger, 1998), or the better known fluid and crys-tallized g of Cattell (1971) and Horn (1982). This usage has quite a different meaning to the differentiation of abilities modeled here. Our modeling is of the possible changes among abilities that contribute to the mechanics of intelligence or fluid g—this model could not apply without qualification to the pragmatics, or crystallized component, of intelligence. This is particularly important considering that the relationship between mechanic/fluid and pragmatic/crystallized components are likely to be different in children and elderly adults.

CONCLUSIONS

Analysis of cross-sectional data from a large elderly sample showed that age impaired performance on all tests that individuals were given, except for some vocabulary tests. However, the amounts of total variance in test performance associated with differences in age between 49 and 92 years were very modest—not exceeding 22%. Nevertheless, nearly all of this age-related variance in performance was predicted by individuals' current scores on the Cattell and Cattell (1960) intelligence test or on either of two simple tasks that index the speed with which individuals can make simple decisions. This is consistent with the speculation that declines in all fluid mental abilities in old age can be parsimoniously described in terms of corresponding declines in speed or *gf*. Further analysis of the data set showed that levels of correlations between scores on intelligence tests and other tests of fluid intelligence, between intelligence tests and other cognitive tests, and between other cognitive tests are consistently higher in a sample aged from 70 to 92 years than in a sample aged from 49 to 69 years. Modeling of a theory of differentiation in children suggests that the most likely explanation of this effect is a decline in some GPCs in elderly adults. However, the consequences of age-related changes in what are usually considered to be "specific" cognitive functions that can have general consequences on cognitive abilities, most obviously executive functions, await further modeling. It may turn out that the distinction between global resources, such as SOP, and specific functions that are commonly used in most cognitive domains will be pivotal in answering the question of whether age-related decline is general or specific.

References

Anderson, M. (1992). *Intelligence and development: A cognitive theory.* Oxford, UK: Blackwell.

Anderson, M. (1999). Project development: Taking stock. In M. Anderson, *The development of intelligence* (pp. 311–332). Hove, UK: Psychology Press.

Anderson, M. (2001). Conceptions of intelligence. *Journal of Child Psychology & Psychiatry, 42*(3), 287–298.

Arbuckle, T. Y., Gold, D., & Andres, D. (1986). Cognitive functioning of older people in relation to social and personality variables. *Psychology and Aging, 1,* 55–62.

Baltes, P. B., Lindenberger, U., & Staudinger, U. M. (1998). Life-span theory in developmental psychology. In, R. M. Lerner (Ed.), *Thoretical models of human development* (5th ed., 1029–1143). New York: Wiley.

Beekman, A. T. F., Deeg, D. J. H., van Tilburg, T., Smit, J. H., & van Tilburg, W. (1995). Major and minor depression in later life: A study of prevalence and risk factors. *Journal of Affective Disorders, 65,* 65–75.

Bent, N. C., Rabbitt, P. M. A., & Metcalf, D. (2000). Diabetes mellitus and the rate of cognitive change. *British Journal of Clinical Psychology, 39,* 349–362.

Birren, J. E., Butler, R. N., Greenhouse, S. W., Sokoloff, L., & Yarrow, M. R. (1963). *Human aging.* Publication no. 986. Washington, DC: US Government Printing Office.

Burgess, P. W. (1997). Theory and methodology in executive function research. In P. M. A. Rabbitt (Ed), *Methodology of frontal and executive function* (pp. 81–116). Hove, UK: Psychology Press.

Cattell, R. B. (1971). *Abilities: Their structure growth and action.* Boston: Houghton Mifflin.

Cattell, R. B., & Cattell, A. K. S. (1960). *The individual or group Culture Fair intelligence test.* Champaign, IL: I.P.A.T.

Deary, I. (2000). *Looking down on human intelligence.* Oxford: Oxford University Press.

Deary, I. J., Egan, V., Gibson, G. J., Austin, E. J., Brand, C. R., & Kellaghan, T. (1996). Intelligence and the differentiation hypothesis. *Intelligence, 23,* 105–132.

Deary, I. J., & Pagliari, C. (1991). The strength of g and different levels of ability Have Detterman and Daniels rediscovered Spearman's Law of diminishing returns? *Intelligence, 2,* 247–250.

Detterman, D. K. (1987). Theoretical notions of intelligence and mental retardation. *American Journal of Mental Deficiency, 92,* 2–11.

Detterman, D. K., & Daniel, M. H. (1989). Correlations of mental tests with each other and with cognitive variables are highest for low-IQ groups. *Intelligence, 13,* 349–359.

Dirken, J. M. (1972). *Functional age of industrial workers.* Groningen, The Netherlands:Wolters-Noordhof.

Duncan, J., Burgess, P., & Emslie, H. (1995). Fluid intelligence after frontal lobe lesions. *Neuropsychologia, 33,* 261–268.

Duncan, J., Emslie, H., Williams, P., Johnson, R., & Freer, C. (1996). Intelligence and the frontal lobe: The organization of goal-directed behavior. *Cognitive Psychology, 30,* 257–303.

Duncan, J., & Owen, A. M. (2000). Common regions of the human frontal lobe recruited by diverse cognitive demands. *Trends in Neurosciences, 23,* 475–483.

Evans, D. A., Beckett, L. A., Albert, M. S., Hebert, L. E., Scherr, P. A., Funkenstein, H. H., & Taylor, J. O. (1993). Level of education and change in cognitive function in a community population of older persons. *Annuals of Epidemiology, 3,* 71–77.

Eysenck, H. J. (1988). The concept of "intelligence": Useful or useless? *Intelligence, 12,* 1–16.

Gur, R. C., Gur, R. E., Orbist, W. D., Skolnik, B. E., & Reivitch, M. (1987). Age and regional cerebral blood flow at rest and during cognitive activity. *Archives of General Psychiatry, 44,* 617–621.

Hasher, L., Quig, M. B., & May, C. P. (1997). Inhibitory control over no-longer relevant information: Adult age differences. *Memory & Cognition, 25,* 286–295.

Hasher, L., Stoltzfus, E. R., Zacks, R. T., & Rypma, B. (1991). Age and inhibition. Journal of Experimental Psychology: Learning, Memory, and Cognition, 17, 163–169.

Haugh, H., & Eggers, R. (1991). Morphometry of the human cortex cerebri and cortex striatum during aging. *Neurobiology of Aging, 12,* 336–338.

Heim, A.W. (1970). *The AH4 group tests of intelligence.* Windsor: NFER/Nelson.

Hertzog, C., Schaie, K. W., & Gribbin, K. (1978). Cardiovascular disease and changes in intellectual function from middle to old age. *Journal of Gerontology, 33,* 872–883.

Hindley, C. B. & Owen, C. F. (1978). The extent of individual changes in IQ for ages between 6 months and 17 years, in a British longitudinal sample. *Journal of Child Psychology and Psychiatry, 19,* 329–350.

Holland, C. M., & Rabbitt, P. M. A. (1991). The course and causes of cognitive change with advancing age. *Reviews in Clinical Gerontology, 1,* 81–96.

Horn, J. L. (1982). The theory of fluid and crystallized intelligence in relation to concepts of cognitive psychology and aging in adulthood. In F. I. M.

Craik & S. Trehub (Eds.), *Aging and cognitive processes* (pp. 183–232). New York: Plenum.

Horn, J. L. (1987). A context for understanding information processing studies of human abilities. In P. A.Vernon (Ed), *Speed of information processing and intelligence* (pp 201–238). Norwood, NJ: Ablex.

Horn, J. L., Donaldson, G., & Engstrom, R. (1981). Application, memory and fluid intelligence decline in adulthood. *Research on Aging, 3*, 33–84.

Jensen, A. R. (1982). Reaction time and psychometric g. In H. J. Eysenck (Ed), *A model for intelligence*. Berlin: Springer-Verlag.

Kimberg, D.Y., & Farah, M. J. (1993). A unified account of impairments following frontal lobe damage: The role of working memory in complex organised behaviour. *Journal of Experimental Psychology: General, 122*, 411–428.

Lachman, R., Lachman, J. L., & Taylor, D. W. (1982). Reallocation of mental resources over the productive lifespan: assumptions and task analyses. In F. I. M. Craik & S. Trehub (Eds), *Aging and cognitive processes* (pp. 96–132). New York: Plenum.

Lamar, M., Zonderman, A. B., & Resnick, S. (2002). Contribution of specific cognitive processes to executive functioning in an aging population. *Neuropsychology, 16*, 156–162.

Lindenberger, U., & Potter, U. (1998). The complex nature of unique and shared effects in hierarchical linear regression: Implications for developmental psychology. *Psychological Methods, 3*, 218–230.

Lowe, C., & Rabbitt, P. M. A. (1998). Test/re-test reliability of the CANTAB and ISPOCD neuropsychological batteries: Theoretical and practical issues. *Neuropsychologia, 36*, 915–923.

Maguire, E., Frackowiak, R. S. J., & Frith, C. D. (1997). Recalling routes around London: Activation of the right hippocampus in taxi drivers. *Journal of Neuroscience, 17*, 7103–7110.

McBride, A. M., & Abeles, N. (2000). Depressive symptoms and cognitive performance in older adults. *Clinical Gerontologist, 21*, 27–47.

McInnes, L., & Rabbitt, P. M. (1997). The relationship between functional ability and cognitive ability among elderly people. In *Facts and research in gerontology* (pp. 34–45). Paris: Serdi.

Parkin, A. J., & Lawrence, A. (1994). A dissociation in the relation between memory tasks and frontal lobe tests in the normal elderly. *Neuropsychologia, 32*, 1523–1532.

Payton, A., Holland, F., Diggle, P., Rabbitt, P., Horan, M., Davidson, Y., Gibbons, L., Worthington, J., Ollier, W. E. R., & Pendleton, N. (2003). Cathepsin D exon 2 polymorphism associated with general

intelligence in a healthy older population. *Molecular Psychiatry, 8*, 14–18.

Pendleton, N., Payton, A., van den Boogerd, E. H., Holland, F., Diggle, P., Rabbitt, P. M. A., Horan, M. A., Worthington, J., & Ollier, W. E. (2002). Apolipoprotein E genotype does not predict decline in intelligence in older adults. *Neurosciences Letters, 324*, 74–76.

Phillips, L. H. (1998). Do "frontal tests" measure executive function? Issues of assessment and evidence from fluency tests. In P. Rabbitt (ed.), *Methodology of frontal and executive function* (pp. 191–194). Hove, UK: Psychology Press.

Piccinin, A. M., & Rabbitt, P. M. A. (1999). Contribution of cognitive abilities to performance and improvement on a substitution-coding task. *Psychology and Aging, 14*, 539–551.

Rabbitt, P. M. (1993). Does it all go together when it goes? *Quarterly Journal of Experimental Psychology, 46*(A), 385–433.

Rabbitt, P., Bent, N., & McInnes, L. (1997). Health, age and mental ability. *Irish Journal of Psychology, 18*, 104–131.

Rabbitt, P. M., Chetwynd, A., & McInnes, L. (2003). Do clever brains age more slowly? Further exploration of a nun result. *British Journal of Psychology, 94*, 63–71.

Rabbitt, P., Diggle, P., Smith, D., Holland, F., & McInnes, L. (2001) Identifying and separating the effects of practice and of cognitive aging during a large longitudinal study of elderly community residents. *Neuropsychologia 39*, 532–543.

Rabbitt, P., Diggle P., Holland, F., & McInnes, L. (2004). Practice and drop-out effects during a 17 year longitudinal study of normal aging. *Journals of Gerontology, Series B., Psychological Sciences and Social Sciences, 59*, P. 84–P97.

Rabbitt, P. M., Donlan, C., Bent, N., McInnes, L., & Abson, V. (1993). The University of Manchester Age and Cognitive Performance Research Centre and North East Age Research longitudinal programmes 1982 to 1997. *Zeitschrift Gerontology, 26*, 176–183.

Rabbitt, P. M. A., Donlan, C., Watson, P., McInnes, L., & Bent, N. (1996). Unique and interactive effects of depression, age, socio-economic advantage and gender on cognitive performance of normal healthy older people. *Psychology and Aging, 10*, 221–235.

Rabbitt, P. M., Watson, P., Donlan, C., Bent, L., & McInnes, L. (1994). Subject attrition in a longitudinal study of cognitive performance in community-based elderly people. In *Facts and research in gerontology* (pp 203–207). Paris: Serdi.

Raz, N. (2000). Aging of the brain and its impact on cognitive performance: Integration of structural and behavioral findings. In F. I. M. Craik & T. Salthouse (Eds.), *Handbook of Aging and cognition (2nd ed)* (pp. 1–90). Mahwah, NJ: Lawrence Erlbaum.

Salthouse, T. A. (1985). *A cognitive theory of aging.* Berlin: Springer-Verlag.

Salthouse, T. A. (1991). *Theoretical perspectives on cognitive aging.* Hillsdale, NJ: Lawrence Erlbaum Associates.

Salthouse, T. A. (1996, April). *Predictors of cognitive aging: What can be learned from correlational research?* Paper presented at the Cognitive Aging Conference, Atlanta, GA.

Savage, R. D. (1984). *Alphabet Coding Task – 15.* Perth, Australia: Murdock University Press.

Schaie, K. W., Labouvie, G. V., & Barrett, T. J. (1973). Selective attrition effects in a fourteen-year study of adult intelligence. *Journal of Gerontology, 28,* 328–334.

Scheibel, M. E., & Scheibel, A. B. (1975). Structural changes in the aging brain. In H. Brody, D. Harmon, and J. M. Ordy (Eds.), *Aging* (Vol. 1, pp. 11–37). New York: Raven Press.

Shallice, T., & Burgess, P. W. (1991). Higher-order cognitive impairments and frontal lobe lesions in man. In H. S. Levin, H. M. Eisenberg, & A. L. Benton (Eds.), *Frontal lobe function and dysfunction* (pp. 43–76). New York: Oxford University Press.

Shilling, V. M., Chetwynd, A., & Rabbitt, P. M. A. (2002). Individual inconsistency across measures of inhibition: An investigation of the construct validity of inhibition in older adults. *Neuropsychologia, 40,* 605–619.

Snowdon, D. A., Kemper, S. J., Mortimer, J. A., Greiner, L. H., Wekstein, D. R., & Markesbery, W. R. (1996). Linguistic ability in early life and cognitive function and Alzheimer's disease in later Life. Findings from the Nun study. *Journal of the American Medical Association, 21,* 528–532.

Sorensenson, H. T. (1997). Birth weight and cognition: A historical cohort study. *British Medical Journal, 315,* 401–479.

Verhaeghen, P., & Cerella, J. (2002). Aging, executive control and attention: A review of meta-analyses. *Neuroscience and BioBehavioral Reviews, 26,* 849–857.

Verhaeghen, P., & De Meersman, L.(1998a). Aging and negative priming: A meta-analysis. *Psychology and Aging, 13,* 435–444.

Verhaeghen, P., & De Meersman, L. (1998b). Aging and the Stroop effect: A meta-analysis. *Psychology and Aging, 13,* 120–126.

Voitenko, V. P., & Tokar, A.V. (1983). The assessment of biological age and sex differences of human aging. *Experimental Aging Research, 9,* 239–244.

White, L. R., Katzman, R., Losonczy, K., et al. (1994). Association of education with incidence of cognitive impairment in three established populations for epidemiological studies of the elderly. *Journal of Clinical Epidemiology. 47,* 363–377.

Yaffe, K., Cauley, J., Sands, L., & Browner, W. (1997) Apolipoprotein E phenotype and cognitive decline in a prospective study of elderly community women. *Archives of Neurology. 54,* 1110–1114.

24

Cognitive Developmental Research from Lifespan Perspectives: The Challenge of Integration

Shu-Chen Li

Paul B. Baltes

Historically, at least two main approaches have been taken to construct lifespan theory (Baltes, 1987). One is to attend to age-specific developmental specialties (e.g., child language development or memory aging) and explore ways of combining them in a cumulative, additive manner. This approach generally yields in-depth coverage of specific mechanisms and processes, such as children's acquisition of cognitive strategies or aging of different memory processes. The challenge here lies in developing general frameworks for comparing and contrasting the universalities and specificities of development across life periods. The other approach is to focus on the entire lifespan and identify general principles of lifelong development within and around which age-specific processes revolve and operate. Such an approach would immediately highlight the "growth–maintenance–decline" dynamic of lifespan cognitive development. The difficulty in this case is the gain of macro understanding at the cost of micro age-specific phenomena. The perspectives presented in this chapter are closer to the latter approach.

Taking the entire lifespan as the conceptual starting point for investigating cognitive development is not easy. The stereotypical agism of "childhood is growth and old age is decline," as well as professional specializations that focus on specific age periods, suggests clear-cut discontinuity. Efforts at integration, therefore, need to overcome such simplistic, conventional expectations. Integration requires a special investment in seeking the common principles with which the universalities and specificities of development across different periods of life can be identified. Therefore, the conceptual efforts of the editors of this volume should be applauded. They took on the task of bridging the conspicuous gaps between child, adult, and aging research by bringing together excellent chapters on child, adult, and aging cognition to open a forum for research on cognitive development across the lifespan. We are convinced that this volume is an important milestone in moving forward the dialogue between researchers who study cognition in different periods of life.

Our aim here is to contribute to this dialogue by outlining a collection of perspectives derived from lifespan psychology that may be helpful for achieving an integrative understanding of lifespan cognition. Following a brief review of key concepts of lifespan psychology, three inter-related perspectives on lifespan cognitive development are outlined. These perspectives are discussed in relation to empirical findings, some covered in this volume. In our view, the goal of "lifespan cognitive psychology" is to shed new insights on (1) the long-term antecedents and consequences of age-specific cognitive processes, (2) the reciprocal co-constructive interactions between neurobiological and socio-cultural influences on cognitive development, and (3) overarching adaptive resource allocation principles that may serve as the backdrop of development in all periods of life. However, we also acknowledge that the broad-brush approach of lifespan cognitive psychology may lose sight of some specific issues that age-specific developmental researchers consider to be important.

CENTRAL CONCEPTIONS
OF LIFESPAN PSYCHOLOGY

Lifespan developmental psychology deals with the study of individual ontogeny from conception to old age (e.g., Baltes, 1987; Baltes, Staudinger, & Lindenberger, 1999; Tetens, 1777; Bühler, 1933; Baltes, Reese, & Lipsitt, 1980). Essentially, the aim of considering human development from a lifespan viewpoint is not only to highlight the notion that development continues beyond childhood and adolescence but also to bring additional content phenomena and principles of development to the foreground. One such principle is the strong interconnection between evolutionary and innate ontogenetic factors and the fact that during the life course these two forces are not always in harmony, but show complex and changing dynamics across the lifespan. Such perspectives have been discussed elsewhere at greater length (Baltes, 1987; Baltes, et al. 1999; Li, 2003; Li & Freund, 2005; Staudinger & Lindenberger, 2003). We draw specific attention to three concepts here (see Table 24.1). Together these concepts generate a family of perspectives for considering the lifespan development of cognitive processes and intellectual abilities across the contextual, behavioral, and neural levels.

Development as Contextualized Selective Lifelong Adaptations

The first central proposition of lifespan psychology is that change processes in individual ontogenesis can occur at any point in the life course from conception to death. Processes of development can operate in early as well as later life periods, thus no age period is dominant in regulating the nature of development (Baltes et al., 1980, 1999; Labouvie, 1982). This stands in contrast to the biological growth and maturation-oriented concept of child development, which assumes a certain end state of maturity that is usually reached by early adulthood (e.g., Harris, 1957; Segalowitz & Rosekrasnor, 1992).

The primary reason for the assumption of development beyond the "biological state of maturity" lies in the strong role that cultural evolution played and continues to play in the development of humankind. The culture-oriented view of human development moves beyond the limits of biological constraints and gives humans further opportunities to "develop" through advances in better and richer biosocial and technological resources. In this vein, lifespan psychology considers development as a lifelong process within and through which individuals selectively adapt to and make use of biological and cultural opportunities and constraints through life. Therefore, the processes of child, adult, and old-age development are not only temporally related, with early periods expressing mostly maturation and later periods expressing mostly decline (cf. Birren, 1964); they are also functionally connected as individuals adapt to, select from, and create the opportunities and constraints that represent the fabric of their life course. A fundamental question of lifespan research is what is possible in principle, despite limited or declining biological capacity at the early and late end of the lifespan, respectively.

In line with other developmental theories (e.g., Bronfenbrenner, 1979; Cole & Cole, 1989, Magnusson, 1988; Nelson, Chapter 12, this volume), lifespan psychology considers individual ontogeny as organized within a relatively open system that is couched within multiple levels ranging from the distal historical context of human evolution to the proximal context of individual ontogeny and the immediate microgenesis at the behavioral, cognitive, and neural levels. Processes at these different levels can form distinct constellations of influences. One general conception of the major forces of development comprises history-graded (general species-typical), age-graded (general cohort-typical and socialization-typical), and idiosyncratic (person-specific) biological and socio-cultural contextual influences on individual develop-ment. A given life course, then, is to be understood in terms of this interwoven system of macro–micro and distal–proximal influences (see Baltes & Smith, 2004, for further discussion).

A key assumption in this line of argument is that developmental trajectories reflect selective adaptation at various levels and that they evince plasticity both intra-individually and inter-individually (see also Lindenberger & von Oertzen, Chapter 21, this vol-ume). There are many possible developmental path-ways, only some of which are realized and expressed owing to contextual influences, person-specific indi-vidual selection, and their interactions. Alongside the plasticity of the individual and the developmental context, viewing development as a lifelong selective adaptation naturally leads the lifespan orientation to explicitly consider the active role of the developing individual (cf. Bell, 1968; Brandtstädter & Lerner, 1999; Heckhausen, 1999; Nelson, 1996; Piaget, 1954). Highlighting individuals' agentic contributions to their own developmental trajectory opens up research questions about the role of self-regulatory and selec-tion processes in cognitive development. Together with developmental plasticity at the individual and contextual level, the individual's active regulation generates a person-specific mixture of biocultural co-constructive developmental influences and outcomes (Li & Freund, 2005).

Pluralistic and Dynamic Nature of Developmental Causes and Consequences

The second central concept of lifespan psychology is recognition that developmental processes are intrin-sically pluralistic and dynamic. Although the physi-cal maturation and senescence aspects of life suggest a seemingly universal lifespan trajectory of growth followed by decline (Baltes, 1987), the forces of cul-tural diversity and opportunities generate diversifica-tion (e.g., more universal social stratifications that are based on class or gender as well as more group-specific influences such as artistic and professional specializa-tions). The simultaneous presence of the relatively more universal and the relatively more diverse sources

of developmental influences, as well as individual-istic selective adaptation, underlie the intrinsically plu-ralistic nature of development. Rather than consider-ing development only as a one-factor (biological maturation) unidirectional (growth-decline) changing function that extends from birth to death, the lifespan orientation considers development as multidimen-sional, multidirectional, and multifunctional. Cogni-tive ontogenesis is thus conceived not only as the outcome of biology-based factors but as the result of complex mixtures of developmental processes that are not necessarily linear and continuous and may be dif-ferentially adaptive (Baltes et al., 1980).

Specifically, cognitive and behavioral development is conceptualized to go through multiple processes (some of which are nonlinear) that include acquisi-tion, maintenance, transformation, and extinction. Considered from the holistic perspective of a person (Magnusson, 1988), the individual's developmental task is inherently multitasking, involving a complex system of processes for differential, collaborative, or interfering resource allocation. In principle, these processes can take place in all life periods, and within each given life period the expressed developmental outcome is the result of dynamic interactions between them. Moreover, changes and continuity can co-ex-ist. "Apparent" no-change at the level of phenotypic expression often results from dynamic changes at the level of the antecedents. Take "maintaining stability" of language communication in old age as an example. It can be a highly dynamic process if one considers that the antecedents (e.g., hearing efficacy) of the "maintained" behavior or function are not invariant. Thus, changes in at least some componential processes of the operating system are necessary to maintain the stability of functioning in other processes. For in-stance, some cognitive and social behaviors acquired in early childhood are maintained in adulthood, but some will be transformed or replaced by other behav-iors as the individuals keep on acquiring new behav-iors that are adaptive to developmental tasks specific to adulthood or old age (Baltes et al., 1999; Eriksson, 1959; Freund & Baltes, 2002; Roisman, Masten, Coatsworth, & Tellegen, 2004; Staudinger, Bluck, & Hertzog, 2003).

Factors contributing to development that differ across individuals also suggest pluralism. Inter-indi-vidual variation not only is important for genetic evo-lution but also is fundamental to societal functioning.

Variations in professional expertise are what make societal functioning possible because effective social systems require different types of competence and roles. Thus, in addition to focusing on normative, group-averaged patterns of developmental trajectories, the lifespan orientation recognizes that individuals differ substantially in the onset, magnitude, rate, and pattern of intra-individual change. The causes of intra-individual changes and variations may not entirely overlap with causes of inter-individual differences in intra-individual dynamics (Baltes & Nesselroade, 1978; Nesselroade, 1991). For instance, individuals, because of their differences in genetic predisposition and culture-based life experiences, may differ in the extent of their functional plasticity (i.e., within-person process and behavioral modifiability) and system robustness (i.e., within-person process and behavioral consistency) of their cognitive and behavioral processes (e.g., Hultsch, MacDonald, Hunter, Levy-Bencheton, & Strauss, 2000; Li, Huxhold, & Schmiedek, 2004).

Development as Adaptive Generation and Regulation of Gains and Losses

A third proposition of the lifespan orientation is the notion that any process of development entails aspects of gain (growth) and loss (decline), although this does not imply that gain and loss exist in equal strength throughout life. Systematic age-related changes in the gain:loss proportion are likely to be present for different domains of functioning. As a whole, with increasing age the proportion of gains and losses in adaptive capacity shift in the direction of lesser gains and more losses (Baltes, 1987; Heckhausen, Dixon, & Baltes, 1989).

Defining gains and losses is not simple. Aside from changes on a predefined scale of higher and lower levels of functioning, there is the issue of measuring consequences in adaptive fitness. This is the multifunctionality argument of lifespan theorists. For instance, a gain in logical ability in children can spell losses in performing other tasks. A telling example is the loss of ability to solve logically "unsolvable" probability tasks while gaining higher order cognitive abilities. Children in such tasks quickly move to a high pay-off option, while adults continue for a long time to seek a perfect (nonexisting) solution and therefore exhibit lower performance than children (Weir, 1964).

Because life is full of nonperfectly solvable tasks, lifespan theorists argue that effective lifespan development requires the acquisition of general-purpose mechanisms that, on average, provide an overall benefit across a wide range of function domains, although partial solutions may be necessary from the standpoint of a single task or domain. Processes that afford ongoing, dynamic interactions of positive (gains) and negative (losses) developmental changes in different functions likely would involve mechanisms that support flexible generation and regulation of developmental resources at the behavioral, cognitive, and neuronal levels. One class of such general mechanisms is the triangulation of processes of selection, optimization, and compensation (the SOC theory; Baltes & Baltes, 1990; Baltes, 1997; Freund & Baltes, 2002). *Selection* implies focusing one's resources on a subset of potentially available options, thereby giving development its direction. Selection thus functions as a precondition for developmental advances. *Optimization* reflects the growth aspect of development. It is defined as the acquisition, generation, refinement, and coordinated application of resources directed at the achievement of higher functional levels. *Compensation* addresses the regulation of loss in development. It involves efforts to maintain a given level of functioning despite decline in, or loss of, previously available resources. In this respect, the theoretical emphasis in lifespan psychology is similar to arguments advanced by psychologists who study behavioral and cognitive heuristics (e.g., Gigerenzer, 2003).

INTEGRATIVE PERSPECTIVES OF LIFESPAN COGNITION

Deriving from the above three concepts of lifespan psychology, we outline a family of interrelated integrative perspectives of lifespan cognition that highlight the co-constructive, pluralistic, dynamic, and adaptive nature of cognitive ontogeny (see Table 24.1). It should be emphasized that these integrative perspectives do not imply identity in causes and consequences of cognitive development in all age periods. Instead, they serve as common frames to align age-specific cognitive research and to show how they can be considered as embedded in a larger overall framework. We define and describe each of these perspectives in turn and then proceed to illustrate their implications for lifespan cognitive research with empirical findings in the remaining of this chapter.

TABLE 24.1. Key Conceptions of lifespan psychology and integrative perspective of lifespan cognition

Concepts of Lifespan Psychology	Integrative Perspectives of Lifespan Cognition	Implications for Considering Causes and Consequences of Lifespan Cognitive Development
Development as contexualized and selective lifelong adaptation	Biocultural co-construction of cognitive development	• Species-typical, socialization-typical, and person-specific influences on neurocognitive development • Co-construction of developmental plasticity at different levels • Individual and age differences in developmental plasticity
Pluralistic and dynamic nature of developmental causes and consequences	Lifespan variations in biological and cultural contributions to cognitive development	• Differential trajectories of processing mechanics and pragmatic knowledge • Differentiation-dedifferentiation of processes and abilities • Developmental differences in within-person dynamics: A person-centered systems view
Development as adaptive generation and regulation of gains and losses	Adaptive functionality of lifespan cognition	• Lifespan variations in cognitive and neurofunctional resource allocation to multiple developmental tasks

BIOCULTURAL CO-CONSTRUCTION OF LIFESPAN COGNITIVE DEVELOPMENT

The Greek philosopher's ancient statement, "All is flux; nothing stays still" (Heraclitus, ca. 500 BC), is not just rhetorical speech but a veridical expression of the nature of many psychological functions and their development. A fundamental fact about human cognition and its associated neurobiological mechanisms is that it involves processes—series of events that are internal or external to the individual occurring simultaneously across different levels in time and across different domains of functions. The human organism is never operating as a single-task (or function) system.

Even standing still requires changes—namely in the determining antecedent forces (e.g., dynamic integration of visual, proprioceptive, and kinetic information). Cognitive development across the lifespan thus entails reciprocal interactions between momentary processing dynamics occurring at the time scales of milliseconds, seconds, hours, days, or weeks across the behavioral, cognitive, and neurobiological levels. The same applies to tasks. We are multitasking organisms. Multitasking, internally and externally, sequentially and simultaneously, is a core feature of systems biology (Groisman & Ehrlich, 2003) and systems psychology (cf. Ford, 1987).

The dynamics across levels and task (function) domains are not always in harmony. Think only of the "unwanted" shift in attention that makes it difficult for a person to stay on task. Cumulatively, these momentary processing dynamics may express various patterns of age differences and changes across the months and years of life. Given reciprocal interactions across levels, behavioral and cognitive changes may be preceded by, paralleled with, or followed by changes at the neurobological levels. Moreover, brain and cognitive development are embedded in the historical phylogenetic context of brain and cognitive evolution and the current socio-cultural context of individual ontogeny.

Species-Typical, Socialization-Typical, and Person-Specific Influences

Extending the notion of contextualized selective development from lifespan psychology to cognitive research implies that cognitive operations at any given life period are outcomes of reciprocal interactions between the individual's neurocognitive processes and the developmental context providing varying degrees and types of supports and constraints for development. Although there are certainly biologically based limits, it is defensible to consider brains as open, dynamic information processors. The basic tenet here is that contextualized experiences shape the structure and functional dynamics of the brain-behavioral reciprocity (e.g., Baltes, Rösler, & Reuter-Lorenz, in press; Li & Lindenberger, 2002). Building on general species-typical neurobiological predispositions evolved through brain evolution, by way of their own experiences embodied in sensory and motor processes and embedded in socio-cultural context, brains obtain information about the world and are shaped by this information as individuals develop.

Therefore, age differences in cognitive operations should not automatically be considered solely as differences in basic information-processing primitives and their neurobiological substrates. Like all individual differences, developmental differences may also reflect the interactions between age differences in three classes of processes: (1) the species-typical neurobiological and cultural evolutionary processes, (2) the normative age-graded socialization-typical ontogenetic processes with which the individual acquires shared pragmatic knowledge (such as basic language and arithmetic skills) of a given social-cultural group, and (3) idiosyncratic (nonnormative) influence of person-specific professional expertise and skills that result, at least in part, from the individual's self-selected and constructed personal life experiences and history. In fact, as inter-individual differences in general have been shown to increase with age (Nelson & Dannefer, 1992), it seems reasonable to argue that the degree of "personalization" of cognition and the brain also increases with age.

RECIPROCAL INTERACTIONS AMONG DEVELOPMENTAL PLASTICITY AT DIFFERENT LEVELS

The individual's active lifelong adaptation to constraints imposed by the multiple levels of developmental context requires flexibility on the part of the developing individual as well as the developmental context. At a conceptual level, such flexibility or plasticity can be defined as the modifiability of the ranges of possible developmental event or processes. We use specific terms to highlight the point that plasticity can originate in the socio-cultural conditions, the behavior of the individual, and the neurobiological substrates. *Societal and cultural plasticity* refers to cultural and societal resources and processes that provide technological, educational, information, and other orga-

nizational opportunities and constraints for individual development. *Behavioral and cognitive plasticity* refers to socialization and learning-dependent behavioral and cognitive processes. *Neuronal plasticity* refers to activity- and experience-dependent neurogenesis, synaptogenesis, and cortical functional organization. *Genetic plasticity* refers to environment and experience-dependent genetic activity and expressions. As schematically depicted in Figure 24.1, there are reciprocal interactions among forms of developmental plasticity across these levels during an individual's lifetime that co-construct brain and cognitive development across the lifespan (see Baltes & Singer, 2001; Li, 2003 for further discussions).

In humans, resources accumulated through cultural evolution (Tomasello, 1999) form a second kind of inheritance (Durham, 1991). In contrast to biological inheritance, culture-based inheritance is more rapid and dissipative. Reflecting cultural resources, the social transmission process in contemporary societies structures the modal experiences that individuals go through in different life periods (e.g., Cole, 1999; Schooler, 1984, 1996).

On the one hand, the initial stages of life are typically more standardized (normative) in their focus on basic competencies. Socio-culturally based basic pragmatic knowledge, such as the knowledge of language and numerical system, is learned by individuals through parent-child interaction and in an age-graded socio-cultural context, such as formal schooling. For instance, in early childhood when language ability is still limited, parental prompting during conversations helps young children produce verbal accounts of their experiences, which in turn may affect how they construct memory (Eisenberg, 1985; Ornstein, Haden, &

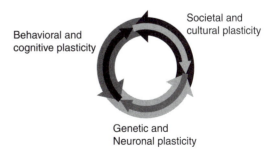

FIGURE 24.1. Schematic representation of biocultural co-construction of developmental plasticity across levels. (Adapted from Li, 2003, with permission of the American Psychological Association.)

Elischberger, Chapter 10, this volume). Schooling plays an important role in structuring and co-constructing (with the individual's active participation; Nelson, 1996) the development of basic language and numerical skills (Palincsar, 1998; Rogoff, 1990). On the other hand, as life unfolds, the influence of individual differences in life histories becomes stronger. Professional skills (e.g., jobs that require different kinds of cognitive skills or levels of self-directedness) and other forms of expertise (e.g., music, chess, or crossword puzzles) reflect increasingly subgroup and person-specific influences that accumulate through the individual's personal life experiences (Baltes et al., 1999). For instance, individuals with different professions or interests may acquire specific knowledge in different domains (e.g., Hambrick, Salthouse, & Meinz, 1999; Salthouse, Chapter 19, this volume; Schooler & Mulatu, 2004).

It should be noted that such individualization does not apply to all aspects of cognition. Some facets of cognitive functioning are more culture-sensitive and culture-exploitive than others, although the relative plasticity across different aspects of cognition has not yet been sufficiently studied. In addition, declines in neurobiological potential during aging may limit the observable behavioral expression of individual differences in lifespan experiences in very old age.

Below we illustrate the influences of acquiring normative pragmatic knowledge and nonnormative, person-specific life experiences on cognitive and neural plasticity. These are the domains for which the ontogenetic time window of cognitive development is longer. Verbal knowledge, for instance, remains well functioning in most people who survive into the eighth decade of life (see further discussion in later sections).

NORMATIVE SOCIAL-CULTURAL INFLUENCES: CO-CONSTRUCTION OF GENERAL PRAGMATIC KNOWLEDGE, COGNITIVE, AND NEURONAL PLASTICITY

Language is perhaps the most ubiquitous socialization-typical pragmatic skill that individuals of a given social-cultural group acquire and apply in daily experiences (Golinkoff & Hirsh-Pasek, Chapter 14, this volume; Kemper, Chapter 15, this volume). Notwithstanding this generality, there are also person-specific influences that could either be due to deficits in species-typical predispositions, assaults to the neurobiological substrates affecting individual differences in language processing, or atypical learning environments (Dennis, Chapter 16, this volume; Caplan & Waters, Chapater 17, this volume). Language-specific linguistic environments affect the development of language processes through formal (e.g., phonology, orthography, and verb morphology) or social-interactive (e.g., parental speech) aspects of language. For instance, infants show better generalizations to phonetic variants around the prototypes contained in their native language, a phenomenon known as the perceptual magnet effect (Kuhl, Williams, Lacerda, Stevens, & Lindblom, 1992). Culture-specific language differences may also influence parental speech and subsequently affect patterns of semantic and cognitive development. For instance, it has been suggested that differences in verb morphology between Korean and English may contribute to the developmental pattern of Korean children acquiring verbs that are relevant to the concepts of planning first and nouns relevant for object categorization second, whereas the order of this developmental pattern is reversed in American children (Gopnik, Choi, & Baumberger, 1996).

Language acquisition may have major implications for the functional architecture of the brain. Recent cognitive neuroscience findings indicate a dynamic shift in cortical organization over the course of language acquisition during childhood (see Neville et al., 1998, for review). Similarly, the progressive developmental history of learning and using languages of different orthographical complexity throughout adult life leaves its trace at the cortical level. For instance, in comparison to the Italian language, English orthography is rather inconsistent, with complicated mappings of letters to sounds. Paulesu and colleagues (2000) recently found that Italian readers showed greater activation in the left superior temporal regions associated with phoneme processing, whereas English readers showed greater activations, particularly for nonwords, in the left posterior inferior temporal gyrus and anterior frontal gyrus, areas associated with word retrieval during both reading and naming tasks. These data suggest that acquiring the rather complex orthographical mapping of the English language impels English readers to invoke additional neurocognitive mechanisms involving word retrieval from semantic memory while reading.

Taken together, the above findings of language-specific experiences and neural plasticity underscore the point that developmental changes in mental representations (Nelson, Chapter 12, this volume; Burke, Chapter 13, this volume) and knowledge (Keil, Chapter 18, this volume; Salthouse, Chapter 19, this volume) are co-constructed by socio-culturally contextualized experiences and neurobiological factors. The evidence that many aspects of language are well preserved into older ages, at least for nonpathological old adults (cf. Kemper, Chapter 15, this volume; Caplan & Waters, Chapter 17, this volume), illustrates how ongoing transactions with the social world nurture long-term developmental proficiency.

PERSON-SPECIFIC SOCIAL-CULTURAL INFLUENCES: OCCUPATION-, EXPERTISE-, AND TRAINING- INDUCED COGNITIVE AND NEURAL PLASTICITY

Throughout, we have emphasized that cognitive development across periods of adult life has an increasingly strong component of individualization that is unlikely to be captured by studies of basic (elementary) tasks of information processing. The case that individual differences in experiences and life histories reflect socio-culturally structured contextual influences can perhaps be best illustrated with respect to occupational contexts. Different types of occupations engender, for instance, job-related stimulus and demand characteristics of varying complexity in the individual's daily job contexts and related experience-based outcomes. At the behavioral level, longitudinal studies have demonstrated reciprocal effects between the complexity of the occupational context and intellectual functioning in older adults (e.g., Schooler, Mulatu, & Oates, 1999; Schooler & Mulatu, 2004).

Another naturalistic setting for considering person-specific social-cultural influences on lifespan cognition is bilingualism (or multilingualism in general). As mentioned above, language is a representative aspect of general pragmatic knowledge that individuals of a given socio-cultural group acquire. However, individuals may differ in their language expertise in terms of whether they need to master more than one language for their daily functioning. Child developmental and aging research studies have shown that the daily experience in processing two or more languages is associated with bilingual individuals' advantage in executive control functions measured by working memory or inhibition tasks (Bialystok, 2001; Bialystok, Craik, Klein, & Viswanathan, 2004).

In addition to contributing to research on the influences of social-cultural context on cognitive plasticity in natural settings, cognitive intervention studies reveal cognitive plasticity in individuals, even individuals in old age (see Kramer & Willis, 2002, for review; Baltes & Lindenberger, 1988). Such research has two major goals. The first is to understand processes that underlie cognitive performance and its ontogeny. The second is to explore the range of what is possible in principle. In terms of memory plasticity in old age, memory-training studies employing the testing-the-limits paradigm (Baltes & Kliegl, 1992) have shown that older adults (from about 60 to 80 years) still displayed a fair level of cognitive plasticity and improved their associative memory by learning a culture-based mnemonic technique (i.e., method of loci).

Aside from the demonstration of performance enhancement by acquiring special skills, these studies exemplified how training research using the testing-the-limits paradigm explores constraints on the zone (range) of potential development (Baltes, 1998). Thus, not unlike contemporary work in childhood, the focus is on maximum limits. Despite the continued plasticity at older ages, it can be shown that the cognitive plasticity of old individuals in the fourth age (i.e., 80 years old and above) is markedly reduced in comparison to young adults (Singer, Lindenberger, & Baltes, 2003). Extending testing-the-limits memory training across the lifespan shows that young children around 10 years of age have greater developmental reserve plasticity than old adults around 70 years of age (Brehmer, Müller, von Oertzen, & Lindenberger, 2004).

In a way, expertise acquisition can be considered to be a long-term testing-the-limit type of training that is implemented in the natural settings of the individual's daily experiences. Expert performance is the result of intense practice extended for a minimum of 10 years for most domains of skill (Ericsson, Krampe, & Tesch-Römer, 1993). In the domain of music expertise, empirical evidence suggests that the long-term extended daily practice of old expert pianists helps to maintain their elite performance, in spite of aging-related decline in basic cognitive processes

(Krampe & Ericsson, 1996). There is also evidence showing that long-term acquisition of expertise leads to experience-induced cortical functional reorganization, in addition to behavioral changes. For instance, it was found that cortical representations of the fingers of the left playing hands of string players were larger than those of the right hand holding the bow, and this was particularly true for individuals who started playing the instrument early in life (Elbert, Pantev, Wienbruch, Rockstroh, & Taub, 1995). Outside the domain of music, Maguire et al. (2000) found that, given their extensive navigation experience, London taxi drivers' posterior hippocampi—regions of the brain involved in storing spatial representation of the environment—were significantly larger in comparison to same-age individuals who did not have as much navigation experience. Furthermore, the number of years spent as a taxi driver correlated positively with hippocampal volume. These data indicate that the adult brain still possesses functional plasticity, allowing the posterior hippocampus to expand regionally in order to accommodate elaboration of environmental spatial representation in individuals who rely heavily on their navigation skills and have achieved a high level of navigation expertise in a particular environment.

The evidence of neurofunctional plasticity in response to socio-cultural influences highlighted above, and other evidence of activity- and experience-dependent neurogenesis synaptogenesis, and myelination (see Gross; 2000; Grossmann, Churchill, Bates, Kleim, & Greenough, 2002; Nelson, 1996, for reviews) together indicate that contextualized experiences play an important role in developmental specification of neurobiological processes of cognition (Johnson, 2001; Taylor, Chapter 2, this volume). Importantly, the effects of contextualized experiences on cognitive processes and their neural substrates are not limited to early development, but also operate during most of the adult lifespan. Context-dependent recruitment of cortical functional circuitry (e.g., Logan, Sanders, Synder, Morris, & Buckner, 2002) has been the focus of neurocognitive aging research in recent years (Buckner et al., Chapter 3, this volume). Such evidence is critical for our appreciation of how biology and culture co-construct development, resulting not only in common features of brain and cognitive development, but also in more "personalized" patterns.

LIFESPAN VARIATIONS OF BIOLOGICAL AND CULTURAL INFLUENCES ON COGNITIVE DEVELOPMENT: CO-CONSTRUCTION IN ACTION

In embracing the propositions of co-constructive and pluralistic developmental processes from the lifespan orientation, research on lifespan cognition requires using a systematic approach. Even when focusing on a specific domain of function, multiple processes are involved. For instance, developmental changes in language processing in children or old adults involve a range of contributing factors (e.g., perceptual, social, and linguistic information) that affect different aspects of language processing to varying degrees (Golinkoff & Hirsh-Pasek, Chapter 14, this volume; Kemper, Chapter 15, this volume). Whereas some domain-general processes may be associated with similar developmental antecedents and exhibit similar onsets, rates, and patterns of development, domain-specific processes have different developmental causes and show distinct and often personalized developmental patterns (cf. Rabbitt & Anderson, Chapter 23, this volume). Moreover, the relation between domain-general and domain-specific processes may vary across the lifespan, as the extent of general processing resources (e.g., species-typical neurobiological potential) applied to the acquisition or expression of specific knowledge and skills varies in different life periods. Think only of the immense range of variations in multi- and sequential task constellations that individuals of different ages face in life.

Developmentalists and lifespan researchers generally appreciate the fact that both biological and socialization processes contribute to individual ontogeny. However, the relative contribution of biology and culture in different periods of life is a topic that is rarely considered. Baltes (1997) made an effort to propose a framework for considering the interplay of biology and culture in lifespan development by specifying three principles (see Figure 24.2).

The first principle suggests that biology-based plasticity decreases after maturity. This is presumably due to the lack of evolutionary selection pressure on survival in the postreproductive phase of life, therefore beneficial evolutionary selection affording optimal functioning (in the sense of basic biological potential) was less operative for later periods of life as genetic evolution proceeded. Second, more and more culture

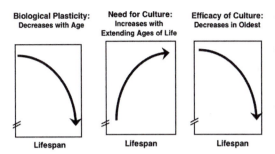

Biological Plasticity: Decreases with Age

Need for Culture: Increases with Extending Ages of Life

Efficacy of Culture: Decreases in Oldest

Lifespan   Lifespan   Lifespan

FIGURE 24.2. Schematic representation of basic facts about the dynamics between biology and culture across the lifespan. (Adapted from Baltes, 1997, with permission of the American Psychological Association.)

is required to extend human development to higher levels of functioning and older ages. By increases in cultural resources, for instance, via the process of cumulative cultural evolution (Tomasello, 1999), the window of ontogenetic time and opportunities can be extended and expanded for more and more individuals, although at the same time the cultural conditions required for reaching increasingly higher levels of functioning and older ages increase as well. The third principle states that cultural impact or efficiency varies by age. Specifically, as the decline in neurobiological functions limits the effectiveness of cultural influences, the efficacy of cultural resources decreases with increasing age. Thus, it takes more and more resources and support to produce the same level of cognitive performance.

Here we illustrate the dynamic interplay between biology and culture by reviewing findings from research on lifespan intelligence. Specifically, we focus on the differential trajectories of the more biology-based cognitive processing mechanics and the more culture-based pragmatic knowledge, as well as the differentiation and dedifferentiation of cognitive abilities (also see Birney & Sternberg, Chapter 22, this volume; Lindenberger & von Oertzen, chapter 21, this volume; Rabbitt & Anderson, Chapter 23, this volume).

DIFFERENTIAL TRAJECTORIES OF PROCESSING MECHANICS AND PRAGMATIC KNOWLEDGE

Dual-component theories of intelligence distinguish between *fluid cognitive mechanics*, which reflect the operations of the relatively more neurobiology-based information-processing mechanisms, and *crystallized cognitive pragmatics*, which are the outgrowth of experience- and culture-based knowledge. Cross-sectional age gradients and longitudinal age trajectories (e.g., McArdle, Ferrer-Caja, Hamagami, & Woodcock, 2002) of these two domains of intellectual abilities generally show a lead-lag pattern across the life course: the relatively more biology-based fluid cognitive mechanics develop and decline earlier than the more culture-based crystallized cognitive pragmatics, consistent with Cattell's investment theory (1971).

As an illustration, the top panel of Figure 24.3 shows the theoretical lifespan age gradients predicted by dual-component theories, whereas the bottom panel shows empirical cross-sectional age gradients covering the age range 6–89 years (Li et al., 2004). The shaded distribution at the end of the theoretical age gradient of the relatively more culture-based cognitive pragmatics is intended to suggest that individual differences in person-specific life experiences, as well as societal opportunities and supports accumulated through life, are likely to produce larger variations between and within persons around the more general age trajectory. Research shows that in current living cohorts the maximum performance levels of cognitive pragmatics are achieved by individuals in their mid-40s and remain stable until 70 years of age, at which point they also decline. Longitudinal findings from the Berlin Aging Study also indicate that some facets of crystallized pragmatics (i.e., verbal knowledge) do not decline until the individuals are in their late 80s (Singer, Verhaeghen, Ghisletta, Lindenberger, & Baltes, 2003).

It is postulated that, despite their greater plasticity, the lifespan trajectory for cognitive mechanics exhibits less variation around the general age gradient than that for cognitive pragmatics. Variations in this category of abilities are more likely to be due to interactions between the individual's level of functioning and task difficulty or to possible confounding with some pragmatic knowledge component, such as test-taking skill. The current findings suggest that the maximum performance levels of cognitive mechanics are achieved by individuals in their mid-20s, and decrements are already visible by age 30.

In general, the rise and fall of cognitive mechanics resemble the lifespan age gradients of other aspects

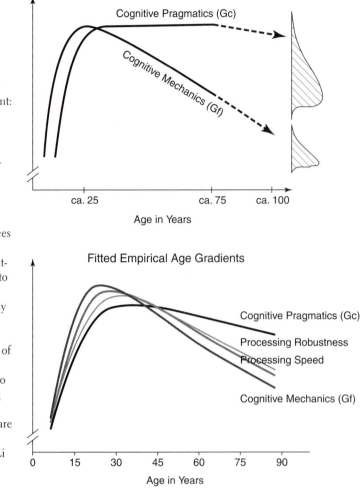

FIGURE 24.3. Two-component theory of intellectual development: Theoretical expectations and empirical findings regarding the fluid cognitive mechanics vs. crystallized cognitive pragmatics. Theoretical age gradients are plotted in the top panel. The dashed lines indicate that fewer empirical findings are available regarding very old age. Differences in the spread of the distributions associated with cognitive pragmatics and mechanics are intended to suggest that age trajectories of cognitive pragmatics are relatively more subject to individual differences in person-specific experiences than the trajectories of cognitive mechanics. Fitted empirical age gradients of the two component of intelligence along with basic processing speed and processing robustness functions are presented in the bottom panel. (Empirical curve adapted from Li et al., 2004, with permission of Karger.)

of cognition such as inhibition, attention, working memory, executive control, and processing speed (e.g., Dempster, 1992; Cepeda, Kramer, & Gonzalez de Sather, 2001; Kail & Salthouse, 1994; Williams, Ponesse, Schachar, Logan, & Tannock., 1999; see also Chapters 4–10, this volume). At first glance, the pervasive inverted U-shaped lifespan functions of various basic information-processing mechanisms seem to suggest similar, if not identical, mechanisms underlying child cognitive development and cognitive aging. The lifespan approach, however, emphasizes that before interpretations of common, universal mechanisms are warranted, potential lifespan age differences in the developmental antecedents of these cognitive mechanisms should be carefully considered. Put differently, the reasons for the rise of cognitive processes in childhood may be different from the causes for the fall of these processes in old age, despite the fact that at the behavioral level the gains and losses in cognitive performance can be quantitatively expressed on the same continuum. For instance, although both children and old adults performed more poorly than young adults in a visual search task, the reasons for the suboptimal performance at both ends of the lifespan were different. Whereas children's poor performance was mainly due to distraction, older adults' performance deficit was specifically sensitive to conditions that triggered more exhaustive search processes (Hommel, Li, & Li, 2004).

DYNAMIC ORGANIZATION OF PROCESSES: DIFFERENTIATION-DEDIFFERENTIATION OF LIFESPAN COGNITION

The conceptual perspective outlined above also has implications for lifespan changes in the organizational structure of cognitive abilities (or tasks). For instance, the idea of increased personalization during adulthood suggests more inter-individual heterogeneity and less covariation of inter-individual differences in abilities. Although traditionally the organization of mental abilities and their underlying cognitive processes was viewed as static, the dual-component theories of intellectual development presented here consider the structure and functional organization of intellectual abilities as dynamic—developing and transforming throughout life. During maturation and senescence, the neurobiological substrates of intellectual functioning apparently grow and decline, respectively; if these changes covary in rate and magnitude, they can be expected to produce more homogeneity across tasks and therefore a new form of high intertask correlation. Thus, both incomplete brain development in childhood and brain aging in old age impose stronger biological constraints on information-processing mechanisms underlying fluid intelligence. However, the specific mechanisms of brain "development" in childhood and processes of brain aging may well differ from each other. Their outcomes regarding individual differences between tasks may be similar, but their biological sources (although they may overlap to some extent) are likely to be distinct.

These differences in specific sources notwithstanding, it is predicted that during childhood and old age, when there are strong biological constraints on information-processing mechanisms underlying knowledge acquisition and expression, strong couplings between basic information-processing mechanisms and fluid and crystallized intelligence are expected. This prediction is supported by recent findings showing that the amount of covariation variance shared among different aspects of intellectual abilities (memory, reasoning, perceptual speed, verbal knowledge and fluency) and the processing speed of a wide range of basic cognitive processes (e.g., visual and memory search, response competition, choice reactions) were higher at both ends of the lifespan (Li et al., 2004). Age differences in the dimensionality of the factor space of intellectual abilities are illustrated here as an example. Extracting principal component factors of the intellectual space that was

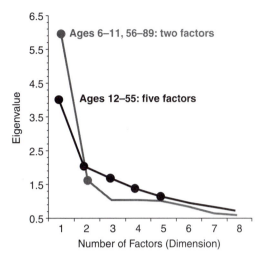

FIGURE 24.4. Less differentiated structure of intelligence in childhood and in old age. As shown in the scree plots of the principal component analyses, only 2 factors were extracted for children and old adult groups, whereas 5 factors were extracted for teenagers and adults.

spanned by 15 psychometric tests of intelligence as an indicator of ability differentiation yielded only two factors for children and old adults. For the middle periods of the lifespan three more factors (that is, five factors in total) were extracted (see Figure 24.4). Similar results of strong correlations between different aspects of intellectual abilities in old age have been observed in cross-sectional and longitudinal analyses of the Berlin Aging Study (e.g., Lindenberger & Baltes, 1997; Ghisletta & Lindenberger, 2003). These findings suggest that the structure of mental abilities is less differentiated—though not necessarily for the same reasons—in childhood and old age than in adulthood (for historical review see Reinert, 1970). This suggests that in old age, when the level of cognitive mechanics reaches a lower-bound threshold, the relatively more biology-based cognitive mechanics constrain the operation of general pragmatic knowledge.

The differentiation and dedifferentiation of intellectual abilities observed at the behavioral level (see also Chapters 22, 21, & 23, this volume) is paralleled by recent evidence showing age differences in the specification of cortical organization during child development (see Johnson, 2001; Chapter 2, this volume, for reviews) and recruitment of additional cortical regions during aging (see Chapter 3, this volume; Cabeza, 2002; Reuter-Lorenz, 2002, for reviews).

LIFESPAN DIFFERENCES IN
INTRA-PERSON DYNAMICS

Recent developments in research on within-person variations of cognitive processing (e.g., Hultsch, MacDonald, & Dixon, 2002; Li, Aggen, Nesselroade, & Baltes, 2001; MacDonald, Hultsch, & Dixon, 2003; Rabbitt, Osman, Moore, & Stollery, 2001; Siegler, 1994) are paralleled by lifespan psychology's emphasis on the dynamic nature of development. Intra-person processing variations are intrinsic to all aspects of human functioning, ranging from neurobiological and sensory aspects to perceptual, cognitive, and emotional processes. According to the lifespan conception of differential intra-individual change dynamics, individuals can differ in the onset, rate, magnitude, and patterns of ontogenetic changes and moment-to-moment microgenetic processes (Nesselroade & Baltes, 1979). Therefore, research on age differences in cognitive efficacy should not only focus on measures of performance level but also on the cognitive system's flexibility, robustness, and resiliency to contextual influences. Such a view is also stimulated by the increasing recognition that everyday cognitive functioning is a continuous stream of multitasking, thus requiring flexible information processing on the part of the individual. However, the tasks and available resources change with age (e.g., Krampe & Baltes, 2003).

Given lifespan variations in the influences of biology, culture, and idiosyncratic life history on cognitive functioning, age differences can be expected in the different aspects of intra-person dynamics, such as functional diversity, functional adaptivity, and processing robustness (Chapters 20 & 21, this volume). For example, basic cognitive processes of young children and old adults tend to be less robust than those of young adults (see bottom panel of Figure 24.3). However, whereas individual differences in the processing robustness of old adults predict the efficacy of the relatively more biology-based cognitive mechanics uniquely beyond processing speed, processing robustness in children is primarily associated with processing speed (Li et al., 2004). Again, such findings underscore the importance of recognizing that, although a given aspect of cognitive processing (or resource) may exhibit a continuous lifespan pattern of rise and fall, antecedents and consequences of the seemingly continuous dimension may not be identical. We also need to study much more carefully the age changes in multitask demands that are a constant backdrop for age differences in any task performance.

Adaptive Functionality
of Lifespan Cognition

Considering cognitive development as the lifelong adaptation to and mastery of the constraints and potentials specific to each life period, we argue that there is no supremacy attached to the cognitive processes associated with any given life period. This stands in contrast to the notion of adult cognition being the "endstate" of cognitive development and that cognitive processes of children and old adults are simply nonoptimal variants of adult cognition. In other words, the operations of cognitive processes are viewed from a functional perspective (e.g., Baltes et al., 1999; Dixon & Baltes, 1986; Glenberg, 1997) that considers the relative match between developmental task demands (and opportunities) with the potential (and limits) of brain capacity and societal plasticity of a given life period. In the theoretical conception of Piaget, cognitive functionality across the lifespan is full of issues of horizontal and vertical decalages. For instance, "immature" behavior and cognition in early life may sometimes be adaptive. Immature sensory systems or limited working-memory capacity during early childhood may be adaptive because they reduce the amount of stimulation young organisms receive, which makes the processes of sensory and cognitive development easier (e.g., Bjorklund, 1997; Mareschal & Shultz, 1996). Similarly, it is adaptive for older adults to trade their reduced processing speed against grammatically less complex sentences to maintain usual conversations (e.g., Chapter 15, this volume), for instance, or to give up full information processing and apply "fast and frugal" heuristics (Gigerenzer, 2003).

Given this functional adaptation principle, it is important to ask the question of whether a given cognitive process (e.g., working memory) serves the same function for individuals in different life periods (Hitch, chapter 8, this volume). The reverse question of whether different processes (or combinations of processes) are involved in implementing similar functions for individuals in different life periods is equally important, albeit age differences in cognitive performance at the behavioral level may only manifest themselves as quantitative differences (e.g., Karmiloff-Smith, 1998).

Adaptive Generation and Allocation of Cognitive Resources

Deriving from the lifespan concept of development as gain-loss dynamics, cognition at any given life period can be considered as (1) resource generation and (2) differential resource allocation over time and between related domains of functions or tasks (Krampe & Baltes, 2003). Successful developmental mechanisms of resource generation and allocation allow individuals to behave and act in ways that are adaptive to the developmental tasks demands and opportunities of the life period that they are in. Cognitive lifespan development consists of a series of sequential, simultaneous, and interactive multitasking situations. The theory of SOC mentioned earlier is an example of general resource generation and allocation mechanisms that facilitate the individual's ability to master the multitasking constellations of life (e.g., Baltes & Baltes, 1990; Baltes, 1997; Freund & Baltes, 2002; Krampe & Baltes, 2003; Li & Freund, 2005). Another related illustration is the average lifespan script of task objectives and the ensuing differences in resource allocation as shown in Figure 24.5. As we study cognitive development across the lifespan and consider issues of external validity, it is important to understand that individuals of different ages are likely to operate under a rather different set of metastrategies and multitask constellations whose fundamental theme is the triangulation of growth, maintenance, and decline.

Regarding the adaptive regulation of cognitive resource, SOC is an effective way to allocate resources among the developmental processes of growth, maintenance, and decline. Differential cognitive resource allocation takes many forms. For instance, given the physical limitations of infants, it is necessary for a substantial amount of behavioral resource to be allocated to sensori-motor processes during infancy. With physical growth and the lessening of physical bodily constraints, more behavioral resources are allocated to the development of basic cognitive functions and complex skill acquisition. At the other end of the lifespan, given the pervasiveness of aging-related cognitive declines, it is important to investigate how old people manage their daily performance by selectively allocating their cognitive resources among different tasks, so that they can best adapt to the bodily and cognitive constraints of old age. In many respects, such general strategies of dealing with a variety of cognitive tasks is closely linked to the topic of executive control (see Chapters 6 & 7, this volume).

Flexible resource allocation is especially important whenever people are faced with multiple tasks or situational constraints and the resources are overtaxed. Evidence from studies that systematically combined sensori-motor tasks of varying difficulty (i.e., walking with or without obstacles) with cognitively demanding tasks (memorization) suggests that older adults invest considerable cognitive resources in the motor

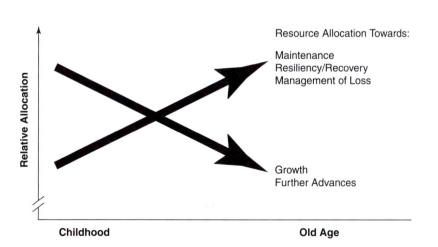

FIGURE 24.5. Lifespan changes in the allocation of resources into growth, maintenance, and management of loss. (Reprinted from Cicchetti, *Developmental Psychopathology 2: Risk, Disorder, and Adaptation*, with the permission of John Wiley & Sons, Inc.)

rather than the cognitive tasks and selectively use external support to compensate for the decreased efficacy of their sensori-motor functions (Lindenberger, Marsiske, & Baltes, 2000; Li, Lindenberger, Freund, & Baltes, 2001). The same may be true for young children when regulating their body movements while performing other tasks. Other evidence from studies examining aspects of older adults' language processing while performing additional concurrent tasks also shows that older adults allocate their resources differently from young adults. For instance, older adults tend to allocate greater resources to conceptual integration when reading (Smiler, Gagne, & Stine-Morrow, 2003) or maintaining sentence complexity and content while talking (Kemper, Herman, & Lian, 2003; see Chapter 15, this volume, for review). It would be intriguing to pursue similar dual- and multitask research in children and adolescents. This would strength the connection between multitask research and ways to manage life development.

Adaptive Generation and Allocation of Neurocognitive Resources

As is inherent in biocultural co-constructivism, the phenomena described always have parallels in brain structure and function. Thus, at the neurobiological level, there is evidence for experiential-based specification of neurocognitive processes during early development. Here we give the example of the neurocognitive development of face processing. In young infants (earlier than 6 months), face processing involves both left and right ventral visual pathways, whereas in adults face processing primarily involves the right ventral visual pathway. While adult brain activity shows specific sensitivity to upright human faces, no such sensitivity for face orientation is observed in young infants. With increasing experience in viewing many human faces, infants of about 12 months of age gradually develop more selective sensitivity to upright human faces (de Haan, Humphreys, & Johnson, 2002; de Haan, Pascalis, & Johnson, 2002).

In comparison to the developmental specification phenomena in childhood, recent work in the cognitive neuroscience of aging suggests aging-related declines in process specification that may involve compensation either as an antecedent or as a consequence. Compared with young adults, who exhibit more clearly lateralized cortical information process-

ing, people in their 60s and beyond showed bilateralized (bihemispheric) activity during memory retrieval and during both verbal and spatial working-memory processing. It seems that in response to aging-related declines in brain efficacy and integrity, tasks with seemingly identical requirements are implemented differently in the aging brain. One view suggests that these data indicate that the aging brain recruits cortical areas in both hemispheres to compensate for neurocognitive declines during aging (see Cabeza, 2002; Reuter-Lorenz, 2002, for reviews of the empirical findings and interpretations). An alternative is to consider such dedifferentiation of neurocognitive processing in old age as the outcome of an aging-related decline in brain integrity. It remains to be seen how much of the cortical functional change reflects neuronal compensatory functional plasticity in the face of losing structural and/or neurochemical integrity; how much reflects the decline in structural, functional, and/or neurochemical integrity itself (e.g., Logan et al., 2002; see Chapter 3, this volume, for reviews); and how much is due to changes in processing strategies at the cognitive and behavioral levels. Answers to these questions may not be straightforward, however, because these different aspects are not independent of each other. Neurocomputational (e.g., Braver et al., 2001; Li, Lindenberger, & Sikström, 2001) and other behavioral computational (Chow & Nesselroade, 2004) models could be useful tools for theoretical investigations of these intertwined relations.

CONCLUDING REMARKS

The present volume is a spirited effort to bring together the work of distinguished cognitive developmental researchers working at different stages of the lifespan. Many of them, most notably the editors in their introductory chapter, have offered their views on how their work may inform research and theory about cognitive development in other periods of life. Our task was to present an approach that derives from lifespan thinking itself. Thus, we have focused on outlining a family of interrelated perspectives of lifespan cognition that originate from central concepts of lifespan psychology. These perspectives suggest that when comparing and contrasting cognitive development across different life periods, the biocultural co-constructive and adaptive nature of cognitive development caution against an immediate interpretation of age differences in cognitive operations as simply driven by the growth and decline of basic information-processing mechanisms and their associated neurobiological mechanisms. The lifespan framework highlights lifespan variations in the relative contributions of biology and culture on cognitive functioning. In early cognitive development, idiosyncratic person-specific experiences tend to play a lesser role, relative to contributions of species-typical neurobiological and age-normative factors. In subsequent phases of lifespan development, however, life-history specific influences may be more significant for understanding adult cognitive development and aging. In old age, because of the pervasiveness of biological decline, processes of greater generality are likely to reenter the system as powerful regulating forces of the developmental trajectories. The evidence reviewed in this chapter provides initial support for these propositions. However, further empirical verifications will require age-comparative, cross-level designs that utilize efficient combinations of different experimental paradigms examining basic cognitive and neuronal processes in well-controlled laboratory settings as well as cognition in everyday functioning using ecologically valid tasks.

Specifically, *training and expertise paradigms* are particularly useful for examining the effects of person-specific life experiences on lifespan neurocognitive development. On the one hand, by holding the amount of practice constant in laboratory settings, researchers performing training studies can help answer questions about lifespan differences in cognitive and neuronal plasticity as well as the relative efficacy of socio-cultural and other contextual contributions to cognitive development. On the other hand, the expertise paradigm allows the influence of individual differences in life experiences to be examined in more ecologically valid domains. As for developmental differences in resource allocation, *simultaneous and sequential multitasking paradigms* may be useful means for understanding the interactions between age differences in the growth–maintenance–decline of processing resources and age differences in resource allocation priorities and strategies.

In summary, obtaining an integrated understanding of the dynamics of contextualized selective cognitive development across different periods is a challenge. To meet this challenge, it is necessary to integrate comparative methods involving systematic comparisons of (1) age, (2) personal experiences that can be experimentally simulated as varying amounts

or types of training or other contextual support, (3) personal experiences that can be more ecologically assessed in terms of expertise, and (4) constellations of multitasking demands. The various theoretical and empirical advances presented in this volume set the scene for achieving that integration.

References

Baltes, P. B. (1987). Theoretical propositions of life-span developmental psychology: On the dynamics between growth and decline. *Developmental Psychology, 23,* 611–626.

Baltes, P. B. (1997). On the incomplete architecture of human ontogeny: Selection, optimization, and compensation as foundation of developmental theory. *American Psychologist, 52,* 366–380.

Baltes, P. B. (1998). Testing the limits of the ontogenetic sources of talent and excellence. *Behavioral and Brain Sciences, 21,* 407–408.

Baltes, P. B., & Baltes, M. M. (1990). Psychological perspectives on successful aging: The model of selective optimization with compensation.In P. B. Baltes & M. M. Baltes (Eds.), *Successful aging: Perspectives from the behavioral sciences* (pp. 1–34).. New York: Cambridge University Press.

Baltes, P. B., & Kliegl, R. (1992). Further testing of limits of cognitive plasticity: Negative age differences in a mnemonic skill are robust. *Developmental Psychology, 28,* 121–125.

Baltes, P. B., & Lindenberger, U. (1988). On the range of cognitive plasticity in old age as a function of experience: 15 years of intervention research. *Behavior Therapy, 19,* 283–300.

Baltes, P. B., & Nesselroade, J. R. (1978). Multivariate antecedents of structural change in adulthood. *Multivariate Behavioral Research, 13,* 127–152.

Baltes, P. B., Reese, H. W., & Lipsitt, L. P. (1980). Lifespan developmental psychology. *Annual Review of Psychology, 31,* 65–110.

Baltes, P. B., Rösler, F., & Reuter-Lorenz, P. (in press). *Brain, mind, and culture: From interactionism to biocultural co-constructivism.* Cambridge, UK: Cambridge University Press

Baltes, P. B., & Singer, T. (2001). Plasticity and the aging mind: An exemplar of the biocultural orchestration of brain and behavior. *European Review, 9,* 59–76.

Baltes, P. B., & Smith, J. (2004). Lifespan psychology: From developmental contextualism to developmental biocultural co-constructivism. *Research on Human Development, 1,* 123–144.

Baltes, P. B., Staudinger, U. M., & Lindenberger, U.

(1999). Lifespan psychology: Theory and application to intellectual functioning. *Annual Review of Psychology*, 50, 471–507.

Bell, R. Q. (1968). A reinterpretation of the direction of effects in studies of socialization. *Psychological Review*, 75, 81–95.

Bialystok, E. (2001). *Bilingualism in development: Language, literacy, and cognition.* New York: Cambridge University Press.

Bialystok, E., Craik, F. I. M., Klein, R., & Viswanathan, M. (2004). Bilingualism, aging, and cognitive control: Evidence from the Simon task. *Psychology and Aging*, 19, 290–303.

Birren, J. E. (Ed.). (1964). *Relations of development and aging.* Springfield, IL: Charles C. Thomas.

Bjorklund, D. F. (1997). The role of immaturity in human development. *Psychological Bulletin*, 122, 153–169.

Brandtstädter, J., & Lerner, R. M. (1999). (Eds.). *Action and self-development: Theory and research through the life span.* London: Sage Publication.

Braver, T. S., Barch, D. M., Keys, B. A., Carter, C. S., Cohen, J. D., Kaye, J. A., Janowsky, J. S., Yahlor, S. F., Yesavage, J. A., & Mumenthaler, M. S. (2001). Context processing in older adults: Evidence for a theory relating cognitive control to neurobiology in healthy aging. *Journal of Experimental Psychology: General*, 130, 746–763.

Brehmer, Y., Müller, V., v.Oertzen, T., & Lindenberger, U. (2004). Episodic memory in childhood and old age: The role of cortical coherence. In A. Mecklinger, H. Zimmer, & U. Lindenberger (Eds.), *Bound in memory: Insights from behavioral and neuropsychological studies.* Herzogenrath, Germany, Shaker Verlag.

Bronfenbrenner, U. (1979). *The ecology of human development.* Cambridge, MA: Harvard University Press.

Bühler, C. (1933). *Der menschliche Lebenslauf als psychologisches Problem* (The human life course as a psychological topic). Leipzig, Germany: Hirzel.

Cabeza, R. (2002). Hemispheric asymmetry reduction in older adults: The Harold model. *Psychology & Aging*, 17, 85–100.

Cattell, R. B. (1971). *Abilities: Their structure, growth and action.* Boston: Houghton Mifflin.

Cepeda, N. J., Kramer, A. F., & Gonzalez de Sather, J. C. M. (2001). Changes in executive control across the life span: Examination of task-switching performance. *Developmental Psychology*, 37, 715–730.

Chow, S.-M., & Nesselroade, J. R. (2004). General slowing or decreased inhibition? Mathematical models of age differences in cognitive *functioning. Journal of Gerontology: Psychological Sciences*, 59B, 101–109.

Cole, M. (1999). Culture in development. In M. H. Bornstein & M. E. Lamb (Eds.), *Developmental psychology: An advanced textbook* (4th ed., pp. 73–123). Mahwah, NJ: Lawrence Erlbaum Associates.

Cole, M., & Cole, S. (1989). *The development of children.* New York: Scientific American Books.

Dempster, F. N. (1992). The rise and fall of the inhibitory mechanisms: Toward a unified theory of cognitive and aging. *Developmental Review*, 12, 45–47.

Dixon, R. A., & Baltes, P. B. (1986). Toward life-span research on the functions and pragmatics of intelligence. In R. J. Sternberg & R. K. Wagner (eds.), *Practical intelligence: Nature and origins of competence in the everyday world* (pp. 203–234). New York: Cambridge University Press.

Durham, W. H. (1991). *Coevolution: Genes, culture and human diversity.* Palo Alto, CA: Stanford University Press.

Eisenberg, A. R. (1985). Learning to describe past experiences in conversation. *Discourse Processes*, 8, 177–204.

Elbert, T., Pantev, C., Wienbruch, C., Rockstroh, B., & Taub, E. (1995). Increased cortical representation of the fingers of the left hand in string players. *Science*, 270, 305–307.

Ericsson, K. A., Krampe, R. T., & Tesch-Römer, K. (1993). The role of deliberate practice in the acquisition of expert performance. *Psychology Review*, 100, 363–406.

Erikson, E. H. (1959). Identity and the life cycle. *Psychological Issues Monograph*, 1. New York: International University Press.

Ford, D. H. (1987). *Humans as self-constructing living systems. A developmental perspective on behavior and personality.* Hillsdale, NJ: Lawrence Erlbaum Associates.

Freund, A. M., & Baltes, P. B. (2002). Life-management strategies of selection, optimization, and compensation: Measurement by self-report and construct validity. *Journal of Personality and Social Psychology*, 82, 642–662.

Ghisletta, P., & Lindenberger, U. (2003). Age-based structural dynamics between perceptual speed and knowledge in the Berlin Aging Study: Direct evidence for ability dedifferentiation in old age. *Psychology and Aging*, 18, 696–713.

Gigerenzer, G. (2003). The adaptive tookbox and lifespan development: Common questions? In U. S. Staudinger & U. Lindenberger (Eds.), *Understanding human development: Dialogues with lifespan psychology* (pp. 423–447). Boston: Kluwer Academic Publishers.

Glenberg, A. M. (1997). What is memory for? *Behavior and Brain Sciences*, 20, 1–55.

Gopnik, A., Choi, S., & Baumberger, T. (1996). Cross-linguistic differences in early semantic and cognitive development. *Cognitive Development, 11,* 197–227.

Groisman, E. A., & Ehrlich, S. D. (2003). A global view of gene gain. Loss, regulation and function. *Current Opinion in Microbiology, 6,* 479–481.

Gross, C. G. (2000). Neurogenesis in the adult brain: Death of a dogma. *Nature Reviews Neuroscience, 1,* 67–73.

Grossman, A. W., Churchill, J. D., Bates, K. E., Kleim, J. A., & Greenough, W. T. (2002). A brain adaptation view of plasticity: is synaptic plasticity an overly limited concept? *Progress in Brain Research, 138,* 91–108.

de Haan, M., Humphreys, K., & M. H. Johnson, M. H. (2002). Developing a brain specialized for face perception: A converging methods approach. *Developmental Psychobiology, 40,* 200–212.

de Haan, M., Pascalis, O., & Johnson, M. H. (2002). Specialization of neural mechanisms underlying face recognition in human infants. *Journal of Cognitive Neuroscience, 14,* 199–209.

Hambrick, D. Z., Salthouse, T. A., & Meinz, E. J. (1999). Predictors of crossword puzzle proficiency and moderators of age-cognition relations. *Journal of Experimental Psychology: General, 128,* 131–164.

Harris, D. B. (Ed.). (1957). *The concept of development.* Minneapolis: University of Minnesota Press.

Heckhausen, J. (1999). *Developmental regulation in adulthood: Age-normative and sociostructural constraints as adaptive challenges.* New York: Cambridge University Press.

Heckhausen, J., Dixon, R. A., & Baltes, P. B. (1989). Gains and losses in development throughout adulthood as perceived by different adult age groups. *Developmental Psychology, 25,* 109–121.

Hommel, B., Li, K. Z. H., & Li, S.-C. (2004). Visual search across the life span. *Developmental Psychology, 40,* 545–558.

Hultsch, D. F., MacDonald, S.W.S., & Dixon, R. A. (2002). Variability of reaction time performance of younger and older adults. *Journal of Gerontology: Psychological Sciences, 57B,* 101–115.

Hultsch, D. F., MacDonald, S.W.S., Hunter, M. A., Levy-Bencheton, J., & Strauss, E. (2000). Intra-individual variability in cognitive performance in older adults: Comparison of adults with mild dementia, adults with arthritis, and healthy adults. *Neuropsychology, 14,* 588–598.

Johnson, M. H. (2001). Functional brain development in humans. *Nature Review Neuroscience, 2,* 475–483.

Kail, R., & Salthouse, T. A. (1994). Processing speed as a mental capacity. *Acta Psychologica, 86,* 199–225.

Karmiloff-Smith, A. (1998). Development itself is the key to understanding developmental disorders. *Trends in Cognitive Sciences, 2,* 389–398.

Kemper, S., Herman, R. E., & Lian, C. H. T. (2003). The costs of doing two things at once for young and older adults: Talking while walking, finger tapping, and ignoring speech or noise. *Psychology and Aging, 18,* 181–192.

Kramer, A. F. K., & Willis, S. L. (2002). Enhancing the cognitive vitality of older adults. *Current Directions in Psychological Sciences, 11,* 173–177.

Krampe, R. T., & Baltes, P. B. (2003). Intelligence as adaptive resource development and resource allocation: A new look through the lenses of SOC and Expertise. In R. J. Sternberg & E. L. Grigorenko (Eds.), *The psychology of abilities, competencies, and expertise* (pp. 31–69). New York: Cambridge University Press.

Krampe, R. T., & Ericsson, K. A. (1996). Maintaining excellence: Deliberate practice and elite performance in young and older pianists. *Journal of Experimental Psychology: General, 125,* 331–359.

Kuhl, P. K., Williams, K. A., Lacerda, F., Stevens, K. N., & Lindbolm, B. (1992). Linguistic experience alters phonetic perception in infants by 6 months of age. *Science, 255,* 606–608.

Labouvie, E. W. (1982). Issues in life-span development. In B. B. Wolman (Ed.), *Handbook of developmental psychology* (pp. 54–62). Englewood Cliffs, NJ: Prentice-Hall.

Li, K. Z. H., Lindenberger, U., Freund, A. M., & Baltes, P. B. (2001). Walking while memorizing: Age-related differences in compensatory *behavior. Psychological Science, 12,* 230–237.

Li, S.-C. (2003). Biocultural orchestration of developmental plasticity across levels: The interplay of biology and culture in shaping the mind and behavior across the lifespan. *Psychological Bulletin, 129,* 171–194.

Li, S.-C., Aggen, S. H., Nesselroade, J. R., & Baltes, P. B. (2001). Short-term fluctuations in elderly people's sensorimotor functioning predict text and spatial memory performance: The MacArthur successful aging studies. *Gerontology, 47,* 100–116.

Li, S.-C., & Freund, A. M. (2005). Advances in lifespan psychology: A focus on biocultural and personal influences. *Research in Human Development, 2,* 1–23.

Li, S.-C., Huxhold, O., & Schmiedek, F. (2004). Aging and attenuated processing robustness: Evidence from cognitive and sensorimotor functioning. *Gerontology, 50,* 28–34.

Li, S.-C., & Lindenberger, U. (2002). Coconstructed functionality instead of functional normality. *Behavioral and Brain Sciences, 25,* 761–762.

Li, S.-C., Lindenberger, U., & Sikström, S. (2001). Aging cognition: From neuromodulation to representation. *Trends in Cognitive Sciences, 5,* 479–486.

Li, S.-C., Lindenberger, U., Hommel, B., Aschersleben, G., Prinz, W., & Baltes, P. B. (2004). Transformations in the couplings among intellectual abilities and constituent cognitive processes across the lifespan. *Psychological Science, 15,* 155–163.

Lindenberger, U., & Baltes, P. B. (1997). Intellectual functioning in old and very old age: Cross-sectional results from the Berlin Aging Study. *Psychology and Aging, 12,* 410–432.

Lindenberger, U., Marsiske, M., & Baltes, P. B. (2000). Memorizing while walking: Increase in dual-task costs from young adulthood to old age. *Psychology and Aging, 15,* 417–436.

Logan, J. M., Sanders, A. L., Synder, A. Z., Morris, J. C., & Buckner, R. L. (2002). Under-recruitment and nonselective recruitment: Dissociable neural mechanisms associated with aging. *Neuron, 33,* 827–840.

MacDonald, S. W. S., Hultsch, D. F., & Dixon, R. A. (2003). Performance variability is related to change in cognition: Evidence from the Victoria Longitudinal Study. *Psychology & Aging, 18,* 510–523.

Magnusson, D. (1988). *Individual development from an interactional perspective: A longitudinal study.* Hillsdale, NJ: Lawrence Erlbaum Associates.

Maguire, E. A., Gadian, D. G., Johnsrude, I. S., Good, C. D., Ashburner, J., Frackowiak, R. S. J., & Frith, C. D. (2000). Navigation-related structural change in the hippocampi of taxi drivers. *Proceedings of the National Academy of Sciences of the United States of America, 97,* 4398–4403.

Mareschal, D., & Shultz, T. S. (1996). Generative connectionist networks and constructivist cognitive development. *Cognitive Development, 11,* 571–603.

McArdle, J. J., Ferrer-Caja, E., Hamagami, F., & Woodcock, R. W. (2002). Comparative longitudinal structural analyses of the growth and decline of multiple intellectual abilities over the life span. *Developmental Psychology, 38,* 115–142.

Nelson, E., & Dannefer, D. (1992). Aged heterogeneity: Facts or fiction? The fate of diversity in gerontological research. *Gerontologist, 32,* 17–23.

Nelson, K. (1996). *Language in cognitive development.* Cambridge, England: Cambridge University Press.

Nesselroade, J. R. (1991). The warp and the woof of the developmental fabric. In R. M. Downs, L. S. Liben, & D. S. Palermo (Eds.), *Visions of aesthetics, the environment and development: The legacy of Joachim Wohlwill* (pp. 213–240). Hillsdale, NJ: Lawrence Erlbaum Associates.

Nesselroade, J. R., and P. B. Baltes (Eds.). (1979). *Longitudinal research in the study of behavior and development.* New York: Academic Press.

Neville, H. J., Bravelier, D., Corina, D., Rauschecker, J., Karni, A., Lalwani, A., Braun, A., Clark, V., Jezzard, P., & Turner, R. (1998). Cerebral organization for language in deaf and hearing subjects: Biological constraints and effects of experience. *Proceedings of the National Academy of Sciences, USA, 95,* 922–929.

Palincsar, A. S. (1998). Social constructivist perspectives on teaching and learning. *Annual Reviews of Psychology, 48,* 345–375.

Paulesu, E., McCrory, E., Fazio, F., Menoncello, L., Brunswick, N., Cappa, S. F., Cotelli, M., Cossu, G., Corte, F., Lorusso, M., Pesenti, S., Gallagher, A., Perani, D., Price, C., Frith, C. D., & Frith, U. (2000). A cultural effect on brain function. *Nature Neuroscience, 3,* 91–96.

Piaget, J. (1954). *The construction of reality in the child.* New York: Basic Books.

Rabbitt, P., Osman, P., Moore, B., & Stollery, B. (2001). There are stable individual differences in performance variability, both from moment to moment and from day to day. *Quarterly Journal of Experimental Psychology: Human Experimental Psychology, 54A,* 981–1003

Reinert, G. (1970). Comparative factor analytic studies of intelligence throughout the life span. In L. R. Goulet & P. B. Baltes (Eds.), *Life-span developmental psychology: Research and theory* (pp. 476–484). New York: Academic Press.

Reuter-Lorenz, P. A. (2002). New visions of the aging mind and brain. *Trends in Cognitive Sciences, 6,* 394–400.

Rogoff, B. (1990). *Apprenticeship in thinking: Cognitive development in social context.* New York: Oxford University Press.

Roisman, G. I., Masten, A. S., Coatsworth, D., & Tellegen, A. (2004). Salient and emerging developmental tasks in the transition to adulthood. *Child Development, 75,* 123–133.

Schooler, C. (1984). Psychological effects of complex environments during the lifespan: A review and theory. *Intelligence, 8,* 259–281.

Schooler, C. (1996). Cultural and social-structural explanations of cross-national psychological differences. *Annual Review of Sociology, 22,* 232–249.

Schooler, C., & Mulatu, M. S. (2004). Occupational self-direction, intellectual functioning, and self-directed orientation in older workers: Findings and implications for individuals and societies. *American Journal of Sociology, 110,* 161–197.

Schooler, C., Mulatu, M. S., & Oates, G. (1999). The continuing effects of substantively complex work on the intellectual functioning of older workers. *Psychology and Aging, 14,* 483–506.

Segalowitz, S. J., & Rosekrasnor, L. (1992). The construct of brain maturation in theories of child development. *Brain and Cognition, 20,* 1–7.

Siegler, R. S. (1994). Cognitive variability: A key to understanding cognitive development. *Current Directions in Psychological Science, 3,* 1–5.

Singer, T., Lindenberger, U., & Baltes, P. B. (2003). Plasticity of memory for new learning in very old age: A story of major loss? *Psychology and Aging, 18,* 306–317.

Singer, T., Verhaeghen, P., Ghisletta, P., Lindenberger, U., & Baltes, P. B. (2003). The fate of cognition in very old age: Six-year longitudinal findings in the Berlin Aging Study (BASE). *Psychology and Aging, 18,* 318–331.

Smiler, A. P., Gagne, D. D., & Stine-Morrow, E. A. L. (2003). Aging, memory load, and resource allocation during reading. *Psychology and Aging, 18,* 203–209.

Staudinger, U. M., & Lindenberger, U. (2003). (Eds.). *Understanding human development: Dialogues with lifespan psychology.* Dordrecht, Netherlands, Kluwer Academic Publishers.

Staudinger, U. M., Bluck, S., & Hertzog, P. Y. (2003). Looking back and looking ahead: Adult age differences in consistency of diachronous ratings of subjective well-being. *Psychology and Aging, 18,* 13–24.

Tetens, J. N. (1777). *Philosophische Versuche über die menschliche Natur und ihre Entwicklung* (The philosophical inquiry about human nature and development). Leipzig, Germany: Weidmanns Erben und Reich.

Tomasello, M. (1999). *The cultural origins of human cognition.* Cambridge, MA: Harvard University Press.

Weir, M. W. (1964). Developmental changes in problem-solving strategies. *Psychological Review, 71,* 473–490.

Williams, B., Ponesse, J., Schachar, R., Logan, G. D., & Tannock, R. (1999). Development of inhibitory control across the life span. *Developmental Psychology, 25,* 205–213.

Author Index

Abdi, H., 267
Abeles, N., 333
Aberg, L., 53
Abrams, C. R., 36
Abrams, L., 196, 197, 202, 233, 246
Abrams, M. T., 28
Abson, V., 332
Acker, J. D., 6, 30, 138
Ackerman, P. L., 194, 199
Adalsteinsson, E., 30
Adams, A., 234
Adams, C., 172, 173, 174
Adams, D., 170
Adams, M. J., 243
Adams, S. E., 72
Adolfsson, R., 30, 164, 165, 166
Adolph, K. E., 288, 291
Ager, J., 16
Aggen, S. H., 304, 311, 356
Aguiar, A., 76
Aguirre, G. K., 32, 194
Ahn, J., 122
Akbudak, E., 30, 31
Akhtar, N., 209, 210
Alajouanine, T. H., 240

Alavi, A., 33
Albert, M. S., 30, 98, 233, 333
Alberts, D. M., 322
Albertson-Owens, S. A., 169
Alderman, N., 98
Aleva, K., 34
Alexander, G. E., 29
Alexander, M. P., 71, 83, 256
Alibali, M. W., 289, 293, 318, 321
Ali-Cherif, A., 260
Alioto, A., 210, 218, 219
Allaire, J. C., 303
Allen, J. B., 169
Allen, P. A., 62, 65
Allen, R., 20
Allison, T., 19
Allport, A., 82
Allport, G. W., 285
Almkuist, O., 53
Alpert, N., 241
Alsop, D. C., 194
Amaral, D. G., 30, 34
Ambridge, B., 118, 121
Amiel-Tison, C., 183
Amso, D., 78, 82

Anagnopoulos, C., 218
Anderson, C., 289
Anderson, J. R., 319, 323, 325
Anderson, M., 333, 335, 338, 339, 340
Anderson, N. D., 22, 34
Anderson, P. A., 195
Anderson, S. W., 97
Andrade, J., 113
Andrassy, J. M., 228
Andres, D., 201, 333
Andrews, G., 320, 321
Anooshian, L. J., 107
Antsey, K. J., 134, 135
Aram, D. M., 241
Arbuckle, T. Y., 201, 230, 241, 333
Ardila, A., 83
Armilio, M. L., 173
Armstrong, I., 83
Arnstein, A. F. T., 36
Arsenault, A., 169
Asburner, J., 28
Aschersleben, G., 8, 99, 107, 139, 304, 305

Ashburner, J., 77, 352
Aslin, R. N., 218
Assad, W. F., 71
Atchley, P., 62
Atkinson, R. L., 128, 129
Atkinson, T. M., 97, 98, 99
Auman, C., 163, 174
Aupée, A. M., 33
Auschutz, L., 286
Austin, A., 173, 196, 201, 202, 241
Austin, E. J., 304, 338
Awh, E., 88
Aylward, E. H., 18

Babcock, R. L., 130
Bach, J., 311
Bachevalier, J., 73, 76
Bäckman, L., 7, 11, 164, 165, 166,
    169, 200, 276, 286, 307
Baddeley, A. D., 9, 87, 112, 113,
    114, 115, 116, 121, 122, 129,
    130, 135, 138, 234, 259
Badecker, W., 257
Badger, A. N., 76
Bahrick, H. P., 166
Bahro, M., 306
Bailey, L., 208
Baillargeon, R., 76, 179
Baker, C., 256, 259
Baker, E., 255
Baker, S., 116, 121
Baker-Ward, L., 143, 144, 145, 146,
    147, 148, 153, 154
Baldwin, D. A., 210, 212
Balinsky, B., 135
Ball, K., 53, 62
Ballard, D., 137, 138
Balota, D. A., 60, 65, 102–103, 163,
    170, 197
Balsamo, L. M., 21
Baltes, M. M., 311, 347, 357
Baltes, P. B., 7, 8, 9, 33, 34, 64, 99,
    107, 134, 135, 139, 193, 198,
    199, 203, 287, 291, 297, 298,
    299, 300, 303, 304, 305, 340,
    344, 345, 346, 347, 349, 350,
    351, 352, 353, 355, 356, 357
Banich, M. T., 63, 65
Barad, V., 63
Barcelo, F., 71
Barch, D. M., 58, 65, 100, 358
Bardell, L., 11, 64, 65
Barker, P. B., 16
Barlow, J. M., 240
Barnes, L. L., 88, 311
Barnes, M. A., 18, 239, 240, 241,
    242, 243, 244, 246, 247
Barnett, A. S., 21, 22, 37
Baron, A., 64, 65
Baron, J.-C., 33

Bar-On, M., 168
Barr, R., 145
Barrett, M. D., 185
Barrett, S. E., 267
Barrett, T. J., 332
Barrouillet, P., 119
Bartolucci, G., 226, 229
Barton, M., 210
Barton, R. M., 234
Bartsch, K., 72
Bartzokis, G., 16
Basili, A., 255
Basso, A., 255
Bastin, C., 166, 167
Bates, E. A., 180, 183, 241, 245
Bates, K. E., 352
Bates, P. B., 195
Batsakes, P. J., 62, 64
Batterman-Faunce, J. M., 145
Batty, M., 19, 20
Bauer, P. J., 143, 145, 184
Baumberger, T., 350
Baumgaertner, A., 246, 247
Bavelier, D., 21, 350
Baving, L., 18
Bayen, U. J., 169
Beach, D. R., 143
Beard, B., 62
Beauvois, M. -F., 256
Bechara, A., 87
Becker, J. T., 34
Becker, M. G., 82
Becker-Caplan, L., 234
Beckett, L. A., 311, 333
Beckmann, J., 325
Beckson, M., 16
Beekman, A. T. F., 333
Beers, S. R., 17
Begy, G., 86
Beier, M.E., 194
Beig, S., 34
Beland, R., 256
Belger, A., 19
Bell, J. A.
Bell, M., 145
Bell, M. A., 72
Bell, R. Q., 346
Bellugi, U., 116, 215
Belopolsky, A. V., 63
Benasich, A. A., 234
Benbow, C. P., 118
Benjamin, B. J., 223
Bennett, D. A., 311
Bennett, D. J., 246
Bennett, P. J., 10
Ben-Shoham, I., 49
Benson, D. F., 33, 97
Bent, L., 332, 333
Bent, N. C., 195, 332, 333
Bentin, S., 19

Benton, A., 97
Berish, D. E., 97, 98, 99
Berk, L. E., 4
Berko Gleason, J., 215, 257
Berkowitz, A. L., 20, 88
Bernardin, S., 119
Berndt, R. S., 242, 255
Bernholz, N., 257
Bernstein, B., 226
Berry, E., 172
Bertenthal, B., 294
Berthaud, I., 215
Bertoncini, J., 183
Bertrand, J., 208, 211
Best, D. L., 152
Beyth, R., 79
Bhakta, M., 32, 33
Bhattacharyya, S., 174
Bialystok, E., 11, 266, 351
Bickerton, D., 226
Bickhard, M. H., 180, 184
Bidell, T. R., 320
Bilker, W., 17
Bill, B., 210
Billington, C., 218
Binet, A., 143, 147, 285
Birch, S., 77
Birmaher, V., 20
Birney, D. P., 319, 320
Birren, J. E., 4, 333, 345
Bishara, A. J., 101, 103, 104
Bishop, D. V., 18
Bixenman, M., 83
Bjorklund, D. F., 143, 145, 148,
    151, 152, 153, 154, 155, 289,
    293, 317, 356
Black, E., 34
Black, J. E., 184
Blanton, R. E., 17
Blaser, S. E., 240, 243, 247
Blazoit, X., 33
Bleckley, M. K., 88
Bleile, K., 241
Blennerhassett, A., 119, 234
Bloom, L., 210, 211
Bloom, P., 77
Bluck, S., 346
Blumenthal, J., 16, 17
Blumstein, S., 255, 256
Boag, C. C., 320, 321
Boden, C., 52
Boileau, R. A., 65
Bojko, A., 63
Boland, A. M., 150, 155
Bookheimer, S. Y., 34
Bookstein, F., 77
Boone, K. B., 107
Booth, J. R., 22
Booth, L., 107
Bopp, K. L., 99, 270

Boring, A. M., 17
Boring, E. G., 318
Borkowski, J. G., 151, 155
Bosman, E. A., 198
Botting, N., 234
Botwinick, J., 226
Bower, G. H., 243
Bowles, R. P., 137
Bowman, C. A., 256
Bow-Thomas, C. C., 289
Boyer, K., 73
Braak, E., 30
Braak, H., 30
Bradford, D. C., 98
Brady, K. D., 18
Braine, M. D. S., 319
Brainerd, C. J., 7, 147
Brand, C. R., 304, 338
Brandimonte, M. A., 117
Brandstädter, J., 346
Brandt, J., 241
Brandt, M. E., 244
Bransford, J. D., 151
Brant, L. J., 16
Brass, M., 76, 77
Braswell, G. S., 293
Braun, A., 350
Braver, T. S., 58, 65, 71, 88, 100, 358
Brehmer, Y., 351
Breier, J. I., 21
Brent, H. P., 19
Brewer, W. F., 267
Briggs, S. D., 6, 30, 34, 138
Bright, P., 247
Brink, J., 98
Brinton, B., 240
Broadbent, D. E., 105, 117, 119, 122
Broadbent, M. H. P., 117, 122
Brodeur, D. A., 47, 52, 53
Brody, B. A., 16, 20
Brody, N., 286, 316
Bronfenbrenner, U., 207, 345
Brooks, P., 82
Brooks, V., 48
Brooks, W. M., 18
Broughton, J., 83
Brown, A. L., 75, 76, 150, 151
Brown, A. S., 195, 196
Brown, D., 49
Brown, G. D. A., 117
Brown, J., 31
Brown, J. E., 18
Brown, R., 7
Brown, R. M., 73
Brown, T. T., 37
Browner, W., 333
Brozoski, T. J., 73
Bruce, D., 241

Bruce, V., 47
Bruck, M., 157, 187
Brunelle, F., 18
Bruner, J. S., 6, 83
Bruni, J., 53, 62
Brunswick, N., 198, 350
Bryant, D., 198, 199
Bub, D., 257
Buchanan, M., 114
Bucht, G., 164, 166
Buckingham, H. W., 256, 258
Buckner, R. L., 28, 29, 30, 31, 32, 33, 34, 35, 139, 144, 197, 352, 358
Budde, M., 22
Buffalo, E. A., 75
Bühler, C., 345
Buitelaar, J. K., 17
Buiten, M. M., 59
Bullmore, E. T., 18
Bundy, D. A., 324, 325
Bunge, S. A., 71, 77, 98
Burack, J. A., 46, 47
Burgess, N., 117
Burgess, P. W., 86, 99, 335
Burgwyn-Bailes, E., 145
Burian, H., 34
Burke, D. M., 7, 9, 118, 173, 193, 195, 196, 197, 198, 201, 202, 229, 233, 241, 246, 247
Burlingham-Dubree, M., 289
Burman, D. D., 22
Burns, H. J., 170
Busa, E., 28, 34, 35
Buss, A. R., 298
Bussiere, J. R., 22
Butcher, S. J., 50
Butler, R. N., 333
Butterworth, B., 258
Buxton, R. B., 22
Byrd, M., 58, 129, 152
Byrne, R. M., 319

Cabeza, R., 7, 8, 11, 22, 32, 34, 135, 306, 355, 358
Cahan, S., 316, 321
Cai, J. X., 36
Caird, J., 49
Caltagirone, C., 255
Cameron, N., 230
Camos, V., 119
Camp, C. J., 286
Campbell, R. A., 18
Campbell, T., 234
Campione, J. C., 151
Caplan, D., 231, 232, 241, 242, 246, 254, 256, 257, 259, 260
Caporael, L., 226
Cappa, S. F., 198, 350
Caramazza, A., 240, 241, 255, 256, 257, 258

Carey, S., 9, 269, 320, 321
Carlin, M. T., 46
Carlson, S. M., 77
Carpenter, M., 210
Carpenter, P. A., 86, 113, 115, 119, 319, 320
Carr, T., 243
Carraher, D. W., 321
Carraher, T. N., 321
Carriger, M. S., 317, 325
Carrillo, M. C., 32
Carroll, J. B., 316, 317, 318, 321
Carstensen, L. L., 11, 163, 174, 194, 200, 201
Carter, C. S., 58, 65, 71, 358
Carullo, J. J., 234
Carver, L. J., 145, 184
Casati, G., 255
Case, R. D., 83, 84, 85, 86, 118, 119, 154, 120, 321
Casey, B. J., 7, 8, 17, 18, 20, 22, 37, 83, 88
Caspi, A., 286
Cassidy, D. J., 150, 151
Cassidy, K. W., 218
Castel, A. D., 168, 172, 174
Castellanos, F. X., 17, 83
Castillo, E. M., 21
Cattell, A. K.S., 332, 335, 336, 340
Cattell, R. B., 193, 298, 304, 316, 332, 335, 336, 340
Cauley, J., 333
Cauley, K. M., 212
Cavanaugh, J. C., 155
Caviness, V. S., Jr., 17
Ceci, S. J., 148, 157, 187, 321, 324
Cepeda, N. J., 63, 83, 354
Cerella, J., 10, 59, 64, 99, 335
Chae, B., 196
Chafee, M. V., 71
Chaix, Y., 21
Chalfonte, B. L., 163, 168, 169, 171, 199
Chambers, D., 79
Chan, D., 28
Chandramallika, B., 99
Chang, B., 267
Chanoine, V., 198
Chapman, S. B., 241
Charles, S. T., 11, 163, 174, 200, 201
Charness, N., 198
Chartier-Harlin, M. C., 31
Chase, W. G., 118, 122
Chason, J., 65
Chasteen, A. L., 174
Chau, W., 11
Chavoix, C., 33
Chelune, G. J., 83
Chen, C. C., 86

Chen, Z., 288, 317, 321
Cherry, K. E., 133
Chetwynd, A., 98, 333
Cheung, H., 227, 228, 232, 234
Chi, M. T. H., 9, 86, 118, 121, 122, 148, 154, 319
Chiappe, P., 234
Chiat, S., 117
Chinsky, J. M., 143
Chiron, C., 18
Chisum, H., 28
Choi, S., 185, 350
Chomsky, N., 244
Chow, S. -M., 358
Christensen, J. R., 18
Christidis, P., 198, 202
Chrosniak, L. D., 169, 171
Chuah, Y. M. L., 116
Chugani, D. C., 16, 18
Chugani, H. T., 16, 18, 73
Chung, M. S., 19
Church, R. B., 293, 294
Churchill, J. D., 352
Churchland, A., 75
Cintron, C. B., 17
Cissell, G. M., 62
Clancy, S. M., 62
Clark, A., 179, 183
Clark, C. A., 30
Clark, E. V., 7, 208, 209, 218
Clark, J. J., 50
Clark, L. A., 285
Clark, R. E., 75
Clark, V., 350
Clasen, L. S., 6
Clifton, C., 243
Clubb, P. A., 143, 146, 148
Clune, M., 79
Coatsworth, D., 346
Coffey, S. A., 21
Coffey-Corina, S. A., 21
Coffman, J. L., 155
Cohen, G., 7, 9, 233
Cohen, J. D., 70, 83, 87, 307, 358
Cohen, M. S., 34
Cohen, N. J., 30, 65, 138, 200, 316, 321
Cohen, S., 83
Cohn, N. B., 98
Colby, A., 286
Colcombe, A., 65
Colcombe, S. J., 8, 65, 163, 173, 174
Cole, B., 51
Cole, M., 155, 266, 345, 349
Cole, S., 345
Collins, D. L., 16
Collins, J. J., 311
Collins, K. W., 234
Colombo, J., 46

Colzato, L., 48, 49
Comalli, P. E., 48
Conant, L. L., 116
Connelly, S. L., 59, 60, 229
Conrad, H., 275, 279
Conrad, R., 114
Constable, R. T., 244
Conti-Ramsden, G., 234
Conturo, T. E., 30, 31
Convit, A., 33
Conway, A. R. A., 87, 88, 99, 113, 115
Conway, M. A., 189
Cook, S., 81
Cooper, J. A., 240
Cooper, P. F., 105
Cooper, P. V., 223
Cooper, R. D., 218
Cooper, W. E., 256
Copeland, D. E., 195
Copeland, K., 244
Coppola, M., 244
Corbetta, D., 288
Corbetta, M., 34
Coren, S., 47, 48
Corina, D., 350
Corkin, S., 200, 244
Cornelius, S. W., 7, 135, 304
Cornoldi, C., 118
Corsale, K., 155
Corte, F., 350
Cortese, M. J., 170, 197
Cosmides, L., 268
Cossu, G., 198, 350
Cotelli, M., 350
Courchesne, E., 28
Covington, J., 28
Cowan, N., 9, 113, 117, 120, 122
Cowles, A., 28
Cox, B., 156
Coyle, T. R., 153, 293, 294
Craik, F. I. M., 6, 7, 9, 11, 22, 29, 53, 58, 64, 107, 129, 148, 151, 152, 166, 168, 169, 171, 173, 199, 200, 266, 307, 351
Crain, S., 234, 242, 265
Crammond, J., 85
Crane, A. M., 73
Crawford, F., 31
Cronbach, L. J., 315
Cronin-Golomb, A., 97
Cross, D., 72
Crow, A., 232
Cruess, L., 75, 81
Crutchfield, J. M., 88
Cruts, M., 165, 166
Culbertson, G. H., 226
Culhane, K. A., 241
Cummings, J. L., 33
Cupit, J., 243, 245

Curiel, J. M., 195
Curtiss, S., 242
Cycowicz, Y. M., 20
Cymerman, E., 202

Dabholkar, A. S., 17
Dagenais, P., 230
Dahl, R. E., 20, 22, 83
Dalton, C., 320, 321
Damasio, A., 87, 97, 188
Damasio, H. 87
Daneman, M., 86, 113, 115, 119, 130, 195, 216, 217, 234
Daniel, M. H., 338, 340
Daniels, K., 87, 102, 106, 107
Dannefer, D., 349
Dark, V. J., 118
Darley, F. L., 256
Daselaar, S. M., 22
Davatzikos, C., 28
Davenport, N. D., 22
Davidi, S., 234
Davidson, J. E., 323
Davidson, M. C., 7, 8, 18
Davidson, N. S., 129, 130, 134, 135, 304
Davidson, P. S. R., 167, 168, 169
Davidson, R. J., 20
Davidson, Y., 333
Davies, L., 154
Davies, M., 215
Davis, G. A., 223
Davis, P., 28
Davis, R. N., 21
Deacon, T. W., 181
Deary, I. J., 22, 304, 315, 318, 335, 338
De Bellis, M. D., 17
Debner, J. A., 100, 102, 106, 107
DeCarli, C., 30
Deeg, D. J. H., 333
de Haan, M., 19, 358
Dehaut, F., 259
De Jong, R., 103
DeKosky, S. T., 34
Delalande, O., 18
de la Sayette, V., 33
D'Elia, L., 107
Delis, D. C., 97, 278
Dell, G. S., 202
Dell, T. C., 64
Della Sala, S., 116
DeLoache, J. S., 76, 150, 151, 187
DeLong, M. R., 29
Delpuech, F., 260
De Meersman, L., 60, 61, 65, 98, 335
Démonet, J.-F., 21, 198
Dempster, F. N., 10, 75, 83, 86, 115, 354
Demuth, K., 218

Denckla, M. B., 18, 28
Denes, G., 256
Denis, J., 53
Dennett, D. C., 179
Dennis, I., 319
Dennis, M., 239, 240, 241, 242, 243, 244, 245, 247
Dennis, S., 319
Denny, M. A., 288
Deouell, L. Y., 32
De Rammelaere, S., 112
DeRenzi, E., 114
Derfuss, J., 76
DeSanti, S., 33
Desgranges, B., 33
Desikan, R. S., 28, 34, 35
Desjardins, N., 210
Desmet, T., 112
Desmond, J. E., 32, 34, 71
D'Esposito, M. D., 32, 71, 137, 138, 168, 194
De Stefano, N., 34
Detre, J. A., 194
Detterman, D. K., 316, 324, 338, 340
Diamond, A., 6, 9, 70, 71, 72, 73, 74, 75, 77, 78, 81, 82, 83, 85
Dick, E., 247
Dickinson-Anson, H., 36
Didow, S. M., 144, 147, 149, 155, 157
Diesendruck, G., 210
Diggle, P., 332, 333
DiGirolamo, G. J., 63
Dimitrovsky, L., 234
Dirken, J. M., 333
Dirksen, C., 32
Dirnberger, G., 71
Dixon, R. A., 7, 11, 165, 166, 233, 276, 303, 304, 311, 347, 356
Dobbs, A. R., 202
Dodd, A., 116
Dogil, G., 244
Doherty, S., 215
Dolan, P. O., 163
Dolan, R. J., 77
Dolcos, F., 22
Dollaghan, C., 234
Don, M., 20
Donald, M., 179, 181, 186, 188, 189
Donaldson, D. I., 71
Donaldson, G., 334
Donlan, C., 332, 333
Dordain, M., 257
Dorfman, J., 32
Dorosz, M., 173
Doussard-Rossevelt, J., 61, 62
Dow, G. A., 184
Dowden, A, 145

Dow-Ehrensberger, M., 155
Drevets, W. C., 20, 22
Driver, J., 47, 82
Dropik, P. L, 143
Drory, A., 51
Druss, B., 194
Ducharme, J. L., 228
Duchek, J. M., 163, 170
Duffy, S. A., 243
Dulaney, C., 60
Dumas, J. A., 169
Dunbar, K., 87
Duncan, J., 71, 86, 96, 98, 335
Dunn, L. M., 233
Dupuis, J. H., 6, 30, 34
Durham, W. H., 349
Duroe, S., 116
Durso, F. T., 88
Durston, S., 17, 18
Dustman, R. E., 98
Dworetzky, B., 256
d'Ydewalle, G., 319
Dywan, J., 98, 169, 229

Eacott, M. J., 76
Eals, M., 21
Earles, J., 130, 134, 139
Eaves, L., 322
Eberhard, J., 53
Eberling, J. L., 31
Eccard, C. H., 20, 22
Eckerman, C. O., 144, 147, 149, 155, 157
Eckman, C. B., 30
Eddy, T., 47
Eddy, W. F., 83
Edelstein, K., 244
Edmonds, G. E., 19
Edvardsson, H., 165, 166
Edwards, J. D., 49, 62
Edwards, N., 16
Egaas, B., 28
Egan, V., 304, 338
Egeth, H. E., 46
Eggermont, J. J., 20
Eggers, R., 335
Ehrlich, S. D., 348
Eichenbaum, H., 30
Eigsti, I. M., 18
Eisdorfer, C., 233
Eisenberg, A. R., 349
Ekelman, B. L., 241
Elavsky, S., 65
Elbert, T., 352
Elliott, R., 77
Ellis, A., 122
Elman, J. L., 22, 180, 183
Embretson, S. E., 316
Emerson, M. J., 96–97, 99, 113, 122
Emery, O., 223

Emslie, H., 86, 98, 335
Endsley, M., 52
Engle, R. W., 9, 77, 87, 88, 99, 102, 103, 106, 113, 115, 129, 234
Engstrom, R., 334
Enns, J. T., 10, 44, 47, 48, 50, 51, 52, 53
Enright, M., 143
Eppler, M. A., 288
Erickson, K. I., 8, 65
Ericsson, K. A., 113, 120, 122, 198, 351, 352
Erikson, E. H., 346
Erkinjuntti, T., 36
Erngrund, K., 164, 166, 200
Estes, W. K., 300
Eustache, F., 33
Evans, A. C., 16, 17
Evans, D. A., 311, 333
Evans, J., 98
Evans, J. D., 166
Evans, J. S. T., 319
Evans, K., 259
Evey, J. A., 208
Ewing-Cobbs, L., 18, 241
Eysenck, H. J., 335

Fabricius, W. V., 286
Fadale, D., 17
Fadda, F., 37
Fadl, Y., 288
Fagan, J. F., III, 75, 212
Fagen, J., 143
Fan, L., 289
Farah, M. J., 194, 335, 877
Farber, K., 240
Farde, L., 307
Farrant, K., 147
Fassbinder, W., 246, 247
Fastenau, P. S., 116
Faulkner, H., 240, 242, 246, 247
Faust, M. E., 60, 65, 87, 102–103, 234, 246, 247
Fazio, F., 198, 350
Federico, A., 34
Feldman, H., 241
Feldman, J. F., 317, 325
Fener, E., 259
Fenner, J., 117
Ferguson, S., 53
Fernald, A., 218
Ferrara, R. A., 151
Ferrari, M., 285, 290
Ferraro, F. R., 246
Ferrell, P., 218
Ferrer-Caja, E., 29, 275, 316, 353
Ferry, P. C., 240
Feuerstein, R., 320, 324
Feyereisen, P., 195
Fidani, L., 31

Field, D. J., 268–269
Filipek, P. A., 17
Finch, D. M., 33
Fine, H. J., 240
Fingeret, A. L., 48
Fink, A., 217
Finter-Urczyk, A., 218
Fischer, F. W., 122
Fischer, K. W., 320
Fischoff, B., 79
Fisher, G. W., 289
Fisk, A. D., 62, 64
FitzGerald, P., 105
Fivush, R., 143, 144, 147, 148, 155, 157, 187, 188
Flavell, E. R., 77
Flavell, J. H., 77, 79, 82, 143, 155, 286
Fleischman, D. A., 165
Fletcher, J. M., 18, 21, 239, 244
Fletcher, P. C., 32, 247
Floden, D., 71
Flynn, E., 77
Flynn, J. R., 316
Fodor, J. A., 178
Fohlen, M., 18
Folds, T. H., 143, 144, 150, 151, 153, 154
Foley, M. A., 171, 187
Folk, C. L., 59
Follmer, A., 146, 148
Foorman, B. R., 21
Footo, M. M., 143, 144, 150, 151, 153, 154
Ford, D. H., 348
Forman, S. D., 83, 88
Forssberg, H., 20, 22
Foster, J. C., 275
Fotenos, A. F., 28
Fournier, P. A., 48
Fowler, C. A., 122
Fox, N. C., 28
Fox, P. T., 88
Frackowiak, R. S. J., 28, 114, 336–337, 352
Francis, D., 21, 244
Frankish, C. R., 122
Franzen, P. L., 7, 8, 20, 88
Frederick, J., 244
Fredrickson, B. F., 200
Freeman, J., 241
Freer, C., 96, 98, 335
Frensch, P. A., 308
Freund, A. M., 64, 287, 291, 345, 346, 347, 357, 358
Friedman, N. P., 96–97, 99, 102, 113
Friesen, C. K., 47, 49
Frieske, D., 130, 133, 134, 139
Fristoe, N. M., 63, 98

Friston, K. J., 28
Frith, C. D., 114, 198, 336–337, 350, 352
Frith, U., 198, 350
Fromhoff, F. A., 147, 148
Frost, C., 28
Frost, S. J., 21
Frustaci, K., 17
Fry, A. F., 86
Frye, D., 9, 79, 326
Fujiki, M., 240
Fujioka, T., 18
Fulbright, R. K., 244
Funahashi, S., 71
Fung, H. H., 174, 180, 181, 182, 187
Funkenstein, H. H., 333
Furst, A., 122
Furtado, E., 146, 154
Fuster, J., 97

Gabaude, C., 53
Gabrieli, J. D. E., 71, 29, 98, 165, 200
Gadian, D. G., 18, 352
Gage, F. H., 36
Gagne, D. D., 358
Gaillard, W. D., 21, 22, 37
Gaines, C., 130, 134, 139
Gainotti, G. B., 255
Gallagher, A., 350
Gallagher, J. M., 267
Galton, F., 285
Gambhir, S. S., 33
Gamst, A., 17
Gangitano, M., 71
Garavan, H., 99, 103, 247
Garcia, J. H., 30
Garcia, R., 179
Garcia-Mila, M., 289
Gardiner, J. M., 103
Garrad-Cole, F., 52
Garrard, P., 245
Garrett, H. E., 304
Garrett, M. F., 256
Garver, K. E., 83
Gathercole, S. E., 115, 116, 117, 118, 121, 122, 234
Gazzaley, A., 32
Gazzaniga, M. S., 49
Geary, D. C., 289
Gelman, R., 208, 266
Gelman, S. A., 267, 270
Genovese, C. R., 83
Gentner, D., 320, 325
Gerhing, H., 227
Gernsbacher, M. A., 87, 88, 234, 246
Gerome, G. J., 65
Gerring, J. P., 18

Gershkoff-Stowe, L., 210
Gerstadt, C., 77, 82
Geschwind, N., 255
Ghatala, E. S., 286
Ghisletta, P., 297, 300, 310, 311, 353, 355
Gibbons, L., 333
Gibbs, J., 286
Gibbs, R. W., 242
Gibson, E., 20
Gibson, E. J., 288
Gibson, G. J., 304, 338
Gibson, J. J., 181
Gibson, K. R., 15
Giedd, J. N., 6, 16, 17, 37, 83
Giffard, C., 33
Gigerenzer, G., 79, 347, 356
Giles, H., 226, 227, 229
Gilhooly, K. J., 122
Gill, S. V., 288
Gilles, F. H., 16, 20
Gillette, J., 215
Gilligan, C., 79
Gimpert, N., 187
Gioia, G. A., 234
Girgus, J. S., 47, 48
Girton, L. E., 28, 31
Gitelman, D. R., 22
Glaser, R., 319
Glass, J. M., 65
Gleason, J. B., 257
Gleitman, H., 215
Gleitman, L., 215
Glenberg, A. M., 356
Glisky, E. L., 29, 167, 168, 169, 171
Glover, G. H., 34, 71
Gmeindl, L., 65
Goate, A., 31
Gobbini, M. I., 19
Godjin, R., 48, 49
Gogtay, N., 6
Gold, D. P., 201, 230, 241, 333
Goldberg, J., 83, 85, 86, 118, 120
Golde, T. E., 30
Goldin-Meadow, S., 289, 293
Goldman, P. S., 73
Goldman-Rakic, P. S., 36, 71, 72, 73, 87
Goldring, J., 83
Goldsmith, M., 104
Goldstein, D., 173
Goldstein, K., 97
Golinkoff, R. M., 208, 209, 210, 211, 212, 213, 218, 219
Gonzalez de Sather, J. C. M., 63, 83, 354
Good, C. D., 28, 352
Goodglass, H., 194, 242, 255, 257
Goodman, G. S., 145

Goodman, J. C., 245
Goodwin, D., 286
Goossens, L., 200
Gopher, D., 63, 65
Gopnik, A., 77, 79, 185, 187, 350
Gordon, B. N., 143, 145, 146, 154
Gordon, L., 212
Gordon, R., 145
Gore, J. C., 244
Gotler, A., 63
Gottlob, L. R., 59
Gould, J., 254
Gow, C. A., 97
Grados, M. A., 18
Grady, C. L., 8, 10, 11, 20, 22, 32, 34, 77
Graesser, A. C., 243
Graf, P., 187
Graham, T., 293
Gramzow, E., 144, 145
Grant, J., 215
Gratch, G., 72
Gravelle, D. C., 311
Graw, T., 49
Gray, J. T., 147
Green, F. L., 77
Green, I., 217
Greenhouse, S. W., 333
Greenhout, A. F., 146
Greeno, J. G., 208
Greenough, W. T., 184, 352
Greenspan, S. L., 243
Greenstein, D., 6
Greenwood, P. B., 29
Greenwood, P. M., 59, 60, 62
Greer, M., 247
Gregory, R. L., 48
Greicius, M. D., 33
Greiner, L. H., 216, 218, 226, 253, 333
Greve, D. N., 28, 34, 35
Gribbin, K., 333
Griffith., E. M., 322
Griggs, D., 62
Grigorenko, E. L., 324, 325
Grober, E., 233
Grodzinsky, Y., 223, 245, 257
Groisman, E. A., 348
Groisser, D. B., 83
Gross, C. G., 352
Grossman, A. W., 352
Growden, J. H., 244
Gubarchuk, J., 227, 228
Guez, J., 6, 168
Guezeldere, G., 32
Gunji, A., 11
Gunning, F. M., 6, 30, 34
Gunning-Dixon, F., 30
Gunter, J. L., 28
Gur, R. C., 17

Gur, R. E., 17, 33
Gustafson, J. E., -316
Gutchess, A. H., 8, 135, 138
Guthke, J., 325
Guttentag, R. E., 117, 143, 144, 150, 151, 152, 153, 154
Guttman, L., 317

Habib, M., 198, 260
Hackney, A., 173
Haden, C. A., 143, 144, 147, 148, 149, 150, 155, 157
Haefele-Kalvaitis, J., 242
Hagen, J. W., 286
Hahn, S., 59, 63, 65
Haider, H., 244
Haig, J. R., 151, 152
Haine, R. A., 143, 147
Hakamies-Blomqvist, L., 53
Hala, S., 77
Hale, S., 86, 130, 133, 246
Halford, G. S., 319, 320, 321, 325
Halit, H., 19
Hall, J., 17
Hall, M., 118
Halle, M., 244
Halliday, M. A. K., 185
Halliday, M. S., 116, 120, 121
Halsted, N., 183
Hamagami, F., 275, 316, 353
Hambrick, D. Z., 63, 64, 275, 279, 350
Hamburger, S. D., 16, 17
Hamer, L., 71, 83
Hamilton, L. B., 155
Hamilton-Wentworth District Health Council, 216
Hanauer, J. B., 82
Hancock, H. E., 106
Hancock, P., 52
Harden, T., 218, 227
Harnishfeger, K. K., 145, 154, 246
Harris, D. B., 345
Harris, H. W., 73
Harris, J. C., 16
Harris, P. L., 72
Harris, R. J., 230
Harrison, C., 65
Harrold, R. M., 195
Harry, J., 311
Hart, B., 18
Hart, S. S., 155
Hartley, A., 34, 138
Hartley, A. A., 57, 59, 60, 63
Hartman, M., 169
Harward, H., 241
Harwood, J., 223
Hasher, L., 9, 10, 29, 58, 59, 60, 61, 86, 87, 98, 99, 106, 112, 135,

136, 137, 145, 154, 163, 169, 172, 173, 174, 201, 229, 230, 234, 246, 247, 335
Hashtroudi, S., 169, 170, 171
Hassol, L., 230
Hatano, G., 266, 269
Haugh, H., 335
Hawkins, R. A., 33
Haxby, J. V., 8, 19, 77, 83
Hay, J. F., 100, 102, 105, 201
Hayashi, K. M., 6
Hayden, M., 70, 75
Hayne, H., 143, 145, 183
Head, D., 6, 30, 31, 34
Healy, M. R., 165, 166, 167, 172
Heathcote, D., 117
Heatherington, C. R., 97
Heaton, R. K., 166
Heberle, J., 79
Heberlein, W., 218
Hebert, L. E., 333
Heckhausen, J., 346
Hedden, T., 29, 129, 130, 134, 135, 137, 304
Hedehus, M., 30
Hedrick, A. M., 144, 147, 150, 155
Heeger, D. J., 32
Heeschen, C., 257
Heger, R., 52
Heim, A. W., 332
Heller, H. S., 233
Heller, R. B., 202
Henderson, A., 77
Henderson, D., 228, 232
Henderson, V. L., 223
Hendrick, E. B., 244
Henkenius, A. L., 17, 18, 28
Hennon, E., 212, 213, 214, 215
Henri, V., 143, 147
Henry, L. A., 119
Henson, R. N. A., 28, 32, 114
Henwood, K., 226, 229
Herman, L., 198, 199
Herman, R. E., 230, 234, 358
Hermon, D. H., 6
Hern, K. L., 240
Heron, A., 119
Herrnstein, R. J., 316
Hertsgaard, L. A., 184
Hertwig, R., 79
Hertzij, M. E., 221
Hertzog, C., 233, 311, 333
Hertzog, P. Y., 346
Hertz-Pannier, L., 18, 21, 22, 37
Hess, T. M., 163, 174
Hessels, S., 101, 103, 104, 270
Hetherington, R., 241, 244
Hewes, A. K., 116
Hickok, G., 244
Hicks, R. E., 307, 308

Hildebrandt, H., 259
Hildebrandt, N., 241, 242, 259
Hill, D. E., 18
Hill, E., 107
Hillis, A., 257
Hills, B., 48, 51
Hindley, C. B., 334
Hindman, J., 228
Hinds, P. J., 77
Hinten, V. J., 139
Hinton, G. E., 319
Hirose, H., 256
Hirsh-Pasek, K., 210, 211, 212, 213, 218, 219, 1914
Hitch, G. J., 86, 87, 112, 113, 115, 116, 117, 118, 119, 120, 121, 122, 129, 135, 138, 139
Hix, H. R., 77
Ho, G., 49, 62
Hobart, C. J., 173
Hochberg, J., 48
Hodges, J. R., 245
Hodson, B. W., 256
Hofer, S. M., 135, 193, 303, 1314
Hoff, E., 216
Hoffman, E. A., 19
Hoffman, H. J., 244
Hoffman, R. R., 240
Hoffrage, U., 79
Holcomb, P. J., 21
Holden, D. J., 144, 153
Hole, G., 49
Holland, A., 241
Holland, C. M., 333
Holland, F., 332, 333
Hollich, G., 210, 211
Hommel, B., 8, 10, 48, 49, 99, 107, 139, 304, 305, 347
Honeck, R. P., 240
Hong, J., 71, 83
Hong, Y., 77, 82
Hood, B. M., 47
Hoogstra, L., 180, 181, 182, 187
Hopkins, S. L., 289
Horan, M. A., 333
Horhota, M., 174
Horn, J. L., 8, 193, 275, 304, 316, 317, 334, 336, 340
Horska, A., 16
Horwitz, B., 8, 32, 77
Houle, S., 32
Houston-Price, C. M. T., 81
Howard, D., 258
Howard, D. V., 195
Howerter, A., 96–97, 99, 113
Howlin, D., 214
Howlin, P., 215
Howse, J. N., 86
Hoyer, W. J., 59, 62, 103

Hsieh, S., 82
Huang, H. W., 33
Huber-Okrainec, J., 240, 242, 243, 247
Hudson, J. A., 147, 148
Huettel, S. A., 32
Hug, S., 77
Hughes, C., 77, 82
Hughes, P., 51
Hughett, P., 17
Huizenga, H. M., 300
Hull, A. J., 114
Hulme, C., 116, 117, 120
Hulme, E., 101, 102, 173, 241
Hulshoff Pol, H. E., 17
Hultsch, D. F., 7, 11, 233, 297, 303, 304, 310, 311, 347, 356
Humphrey, D. G., 58, 59, 60, 61, 62, 65, 98
Humphreys, G. W., 62
Humphreys, M. S., 319
Humphreys, R. P., 244
Hunt, C., 138
Hunt, E., 285
Hunter, L., 257
Hunter, M. A., 347
Hunter, W. S., 143
Huppi, P. S., 30
Husmann, R., 244
Hussain, Z., 168
Hutchinson, J. E., 209
Huttenlocher, J., 118, 202, 208
Huttenlocher, P. R., 17
Hutton, U., 86, 118, 119, 120, 122, 139
Huxhold, O., 298, 299, 347, 353, 354, 355, 356
Hyde, M. R., 257
Hyle, M., 50
Hyltenstam, K., 223
Hynd, G. W., 82, 240

Iarocci, G., 47
Ibrahim, Z., 21
Igvar, M., 32
Iidaka, T., 20
Inagaki, K., 266, 269
Inhelder, B., 7, 77, 265
Insausti, R., 33
Intieri, R. C., 300, 403
Intons-Peterson, M. J., 173
Ippel, M. J., 315, 318
Irwin, D. E., 62
Irwin, J. M., 210
Isaac, W., 82
Isaacowitz, D. M., 11, 200, 201
Isaacs, E. B., 118
Ishii, R., 11
Isquith, P. K., 234
Itier, R. J., 19, 20, 22

Itoh, M., 256
Izukawa, D., 71, 83

Jacennik, B., 241
Jack, C. R., Jr., 28, 30
Jackson, J. H., 223, 245
Jacobs, J., 143
Jacobsen, C. F., 97
Jacoby, L. L., 29, 77, 100, 101, 102, 103, 104, 167, 270
Jagust, W. J., 31, 58, 65
Jahanshahi, M., 71
Jakobsen, R., 223
Jambaque, I., 18
James, L. E., 7, 9, 173, 195, 196, 201, 202, 233, 241, 247
James, M., 98
Janisse, J. J., 16
Janke, M., 53
Janowsky, J. S., 58, 65, 358
Janssen, J. C., 28
Jarrold, C., 116
Jarvik, M. E., 76
Java, R. I., 98, 167
Jeffries, N. O., 17
Jenkins, L., 130, 133
Jenner, A. R., 21
Jennings, J. M., 6, 9, 29, 100, 102, 105, 129, 167, 200
Jensen, A. R., 316, 318, 335
Jernigan, T. L., 17
Jerrams-Smith, J., 117
Jezzard, P., 350
Joanette, Y., 256, 260
Joanisse, M., 117
Job, R., 240, 255
Joerding, J. A., 130, 133
Joffe, K. M., 62
Johansson, K., 53
Johnson, M. B., 316
Johnson, M. H., 19, 180, 183, 202, 358
Johnson, M. K., 71, 138, 163, 168, 169, 170, 171, 199
Johnson, M. V., 19
Johnson, R., 96, 98, 335
Johnson, S., 240
Johnson, S. P., 270
Johnson, T., 155
Johnson-Laird, P. N., 152, 319, 321
Johnsrude, I. S., 28, 352
Johnston, M. V., 18
Jokel, R., 243, 245
Jolesz, F., 30
Jones, C. J., 311
Jones, D., 195
Jones, D. K., 30
Jones, H. E., 275, 279
Jones, L. B., 83
Jones, S., 32

Jones, S. S., 210
Jonides, J., 34, 88, 114, 130, 133, 138
Joseph, S., 50
Josephs, O., 77
Jou, J., 230
Juhasz, C., 16
Jukes, M., 324, 325
Jurica, P. J., 130
Jusczyk, P. W., 183, 194, 218
Just, M. A., 113, 119, 319, 320

Kahn, I., 77
Kahn, J., 228
Kail, R., 10, 86, 120, 154, 354
Kalaria, R. N., 30
Kalimo, H., 30
Kane, M. J., 9, 60, 61, 87, 88, 99, 102, 103, 106, 129, 136, 137
Kaplan, B., 265
Kaplan, E., 97, 98, 278
Kapur, S., 32, 34
Karlsson, S., 164, 166
Karmiloff-Smith, A., 7, 9, 179, 180, 183, 184, 185, 194, 215, 356
Karni, A., 350
Karpel, M. E., 103
Karzon, R. G., 218
Kaszniak, A. W., 7, 169, 199
Katz, D., 71
Katz, L., 21
Katz, R. B., 122
Katz, W., 256
Kaufman, A. S., 278
Kaufman, N. L., 278
Kaufmann, W. E., 16
Kausler, D. H., 130
Kavé, G., 243, 245
Kaye, J. A., 358
Kaysen, D., 17
Kean, M. - L., 257
Kee, D. W., 154
Keefe, D., 246
Keefe, K., 241
Keightlry, M. L., 34
Keil, F. C., 266, 267, 269, 270
Keleman, D., 266
Kellaghan, T., 304, 338
Keller, E., 2526
Kelley, C. M., 77
Kelley, W. H., 32
Kelly, K., 79
Kemler-Nelson, D. G., 194, 218
Kemper, S. J., 195, 199, 201, 216, 218, 223, 226, 227, 228, 230, 231, 232, 233, 234, 253, 333, 358
Kemper, T. L., 30, 36
Kempler, D., 246
Kemps, E., 112
Kemtes, K. A., 199, 231, 232

Kenemans, J. L., 59
Kennedy, D. N., 17
Kennedy, K. M., 30
Kennedy, L., 194
Kensinger, E. A., 170
Kent, R., 256–257
Kenworthy, L., 234
Kerkman, D. D., 292
Kertesz, A., 258
Keshavan, M. S., 17, 83
Keys, B. A., 58, 65, 358
Keysar, B., 246
Khanna, M. M., 88
Kieley, J. M., 59, 60, 63
Kieras, D. E., 65
Kihlstrom, J. F., 7, 199
Killgore, W. D., 17
Killiany, R. J., 30
Kim, S., 33
Kimberg, D. Y., 87, 335
King, S. W., 20
Kingstone, A., 47, 49
Kinney, H. C., 16, 20
Kinsbourne, M., 8, 307, 308
Kintsch, W., 113, 120, 122, 137, 183, 240–241, 245
Kirkham, N. Z., 75, 81, 82
Kitcher, P. S., 269
Kleim, J. A., 352
Klein, R., 53, 351
Klein, S. K., 240
Kliegl, R., 64, 199, 203, 351
Klingberg, T., 20, 22
Kloman, A. S., 16, 20
Kloo, D., 77, 82
Knight, R., 71
Knopman, D. S., 28
Knowlton, B., 244
Koenderink, M. J. T., 72, 73
Koeppe, R., 138
Kohlberg, L., 77, 286
Kohn, B., 241, 242
Kohn, S. E., 256
Koinis, D., 77, 79
Kok, A., 59
Kolb, B., 20, 29
Kondoh, Y., 33
Konner, M., 16, 20
Koriat, A., 104
Koroshetz, W. J., 244
Kosaka, H., 20
Koski, L., 71
Kosowski, T. D., 209
Koutstaal, W., 169, 170, 171, 172
Kowalska, D. M., 76
Kozuch, P. L., 17
Kramer, A. F. K., 8, 11, 58, 59, 60, 61, 62, 63, 64, 65, 83, 98, 351, 354
Kramer, J. H., 97, 278
Kramer, J. J., 286

Krampe, R. T., 198, 304, 311, 351, 352, 356, 357
Krasnegor, N. A., 97
Krause, B. J., 71
Kraut, M. A., 28
Kray, J., 63
Kreuger, S., 6
Kruglanski, A. W., 79
Kuczaj, S. A., 289
Kuhl, D. E., 33
Kuhl, P. K., 350
Kuhn, D., 289
Kuhn, H. G., 36
Kuhn, J., 145
Kunz, K., 7, 8
Kurland, D. M., 83, 85, 86, 118, 120
Kwon, H., 20, 22
Kwong, B., 20
Kynette, D., 201, 223, 230

LaBerge, D., 243
Labouvie, E. W., 345
Labouvie, G. V., 332
Labouvie-Vief, G., 173, 174
Lacerda, F., 350
Lachman, J. L., 332
Lachman, R., 332
Lahar, C. J., 228, 232
Lain, C. H. T., 358
Lalevée, C., 33
Lalwani, A., 350
Lamar, M., 335
Lambertz, G., 183
Landau, B., 210
Landerl, K., 198
Lang, B., 77
Lange, G., 144, 154
Lange, N., 17
Langenecker, S. A., 247
Langham, M., 49
Langley, L. K., 59
Langston, M. C., 243
Langton, S. R. H., 47
Lapointe, S., 256, 257
Larish, J. F., 11, 58, 59, 60, 61, 64, 65, 98
Larsson, M., 169
Larus, D. M., 143, 146
Lasserson, D., 33
Lauber, E. J., 65
Laucht, M., 18
Lauer, R. E., 116
Laughlin, J. E., 113, 115
Launer, L. J., 30
Lautenschlager, G., 129, 130, 134, 135, 304
Lautrey, J., 311
Lavenex, P., 30
Laver, G. D., 198, 233

Lavie, N., 59, 60
LaVoie, D. J., 165, 166, 167, 169, 172
Lawrence, A., 335
Lawrence, L. D., 98
Lawrence, W. A., 116, 120
Lawson, M. J., 289
Lazar, R. T., 240
Leal, L., 155
Lease, J., 137, 138
Leathem, J., 240
Leather, C. V., 119
Lebiere, C., 319
Le Bihan, D., 18, 21, 22, 30, 37
Lecours, A.-R., 16, 20, 256, 257, 256, 258
Lederer, A., 215
Lee, C., 50
Lee, E. -Y., 75
Lee, J. R., 21
Lee, M., 17
Leeevers, H. J., 234
Leekam, S. R., 77, 79
Le Grand, R., 19
Lehman Blake, M., 246, 247
Lehto, J., 98
Lei, Z., 22
Leighton, E., 172
Leinbach, J., 244
Leirer, V. O., 228
Le Mestric, C., 33
Leon, M. J., 33
Leonard, G., 16
Leonard, J. S., 228
Lerner, R. M., 346
Lesser, I. M., 107
Levelt, W. J. M., 201, 240, 255
Levin, D., 270
Levin, D. T., 50
Levin, H. S., 18, 241
Levin, J. R., 286
Levine, B., 71, 83
Levine, S., 202
Levitt, J. G., 17
Levy, B. A., 243
Levy, E., 186
Levy, E. T., 256
Levy, Y., 214
Lewandrowski, K. U., 33
Lewis, D. A., 73
Lewis, J. L., 293
Lewis, P., 33
Lewis, V. J., 114, 116
Lhermitte, F., 7, 97, 240, 256
Li, K. Z. H., 10, 63, 64, 98, 145, 163, 169, 287, 291, 303, 304, 311, 347, 358
Li, S.-C., 8, 10, 99, 107, 139, 298, 299, 302, 304, 305, 306, 307,

308, 310, 311, 345, 346, 347, 349, 353, 354, 355, 356, 357
Li, W., 22
Lian, C. H. T., 230
Liberman, I. Y., 122
Liberty, C., 151, 152
Lidow, M. S., 73
Lidz, C. S., 320, 324
Lieberman, M., 286
Light, L. L., 9, 29, 165, 169, 193, 194, 195
Liker, J., 321
Lillo-Martin, D., 265
Lim, K. O., 28, 30
Lima, S. D., 246
Lincourt, A. E., 59, 62
Lindenberger, U., 7, 8, 34, 63, 64, 99, 107, 134, 135, 139, 193, 198, 287, 291, 297, 298, 300, 302, 303, 304, 305, 307, 308, 310, 311, 336, 340, 345, 349, 351, 353, 355, 358
Linderholm, T., 245
Lindsay, D. S., 102, 103, 170
Linebarger, M. C., 241, 258, 259
Lipsitt, L. P., 345, 346
Lipsitz, L. A., 30, 311
Little, D. M., 65
Littler, J. E., 116, 120, 121
Liu, H., 17
Livesey, D. J., 77, 83
Livesey, P. J.
Lloyd, S. A., 118
Lobaugh, N. J., 20
Locantore, J. K., 22, 34, 196
Lockhart, K. L., 267
Loesnner, M., 33
Loewen, E. R., 29
Loftus, E. F., 103, 170
Logan, G. D., 10, 98, 354
Logan, J. M., 32, 34, 139, 352, 358
Logie, R. H., 113, 114, 115, 118, 122
Lohman, D. F., 315, 317, 318
Loken, W. J., 6
Longoni, A. M., 116
Look, R. B., 137–138
Lorusso, M., 350
Lövdén, M., 98, 170, 171, 300, 310
Love, T., 241
Loveless, M. K., 228
Lovett, M. W., 241
Lowe, C., 98, 335
Lu, P. H., 16
Lucas, D., 143
Lucchelli, F., 246, 247
Lucero, A. A., 288
Luciana, M., 117
Luck, S. J., 114
Lugar, H. M., 37
Lukas, K. E., 64

Lum, J., 47, 52
Luna, B., 83
Lundberg, C., 53
Luria, A. R., 82, 97
Lusk, L., 6
Lustig, C., 32, 33, 137
Luszcz, M. A., 134, 135
Lutz, D. J., 320
Lyons, G. R., 97
Lyons, K., 218

MacAuley, E., 120, 122
MacDonald, A. W., III, 71
MacDonald, S. W. S., 297, 303, 310, 311, 347, 356
MacKay, D. G., 193, 195, 196, 197, 200, 202, 233, 246, 247
Mackey, T., 240
Mackworth, J. F., 86
MacLean, R. D., 20
MacLeod, C. M., 48, 71
Macmillan, M. B., 97
Macnamara, J., 3
MacWhinney, B., 244
Madden, D. J., 59, 62, 195
Maercker, A., 9
Magnor, C., 198, 199
Magnus-Petersson, K., 32
Magnusson, D., 299, 345, 346
Maguire, E. A., 336–337, 352
Maguire, M., 212
Maisog, J. M., 8, 32
Maitland, S. B., 165, 166, 300, 304
Majovski, L. V., 16
Makris, N., 259
Malecki, J., 48
Maloney, L. M., 245
Mandell, D. J., 77
Mandler, J. M., 179, 184, 185, 186, 266
Mangin, J. F., 30
Marchman, V. A., 241, 270
Marcoen, A., 200
Marcovitch, S., 9
Mareschal, D., 356
Margaret, A., 230
Marin, O., 255, 259
Mark, L. S., 122
Mark, R. E., 167
Markesbery, W. R., 226, 253, 333
Markley, R. P., 286
Markman, E. M., 208, 210
Marks, W., 138
Markson, L., 210
Markus, H. S., 30
Marquez, D. X., 65
Marquis, J. G., 216, 218, 223, 226
Marsden, P., 33
Marshalek, B., 317
Marshuetz, C., 34, 135, 138

Marsiske, M., 64, 303
Martell, C., 53
Martin, A., 117, 240, 255
Martin, C. L., 285
Martin, N., 256
Martin, R., 259
Masalehdan, A., 17
Masten, A. S., 346
Masullo, C., 255
Masur, D., 240
Mathalon, D. H., 28
Mather, M., 163, 169, 170, 171, 174
Matsui, M., 17
Matsumoto, K., 77
Matthews, P. M., 34
Mattila, W., 64, 65
Maurer, D., 19
May, C. P., 9, 60, 61, 99, 106, 136, 137, 172, 173, 229, 246, 247, 335
Maybery, M. T., 116
Maylor, E. A., 9, 59, 62, 195
Mayr, U., 63, 64
Mazzarella, M. M., 48
Mazziotta, J. C., 16, 34, 73
Mbise, A., 324, 325
McAdams, D. P., 189
McArdle, J. J., 275, 316, 353
McAuley, E., 65
McAuley, R., 154
McAvoy, M., 32, 33
McBride, A. M., 333
McCabe, A., 143, 147, 148, 155
McCall, L. E., 155
McCall, R. B., 317, 325
McCarthy, G., 19, 32
McCarthy, R., 255, 256, 259
McClelland, J. L., 87, 202, 270, 319
McCollam, K., 316
McCracken, J. T., 17
McCrory, E., 198, 350
McDaniel, M. A., 234, 246
McDermott, K. G., 170
McDonough, L., 184, 185, 186
McDougall, S., 122
McDowd, J. M., 53, 57, 63–64, 98, 166
McElree, B., 103
McEvoy, C. L., 246
McEwen, B. S., 36
McGilly, K., 289, 290, 293
McGinnis, D., 216, 217, 219
McGrew, K. S., 278
McGuigan, F., 149
McGuthry, K. E., 63
McGwin, G., 49
McInnes, L., 98, 195, 332, 333
McIntosh, A. R., 8, 10, 22, 32, 34, 77, 306
McIntyre, J. S., 7, 199
McKoon, G., 297, 310

McLellan, K., 173
McLeod, P., 114
McNamara, D. S., 234
McNeil, M. R., 257
McNeill, D., 256
McQuain, J. M., 6, 30, 34
McVey, K. A., 155
Mead, G., 169
Means, B., 266
Medin, D., 270
Medlin, R. G., 152
Meguro, K., 33
Mehler, J., 183, 257
Meinz, E. J., 86, 98, 199, 275, 279, 350
Meir, M., 49
Meiran, N., 83
Meltzoff, A. N., 143
Menard, W. E., 198, 199
Mencl, W. E., 21, 244
Mendelsohn, D., 241
Menn, L., 242, 257
Menna, R.
Menon, V., 20, 22, 33
Menoncello, L., 350
Mentis, M. J., 32
Merian, N., 63, 82, 83
Merikle, P. M., 115
Merriam, E. P., 83
Merriman, W. E., 208
Merritt, K. A., 145, 146, 154
Mervielde, I., 79
Mervis, C. B., 208, 209, 211, 215
Mesulam, M.-M., 22, 97, 253
Metcalf, D., 333
Metis, M. J., 8
Metsala, J. L., 117
Meyer, D. E., 65
Meyer, J. R., 22
Mezenge, F., 33
Miceli, G., 255, 257
Miezin, F. M., 37
Mikels, J. A., 34, 135, 138
Milberg, W., 233
Miles, C., 86
Milham, M. P., 63
Milinder, L. A., 228
Miller, A., 34, 138
Miller, B. L., 107
Miller, B. T., 71
Miller, D., 50
Miller, D. G., 170
Miller, E. K., 70, 76, 77, 98, 307
Miller, G. A., 117, 180, 181, 182, 187
Miller, J., 30
Miller, K. F., 289
Miller, L. T., 86
Miller, P. H., 153, 286
Miller, P. J., 180, 181, 182, 187
Miller, R., 62

Miller, S. A., 286
Miller, S. W., 166
Millien, I., 33
Mills, D. L., 21
Mills, J., 44
Milne, A. B., 86
Milner, B., 114, 130
Milson, R., 319
Minear, M., 8, 306, 308
Minshew, N. J., 83
Mintun, M. A., 34
Mintz, J., 16, 180, 181, 182, 187
Mishkin, M., 18, 76
Mitchell, K. J., 71, 138, 168, 169, 170, 171
Mitchum, C. C., 242
Mitzner, T. L., 216, 218, 226
Miyake, A., 96–97, 99, 102, 113, 115, 119, 122, 129
Moely, B. E., 155
Molchan, S. E., 306
Molenaar, P. C. M., 300
Molko, N., 30
Momenthaler, M. S., 58, 65
Mondloch, C. J., 19
Monk, A., 122
Monsell, S., 63, 82
Montgomery, J., 234
Montie, J., 212
Moore, B., 195, 310, 311, 356
Morgan, B. G., 15
Morgan, G. A., 77, 83
Morgan, J., 218
Morgan, M. J., 86
Mormino, E. C., 17
Morrell, R. W., 134
Morris, E. D. M., 86
Morris, J. C., 28, 31, 32, 33, 34, 139, 352, 358
Morris, L. W., 29
Morris, P. A., 207
Morris, R. G., 29, 30
Morrison, F. J., 155, 322
Morrow, D. G., 198, 199, 228, 243
Mortilla, M., 34
Mortimer, J. A., 226, 253, 333
Moscovitch, M., 29, 171, 201
Moseley, M., 30
Moses, L. J., 77
Moss, F., 311
Moss, H., 247
Moss, H. E., 240
Moss, M. B., 30, 36
Most, R. B., 325
Mott, S. H., 21, 22, 37
Mottaghy, F. M., 71
Mottron, L., 46, 47
Mozley, D., 33
Mrzljiak, L., 72, 73
Muggia, S., 246, 247

Muir, C., 116, 120
Muier-Broaddus, J. E., 154
Mukherjee, P., 30
Mulatu, M. S., 350, 351
Mullan, M., 31
Müller, H. J., 58
Muller, R. A., 18
Muller, U., 9
Müller, V., 351
Multhaup, K. S., 246, 247
Mumenthaler, M. S., 358
Munakata, Y., 87, 202
Mungas, D., 31
Munoz, D. P., 83
Murachver, T., 145
Murata, T., 20
Murnane, K., 169
Murphy, B. L., 36
Murphy, G. L., 267, 270
Murphy, K. J., 71, 83, 99, 103, 173
Murphy, W. E., 229
Murray, A. D., 22
Murray, C., 316
Murray, D. J., 114
Murray, E. A., 75
Murray, R., 322
Musen, G., 244
Muzik, O., 16
Myers, J., 144, 145
Myers, J. T., 146
Myers, S. D., 227, 230
Myerson, J., 130, 133, 246

Nagell, K., 210
Naidu, S., 16
Naigles, L., 216
Nanayakkara, N., 226
Nartowitz, J., 234
Nash, C., 138
Naus, M. J., 144, 151, 152, 153,
    154, 155
Naveh-Benjamin, M., 6, 163, 168,
    169, 171, 308
Neely, A. S., 286
Neil, J., 30
Neill, W. T., 60, 61
Neisser, U. 128
Nelson, C. A., 117, 1415
Nelson, E., 349
Nelson, J. K., 88
Nelson, K., 143, 147, 149, 152, 181,
    182, 183, 184, 185, 186, 187,
    188, 189, 200, 201, 207, 209,
    346, 350, 352
Nespoulous, J. L., 256, 257
Nesselroade, J. R., 7, 135, 300, 302,
    303, 304, 310, 311, 347, 356,
    358, 399
Nestor, P., 53
Neumann, J., 76

Neves, D. M., 319, 323, 325
Neville, H. J., 21, 350
Newcombe, N. S., 208
Newell, A., 319
Newman, J., 241
Newman, M. C., 169
Newman, R. S., 155
Ngrosho, D., 324, 325
Ni, W., 242, 244
Nichelli, P., 114
Nichols, T., 34
Nicholson, C. B., 240
Nielson, K. A., 247
Niemi, J., 311
Nieminen, T., 49
Nilsson, L.-G., 30, 98, 164, 165,
    166, 200
Nissen, H. W., 97
Nix, L. A., 195
Nixon, P. D., 76
Nokes, C., 324, 325
Noll, D. C., 20, 83, 88, 38
Noll, J., 17
Norman, D. A., 97, 325
Norman, K. A., 171
Norman, M. A., 166
Norman, S., 201
Nougier, V., 52
Nuechterlein, K. H., 16
Nugent, T. F., 6
Nuñes, T., 321
Nyberg, L., 22, 30, 32, 34, 164, 165,
    166, 200
Nyquist, L., 173, 174
Nystrom, L. E., 83, 88

Oates, G., 351
Obler, L. K., 223, 233, 242, 257
O'Brien, K., 223, 230
O'Brien, K. C., 32, 33
O'Brien, P. C., 28, 30
Ochsner, K. N., 71
Odell, K., 257
Oertzen, T. V., 311, 351
Ogle, L. T., 243
O'Hara, R., 34
Okada, T., 20
O'Kane, G., 230
Ollier, W. E. R., 333
Olofsson, U., 200
Olshausen, B. A., 268–269
Olson, C. R., 33
O'Malley, C., 77
Omori, M., 20
O'Neil, C., 49
O'Regan, J. K., 50
Orendi, J. L., 83
Ornstein, P. A., 143, 144, 145, 146,
    147, 149, 150, 151, 152, 153,
    154, 155, 156, 157

Osman, P., 310, 311, 356
Osowiecki, D., 199
Ostrin, R., 257
O'Sullivan, M., 30
Othick, M., 227
Overman, W. H., 73
Overmeyer, S., 18
Owen, A. M., 71, 98, 137–138, 335
Owen, C. F., 334
Owens, J. L., 145
Owsley, C., 53, 62

Padilla, F., 122
Padowska, B., 82
Pagliari, C., 338
Paivio, A., 116
Palfai, T., 326
Palincsar, A. S., 350
Palmer, S., 116
Palumbo, C., 71, 83
Pang, E. W., 20
Pantev, C., 11, 18, 352
Pantoni, L., 30
Papagno, C., 117, 122, 246, 247
Papanicolaou, A. C., 21
Pappata, S., 30
Paquier, P., 240, 241
Parasuraman, R., 53, 59, 60, 62
Paredes, D. R., 289
Paris, S. G., 155
Parisi, D., 180, 183
Park, D. C., 8, 32, 33, 34, 98, 129,
    130, 133, 134, 135, 137, 138,
    139, 163, 164–165, 304, 306, 308
Park, R., 8, 306, 308
Park, Y., 120
Parkes, K. R., 105
Parkin, A. J., 98, 167, 335
Parrish, T. B., 22
Pascalis, O., 358
Pascual-Leone, A., 71
Pascual-Leone, J., 320, 321
Passarotti, A. M., 22
Passingham, R. E., 76, 77
Passler, P. A., 82
Pasupathi, M., 11, 173, 174, 201
Pate, D. S., 256
Patterson, K., 245
Paul, B. M., 22
Paul, S. T., 199
Paulesu, E., 114, 198, 350
Paus, T., 16, 17
Pauzie, A., 53
Payer, D.
Payne, B. K., 106
Payton, A., 333
Peaker, S. M., 116, 122, 139
Pearson, D. G., 118
Pedelty, L. L., 256
Pedroza, M. J., 197, 202

Pellissier, J., 260
Pendleton, N., 333
Pennington, B. F., 83
Penpeci, C., 10
Perani, D., 350
Perez, E., 19
Perfetti, C. A., 243
Pericak-Vance, M. A., 34
Perlman, A., 63
Perlmutter, M., 144, 155, 173, 174
Perner, J., 77, 79, 82, 180
Perrig, P., 144
Perrig, W. J., 144
Perron, C., 257
Perry, M., 293
Pesenti, S., 350
Peters, A., 36
Peters, L., 195
Petersen, R. C., 30
Petersen, S. E., 34, 37, 88
Peterson, B. S., 17, 18, 28
Peterson, C., 143, 145, 147, 148, 155
Peterson, J. R., 17
Peterson, M. S., 63
Petrides, M., 71, 130, 137–138
Petropoulos, H., 18
Peuster, A., 73
Pfefferbaum, A., 28, 30
Pham, D. L., 28
Phelps, M. E., 16, 33, 73
Phillips, L. H., 20, 335
Phillips, S., 319, 320, 321, 325
Piaget, J., 5, 6, 7, 71, 77, 179, 193, 265, 286, 320, 346
Piccinin, A. M., 336
Pichora-Fuller, M. K., 195, 216, 217
Pickering, S. J., 115, 116, 117, 122
Pickles, A., 322
Pierce, T. W., 59, 62
Pietrini, P., 8
Pike, B., 16
Pilgrim, L., 247
Pillon, B., 7
Pinker, S., 209, 214, 244, 266, 268, 270
Piñon, D. E., 77, 79
Pipe, M.-E., 145
Platzak, C., 242, 247
Pleydell-Pearce, C. W., 189
Plude, D., 47, 52, 53, 61, 62
Plunkett, K., 180, 183, 210, 270
Polk, T. A., 8, 34, 135, 138, 194, 306, 308
Pollio, H. R., 240
Pollio, M. R., 240
Polster, M. R., 29, 168, 171
Poncet, M., 260
Ponesse, J., 10, 354
Ponton, C. W., 20

Poon, L. W., 199
Posner, M. I., 58, 83, 88, 114
Postle, B. R., 137, 138
Potter, U., 336
Potts, R., 180, 181, 182, 187
Poupon, C., 30
Povinelli, D., 47
Power, K. G., 86, 114, 118
Prather, P., 230, 231, 241
Pratt, C. C., 289
Pratt, J., 47, 48, 49, 52
Pratt, M. W., 201
Premack, D., 77
Prenovost, K., 216, 218, 226
Pressley, M., 151, 286
Preusser, D., 53
Pribram, K. H., 97
Price, C., 350
Prill, K. A., 64
Prince, S. E., 22
Principe, G. F., 144, 146, 147, 154
Pringle, H., 62
Printz, H., 307
Prinz, W., 8, 99, 107, 139, 304, 305
Priplata, A. A., 311
Prull, M. W., 34, 98, 165, 166, 167, 172
Puce, A., 19
Pugh, K. G., 30
Pugh, K. R., 21, 244
Pullara, O., 228
Punto, M., 49
Pye, C., 234

Quas, J. A., 145
Quig, M. B., 335
Quine, W. V. O., 208, 270

Rabbitt, P. M. A., 58, 98, 99, 195, 310, 311, 332, 333, 334, 335, 336, 356
Rabinowitz, M., 154
Race, E. A., 34
Rademacher, J., 17
Radvansky, G. A., 195
Raffone, A., 114
Rahhal, T. A., 61, 163, 172, 173, 174, 199
Raichle, M. E., 32, 33, 34, 88
Rainer, G., 71
Raininko, R., 36
Rajah, M. N., 10
Rajapakse, J. C., 16, 17
Rakic, P., 73
Ramey, C. T., 321, 324
Ramey, S. L., 321, 324
Ramnani, N., 77
Randolph, B., 46, 47
Rao, N., 155
Rapin, I., 240

Rapoport, J. L., 6, 16, 17, 83
Rapoport, S. I., 77
Rapp, B., 256
Rapus, T., 79
Rash, S., 201, 223, 230
Rastle, K. G., 202
Ratcliff, R., 297, 310
Ratner, H. H., 187
Rattermann, M. J., 320, 325
Rauschecker, J., 350
Rawles, J. M., 28
Raye, C. L., 71, 138, 168, 171
Raz, N., 6, 7, 11, 30, 34, 58, 98, 133, 138, 168, 169, 306, 307, 335
Read, S., 246
Reader, M. J., 18
Reason, J., 52, 105
Redbond, J., 81
Reddy, H., 34
Reder, L. M., 319
Reed, B. R., 31, 58, 65
Reed, L. J., 33
Rees, E., 319
Reese, E., 147, 148, 155, 157
Reese, H. W., 299, 300, 345, 346
Reilly, J. S., 241
Reinert, G., 304
Reisberg, D., 79
Reiss, A. L., 18, 20, 22, 28, 33
Renaux-Kieffer, V., 18
Rensink, R. A., 50
Resnick, S., 335
Resnick, S. M., 28
Ress, D., 32
Reuchlin, M., 299
Reuter-Lorenz, P. A., 34, 88, 135, 138, 349, 355, 358
Reyna, V. F., 7, 147
Reynolds, J. R., 71
Reznick, J. S., 77, 79
Ricciardi, M. M., 48
Rice, C., 77, 79
Rice, K., 227, 228
Rice, M. L., 214
Richards, J. R., 47, 52
Richardson, D., 266
Richardson-Klavehn, A., 103
Richelme, C., 17
Richter, P., 52
Riddlesberger, M. M., 145
Ridolfo, H. E., 198, 199
Riggs, K. J., 82
Rimmo, P., 53
Ripoll, H., 52
Rips, L., 319
Ristic, J., 47, 49
Rittle-Johnson, B., 289, 318, 321
Rizzo, S., 246, 247
Robbins, T. W., 98
Roberts, M. J., 319, 321

Roberts, R. D., 318
Robertson, B. A., 166
Robertson, R. R. W., 234, 246
Robins, S. L., 201
Rocchi, P., 173
Rochat, P., 183
Roche, R. A. P., 99, 103
Rochon, E., 243, 245, 246
Rockstroh, B., 352
Rockwell, T., 48
Rodrigue, K. M., 30
Roediger, H. L., III, 170
Roenker, D. L., 53, 62
Rogan, J. D., 64
Rogers, R. D., 63, 82
Rogers, W. A., 60
Rogoff, B., 6, 155, 350
Roisman, G. I., 346
Rokeach, M., 174
Rolfhus, E. L., 199
Romani, C., 257
Romine, L., 138
Roncadin, C., 241
Rönnlund, M., 98, 165, 166
Roodenrys, S., 117
Rosati, A., 77, 79
Rose, A. S., 317, 325
Rose, D. F., 241
Rosekrasnor, L., 345
Rosen, A. C., 34
Rosen, B. R., 137–138
Rosen, M. J., 199, 227
Rosen, V. M., 102
Rosenbek, J. C., 256–257
Rosenberg, D., 73
Rosenblum, K. E., 289
Rosene, D. L., 36
Rosengren, K. K., 293
Rosengren, K. S., 289
Rösler, F., 349
Rosman, H., 82
Ross, B., 18
Ross, E., 75
Ross, J. L., 28
Ross, T. J., 99, 103
Rosselli, M., 83
Rossetti, Z. L., 37
Rosvold, H. E., 73
Rothbart, M. K., 83
Rouillon, F., 258
Rourke, S. B., 215
Routhieaux, B. C., 29, 168, 171
Rovee-Collier, C., 143, 144, 183
Rozenblit, L., 267
Rozin, P., 270
Rubin, D. C., 30, 199
Rubin, S. R., 168, 169
Ruble, D. N., 285
Ruchoux, M. M., 30
Ruffman, T., 20

Rugg, M. D., 166, 167, 168
Ruiz, A., 321
Rulf, S., 289
Rumelhart, D. E., 270, 319, 325
Rumsey, J. M., 16, 17
Rushworth, M. F. S., 76
Rusinek, H., 33
Rutter, M., 322
Ruz, M. L., 198, 202
Ryalls, J. H., 256
Ryan, E. B., 120, 122, 223, 226, 229, 266
Ryan, J., 138
Ryan, N. D., 20, 22
Ryan, S., 228
Rypma, B., 32, 60, 138, 335

Sachs, B. C., 21
Sadato, N., 20
Saffran, E. M., 255, 256, 258, 259
Sahakian, B. J., 98
Saito, S., 119
Salat, D. H., 28, 34, 35
Salmon, K., 149
Salmon, W. C., 269
Salthouse, T. A., 10, 29, 34, 58, 63, 64, 86, 97, 98, 99, 106, 130, 133, 134, 135, 137, 163, 198, 199, 225, 227, 275, 276, 279, 280, 281, 283, 297, 300, 302, 303, 310, 318, 350, 354
Samuels, J., 243
Samuels, S. J., 86
Samuelson, L. K., 210
Sanborn, A., 198, 199
Sandblom, J., 32
Sanders, A. L., 32, 34, 139, 352, 358
Sandor, T., 30
Sands, L., 333
Sanford, A. J., 247
Sanft, H., 173
Santiago, J., 198, 202
Santosh, P. J., 18
Santulli, K. A., 155
Sarna, S., 36
Sartori, G., 240, 255
Sasanuma, S., 256
Sattler, J. M., 317
Saults, J. S., 130
Saunders, A. M., 34
Savage, A., 8, 306, 308
Sawaguchi, T., 73
Scahill, R. I., 28
Scalf, P., 65
Scalf, R., 8
Scalisi, T. G., 116
Schaafstal, A., 116, 121
Schachar, R., 10, 354
Schacht, T., 234

Schacter, D. L., 7, 144, 169, 170, 171, 199
Schaeffer, J., 242
Schaeken, W., 319
Schaie, K. W., 11, 195, 199, 234, 300, 304, 332, 333
Schaner-Wolles, C., 244
Schapiro, M. B., 8
Schatz, J., 34
Schauble, L., 289
Schechter, A., 143
Scheibel, A. B., 332
Scheibel, M. E., 332
Scheltens, P., 30
Scherr, P. A., 333
Schiano, D. J., 116
Schiller, P. H., 48
Schlaggar, B. L., 37
Schlagmüller, M., 155
Schliemann, A. D., 321
Schmalhofer, F., 246
Schmidt, M. H., 18
Schmiedek, F., 298, 299, 347, 353, 354, 355, 356
Schmitter-Edgecombe, M., 100, 195
Schneider, B. A., 195, 216, 217
Schneider, J. A., 311
Schneider, W., 44, 143, 151, 153, 154, 155, 157, 323
Scholey, K. A., 114
Scholl, B. J., 50
Schonfield, D., 166
Schooler, C., 349, 350, 351
Schott, J. M., 28
Schraagen, J. M., 116, 121
Schreurs, B. G., 306
Schroots, J. F., 4
Schroyens, W., 319
Schubert, A. B., 83
Schulte, M., 18
Schultz, M., 18
Schumacher, E. H., 65
Schunn, C. D., 319
Schwartz, M. F., 255, 257, 258, 259
Schwartz, N., 130, 133
Schwartzman, A., 201
Schweikert, R., 117
Schwimmer, J., 33
Scialfa, C. T., 62
Scott, J. H., 86, 114, 118
Scribner, S., 155
Segalowitz, S. J., 98, 169, 345
Seidenberg, M. S., 117
Seier, W. L., 286
Sekuler, A. B., 10
Sekuler, R., 10
Selkoe, D. J., 30
Semenza, C., 194, 256
Semrud-Clikeman, M., 240

Serdaru, M., 7
Sergent-Marshall, S. D., 197
Serna, R., 46
Servan-Schreiber, D., 307
Service, E., 117, 122
Shaffer, D. R., 3–4
Shah, P., 113, 115, 129
Shallice, T., 70, 97, 114, 255
Shaner, T. L., 64
Shankweiler, D., 122, 234, 242, 243, 244
Shapiro, K., 52
Shapiro, L. R., 146, 148
Shapiro, T., 221
Shaw, L. K., 186
Shaw, R. S., 57, 63–64
Shaywitz, B. A., 21, 244
Shaywitz, S. E., 21, 244
Sheldon, N., 33
Shephard, D., 212
Shewan, C. M., 223
Shields, P., 143
Shiffrin, R. M., 44, 128, 129, 323
Shifren, K., 134
Shilling, V. M., 98
Shimamura, A. P., 130
Shimony, J. S., 30, 31
Shinar, D., 48, 49, 51
Shinnar, S., 240
Shipley, C., 290, 292
Shipley, W. C., 130, 233
Shisler, R. J., 88
Shiung, M. M., 28
Shore, D., 50
Shrager, J., 289, 290, 292
Shultz, T. R., 289
Shultz, T. S., 356
Shutts, K., 75
Shyi, G. C.-W., 143
Siakaluk, P. D., 62
Siegel, L. S., 86, 120, 122, 234
Siegler, I. C., 233
Siegler, R. S., 7, 154, 202, 286, 288, 289, 290, 292, 293, 298, 317, 318, 321, 356
Siemens, L., 152, 154, 156
Sikström, S., 297, 306, 307, 308, 358
Silva, P. A., 286
Silveri, M. C., 255, 257
Silverman, D. H., 33
Simmons, A., 18
Simon, E. W., 7
Simon, H. A., 118, 319
Simon, T., 285, 319
Simons, D. J., 50, 270
Simos, P. G., 21
Simpson, A., 82
Simpson, R. K., 256
Singer, H. S., 18, 28

Singer, L., 212
Singer, T., 297, 300, 303, 349, 351, 353
Sit, R. A., 64
Ska, B., 257
Slabach, E. H., 59, 63
Slagter, H. A., 20
Sliwinski, M. J., 233, 303
Sloane, M., 53
Sloane, N., 62
Sloman, S. A., 270
Slomine, B. S., 18
Small, B. J., 233, 304
Small, G. W., 33
Smiler, A. P., 358
Smiley, A., 51
Smit, J. H., 333
Smith, A. D., 129, 130, 134, 135, 304
Smith, A. F., 65
Smith, C. S., 270
Smith, D., 332, 333
Smith, E. E., 34, 114, 130, 133, 138
Smith, J., 7, 9, 199, 203, 346
Smith, L. B., 155, 210, 299
Smith, M. C., 173, 174
Smith, M. R., 8, 306, 308
Smith, P. K., 129, 130, 134, 135, 3034
Smith, S. A., 234
Smyth, M. M., 114
Snell, J. W., 17
Snow, C. E., 218
Snow, R. E., 317
Snowdon, D. A., 226, 253, 333
Snowling, M., 117
Snyder, A. Z., 28, 31, 32, 34, 35, 139, 352, 358
Söderlund, H., 30
Sodian, B., 155, 157
Soederberg, L. M., 228
Soederberg Miller, L. M., 228
Sokoloff, L., 333
Somberg, B. L., 64
Song, J., 241
Sonke, C. J., 59
Sorensenson, H. T., 333
Souder, E., 33
Southwood, M. H., 230
Sowell, E. R., 17, 28
Sparing, R., 71
Sparks, G., 241
Spearman, C., 285
Spelke, E. S., 48, 76, 180, 208
Spencer, D. D., 19
Spencer, J. P., 288
Spencer, W. D., 7, 169
Sperry, S., 65
Spicker, B., 145, 146
Spieler, D. H., 60, 65, 102–103, 297, 310

Spiro, A., 7, 304
Sporty, M. L., 17
Spreen, O., 130
Sprott, R., 223, 230
Squire, L. R., 30, 75, 244
Srivastava, G., 33
Staff, R. T., 22
Stallcup, M., 194
Stanhope, N., 33
Stankov, L., 318
Stark, R. E., 241
Stattin, H., 299
Stauder, J. E. A., 46
Staudinger, U. M., 7, 9, 11, 193, 198, 304, 340, 345, 346, 350, 356
Stebbins, G. T., 32
Stefanacci, L., 75
Stein, E. A., 99, 103
Stein, J.-F., 52
Stemerdink, N., 83
Stenger, V. A., 71
Stern, C. E., 137–138
Stern, P., 194
Sternberg, R. J., 285, 290, 315, 316, 318, 319, 320, 322, 323, 324, 325
Stern, Y., 34
Stevens, K. N., 350
Stevenson, N. J., 321
Stewart, J., 53
Stigsdotter-Neely, A., 32
Stiles, J., 22
Stine, E. A. L., 133, 199, 227, 228, 230, 232
Stine-Morrow, E. A. L., 194, 195, 198, 199, 228, 358
Stojwas, M. H., 34
Stollery, B., 310, 311, 356
Stoltzfus, E. R., 60, 61, 173, 335
Stone, B. P., 152
Story, T., 267
Strauss, E., 130
Strayer, D. L., 60, 64, 65, 98
Strick, P. L., 29
Stromswold, K., 241
Stroop, J. R., 71
Strosberg, R., 210
Stuart, G., 117
Sturt, P., 247
Stuss, D. T., 71, 83, 97
Stutts, J., 53
Styles, E. A., 82
Suckling, J., 18
Suengas, A. G., 171
Sulkava, R., 36
Sullivan, E. V., 28, 30
Sullivan, K., 77, 79
Sullivan, M. P., 60
Sullivan, M. W., 143
Sullivan, S., 20

Summala, H., 49
Summers, P. E., 30
Sun, R., 179, 184, 185
Sunderland, T., 306
Suprenant, A. M., 162
Suzuki, W. A., 30, 33, 77
Svetina, M., 289
Svoboda, E., 201
Swales, M., 96, 98
Sweeney, J. A., 83
Swinney, D., 230, 231, 241

Tager-Flusberg, H., 77, 79
Tallal, P., 234
Tam, R., 174
Tanaka, K., 77
Tangalos, E. G., 30
Tannock, R., 10, 354
Tantufuye, E., 324, 325
Tardif, T., 115
Tarshish, C. Y., 33
Taub, E., 352
Taylor, C., 77, 82
Taylor, D. W., 332
Taylor, E., 18
Taylor, E. M., 246
Taylor, G. A., 275
Taylor, J. K., 195
Taylor, J. O., 333
Taylor, L., 20
Taylor, M. J., 18, 19, 20, 21, 22
Taylor, S. F., 34, 58, 65, 135, 138
Tellegen, A., 285, 346
Teller, T., 198, 199
Teng, E., 75
Tesch-Römer, K., 351
Tessler, M., 149
Tessner, K. D., 17
Tetens, J. N., 300, 304, 345
Teuber, H. L., 97
Thaler, D. S., 297, 302
Thelen, E., 288, 299
Theodore, W. H., 21, 22, 37
Thom, D., 52
Thomas, D. M., 62
Thomas, K. M., 7, 8, 17, 18, 37, 88
Thompson, L. L., 83
Thompson, M., 216, 223
Thompson, M. A., 243
Thompson, N., 116, 120
Thompson, P. M., 6, 17, 18, 28
Thompson, R. A., 2825
Thompson, W. W., 304
Thomson, D. M., 19
Thomson, N., 114
Thornton, A. E., 6
Thulborn, K. R., 83
Tidball, G., 210
Tieman, J., 30
Tigges, J., 36

Tikhomirov, O. K., 83
Tilvis, R., 36
Tipper, S. P., 60, 61
To, D., 17
Toga, A. W., 6, 17, 28
Toglia, M. P., 103
Tokar, A. V., 333
Tomasello, M., 184, 185, 209–210, 210, 349, 353
Tompkins, C. A., 246, 247
Toni, I., 77
Tooby, J., 266
Toth, J. P., 100, 101, 103, 104, 106
Tottenham, N. T., 18
Towle, C., 73
Townsend, J., 28
Towse, J. N., 81, 118, 119, 120, 122, 139
Trabasso, T., 152
Tracey, I., 137–138
Trainham, T. N., 103
Trainor, L. J., 18
Trainor, R. J., 83
Tranel, D., 87, 97
Trauner, D. A., 17
Trick, L., 10, 44, 51, 52, 53
Troen, B. R., 27
Trommer, B. L., 22
Tsai, S. Y., 33
Tsang, P. S., 64
Tuholski, S. W., 88, 113, 115, 129
Tulving, E., 32, 34, 163, 183, 200
Tun, P. A., 199, 227, 230
Turetsky, B. I., 17
Turner, D. A., 32
Turner, M., 73
Turner, R., 350
Tyler, L. K., 240, 247, 258
Tzeng, Y., 245

Udwin, O., 215
Ullman, M. T., 244, 270
Ulmen, R., 53
Ulug, A. M., 18
Ulyings, H. B. M., 72, 73
Underwood, B. J., 146
Ungerleider, L. G., 8, 32
Unsal, A., 98
Ushijima, T., 256

Vaituzis, A. C., 6, 16, 17
Vakil, E., 65
Valdes, L., 60
Valdiserri, M., 7, 199
Valencia-Laver, D., 169
Valentine, T., 122
Vallar, G., 114, 116, 122, 259
Valsiner, J., 156
Van Broeckhoven, C., 165, 166
Van de Moortele, P. F., 18

van den Boogerd, E. H., 333
van den Broek, P., 245
Vandeputte, D., 227, 228
Van der Linden, M., 166, 167
van der Meere, J., 83
van Dijk, T. A., 240–241
Van Dongen, H. R., 240, 241
van Engeland, H., 17
Van Hiel, A., 79
Van Hout, A., 240
Vanier, M., 256
Van Lancker, D., 246
van Tilburg, T., 333
van Tilburg, W., 333
Vargha-Khadem, F., 18, 118
Vasa, R., 18
Vasilyeva, M., 202
Vauss, Y. C., 17
Vavrik, J., 44
Vecchi, T., 118
Verhaeghen, P., 60, 61, 64, 65, 98, 99, 133, 195, 197, 200, 297, 335, 353
Veriejken, B., 288
Vernon, P. A., 86
Verstynen, T., 71
Vesneski, M., 195
Viader, F., 33
Vigil, J., 18
Vignolo, L. A., 255
Viitanen, M., 30
Villa, G., 255
Vining, E. P., 241
Vires-Collins, H., 65
Vise, M., 155
Vishton, P. M., 76
Visscher, K. M., 37
Viswanathan, M., 351
Vitolo, L., 173, 174
Vogel, E. K., 114
Vogt, B. A., 33
Voitenko, V. P., 333
von Cramon, D. Y., 76, 77
von Eye, A.E, 7
Vosniadou, S., 267
Vygotsky, L. S., 6, 179, 180, 265, 320, 324

Wade, E., 195, 196, 202, 233
Wadley, V. G., 62
Wager, T., 113
Wagner, A. D., 77
Wagner, D. A., 155
Wagner, L., 144, 145
Wagner, P., 52
Wahlin, A., 165, 166
Walker, C. H., 243
Walker, P., 117
Wallace, C. S., 184
Wallis, J. D., 76, 77

Walter, B. M., 98, 167
Wang, P. P., 116, 215
Wapner, S., 48
Ware, A., 184
Warren, J., 227
Warrington, E. K., 114, 255, 256, 259
Warr-Leeper, G. A., 240
Wason, P., 321
Waters, G. S., 231, 232, 246, 259, 260
Watkins, M. J., 116
Watson, D., 285
Watson, D. G., 62
Watson, P., 332, 333
Watt, R., 47
Waxman, S. R., 209
Wayland, S., 242
Wearing, H., 118, 121
Webb, A., 63, 65
Weber, T.A., 11, 64, 65
Webster, D. M., 79
Wechsler, D., 129, 166, 226, 230, 233, 276, 278
Wecker, N. S., 97
Weigand, S. D., 28
Weinstein, H., 53
Weir, M. W., 347
Weise, G., 52
Weisper, S., 247
Weissman, D. H., 63
Wekstein, D. R., 226, 253, 333
Welch-Ross, M. K., 187
Welcome, S. E., 17, 18, 28
Welford, A. T., 275, 276, 277, 280, 307
Wellman, H. M., 72, 150, 151, 153, 155
Welsh, M. C., 83
Welsh, R. C., 138
Welsh, T. F., 20
Wenger, N., 208
Wenner, J. A., 143
Wenner, M., 240
Werner, H., 48, 265
Werner, N. K., 246
Wernicke, K., 255
West, R. L., 29, 58, 65, 98, 163, 173
West, T., 173
Westerberg, H., 20, 22
Wewerka, S. S., 143
Whalen, P. J., 20, 22
Whalley, L. J., 22
Whishaw, I. Q., 29
Whitaker, H. A., 241, 242
White, K. K., 196, 233
Whitney, P., 243

Wickens, D., 137
Widing, G., 164, 166
Wiegel-Crump, C. A., 245
Wienbruch, C., 352
Wiesenfeld, K., 311
Wiig, E. H., 234
Wikman, A., 49
Wilblad, B., 164, 166
Wiles, J., 319
Wilkie, F., 233
Wilkinson, M., 240, 242, 246, 247
Willen, J. D., 47
Williams, A., 53
Williams, B., 10, 354
Williams, K. A., 350
Williams, L., 77
Williams, L. E., 30, 31
Williams, P., 335
Williams, S. C., 18, 30
Willis, C. S., 117, 234
Willis, S. L., 7, 11, 135, 300, 304, 351
Willoughby, T., 3–4
Wilson, B., 20
Wilson, B. A., 98
Wilson, J. T. L., 86, 114, 118
Wilson, R. S., 311
Wilson, W. H., 319, 320, 321, 325
Wimmer, H., 77, 79
Wingfield, A., 133, 194, 195, 199, 227, 228, 230, 231, 232
Winner, E., 77, 79
Winocur, G., 29, 171, 201, 243, 245
Wiseman, M. B., 34
Wisniewski, A., 97
Witzki, A. H., 96–97, 99, 113
Wohlwill, J. F., 300
Wolf, O. T., 33
Wolfe, J. M., 50
Wolters, G., 114
Wong, E. C., 22
Wood, D., 77
Wood, E., 3–4
Wood, J., 53
Woodard, J. L., 98, 106
Woodcock, R. W., 275, 278, 316, 353
Woodin, M. E., 116, 121
Woodruff, G., 77
Woodward, A., 210
Worden, P. E., 152
Worsley, K., 16
Worthington, J., 333
Worthley, J. S., 195, 196, 202, 233
Wright, E. A., 28
Wright Cassidy, K., 194

Wszalek, T. M., 63, 138
Wu, C. C., 31
Wulf, G., 52
Wynn, C., 122
Wynn, V., 116

Xu, B., 21

Yaffe, K., 333
Yahlor, S. F., 358
Yakolev, P. I., 16, 20
Yan, M., 17
Yang, Y., 18
Yantis, S., 46, 58
Yarrow, M. R., 333
Yekovich, F. R., 243
Yeni-Komshian, G., 255
Yeo, R. A., 18
Yerys, B. E., 170
Yesavage, J. A., 58, 65, 358
Ylikoski, A., 36
Yngve, V., 230
Yonekura, Y., 20
Yonelinas, A. P., 166, 167, 168
Yoon, C., 173, 229
Yoshioka, H., 256
Young, M., 245
Younkin, S. G., 30
Yule, W., 214
Yurgelun-Todd, D. A., 17

Zacks, R. T., 9, 10, 29, 60, 87, 88, 98, 99, 106, 113, 135, 136, 145, 154, 163, 169, 173, 201, 229, 230, 246, 247, 335
Zaitchik, D., 77
Zamora, L., 18
Zarahn, E., 32
Zeef, E. J., 59
Zeidner, M., 325
Zelazo, P. D., 9, 79, 107, 326
Zelinski, E. M., 216, 217, 219
Zeman, B. R., 155
Zhang, L., 241
Zielinski, T., 320, 321
Zijdenbos, A., 16, 17
Zingeser, L. B., 255
Zipursky, R. B., 28
Zohar, A., 289
Zola, S. M., 75
Zonderman, A. B., 28, 335
Zurbriggen, E. L., 65
Zurif, E. B., 230, 231, 241, 256, 258
Zwaan, R. A., 195
Zwahr, M. D., 130, 134, 139
Zwann, R. A., 243

Subject Index

Abilities, as competencies, 324
Abstract attitude, 98
Abstract thought, in childhood, 265–267
Access, as inhibition subprocess, 99
Accessibility bias, 100
Accommodation, 320
Achievement, learning and, 318
Acoustic-phonetic processing disorders, 255
ACT (Adaptive Control of Thought), 319, 320, 323
Activity, goal-directed, 71
Adaptation
  brain plasticity and, 11
  epistemological theories and, 320
  functional, in cognitive development, 356
Adaptive Control of Thought (ACT), 319, 320, 323
ADHD (attention deficit hyperactivity disorder), 18
Adult development theories, cognition components and, 193
Adulthood
  adaptive developmental tasks in, 346–347
  cognition, inter-individual differences, 292
  intellectual development determinants, 325
  semantic representation during, 194–198
  strategy use and choice, 290–291

Age/aging
  advanced, 37
  behavioral, 308t
  binding differences and, 172–173
  differentiation of cognitive abilities and, 331–341
  effects on efficiency of basic cognitive processes, 277–279
  intuitive theories and, 267–268
  language impairments after stroke and, 253, 254
  memory and, 163–166, 164f
  neural, 308t
  normal, brain volume reduction in, 28
  representation and, 193–203
  suppression deficits, 247
  vs. cognitive development, 270–271
Age-related changes
  in analytical reasoning, 274–276, 275f
  in cognitive behavior, working memory and, 134–135
  decline patterns, 9–11
  differentiation, in fluid ability test performance, 337–338, 338t
  in domain specificity, 269
  in knowledge, 282–283, 284
  in language dissolution, vs. child-hood brain injury, 244–247

Age-related changes (*continued*)
  in meaning, 245–247
  mechanisms of, 281–282
  patterns of, 271
  in speed of processing, 332
  in strategy use and choice, 290–291
  within-person variations in, 356
  working memory effect on, 133–134
Age trajectory, 275–276
Agrammatism, 242, 244, 256, 257–258
AH4-1 intelligence test scores, age-related variance in,
    337–338, 338*t*
Alzheimer's disease
  amyloid, emergent maladaptive development and, 37
  amyloid deposits, 30
  brain volume loss in, 28
  declarative memory deficits in, 29, 30, 244
  early-onset forms, 31
  hypometabolism in, 33
  low P-density in, 226
  meaning dissolution and, 245–247
  medial temporal lobe in, 30, 33
  recruitment patterns and, 34
  tau, 30
Ambiguous figures, 79
Amygdala, sex differences in, 17
Amyloid deposits, 30, 37
Anagrams, 279
Analytical reasoning, age-related changes in, 274–276, 275*f*
Anomia, 240
A-not-B task
  description of, 100–102, 101*f*, 102*t*
  error, in infants, 72, 74*f*
Aphasia, 253–254
  auditory, 256
  childhood, 239
    cognition theories and, 243–244
    language theories and, 243–244
    symptoms of, 240
  conduction, 260
  in focal vascular disease, 255–260
  jargon, 258
  posterior, 244
  symptoms of, 240
Appearance-reality tasks, 79
Applications, 323
Apraxia, 256–257
Articulation disorders, 256
Assimilation, 320
Associative deficit hypothesis, 168–169, 170
Attention
  age-related differences, 22, 29
  control of, 10
  definition of, 44
  divided. *See* Divided attention
  executive processes in, 100
  focus, 144
  goal-directed, 57
    spatial cueing and, 58–59
    visual search and, 61–62

  memory development and, 154–155
  prefrontal cortex and, 29
  selective. *See* Selective attention
  spatial orienting and, 46–47
  stimulus-driven, 57–58
    spatial cueing and, 58–59
    visual search and, 61–62
Attentional inertia, 81–82
Attention deficit hyperactivity disorder (ADHD),
    18
Attribution Threshold model, 104, 105*f*
Auditory aphasia, 256
Auditory moving window paradigm, 232
Autism, 47, 214–215
Autobiographical memory, 188, 200–201
Automaticity, selection and, 44, 44*f*
Awareness, selection and, 44
Awkward reach, 73*f*

Baby talk, 218
Background knowledge, reading strategies and,
    228
Balance beam problem, 7
Basal ganglia, 29
Basic processing mechanism (BPM), 338–339
BCA (broad cognitive abilities), 316
Behavioral plasticity, 349, 349*f*
Bilaterality, 8
Bilingualism, 351
Binding, age differences in, 172–173
Binding-deficit hypothesis, 170
Binding deficits, 199
Biology
  compensation in, 11
  differentiation of cognitive abilities and, 334–335
  lifespan cognitive development variations and, 352–
    353, 353*f*
  lifespan variations in, 356
  naïve, 266
Block design test, 277–279, 277*t*, 278*f*
BPM (basic processing mechanism), 338–339
Brain. *See also specific brain regions*
  age-related changes, 27–38
    compensatory recruitment, 33–34
    "first-in, last-out" models, 34
    functional changes, 22, 32–34
    in neurocognitive processing, 358
    in recruitment, 33–34
    structural changes, 28–32, 31*f*
    systems affected by, 29
  development
    brain aging processes and, 355, 355*f*
    physiological measures of, 15–16
  frontal lobes, 6–7
  function, compensatory mechanisms, 8
  lesions, accumulated, 36–37, 36*t*
  metabolic needs of, 15–16
  plasticity. *See* Plasticity, neuronal
  senescence, 307
  size, 15

structure
    adult-child similarities, 3
    age-related changes, 22
    language acquisition and, 350
systems, vulnerability, in aging, 34
volume
    in attention deficit hyperactivity disorder, 18
    childhood reductions, 22
    reduction across lifespan, 28
weight, 15
Brain biopsy, language symptoms and, 253
Brain damage
    childhood
        language dissolution and, 244–247
        language form disorders and, 241–242
    congenital, 244–247
    early, meaning and, 245–247
    in language areas, 253–254
    localized/focal
        childhood recovery from, 18
        familiarity and, 167–168
        recollection and, 167–168
    meaning disorders from, 239–241
    traumatic, childhood recovery from, 18
Brain imaging, functional, 32–34, 194. *See also*
    Functional magnetic resonance imaging
Broad cognitive abilities (BCA), 316
Broca's aphasia, 260

CADASIL, 30–31, 34
Card sorting test, 277*t*
Caretaking routines, infant's knowledge of, 184
Cattell Culture Fair test, age-related variance in, 336, 337*t*
Caudate, 17, 29
Change detection task, visual exploration and, 50–51
Childhood amnesia, 188
Children. *See also* Infants
    abstract-to-concrete progressions in, 265–267
    brain development, brain aging processes and, 355, 355*f*
    brain structure similarity with adults, 3
    cognitive abilities
        inter-individual differences, 291–294
        intra-individual differences, effect on inter-individual differences, 292–294
        modeling, psychometric measures for, 339
        specific, 339–340
    development, 37. *See also specific developmental areas*
        definition of, 4
        experience and, 17–18
        neural, functional measures of, 17
    executive function in
        age 1–2, 73, 75
        ages 3–5 years, 77, 78*f*, 79, 80*f*, 81–83
    intellectual development, determinants of, 325–326
    memory development in. *See* Memory, development
    nervous system development
        of face processing, 19–20
        of language skills, 20–21

preschool
    abstract thought and, 265, 266
    biological thought and, 269
    strategy use and choice, 289
representational development
    age 1 to 4 years, 185–187
    cognitive mechanisms for, 202
school-age
    rehearsal protocols, 151–152, 151*t*
    representation development and, 188–189
    strategy choice process, 289–290
    strategy use and, 289–290
    working memory structure in, 121
Choice/no-choice design, 290–291
Chunking, 117–118, 122
Circadian arousal patterns, 173
Circumlocutions, 240
Closed head injuries, reading abilities and, 243
Co-constructivism, 7
Cognition
    age-related changes, working memory and, 134–135
    age-related declines, mechanisms of, 58
    in aging, two-factor assessment framework, 29
    control. *See* Executive functions
    dependence on knowledge, 283
    development. *See also* Lifespan cognitive development
        abstract-to-concrete progressions, 265–267
        context in, 5–7
        domain specificity and, 268–269
        functional changes, 19
        multidimensional/multidirectional, 346
        neural bases of. *See* Brain; Nervous system
        patterns, 264
        research on, 344–358
        socialization and, 350
        vs. aging, 270–271
    developmental theories, childhood aphasia and, 243–244
    differentiation, in elderly, 340
    general slowing, dual-task processing and, 63–65
    higher-order, working memory function and, 139
    inter-individual variability. *See* Inter-individual variability
    intra-individual variability. *See* Intra-individual variability
    processes, basic, age-related changes in efficiency of, 277–279
    slowing, older adults' language processing and, 227–228
Cognitive aging, 3, 4
Cognitive capacity, intellectual development and, 325–327
Cognitive modifiability, 324
Cognitive resources
    adaptive generation/allocation of, 357–358, 357*f*
    differentiation of, 135–136, 136*f*
Cognitive strategies, domain specific, 271
Cognitive tests, of executive function, 98–99
Compensation
    biological *vs.* social, 11
    definition of, 33, 347
    in reading, 21

Competencies, developing, 323–324
Concept formation test, 277–279, 277t, 278f
Concrete operationalism, 82
Concrete-operations period, 320
Concrete thought, in childhood, 265–267
Conduction aphasia, 260
Congenital brain damage, 244
    meaning dissolution and, 245–247
    suppression deficits, 247
Context
    in cognitive development, 5–7
    in memory development, 152–153, 157
Contextualist theories of intellectual development, 316, 321–322
Continuous adaptive development, 35–36, 36t
Control processes
    in cognitive development, 8–9
    selection and, 44, 44f
Conventionality, 208–209
Conversations, adult-child
    elaboration in, memory encoding and, 147–148
    during ongoing events, 148–150
Coordination of attention, age-related differences
    in general switch costs, 63
    in specific switch costs, 63
    in task switching, 62–63
Corpus callosum
    agenesis, 247
    anterior, age-related changes, 30
Corsi span procedure
    developmental trajectory and, 130, 131f–132f
    for working memory measurement, 114, 116, 118
Cortical thickness differences, age-related, 35, 35f
Counting span, 118, 119
Covert orienting, 46–48
Creativity, 323
Crossword puzzle solving, age-related changes in, 274–275, 275f, 280
Crystallized intelligence
    development of, 316
    differentiation/dedifferentiation of, 304, 305f, 306
    mechanisms of, 353–354, 354f
    vs. fluid intelligence, 193, 333–334, 340
Cue-to-target interval (CTI), 63
Cultural plasticity, 349
Culture
    knowledge acquisition, 189
    lifespan cognitive development variations and, 352–353, 353f
Culture Fair intelligence tests, age-related variance in, 332, 332f, 335–336, 336t, 337t
Curiosity, 267
"Curse of knowledge" tendency, 77, 79

Day-night task, 82
DCCS (Dimensional Change Card Sort task), 77, 79, 80f–81f, 81–82
Declarative memory (explicit), 163, 164f
    age-related changes, 29
    deficits, in Alzheimer's disease, 29, 30

definition of, 163
    episodic, 163, 164f
    impairments, 244
    lexicon and, 244
    semantic, 163, 164f
Dedifferentiation, of cognitive function, 8, 139
Dedifferentiation. See also Differentiation/dedifferentiation hypothesis
Deese-Roediger-McDermott procedure (DRM), 170
Delayed nonmatching to sample (DNMS), 73, 75–76, 75f, 77
Deletion, as inhibition subprocess, 99
Deliberation
    age-related changes in, 46
    selection and, 45f, 46
    visual, 51–53
Delis-Kaplan Executive Function Test, 277–279, 277t, 278f
Dementia
    meaning and, 245–247
    suppression deficits, 247
Demyelination, age-related changes in, 11
Dependency, age-related changes in, 6
Detour reaching, 71, 72f–73f
Detterman effect, 338, 339
Developing-expertise model, 323–324
Developing mind, theories of, 315–319
Development, human. See also specific types of human development
    as adaptive generation, 347, 348t
    commonalities with aging, 3–5
    as contextualized selective lifelong adaptation, 345–346, 348t
    culture-oriented view of, 345
    definition of, 4
    differences with aging, 5
    gain-loss regulation and, 347, 348t
    model of, 340
    patterns of, 9–11
    pluralistic and dynamic processes of, 346–347, 348t
    theories, 345
    trajectories, selective adaptation and, 345–346
Developmental psychology, definition of, 4
Differential psychology, 315
Differentiation/dedifferentiation hypothesis
    in child development, 7–8
    of cognitive resources, 135–136, 136f
    description of, 303–304
    of emotions, 20
    lifespan cognition and, 355, 355f
    neuronal level, 306
    processing fluctuations and, 304, 305f, 306
    representation and, 307
Differentiation of cognitive abilities, aging and, 331–341
    protective factors, 333–334
    rate of change and, 332–333
    vs. other variance factors, 334–337, 336t
Diffusion tensor imaging, of white matter changes, 30, 31f

Digit span, 115
    backwards, 129, 130, 131*f*–132*f*
    forwards, 130, 131*f*–132*f*
Digit symbol test, 277–279, 277*t*, 278*f*
Dimensional Change Card Sort task (DCCS), 77, 79,
    80*f*–81*f*, 81–82
Discontinued development, 36, 36*t*
Dissociation, between frontal-striatal and hippocampal
    changes, 31
Distraction
    response compatible paradigm, 59–60
    selective attention and, 59–61
Distractor inhibition model, 61
Divided attention
    age-related differences
        in coordination, 62–65
        in dual-task processing, 63–65
        in task switching, 62–63
    definition of, 57
DNMS (delayed nonmatching to sample), 73, 75–76,
    75*f*, 77
Dog-pig manipulation, 82
Domains
    of representation, 199–200
    specificity of
        knowledge growth and, 268–269
        in working memory, 119–120
Domain-specific constraints theories, 208
Dopamine, in dorsolateral prefrontal cortex, 73
Dopamine receptor density, age-associated differences
    in, 307
Dorsolateral prefrontal cortex, 72–73
Down syndrome, 116
Driving performance
    perceptual illusions and, 48
    visual exploration and, 51
    visual habit and, 49–50
DRM (Deese-Roediger-McDermott) procedure, 170
Dual-coding model, 116
Duality of mind theories, 179
Dual-process models
    cognitive control in, 100
    of recollection and familiarity, 166–168
Dual-task processing
    age-related differences, 63–65
        task priority and, 64
        training/practice effects on, 64
    procedures, 114
Dyadic communication
    childhood memory development and, 144, 145
    in memory development, 147–150, 149*f*
Dynamic-assessment paradigm, 324
Dysarthria, 256–257
Dyslexia, 21, 22

ECM. *See* Emergentist coalition model
Education
    developmental plasticity and, 350
    formal, cognitive-ability test scores and, 322
Effort, memory performance and, 154–155, 156

Elderly
    abstract *vs.* concrete thought and, 266–267
    expertise development in, 326–327
    rulelike representations and, 270
Elderspeak, 218–219, 226–227
Emergentist coalition model (ECM), 211–219
    coincident condition and, 213
    conflict condition and, 213
    evidence for, 212–213, 212*f*
    implications of, 214–216
    language in elderly populations and, 216–219
    principle of reference and, 213–214
Emergent maladaptive development, 36*t*, 37
Emotions
    differentiation of, 20
    processing from facial expressions, 20
Encoding process
    for childhood memories, 146
    deficits, 170
English verbs, past-tense inflections, 270
Environmental support, decreasing reliance in children,
    6
Episodic memory, 163, 164*f*
    age differences, 165–166
        in context *vs.* content, 169
        for individual items/associations, 168–169
        in memory errors, 170–171
        recollection/familiarity and, 166–168
        source memory and, 169
    age-related changes in, 200
    long-term memory and, 164–165, 164*f*
    moderating factors, in older adults, 172–174
    retrieval, 11
    retrieval model of, 61
Epistemological theories of cognitive development, 320–
    321, 324
Epistemological metaphor, of intelligence, 315–316
ERPs. *See* Event-related potentials
Essentialism, naïve, 266
Evaluative-flanker task, 106
Event-related memory
    child development of, 145–147
    establishing event representation, 146–147
Event-related potentials (ERPs)
    face processing, 19
    reading-related tasks, 21
    utility for developmental studies, 17
Events
    ongoing, adult-child conversations during, 148–150
    perception of, 181, 182*t*
    representation, in infancy, 184
Evolution, innate ontogenetic factors and, 345
Exclusion tests of memory, 167
Executive functions
    age-related changes, 9, 29, 107–108
    in children
        infants, 71–73, 72*f*–74*f*
        ages 1–3, 73–77
        ages 3–5 years, 77, 78*f*, 79, 80*f*, 81–83
        ages 5–11, 83–86

Executive functions (*continued*)
  component cognitive abilities
    flexibility, 70
    inhibition, 70
    working memory. *See* Working memory
  definition of, 96
  development, early, 106–107
  frontal lobe and, 9
  frontal-striatal circuit age-related changes and, 30
  latent-variable techniques, 99
  mediation, brain areas in, 71
  mirrored-pattern of control, 10
  origin of concept, 97
  portion-of-variance problem, 99
  prefrontal cortex and, 29
  problems with measuring, 98, 99–100
  process-dissociation measures, 97, 100, 107
    of individual differences, 105–106, 108
    "I told you . . ." procedure, 103–105, 104*t*, 105*f*, 108
    of recollection over proactive interference, 100–
      102, 101*f*, 102*t*
    in retroactive interference, 103–105, 104*t*, 105*f*
  situations requiring, 70
  task-based measures, 96
    cognitive, 98–99
    limitations of, 98, 99
    neuropsychological, 98
    Stroop task, 71, 98
  terminology, 70
  unity/diversity of, 98–99, 100
Experience
  age and, 279
  child development and, 17–18
  cognitive-ability test scores and, 322
  contextualized, brain-behavioral reciprocity and, 348–
    349
  infant strategy choice and, 288
  intellectual development and, 325–327
  knowledge and, 283
  neural network formation and, 22
  occupational, cognitive development and, 351
  representation and, 197–198
  representation during infancy and, 184
  salient, children's memories of, 145–146
Experience-expectant neural developmental processes,
  184
Experimental psychology, 315
Expertise
  acquisition, neuronal plasticity and, 352–352
  development, theory of, 323–324
  development of, in old age, 326–327
  paradigms, 359
  person-specific professional, 349
Explicit memory. *See* Declarative memory
Exploration
  age-related changes in, 46
  selection and, 45–46, 45*f*
  visual, 50–51
Extendibility, 212

Eye gaze
  cueing effects, in autism, 47
  spatial orienting and, 47
  for word learning, 211
Eye-tracking, of language processing, 232–233

Face, human
  direction of gaze in, 47
  processing development, neural correlates of, 19–20
False-belief task, 79
False memories, 170
Familiarity
  memory errors and, 170–171
  recollection and, 166–168
  working memory and, 117–118
Fast-mapping situation, age-related decline in language
  learning and, 216–217
Feature binding deficit view, 168–169
Figural fluency test, 277*t*
Finger movements, non-music-related *vs.* music-related,
  198–199
Flexibility, cognitive, definition of, 70
Fluid intelligence
  ability test performance, age-related differentiation in,
    337–338, 338*t*
  age-related decline in, 332
  biological factors and, 316
  differentiation/dedifferentiation of, 304, 305*f*, 306
  experiential subtheory and, 323
  mechanisms of, 353–354, 354*f*
  vs. crystallized intelligence, 193, 333–334, 340
fMRI. *See* Functional magnetic resonance imaging
Focal vascular disease, language disorders in, 255–260
Focused reduced relative clause sentence, 232
Focus switching, 99
Formal-operations period, 320
Frontal aging hypothesis, 335–336
Frontal lobe
  activation, 22
  atrophy, 32
  bilateral recruitment, 34
  executive functions and, 9
  in face recognition, 20
  familiarity and, 168
  myelination, 20
  pathology, 6–7
  recollection and, 168
  retrieval age-related deficits and, 170
  underrecruitment in aging, 32–33, 33*f*
  ventral regions, working memory and, 137–138
  volume, age-related decreases, 138
Frontal-lobe hypothesis of cognitive aging, 98
Frontal-striatal circuits
  cognitive aging and, 30
  deficits, in attention deficit hyperactivity disorder, 18
  functions of, 29
  genetic mutations effects on, 30–31
  recruitment and, 34
Functional adaptation principle, 356

Functional magnetic resonance imaging (fMRI), 32
  of Alzheimer's disease, 33
  DNMS, 77
  in face-identification task, 19–20
  frontal cortex underrecruitment in aging, 32–33, 33f
  of verbal fluency, 21

Game knowledge, children and, 184
"Garden path" effect, 232
Gaze orienting reflex, 47
General-purpose mechanisms, 347
Genetic mutations, effects on frontal-striatal circuits, 30–31
Genetic plasticity, 349, 349f
Global Functional Performance Characteristic (GPC),
      326, 335–340
Glucose metabolism
  age-related changes in, 16
  in dorsolateral prefrontal cortex, 73
Go/no-go task, 83
GPC (Global Functional Performance Characteristic),
      326
Graduate Record Examination, 274
Grammatical complexity, age-related decline in, 223–
      226, 224f, 225f
Grasping connections, 76
Gray matter
  childhood development, 38, 38f
  maturation, 16–17
  volume changes, 28
    in attention deficit hyperactivity disorder, 18
    developmental continuity and, 34–35, 35f

Habits
  age-related changes in, 46
  selection and, 45, 45f
  visual, 48–50
Hearing semantic elaborations, 219
Hemispherectomy, language impairments after, 242
Hippocampal formation, 29–30
  age-related changes in, 335
  cognitive aging and, 30
  neural activation, working memory and, 138
  preferential vulnerability, 31–32
  sex differences in, 17
  volume, navigation skills and, 352
  volume reduction, 31
Hormones, gray matter maturation and, 17
Hydrocephalus
  language disorders in, 241, 243
  reading comprehension and, 243
  sentence and text comprehension impairments and, 246
Hypertension, 30

Idioms
  comprehension, in Alzheimer's disease, 246
  comprehension impairments, 240
  decomposable, 243
  definition of, 240
  nondecomposable, 243

Idiosyncratic influences, on development, 349
IFJ (inferior frontal junction), 76
Imitation
  delayed, 184
  infants and, 183–184
Inclusion tests of memory, 167
Infancy, cognition, inter-individual differences, 291
Infant-directed speech, 218
Infantile amnesia, 188
Infants
  executive function in, 71–73, 72f–74f
    A-not-B error and, 72, 74f
    delayed nonmatching to sample and, 73, 75–76,
        75f
    physical connection, 76
  intellectual development, determinants of, 325–326
  intra-individual variability in cognition, 287–289
  representation and, 183–185
  representation formation in, 270
Inferencing, 243
Inferior frontal junction (IFJ), 76
Information processing, default mode, 98
Information-processing theories of intelligence
      development, 315, 319–320, 324
Inhibition
  age-related changes in language and, 229–230
  control, 246
  deficits, 229–230, 234
  definition of, 70
  in Stroop task control, 102–103
  subprocesses, 99
  working memory and, 71
Inhibition of return effects (IOR), 59
Inhibitory deficit theory, 229–230
Inquiry, patterns of, 267
Integration, theoretical, 344
Intelligence
  competency development and, 324–325
  conceptualization of, 318, 324–325
  dedifferentiation, 355, 355f
  definition of, 318, 324
  development
    cognitive capacity and, 325–327
    contextualist theories of, 321–322
    epistemological theories of, 320–321
    experience and, 325–327
    information-processing perspective of, 319–320
    from psychometric tradition perspective, 316–319,
        317f
  differentiation, 355, 355f
  differentiation/dedifferentiation hypothesis, 303–304
  dual-component theories of, 353–354, 354f
  fluid vs. crystallized, 8
  hierarchy of abilities, 316
  mechanics vs. pragmatics, 8
  priority assumption of, 316, 318–319
  stability assumption of, 316–318, 317f, 324–325
  triarchic theory of, 322–324
  youthful, sustained competence and, 333–334

Intelligence theories, synthesizing, 324–325
Interactive Preferential Looking Paradigm (IIPLP), 212, 212*f*
Interference, of working memory with age, 136–137
Interhemispheric integration, 247
Inter-individual variability, 287, 308, 346–347
  demographic, 285
  in extrapolating intra-individual variability, 300–301
  in infancy, 291
  intra-individual variability and, 292–294
  longitudinal stability, 286
  predictive validity, 286
  qualitative, 285
  quantitative, 285
Intra-individual variability, 291, 347
  effect on inter-individual differences, 292–294
  during infancy, 287–289
  measurement of, by extrapolation, 300–301
Intuitive theories, 267–268
IOR (inhibition of return effects), 59
IQ, 339
IQ tests, 338
Irony, 217
"I told you . . ." procedure, 103–105, 104*t*, 105*f*

Jargon, phonemic, 240
Jargon aphasia, 258

Kaufmann Adolescent and Adult Intelligence Test, 277–279, 277*t*, 278*f*
"Knew it all along" effect, 77, 79
Knowledge
  acquisition, 9, 122–123
    components of, 323
    skills for, 323
  age-related changes in, 279, 282–283
  cognitive capacity and, 321
  cognitive dependence on, 283
  conceptual, aging and, 195
  construction, influences on, 350–351
  domain-specific, development of, 188–189
  effects on working memory, 117–118
  experience and, 283
  growth
    domain specificity and, 268–269
    frequency-based information and, 269–270
    intuitive theories and, 267–268
    patterns of, 264–271
  pragmatic, mechanics of, 353–354, 354*f*
  prior, memory performance and, 153–154, 156
  processing efficiency and, 279–281
  representations
    development of, 8–9
    organization of, 9
  stored, accessibility of, 9
  thought and, 280
  utilization, difficulties in children, 9
  vs. representation and memory, 183
  working memory and, 117–118, 122–123
Knowledge-acquisition algorithms, 338

LAD (language acquisition device), 6
Language
  abilities, after stroke, premorbid language function and, 260
  acquisition
    abstract thought and, 265
    brain architecture and, 350
    ERP studies, 21
  in adulthood, 223–234
  age-related changes in
    cognitive slowing effects, 227–228
    inhibitory deficits and, 229–230
    language-specific deficits and, 233
    working memory and, 230–233
  comprehension, aging and, 195
  development, 185–187
    atypical, 214–216
    culture-specific, 350
    regression hypothesis of, 223
    socialization and, 350
  dissolution, 244–247
  in elderly populations, 216–219
  evolution, levels of representation and, 181–182
  experience, early, 186–187
  lateralization, 21
  learning, age-related decline, emergentist coalition model and, 216–219
  processes, aging and, 195
  recovery after stroke, age and, 254
  as representational system, 178–179, 180
  simplification, in older adults, 223
  skills development, neural correlates of, 20–21
  tasks, recruitment patterns and, 34
Language acquisition device (LAD), 6
Language acquisition support system (LASS), 6
Language disorders
  from brain injury, 239
  causes in older age, 253
  childhood-acquired, 239
  from congenital malformations, 239
  in focal vascular disease, 255–260
  of form, after childhood brain injury, 241–242
  of meaning, after childhood brain injury, 239–241
  post-stroke. *See* Aphasia
  production deficits, cross-cultural comparison of, 198
  from traumatic brain injury, in preschool children, 18
Language-specific deficits, age-related changes in language and, 233
Language theories, childhood aphasia and, 243–244
LASS (language acquisition support system), 6
Lateralization, of language, 21
Leadership, age and, 279
Learning
  achievement and, 318
  difficulties, working memory impairments and, 122
  skills, 323
  tasks, age-related variance in, 336–337
  in triarchic model, 326
  within-task, 318
Left hemisphere, syntax and, 241–242

Letter-number sequencing test, 277–279, 277t, 278f
Letters, visual recognition of, 194
Lexicon, declarative memory and, 244
Life history influences, variations in, 356
Lifespan cognitive development
    accumulated lesions of, 36–37, 36t
    adaptive functionality of, 356
    biocultural co-construction of, 348–349
    biological variations, 352–353, 353f
    continuous, maladaptive consequences of, 36, 36t
    continuous adaptive, 35–36, 36t
    convergent responses during, 37
    cultural variations, 352–353, 353f
    discontinued, 36, 36t
    emergent maladaptive, 36t, 37
    expertise and training influences, 351–352
    fictional depiction of, 38, 38f
    forms of, 36t
    integrative perspectives of, 4–5, 347, 348t
    intra-person dynamics, 356–358
    occupational influences, 351–352
    person-specific influences, 351–352
    resources, adaptive generation/allocation of, 357–358,
        357f
    social-cultural influences, 351–352
    trajectories, 9–11, 58
        differential, of processing mechanics and pragmatic
            knowledge, 353–354, 354f
        of growth, 346
        of working memory, 130, 131f–132f, 133, 138–139
Lifespan developmental psychology
    central concepts, 345–347
    goal of, 345
Lifespan theory, approaches for, 344
Linguistic structure, of spontaneous speech
    D-level, 223–224, 224f
    P-density, 223, 224, 224f
Liquid conservation task, 82–83
Listening span, 119, 120
Loftus post-event misinformation paradigm, 170
Logical reasoning, sequential development of, 321
Logical steps test, 277–279, 277t, 278f
Long-term memory
    aging and, 162
    biological factors and, 162
    concept of, 128
    episodic memory and, 164–165, 164f
    participant characteristics and, 162
    phonological, 117
    repetition priming and, 164–165, 164f
    semantic memory and, 164–165, 164f
    social/emotional variables and, 162
    working memory and, 113
Luria's hands test, 82
Luria's tapping test, 82

Magnetic resonance imaging. See also Functional
        magnetic resonance imaging
    brain volume reduction, 28
    white matter maturation, 16

Main clause sentences, 232
Maladaptive consequences of continuous development,
    36, 36t
Mapping problems, 208, 258–259
Matrix reasoning test, 276, 277–279, 277t, 278f
Meaning
    age-related changes in, 245–247
    capacity constraints on, 245–246
    disorders
        after childhood brain injury, 239–241
        dissociations within language and, 242–243
    dissociation, vs. form dissociation, 245
    dissolution, dementia and, 245–247
    in early brain damage, 245–247
    figurative, 240
    lexical, 240
    textual, 240–241
Medial temporal lobe
    in Alzheimer's disease, 30, 33
    damage, 30
    familiarity and, 168
    functions of, 29–30
    memory system
        maturation of, 75
        recruitment and, 34
        recollection and, 168
Memorization, intentional, frontal cortex in, 32
Memory. See also specific types of memory
    age-related changes, 22, 29, 163–166, 164f
    for block designs, 277t
    context and, 6
    declarative. See Declarative memory
    declarative-procedural distinction, 244
    deficits, individual differences in, 105–106
    development, 143–145
        context specificity in, 152–153, 157
        determinants of, 155–156
        dyadic communication and, 144, 145, 147–150,
            149f
        effective strategy use and, 153
        effort and, 154–155, 156
        event-related, 145–147
        for event-related material, 145–147
        mediators of, 147
        metamemory and, 155
        mnemonic competence and, 143–144
        organization and, 151–152
        prior knowledge and, 153–154
        rehearsal and, 151–152, 152t
        schooling effects on, 155
        strategy usage and, 150–151
    early forms of, 183
    encoding, 32
    errors, age differences in, 170–171
    executive processes in, 100
    explicit. See Declarative memory
    implicit or nondeclarative, 163, 164
    importance of, 162
    load, task switching and, 63
    mnemonic systems for, 286

Memory (*continued*)
  for new information related to area of expertise, 199
  performance, determinants of, 155–156
  strategies
    effective use of, 153
    effort requirements for, 154–155
    organizational, 151–152
    prior knowledge and, 153–154
    rehearsal, 151–152, 152*t*
  strategies, development, schooling effects on, 155
  tasks, age-related variance in, 336–337
  training, cognitive plasticity and, 351
  vs. representation and knowledge, 183
Memory Characteristics Questionnaire (MCQ), 170
Memory tests
  exclusion-type, 167
  inclusion-type, 167
  performance
    prior instructions and, 173–174
    time perspective and, 174
Meningomyelocele. *See* Spina bifida meningomyelocele
"Mental gymnastics" exercises, 277
Mental representation. *See* Representation
Metabolism
  age-related changes in, 33
  resting, in Alzheimer's disease, 33
Metacognitive skills, 323
Metacomponents (executive processes), 323
Metalinguistic awareness, 266
Metamemory, memory performance and, 155, 156
Meta-representational level, 187
Mimesis, 181, 182*t*
  infants and, 183–184
Mind, human, as hybrid, 182
Minimal cognitive architecture theory, 338
Mnemonic systems, for memory improvement, 286
Modality-specific anomia, 240
Monkey, periarcuate region, 76
Moral reasoning, 77, 79, 286
Morphological processing, disturbances in, 257
Morphology disorders, 242
Mother-child conversational interaction
  elaboration in, 147–148
  of ongoing events, 148–150
Mother-infant relationship, human *vs.* nonhuman primate, 184
Motivation, developing-expertise model and, 323
Multiple-strategy use, by children, 289
Multitasking, 348, 359
Music expertise acquisition, neuronal plasticity and, 352–352
Mutual exclusivity principle, 208, 209
Myelination, 16, 20
Mystery codes test, 277*t*
Mythic narratives, 181–182, 182*t*

Narratives, mythic, 181–182, 182*t*
Navigation skills, hippocampal volume and, 352
Negative priming paradigm, 60–61
Neologisms, 240

Neo-Piagetian theories of cognitive development, 320–321
Nervous system. *See also* Brain
  development
    of face processing, 19–20
    of language skills, 20–21
  differentiation/dedifferentiation hypothesis and, 306
Neural activations, in working memory, age differences in, 137–138
Neurocognitive deficits, language-specific effects of, 198
Neurocognitive resources, adaptive generation/allocation of, 358
Neuronal plasticity, 349, 349*f*, 350–352
Neuropsychological tests, of executive function, 98
Neurotransmitters, 16
Node Structure Theory (NST), 196, 196*f*, 199
Noise, in aging systems, 307, 311
Nonword repetition task, 116
Noun-category bias, 209
Novel name-nameless category (N3C), 208, 209
NST (Node Structure Theory), 196, 196*f*, 199
Number conservation strategies, 286
Numbers, visual recognition of, 194

Occupation, cognitive development and, 351
Off-topic speech, 241
Ontogenetic factors, evolution and, 345
Ontogenetic processes, socialization-typical, 349
Operation span, 118, 120
Optic aphasia, 256
Optimism, irrational, of young children, 267
Optimization, 347
Organic capacities, 276–277, 280, 281
Organization
  definition of, 320
  differences in, 7
  techniques, of school-age children, 151–152
Orienting, exogenous, spatial cueing and, 58
Original associative similarity, 270
Original inhibitory deficit hypothesis, 58
Orthographic representations, age-related changes in, 197
"Over-extensions," 186
Overt orienting, definition of, 46
Oxygen consumption, by brain, 15

Paragrammatism, 242, 257–258
Parallel processing, 121
Paraphasias
  phonemic, 240, 256
  semantic, 240
Parietal lobe
  activation, 22
  myelination, 16
  posterior, reduced resting metabolism in Alzheimer's, 33
Parkinson's disease, 244
Pauses, 240
P-density. *See* Propositional density
Perceptual cues, for word learning, 211
Perceptual grouping, 48

Perceptual processing deficit hypothesis, 58
Perceptual salience, 211, 215, 217
Performance components, 323
Performance-operating characteristic (POC), 64
Periarcuate region, in monkey, 76
Perpetual set, 44
Perspective, ambiguous figures and, 79
Perspective-taking, 82
PET. *See* Positron emission tomography
PFC. *See* Prefrontal cortex
Phonemic-similarity effects, in memory tasks, 116
Phonological loop, 116
    functions of, 117, 122
    impairments, 122
    in working memory, 129
Phonological recoding, 116–117
Phonological representations
    aging and, 195–196
    Node Structure Theory, 196, 196*f*
    weak connections and, 196–197, 196*f*
Phonological-similarity effect, 114
PI. *See* Proactive interference
Piaget's theory of intellectual development, 320
Picture-homophone matching, 255–256
Picture perception, "dual reality" of, 47–48
Pidgins, 226
Planning articulation, 256
Plaques, in Alzheimer's disease, 30
Plasticity
    biology-based, age-related changes in, 352–353, 353*f*
    cognitive, 349, 349*f*
        occupational influences, 351
        social-cultural influences, 351
    developmental, 346
        reciprocal interactions in, 349–350, 349*f*
    neuronal, 11, 349, 349*f*, 350–352
        functions of, 18
        impairments of, 18
        in old age, 22
    societal, 349
Positron emission tomography (PET), 32
    DNMS, 77
    frontal cortex underrecruitment in aging, 32
Posterior cingulate, reduced resting metabolism in
        Alzheimer's, 33
Practical intelligence, 323
Practice
    age-related decline in skill representations and, 198–
        199
    expert, 198–199
Pragmatic constraint of contrast, 209
Prefrontal cortex (PFC)
    age-related changes in, 335
    damage, 29, 98
    dorsolateral
        dopamine in, 73
        glucose metabolism in, 73
        neural activation, working memory and, 138
    functions of, 29
    ventrolateral, 76

Preoperational period, 320
Preoperational stage, 82
Preserved memory, 172–173
Principles/constraints theories of word learning, 208–209
Priority assumption, of intelligence, 316, 318–319
Proactive interference (PI), 100–102, 101*f*, 102*t*
    age-related changes, 106–107
    with working memory, age and, 136–136
Problem-solving ability, 7, 285–293
Problem space, word learning and, 208–211
Process-dissociation measures, 97, 100, 107, 167
    of individual differences, 105–106, 108
    "I told you . . ." procedure, 103–105, 104*t*, 105*f*, 108
    of recollection over proactive interference, 100–102,
        101*f*, 102*t*
Processing
    cultural evolutionary, 349
    dynamic organization of, 355, 355*f*
    efficiency, knowledge and, 279–281
    fluctuations, 302–304, 305*f*, 306
    mechanics, 353–354, 354*f*
    robustness, differentiation/dedifferentiation of, 304,
        305*f*, 306, 306*t*
    species-typical neurobiological, 349
    speed. *See* Speed of processing
Production system, rule-based, 319
Programmatic speech, 257
Propositional content, difficulties in, 258
Propositional density (P-density)
    age-related decline in, 223–226, 224*f*, 225*f*
    in Alzheimer's disease, 226
    in young adulthood, 226
Psychological refractory period paradigm (PRP), 64–65
Psychological theories, 315
Psychometric tests, 338–339
Psychometric theories, 315, 316, 324
    of intellectual development, 316–319, 317*f*
    modeling of ability in children, 339
Putamen, 17, 29

Quinean conundrum, 208–210

RADEX model, 317
Raven's Progressive Matrices, 106
Reaction time task (RT), 10
Reading
    language lateralization and, 21
    learning, phonological loop and, 122
    textual meaning disorders and, 240–241
    time, cognitive slowing and, 228
    working memory and, 119–120
Reading bottleneck hypothesis, 243
Reading comprehension
    semantic activation and, 246–247
    suppression and, 246–247
    word decoding, processing speed and, 243
Reading span task
    developmental trajectory and, 130, 131*f*–132*f*
    for working memory measurement, 115, 118, 119–
        120, 130

Reasoning abilities, age-related changes in, 29
Rebus learning, 277t
Recalling nameable drawings task, 116
Recollection (recall), 170–171
  differentiation and, 7
  familiarity and, 166–168
Recollection/Accessibility-Bias model, 100–102, 101f, 102t
Recruitment
  age-related changes in, 33–34
  frontal, 37
Reduced relative clause sentences, 232
Referential cohesion impairments, 241
Reflexes
  age-related changes in, 46
  selection and, 44–45, 45f
  visual, 46–48
Regression-based analytical approach, 280–281
Rehearsal protocols, school-age children, 151–152, 151t
Relative-clause construction, 231
Remember-know procedure, 167
"Reminiscence bump," 189
Repetition priming, 164
  age differences in, 165
  associative, 165
  item, 165
  long-term memory and, 164–165, 164f
Representation
  across lifespan, 190
  aging and, 193–203
  autobiographical memories, aging and, 200–201
  creating, 184
  development
    age-related changes in, 350–351
    in childhood, 202
    in children age 1–4 years, 185–187
    in infants, 183–185
    of literate meta-cultural level, 188–189
    in old age, 201, 202–203
    of self and self memory, 187–188
  developmental theories of, 179–181, 180t
  domains of, 199–200
  domain specificity and, 194
  experience and, 193–194
  formation in infants, 270
  function of, 178
  in infancy, 183–185
  levels of, 179
    developing, 182–189
    in phylogeny and ontogeny, 181–182, 182t
  neurocognitive factors and, 193–194
  rulelike, 270
  semantic, aging and, 194–198
  of skill, aging and, 198–199
  vs. memory and knowledge, 183
Representational dedifferentiation theory, 307
Resistance to distraction, selective attention and, 59–61
Response compatible paradigm, for distraction testing, 59–60
Resting metabolism, age-related changes in, 33

Restraint, as inhibition subprocess, 99
Retrieval
  age-related deficits, 170
  failures, 195
Retroactive interference
  executive functions in, 103–105, 104t, 105f
  with working memory, age and, 136–136
Rett syndrome, 18
Role disorders, 241–242
RT (reaction time task), 10

SAM (specific abilities model), 339–340
Sarcasm, 217
Scaffolding, 6
  of children's memories, 148
  representation during infancy and, 184
Schematic structure, problems with, 241
Schematic support, decreasing reliance in children, 6
Schizophrenia, 17
Schooling. See Education
Selection, 347
Selective attention (selection), 43–53
  age-related differences, negative priming paradigm, 60–61
  automatic, 44
  awareness and, 44
  control and, 44
  definition of, 58
  endogenous, 44
  exogenous, 44
  modes of, 44–46, 45f. See also Deliberation; Exploration; Habits; Reflexes
    age-related changes in, 46–53
    model of, 44, 44t
  resistance to distraction and, 59–61
  types of, 44
  visual, spatial cueing and, 58–59
Self-awareness, 187–188
Self-ordered Pointing Task, 130
Semantic disorders, category-specific, 240
Semantic knowledge, level of, aging and, 200
Semantic memory, 163, 164f
  age differences in, 165
  long-term memory and, 164–165, 164f
Semantic priming, 229–230, 246
Semantic representations, 246–247
  during adulthood, 194–198
  after early brain damage, 247
  deficits, category-specific, 255
  new factual, age-related declines in learning, 199–200
  Node Structure Theory, 196, 196f
  preservation, autobiographical descriptions of, 201
  weak connections and, 196–197, 196f
Seniority, 279
Sensorimotor memory, in infancy, 183
Sensorimotor period, 320
Sensory development, 16
Sensory function, higher-order cognition and, 135

Sentence-processing problems, working-memory
      limitations and, 231
Serial processing, 121
Sex differences, in gray matter maturation, 17
Short-term memory, 113
   concept of, 128
   disorders of, 259–260
   phonological, 117
Skill representation, aging and, 198–199
SLI (specific language impairment), 214
SOA (stimulus onset asynchrony), 64–65
Social compensation, *vs.* biological compensation, 11
Social cues, for word learning, 211
Socialization, cognitive development and, 350
Societal plasticity, 349
Socioemotional selectivity theory, 200
SOC theory, 287, 311
Sonorance hierarchy, 257
SOP. *See* Speed of processing
Sound-planning problems, 256
Source memory, 169
Spanish, production deficits, in old age, 198
Spatial cueing
   endogenous, 59
   exogenous, 58–59
   visual selective attention and, 58–59
Spatial orienting, 46–47
Spatial processing, age-related changes in, 29
Spatial relations test, 277–279, 277t, 278f
Specific abilities model (SAM), 339–340
Specific language impairment (SLI), 214
Speech registers
   of older adults
      for different partners, 227
      simplified, overall decline in processing speed and,
         228
      simplified in older adults, 226
Speed of processing, 234
   differentiation/dedifferentiation of, 304, 305f, 306,
      306t
   word decoding, reading comprehension and, 243
Speed of processing (SOP), 326, 335–340
   accuracy and, 319
   age-related changes in, 29, 332
   cognitive abilities and, 318–319
   mechanism of, 135–136
   working memory and, 120–121, 134–135, 139
Spina bifida meningomyelocele
   language disorders in, 240, 241, 243
   learning and, 244
   procedural memory and, 244
   reading comprehension and, 243
   semantic representations in, 246
   sentence and text comprehension impairments and,
      245–246
   suppression deficits, 247
Stability assumption, of intelligence, 316–318, 317f
Static tests, 318
Stimulus onset asynchrony (SOA), 64–65

Story-telling, 173
Strategy
   choice
      during childhood, 289–290
      during infancy, 287–289
      process of, 286–287
      by younger *vs.* older adults, 290–291
   use
      during childhood, 289–290
      during infancy, 287–289
      by younger *vs.* older adults, 290–291
Stroke patients
   adult, language disorders in, 245
   childhood, language disorders in, 244, 245
   recognition of spoken word, 255
   speech production disorders, 255–256
   word meaning disturbances, 255
Stroop effect, 48–49, 60, 65
Stroop task, 103–104, 335
   color-naming effect, 48–49
   color-word, executive function and, 71, 98
   color word condition, 60
   inhibitory control in, 102–103
   negative-priming, executive function and, 98
   spatial, 106
   working-memory capacity and, 106
Subject-relative clause construction, 231
Suppression, 246
Suppression deficits, 247
Switch costs
   general, 63
   specific, 63
Syntactic complexity, reducing, 219
Syntactic comprehension deficits, 241–242, 259
Systems-based language theory, 215–216

Tag questions, problems with, 242
Task-switching hypothesis, 119
Task-switching processes
   age-related differences, 62–63
   global, 99
   local, 99
Taxonomic assumption, 209
Teratogens, 36
Text macrostructure, problems with, 241
Text representation, 243
Theories of representation, 182, 182t, 183
Theory-of-mind tasks, 77, 78f
Thinking/athlete analogy, 281
Thought
   aging and, 274–283
   definition of, 274
   knowledge and, 280
   thinking skills, 323
Time concepts, development of, 188
Tip-of-the tongue phenomenon (TOT), 195–197, 233
TOT (tip-of-the-tongue phenomenon), 195–197, 233
Tower of Hanoi, 277t
Training paradigms, 359

Transmission-deficit principle, 196–199, 233
Traumatic brain injury, long-term language skills impairment from, 18
Triarchic theory of intelligence, 322–324
    componential subtheory, 322–323
    contextual subtheory, 323
    experiential subtheory, 323
20 questions test, 277–279, 277t, 278f
Two-stages-of-life perspective, 4

Utilization deficiency, 286

Variability
    in cognitive aging, 297–311
        empirical findings, 302–303
        formal model of, 307–308, 308t, 309f, 310, 310f
        future research directions, 310–311
        inter-individual, vs. intra-individual, 301–302, 301f, 301t
        intra-individual, vs. inter-individual, 301–302, 301f, 301t
        measurement of, 299–302
        microgenetic, 303
        sample homogeneity, 300
        variation equivalence, 300
        within-person, taxonomy of, 298, 299t
    of cognitive aging, differentiation/dedifferentiation hypothesis, 303–304
Variability of performance, 4
Vascular compromise, 30
Verbal fluency, 21
Verbal span tasks, 114–116
Verbal subsystems, differentiation of, 135–136, 136f
Visual auditory learning test, 277–279, 277t, 278f
Visual-geometric illusions, 47–48
Visual marking, age differences in, 62
Visual matching test, 277–279, 277t, 278f
Visual processing
    exploration, 50–51
    habits, 48–50
    reflexes, 46–48
    in Williams syndrome, 215
Visual recognition, of numbers/letters, 194
Visual search
    age-related effects in, 10–11, 61–62
    infants and, 71–72
    oddball or pop-out tasks, 50
    Stroop effect and, 48–49, 60, 65
    training effects, 62
Visuo-spatial measures, of working memory, 130
Visuo-spatial span tasks, 115
    complex, 114
    simple, 114, 118
Visuo-spatial subsystems, differentiation of, 135–136, 136f
Visuospatial tasks, Self-ordered Pointing Task, 130
Vocabulary
    development, in Williams syndrome, 215
    knowledge, aging and, 195

Voiding cystourethrogram, memory encoding for, 146–147
Vulnerability, differential, to accumulated lesions, 37

WAIS (Wechsler Adult Intelligence Scale), 129, 277–279, 277t, 278f
Wason Selection Task, 321
Wayfinding, 117
Wechsler Abbreviated Scale of Intelligence (WASI), 276, 276f
Wechsler Adult Intelligence Scale (WAIS), 129, 277–279, 277t, 278f
Wechsler Intelligence Scale for Children (WISC), 115
Wechsler Memory Scale Letter-Number Sequencing task, 129–130
Wernicke-Geschwind model of language, 35, 35f
Wernicke's aphasia, 260
White matter
    age-related changes
        diffusion tensor imaging of, 30, 31f
        frontal recruitment and, 32
    in Alzheimer's disease, 30, 31f
    damage, 30, 31
    maturation, 16
    volume
        in attention deficit hyperactivity disorder, 18
        reductions in, 28
Williams syndrome, 116, 215
WISC (Wechsler Intelligence Scale for Children), 115
Wisconsin Card Sort Test (WCST), 79, 98
Woodcock-Johnson tests, 277–279, 277t, 278f, 316
Word decoding, processing speed, reading comprehension and, 243
Word-finding failures, 195, 233, 234, 240
Word forms
    accessing from concepts, impairments of, 240, 256
    activating from concepts, disturbances in, 255–256
    errors, 244
Word-learning principles, 211
Word-length effects, in memory tasks, 114, 116
Word meaning disorders, 255
Word production, 196
Word retrieval failures, 233
Words
    ambiguous, meaning of, 246
    learning
        coordinating information sources for, 217
        early stage, 185–186
        emergentist coalition model of. See Emergentist coalition model
        multiple outputs for, 211, 211f
        theories of, 208–211, 209f
        in Williams syndrome, 215
    meaning of. See Meaning
Word-sound planning, impairments of, 240
Word switch task, 279
Working attention, 9
Working memory, 9, 71, 102
    age-related changes in language and, 230–233
    age-related effects, 20

capacity, 106, 133–134
central executive system of, 129
characteristics of, 113, 128
cognitive behavior age-related changes and, 134–135
complex span tasks, 112, 115
  cognitive abilities and, 119
  domain specificity and, 119–120
  reading/arithmetic attainment and, 122
  theoretical accounts, 118–119
concept of, 112–113
definition of, 70, 113
developmental changes
  in adulthood, 130, 131f–132f, 133
  in childhood, 115–120
examples of, 128–129
familiarity effects, 117–118
functions of, 122
impairments, 122
interference with age, 136–137
knowledge acquisition and, 122–123

knowledge effects, 117–118
lifespan perspective, 138–139
limitations, 234, 245–246
long-term memory and, 113
measures of, 129–130
model, initial, 129
multicomponent approach, 113
neural activations, age differences in, 137–138
processing speed and, 120–121
simple span tasks, 112, 114, 115–116
  phonological loop and, 117
  phonological recoding, 116–117
  verbal, 114, 116
  visuo-spatial, 118
subprocesses, 113
system, structure of, 121
unitary approach, 113
visuo-spatial measures, 130

Yngve depth, 230